Landscape and Land Use in
First Millennium BC
Southeast Italy

Amsterdam Archaeological Studies 25

Other titles in the AAS series:

1. N. Roymans (ed.): *From the Sword to the Plough. Three Studies on the Earliest Romanisation of Northern Gaul*
   Open Access edition: http://dare.uva.nl/record/19675

2. T. Derks: *Gods, Temples and Ritual Practices. The Transformation of Religious Ideas and Values in Roman Gaul*
   Open Access edition: http://dare.uva.nl/aup/en/record/172370

3. A. Verhoeven: *Middeleeuws gebruiksaardewerk in Nederland (8e – 13e eeuw)*
   Open Access edition: http://dare.uva.nl/aup/en/record/172373

4. F. Theuws / N. Roymans (eds): *Land and Ancestors. Cultural Dynamics in the Urnfield Period and the Middle Ages in the Southern Netherlands*
   Open Access edition: http://dare.uva.nl/aup/en/record/172372

5. J. Bazelmans: *By Weapons made Worthy. Lords, Retainers and their Relationship in* Beowulf
   Open Access edition: http://dare.uva.nl/aup/en/record/172337

6. R. Corbey / W. Roebroeks (eds): *Studying Human Origins. Disciplinary History and Epistemology*
   Open Access edition: http://dare.uva.nl/aup/en/record/172272

7. M. Diepeveen-Jansen: *People, Ideas and Goods. New Perspectives on 'Celtic barbarians' in Western and Central Europe (500-250 BC)*
   Open Access edition: http://dare.uva.nl/aup/en/record/172273

8. G. J. van Wijngaarden: *Use and Appreciation of Mycenean Pottery in the Levant, Cyprus and Italy (ca. 1600-1200 BC). The Significance of Context*
   Open Access edition: http://dare.uva.nl/aup/en/record/172274

9. F.A. Gerritsen: *Local Identities. Landscape and community in the late prehistoric Meuse-Demer-Scheldt region*
   Open Access edition: http://dare.uva.nl/aup/en/record/172820

10. N. Roymans: *Ethnic Identity and Imperial Power. The Batavians in the Early Roman Empire*
    Open Access edition: http://dare.uva.nl/aup/en/record/172930

11. J.A.W. Nicolay: *Armed Batavians. Use and significance of weaponry and horse gear from non-military contexts in the Rhine delta (50 BC to AD 450)*
    Open Access edition: http://dare.uva.nl/aup/nl/record/397232

12. M. Groot: *Animals in ritual and economy in a Roman frontier community. Excavations in Tiel-Passewaaij*
    Open Access edition: http://dare.uva.nl/aup/en/record/301888

13. T. Derks & N. Roymans (eds): *Ethnic Constructs in Antiquity. The role of power and tradition*
    Open Access edition: http://dare.uva.nl/aup/en/record/301890

14. T. D. Stek: *Cult places and cultural change in Republican Italy. A contextual approach to religious aspects of rural society after the Roman conquest*
    ISBN 978 90 8964 177 9

15. P. A.J. Attema, G.-J. L.M. Burgers & P. M. van Leusen: *Regional Pathways to Complexity. Settlement and land-use dynamics in early italy from the bronze age to the republican period*
    ISBN 978 90 8964 276 9

16. E.M. Moormann: *Divine Interiors. Mural paintings in Greek and Roman sanctuaries*
    ISBN 978 90 8964 261 5

17. N. Roymans / T. Derks (eds): *Villa Landscapes in the Roman North. Economy, Culture and Lifestyles*
    ISBN 978 90 8964 348 3

18. N. Roymans / G. Creemers / S. Scheers: *Late Iron Age Gold Hoards from the Low Countries and the Caesarian Conquest of Northern Gaul*
    ISBN 978 90 8964 349 0

19. D. S. Habermehl: *Settling in a Changing World. Villa development in the northern provinces of the Roman Empire.*
    ISBN 978 90 8964 506 7

20. D. G.Yntema: *The Archaeology of South-East Italy in the first millenium BC. Greek and native societies of Apulia and Lucania between the 10th and the 1st century BC.*
    ISBN 978 90 8964 579 1

21. Manuel Fernández-Götz: *Identity and Power. The Transformation of Iron Age Societies in Northeast Gaul.*
    ISBN 978 90 8964 597 5

22. N. Roymans / T. Derks and H. Hiddink (eds): *The Roman Villa of Hoogeloon and the Archaeology of the Periphery.*
    ISBN 978 90 8964 836 5

23. A. Van Oyen: *How Things Make History. The Roman Empire and its Terra Sigillata Pottery.*
    ISBN 978 94 6298 054 9

24. M. Groot: *Livestock for Sale: Animal Husbandry in a Roman Frontier Zone.*
    ISBN 978 94 6298 080 8

Landscape and Land Use in First Millennium BC Southeast Italy

PLANTING THE SEEDS OF CHANGE

DAPHNE LENTJES

AMSTERDAM UNIVERSITY PRESS

This book meets the requirements of ISO 9706: 1994, Information and documentation – Paper for documents – Requirements for permanence.

Cover illustration: *Harvest in Provence*, Vincent van Gogh, 1888

Cover design: Kok Korpershoek, Amsterdam
Lay-out: Bert Brouwenstijn, Almere

ISBN   978 90 8964 794 8
e-ISBN   978 90 4852 613 0 (pdf)
NUR   682

© Daphne Lentjes, Amsterdam University Press, Amsterdam, 2016

All rights reserved. Without limiting the rights under copyright reserved above, no part of this book may be reproduced, stored in or introduced into a retrieval system, or transmitted, in any form or by any means (electronic, mechanical, photocopying, recording, or otherwise), without the written permission of both the copyright owner and the editors of this book.

CONTENTS

PREFACE ... IX

1 INTRODUCTION ... 1
1.1 Archaeological research of landscape and land use in southeast Italy ... 1
1.2 Aims and research questions ... 4
1.3 Research method ... 6
1.4 Structure of the book ... 7

2 CASE STUDY 1: L'AMASTUOLA ... 9
2.1 Introduction: The site and its surroundings ... 9
2.2 History of research ... 10
2.3 The archaeological research ... 12
    2.3.1 Diachronic overview ... 12
    2.3.2 Specific contexts ... 14
2.4 The archaeobotanical research ... 26
    2.4.1 Sampling methods and data ... 26
    2.4.2 Charcoal ... 27
    2.4.3 Seeds and fruits ... 31
2.5 The archaeobotanical research: Interpretations ... 33
    2.5.1 The use of wood ... 33
    2.5.2 Food preparation and diet ... 37
    2.5.3 Grape and olive cultivation ... 45
    2.5.4 The use of plants in ritual activities ... 47
2.6 Summary and conclusion ... 49

3 CASE STUDY 2: MURO TENENTE ... 53
3.1 Introduction: The site and its surroundings ... 53
3.2 History of research ... 53
3.3 The archaeological research ... 54
    3.3.1 Diachronic overview ... 54
    3.3.2 Specific contexts ... 58
3.4 The archaeobotanical research ... 63
    3.4.1 Sampling methods and data ... 63
    3.4.2 Charcoal ... 63
    3.4.3 Seeds and fruits ... 66
3.5 The archaeobotanical research: Interpretations ... 68
    3.5.1 The use of wood ... 68
    3.5.2 Food preparation and diet ... 74
    3.5.3 Grape and olive cultivation ... 78
    3.5.4 The use of plants in ritual activities ... 81
3.6 Summary and conclusion ... 84

4	**MESO LEVEL: LANDSCAPE AND LAND USE AROUND L'AMASTUOLA AND MURO TENENTE**	87
4.1	Introduction	87
4.2	L'Amastuola	88
	4.2.1 The landscape	88
Box 1: Mediterranean plant communities		91
	4.2.2 Land use	94
Box 2: The storage capacity of the grain silos at l'Amastuola		98
4.3	Muro Tenente	102
	4.3.1 The landscape	102
	4.3.2 Land use	105
Box 3: Confronting the grape measurements from Muro Tenente (unit 89) with the statistical analysis program SPSS		109
4.4	Conclusion: Landscape and land use at l'Amastuola and Muro Tenente compared	109
5	**MACRO LEVEL: PART ONE**	111
5.1	Introduction	111
5.2	A short introduction to archaeobotanical research in southeast Italy, and the archaeological sites	112
5.3	Research aspects	117
	5.3.1 The use of wood	117
	5.3.2 Food preparation and diet	119
	5.3.3 Grape and olive cultivation	131
	5.3.4 The use of plants in ritual activities	147
Tables chapter 5		160
6	**MACRO LEVEL: PART TWO**	185
6.1	Introduction	185
6.2	The Final Bronze Age (c. 1200-1000 BC)	186
6.3	The Early Iron Age (c. 1000-600 BC)	189
6.4	The Archaic/Classical periods (c. 600-325 BC)	196
6.5	The Early Hellenistic Period (c. 325-200 BC)	207
6.6	Epilogue: Southeast Italy in the Late Hellenistic/ Early Roman period (200-30 BC). Nothing but sheep and olive trees?	214
7	**CONCLUSIONS**	217
7.1	Introduction, restatement of research aims and method	217
7.2	Long-term developments in landscape and land use	217
7.3	Long-term developments in the scale and organization of agricultural production: Expansion, rationalization, specialization	219
7.4	The effect of Greek colonization	222
7.5	Future research	223
LIST OF FIGURES		225
BIBLIOGRAPHY		229

APPENDIX 1 ARCHAEOBOTANICAL SAMPLE PROCESSING 253
A 1.1 Methodology: General introduction 253
A 1.2 Archaeobotanical sampling at l'Amastuola, Muro Tenente and Li Castelli 254
A 1.3 Recommendations 254

APPENDIX 2 ARCHAEOBOTANICAL ANALYSES FROM L'AMASTUOLA,
COMPLETE RESULTS 257
A 2.1 Results: Seeds and fruits 257
A 2.2 Results: Charcoal 261

APPENDIX 3 ARCHAEOBOTANICAL ANALYSES FROM MURO TENENTE,
COMPLETE RESULTS 267
A 3.1 Results: Seeds and fruits 267
A 3.2 Results: Charcoal 270

APPENDIX 4 ARCHAEOBOTANICAL ANALYSES FROM LI
CASTELLI DI SAN PANCRAZIO SALENTINO, COMPLETE RESULTS 272
A 4.1 Introduction to the site 272
A 4.2 Results: Seeds and fruits 274
A 4.3 Results: Charcoal 275

APPENDIX 5 GRAPE MEASUREMENTS MURO TENENTE AND L'AMASTUOLA 277
A 5.1 Morphometric analysis methods to distinguish between cultivated and wild grapes
(*Vitis vinifera* var. *vinifera* vs *Vitis vinifera* var. *sylvestris*) 277
A 5.2 Results: Muro Tenente 278
A 5.3 Results: L'Amastuola 281

APPENDIX 6 ANCIENT WRITTEN TEXT FRAGMENTS 282

INDEX 291

Preface

The period under study here roughly covers the Early Iron Age and the Archaic, Classical and Early Hellenistic periods. While some variation is noticed in the dating of these periods and the exact time frame that they represent, this study will largely follow the chronological scheme proposed by Attema, Burgers and Van Leusen (2010), with some minor changes:

Early Bronze Age	c. 2300-1700 BC
Middle Bronze Age	c. 1700-1350 BC
Recent Bronze Age	c. 1350-1200 BC
Final Bronze Age	c. 1200-1000 BC
Early Iron Age	c. 1000-600 BC
Archaic Period	c. 600-480 BC
Classical Period	c. 480-325 BC
Early Hellenistic Period	c. 325-200 BC
Late Hellenistic / Early Roman Period	c. 200-30 BC

All dates in this study should be considered as years BC, unless otherwise stated.
The descriptions of the characteristics of wild plants that I use are based on Pignatti (1982), Polunin and Huxley (1974) and Polunin (1969). All scientific names can be found in *Tables 5.1-5.5*.

Chapter 1 – Introduction

1.1 ARCHAEOLOGICAL RESEARCH INTO LANDSCAPE AND LAND USE IN SOUTHEAST ITALY

The research presented in this book is concerned with the period between the end of the Final Bronze Age and the beginning of the Late Hellenistic Period in southeast Italy. *Figure 1.1* shows the part of Italy that constitutes the research area. It consists of the regions around the Gulf of Taranto, including the Salento Isthmus in the southern part of Apulia, the Basilicata (or ancient Lucania) region, the southernmost tip of Campania and the north of Calabria. This area is rather varied in terms of relief, hydrology, and vegetation patterns. This partly explains the variation in land use at the sites I will discuss in the pages to follow. The Salento district is largely made up of a slightly undulating plain with light arable soils, which, starting from the Adriatic, rises very gradually to approximately 60 m above sea level. The coastal zone consists mostly of dunes, low cliffs, and lagoons. Towards the south, the plain merges into the hillier calcareous landscape of the Serre Leccesi. To the west and north, the Brindisi district encompasses some of the hard limestone spurs of the Murge uplands, a plateau which gradually merges into the Apennine mountain chain.[1] Basilicata, on the other hand, is the most mountainous region in the south of Italy, as it covers an extensive part of the southern Apennines. It is bordered on the east by a large part of the Bradano river depression, which is traversed by numerous streams and declines to the south-eastern coastal plains on the Ionian Sea.[2] The north of Calabria consists largely of an alluvial plain, which is delimited in the north by a crescent-shaped mountain range, with few access points to the mountainous hinterland. Inland routes are largely restricted to the wide river beds of the streams entering the plain from the mountains.[3]

This research covers the entire first millennium BC except for the last two centuries, which represent the Late Hellenistic period. A decision was made to omit this period because of the unprecedented changes that took place when southern Italy was incorporated in the Roman state.[4] This study fits into a well-established tradition of archaeological research in southeast Italy. The processes of urbanization and Greek colonization in particular have long since fascinated archaeologists. Starting in the 8th century BC, small groups of Greek migrants settled along the coast of southern Italy ('Magna Graecia') and established colonies, including Taras (modern Taranto), Metapontion (Metaponto), Siris/Herakleia (Policoro), and Sybaris (Sibari). The archaeological study of this Greek colonization movement has already spawned a huge bibliography,[5] which is mostly concerned with the colonial Greek cities and the diffusion of Greek art, architecture, and town planning.[6]

However, in the past few decades, research on the contemporary indigenous regions has also made a giant leap forward. The investigations by Renato Peroni and Francesco D'Andria in particular have led to important new insights into the processes of urbanization and growing social and economic

---

[1] Van Joolen 2003, pp. 5-8; Attema *et al.* 2010, p. 5.
[2] Attema *et al.* 2010, p. 5.
[3] Van Joolen 2003, pp. 13-14; Attema *et al.* 2010, p. 5.
[4] Yntema 2006.
[5] Nenci and Vallet 1977-2005.
[6] Cf. Attema et al. 2010, p. 119. See in particular Dunbabin 1968; Boardman 1998.

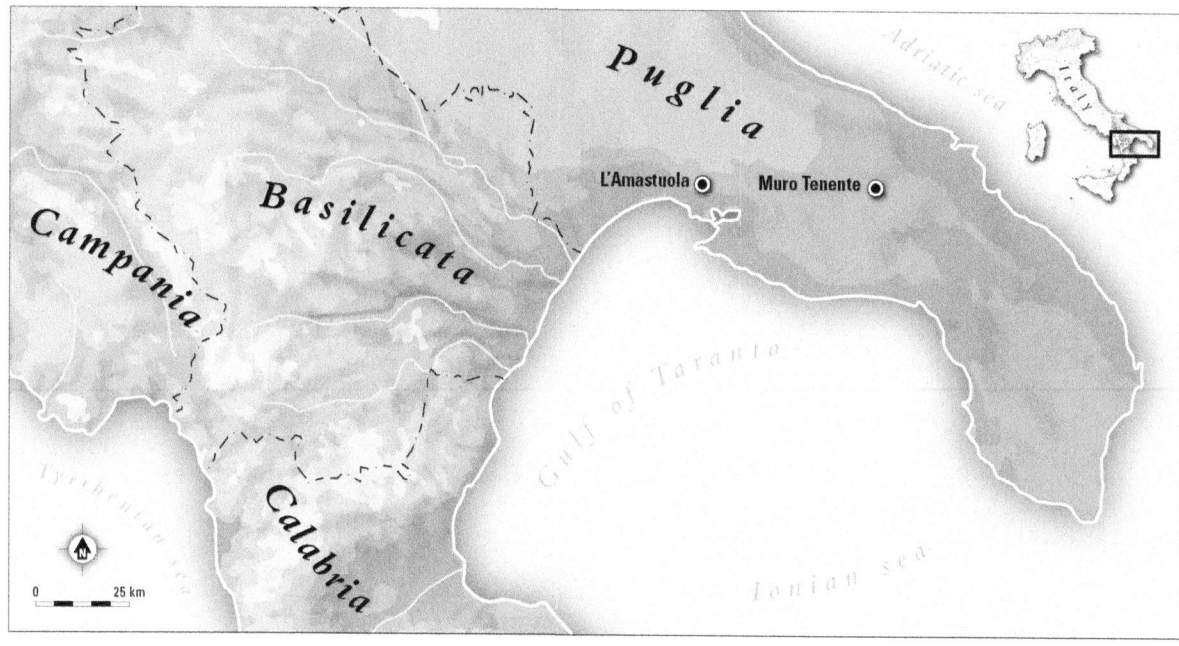

Fig. 1.1. The research area of this study. Map by Bert Brouwenstijn.

complexity in the inland areas of Basilicata, Calabria, and Salento (southern Apulia).[7] Moreover, the aforementioned focus on urban contexts is currently counterbalanced by an increase in the number of excavations of rural sites and of archaeological field survey projects.[8] Intensive field survey has proved to be a particularly useful tool in reconstructing the organization of the landscape and changes in settlement patterns and settlement hierarchy.[9] Italy has a long research tradition of topographical studies (which are mainly concerned with the recording of standing structures[10]), but since the early 1980s, the research method of field survey has truly come of age here.[11] Notable examples of field surveys in southeast Italy are the projects in the Basentello valley,[12] around the Roman villa sites of San Giovanni di Ruoti[13] and *masseria* Ciccotti,[14] and the Lucanian site of Roccagloriosa.[15] The territory (or *chora*) of the Greek colony of Metapontion has been especially intensely surveyed.[16]

[7] For example, Peroni 1984, 1994; D'Andria 1988, 1990, 1996. Other overviews of the pre-Roman phases in southeast Italy were produced by Adamesteanu 1974; Pontrandolfo Greco 1982; De Juliis 1988; D'Agostino 1989.

[8] Cf. Renfrew and Bahn 2004, pp. 67-110.

[9] Intensive surveys include the complete or near-complete coverage of an area at a high resolution, usually by means of systematic field walking. Extensive survey, on the other hand, is characterized by a low-resolution approach in which only selected parts of a larger study area are visited.

[10] A typical example is the Forma Italiae project, a long-term series of surveys initiated by the University of Rome in the 1950s and 1960s. These studies concentrate on contiguous survey areas, the so-called a tappeto-method, systematically exploring an entire study area to record archaeological sites. Terrenato (2000, pp. 22-23) has argued that methodological differences between Italian and foreign survey research are still visible today. Whereas the Dutch, British, Canadian, and American projects attempt to measure the density of artefact scatters all over the sampled area, most Italian projects use a simpler site-based approach. In other words, Italian survey projects often disregard off-site artefact scatters and focus on the identification of settlements. According to Terrenato, these different approaches often stand in the way of ambitions to standardize field survey techniques, which would be an important step forward in Italian landscape archaeology.

[11] Cf. Barker 1995a, pp. 5-9 for a short overview of the development of survey archaeology in Italy.

[12] Small *et al.* 1988; Small 2001.

[13] Roberto *et al.* 1985; Roberto and Small 1994.

[14] Gualtieri and Fracchia 1993.

[15] Gualtieri and Fracchia 1990; Gualtieri and De Polignac 1991; Fracchia and Ortolani 1993.

[16] Carter 2001; De Siena 2001; Carter 2006; Carter, Prieto and Trelogan 2011.

The Dutch archaeological projects in southeast Italy have also contributed to this development. Since the early 1980s, the Archaeological Centre of VU University Amsterdam (ACVU) and the Groningen Institute of Archaeology (GIA) have conducted a series of excavations and field survey projects in southeast Italy. A large part of this research was carried out within the context of the multidisciplinary Regional Pathways to Complexity (RPC) project (1997-2009), a comparative assessment of processes of centralization and urbanization in three Italian regions (the Pontine region in Latium, the Salento Isthmus in Apulia, and the Sibaritide in Calabria) during the first millennium BC.[17] VU University Amsterdam also undertook smaller-scale survey and excavation projects in the Brindisino and Tarantino, including surveys and excavations in and around the settlements of Muro Tenente and l'Amastuola.[18]

It is mainly due to this surge in survey projects that ancient landscapes—as opposed to urban contexts—have become an increasingly important research topic in the archaeology of southeast Italy.[19] This type of research is often referred to as 'landscape archaeology'. The dominant perspective on current landscape studies in the Mediterranean has been inspired by the historian Fernand Braudel.[20] Braudel's theories became the cornerstone of the French school of Annales history, focusing on the interplay between different kinds of histories operating at different timescales, dubbed *événements* (short-term occurrences in political or military history), *conjonctures* (the medium-term change of demographic and economic cycles), and *longue durée* (long-term processes of change of 'structures' and the landscape). The goals of landscape archaeology are much the same as those of Annales history, especially on the level of *conjonctures* and *longue durée*.[21] Several archaeological case studies have shown the potential of the Annales paradigm for landscape archaeology.[22] However, Braudel's ideas have also been criticized by both later generations of Annales historians and post-processual archaeologists. Braudel regarded landscape and social structures as much more important to change than individual human agency, a viewpoint that many considered as a form of environmental and structural determinism. Critics argued that humans can also create, reproduce, and cause long-term transformations.[23] Indeed, later generations of landscape archaeologists such as Leroy-Ladurie have fine-tuned Braudel's timescale and were keen to link persons, events, and mentalities into medium- and longer-term time processes.[24]

Nevertheless, the debate about the best strategy for the study of ancient landscapes in Italy continues to this day. The balance between the role of the landscape itself on the one hand, and human agency on the other still forms an important point of discussion. In spite of the great advances in landscape archaeology in the past few decades, no single study exists that considers the *mutual* relationship between man and landscape in long-term processes of change. Human choices affect the landscape, but the natural environment can also determine human behaviour, for instance the choice of settlement locations and land use. Indeed, from the 1970s onwards, archaeological research in the Mediterranean basin started to pay increasing attention to the

---

[17] Attema *et al.* 2010.

[18] For Muro Tenente and l'Amastuola, see chapters 2 and 3. Other field surveys and excavation projects by the ACVU were carried out around the settlement of Oria (1981-1983, final report: Yntema 1993), Valesio (1984-1992, final reports: Boersma and Yntema 1987; Boersma *et al.* 1995; Yntema 2001), Muro Maurizio, San Pancrazio and Cellino San Marco (1992-1995, final report: Burgers 1998) and Ostuni (1999-2000, report: Burgers *et al.* 2010).

[19] See most recently Attema et al. 2010.

[20] Bintliff 1989, with further references.

[21] Braudel 1949; cf. Barker 1991, 1995a, b, Bintliff 1989, with further references.

[22] For example, the Boeotia Survey project in Greece, directed by Bintliff and Snodgrass, see Bintliff *et al.* 1991.

[23] Barker 1991, p. 3.

[24] Leroy-Ladurie 1966, 1975; cf. Bintliff 1989, with further references; Bintliff 2004.

natural landscape,²⁵ since the integration of bioarchaeological data into archaeological research is essential for the study of landscape and settlement dynamics.

1.2 AIMS AND RESEARCH QUESTIONS

In short, a closer look at the history of archaeological research shows a change of perspective. Until recently, archaeologists studying the first millennium BC in southeast Italy tended to focus on Greek rather than on indigenous material culture. In recent decades, this imbalance has been corrected. A large and growing body of literature records studies of the inland areas of Basilicata, Calabria, and southern Apulia, and the relationships between the indigenous populations living in these areas with the Greek colonial settlements on the coast. A more recent trend in archaeological research in southeast Italy involves the investigation of ancient landscapes, which is illustrated particularly well by the growing number of archaeological field survey projects and excavations of rural sites. Thanks to this development, archaeological research was able to change its focus from short-term historical events (or, in Braudelian terms, événements) to long-term developments (*conjonctures* and *longue durée*).

However, these studies generally have one important limitation. Whereas our knowledge of habitation patterns and human impact on the landscape in this area has increased enormously, the basic understanding of what this landscape looked like and how it was used—besides for settlement building—has lagged behind. This was the main reason why, in 2003, it was decided to incorporate archaeobotanical research (the study of archaeological plant remains) into VU University's archaeological projects in southeast Italy. The results can be found in this book. In this study, I intend to use a different approach to study the occupational history of pre-Roman southeast Italy. Rather than focusing solely on human activities, I will attempt to put the archaeological research data in a broader perspective of developments in landscape exploitation, agricultural production, and human impact on the natural landscape. The primary aim of this book is to explore how the opportunities offered by the landscape influenced human strategies and how humans altered the landscape in order to adapt it to their needs.

My second aim is of a methodological nature: I wish to show that archaeobotany offers major opportunities for studies of ancient landscapes and their exploitation. Indeed, archaeobotany is a field of research that is slowly coming of age and developing into an independent discipline in Italy and other Mediterranean countries. The first important steps in this process were taken in the 1970s and early 1980s, when archaeobotanical research concentrated on the need to catalogue the finds, and create a general image of the available species.²⁶ Today, this phase of collecting information is slowly coming to an end, making way for synthesizing, regional studies. The research presented in this study clearly fits into this trend, but also wishes to take a step forward, integrating archaeobotanical data into a multidisciplinary research framework.

---

[25] See for example Karl Butzer's geoarchaeological studies in Spain (1985), Portugal (1967), and Cyprus (2007). In addition, many palaeoenvironmental data from Mediterranean countries were gathered by members of the Cambridge Palaeoeconomy movement of the 1970s-1990s. Notable examples are Graeme Barker's survey research in Yugoslavia (1975) and Italy (1991, 1995a, 1995b) and Bintliff and Snodgrass' project in Boeotia. The Cambridge School focused more on the economic aspects of archaeology, for instance in the work of Michael Jarman (1971, 1975), Iain Davidson (1981, 1983), Robin Dennell (1983), and Eric Sidney Higgs (1975). The latter is mainly known for the development of a method to evaluate the setting of each site (Site Catchment Analysis), together with geologist Claudio Vita-Finzi (1970).

[26] For example, Castelletti 1972, 1976, 1978; Costantini 1979, 1980, 1983a, 1983b, 1983c; Follieri 1971, 1973, 1975; Follieri and Coccolini 1979; Hjelmqvist 1977; LaCroix Phippen 1975; Pals and Voorrips 1979.

There is another good reason for this incorporation, namely to avoid certain factors that create bias in archaeobotanical research. As with all archaeological remains, the interpretation of archaeobotanical data should be treated with caution.[27] Although the archaeobotanical assemblage from a given site can provide much information, it is not necessarily representative of the actual range of species that may have been present at the time. Indeed, certain plant types are found much more frequently than others because they were more commonly used. This is particularly true for edible plants, but also for species that are used as medicine, fuel, construction material, etc. Moreover, the majority of archaeobotanical assemblages discussed in this study consists of carbonized plant remains. The interpretation of carbonized archaeobotanical remains brings its own set of problems, since not all plant remains have the same chance of survival. A great deal of literature has been dedicated to these complications.[28] Plant species that had no economic value, such as wild herbs, are less likely to have been preserved in the archaeobotanical assemblage. In order to overcome these biases, this study will integrate archaeobotanical studies with information from archaeological excavations, field surveys, ancient written sources, and archaeozoological studies.

To achieve the underlying aims, this study will focus on three major research themes in particular.

1. Long-term developments in landscape and land use that took place in southeast Italy between c. 1000 and 200 BC. In this period, the region underwent major processes of change connected to Greek colonization, urbanization, and the arrival of the Romans. These developments must have had far-reaching consequences for the natural landscape: new settlements and roads were built, previously untilled grounds were cultivated, and existing fields were used more intensively. At the same time, it is important to consider that the opportunities offered by the landscape, determined by factors such as soil quality, water availability, and relief, must have imposed limitations on these developments.

2. Long-term developments in the scale and organization of agricultural production. It can be assumed that the processes of urbanization, increasing interconnectivity, and increasing social complexity, resulted in changes in consumer-producer relations. By the time southeast Italy was incorporated in the Roman state (around the middle of the 3rd century BC), a relatively highly developed rural economy had emerged producing, among other products, wine and olive oil, on a scale that was large enough to export surplus to other parts of Italy and markets overseas. Clearly, this degree of socio-economic complexity did not develop overnight. However, when do we detect the first indications of an increase in the scale of agricultural production? I will investigate this process focusing on the following key terms:

a) Agricultural expansion, by which I mean an enlargement of the area that is used for agriculture, but also the increasing investment in the means of production per unit of ground area or, in animal husbandry, per head of livestock;

b) Agricultural rationalization, i.e. the introduction of rational, calculated motivations for the organization of land use;

c) Agricultural specialization, i.e. the introduction of a production method with which a settlement focuses on the production of a limited scope of agricultural products in order to gain a greater degree of productive efficiency. This is usually done with the aim of selling part of the produce on a market.

3. The effect of Greek colonization on landscape and land use. This is basically a sub-theme of the other two, to which I will pay particular attention. The coastal lands of southern Italy apparently appealed to Greek settlers.[29] At a specific point in time, colonial towns developed with strictly organized agricultural territories. What was the basis of subsistence for these towns? What did their agricultural territories look like and how did these *chorai* develop? Although we will see in the fol-

---

[27] Willerding 1971, 1991.

[28] For example, Hillman 1981, 1984; Boardman and Jones 1990; Van der Veen 2007.

[29] See Crielaard 2013 for the attitudes in the Greek epics towards sailing, travelling and other overseas activities.

lowing chapters that the traditional perspective on Greek colonization (with an active, 'civilizing' role for the colonists) has not escaped criticism, there can be no doubt that the process of defining colonial territories and intensifying agricultural production around the colonial towns affected land use practices elsewhere in southeast Italy. For example, it has often been assumed that Greek migrants introduced grape and olive cultivation to southern Italy.

1.3 RESEARCH METHOD

Micro level

To carry out this investigation, I discern three levels of interpretation: the micro, meso and macro levels. The first one is demonstrated in two case studies, i.e. the plant remains of the sites of l'Amastuola and Muro Tenente (for the location of these sites, see *Figure 1.1*). These sites were excavated in the 1990s and 2000s by VU University Amsterdam in collaboration with the Soprintendenza per i Beni Archeologici della Puglia. The excavations at l'Amastuola yielded remains of both Greek and indigenous[30] occupation, dating to the period between the late 8th and the first half of the 5th centuries BC. The settlement of Muro Tenente was continuously occupied from the 8th until the 1st century BC. These two sites were selected as case studies for the following reasons. Firstly, their occupational history covers most of the first millennium BC, the period under study. More importantly, the sites contain archaeological traces of some of the most important processes of change that characterize the first millennium BC. L'Amastuola has been interpreted as a mixed Greek-indigenous settlement, located outside the territory of the Greek colony of Taras. This makes it an excellent case for investigating the effects of the earliest phase of the Greek colonization and indigenous Greek relationships. The period represented by the excavations at l'Amastuola covers the late 8th until the first half of the 5th century BC. In the subsequent period, Muro Tenente had its most significant phase of growth. In the Early Hellenistic period, the settlement area expanded considerably and isolated farmsteads started to appear in the countryside around the site. These phenomena make the site of Muro Tenente particularly suited to studying the processes of rural landscape infill and urbanization that took place in large parts of southeast Italy between the late 4th and 3rd centuries BC.

In the first two chapters of this book, I will present the archaeobotanical evidence extracted from the sites of l'Amastuola and Muro Tenente. Combining this information with archaeological and archaeozoological data, I will attempt to shed light on several important aspects of everyday life at these settlements. I will focus on four research aspects: 1) the use of wood; 2) food preparation and diet; 3) the cultivation of grapes and olives; and 4) the use of plants in ritual activities. The discussion will be structured around these research aspects, which means that I will pay only limited attention to chronological differences.

Meso level

After these two case studies, I will proceed with the interpretation on a meso level. At this stage of interpretation, the case studies will be put into a wider spatial and chronological context. I will discuss the regional landscapes that were exploited by the inhabitants of l'Amastuola and Muro Tenente.

---

[30] The labels 'Iapygians' and 'Messapians' for the peoples that inhabited these parts of southern Italy derive from the accounts by ancient Greek authors. For example, the Greek historian Diodorus Siculus (1st century BC) notes that the oracle of Delphi made the following promise to the Spartan party that was going to settle at Taras in 706 BC: 'I have given to you Satyrion and Taras, a rich country to dwell in and to be a plague to the Iapyges' (after Burgers and Crielaard 2007). For a discussion of the ethnic background of these people, see Yntema 2009.

Archaeological and archaeobotanical research data will be used to reconstruct agricultural strategies and methods of land use. I will pay special attention to chronological developments in both sites' rural economies and attempt to detect specific differences. In addition, I will focus on the natural landscape around the sites. Where did the inhabitants of l'Amastuola and Muro Tenente go to hunt, collect fire and construction wood, and gather wild food and other natural resources? What did the landscapes surrounding these two sites look like?

Macro level (a)
Finally, the analysis will be brought to a macro level, which represents both a regional and a diachronic level of interpretation. In other words, the final purpose of this study is to create an overview of long-term developments in the way land use in southeast Italy developed in the course of the roughly eight centuries under study. This overview will also include research data from the Recent and Final Bronze Age, which are essential to our understanding of the following centuries. The overview will be based on archaeobotanical studies from all sites in southeast Italy inhabited during the first millennium BC for which such studies have been carried out. These results will be integrated into a multidisciplinary framework by including the results of other types of research, including:
1. Archaeological excavation data;
2. Field survey data;
3. Archaeozoological data;
4. Ancient written texts.

Combining these results, I will discuss the same research aspects I focused on in the analysis on a micro level (i.e. the use of wood, food preparation and diet, the cultivation of grapes and olives, and the use of plants in ritual activities).

Macro level (b)
In the second part of the macro level analysis, I will integrate the results from the sites in southeast Italy into a diachronic overview of changes in landscape and land use in southeast Italy between c. 1000 and 200 BC.

1.4 STRUCTURE OF THE BOOK

This study is divided into seven chapters. Chapters 2 and 3 deal with the case studies of l'Amastuola and Muro Tenente, i.e. the interpretation on a micro- or site level. In chapter 4, the focus will be widened to the meso level, putting the results from the case studies into a broader spatial context. This will result in an analysis of the rural economies and exploitation of the surrounding landscape at l'Amastuola and Muro Tenente. The macro level of research is discussed in chapters 5 and 6. Chapter 5 includes the archaeobotanical research data from southeast Italy and their interpretation. It focuses on recurring research aspects, including the use of wood, diet and food preparation, the cultivation of grapes and olives, and the use of plants in ritual activities. In chapter 6, I will review the research conducted on landscape and settlement dynamics in pre-Roman southeast Italy and compose an overview of long-term developments, i.e. the interpretation on a macro level. The last chapter (7) summarizes the results of this study and offers suggestions for further research. Finally, a catalogue of the archaeobotanical research data and a separate Appendix with tables and figures is attached.

Chapter 2 – Case study 1: L'Amastuola

2.1 INTRODUCTION: THE SITE AND ITS SURROUNDINGS

The site of l'Amastuola is located on a flat-topped, elongated ridge about 220 metres above sea level (see *Figures 2.1 and 2.2*). The site derives its name from the *masseria* (landed estate) that occupies the hilltop; the ancient name is unknown. The nearest modern towns are Massafra and Statte, and the site is no more than 15 kilometres away from Taranto, the former Spartan colony of Taras. The l'Amastuola hill offers a good view of the surrounding countryside and of the coastline of the Gulf of Taranto. The slopes are relatively steep, especially on the south and south-west sides of the hill. This steepness makes access rather difficult to the so-called 'south terrace', where the archaeological excavations have taken place. An extensive *necropolis* is located approximately a kilometre south of the l'Amastuola hill.

In Ester van Joolen's evaluation of land systems, l'Amastuola is placed in the *Mottola undulating sloping land system*.[1] She describes the area as a landscape of relatively small valleys and hills that are traversed by canyon-like river valleys (*gravine*). One such canyon-like river valley can be found near the site and is aptly named Gravina dell'Amastuola. In the undulating sloping land system, a wide variety of rock formations and sediments occur, probably formed by differential erosion. The landscape along the coast is very different from the hilly inland. This strip of land, which Van Joolen named the *Taranto coastal land system*, is characterized by a coastal landscape of mobile dunes, interspersed with lagoons and the occasional steep cliff.[2] According to Van Joolen, the dunes and the soils in the dry lagoons are not suitable for agriculture because of their high salt and low clay content. However, landscape reconstruction based on lithological and (micro)faunal criteria in the central part of the Taras floodplain by Ruben Lelivelt[3] has shown that between the Early Bronze Age and late Roman times the Tarantine coastline consisted of a peat land that was probably periodically flooded. These lagoons may have been used for fishing and gathering of shellfish in the past. Lelivelt also concluded that the salinity levels were low enough to have allowed farming in the marshes.[4]

The *masseria* on the l'Amastuola hill was used in sub-recent times for a mixed farming system with crop cultivation (cereals, fruits, and vegetables) and livestock (cows and sheep/goats). In the surrounding countryside, olives, cereals, citrus fruits, watermelons, and figs were cultivated. The *masseria* l'Amastuola and its surrounding arable grounds were recently purchased by the Kikau group, a company that produces aluminium window shutters. It aims to create a historical landscape park in the area. As a first step, the olive trees around the l'Amastuola hill have been replaced with an extensive vineyard, and a large number of olive trees was imported from elsewhere to be placed along the roads.[5]

---

[1] Van Joolen 2003, pp. 55-58, Figure 3.8.
[2] Van Joolen 2003, pp. 49-51, Figure 5.5.
[3] Lelivelt 2013.
[4] Lelivelt 2013, p. 101.
[5] www.kikau.it. In the near future, the various buildings of the masseria complex are to be restored and used for exhibitions, wine tastings, and a small museum dedicated to the archaeological site will be opened.

Fig. 2.1. Aerial view of the l'Amastuola hilltop. Photo: Società Kikau.

2.2 HISTORY OF RESEARCH

The archaeological research at l'Amastuola hill started in 1988, when G.A. Maruggi of the Soprintendenza per i Beni Archeologici della Puglia investigated the above-mentioned *necropolis* some 800 metres south of the l'Amastuola hill. It is estimated to have contained over 1,000 burials, consisting of rectangular cut-outs in the limestone rock, the vast majority of which have been emptied by grave robbers. A total of 154 tombs were excavated by Maruggi, who concluded that the earliest graves are located in the western part of the cemetery area and date to the second quarter of the 7th century BC. Later, the *necropolis* expanded further to the east; it continued to be used for burials until the early 5th century BC. According to Maruggi, both the grave goods and the burial practices testify to an exclusively Greek milieu.[6] In 1991, the Soprintendenza started archaeological research on the south terrace of the l'Amastuola hill. The excavations unearthed a series of buildings that yielded evidence of both indigenous and Greek inhabitation. In Maruggi's view, the earliest indigenous settlement was destroyed in the early 7th century BC and replaced by Greek-style houses of people who used Greek pottery. This suggests that the new inhabitants were Greek colonists, who arrived at l'Amastuola one generation after the foundation of Taras.[7] This view also ties in with the finds in the *necropolis*, which appeared to be exclusively Greek.

The fieldwork at l'Amastuola was continued in 2003 by VU University, in collaboration with the Soprintendenza.[8] Between 2003 and 2008, seven trenches were opened on the south terrace (*Figure*

[6] Maruggi 1996, p. 201.
[7] Maruggi 1996, pp. 215-217.
[8] Preliminary reports: Burgers and Crielaard 2007; Crielaard and Burgers 2012. Final report: Burgers and Crielaard 2011.

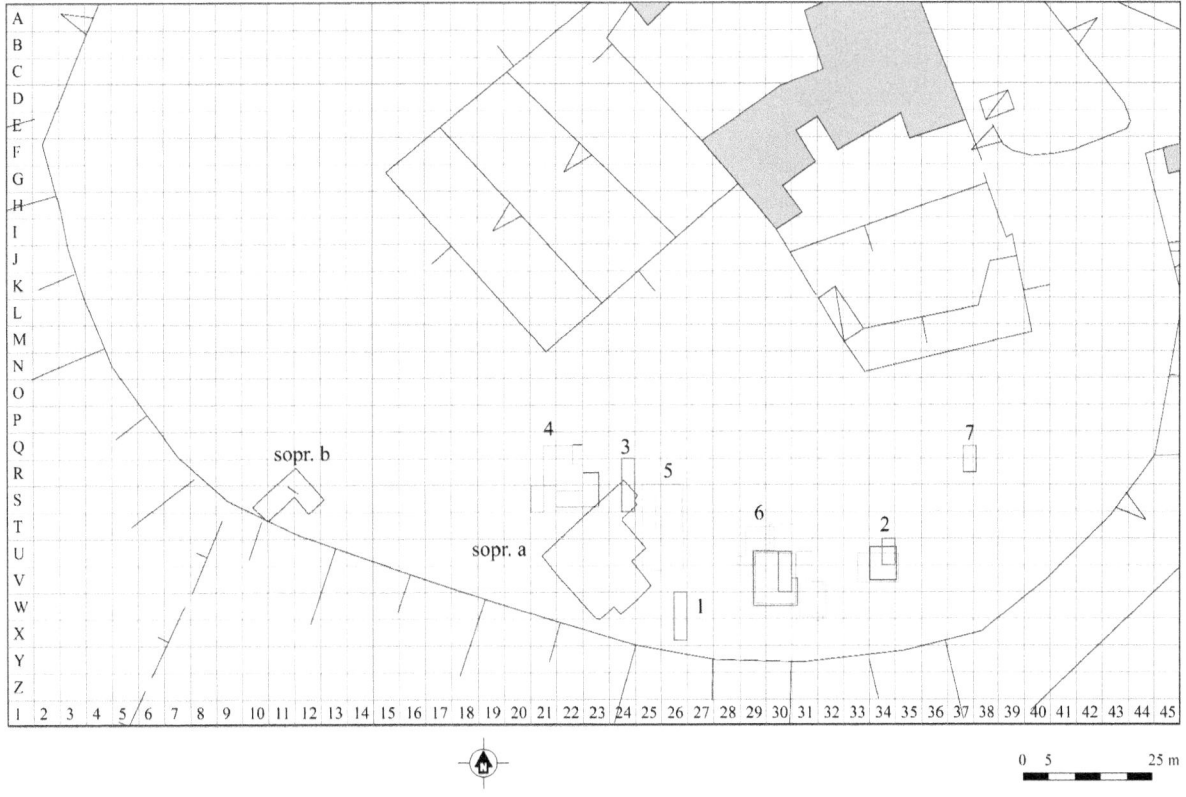

Fig. 2.2a. L'Amastuola, south terrace: Location of the excavation trenches. Map by Jaap Fokkema.

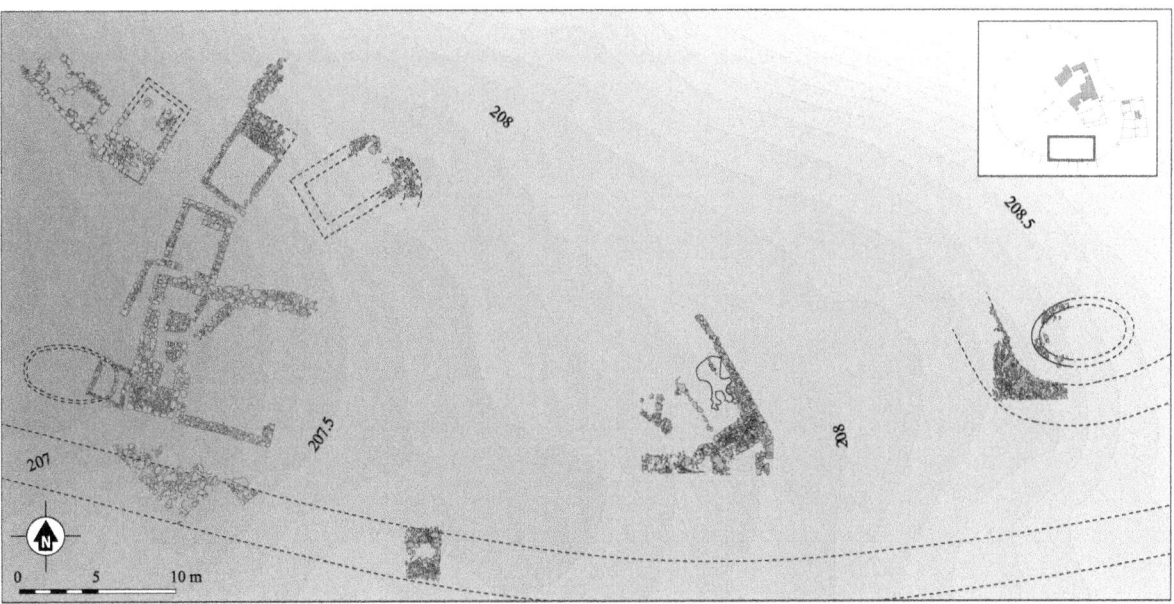

Fig. 2.2b. L'Amastuola, south terrace: Location of the excavation trenches. Map by Bert Brouwenstijn.

2.2), accompanied by field surveys (both on-site and in the surrounding area), non-destructive geophysical surveys, geo-archaeological and archaeobotanical analyses, and further exploration of the *necropolis* area. Based on these investigations, G.-J. Burgers and J.P. Crielaard reached different conclusions about the settlement on the l'Amastuola hill. In their view, the evidence supplied by domestic architecture, material culture, and burial practices is not indicative of a hostile takeover of the indigenous settlement by Greek colonists. For instance, it was discovered that the indigenous fortification wall was built around 670 BC, which is a few decades later than the date proposed by Maruggi. This later date contrasts with the idea that the indigenous habitation met a violent end in the early 7th century BC. Clearly, it would be odd to construct an indigenous-type defence system around a settlement that is part of the territory of a Greek *polis*. Instead, Burgers and Crielaard argue that during most of the 7th and 6th centuries BC, the south terrace housed a mixed Greek-indigenous community that was orientated towards its (indigenous) neighbours in the west (especially l'Incoronata and Siris), rather than the Greek colony of Taras in the east.[9] As these authors have shown, the adaption of Greek customs was probably a long-term process at l'Amastuola. Combining the survey data with the excavation results, Burgers and Crielaard proposed as a working hypothesis that the l'Amastuola area was incorporated in the Tarentine *chora* only in the course of the 5th century BC, not in the early 7th century.[10] Around this time, both the settlement on the l'Amastuola hill and the south *necropolis* were abandoned. At the same time, small rural sites started to appear in the surrounding countryside. This development may be related to the northward and westward expansion of the Tarentine *chora*.

Evaluating the different views on the settlement on the l'Amastuola hill, it is clear that this site is of special interest for the ongoing debate on early Greek migration in southern Italy. As a mixed Greek/indigenous site at a close distance to the colony of Taras, l'Amastuola is an excellent case study for investigating the nature of the relationships between Greek and indigenous populations. The site also has other attractive features that make it well-suited for this study. As we will see in chapter 5, archaeobotanical samples from the formative stages of the Greek colonization process are relatively rare. Since the effect of this process on the exploitation and organization of the landscape is one of the main research themes of this study, the archaeobotanical data from l'Amastuola are of crucial importance.

2.3 THE ARCHAEOLOGICAL RESEARCH

Before discussing the results of the archaeobotanical analysis at l'Amastuola, a more detailed introduction to the history of the settlement is required. First, I will present a short diachronic overview of the results of the archaeological investigations. I will then focus on a number of different types of contexts that were either intensively sampled and contained interesting archaeobotanical material, or are of specific interest for the interpretation of the site.

2.3.1 DIACHRONIC OVERVIEW

According to Burgers and Crielaard, the l'Amastuola hill was occupied from the late 8th century onwards.[11] The first traces of occupation on the south terrace are represented by the scant remains of three curvilinear huts, the outer *agger* and a second, inner *agger*-type fortification wall, together with impasto and matt-painted pottery, some metal objects, and remains of building material. The site has also supplied

---

[9] Burgers and Crielaard 2007, pp. 106-107. In fact, there is a large volume of published studies describing the extremely complex and much-debated use of material culture to attribute archaeological evidence to a certain ethnic group. Many scholarly publications have been dedicated to the possible interpretation of 'native' and 'Greek' material culture in south-eastern Italy; see for example Morel 1984; Whitehouse and Wilkins 1989; Yntema 2000; Burgers and Crielaard 2007; Crielaard and Burgers 2012.

[10] Burgers and Crielaard 2007, p. 107.

[11] This diachronic overview is based on the preliminary reports of the investigations at l'Amastuola, i.e. Burgers and Crielaard 2007, 2011; Crielaard and Burgers 2012.

Fig. 2.3. L'Amastuola, trench 6: Digital reconstruction of the cultic structure by Bert Brouwenstijn.

evidence of cultic activities from this earliest phase, including the remains of a one-time cultic event, probably a ritual feast, and another large deposition of votive material in one of the huts. A third context of ritual origin was found about 15 metres to the southeast of the latter deposition. Here, a large number of votive offerings was found with an exceptionally long chronological range (c. 400 years), indicating that this location was already in use for cultic activities as early as the first half of the 7th century BC.

Greek influences became increasingly apparent at l'Amastuola during the later 7th and 6th centuries BC. This development is particularly evident in the south *necropolis*, which came into use around 675 BC. Its location, tomb types, manner of deposition, and grave inventories are all in line with Greek traditions.[12] In addition, the huts in the settlement were replaced by rectangular, Greek-style houses (*oikoi*). It is clear that this replacement happened gradually and should not be interpreted as a clear break in the site's settlement history, since some of the huts continued to be inhabited when the first rectangular houses were already in use.[13] Other changes in material culture are also visible in this period, such as the replacement of impasto and matt-painted wares by pottery of a Greek type. By the end of the 6th century, or perhaps even earlier, Greek-style pottery was indeed produced on site in a potter's workshop. The presence of this workshop, and a smithy producing iron objects, suggests that the settlement belonged to a largely self-sufficient community.

---

[12] However, the find of a human-size *stele* of local stone in the *necropolis* area strongly suggests that burial traditions were not exclusively of the Greek type. It is distantly related to the well-known Daunian *stelai*, but has its closest parallels in examples from indigenous sites in Salento, such as Cavallino, Mesagne and Muro Tenente. For this reason, Burgers and Crielaard (2007, p. 100) have argued that it is at odds in an otherwise Greek-type funerary context, and may be considered an expression not only of ethnic identity but also of gender, status, and elite solidarity with peer groups in indigenous Salento.

[13] For example, there is a chronological overlap between the hut remains found in Trench 2 and Maruggi's *oikoi* β and γ. Burgers and Crielaard 2007, p. 106.

Both the surveys and the excavations indicate that the settlement was largely abandoned before the middle of the 5th century BC. The survey data show that a new settlement was laid out on the lower terraces north and east of the hilltop.[14] This new settlement, which has not been excavated, was apparently much larger than the one on the south terrace. The finds of large, carefully dressed blocks indicate that it was also characterized by a different, more monumental type of architecture. In the same period, the settlement pattern around the l'Amastuola hill changed dramatically. The landscape around the site had been almost void of other settlements in the Archaic and Classical periods, but as the surveys showed, numerous small rural sites started to appear all over a relatively large area covering the terraces below the l'Amastuola hill in the 4th century BC.

Meanwhile, mud slides quickly covered most of the archaeological structures on the south terrace with layers of washed-down earth and debris.[15] However, not all activities on the l'Amastuola hill came to a halt. Cultic activities continued on the same location where the deposition of votive offerings had started in the early 7th century BC. At some point, probably in the 4th century BC, a tomb-like cultic structure made of large, stone blocks was built here (*Figure 2.3*), which may have been dedicated to the *Dioskouroi* (see below, section 2.5.4).[16] Assuming that the l'Amastuola hill had been incorporated into the Tarantine *chora* at this point, Crielaard and Burgers have suggested that the building could have been erected by the Tarentines as a territorial marker.[17] Judging from the latest datable votive material, the cult came to an end in the early 3rd century BC. The cultic structure was destroyed and a large pit was dug to dump the stone blocks. A possible explanation for this course of events may be found in the Roman conquest of southern Italy around this time. The burying of the blocks is then taken to symbolize the clearance of signs of Tarentine domination in the area.

2.3.2 SPECIFIC CONTEXTS

Iron Age huts
The earliest habitation remains on the south terrace consisted of curvilinear huts with stone plinths and possibly wattle-and-daub and/or mud brick walls, which can be dated to the late 8th and 7th centuries BC. Three such huts were excavated on the south terrace of the l'Amastuola hill; one by the Soprintendenza and two by the VU University team (*Figures 2.6, 2.8a,* and *2.9a*).[18] The hut in trench 5 (*Figure 2.9a*) was about 5 metres long and 3 metres wide, with a stone base that was constructed directly on top of the bedrock. In the northeast corner of the hut in trench 2, many burned high-quality matt-painted pottery shards were found, along with a few other artefacts that can be associated with wool production, including a spindle whorl, a loom weight, and a terracotta 'spool' that may have been used for tablet weaving.[19] The combination of these specific artefacts and other objects with burnt organic

---

[14] Burgers and Crielaard 2007, pp. 92-99.

[15] Mud slides created two distinct layers that are referred to as colluvium 1 and 2. Colluvium 1 was found mainly in trench 2 and was probably deposited in the 6th century BC. It contained pottery and architectural elements such as mud brick, which were probably washed down from higher grounds towards the top of the hill. Geochemical analyses showed that the upper part of colluvium 1 was rich in phosphates, suggesting that the washed-down earth was manured in later times. Its presence in trench 2 might indicate that the occupation of that part of the terrace had already come to an end by this time. Colluvium 2, on the other hand, can almost certainly be linked to the phase of abandonment of the south terrace in the 5th century BC. Burgers and Crielaard 2007, pp. 101-102.

[16] Crielaard 2011, p. 88.

[17] Crielaard and Burgers 2012, p. 87.

[18] Maruggi 1996, pp. 216-217 (Fig. 19); Burgers and Crielaard 2007, p. 86; Crielaard and Burgers 2012, pp. 71-72.

[19] Crielaard 2011, p. 50. As explained by Gleba (2008, pp. 103-104, 127-128, 140-143), these three types of objects represent different stages in the process of textile production. A spindle whorl is positioned on a spindle and provides weight and tension for spinning fibres into

Fig. 2.4. L'Amastuola, trench 4: Burnt loam showing wood impressions. Burgers and Crielaard 2007, 89 (Fig. 16).

remains suggest that this was an intentional deposition, possibly of a ritual nature.[20] Outside this hut, a thin band of burnt clay was uncovered that may have been associated with an open fireplace or hearth.

In addition, traces of Iron Age occupation were also excavated in trenches 3, 4, and 6.[21] In trench 3, pieces of burnt loam and traces of burning were found, as well as fragments of smashed matt-painted vases (datable mostly to the 7th century BC) and the lower part of a small, undecorated container or storage jar (*Figure 2.25*) that contained charred botanical material. In trench 6, the possible remains of the cooking facilities of a hut were uncovered (*Figure 2.10a*). The area was much disturbed and did not reveal any walls from the Early Iron Age phase, but contained many animal bone fragments, a hearth, an oven and a few other fireplaces that were probably used for low-temperature cooking. A layer (unit 620) that was possibly connected to the same 'hut', but may also represent another domestic context from the Early Iron Age phase, is situated to its southwest. Here, traces of burning were found, as well as a spindle whorl, an iron nail, some loom weights, and much pottery, mostly matt-painted and impasto wares. Finally, some probable remains of walls or roofs were found in trench 4, in the levelling material that was used to prepare the area for later construction activities.[22] They consisted of lumps of burnt loam with impressions of branches

thread. Loom weights keep the warp of a warp-weighted loom taut during weaving. Spools (Italian *rocchetti*) are small cylindrical objects, made of terracotta and ranging in length between 3 and 10 cm. Although their function is still widely debated, most scholars agree that they are in some way associated with textile production. Ræder Knudsen (2002, pp. 228-229) and Gleba (2008, p. 141) have argued that they performed a similar function as loom weights on a standing loom. Spools, however, may have been used as small weights for the sets of threads passing through tablets representing a different weaving method, so-called tablet weaving.

[20] Burgers and Crielaard 2007, p. 86.
[21] Burgers and Crielaard 2007, p. 89, Crielaard and Burgers 2012, pp. 70-71 and pp. 89-90.
[22] Burgers and Crielaard 2007, p. 89.

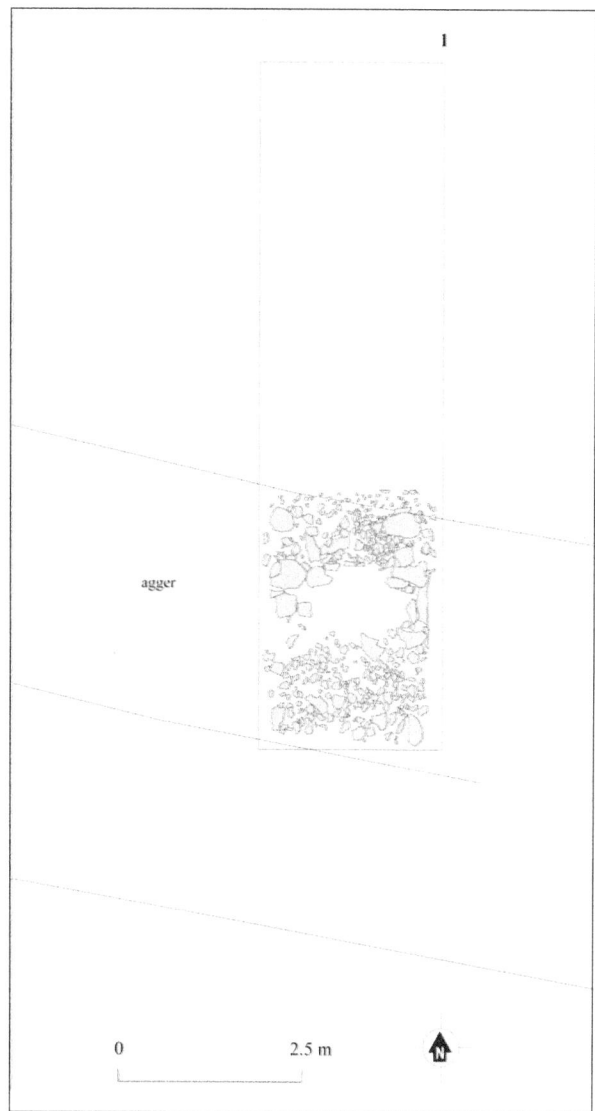

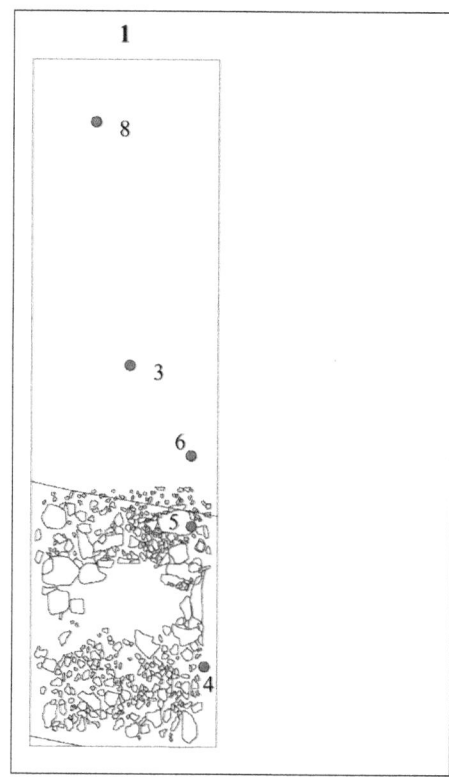

Fig. 2.5b. L'Amastuola, trench 1: Location of the archaeobotanical samples. Drawing by Jaap Fokkema.

Fig. 2.5a. L'Amastuola, trench 1: Location of the archaeological finds. Drawing by Jaap Fokkema.

or stalks (*Figure 2.4*). The imprints seemed to belong to both smaller plants or trees and larger branches, but were generally too large in diameter (between 3 and 4 centimetres) to have been made by reed.[23]

The ritual deposition in trench 6

In the north-east part of trench 6, a circular feature of hard-packed clay (unit 509) was uncovered (*Figure 2.10a*). Underneath this layer, a black semi-circular area was found that had a hard whitish band around it (units 501 and 510, *Figure 2.11*). This feature contained a huge amount of pottery, both burnt and unburnt shards, sometimes belonging to the same pots, of a variety of shapes that can mostly be related to the communal consumption of food and wine.[24] As a possible interpretation, Crielaard has

[23] Research of reed varieties from all over the world that was carried out by Laura Kooistra (pers. comm.) has shown that reed stalks rarely grow thicker than 2 or 3 centimetres. This seems to be confirmed by the descriptions of the Gramineae, Cyperaceae and Typhaceae families in Tutin *et al.* 1980, pp. 118-267 and pp. 275-323.

[24] Preliminary results pottery analyses: Crielaard and Burgers 2010; Crielaard 2011, pp. 69-75, Figures 3-33, 3-34, 3-35, 3-36, 3-37, Tabella 2.

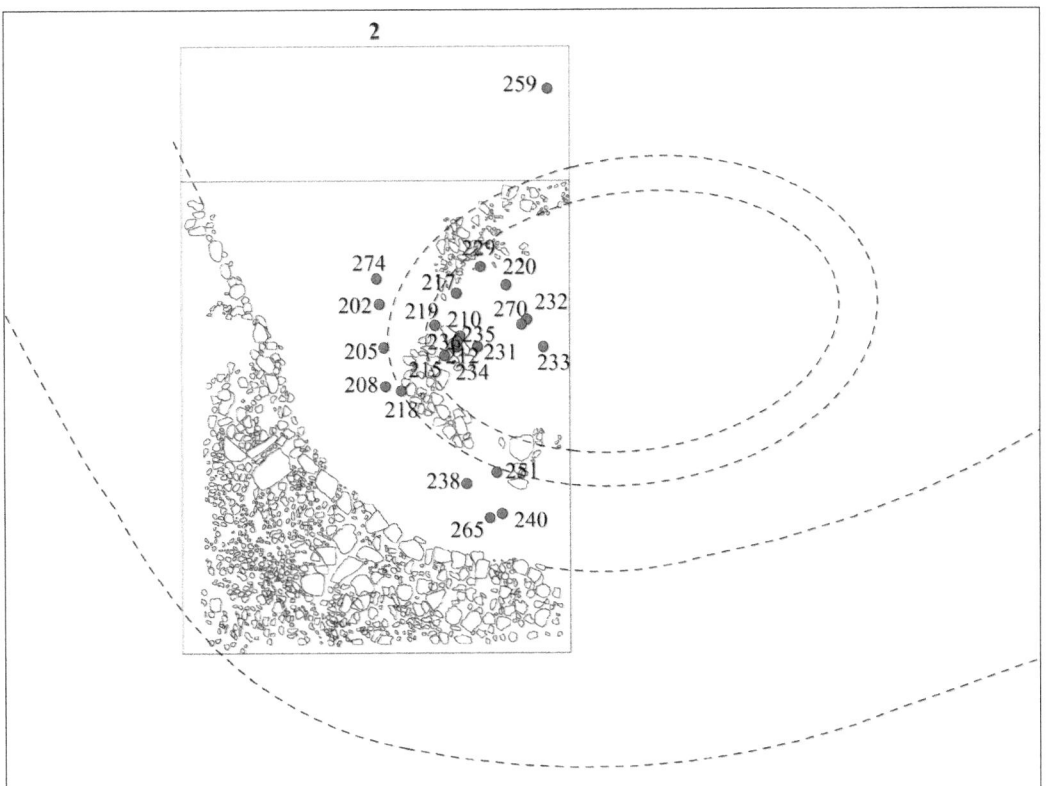

Fig. 2.6a. L'Amastuola, trench 2: Location of the archaeological finds. Drawing by Jaap Fokkema.
Fig. 2.6b. L'Amastuola, trench 2: Location of the archaeobotanical samples. Drawing by Jaap Fokkema.

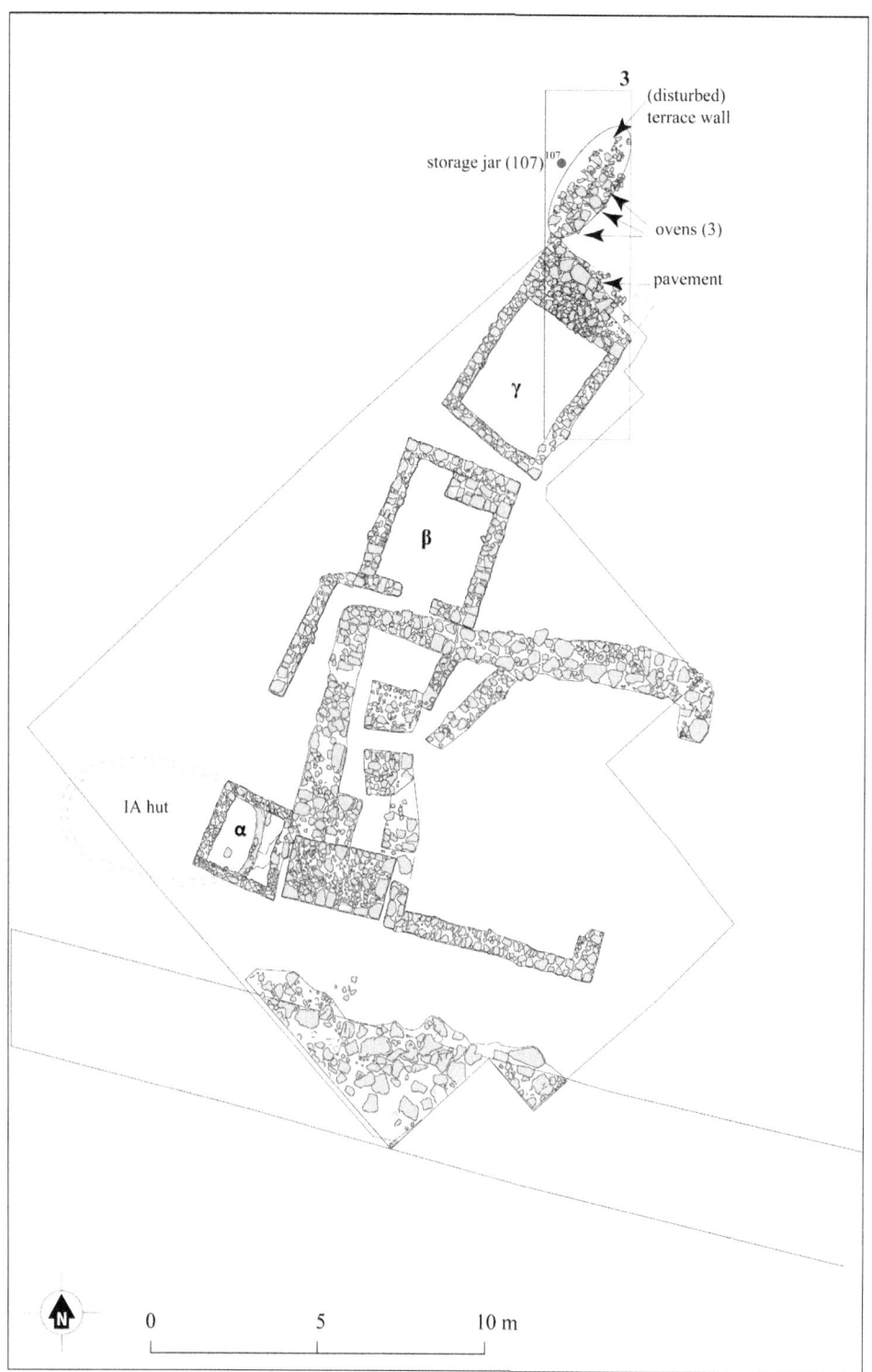

Fig. 2.7a. L'Amastuola, trench 3: Location of the archaeological finds. Drawing by Jaap Fokkema.

suggested that after the ritual consumption of food and drink, the vases were smashed and the fragments left in the ashes.[25] The black area also contained much charcoal and several domestic objects, including a grinding stone and terracotta loom weights, 'spools', a marble, a spindle whorl, and a conical object of unknown function. The evidence suggests that the ritual might have been a one-time

[25] Crielaard 2011, pp. 72-73.

Fig. 2.7b. L'Amastuola, trench 3: Location of the archaeobotanical samples. Drawing by Jaap Fokkema.

event. Since the pottery comprised especially Sub-Geometric fine wares (with a minority of coarse wares and handmade wares, including matt-painted), this event is likely to have taken place in the first half of the 7th century BC. This means that it can be related to an early stage in the settlement's occupation history, probably not long after Greeks had settled at l'Amastuola.[26]

Greek-style buildings/oikoi

The first three Greek-style structures, building α and *oikoi* β and γ, were excavated by the Soprintendenza in the 1990s (*Figure 2.7a*).[27] The VU excavations also unearthed several rectangular, one-room houses, *oikoi* ε and η and buildings δ, ζ and θ (*Figures 2.8a* and *2.9a*).[28] VU-trench 3 was located directly north of *oikos* γ; in this area, a much-disturbed terrace wall was found that seemed to be a continuation of the north-west wall of *oikos* γ (*Figure 2.5*).[29] In niches in the south-eastern face of this wall, the remains of two or three small (bread?) ovens were discovered. The pottery associated with these ovens was mainly of Greek colonial type. This trench also contained a pavement of large flagstones, already partly uncovered by the Soprintendenza, which was probably in use until the late 6th century BC.

This occupation period, between the late 7th and late 6th centuries BC, seems to be roughly the same for all the Greek-style buildings on the south terrace. Building δ was uncovered in the western part of the trench 4 (*Figure 2.8a*).[30] It had a tile roof and a floor of beaten earth mixed with lime. Inside the room, a hearth, a stone mortar, and fragments of a storage vessel and the upper parts of water contain-

[26] Crielaard 2011, p. 73.
[27] Maruggi 1996, pp. 203-214.
[28] Burgers and Crielaard 2007, pp. 89-92; Crielaard and Burgers 2012, pp. 70-90.
[29] Burgers and Crielaard 2007, pp. 87-89.
[30] Burgers and Crielaard 2007, pp. 89-90; Crielaard 2011, pp. 57-59.

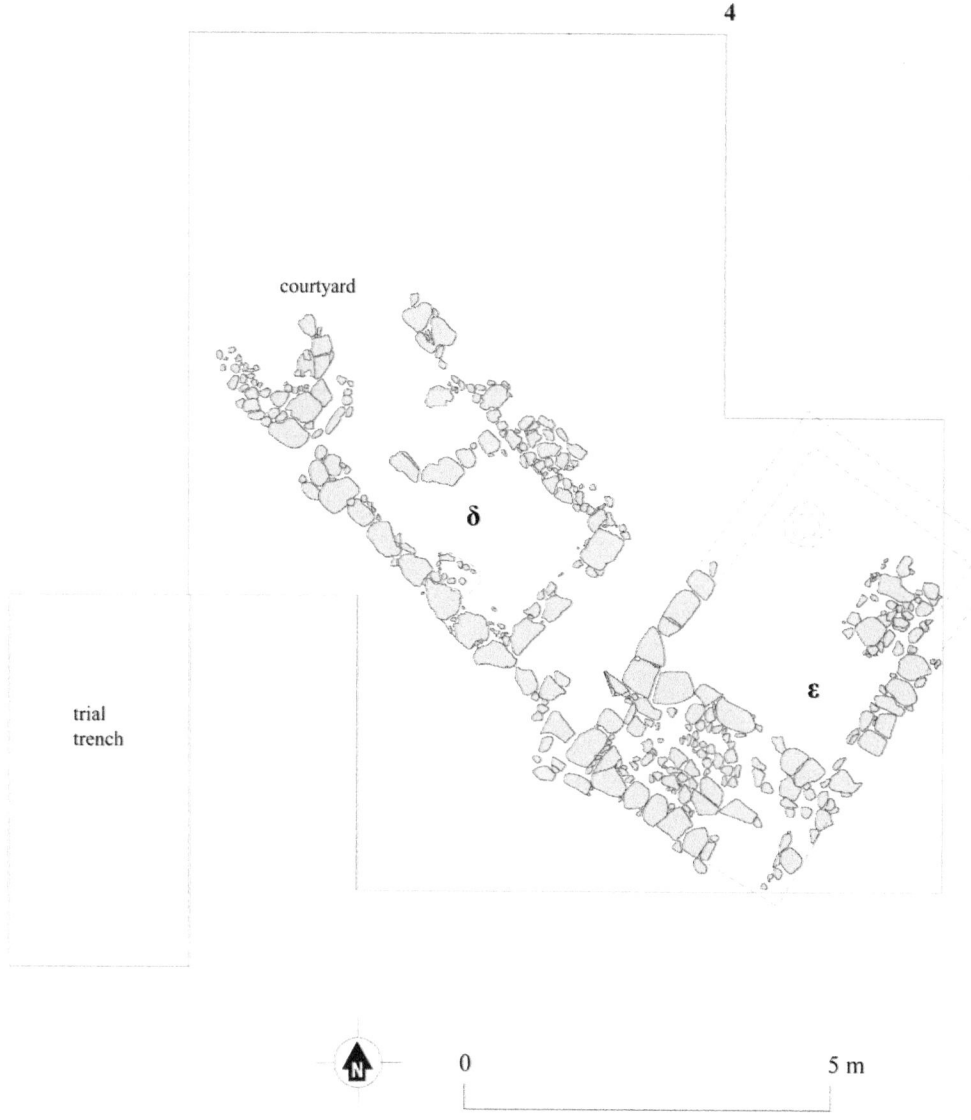

Fig. 2.8a. L'Amastuola, trench 4: Location of the archaeological finds. Drawing by Jaap Fokkema.

ers (*hydriai*) were found. These *hydriai* were dug into the floor and could have been used as pot stands. Considering its inventory and the fact that it seems too small (2.9 x 4.8 m) to be an independent house, building δ was interpreted as a kitchen facility. It may have been part of a larger building complex, possibly a courtyard house. South-east of this building, the foundations of *oikos* ε were unearthed. As I mentioned above, this structure seems to have housed a smithy. It consisted of a stone-paved antechamber and an inner room that contained both objects for domestic use (such as spindle whorls and a grinding stone) and various iron objects. The oven that might have been used to heat the metal was situated in the northern part of the room. To the southeast of this oven a stone workbench was discovered. Small pieces of metal bloom were found scattered outside the building.

Three other rectangular structures, buildings ζ, θ and η, were uncovered in trench 5 (*Figure 2.9a*).[31] All three buildings were probably covered with roof tiles. Building ζ was constructed on top of the

[31] Burgers and Crielaard 2007, pp. 90-91; Crielaard 2011, pp. 62-67.

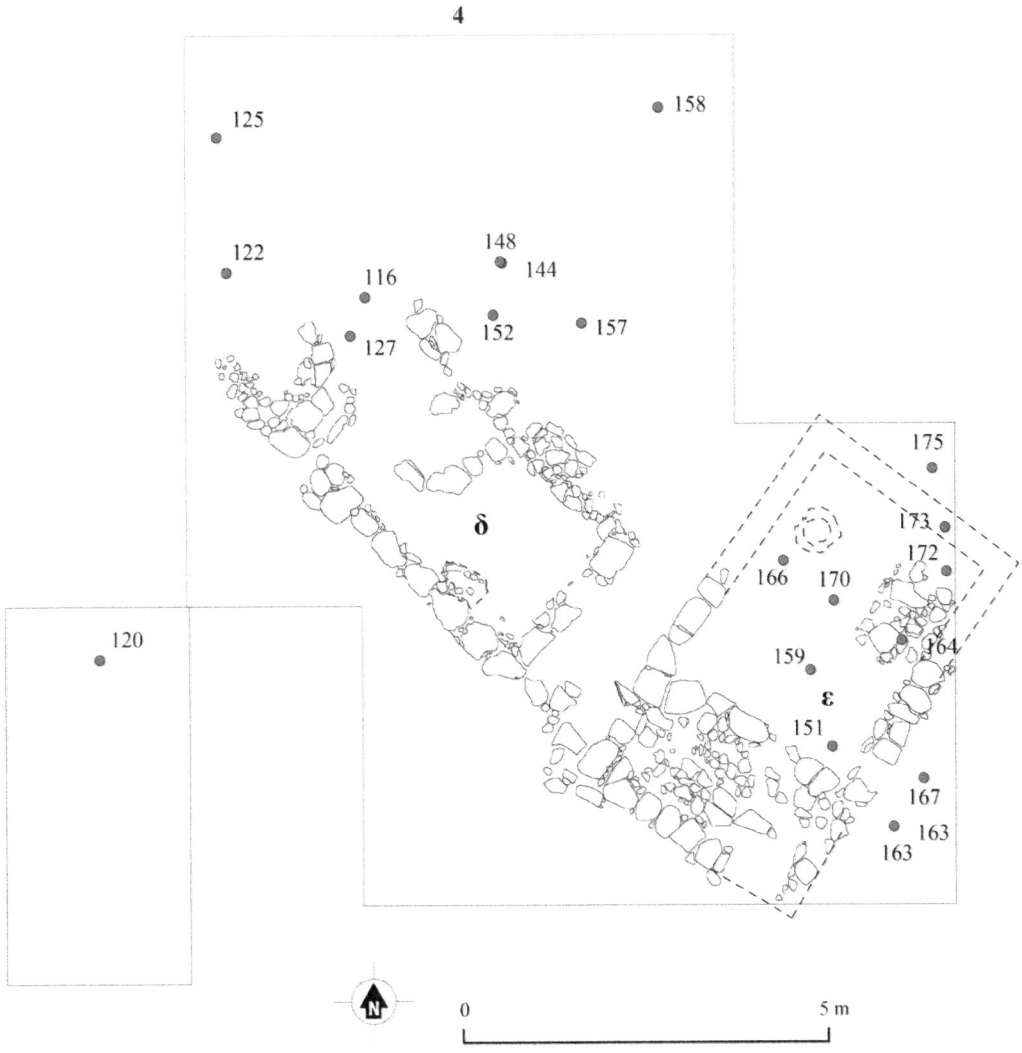

Fig. 2.8b. L'Amastuola, trench 4: Location of the archaeobotanical samples. Drawing by Jaap Fokkema.

Iron Age hut in this trench, partly re-using the hut's foundation stones. Associated pottery from this structure comprised 'colonial' fine wares, impasto, a Corinthian type-A transport amphora, and storage jars. Inside this structure, a burnt layer was uncovered that may have been associated with a pyrotechnic feature, probably an open fireplace. Building θ was built against the south side of ζ, somewhere in the later 7th century BC. The floor matrix provided an interesting array of finds, including carbonized plant remains, burnt loam, a trapezoidal and a rounded cone-shaped spindle whorl, a loom weight, a bronze arrow head, and an iron double axe. A piece of antler and bones of red deer (*Cervus elaphus*) were found inside and just outside this building.

Oikos η was located to the southeast of buildings ζ and θ. Only the western wall and part of what seems to be a portico and entrance on the south side were excavated. The pottery finds from the floor levels (coarse cooking ware, 'colonial' wares, *hydriai*, a Corinthian type-A transport amphora and *pithoi*, but no matt-painted ceramics) indicate that it was slightly later in date than the other two buildings, ζ and θ. The *oikos* complex was completed by an outside area between buildings θ and η. Here, two circular stone platforms were located that have been interpreted as silos for grain storage

Fig. 2.9a. L'Amastuola, trench 5: Location of the archaeological finds. Drawing by Jaap Fokkema.

(*Figure 2.12*).[32] Both platforms had a diameter of almost two metres and were constructed of mainly small stones, delineated by a ring of medium-sized stones, some of which were found standing in a vertical position, suggesting that the platforms supported some kind of superstructure. Bands of yellowish soil, which can probably also be connected to this superstructure, were found surround-

[32] This interpretation is based on parallels with similar structures from Greece and western Anatolia which were also interpreted as silos. For a detailed discussion, see *Box 2*.

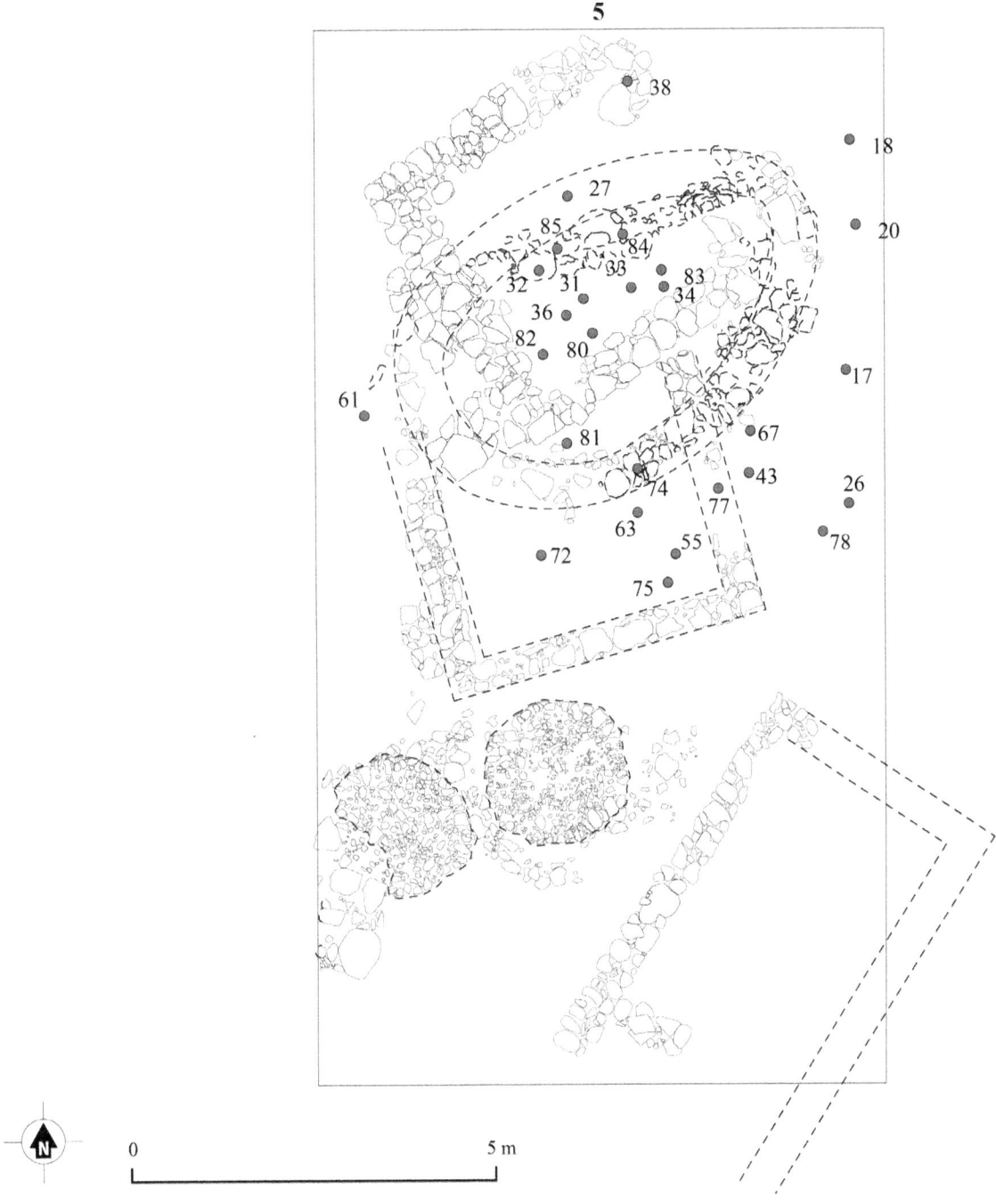

Fig. 2.9b. L'Amastuola, trench 5: Location of the archaeobotanical samples. Drawing by Jaap Fokkema.

ing each of the platforms. Unfortunately, the structures contained very little datable material and no botanical macroremains, but the find of a hydria handle from the yellowish soil suggests that the platforms were in use in the same period as buildings θ and ζ.

Potter's workshop

The workshop that was uncovered in trench 6 belongs to the same phase as the *oikoi* in the occupational history of the south terrace. It appears to have been in use between the late 7th and the early 5th

Fig. 2.10a. L'Amastuola, trench 6: Location of the archaeological finds. Drawing by Jaap Fokkema.

century BC (*Figure 2.10a*).[33] The workshop contained two levigation tanks and at least three kilns, a large one in the south-east part (kiln D) and two smaller (kiln C and E) on the other side. However, during the excavations in 2007 it became clear that not all kilns were in use at the same time and that the workshop was modified and restructured during at least three building phases. Phase 1 is represented by a floor constructed with the help of large flagstones, kiln D, and possibly also kiln E. In phase 2, a courtyard wall was constructed, running north-west/south-east and delineating the

[33] Crielaard 2011, pp. 75-76.

Fig. 2.10b. L'Amastuola, trench 6: Location of the archaeobotanical samples. Drawing by Jaap Fokkema.

workshop in the east. In the south-east and south, the stone levigation tank and two rounded basins were placed. Kiln C was also in use in phase 2. Phase 3 belongs to the youngest habitation phases on the south terrace, and can be placed in the first half of the 5th century BC. In this period, the working area was levelled with a new, thick floor (unit 313) that contained a hearth and several objects that can be associated with a typical domestic context, such as loom weights, kitchenware, an iron object that was interpreted as a roasting spit (*obelos*), and a cooking pot with the carbonized remains of a sort of gruel (see below).

Fig. 2.11. L'Amastuola, trench 6: Black semicircular area (units 501 and 510). Burgers and Crielaard 2011, 69 (Figures 3-32).

To the northwest of the workshop structure, a half-open space was excavated that probably had a domestic function.[34] The structure contained a succession of floors or surfaces, mainly dating to the 6th century BC, with numerous domestic objects such as grinding stones, a pounder, a whetstone, and loom weights. One of the lower surfaces included two cooking areas that consisted of a hearth or fireplace (unit 538), and another fireplace on top of a flat stone (unit 540), probably for high-temperature cooking. To the east of this walled space, the remains of another pottery kiln (unit 537) were uncovered. In sum, it seems that the potter's workshop was part of a larger area devoted to ceramic production.

2.4 THE ARCHAEOBOTANICAL RESEARCH[35]

2.4.1 SAMPLING METHODS AND DATA

Archaeobotanical sampling occurred in a more or less systematic way from the first VU excavation campaign onwards. Soil samples were taken from all the excavated trenches, i.e. from five units in trench 1, 24 in trench 2, six in trench 3, 20 in trench 4, 29 in trench 5, 38 in trench 6, and two in trench 7. A detailed description of the sample processing method, the complete results of the archaeobotanical analyses, and the locations of the sampled units can be found in appendices 1 and 2 and *Figures 2.5-2.10*, respectively. The archaeobotanical sample yielded a total of 3,114 charcoal fragments and 8,947 seeds and fruits, most of them carbonized. The results of the charcoal analysis are visualized

---

[34] Crielaard 2011, p. 77.

[35] The archaeobotanical finds from l'Amastuola have already partly been published in Lentjes 2011.

Fig. 2.12. L'Amastuola, trench 5: Possible silos for grain storage. Burgers and Crielaard 2011, 65 (Figures 3-28).

in *Figures 2.13* and *2.14*, the seeds and fruits in *Figures 2.15* and *2.16*. In these figures, no chronological or contextual differences are distinguished. The archaeobotanical data from l'Amastuola will now be discussed by theme, and not necessarily chronologically.

2.4.2 CHARCOAL

Charcoal is what is left of wood after it carbonizes, i.e. when it is heated in the (near) absence of oxygen. The black residue consists of impure carbon, which is not affected by bacteria or fungi. The charcoal assemblage from l'Amastuola includes thirteen different wood species.[36] It is logical to think of archaeological charcoal as the remains of firewood, but not all trees provide suitable fuel. In fact, certain species are traditionally used as firewood, whereas others are much more suited to construction, to produce small wooden objects, or as decoration. In the following, the different wood species that were found at l'Amastuola will be separately discussed, focusing on their characteristics and practical use.

Figures 2.13 and *2.14* make it clear that the great majority of charcoal fragments, both in absolute numbers (1,084 fragments) and in terms of frequency (in 85 units), belong to various oak species, both evergreen (*Quercus* cf. *ilex*) and deciduous types. There are more than ten different oak species that grow in Apulia today, including Macedonian oak (*Quercus trojana*), Turkey oak (*Quercus cerris*) and Vallonea oak (*Quercus macrolepis*).[37] Olive wood (*Olea europaea*) occurs only slightly less frequently

---

[36] Unless indicated otherwise, all botanical characteristics from the plant species that are discussed in this chapter were taken from Pignatti 1982 and Minelli 2002.

[37] Pignatti 1982, pp. 113-120. One gigantic Vallonea oak that is at least 600 years old can be admired at Tricase.

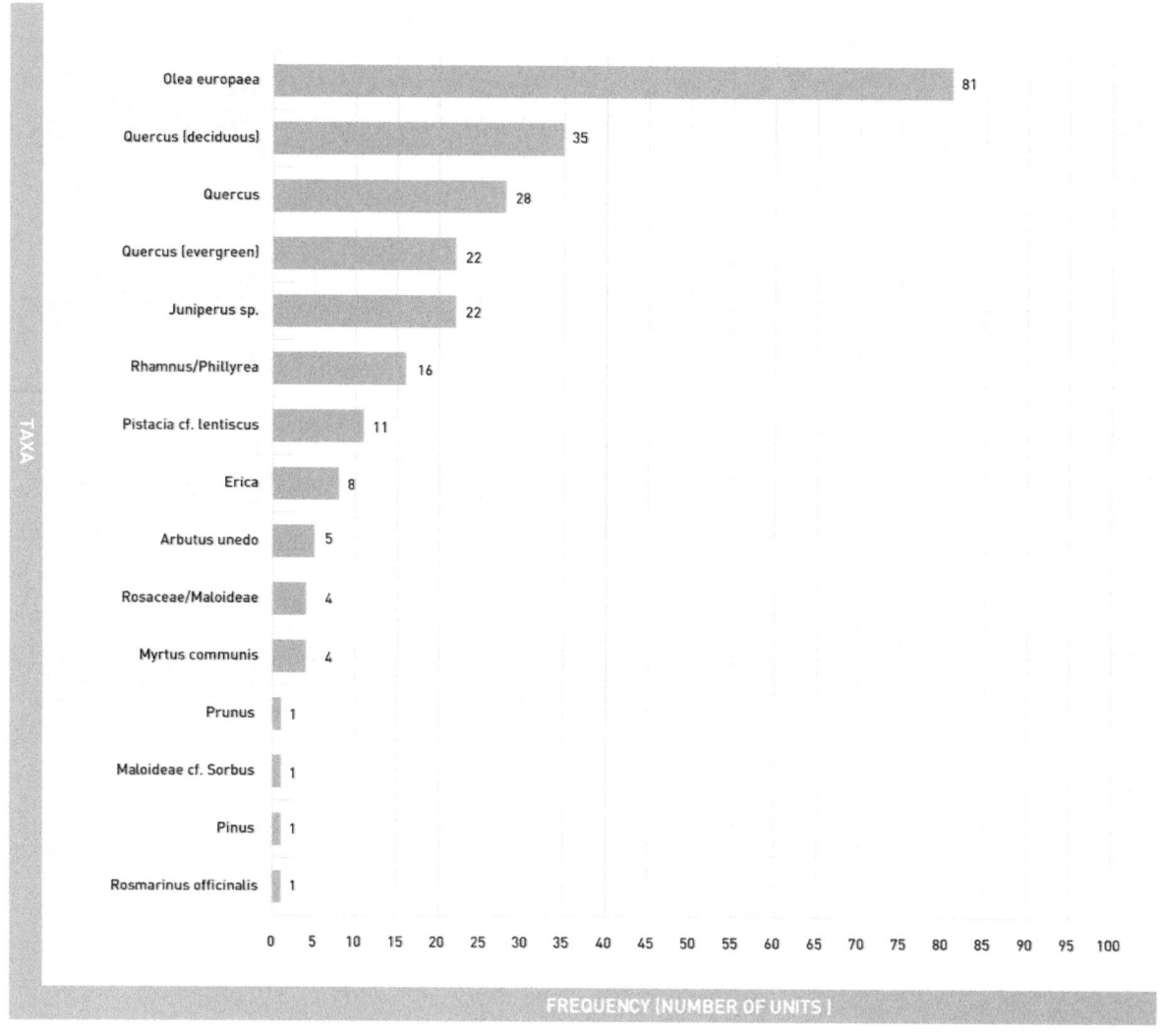

Fig. 2.13. L'Amastuola, results of the charcoal analysis: Frequency of wood taxa (i.e. the number of stratigraphical units in which it was found). Chart by Bert Brouwenstijn.

at l'Amastuola, in 81 units, and its 1,008 fragments make up 39% of the total amount of identified charcoal pieces. Olive trees can reach hundreds of years of age and tend to become hollow and dead on the inside, and split into multiple smaller trunks on the outside. This typical form makes the wood less suitable for use as construction material.[38]

Today, wild olive trees (*Olea europaea* ssp. *sylvestris*) and evergreen oaks can mostly be found in Mediterranean *macchia*. *Macchia* is essentially a type of shrub land that is characteristic of the Mediterranean region, typically consisting of densely growing evergreen shrubs.[39] Although *macchia* is by definition a natural vegetation type, in many places its appearance is due to destruction of forest cover, mainly by frequent burning that prevents young trees from maturing. In addition, it grows in arid, rocky areas where only drought-resistant plants are likely to prosper. In most cases, Mediterranean *macchia* is the result of human impact on the landscape. I will discuss this vegetation type and other characteristics of Mediterranean ecosystems in more detail in chapter 4 (*Box 1*).

[38] Gale and Cutler 2000, p. 171.

[39] Smith and Gillett 2000, p. 6.

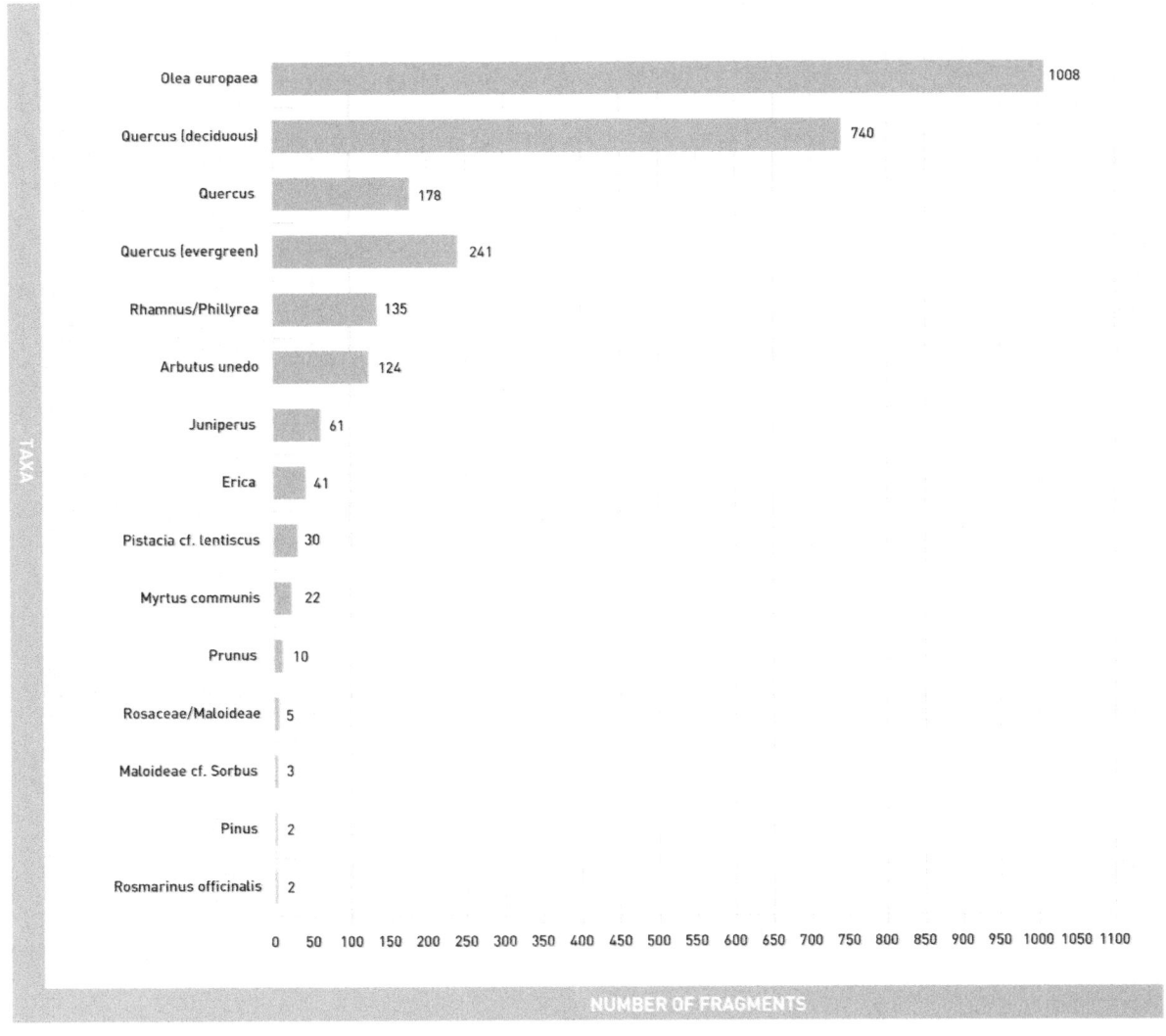

Fig. 2.14. L'Amastuola, results of the charcoal analysis: Total number of fragments of wood taxa. Chart by Bert Brouwenstijn.

The other charcoal species, which make up significantly less dominant parts of the charcoal assemblage, include *Rhamnus/Phillyrea* (5.2%), *Arbutus unedo* (4.8%), *Juniperus* sp. (2.3%), *Erica* sp. (1.6%) and *Pistacia* sp. (1.15%). The wood anatomy of the genera *Rhamnus* and *Phillyrea* is almost indistinguishable, but both include common *macchia* species such as Italian buckthorn (*Rhamnus alaternus*) and mock privet (*Phillyrea angustifolia*). Italian buckthorn wood is suitable for the turned components of furniture, but starts to release a foul smell when it is worked (*legno puzzo* or 'stinking wood'). The leaves and berries can be used as a natural dye: the leaves and branches provide yellow, the fruits green. The strawberry tree (*Arbutus unedo*) is an evergreen shrub or small tree that is characteristic of *macchia* vegetation in the Mediterranean region.[40] The fruit, a small pinkish-red berry, is edible. In some countries, arbutus berries are used to make jam and liqueurs (Portuguese 'medronho', Corsican 'liqueur a l'arbouse', Sardinian 'fior di corbezzolo'). The charcoal fragments of juniper (*Juniperus* sp.) may belong to common juniper (*Juniperus communis*), prickly juniper (*Juniperus oxycedrus*), or Phoenicean juniper (*Juniperus phoenicea*). The latter two grow on dry soils and in *macchie*; common juniper can be found throughout the northern hemisphere in heath lands and arid forests. Tree heath (*Erica arborea*) reaches

[40] Pignatti 1982, p. 261; Renfrew 1973, p. 152.

a typical height of 1 to 4 metres and has white flowers; Mediterranean heath (*Erica multiflora*) becomes 50-180 centimetres tall and its flowers are pink. Both species prefer acid soil and are found mostly in the *macchia*, the dry evergreen shrublands that can be found throughout the Mediterranean region (see the discussion of *macchia* in *Box 1*). Until recently, tree heath was often used for charcoal production, to make brooms and to cover the roofs and walls of houses.[41] The charcoal fragments of *Pistacia* may belong to either *Pistacia lentiscus* or *Pistacia terebinthus* (which is not the pistachio tree that is now widely cultivated in the Mediterranean region for its edible nuts, *Pistacia vera*). *Pistacia terebinthus*, terebinth, can be tapped for turpentine. Terebinth resin was widely used as a preservative in ancient wine because it has the ability to kill bacteria. *Pistacia lentiscus* supplies mastic resin.[42] Mastic trees are a typical part of middle/high Mediterranean *macchia*, especially along the coasts. The wood is hard and robust but not very usable as timber because mastic trees are often a bit crooked and rarely grow higher than 5 metres. It is, however, excellent wood for charcoal production.

Finally, a small number of fragments belonging to the Rosaceae or Maloideae family (including the genera *Prunus* and *Sorbus*) and myrtle (*Myrtus communis*) were found, in addition to pine tree (*Pinus*) and rosemary (*Rosmarinus officinalis*). *Prunus* is a genus of trees and shrubs that includes plums (*Prunus domestica*), cherries (*Prunus avium*), peaches (*Prunus persica*), apricots (*Prunus armeniaca*), and almonds (*Prunus dulcis*; synonym: *Amygdalus communis*). But the charcoal from l'Amastuola is more likely to belong to a wild species, as most of these varieties were not introduced in Italy before Roman times. The genus *Sorbus* also includes several hundred species of trees and shrubs (in the subfamily Maloideae of the Rosaceae family), such as whitebeam (*Sorbus aria*) and rowan (*Sorbus aucuparia*).

Myrtle is an evergreen shrub or small tree that can become up to 5 metres tall. Myrtle is widespread in the Mediterranean region and is one of the most common components of Mediterranean *macchia*. The leaves and berries contain a fragrant oil that is still used in modern Sardinia and Corsica to produce an aromatic liqueur called 'mirto'. The fragments of pine wood could not be identified on the species level, but probably belong to either umbrella pine (*Pinus pinea*) or Aleppo pine (*Pinus halepensis*), since these are the two most common species in this part of Italy. Both these pines can become quite tall, up to 25 metres, and are most commonly found along the coast, in pine bushes (*pinete*), *garighe* (see chapter 4), in *macchia* and on arid slopes. The cones of the umbrella pine contain edible seeds (pine nuts). Much like *Erica*, pine trees are very flammable but well-adapted to fire. The trees die, but grow back very swiftly from the popped seeds released from their cones.[43]

Rosemary is a woody perennial herb that is best known for its fragrant evergreen needle-like leaves that are used frequently in traditional Mediterranean cuisine. Being quite resistant and drought-tolerant, rosemary is often part of low Mediterranean *macchie* and *garighe*.

---

[41] Gaudenzio and Peccenini 2002, p. 36.

[42] Tree resin can prevent wine from turning into vinegar, and is still used for this purpose in Greek resinated wine, *retsina*. In ancient Rome, myrrh, frankincense, pine and cedar resin were the preferred wine additives. But since myrrh and other exotic tree resins were not widely available in Italy, the Romans – and presumably also other ancient peoples that had no access to the major trade routes from Africa and the Arabian Peninsula – often had to be content with terebinth tree resin. The terebinth tree (*Pistacia terebinthus*) and mastic (*Pistacia lentiscus*) can yield up to 2 kilograms of resin in late summer or fall, at just about the same time that grapes are ready to be picked. Today, terebinth resin is still used to make chewing gum, perfume, drinks and sweets in the Near and Middle East. Although the word turpentine actually derives from terebinth, the natural resin, unlike the concentrated distillate, is not offensive in taste and smell. McGovern 2003, pp. 70-71.

[43] Grove and Rackham 2001, pp. 219-220.

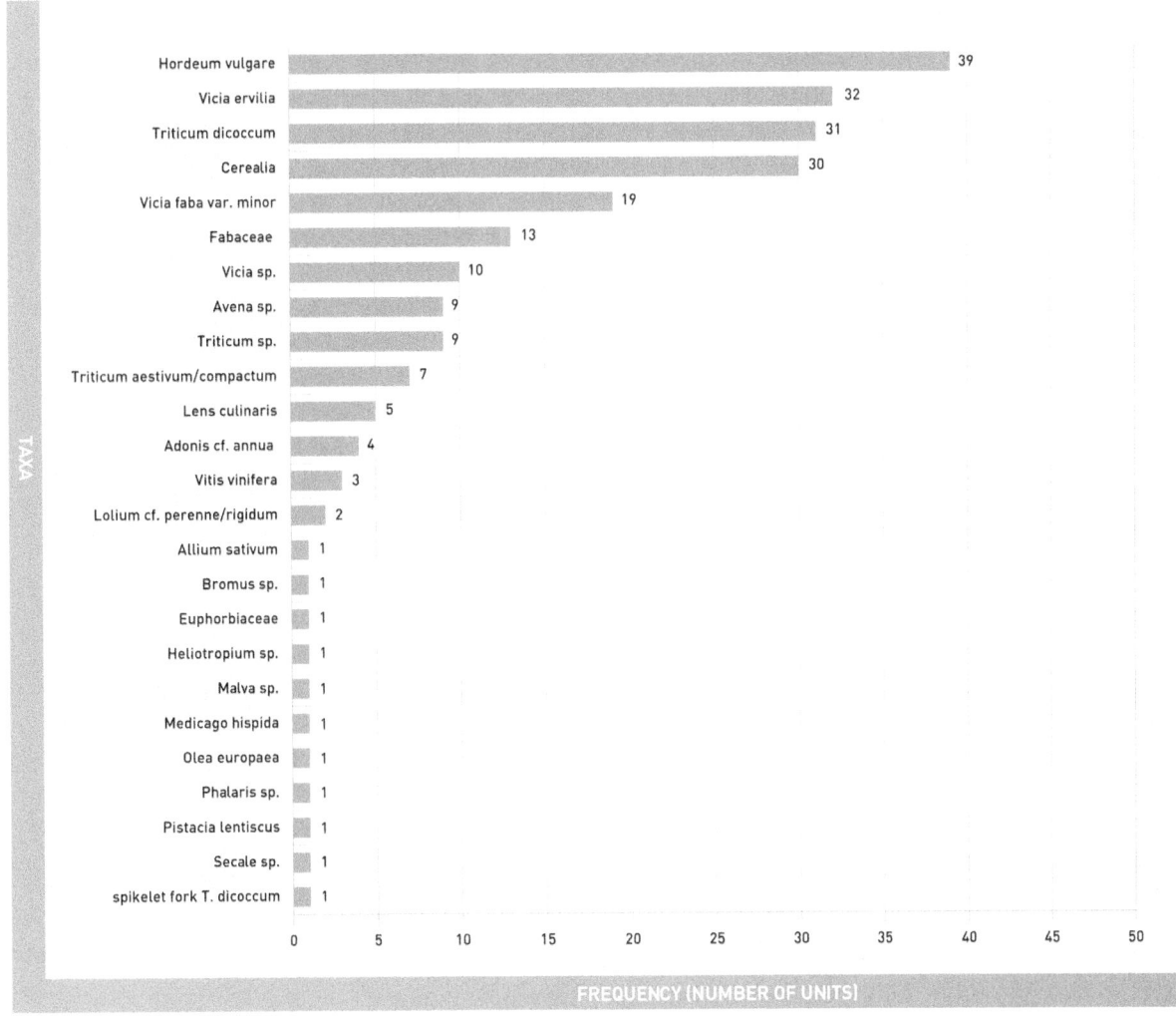

Fig. 2.15. L'Amastuola, results of the analysis of seeds and fruits: Frequencies. Chart by Bert Brouwenstijn.

2.4.3 SEEDS AND FRUITS

The samples mainly included cereals, the great majority of them being hulled barley (*Hordeum vulgare*).[44] Emmer wheat (*Triticum dicoccum*) is less common, but did provide a few spikelet forks (or rachis internodes, the stem portion between the nodes). In contrast to the cereal finds from Muro Tenente (see chapter 3), free-threshing wheat (*Triticum aestivum/compactum*) is quite rare at l'Amastuola, and naked barley was not found at all. The samples also contained quite a few charred seeds of weeds that might have grown in the cereal fields: oat (*Avena*), brome (*Bromus* sp.), rye (*Secale cereale*), autumn adonis (*Adonis* cf. *annua*), ryegrass (*Lolium* cf. *perenne/rigidum*), mallow (*Malva* sp.), a few seeds from the

[44] At least one sample, from unit 534, contained both six-rowed barley (*Hordeum vulgare* L. ssp. *vulgare*) and two-rowed barley (*Hordeum vulgare* L. ssp. *distichum*). According to Jacomet (2006) and Bouby (2001), six-rowed barley has three fertile spikelets per rachis segment, whereas two-rowed barley has only one (the two outer ones are sterile). However, this distinction is very difficult to make with charred cereal remains, since the process of carbonization often causes the grains to become corroded or pressed, and therefore deformed (see most recently Ruas and Bouby 2010, with further references). For these reasons, it was decided to refer to the barley grains from l'Amastuola and Muro Tenente as *Hordeum vulgare*.

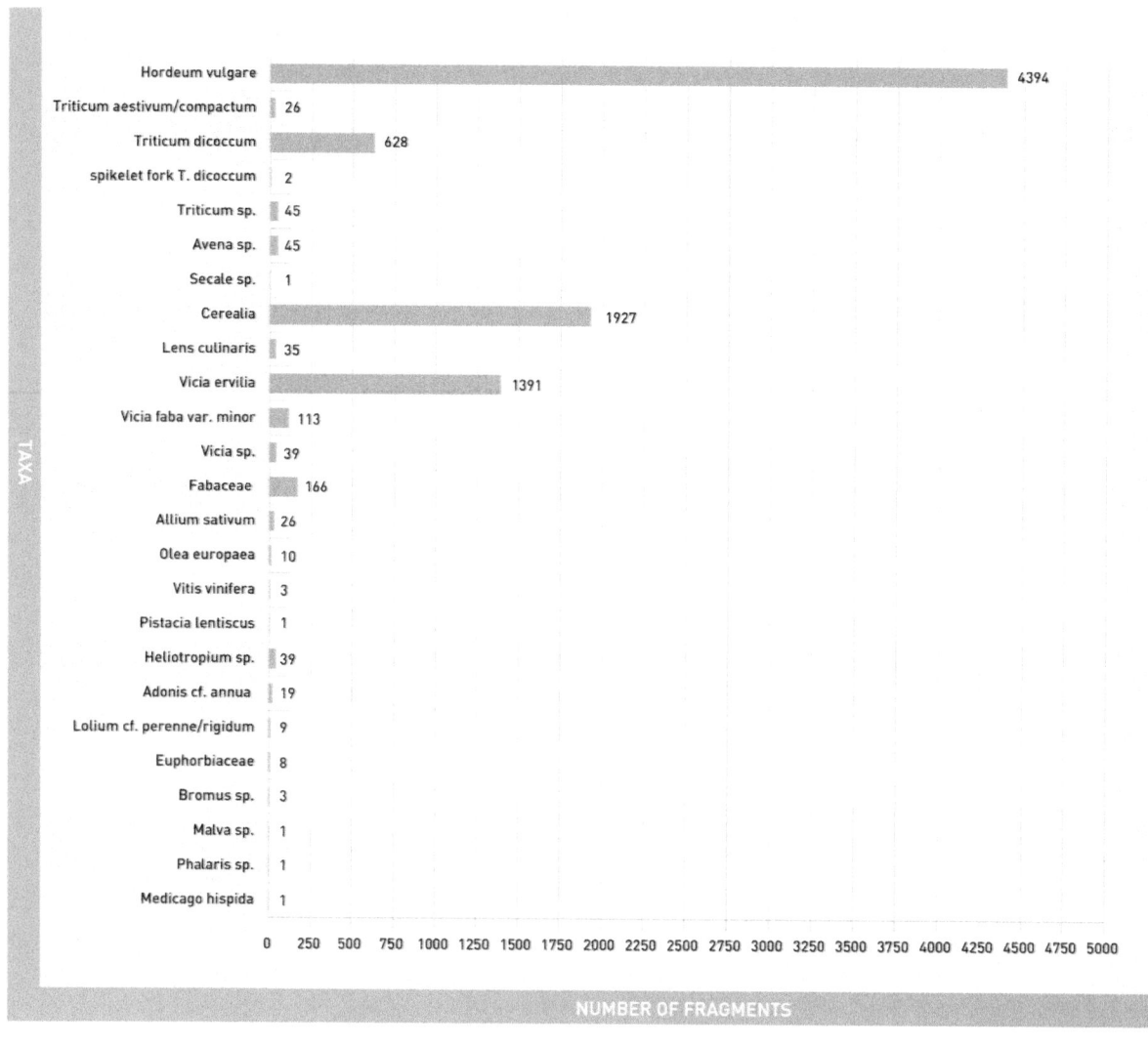

Fig. 2.16. L'Amastuola, results of the analysis of seeds and fruits: Total number of fragments. Chart by Bert Brouwenstijn.

Spurge family (Euphorbiaceae), héliotrope (*Heliotropium* sp.), and bur medick (*Medicago hispida*). Apart from the charred weeds, the soil samples also contained a number of 'fresh' (i.e. not carbonized) seeds that were probably modern contaminations.[45] Because of their questionable provenance, these seeds have been left out of the graphics. Fruit remains are rare: only a few olive stones, three grape pips (*Vitis vinifera*), and a mastic berry (*Pistacia lentiscus*) were found. Pulses, on the other hand, abound: lentils (*Lens culinaris*) and broad beans (*Vicia faba* var. *minor*) are both part of the archaeobotanical assemblage, but the most dominant legume species is bitter vetch (*Vicia ervilia*). Finally, a most unusual find was made in the ritual deposition in trench 6; the burnt remains contained carbonized garlic cloves (*Allium sativum*).

[45] Among these not-carbonized seeds were field mustard (*Brassica rapa*), coastal sandbur (*Cenchrus pauciflorus*), goosefoot (*Chenopodium* sp.), spiny spiderflower (*Cleome spinosa*), hawthorne (*Crataegus* sp.), viper's bugloss (*Echium* sp.), sun spurge (*Euphorbia helioscopia*), and small burnet (*Sanguisorba minor*).

2.5 THE ARCHAEOBOTANICAL RESEARCH: INTERPRETATIONS

In the following paragraph, I will discuss the archaeobotanical data from l'Amastuola and the information they provide about a number of research aspects. I will start by reviewing the evidence of local plant use, discussing the use of wood. Subsequently, the information about food preparation and diet, the cultivation of grapes and olives, and the use of plants in ritual activities will be reviewed.

2.5.1 THE USE OF WOOD

Table 2.1 and *Figure 2.17* compare the charcoal from fourteen contexts associated with fuel, including hearths and fireplaces, namely the area outside the Iron Age hut in trench 2, the interior of buildings ζ and δ, one of the (bread?) ovens in *oikos* γ, and the various kilns that were excavated in and around the potter's workshop in trench 6. The locations are indicated in *Figure 2.18*. Obviously, these charcoal assemblages only provide a partial impression of which species were preferred as fuel. In addition, the archaeological contexts from which they were collected represent different types of pyrotechnic structures, including closed ones such as ovens and furnaces, as well as open fireplaces. There is a large number of publications considering the different types of fuel that can be used in structures of these types.[46] Charcoal can be the residue of heating or cooking fires, but it can also be produced to use as a fuel to generate higher temperatures, particularly for industrial processes such as metallurgy and pottery production. Determining the purpose of charcoal assemblages from archaeological contexts can be particularly difficult.[47] The interpretation often depends on clues provided by the context, although recent research has highlighted the use of physical and chemical characteristics of charcoal to provide information about the nature of the fuel and the temperatures that are generated during combustion.[48] However, this type of analysis has not been carried out at l'Amastuola. Moreover, the archaeological context of most of the charcoal finds often provided only limited information about its use. Therefore, the following overview of fuel use at l'Amastuola concerns only the wood types and possible differences of wood use between different pyrotechnic structures.

More than two thirds of the charcoal collection consists of olive wood (31%) and oak wood (mostly deciduous, but also a small part evergreen oak, 39%). This outcome is not surprising, since olive and oak trees are generally much bigger than the other species that occurred in these samples, which included *Erica* sp. (8%), *Rhamnus/Phillyrea* (3%), juniper (2%), *Pistacia* sp. (0.75%), and strawberry tree (0.5%). In comparison to these middle-high *macchia* species, oak and olive trees are more likely to provide large quantities of firewood.[49] Moreover, oak and olive also provide suitable fuel. They are still often used in hearths, ovens, and stoves in southern Italy today. Both species have high calorific values and provide long-lasting fuel,[50] which would have been particularly needed in the pottery and metal kilns at l'Amastuola. Indeed, the metal oven (units 166 and 170) in trench 4 contains mostly olive and oak wood, with a few fragments of juniper. Unfortunately, only a limited amount of charcoal was found in and around the oven (16 fragments). The same applies to the sample from kiln D (unit 346), which contained one single fragment of olive wood and three of *Rhamnus/Phillyrea*. The kiln that was found northeast of the potter's workshop (unit 537, 542) provided a richer charcoal sample, which mostly contained oak (75%) and olive wood (17%) with a little *Rhamnus/Phillyrea* (1.5%). Kiln E (units

---

[46] See especially Vernet 1997; Théry-Parisot 2001; Dabas et al. 2002; Thiébault 2002; Fiorentino and Magri 2008; Keeley 2009; Scott and Damblon 2010.

[47] Scott and Damblon 2010, p. 3.

[48] McParland *et al.* 2009a, b.

[49] Chabal 1994, pp. 323-324.

[50] Gale and Cutler 2000, pp. 173, 205.

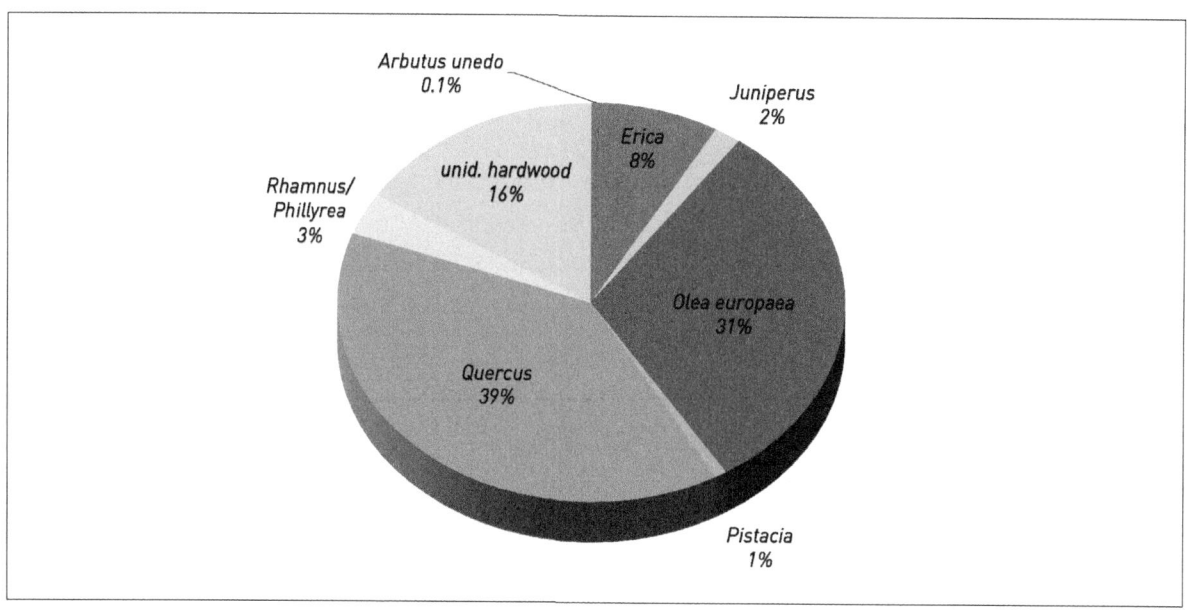

Fig. 2.17. L'Amastuola, results of the charcoal analysis: Wood taxa from hearths and fireplaces (fuel?). Chart by Bert Brouwenstijn. L'Amastuola, south terrace: Location of the samples from hearths and fireplaces (units 265, 274, 112, 148, 166, 170, 32, 33, 332, 335, 346, 373, 537, 542). Drawing by Jaap Fokkema.

335, 373 and 332) yielded a sample in which a relatively wide variety of species are represented, with strawberry tree (1%), juniper (3%), *Pistacia* (3%), and *Rhamnus/Phillyrea* (9%) in addition to the 'usual' olive wood (38%) and oak (32%).

It is questionable whether this material represents the residues of heating or cooking fires or of fuel that was carbonized before (industrial) use. Charcoal is still used in a range of industrial processes as a heat source, both on a small- and a large scale.[51] Charcoal would have been the preferred type of fuel instead of wood in the pottery and metal workshops in trenches 6 and 4, since it can reach much higher temperatures. Charcoal is produced in so-called charcoal burners, in which wood is carbonized in a reducing atmosphere (i.e. with as little oxygen as possible) to prevent it from burning and turning to ashes. In this way, the wood becomes completely dry and compact, greatly increasing its heating value and limiting the production of smoke.[52] There are no archaeological indications of the use of charcoal burners at l'Amastuola, but such structures can be archaeologically invisible.[53] In modern northern Africa, for instance, charcoal is produced in a shallow pit with a levelled base. The wood is laid out in a neat stack inside the pit, then covered with vegetation or straw and loose earth before it is ignited. This earth cover is kept wet during the burning process, which can take ten to fifteen days.[54] After the charcoal is collected and taken elsewhere, it is unlikely for the remaining structure to survive in the archaeological record. Even if it did, a charcoal burner is unlikely to be located inside the settlement, as the smoke would cause nuisance and even fire hazard. This means that it would not be picked up by urban-based excavations.

There is no more clarity about the use of wood as construction material.[55] The lumps of burnt loam with impressions of branches that were found in trench 4 show that vital parts of the Iron Age huts or

[51] Syred and Griffiths 2006.
[52] Horne 1982, p. 6.
[53] For the use of charcoal as fuel in archaeological contexts, see section 5.3.1, as well as discussions in Théry-Parisot 2001; Pye and Ancel 2006; Braadbaart and Poole 2008.
[54] Kelley 2002, p. 4.
[55] The volume of published studies describing the role of wood in construction in pre-Roman Italy is remarkably small, but some relevant information can be found in Richter 1966; Meiggs 1982 and most recently Gale and Cutler 2000.

Trench	2	2	3	4	4	4	5	
Unit	265	274	112	148	166	170	32	
Context	hearth?	fill of	furnace	oven	= /170\	oven	hearth	
Structure	IA hut	/265\	oikos γ	building δ		oikos ε	building ζ	
Date	VIII-VII BC		VI BC	VI BC		VI BC	VI BC	
Taxa								common name
Arbutus unedo	1							strawberry tree
Erica sp.		31						heath
Juniperus sp.					4			juniper
Olea europaea	18	5	6	12	3	6	11	olive
Quercus (deciduous type)							3	oak
Quercus (evergreen type)	1	1					3	oak
Quercus sp.	2				3			oak
Pistacia cf. lentiscus.								mastic
Rhamnus/ Phillyrea		1						Rhamnus/ Phillyrea
indet. Hardwood	5	36						indet. Hardwood

Trench	6	6	6	6	5	6	6	
Unit	332	335	346	373	33	537	542	
Context	= /335\	kiln E	ash kiln D	ash kiln E	fireplace	kiln?	ash connected with	
Structure		workshop	workshop	workshop	building ζ	-	/537\	
Date		VI BC	VI BC	VI BC	VI BC	?	?	
Taxa								common name
Arbutus unedo		1						strawberry tree
Erica sp.								heath
Juniperus sp.	3							juniper
Olea europaea	17		1		13	19	5	olive
Quercus (deciduous type)					2		118	oak
Quercus (evergreen type)								oak
Quercus sp.						28		oak
Pistacia cf. lentiscus.	3							mastic
Rhamnus/ Phillyrea	3	4	3			1	2	Rhamnus/ Phillyrea
indet. Hardwood		2		10		11	1	indet. Hardwood

Table 2.1 L'Amastuola, charcoal from contexts that can be associated with hearths or furnaces.

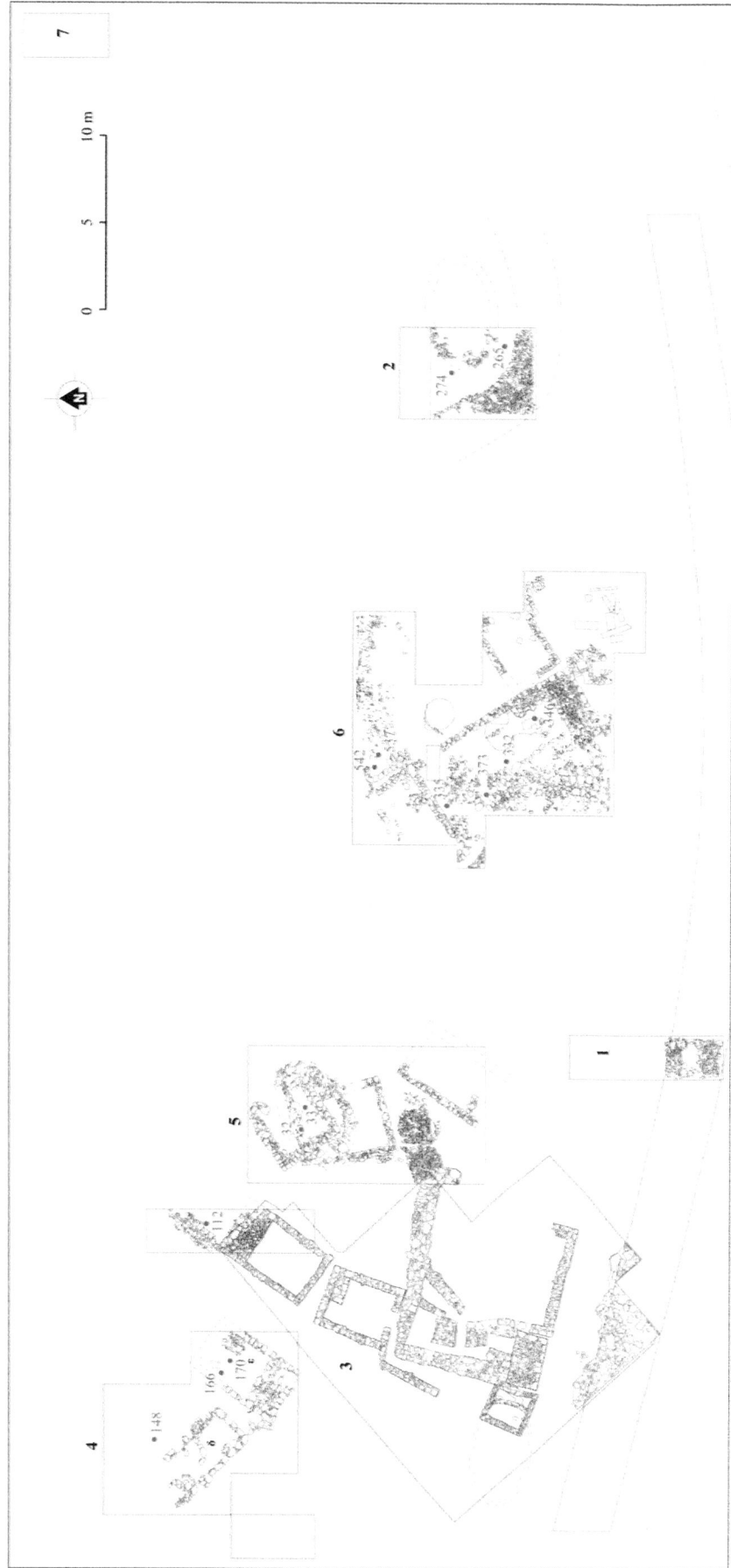

Fig. 2.18. L'Amastuola, south terrace: Location of the samples from hearths and fireplaces (units 265, 274, 112, 148, 166, 170, 32, 33, 332, 335, 346, 373, 537, 542). Drawing by Jaap Fokkema.

houses were made of wood. The stalks were probably part of the wattle-and-daub walls or roof. Unfortunately, it is unclear what kind of wood the impressions belong to. A varied charcoal assemblage was found in the same context (unit 122), including *Erica*, juniper, olive, mastic, *Phillyrea*, oak (deciduous and evergreen) and fruit trees, which makes it all the more likely that the area was used to dump refuse of all sorts and does not exclusively contain building material. There are some other contexts that might contain traces of building wood, such as the levelling layer that was deposited on top of the Iron Age hut in trench 2 (that included olive, oak and juniper wood), but the quantities are too small and their provenance too questionable to reach any valid conclusions about construction wood at l'Amastuola.

2.5.2 FOOD PREPARATION AND DIET

The analysis results of all the seeds and fruits that were found at l'Amastuola can be found in *Figures 2.15* and *2.16* and Appendix 2. It can be concluded that a considerable part of everyday meals probably consisted of cereals. They could have been consumed in various ways, in the form of watery gruels (see below), or milled to produce flour to make bread. A series of three small ovens, dating to the 6th century BC, was found in niches in the south face of the much disturbed 'terrace wall' in trench 3. This wall is a continuation of the north-west wall of *oikos* γ. The size and location of the ovens suggest that they were used in connection with food preparation, possibly bread baking. Unfortunately, no direct archaeobotanical evidence for the processing of cereals was found here. The sample that was taken from one of the ovens (unit 112) did not include any macroremains, nor did the archaeological contexts around them, with the exception of unit 105, which represents an ancient outdoor surface to the south and east of the ovens. A single barley grain and one of emmer were found here. In *Table 2.2*, the data from another possible oven are added. This one was set against the exterior wall of building δ (unit 148) and will therefore be referred to as oven δ. This oven also contained no more than a single grain of emmer. However, the ashy refuse dump next to it (unit 144[56]) is especially rich in macroremains, including 122 carbonized grains of hulled barley, 24 of emmer wheat and 39 other unidentified cereal grains. Considering the location and the pottery finds from this dump (including some 7th century BC pottery), it can be hypothesized that it was used to deposit burnt refuse from the oven, such as cereals that had accidentally been carbonized during processing.

It appears that most of the cereals that were found at l'Amastuola were hulled, although it should be added that naked cereals are often underrepresented in archaeobotanical assemblages.[57] In any case, cereal parching must have been a common part of everyday food preparation.[58] Parching was probably done using mortars and pestles.[59] Two such mortars were found during the excavations, in building δ (*Figure 2.19*), and in one of the colluvium layers that covered the Iron Age hut in trench 2 (*Figure 2.20*). The excavations also uncovered several grinding stones, for example in *oikos* ε (*Figures 2.21a and*

[56] Burgers and Crielaard 2007, p. 89.
[57] Hulled cereals often require a process of parching before they can be completely threshed and processed, and there is a good chance that they accidentally carbonize in a fire. These carbonized hulled cereals often represent a large part of the macroremains assemblage from Mediterranean countries, because other environmental factors that allow preservation, such as permanent wetness or drought, are usually lacking. Therefore, species that are less likely to be carbonized, either because they do not require such a preparation process (vegetables, fruits) or because they are destroyed by the fire (oily seeds such as flax), will probably be under-represented among the macroremains. Cf. Hillman 1981, p. 142; Jacomet 2006, p. 5; Van Der Veen 2007, p. 977.
[58] We know from ethnographic evidence that hulled wheats are usually stored as spikelets and dehusked when required, which was likely to be a time-consuming daily chore. Hillman 1984, p. 8.
[59] For a discussion of the efficiency of mortars for grain dehusking in comparison with a saddle-quern, see Meurers-Balke and Lüning 1992, pp. 346-357.

Trench	3	4	4	
Unit	105	144	148	
Context	outdoor surface near oven	refuse dump oven	oven	
Structure	oikos γ	building δ	building δ	
Date	VI BC	VI BC	VI BC	
Taxa				common name
Hordeum vulgare	1	112		hulled barley
Triticum aestivum/compactum		1		free-threshing wheat
Triticum dicoccum	1	24	1	emmer wheat
Cerealia		39		cereals
Lens culinaris		1		lentil
Vicia ervilia		8		bitter vetch
Vicia sp.		5		vetch
Avena sp.		13		oat
Medicago hispida		1		bur medick

Table 2.2 L'Amastuola, macroremains from contexts that can be associated with possible ovens in oikos γ and building δ.

b). Figurative evidence for the use of mortars and pestles can be seen on the Daunian *stelai* depicted in *Figures 2.22a* and *b*.[60] Furthermore, Hesiod (c. 750-650 BC) describes the manufacture of a wooden mortar of considerable dimensions (c. 90-100 cm in height) in *Works and Days*.[61] Interestingly, a stone mortar of a similar size was found on the slope of the l'Amastuola hill (*Figure 2.23a*). However, since this tool was found out of context, it is unclear whether it derived from the ancient settlement; in fact, it may have been used at the *masseria* l'Amastuola on the hilltop. Mortars of this type were still in use until the middle of the 20th century in this part of Italy (*Figure 2.23b*).

Weeds make up a significant part of the macroremains assemblage at l'Amastuola, and include species that grow in cornfields (*Avena* sp., *Bromus* sp., *Secale cereale*, *Adonis* cf. *annua*) and other cultivated grounds (*Malva* sp., *Heliotropium* sp., *Medicago hispida*), including waste places and waysides.[62] In contrast, chaff remains are scarce at l'Amastuola. Only two rachis internodes were found, both of them among the remains of Iron Age habitation in trench 6.

Given the abundance of cereal weeds, the scarcity of chaff remains is striking. Three possible explanations can be proposed to explain this contrast. The first one is connected to a general problem with the interpretation of carbonized plant assemblages. As Hillman[63] has pointed out, the only components that are likely to survive in charred form are the small, dense items able to drop quickly through the flames and into the ashes without being burned themselves. Light chaff remains such as straw and rachis fragments are the first components to be lost.[64] Apart from this first explanation, the mesh width of the smallest sieve in the flotation machines that were used at l'Amastuola may have also influenced the find. The largest sieve had meshes of 2.5 and the smallest of 1 millimetre, which

[60] Nava 1980, fig. CCLVII and CCCLXXXI. Numerous examples of this type of *stelai* are known from northern Apulia, where they came to light during plough activities in the arable fields near the modern town of Manfredonia. Since they were obviously found out of context, it is difficult to associate them with a precise chronological period. However, according to D. Yntema the figurative style on the *stelai* that are mentioned in this chapter suggests a date between c. 650 and 580 BC.

[61] *W&D* 420.

[62] Polunin 1969.

[63] Hillman 1981, p. 140.

[64] Cf. Boardman and Jones 1990.

Fig. 2.19. L'Amastuola, trench 4: Stone mortar from building δ. Burgers and Crielaard 2011, 150 (Figures 8-14).

is a good measure for the gathering of charcoal fragments, but too large for most chaff remains and small weed seeds. Nevertheless, it can be argued that spikelet forks were apparently big enough to be collected in the small sieve, and they do not abound in the archaeobotanical assemblage either. A third explanation, then, is that the waste products from cereal cleaning are only rarely found in soil samples from l'Amastuola because this process usually took place outside the settlement.[65] The finds of mortars and grinding stones indicate that cereals were probably cleaned at the household level, but these tools might have been used for the last cleaning stage only. The cereal weeds that were found at this site all have roughly the same grain size as wheat and barley. It is possible that they were already partially cleaned, and mixed with the odd weed grain that had escaped the cleaning process of sieving. Such sieving processes only remove weeds that are smaller than the cereal grains.[66] Apparently, the remaining weeds did not bother the inhabitants of l'Amastuola, as they did not remove them when they used cereals to prepare their meals. We have direct evidence of this in the form of a cooking pot with carbonized contents. This pot, with a rounded base and a relatively narrow neck, was found on the most recent floor level in the potter's workshop (unit 313, *Figure 2.24*). It contained ten fragments of charred olive stones along with 170 seeds of hulled barley, emmer wheat, pulses (*Vicia* sp.), grains of wild grass (*Bromus* sp.) and free-threshing wheat in what seems to be a sort of gruel (see *Table 2.3*).

---

[65] On the basis of ethnographic research in Turkey, Hillman (1984, p. 8) has argued that in dry areas it is common practice to store the partially cleaned grain into bulk storage. In areas with wet summers, however, it is the complete spikelets that are put into storage.

[66] See especially Hillman 1981, 1984; Boardman and Jones 1990 and more recently Valamoti 2005; Van Der Veen 2007 on the reconstruction of cereal husbandry from charred crop remains.

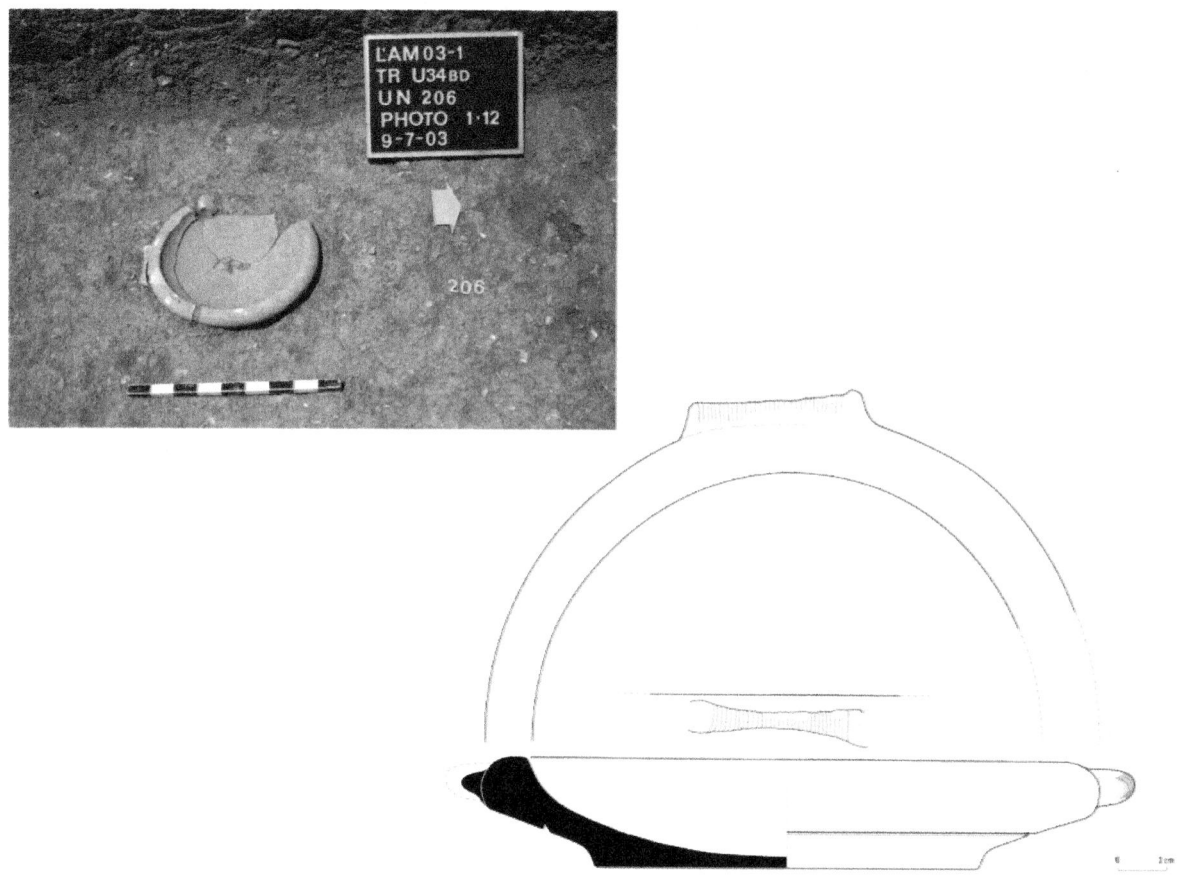

Fig. 2.20. L'Amastuola, trench 2: Terracotta mortar from the colluvium layer. Burgers and Crielaard 2007, 102 (Figure 39e).

Another interesting find for our understanding of the inhabitants' diet was made in a storage jar (unit 107 lot 275) from the partially burned layer northwest of the 'terrace wall' in trench 3 (*Figure 2.25, Table 2.3*). This jar is datable to the middle of the 7th century BC, and contained 685 seeds of bitter vetch, but no other crop remains. As its name implies, the seeds of bitter vetch are bitter and toxic to humans and to some animals. The poisonous substance can, however, be removed by soaking the seeds in water.[67] The discovery of the storage jar full of seeds next to fine matt-painted pots used for household purposes seems to indicate that this vetch was actually used for human consumption here. Bitter vetch is omnipresent in all chronological phases at l'Amastuola, indicating that they remained an important part of the diet throughout the settlement's occupation period. On the whole, pulses seem to have been the predominant crops beside cereals. In addition to bitter vetch, lentils and broad beans occur frequently in the samples. Broad beans were found in all habitation phases.[68] Lentils only occurred in the samples that were datable to the 6th century BC, but that could be coincidental. It is possible that the lentil was not much in use in the earliest phases, but it seems unlikely that it was part of the human diet in the 6th century and stopped being consumed in the 5th century BC. The absence of chickpeas (*Cicer arietinum*) in the samples from l'Amastuola is remarkable (see section 5.3.2 on the occurrence of these species at other contemporary sites in southeast Italy), but probably purely coincidental. Pulses are notoriously underrepresented in archaeological soil samples, as they are less likely to come into contact with fire and therefore have less chance to of being carbonized.[69]

[67] Zohary and Hopf 2000, p. 116.

[68] According to Forti and Stazio (1983, p. 673) the broad beans from Taras were known for their exceptional quality.

[69] See above, note 57.

Trench	3	6	
Unit	107	313	
Container	storage jar	cooking pot	
Structure	-	Living space	
Date	Mid VII BC	V BC	
Taxa			common name
Hordeum vulgare		170	hulled barley
Triticum aestivum/compactum		1	free-threshing wheat
Triticum dicoccum		20	emmer wheat
Triticum sp.		2	wheat
Cerealia		70	cereals
Olea europaea		10	olive
Vicia faba var. Minor		1	broad bean
Vicia ervilia	685	1	bitter vetch
Fabaceae		4	legumes
Bromus sp.		3	brome

Table 2.3 L'Amastuola, macroremains from cooking pot and storage jar.

The location of the above storage jar and others that were found within the settlement suggests that crop storage took place mostly at the household level at l'Amastuola. Storage vessels and amphorae were found in various other contexts, such as building δ and the upper floor of the potter's workshop. The distribution of these storage vessels could possibly offer more insight into crop storage patterns in the settlement, but it is important to point out that such vessels were also frequently re-used. An amphora that originally contained olive oil or wine could be used for years afterwards, for example to store water.[70]

Obviously, the daily menu would have included animal products as well. Unfortunately, our information about livestock keeping at l'Amastuola is limited, since the archaeozoological remains have not been systematically analysed yet. The preliminary excavation reports frequently mention finds of sheep/goat bones, as well as some remains of cattle.[71] Evidently, the inhabitants' diet included the occasional consumption of meat, which can also be deduced from the roasting spit that was used in the most recent phase of the potter's workshop in trench 6. Shells and fish bones, however, are very rare among the faunal remains. The only indication of exploitation of the maritime environment is a large bronze fish hook, which was found in the same context as the deer bones in trench 6.

[70] Cf. Notarstefano 2012, p. 67.
[71] Burgers and Crielaard 2007, p. 110. Crielaard (2011, p. 61), mentions the find of an almost complete leg of a goat or sheep under the south wall of *oikos* ε. Unfortunately, no exact numbers can be given yet.

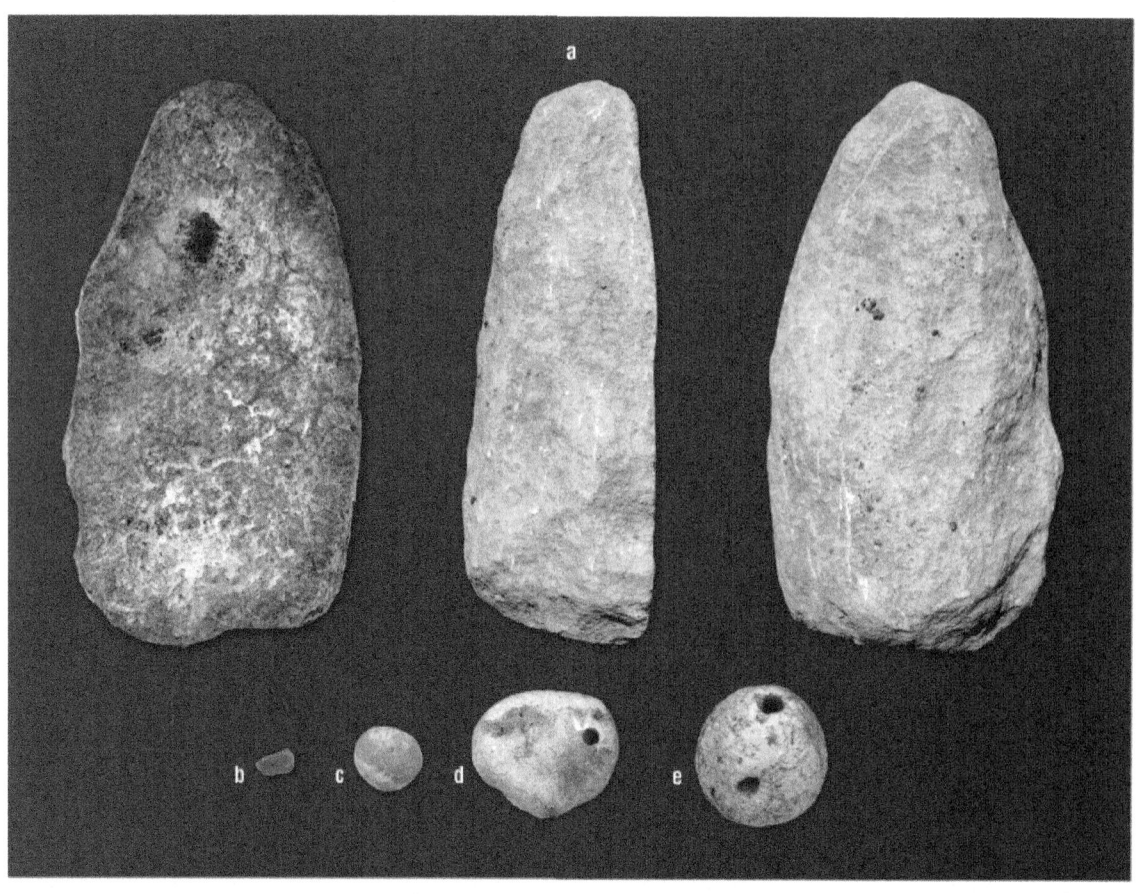

Fig. 2.21. L'Amastuola, all trenches: Grinding stones. Burgers and Crielaard 2011, 151-152 (Figures 8-15).

Fig. 2.22. Decorations on Daunian stelai showing cereal parching with mortars and pestles. Nava 1980, Figures CCLVII (775B) and CCCLXXXI (1157AB). Cf. Burgers and Crielaard 2011, 153 (Figures 8-17b).

Fig. 2.23a. L'Amastuola, south of the hill: Stone mortar. Photo by Jan Paul Crielaard (cf. Burgers and Crielaard 2011, 153 (Figures 8-17a).

Fig. 2.23b. San Pancrazio Salentino, Apulia: Stone mortar of unknown origin. Photo by the author.

	Minimal length (mm)	Minimal width (mm)
Fragment 1	7	4
Fragment 2	5.5	5
Fragment 3	3.5	5

Table 2.4 L'Amastuola, measurements of olive stone fragments from unit 313 lot 877 (cooking pot, 5th century BC).

2.5.3 GRAPE AND OLIVE CULTIVATION

Archaeological evidence for the production of olive oil and wine, such as pressing stones and fermentation tanks, is absent at l'Amastuola. But it is important to keep in mind that archaeological remains of olive oil and wine production (indeed, of all agricultural production processes) are notoriously scarce anywhere in the Mediterranean.[72] Furthermore, there are a few indications of olive and grape *consumption*. This evidence is primarily found in the form of transport amphorae, which were used to import liquid bulk goods, probably wine and olive oil, from eastern Greece.[73] Small oil flasks, which are likely to have contained perfumed oil, were also among the finds.[74] Furthermore, almost all of the pottery finds from the burnt deposit in trench 6 represent vase shapes that can be associated with wine consumption. According to Burgers and Crielaard, imported wine, which no doubt was often consumed in connection with imported drinking services, may have been a luxury item that was associated with an elite, 'internationally' oriented lifestyle.[75]

As we have seen above, olive charcoal is omnipresent at l'Amastuola. However, in order to establish whether these olives were cultivated or wild, biometric studies on olive stones are required. Olive macroremains are surprisingly rare at this site and were only found in one context, the cooking pot from the potter's workshop in trench 6. The olive stones in this pot were fragmented (*Figure 2.26*), which could indicate that they were pounded in order to extract some of the oil, although this would be a very crude way indeed to produce olive oil.[76] Unfortunately, the stone fragments were too small to carry out any significant biometric measurements. It was not possible to measure the exact length

[72] Foxhall (1993) has given several reasons why olive crushers are seldom recovered in ancient Greek contexts. First, the presses were probably located in the countryside near the olive groves, whereas archaeological research is often focused on settlement areas. Second, much equipment has probably vanished when it was re-used, especially in areas where easily workable stone is scarce. Third, it is also possible that people did not always use archaeologically recognizable olive presses. Depending on their economic circumstances, they might just have used a hole in the ground with pebbles in it, which, after use, would remain virtually invisible in the archaeological record. See also Brun 2004.

[73] There is a variety of imported amphorae among the pottery finds from l'Amastuola, originating primarily from the Gulf of Corinth (Corinthian type A amphorae), but also from adjacent regions in southern Italy (Corinthian type B amphorae, see paragraph 5.3.3). Burgers and Crielaard 2007, pp. 102-104.

[74] See, for example, the ovoid *aryballoi* from Trench 2 and Trench 6. Burgers and Crielaard 2007, p. 103; Crielaard and Burgers 2012, p. 84 (*Figure 30e*).

[75] Burgers and Crielaard 2007, p. 110.

[76] Olive oil production involves a long process of grinding, pressing, resting and filtering. Simply grinding a few olives would result in a hardly edible olive paste. Grinded olives need to be pressed to separate the vegetal liquid from the paste, and this liquid still contains a significant amount of water. Traditionally, the olive oil is shed from the water by letting the liquid steep in a container for a certain amount of time, during which the oil will sink and the water float on top. The oil can then be tapped from the bottom of the container, or the water can be skimmed off the top.

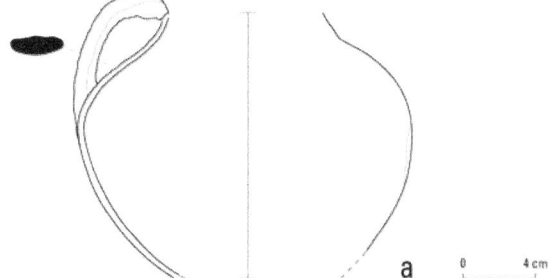

Fig. 2.24. L'Amastuola, trench 6: Cooking pot with rounded base and relatively narrow neck. Burgers and Crielaard 2007, 102 (Figure 39a).

and width of most of the fragments either. The dimensions of the three largest fragments are included in *Table 2.4*. It can be observed that the minimum width of these fragments is relatively constant – perhaps suggesting that the olives' overall dimensions did not show much variety, which is a typical feature of olives that are grafted (i.e. cultivated) rather than grown from seeds.[77] But that suggestion is based on three measurements only, and obviously needs to be treated with much caution. In sum, it must be concluded that, on the basis of the present data, it is impossible to say whether the olive stones that were found at l'Amastuola belonged to the cultivated or wild variety.

Grape remains are equally rare at l'Amastuola. No *Vitis* charcoal at all and only three grape pips (in units 159, 626, and 627) were found. Traditionally, cultivated grapes are distinguished from wild ones by measuring them and calculating the so-called Stummer index.[78] However, the problem is that the ratios differ between regions, and the extent of overlap between cultivated and spontaneous *Vitis* can be considerable. Furthermore, in the archaeological record seed dimensions can be deformed by different processes of preservation, such as carbonization or mineralization. These problems have caused some authors to express their doubts about the value of the Stummer index for the identification of wild or cultivated grapes.[79] Indeed, to overcome this problem Mangafa and Kotsakis started an investigation of modern populations of wild and cultivated vines and their carbonization under differing charring conditions.[80] Their experiments resulted in a new series of formulas, which are particularly useful for the analysis of macroremains that fall within the overlap zone of Stummer's index, and seem to lead to more reliable results.[81] Unfortunately, one of the three grape pips (from unit 627) was too fragmented to be measured. The other two were relatively small and thin, measuring 5 x 3.2 mm and 4.3 x 2.5 mm, respectively. These measurements make them unsuitable for the Stummer index (scores: 64 and 58), but the formulae by Mangafa and Kotsakis seem to qualify them as belonging to the wild variety.[82] Although the suitability of these formulae can be questioned (see section 4.3.2 and *Box 3*), the evidence for grape cultivation at l'Amastuola remains inconclusive.

---

[77] Cf. Kislev 1994-1995, p. 137. See section 5.3.3 for more recent bibliographical references about biometrical analysis of olive stones.

[78] By calculating the breadth (B) and length (L) index and dividing the two, Stummer (1911) stated that indices between 44 to 53 characterize wild vines and indices between 76 to 83 cultivated ones. Seeds with indices from 54 to 75 could belong to either subspecies.

[79] Smith and Jones 1990, p. 322.

[80] The four formulae by Mangafa and Kotsakis (1996) require measurements of length (L), breadth (B), length of the stalk (LS) and the distance from the base of the chalaza (the spoon-shaped structure on the dorsal side of a grape pip), to the tip of the stalk (PCH). See *Box 3* and Appendix 5.

[81] Mangafa and Kotsakis 1996, p. 418.

[82] The pips from unit 159 and unit 626 scored -2.2 and -1.6, respectively, for Mangafa and Kotsakis' Formula 1 (lower than -0.2: definitely wild), -2.2 and -1.2 for Formula 2 (lower than -0.2: definitely wild), -2.0 and -1.3 for Formula 3 (lower than 0: definitely wild) and -2.3 and -2 for Formula 4 (lower than -0.9: definitely wild).

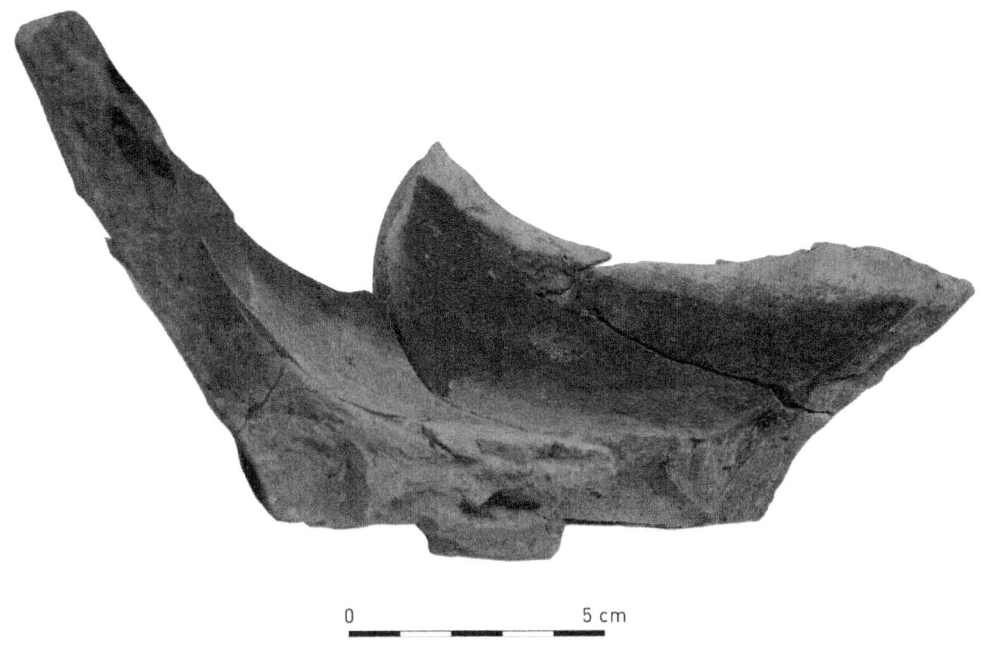

Fig. 2.25. L'Amastuola, trench 3, unit 107: Storage jar. Photo by Jan Paul Crielaard.

2.5.4 THE USE OF PLANTS IN RITUAL ACTIVITIES

The excavations on the l'Amastuola hill revealed two deposits, in trenches 2 and 6, which appeared to be of ritual origin.[83] They are represented in the archaeobotanical analysis by four sampled archaeological units, 509, 513, 229, and 233 (see *Table 2.5*). Both locations seem to have been used more or less in the same period (i.e. the first half of the 7th century BC) for rituals that involved communal eating and drinking, food sacrifices, and the ritual destruction of dining equipment. However, it is interesting to note the differences in the type of pottery that was deposited (sub-geometric vs matt-painted) and the nature of the location (inside vs outside). Crielaard and Burgers have argued that these differences can perhaps be associated with cultural or ethnic affiliations or identities, meaning that during this early stage of cohabitation at l'Amastuola, Greeks and indigenous populations held their celebrations separately.[84]

Among the macroremains from the deposit in the Iron Age hut in trench 2 were two grains of free-threshing wheat, one of emmer, and three seeds of bitter vetch. However, the most surprising discovery was made in trench 6, i.e. 27 carbonized cloves of garlic, which are the earliest finds of this type in Italy (*Figure 2.27a*).[85] The morphology of these specimens, especially the cell anatomy (which was studied under a Scanning Electron Microscope (SEM)), leaves no doubt about their identification.[86] As

[83] Burgers and Crielaard 2007, pp. 86-87; Crielaard 2011, pp. 68-75.
[84] Crielaard and Burgers 2010; 2012, p. 98.
[85] Helmut Kroll's database of literature (1981-2004) on archaeological plant remains (www.archaeobotany.de) only reports finds in Medieval (Castiglioni *et al.* 1999) and Roman (Castelletti *et al.* 2001; Rottoli 2002, p. 237) northern Italy. Prof. Mauro Rottoli of the Laboratorio di Archeobiologia dei Musei Civici di Como informed me that to his knowledge, the earliest garlic finds in northern Italy are from Roman Imperial times. Additional bibliographical research only yielded one garlic find in southern Italy, from the Casa dell'Alcova at Herculaneum (Jashemski and Meyer 2002, pp. 87-88). The cloves from l'Amastuola are more than 600 years older.

Trench	2	2	6	6	
Unit	229	233	509	513	
Context	Ritual deposition	= /229\	Around/beneath /513\	Ritual deposition	
Structure	IA hut	IA hut	ritual meal deposition	ritual meal deposition	
Date	Mid VII BC	Mid VII BC	1st half VII BC	1st half VII BC	
Charcoal					common name
Olea europaea	13		2		olive
Quercus (deciduous type)		5			oak
Quercus (evergreen type)		1		158	oak
Quercus sp.	4				oak
indet. Hardwood				19	indet. Hardwood
seeds and fruits					
Allium sativum				27	garlic
Triticum aestivum/compactum	2				free-threshing wheat
Triticum dicoccum	1				emmer wheat
Vicia ervilia	3				bitter vetch

Table 2.5 L'Amastuola, charcoal and macroremains from ritual depositions

can be seen in *Figures 2.278b and c*, the SEM photos show a pattern of elongated cells on the surface of the garlic cloves, with straight short cell walls that narrow to one point. The latter feature is diagnostic for *Allium* epidermis, but it is difficult to specify whether the specimens should be identified as garlic (*Allium sativum*), onion (*Allium cepa*) or leek (*Allium porrum*).[87] Yet, if we combine this feature with the clove-like form and the clear stem attachment scars (which are left after the cloves are separated from the stem disc on one end, see *Figure 2.27d*), there can be no doubt that these macroremains should, indeed, be identified as garlic.

Garlic is a member of the onion family, Alliaceae, and has been used throughout history for both culinary and medicinal purposes. The wild ancestry of garlic has not been definitely established, but according to Zohary and Hopf, the plant is likely to have originated in the Near East (Turkey, Iran, and Central Asia).[88] Its presence at l'Amastuola indicates that the use of garlic was known long before the arrival of the Romans in southern Italy, although we do not know whether it was cultivated here, imported, or gathered from the wild. The garlic cloves may be interpreted as a food product that was part of the ritual feast that was celebrated here. However, the fact that the ash deposition contained no other macroremains seems to indicate that the garlic cloves had some sort of ritual significance.

In short, these contexts at l'Amastuola show that the ritual offering of food was not uncommon. Indeed, similar food offerings have been found at many other sites in southeast Italy and Greece. I will discuss these in chapter 5, where I will also elaborate on the possible ritual significance of particular foodstuffs, including garlic.

---

[86] The SEM photos were made by Lucy Kubiak-Martens, to whom I am much obliged.

[87] Cf. Kubiak-Martens 2002, Figure 2b; Tomlinson 1991.

[88] Zohary and Hopf 2000, pp. 195-196.

Fig. 2.26. L'Amastuola, trench 6: Fragmented olive stones from cooking pot. Photo by the author.

2.6 SUMMARY AND CONCLUSION

The results of this first case study supply information about several important aspects of everyday life at l'Amastuola. I focused on a combination of archaeological, archaeobotanical, and archaeozoological data to demonstrate what use the inhabitants made of plants, animals, and vegetable products. The first research aspect I discussed was the use of wood. As we have seen, the charcoal assemblage in hearths and fireplaces suggests that olive and oak wood were possibly deliberately selected as fuel. More than two thirds of the charcoal collection consists of these wood types. Other species that were found included *Erica, Rhamnus/Phillyrea, Juniperus, Pistacia,* and *Arbutus unedo*. Unfortunately, the indications for the use of wood as construction material are too scant to draw firm conclusions. The same holds true for the possible evidence of charcoal production at l'Amastuola.

The archaeobotanical data also supplied information about the consumption and preparation of food at l'Amastuola. The plant part of the diet seems to have consisted mainly of hulled barley and wheat, and fruits such as olives and possibly grapes, strawberry tree berries, and crab apples. Pulses were also found in considerable amounts, most notably bitter vetch, which seems to have been a regular part of everyday meals. Hulled cereals probably played a more important role than free-threshing wheat. Cereal weeds also made up a rather significant part of the macroremains assemblage, but only weeds of roughly the same grain size as wheat and barley were found, perhaps indicating that these escaped the cleaning process of sieving. In any case, the find of some bromegrass seeds in a cooking

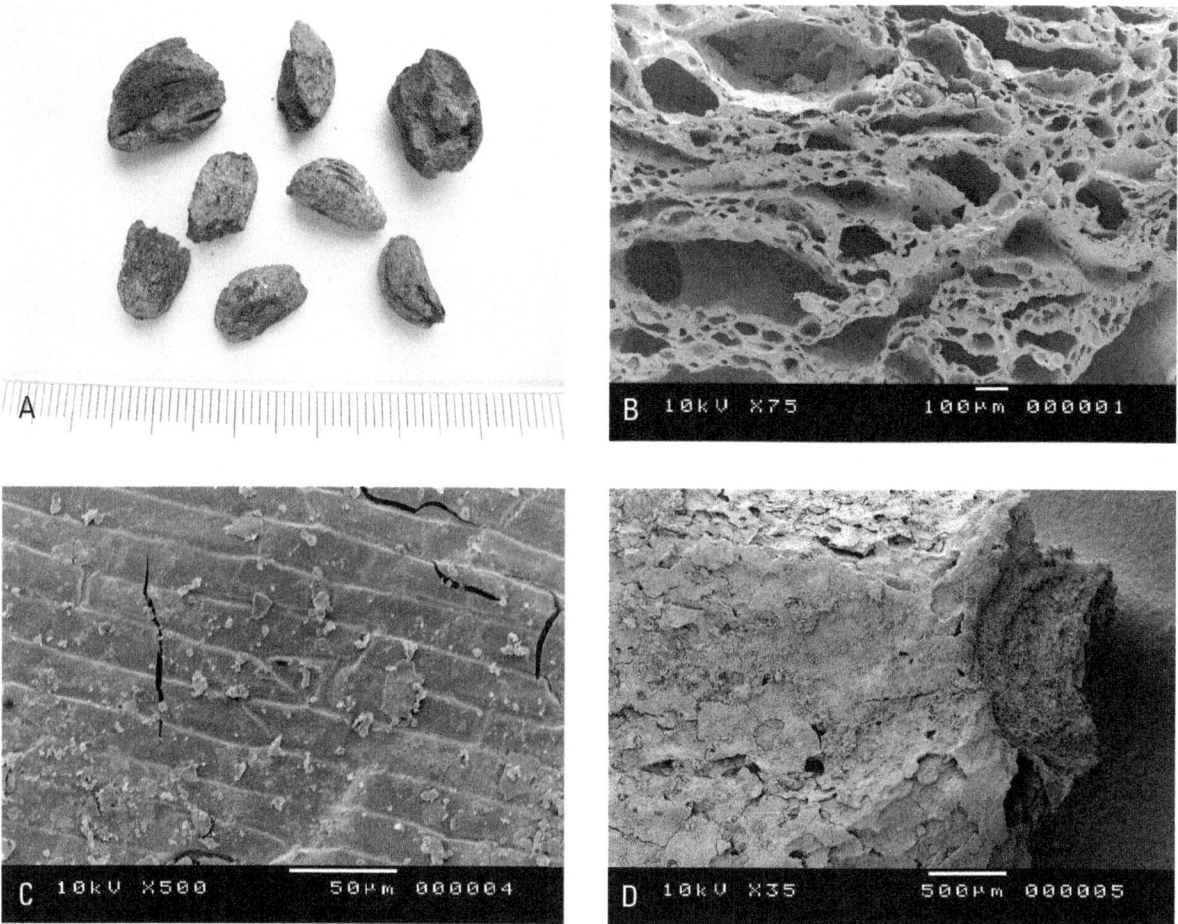

Fig. 2.27. a L'Amastuola, trench 6: Carbonized garlic cloves (*Allium sativum*). Photo by Mark van Waijjen, courtesy of Biax consult; b SEM image showing epidermal surface. Photo by Lucy Kubiak-Martens, courtesy of Biax consult; c SEM image showing epidermal surface. Photo by Lucy Kubiak-Martens, courtesy of Biax consult; d SEM image showing attachment scar. Photo by Lucy Kubiak-Martens, courtesy of Biax consult.

pot indicates that weed grains were not always removed, and were consumed together with cereals.

The presence of transport amphorae leaves little doubt that wine and olive oil were also consumed at l'Amastuola. However, there is no archaeological evidence of local olei- and viticulture. The archaeobotanical evidence also remains inconclusive, especially with regard to wine production, since no *Vitis* charcoal and only three grape pips were found. Olive macroremains are equally rare. Olive charcoal, on the other hand, is omnipresent at l'Amastuola. There are two possible explanations for this phenomenon. Either this olive wood was collected from wild trees, or it consisted of prunings from cultivated olive trees. I will return to this issue in chapter 4, when I discuss the surrounding landscape and rural economy of l'Amastuola.

Finally, I discussed the use of plants in ritual activities by comparing two intentional deposits that appeared to be of cultic character, in trench 2 and trench 6. Although these two deposits are considerably different in nature, their presence shows that food sacrifices were common during the early habitation phases of l'Amastuola. In these cases, the offerings included cereals, pulses and garlic.

In conclusion, the picture that emerges from the results at l'Amastuola is that of a small community that cultivated a wide array of crops (cereals, pulses, fruits). While it is true that most of the charcoal collection consisted of olive and oak wood, the presence of at least five other wood types suggests that the inhabitants did not go to great lengths to collect or import suitable fuel wood. These results give rise to a number of questions. Now that we have seen what types of crops were consumed and how these were prepared, we should take a look at where they were grown. Was the settlement at l'Amastuola surrounded by arable fields? What did these fields look like? What was the scale of production on these fields? Did agricultural production aim at subsistence, or was an agricultural surplus produced? Moreover, the findings about the use of wood as fuel also pose several questions. Where was this wood collected? Why were these particular wood species selected? If there were others, which ones? These issues will be discussed in chapter 4, in which I take a closer look at the landscape and land use at l'Amastuola.

Chapter 3 – Case study 2: Muro Tenente

3.1   INTRODUCTION: THE SITE AND ITS SURROUNDINGS

The archaeological site of Muro Tenente (*Figures 3.1* and *3.2*) is located between the modern towns of Latiano and Mesagne, some 20 kilometres south-west of Brindisi. The site is located in a slightly elevated position (c. 5 metres higher than the surrounding landscape) in the Brindisino plain, a relatively flat area in southeast Apulia. The settlement's ancient name is unknown; the site is probably called Muro Tenente after what is today its most conspicuous feature, the 2.7 kilometres long fortification wall (*Figure 3.3*), and the nearby *masserie* Muro and Tenente.[1] In Ester van Joolen's evaluation of the land systems in the Salento Isthmus, Muro Tenente is placed in the *Brindisino-plain land system*, a flat or almost flat ('terraced') landscape that shows no or relatively minor relief and is intersected by river valleys and depressions.[2] Today, olive orchards are the principal form of land use in the Brindisino, together with grapes and cereals (wheat and barley), and occasionally tomatoes, eggplants, melons, citrus fruits, and figs.

3.2   HISTORY OF RESEARCH

The first systematic excavations at Muro Tenente were carried out by the Soprintendenza per i Beni Archeologici della Puglia in the 1960s and 1970s. Among the first discoveries were a large number of graves and parts of a domestic quarter, dated to the 4th century BC.[3] In 1992, a survey team from VU University Amsterdam started to investigate the settlement area.[4] The surface scatters revealed that the site was occupied from the Early Iron Age until the Early Imperial period (1st century AD). The survey results showed that the intra-mural settlement area was not completely used for habitation; domestic complexes and burial locations were grouped in nuclei, with large open spaces in between. The settlement appeared to be fairly small in the early periods of its existence, and it did not expand significantly until the Early Hellenistic period. In 1993, VU University started excavations at Muro Tenente as part of the long-term research of regional settlement patterns in the Brindisi district in southeast Italy. This so-called Brindisino project also included excavations and surveys in other sites in the area, such as Oria, Masseria Mea (Cellino San Marco), Muro Maurizio, San Pancrazio Salentino, and Valesio.

The excavations at Muro Tenente continued annually until the summer of 2002. A few years later, the municipality of Mesagne started a project to create an archaeological park in the area, including the building of facilities to make the park more accessible to the public and the re-opening and cleaning of the central part of the site, while excavations began again in the spring of 2007.[5] This project was financed by the European Union and carried out by the Royal Netherlands Institute in Rome in collaboration with the Università del Salento in Lecce and VU University. More recently, three one-month summer campaigns were carried out in 2008, 2009, and 2010.

---

[1] Burgers 1994, p. 146.
[2] Van Joolen 2003, pp. 52-54.
[3] Lo Porto 1976; Russo Tagliente 1992, pp. 118-120.
[4] Burgers 1994, 1996, 1998, pp. 53-94; Burgers and Yntema 1998, 1999; Burgers and Napolitano 2010.
[5] Burgers 2010, pp. 12-13.

Fig. 3.1. Aerial view of Muro Tenente, showing the outlines of the Early Hellenistic fortification wall (cf. Figure 3.2). Burgers and Napolitano 2010, 8.

3.3 THE ARCHAEOLOGICAL RESEARCH

I will discuss the site of Muro Tenente in much the same way as I discussed l'Amastuola in the previous chapter. First, the excavation results will be presented diachronically, starting with the scarce traces of Early Iron Age habitation and ending with the site's abandonment around the 1st century AD. Subsequently, I will focus on specific contexts that were either intensively sampled and contained interesting archaeobotanical material, or are otherwise of specific interest for the interpretation of the site.

3.3.1 DIACHRONIC OVERVIEW

The survey of the settlement area has shown that the earliest Iron Age habitation was located in the centre of the walled area (*Figure 3.2*, trench C).[6] The central area is the most elevated point of the site, at about 100 metres above sea level (*Figures 3.2, 3.5*).[7] Apart from this central nucleus, a few other minor scatters of impasto pottery were detected, covering an area of some 15 hectares in total. This indicates that the settlement had a fairly dispersed character in this period. However, only a few Iron

---

[6] Burgers 1998, p. 61.

[7] This higher location also caused a greater degree of erosion in this part of the site, resulting in a considerably thinner plough zone covering the archaeological strata. In fact, some of the upper archaeological strata in the central excavation trench have already disappeared. Burgers and Yntema 1999, p. 121.

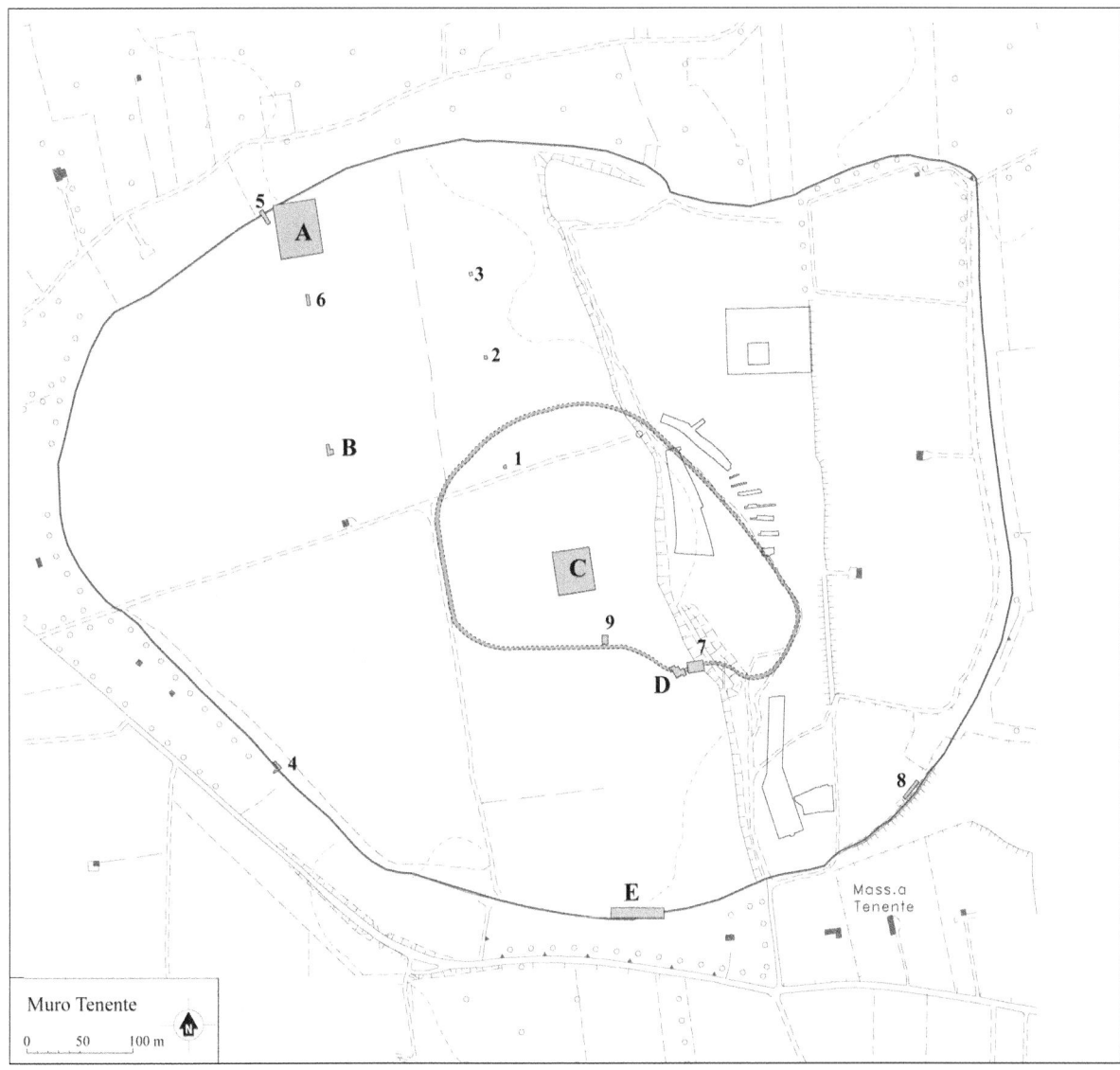

Fig. 3.2. Muro Tenente, location of the excavation trenches and soundings. Map by Jaap Fokkema.

Age features were actually discovered during the excavations, which suggests that most traces of Iron Age origin had already been removed (or built over) in antiquity. Possible remains of an Iron Age hut were found in one of the test trenches that were dug in 1992 (*Figure 3.2*, sounding nr. 1[8]). A great deal of Iron Age pottery was among the finds from the north-east and east area of the central excavation trench, but there were no architectural remains.[9]

The surveys indicate that habitation continued in the central area in the following centuries.[10] At some point in time,[11] this centre was surrounded by a fortification wall, suggesting that the enclosed

---

[8] Burgers 1996, p. 109.

[9] A rectangular structure built with upright flat stones located southeast of room 3 (*Figure 3.5*, 'IA hut?') was initially interpreted as an Iron Age storage room for agricultural products (Burgers, Crielaard and Yntema 2010, p. 19). However, later on, a closer examination of this structure indicated that an Iron Age date is highly unlikely (J.P. Crielaard, pers. comm.).

[10] Burgers 1998, p. 63.

[11] The exact date of the oldest phase (when the structure probably served as a terrace wall) is still unclear, but finds of diagnostic potter from the 6th century BC is indicative of a *terminus postquem* around that period. Pers. comm. Raphaëlle-Anne Kok-Merlino, who directed the excavation of the fortification wall in 2008.

Fig. 3.3. Muro Tenente, inner face of the southern section of the fortification wall. Burgers and Napolitano 2010, 43.

area (c. 8 hectares) had some sort of special status.[12] Only a small part of this wall was excavated (*Figure 3.2*, trench D), but its course can be followed on aerial photos. The fortification wall around the central area was apparently built and modified during several construction phases. In the latest one, between the end of the 4th and beginning of the 3rd century BC, at least one tower was added.[13] At about the same time, another fortification wall was constructed surrounding the whole settlement area. As already mentioned, this outer fortification circuit is still the best visible ancient structure at Muro Tenente. Almost the entire length of the course of the fortifications can be followed, enclosing an area of c. 52 hectares. On the basis of the ceramic evidence, it was concluded that the wall was erected in a single building phase, at some point in the early 3rd century BC.

Most of the structures in the central habitation area date to the Early Hellenistic phase, and include stone walls that seemed to define three rooms, a central courtyard, but also two roads and several clusters of graves (*Figure 3.5*). The whole complex appeared to have grown 'organically', rather than having been built according to a predefined layout. The most characteristic feature of the building complex was the so-called north wall, a particularly thick (1.5 metre) structure that was apparently built during various phases or instances, resulting in several 'shells' with a different width and construction technique. The north side of this wall was flanked by a road, paved with crushed limestone (*tufina pressata*). Against the south side of the wall, three individual rooms were built (*Figures 3.5*, rooms 1, 2, and 3), and south of these rooms, a large (140 m^2) courtyard was located. The area to the east was interpreted as a somewhat peripheral area, where fires were lit and refuse was dumped. However, the discovery of

---

[12] Burgers and Yntema 1999, p. 120.

[13] Kok 2010, pp. 34-36.

Fig. 3.4. Muro Tenente, northern excavation trench (A). Burgers and Yntema 1999, 114 (Figure 3), with additions by Jaap Fokkema.

a pit grave (*Figure 3.5*, grave 30), indicated that this area was also used for burials. In the south-eastern part of the central habitation area, another cluster of 13 graves was found.[14]

The excavations revealed two habitation quarters that were newly built in the Early Hellenistic Period. The first was located on the inner side of the northern section of the fortifications (trench A on *Figure 3.2*, see also *Figure 3.4*), the second in the southern section (*Figure 3.6*, trench E on *Figure 3.2*). In contrast to the buildings in the centre, the houses in these parts of the settlement appeared to have been built according to a predefined, regular layout, consisting of series of adjoining houses that make up a kind of *insulae*, separated from each other by paved streets. This predefined pattern might suggest that the new houses were built in a period when the settlement's population was growing rapidly, creating a need for quickly built, rationally planned new living quarters.

Despite the new building activities in this phase, the settlement's spatial and functional structure continued to have a rural character. The surveys have detected numerous isolated, fairly small scatters (c. 500 m² on average) that started to appear in the Early Hellenistic period in the area surrounding the site. It seems that, in this period, part of the population lived in farmsteads in the nearby countryside. Occasionally, fragments of funerary wares were also found at or in close proximity to these sites, indicative of small rural *necropoleis*. The extra-urban occupation seems to have consisted of isolated farm sites, mostly located at a distance of at least one kilometre from the city walls.

The period of building activities apparently ended less than a century later, when the houses in the northern periphery were abandoned. Some of the structures in the south were destroyed by fire, but this area remained partly in use. Two rectangular structures were built parallel to the fortification wall (*Figure 3.6*, ambiente 1 and 2), but they may have been seasonal refuges and not permanently inhabited houses.[15] The presence of nine large tufa blocks close to the fortification wall has been interpreted as a sign that some restoration work on the wall was carried out. The necessity to reinforce the fortification wall might be connected to events during the Second Punic War (218-201 BC), when Hannibal pillaged large parts of Apulia.[16] After the abandonment of the domestic quarters in the periphery, the site was reduced to a much smaller building nucleus in the former town centre. Habitation continued here until the early Imperial period. The peripheral zones were no longer used for housing, but for agricultural purposes and, occasionally, burials.

3.3.2 SPECIFIC CONTEXTS

Central area (Figures 3.5 and 3.9)
The walls of the three rooms that were excavated in the central excavation trench all had stone foundations with mud brick superstructures, and plaster or clay floors. Only the room in the middle (room 2) was completely covered with a tiled roof. Inside, traces of pyrotechnical activity were found: a hearth and, in a later phase, a small oven or furnace. Both features probably had a domestic function. The hearth could be used to heat the room and prepare food at high temperatures, whereas the furnace was probably utilized to cook food at a low fire.[17] The easternmost room (room 3) housed a small well (unit 450), consisting of a square pit that was lined with stone slabs. Room 1 on the west side was probably a semi-indoor area, that was used for household activities. It was named the 'entrance room' after the large, rectangular 'threshold' of limestone that is incorporated in the north wall.[18] On its west

[14] Tetteroo and Waagen 2010, pp. 111-140.

[15] Di Noi and Burgers 2010, p. 48.

[16] Di Noi and Burgers 2010, p. 52.

[17] Units 1675 and unit 1775, not sampled. Crielaard, unpublished preliminary report of the 2001 campaign at Muro Tenente, p. 7.

[18] Although the excavation of the wall clearly showed that this limestone block is part of the outer face, and the entrance of Room 1 was probably on the south side.

Fig. 3.5. Muro Tenente, central excavation trench (C). Burgers and Napolitano 2010, 4, with additions by Jaap Fokkema.

side, another paved road was located that reached a dead-end against the north wall. Overall, the three rooms give the impression of small, very modest living and working areas.

As the survey and test trenches had already indicated, the settlement area was not completely used for habitation. Large open spaces existed in between the habitation nuclei. It seems that this pattern was repeated on a smaller scale at the level of individual households, as the excavated houses were also separated by open spaces. The function of these open spaces is unclear, but it is possible that they were used for various domestic activities, for example to keep animals, grow fruit and vegetables, and store and process crops. In the courtyard south of the three rooms, a small water channel was located, which consisted of three worked stone blocks that were heavily damaged by recent ploughing activities. In the area south of the courtyard, a layer with much charcoal (units 455, 458, 459, and 1702) was found.[19] The latest datable pottery from this stratum could be attributed to the late 4th century BC. The charcoal may have been scooped out of a nearby structure that was interpreted as a kiln (units 841 and 598), possibly for the production of pottery, or indeed charcoal (see section 3.5.1).

In the open area east of the three rooms, two deep pits were excavated that yielded evidence of pyrotechnic activities *in situ* (units 1630, 1635, and unit 1663). Other finds included an ash deposit (unit 503, dating to the 4th century BC), and some bones and a skull of a sheep/goat (unit 1620). The area also contained a tomb (grave 30). About 50 centimetres northeast of this grave a black spot was found, containing a large quantity of carbonized grape remains. There seems to be no stratigraphic connection between grave 30 and this grape deposit.

Funerary remains (Figures 3.22 and 3.23)
Clusters of graves were excavated in the central and northern excavation trenches.[20] Unfortunately, the majority had been plundered during recent looting activities. The earliest graves are of the *fossa* (pit) type, dating to the 5th century BC. Four graves in the central trench are more elaborate cist tombs, which are also datable to the 5th century BC. The graves in the centre seem to be clustered in small nuclei, with enclosure walls delineating the different burial plots. The wall structures in the southeast corner of the same trench can probably be interpreted as the foundations of similar burial enclosures. Although the tombs at Muro Tenente are clustered and not randomly dispersed over the settlement area, it is not appropriate to refer to them as *necropoleis*,[21] since they do not form a separate 'city of the dead' outside the living quarters.

In 2001, osteological analyses were carried out on 28 skeletons (found in graves excavated between 1995 and 2001) by Erik Akkerman.[22] The average body height of the deceased inhabitants in these graves was around 155 centimetres for adult women and 163 centimetres for men.[23] Most of the adults suffered from degenerative arthritis, a joint disorder that is caused by daily wear, usually presenting itself in old age. However, since the average age at death of the individuals in this sample was only 26.5 years old for women and 33.5 years old for men, the presence of arthritis might indicate that these individuals continuously carried out heavy physical labour. This seems to be confirmed by the discovery that the muscle attachments on the bones of most individuals were quite large, suggesting a well-developed muscular system. Overall, it can be said that the skeleton remains are indicative of a hard-working peasant population.

The northern Early Hellenistic habitation quarter (Figure 3.4)
The different layout of the houses in the Early Hellenistic complex located next to the northern fortification wall, compared to the buildings in the centre, was perhaps the result of rational planning. Geophysical research indicated that the soil underneath the houses was probably used for agricultural purposes prior to the construction of the habitation quarter. The complex was built in the early 3rd century BC, and abandoned in the final quarter of the same century. Some small and scattered cemeteries were also discovered, mostly datable to the 4th century BC.[24] The houses consisted of stone plinths carrying mud brick superstructures and tiled roofs of which the scatters were found on the earthen floors. Most houses had several rooms, some of them with clearly defined functions, such as one of the northernmost rooms (IX) that contained a series of large storage vessels (*dolia*) still *in situ*, probably for the storage of agricultural produce.[25] One of the other rooms (VIII) had plastered walls, and in one

---

[19] Unit 458 is described in the find administration as 'small black charcoal spots forming some sort of construction: postholes?' But considering their location among the other charcoal depositions, it seems likely that these spots are also related to the nearby kiln.

[20] Tetteroo and Waagen 2010.

[21] As, for example, Burgers and Yntema (1999, p. 121) call it.

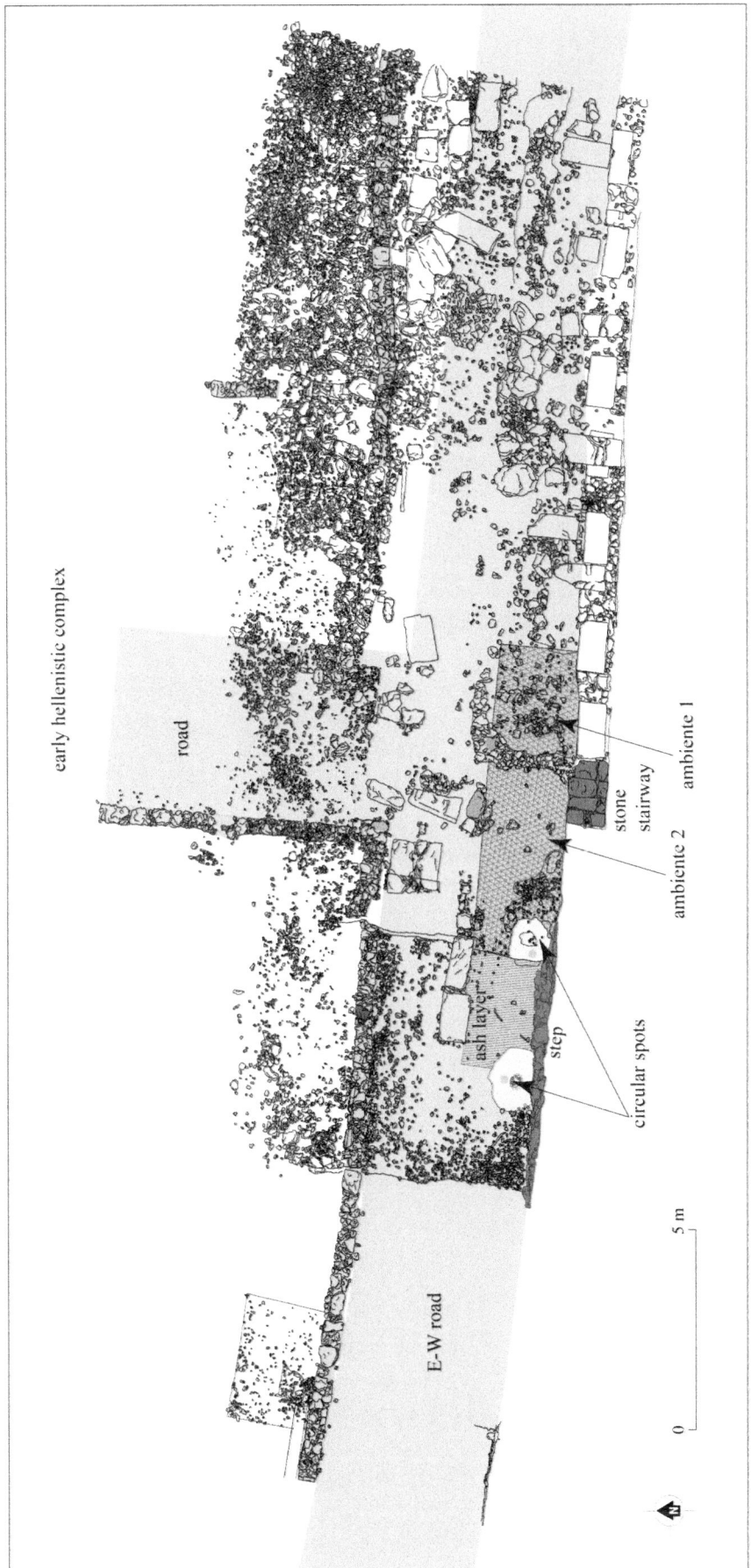

Fig. 3.6. Muro Tenente, southern excavation trench (E). Drawing by Jaap Fokkema.

of its corners, a concentration of 36 pyramidal loom weights was found. Another indication of small-scale craft activities came from the supposed courtyard at the eastern side of this room, where a large quantity of misfired shards suggests that this zone was used for pottery production.[26]

The southern Early Hellenistic habitation quarter (Figure 3.6)
This part of the settlement probably housed a habitation quarter that is contemporary to the one along the northern fortification wall, but only a very small part of it has been excavated. The investigations so far have unearthed a stone stairway that gave access to the fortifications, a road that ran along the inside of the wall, and another road that probably connected the wall with the centre of the settlement. The Early Hellenistic building complex was built next to this north-south orientated road, in a similar style as the houses in the northern trench, with stone walls and tile roofs.

In the eastern corner of the southern trench, a step in the fortification wall was found, and a thick, charcoal-rich layer ('ash layer') that extended over a more or less rectangular area of 5 x 2 metres. This layer was sampled thoroughly, resulting in 18 soil samples.[27] It has been interpreted as the remains of a wooden structure, which may have been in use shortly after the abandonment of the peripheral living quarters along the northern and southern part of the fortification wall.[28] The exact period of occupation, however, is not entirely clear, so the structure could also be contemporaneous to the living quarters. The burnt layer was cut by two large brownish circular spots, which were initially thought to have contained large storage vessels. In the middle, a smaller dark circle was visible that looked like a posthole. In 2008, one of the two '*pithoi*'-pits (unit 20056) was excavated (the other one was too shallow), only to reveal that it hardly contained any archaeological material. The smaller 'posthole' in the middle included a few hard-baked pottery shards, that were placed upright in the hole, presumably to hold a wooden pole.[29] Unfortunately, neither the '*pithoi*', nor the posthole spots contained any datable pottery, so we can only conclude that these features date from a period posterior to the burnt layer.

This part of the settlement was abandoned in the same period as the habitation quarter in the north, i.e. around the last quarter of the 3rd century BC. The two small rooms that were built parallel to the fortification wall (*ambiente* 1 and 2) belong to the most recent traces of habitation. Only one of these 'rooms' (1) has been excavated, revealing several occupational layers and a fireplace. To judge from the reinforcement of the fortification wall in this period, the later 3rd and 2nd centuries BC may have been eventful periods for the inhabitants of Muro Tenente.

---

[22] Akkerman 2002.

[23] This is shorter than the average modern Italian (165 cm for women and 176 cm for men (Garcia and Quintana-Domeque 2007), but similar to southern Italy's peasant population before the Second World War (Carter 2006, p. 42).

[24] Burgers and Yntema 1999, p. 122.

[25] Burgers 1998, p. 118.

[26] Burgers and Yntema 1999, p. 120.

[27] Unfortunately, the exact location where the samples were taken was not marked in the excavation report.

[28] Di Noi and Burgers 2010, p. 47. This abandonment probably took place in the final quarter of the 3rd century BC; the ash layer contained the base of a black gloss vase that provided a date in the late 3rd or early 2nd century BC.

[29] Pers. comm. from Lucia di Noi, who directed the excavations in the southern excavation trench in 2007.

3.4 THE ARCHAEOBOTANICAL RESEARCH[30]

3.4.1 SAMPLING METHODS AND DATA[31]

During the first years of excavation (1992-2000), archaeobotanical sampling was conducted only occasionally. For this reason, there is only a limited quantity of plant material from the parts of the settlement that were excavated before 2001, particularly the domestic complex in the northern periphery (trench A, excavated 1992-1998). Only seven units were sampled, seemingly at random (their locations are indicated in *Figure 3.7*). One single sample was taken in test trench B (*Figure 3.8*). In the central excavation area (trench C), samples were taken from 47 units. Seven of them derived from burials; the other samples were collected in a variety of other contexts, all datable to the Early Hellenistic period (*Figure 3.9*). During the excavations in 2007 along the interior of the southern fortification wall (trench E), a total of 41 soil samples were taken from eleven stratigraphic units (*Figure 3.10*). The archaeobotanical analyses yielded a total of 5158 charcoal fragments and 5628 carbonized seeds and fruits. The complete results can be found in Appendix 3, *Figures 3.12* and *3.13* (charcoal), *Figures 3.14* and *3.15* (seeds and fruits). In the figures, no chronological or contextual differences have been distinguished.

3.4.2 CHARCOAL

Figures 3.12 and *3.13* make it clear that the great majority of charcoal fragments from Muro Tenente, at least in absolute numbers (792 fragments), belongs to the genus *Erica*, including tree heath and Mediterranean heath fragments. However, in terms of frequency (i.e. how often a taxon is found in different units), *Olea europaea* heads the list (19 units). Another wood taxon that occurs quite frequently is oak, including both evergreen and deciduous types. *Juniperus* sp. was found in large numbers, but all these fragments came from a single context, in contrast to *Pistacia* sp., which appeared in modest amounts, but in quite a few different units. In addition to the carbonized wood of *Pistacia lentiscus*, several fruits were found. Other taxa that were identified include pine wood, myrtle and *Rhamnus/Phillyrea*. Finally, a few fragments of charcoal from an apple or pear genus (*Pyrus/Malus*) were found. A short description of the main characteristics of all these species was given in chapter 2, where the results of the archaeobotanical analyses at l'Amastuola are discussed. However, a few plant species were found at Muro Tenente that did not occur in the samples from l'Amastuola. These include pomegranate (*Punica granatum*), which was found in one context only and appeared too damaged to provide a secure identification. A few small fragments of sage (*Salvia*) were found in one context. *Salvia* is the largest genus in the mint family, Lamiaceae, with a few dozen species of shrubs, herbaceous perennials, and annuals. *Ephedra* (Mormon-tea) is a small (20-150 cm) plant that occurs in dry climates over a wide area across southern Europe, mostly on beaches and on dry calcareous soils. The fragments of *Populus/Salix* are a bit of a surprise in this context, as neither poplar (*Populus*), nor willow (*Salix*) are *macchia* species. They are both found primarily on moist soils along water courses, none of which can be found around the site of Muro Tenente today. Wild apples and pears (*Pyrus pyraster, Pyrus amygdaliformis, Malus sylvestris*) can still be found throughout the Mediterranean region in forests, *macchie* and *garighe*. The cultivated species are *Pyrus communis* and *Malus domestica*, but on the basis of the anatomy of these charcoal fragments, it is not possible to determine whether the wood belonged to a cultivated variant.

---

[30] The archaeobotanical finds from Muro Tenente have already partly been published in Burgers and Lentjes 2008 and Lentjes 2010 (all macroremains).

[31] A detailed description of the sample processing method and the complete analysis results can be found in the appendix.

Fig. 3.7. Muro Tenente, archaeobotanical samples from the northern excavation trench (A). Drawing by Jaap Fokkema.

Fig. 3.8. Muro Tenente, archaeobotanical sample from test trench B. Drawing by Jaap Fokkema.

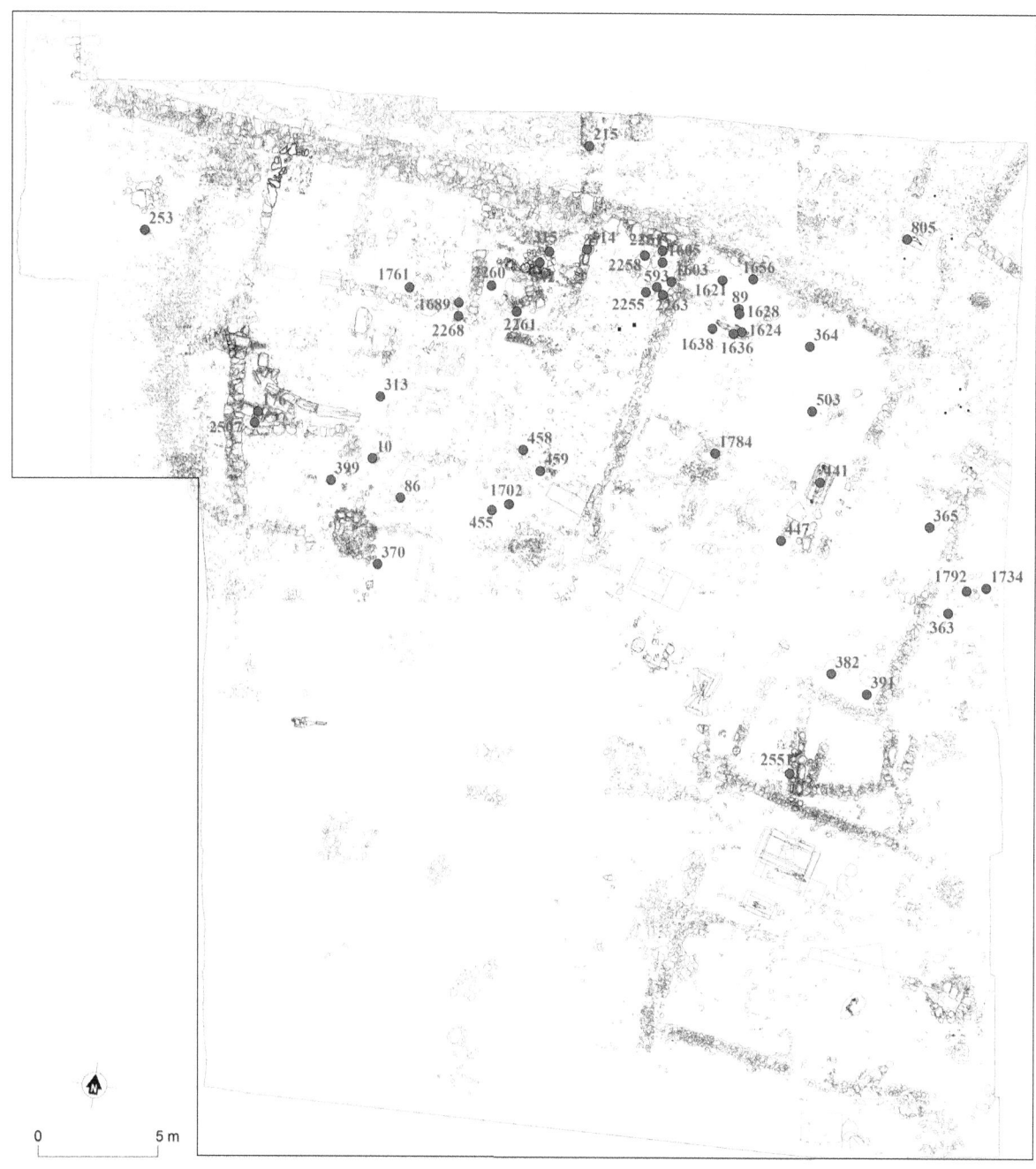

Fig. 3.9. Muro Tenente, archaeobotanical samples from the central excavation trench (C). Drawing by Jaap Fokkema

3.4.3 SEEDS AND FRUITS

The sample from Muro Tenente mostly consisted of cereals, the majority of them free-threshing wheat and barley, both naked and hulled (see *Figures 3.14* and *3.15*). Other cereals that were found at Muro Tenente include rye, oat, and emmer wheat. The only rachis internodes that were found at Muro Tenente belong to the latter cereal type. Pulses were found mostly in burial contexts. Broad bean and bitter vetch are the most common types. Fruit remains are quite rare, with the exception of the large deposition of carbonized grapes that was located next to grave 30. Olive stones were also found, as well as two mastic berries and two unknown fruits from the Rosaceae family.

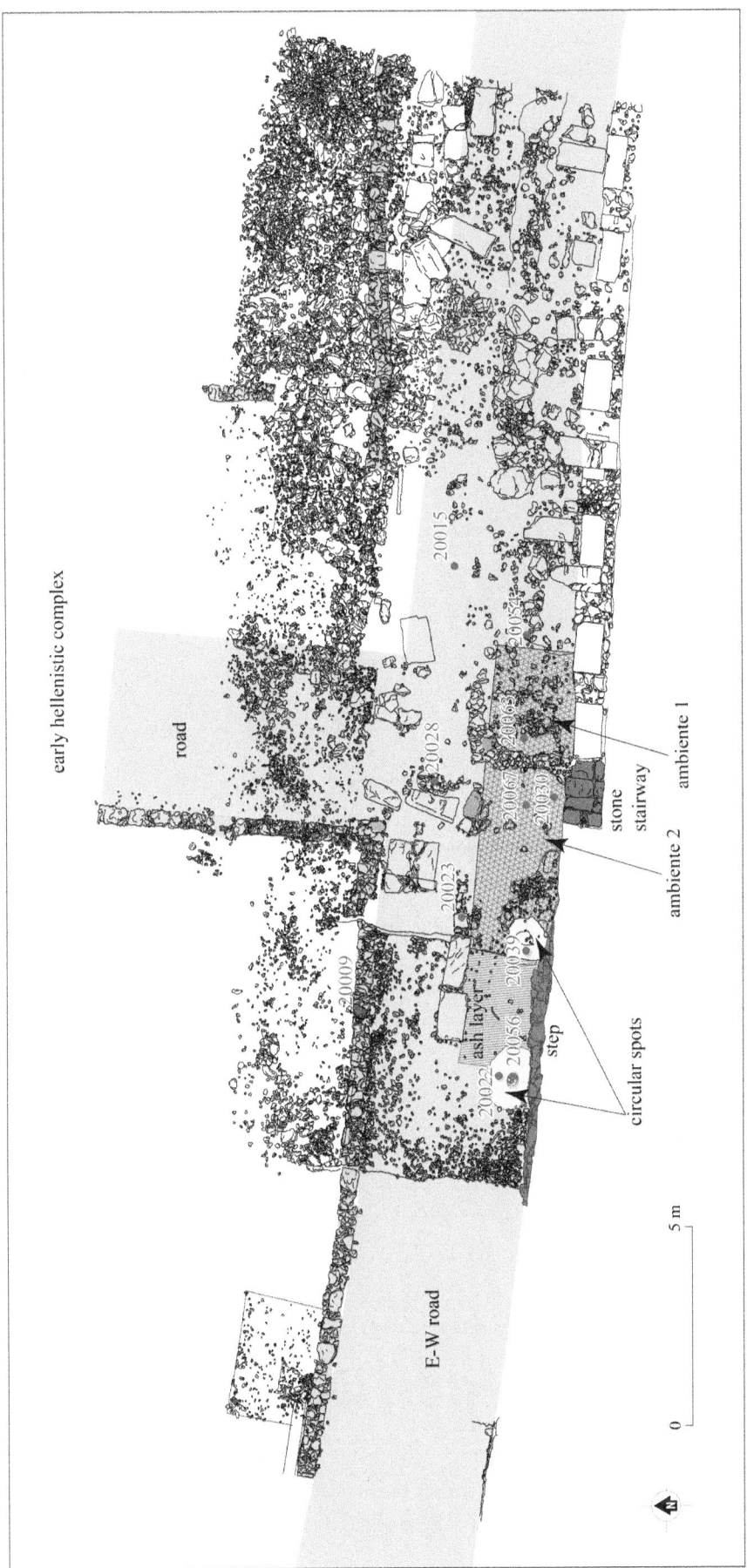

Fig. 3.10. Muro Tenente, archaeobotanical samples from the southern excavation trench (E). Drawing by Jaap Fokkema.

Fig. 3.11. Muro Tenente, ashy layer in the southern excavation trench (E), units 20009 and 20011. Photo by Lucia Di Noi.

3.5 THE ARCHAEOBOTANICAL RESEARCH: INTERPRETATIONS

To facilitate the comparison with l'Amastuola, the following pages are organized in the same way as section 2.5, starting the discussion of the archaeobotanical data from Muro Tenente with a review of the use of wood, followed by discussions of food preparation and diet, the cultivation of grapes and olives, and the use of plants in ritual activities.

3.5.1 THE USE OF WOOD

In *Table 3.1* and *Fig. 3.16*, charcoal from six contexts that can be associated with hearths or furnaces are compared in order to form a general picture of which firewood was used. The same restrictions that were expressed in Chapter 2 obviously hold true for the charcoal assemblage of Muro Tenente. In other words, it only provides a partial impression of which species were preferred as fuel and/or produce ash, with no distinction between different types of pyrotechnic structures. Just like the charcoal assemblage from l'Amastuola, the fuel species at Muro Tenente included olive and oak wood. Other wood types that were used as fuel include *Pistacia* and members of the Pomoideae family. Interestingly, oak does not abound in the fuel assemblage; a large quantity of fragments was found in unit 458, but

Trench	C	C	C	
Unit	253	455	458	
Context	refuse dump	charcoal deposit	charcoal deposit	
Structure	-	kiln	kiln	
Date	IV-III BC	2nd half IV BC	2nd half IV BC	
Taxa				common name
Erica sp. (incl. Erica cf. multiflora and Erica cf. arborea)	23	65	100	Mediterranean/ tree heath
Olea europaea	49			olive
Pistacia sp.	19			mastic
Pomoideae (Pyrus/Malus)				pear/ apple
Quercus sp.			201	oak
unidentifiable hardwood	136	70	364	unidentifiable hardwood
Trench	C	C	C	
Unit	459	503	1702	
Context	charcoal deposit	ash deposit	charcoal deposit	
Structure	kiln	-	kiln	
Date	2nd half IV BC	IV BC	2nd half IV BC	
Taxa				common name
Erica sp. (incl. Erica cf. multiflora and Erica cf. arborea)	10	10	467	Mediterranean/ tree heath
Olea europaea				olive
Pistacia sp.				mastic
Pomoideae (Pyrus/Malus)			7	pear/ apple
Quercus sp.				oak
unidentifiable hardwood		28	1650	unidentifiable hardwood

Table 3.1: Muro Tenente, charcoal from contexts that can be associated with hearths or furnaces

Trench	E	E	
Unit	20011	20056	
Context	ashy layer	post hole	
Structure	burnt structure?	?	
Date	Late Hellenistic	Late Hellenistic	
Taxa			common name
Erica sp.	5		heath
Juniperus sp.		373	juniper
Olea europaea	55	10	olive
Pinus sp.		10	pine
Pistacia cfr. lentiscus	4		mastic
Rhamnus/Phillyrea			Rhamnus/Phillyrea
Quercus cf. evergreen type	62		oak
Quercus sp.	91		oak
indet. hardwood	53		indet. hardwood

Table 3.2: Muro Tenente, charcoal from contexts that can be associated with construction material

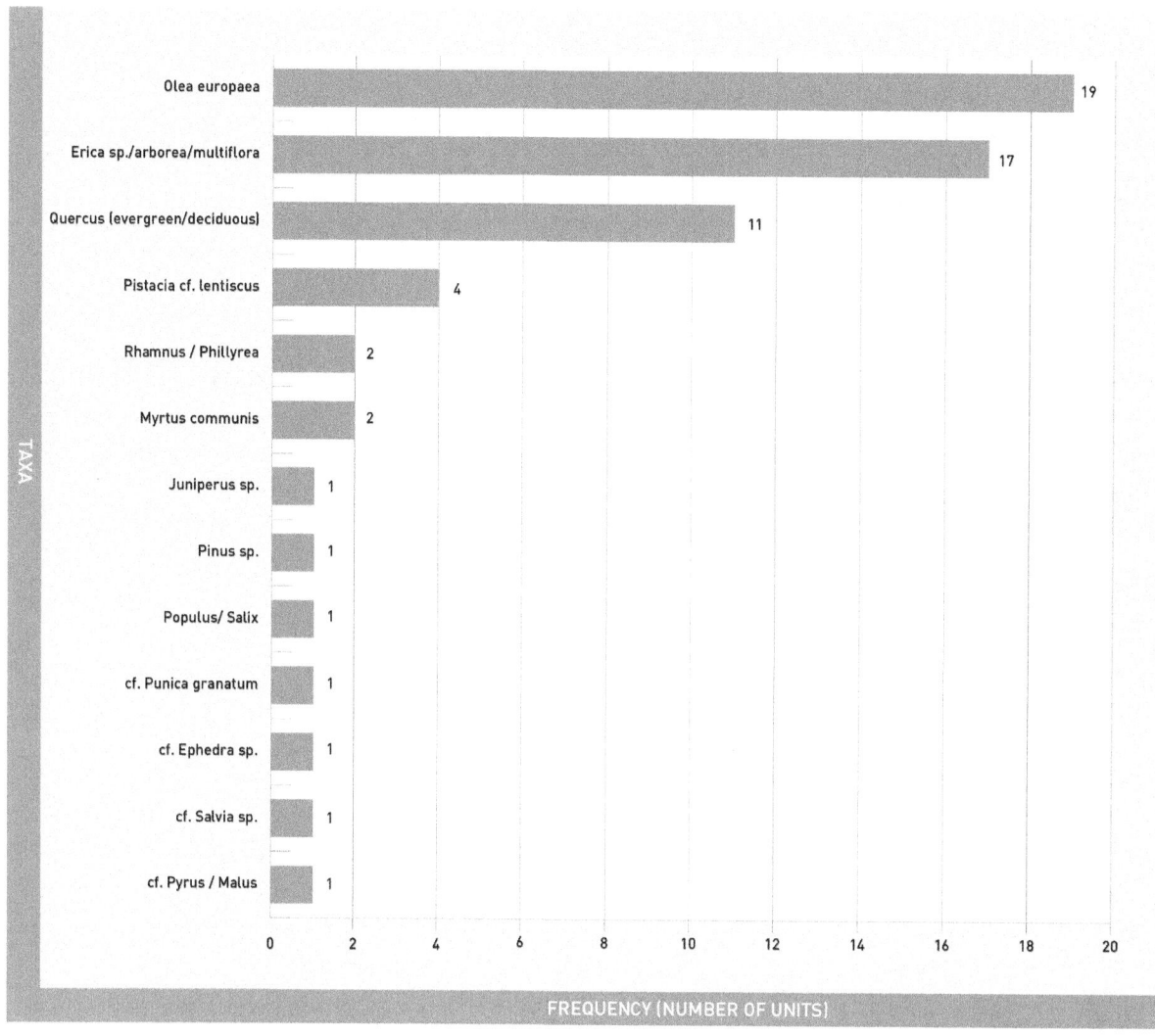

Fig. 3.12. Muro Tenente, results of the charcoal analysis: Frequency of wood taxa (i.e. the number of stratigraphical units in which it was found). Chart by Bert Brouwenstijn.

none of the other units contained oak charcoal. A possible explanation is that oak wood would have been difficult to obtain, if there were no oak forests within easy reach of the settlement.

As we have seen above, *Erica* wood abounds in the archaeobotanical assemblage from Muro Tenente. Apparently, it was also regularly collected to use as firewood. *Erica* wood is, indeed, a good choice to light a fire, but it is not very suitable to maintain it and to reach a high temperature. While doing some ad hoc experiments with *Erica* twigs and fire, I found that small, sun-dried twigs in particular took no time at all to burn and turn to ashes. It is possible that the *Erica* branches that were used as fuel for fires at Muro Tenente were thicker and contained more water, or even that most of the *Erica* wood was entirely consumed by the fire.

Interestingly, the excavations at Muro Tenente revealed two deposits of ash that were not associated with pyrotechnic structures (units 253 and 503). Since ash can be used for a variety of purposes,[32] it is possible that it was collected and stored here on purpose. In fact, ash production could very well

[32] The alkalic properties of ash make it especially effective as a whitening agent to wash clothes, but also to use as a fertilizer for agricultural fields. Hakbijl (2002) also reports its effectiveness as an insecticide.

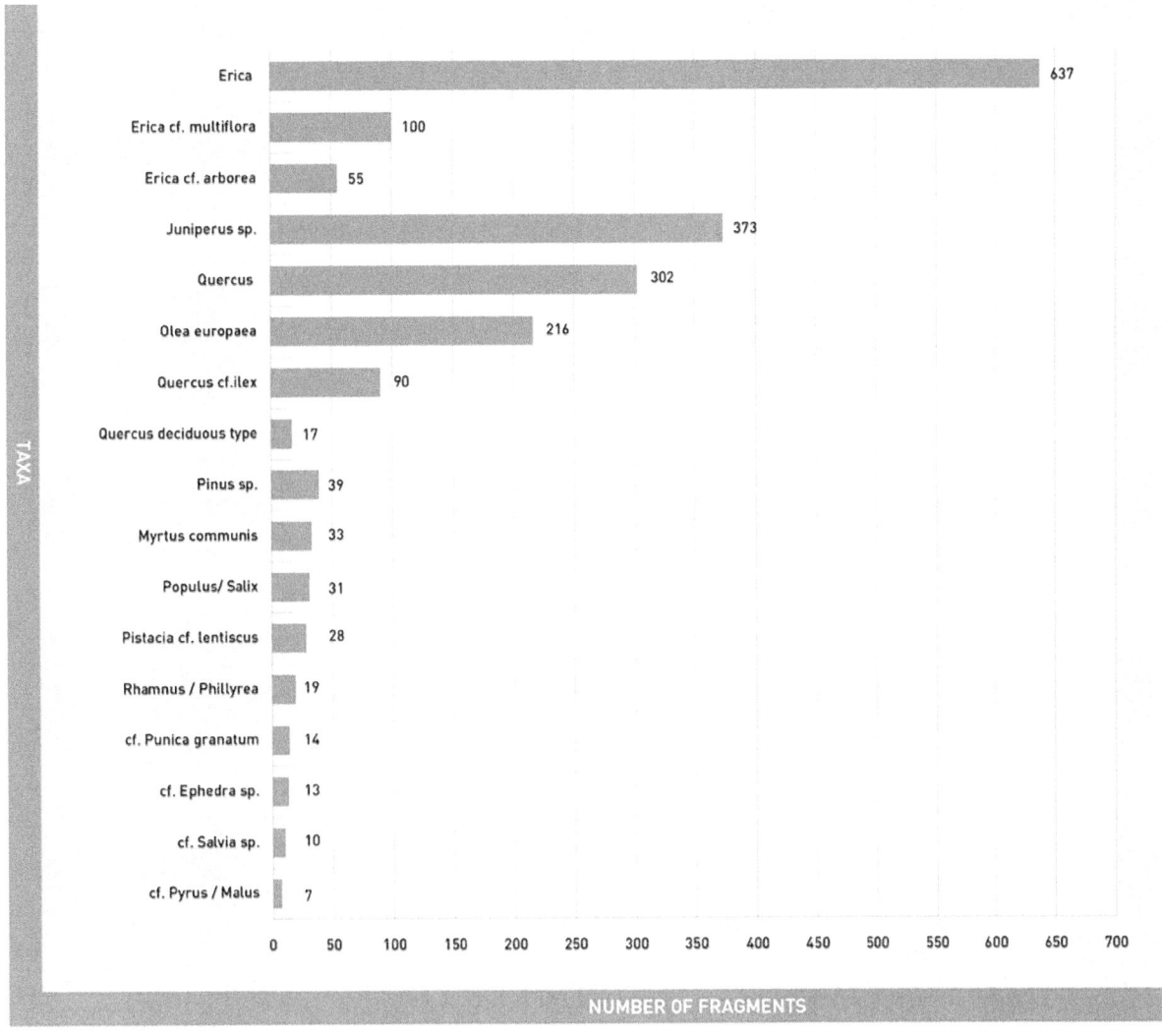

Fig. 3.13. Muro Tenente, results of the charcoal analysis: Total number of fragments of wood taxa. Chart by Bert Brouwenstijn.

have been part of the settlement's routine craft activities. The same can be argued for the production of charcoal. There are no archaeological indications of the use of charcoal burners at Muro Tenente, but, as I explained in Chapter 2, such structures can be archaeologically invisible. Most of the charcoal that was collected in the areas around the 'kiln' structure in the area south of the rooms[33] and in the courtyard in trench C[34] (*Fig. 3.9*) showed severe heat damage and vitrification, as can be seen on *Fig. 3.17*. This damage could indicate that the fuel was already carbonized before use[35] (i.e. that it was charcoal instead of wood), especially since the 'kiln' may have been used for pottery production or metal smelting, which requires high temperatures. Indeed, it could even be hypothesized that this kiln was especially used for the production of charcoal, which would explain the abundant presence of (heavily damaged) charcoal fragments in this part of the courtyard.

To complete the discussion of the use of wood, a few observations can be made about wood as construction material (see *Table 3.2*). The recent excavations along the southern fortification wall (trench E) supplied two possible examples of charcoal remains from buildings. Unfortunately, no comparable

[33] Units 253, 455, 458, 503, and 1702.
[34] Units 841 and unit 598.
[35] Although recent studies (McParland *et al.* 2010) show that vitrified charcoal does not always result from high temperature charring.

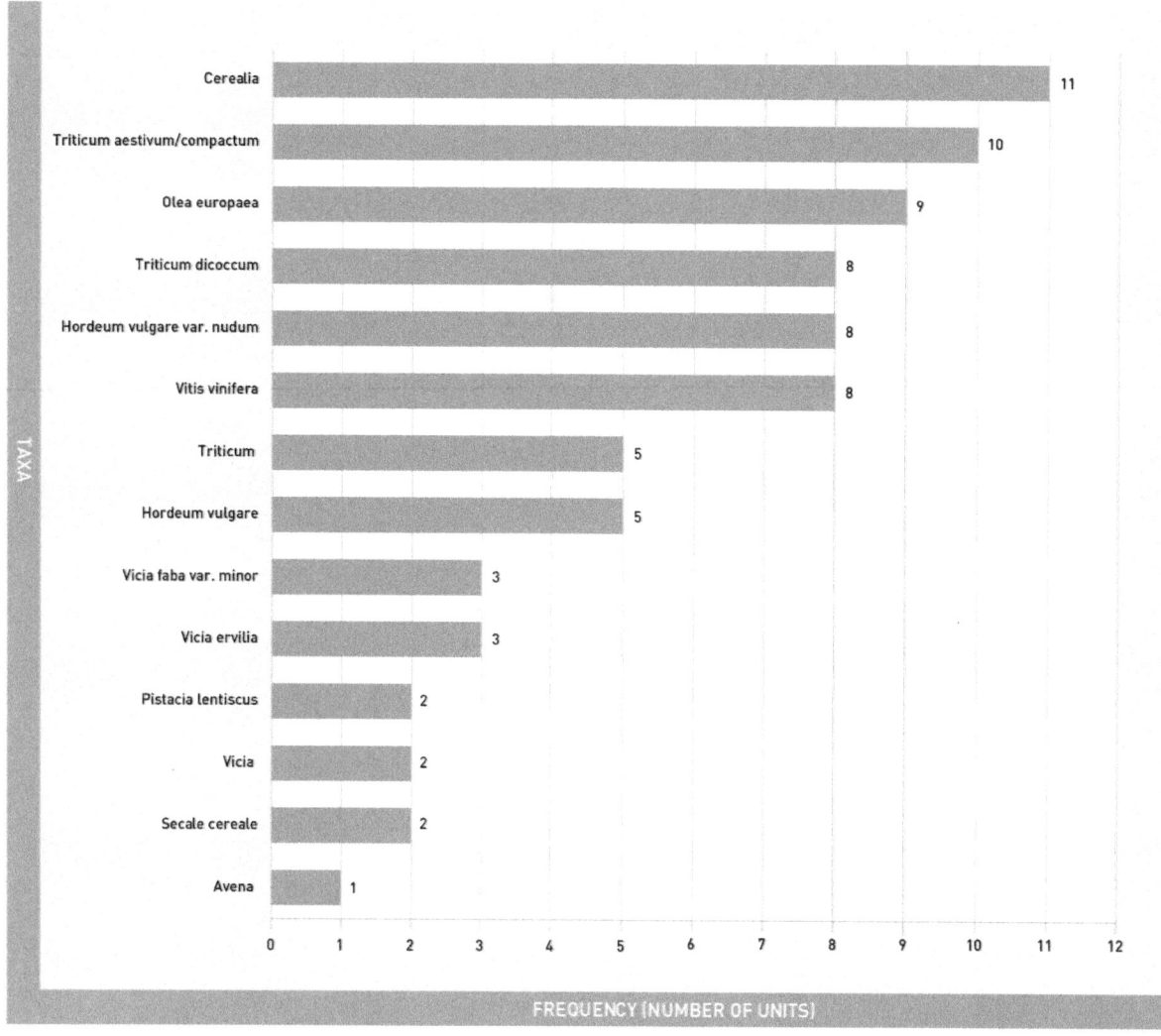

Fig. 3.14. Muro Tenente, results of the analysis of seeds and fruits: Frequencies. Chart by Bert Brouwenstijn.

contexts were found in the other excavation trenches. The remains from the southern trench can both be associated with the charcoal-rich layer in the eastern corner ('ash layer' on *Figure 3.6*, see also *Figure 3.11*) and were retrieved from the ash layer itself (unit 20011) and from one of the post holes (unit 20056) that was found in it. As I described above in section 3.3.2, this posthole spot dates to a period posterior to the burnt layer.

The charcoal from unit 20056 is the only context in Muro Tenente where *Juniperus*-wood was found. The wood of Mediterranean juniper (*Juniperus communis*) is known for its excellent qualities, since it is robust, easy to work, fragrant and takes a good polish. Indeed, juniper wood was highly praised as construction wood by the Romans.[36] It is unclear, however, whether it was used as a wooden post here or for some other part of the structure, such as the roof or the floor.

The charcoal from the ashy layer included oak, olive, mastic, and *Erica* wood (*Figure 3.19*). I would argue that the relatively large amount of oak (153 fragments out of 270, i.e. 57%) derived from the timber used for this structure, including one of the central posts that supported the roof. Oak trees generally produce excellent timber.[37] The roof was possibly covered with heather twigs (*Erica*), and could even have been supported by beams made of olive wood, although olive is not particularly

[36] Meiggs 1982.

[37] Gale and Cutler 2000, p. 204.

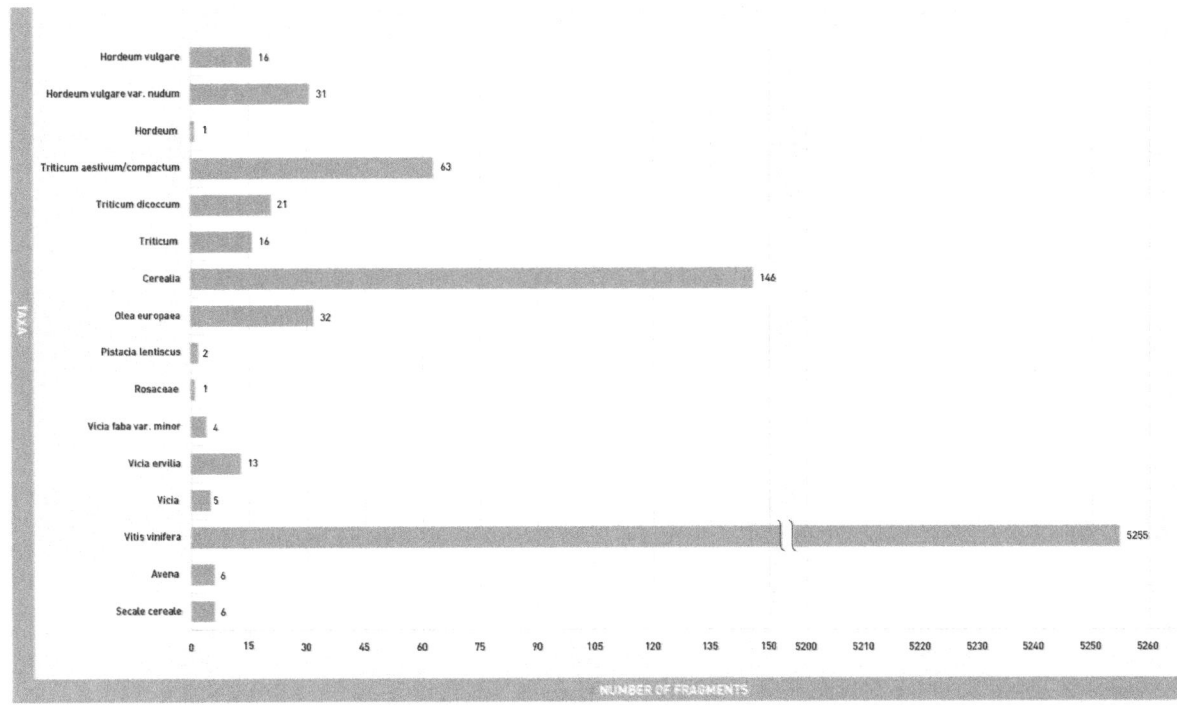

Fig. 3.15. Muro Tenente, results of the analysis of seeds and fruits: Total number of fragments. Chart by Bert Brouwenstijn.

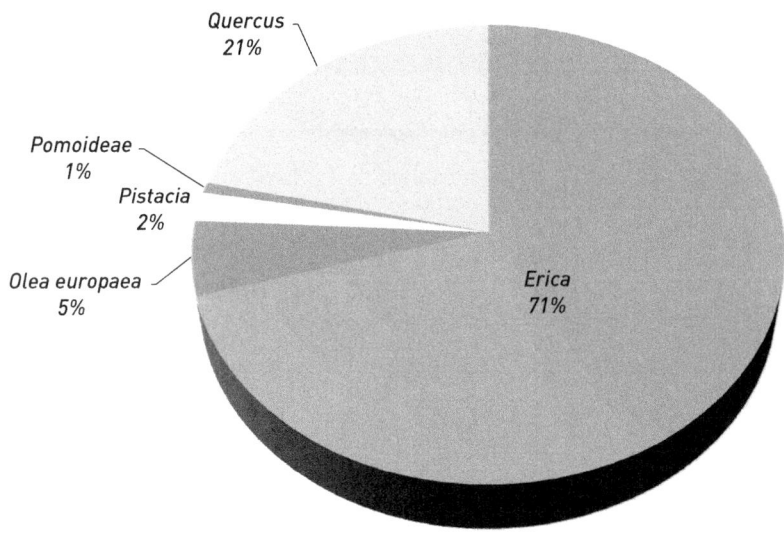

Fig. 3.16. Muro Tenente, results of the charcoal analysis: Wood taxa from hearths and fireplaces (fuel?). Chart by Bert Brouwenstijn.

suitable for construction. However, it is also possible that the olive wood, together with mastic, *Erica* and various cereals, fruits and pulses that were found in the same context, were the remains of either a refuse dump or storage facility in this area (see section 4.3.2). Summarizing, very little can be said about wood as construction material at Muro Tenente, because there is too little charcoal from associated contexts. It appears that *Erica*, juniper, olive, mastic, and oak wood were all used in house building, but it is unclear for which parts of the structures.

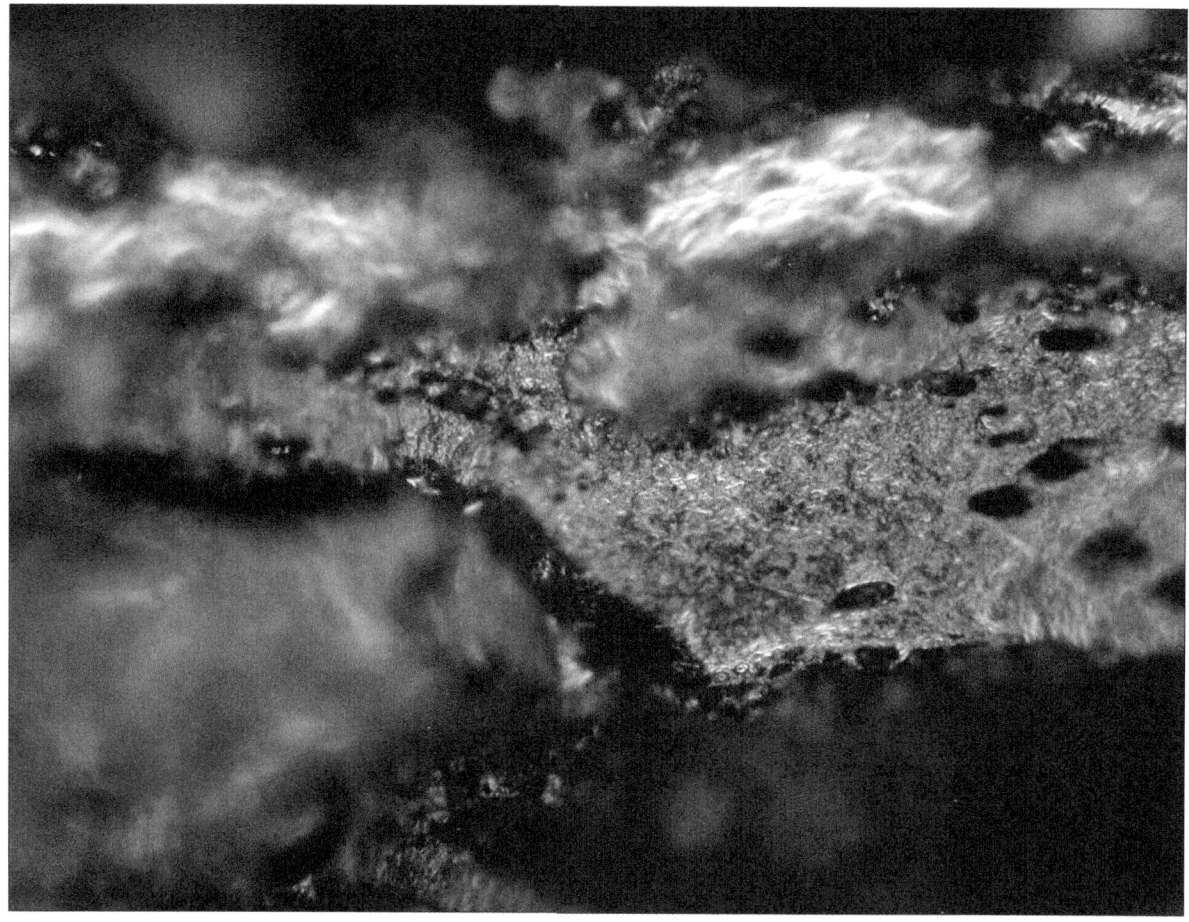

Fig. 3.17a. Muro Tenente, charcoal fragment from unit 455. Photo by the author.

Fig. 3.17b. Muro Tenente, charcoal fragment from unit 455, 100x magnification. Photo by the author.

3.5.2 FOOD PREPARATION AND DIET

The cereal spectrum at Muro Tenente differs somewhat from the one at l'Amastuola. Free-threshing wheat abounds, as well as naked barley. Considering that free-threshing cereals are usually underrepresented because there is less chance that they get carbonized in the cleaning process, it may be assumed that free-threshing wheat and naked barley were an important part of everyday meals at Muro

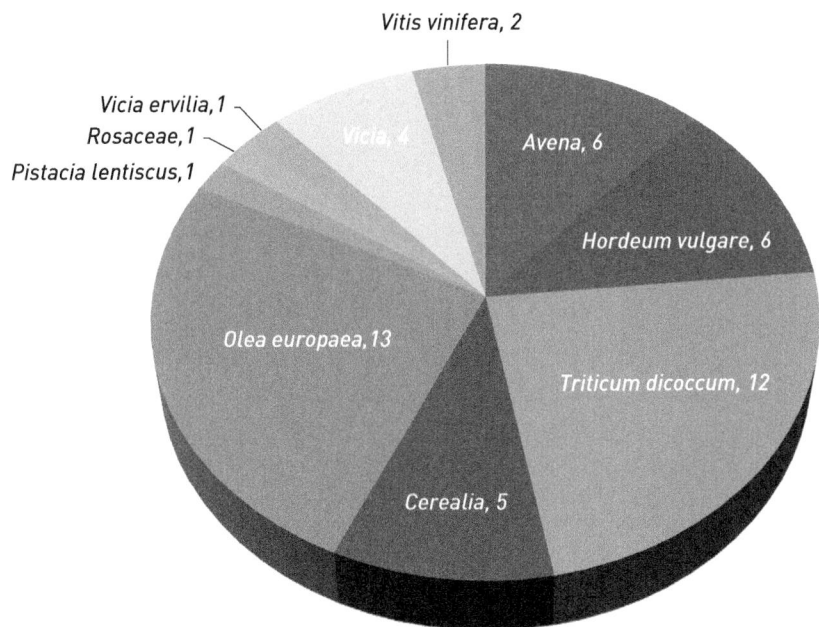

Fig. 3.18. Muro Tenente, results of the analysis of seeds and fruits from unit 20011. Chart by Bert Brouwenstijn.

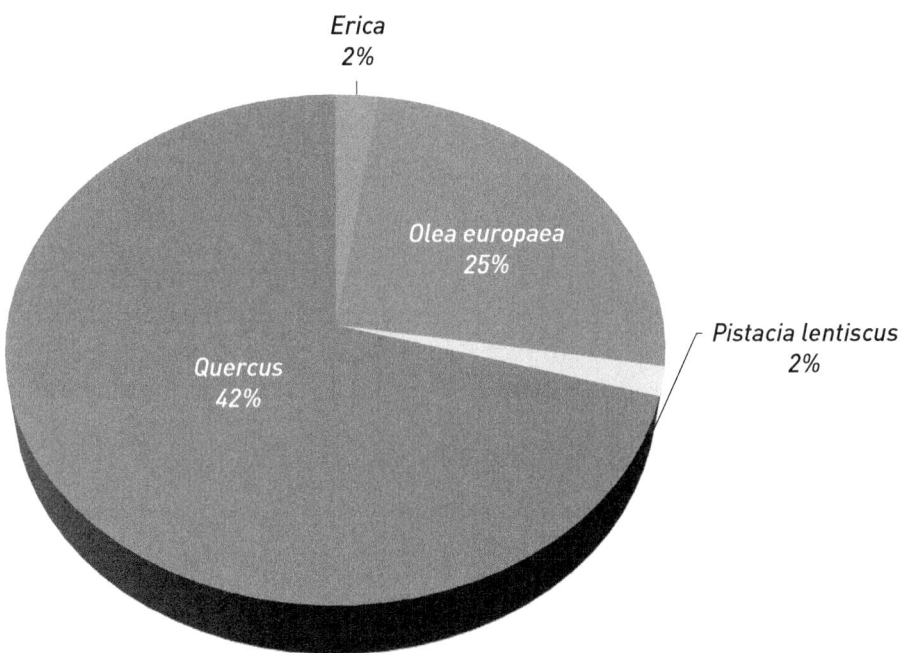

Fig. 3.19. Muro Tenente, results of the charcoal analysis from unit 20011. Chart by Bert Brouwenstijn.

Tenente. This means that, in contrast to l'Amastuola, a considerable part of the cereal crops did not need parching. That said, mortars and pestles were occasionally found at the site, as well as millstones, although generally out of context. Until recent times, stones were often removed from the fields and piled up elsewhere by local farmers to prevent them causing damage to the plough.[38]

The absence of weeds and scarcity of chaff in the samples from Muro Tenente is remarkable. The few grains of oat and rye can probably be regarded as weedy admixtures[39] in the wheat and barley

---

[38] Burgers 1998, p. 254.

[39] Cf. Hopf 1991, p. 247.

Fig. 3.20. Muro Tenente, location of archaeobotanical samples that contained chaff remains. Drawing by Jaap Fokkema.

yields, and a total of ten spikelet forks from emmer wheat from six different units represent the only chaff remains. The units in which the spikelet forks were found are indicated in *Figure 3.20*. Four of these find contexts were probably refuse dumps, but unit 1636 and unit 1638 are the upper and lower layer of the fill of grave 30. The scarcity of chaff and weed remains at Muro Tenente may be due to the sampling method,[40] but it is also possible that cereal cleaning usually took place outside the settlement.

---

[40] As I pointed out in Chapter 2, light chaff remains are usually rare in carbonized archaeobotanical assemblages, because they are unlikely to survive in charred form. The mesh width of the smallest sieve in the flotation machines may have been a factor here.

Cereals may have been the most important component of the crop collection in Muro Tenente, but pulses were clearly also part of the everyday diet, even though broad beans and bitter vetches were the only two types of beans among the archaeobotanical macroremains. Other pulses are conspicuously lacking; in particular, the absence of chickpeas and lentils is remarkable. As we have seen in the previous chapter, chickpeas were also absent in the samples from l'Amastuola. Why they were not found at Muro Tenente is unclear, but it probably has to do with the relatively small number of samples.

The cereals could have been eaten whole, in porridges and gruels, or milled to flour to bake bread, although no clear evidence for bread baking was found at Muro Tenente. Pulses can be eaten fresh or dried, or ground into bean flour to bake bread. Pliny describes how bakers used broad bean flour (*lomentum*) mixed with wheat flour to increase the bread weight.[41] Pulses, on the other hand, can also be grown to enrich the soil as a green crop, or as a complement in fodder. As far as fruit and vegetables are concerned, only the consumption of grapes and olives is clearly demonstrated at Muro Tenente. In addition, there is some charcoal from pomegranate, apple (*Malus*) and pear (*Pyrus*) trees. It remains uncertain whether these fruits were cultivated or gathered in the wild.

As far as the food products originating from animals are concerned, the stable isotope analysis on five human skeletons from Muro Tenente showed that meat did not play a large role in the inhabitants' diet.[42] Sheep and goats' milk would have been a much-needed source of protein and animal fat.[43] Indeed, observations in the excavation reports indicate that a large part of the archaeozoological material consisted of sheep (*Ovis aries*) and/or goat (*Capra hircus*) bones. We have to rely on these notes to get an impression of what kind of animal bones were found at Muro Tenente, since the bone material is now lost due to a flood that a few years ago partially destroyed the archaeological storage depot of the Museo Nazionale Archeologico di Egnazia, where the finds from Muro Tenente are stored.

---

[41] Ciaraldi 1999, p. 83: Plin. *Nat.* 18.30.117.

[42] Akkerman (2002, p. 46) subjected bone material from five Muro Tenente skeletons (two male, three female) to stable isotope analysis. Nitrogen is a stable isotope that is often used in osteological research, because its values can reflect the ratio between diet components of marine and terrestrial origin. Nitrogen enters the food chain from soil or seawater, taken up first by plants, then passed up the food chain to animals. In groups of humans subsisting on land plants and animals, the collagen in their bones contains relatively low levels of $\delta^{15}N$, while those groups relying on freshwater or marine animals will have higher $\delta^{15}N$ values. These differences can be explained by the fact that water, and therefore also fish and water mammals, are naturally high in nitrogen. The quantities of the different isotopes can be measured by mass spectrometry and compared to a standard; the result (e.g. $\delta 13C$, $\delta 15N$, δ = delta) is expressed as parts per thousand (‰ or ppm). The $\delta^{13}C$ values from the skeletons at Muro Tenente were normal, but low $\delta^{15}N$ values suggested that these individuals lived on a modest, primarily vegetarian diet. Another common feature was the relatively bad condition of the teeth; a high percentage showed caries and teeth rot. Nevertheless, apart from a single case of rickets (a childhood disease caused by vitamin D deficiency, leading to softening of bones and potentially fractures and deformity), there were hardly any traces found of severe illnesses. Signs of growth arrest due to starvation, which can be witnessed by Harris' lines (dense lines parallel to the growth plates of long bones, representing temporary slowing or cessation of longitudinal growth) were equally rare.

[43] Milk and dairy products were probably obtained from goats and sheep and not from cows, as, until recently, drinking cow milk was very unusual in Mediterranean countries. Sheep and goats are much better adapted to heat and drought than cattle, which is one of the reasons why they play such an important role in the economy of Mediterranean countries. Goats eat practically anything: they can thrive on dry *macchia* vegetation and still produce plenty of milk. This is why modern Mediterranean farmers often keep a few goats with a flock of sheep for the milk, and also because the goats can lead the way for flocks of sheep on the move. Barker 1985, pp. 30-31, 43; De Grossi Mazzorin 2001.

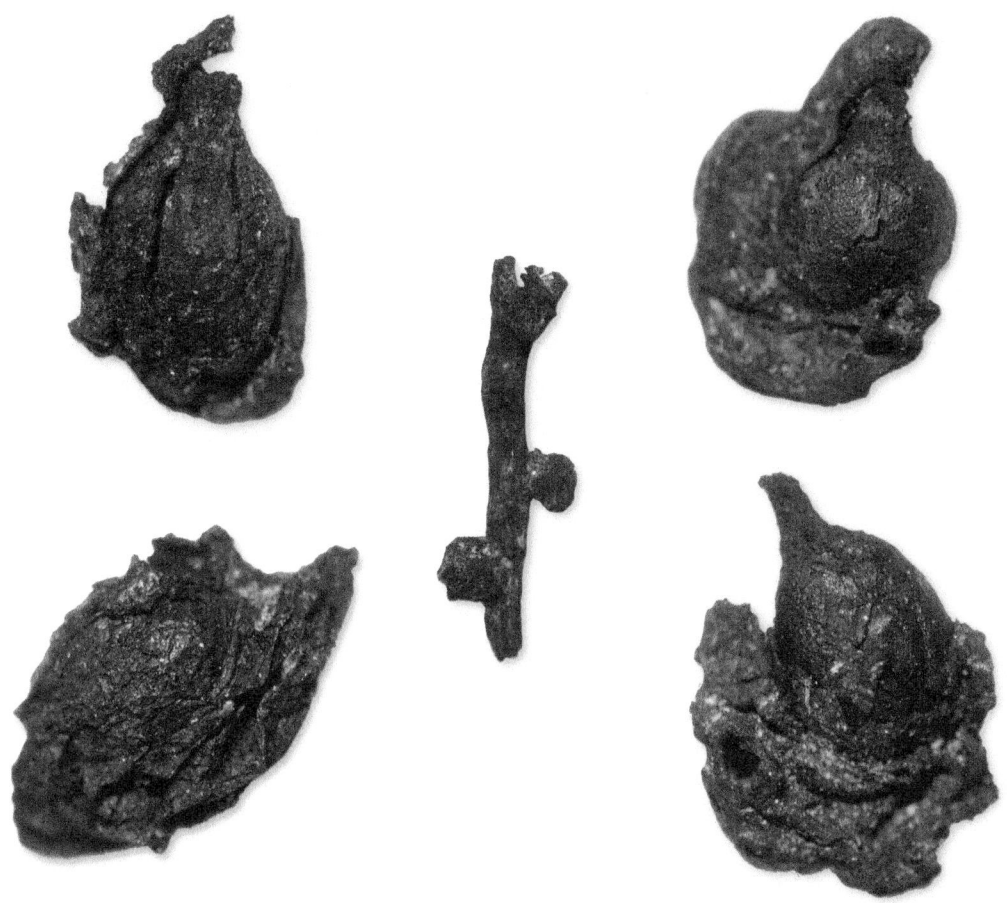

Fig. 3.21. Muro Tenente, carbonized grape (*Vitis vinifera*) remains from unit 89. Photo by the author.

3.5.3 GRAPE AND OLIVE CULTIVATION

The excavations at Muro Tenente have supplied little direct archaeological evidence for the production of wine and olive oil, but, as I have already pointed out in the previous chapter, this shortage is hardly surprising, since it is quite exceptional to find archaeological remains of olive oil and wine production in Mediterranean contexts.[44] Significantly, dense concentrations of transport vessels for wine and/or olive oil were recovered during the urban survey of Muro Tenente. The finds also included fragments of olive/wine presses, but, as is the case with most millstones and other heavy agricultural processing equipment, they were generally found out of context. As a result, they cannot be held to refer to wine and olive oil production in a specific period of time.[45] The archaeobotanical evidence for olive and grape cultivation at Muro Tenente is fragmented, but does provide some valuable information. Olive wood is ubiquitous at Muro Tenente. Olive stones were found in modest quantities, but they

---

[44] Cf. Foxhall 1993 (see section 2.5.3). Especially the reuse of the pressing equipment may be a factor here. Some pressing stones were picked up during the surveys, but they were rarely found in context during the excavations. Furthermore, it must also be pointed out that only a small part of the settlement has been excavated. It is quite possible that there are still wine and olive presses waiting to be uncovered.

[45] Cf. Burgers 1998, p. 254.

Fig. 3.22. Muro Tenente, central excavation trench (C) with the location of graves 22, 25, 27 and 30. Drawing by Jaap Fokkema.

appeared all over the settlement in various types of contexts, including graves, ritual contexts, and refuse dumps.[46]

Grape remains, on the other hand, occur in abundance at Muro Tenente. The most interesting find was made in one particular context located a little to the northeast of grave 30 in the central excavation trench (C). The soil sample from the black spot that was uncovered here contained 9 olive stones and 5175 grape pips, together with grape stems, skins, and flesh (*Figure 3.21*). The presence of the latter

[46] Units 89, 253, 805, 1624, 1636, 1638, 2551, 20011, and 20067.

Fig. 3.23. Muro Tenente, northern excavation trench (A) with the location of grave 45. Drawing by Jaap Fokkema.

indicates that the grapes were not fresh when they were carbonized, as fresh grapes contain much water and tend to explode when they are exposed to fire, leaving hardly any trace of their skins and pips. It takes no more than a few minutes for a grape to burn away in smothering ashes. Therefore, if the grapes from Muro Tenente had been fresh, they could not have been exposed to the fire for more than a few minutes. Otherwise, there would not have been so many pips left. A more plausible explanation is that they were dried, or in some other way drained of their liquid contents. It is possible that the fruits were raisins,[47] but it rather looks like they were pressed. Some of the finds consist of grape-skins attached to the pips, and the abundant presence of loose, 'empty' skins also strongly suggests juice extraction. Furthermore, the fruit remains show a clear resemblance to pressed grapes from other archaeological sites, such as the Neolithic site of Dikili Tash in northern Greece[48] and Early Hellenistic Komboloi in Southern Macedonia.[49] In short, I would argue that the archaeological remains of the grapes from Muro Tenente morphologically resemble 'wine-pressings'. The deposition could represent the remains of grape juice residue after fermentation, possibly – but not necessarily – with wine as the desired end product. The grape pressings may have been dumped and carbonized after sieving. It is possible that their carbonization is due to use as fuel (see section 5.3.1). However, even if the hypothesis is accepted that this grape deposit represents the remains of wine production, it still supplies no conclusive evidence of grape cultivation at Muro Tenente. The idea that wild grapes can be used to produce wine is now widely accepted.[50] I will return to this issue in the next chapter, when I discuss the possibilities of grape and olive cultivation at Muro Tenente in more detail.

3.5.4 THE USE OF PLANTS IN RITUAL ACTIVITIES

Some of the most significant finds of archaeobotanical material at Muro Tenente derive from graves (*Figures 3.22* and *3.23*). Unfortunately, in only five out of the 29 tombs that were excavated soil samples were taken. Four of these graves (22, 25, 27, and 30) are located in the central excavation trench, and one in the northern trench (45).[51] The information on the graves, including the results of the archaeobotanical analyses, is collected in *Table 3.3*.

---

[47] Cf. Cartwright 2003.

[48] Valamoti *et al.* 2007.

[49] Margaritis and Jones 2006.

[50] The process of wine making was apparently invented before the cultivation of the grape: finds of tartaric acid in vessels from astonishingly early contexts in the Near East has led to the discovery that the presence of cultivated grapes is not necessarily a conditio sine qua non for wine making. Tartaric acid is one of the main acids found in wine, but it also occurs naturally in grapes and many other plants, so the substance in these vessels could, theoretically, also have been grape juice. Such ancient grape juice, or wine, has been found in vessels from Hajji Firuz Tepe and Godin Tepe in Iran that date to the 6th millennium BC, and the Macedonian tell-site Dikili Tash/Philippoi (Valamoti et al. 2007). Some of the burnt houses from the latter site, dating to the end of the 5th millennium BC, contained the remains of charred grape pips with skins, clearly used for the extraction of juice. Measurements carried out on the grape pips suggest that they were morphologically wild. Since the region of the Drama plain, where the site is located, is within the geographical distribution zone of the wild vine, it is possible that these grapes were harvested from wild plants. Another possibility would be that the grapes represent a 'transitional phase' in cultivation, originating from plants at a very early stage of tending or cultivation (before the development of pips bearing the morphological characteristics of domestication).

[51] All information on the graves is derived from Tetteroo and Waagen 2010, except for grave 30 (Crielaard 2001, p. 9). As will be clear from the descriptions above, there is generally more information available on the more recently excavated tombs than of the ones that were excavated at an earlier stage. Note that the original grave numbers do not match with the numbers in the published catalogue. Grave 25= burial 26 in the catalogue; 27= burial 28; 30= burial 29, 45= burial 15a. Grave 22 is not included in the catalogue.

Trench	A	C	C	C	C	
Unit	34	441	447	805	1624	
Context	grave fill	grave fill	around grave	fill + grave gifts	grave fill	
Structure	grave 45	grave 25	grave 22	grave 27	grave 30	
Date	Early Hellenistic	Early Hellenistic	Early Hellenistic	Early Hellenistic	Early Hellenistic	
charcoal						common name
Erica sp.		8		11		heath
Olea europaea			7	2		olive
Pinus pinea/ halepensis				29		umbrella/ Aleppo pine
Punica granatum	14					pomegranate
indet. hardwood	12	21	16	23		indet. hardwood
indet. softwood				107		indet. softwood
seeds and fruits						
H. vulgare var. nudum					1	naked barley
Olea europaea				2	8	olive
Triticum aestivum/ compactum			2		1	free-threshing wheat
Triticum dicoccum					1	emmer wheat
Triticum sp.		1				wheat
Cerealia		7			2	cereals
Vicia faba var. minor					2	broad bean
Vicia sp.		1				vetch
Vitis vinifera					30	grape

Trench	C	C	C	C	
Unit	1636	1638	1689	2551	
Context	upper layer grave fill	lower layer grave fill	contents drinking cup	contents plainware pot	
Structure	grave 30	grave 30	wall *necropolis*	wall *necropolis*	
Date	Early Hellenistic	Early Hellenistic	Early Hellenistic	Early Hellenistic	
charcoal					common name
Erica sp.				49	heath
Olea europaea		1			olive
Pinus pinea/halepensis					umbrella/ Aleppo pine
Punica granatum					pomegranate
indet. hardwood		29	8		indet. hardwood
indet. softwood					indet. softwood
seeds and fruits					
H. vulgare var. nudum					naked barley
Olea europaea	1	1		1	olive
Triticum aestivum/ compactum					free-threshing wheat
Triticum dicoccum		1			emmer wheat
Triticum dicoccum *spikelet fork*	2	1			emmer wheat
Triticum sp.			1		wheat
Cerealia	4				cereals
Vicia ervilia	11				bitter vetch
Vicia faba var. minor	1				broad bean
Vicia sp.					vetch
Vitis vinifera	36	2			grape

Table 3.3: Muro Tenente, grave contexts and possible ritual depositions

The differences between the archaeobotanical data from graves – some contained considerably more plant remains than others – can probably be attributed to problems of sampling and post-depositional processes. For example, grave 30 was excavated in 2001, when archaeobotanical sampling was carried out much more meticulously than during the earlier excavation campaigns. Nevertheless, there are also some interesting finds from the graves of earlier excavations. For instance, grave 45, which was excavated in the northern excavation trench (A) in 1997, did not contain any macroremains, but it is the only context at Muro Tenente where carbonized pomegranate wood was found, although the charcoal fragments were heavily damaged, making it difficult to positively identify them.

Grave 22 was not excavated because it appeared to be disturbed, but a soil sample was taken from the area around it. It is possible that there is no relation between the grave and the area of the sample, which contained some wheat (*T. aestivum/compactum* and *Triticum* sp.), a vetch (*Vicia* sp.), and some unidentified cereals. Among the charcoal fragments were olive wood and unidentifiable hardwood.

Only two soil samples were taken from grave 25, a pit (*fossa terragna*) grave that was excavated in 2000. One sample was taken from the grave fill (unit 560), and one smaller sample of a charcoal spot within the fill (unit 441). The sample from the grave fill did not contain any botanical material, probably due to the ploughing (?) damage that was caused to the grave, resulting in the removal of the cover stones and parts of the skeleton. The charcoal sample from the fill yielded only a tiny quantity of fragments of *Erica* sp.

Grave 27 is another pit grave that was excavated in the same year, from which five samples were taken: two from the grave fill and three from the contents of a black gloss *kantharos*, a Gnatia *kantharos*, and one of several small black gloss cups that belonged to the grave gifts from inside the tomb. The samples yielded a modest amount of macroremains, consisting of two olive stones, which were possibly part of a food offering. An interesting aspect of the plant remains from this grave was the discovery of pine wood. *Pinus pinea* and *Pinus halepensis* are not distinguishable from one another on the basis of their wood anatomy, but these are the most common pine species in the Mediterranean region. Unfortunately, no pine cones or nuts were encountered. These might have had a symbolic value (see section 5.3.4 for the association of the pine cone with Dionysus).

Grave 30 contained the remains of a female between 20 and 23 years of age. The deceased woman's right hand seemed to have held three small, rounded stones and next to the left hand a bigger stone (a pestle?), and a smaller, round stone were found. According to the preliminary osteological analysis, the woman was c. 1.48 metres tall (measured *in situ*).[52] Her teeth show clear signs of extreme decay, while the bones bear evidence to the first stages of degenerative arthritis. The ceramic grave gifts date between 280 and 230 BC, so the burial took place in a period when the nearby rooms were still in use. The soil samples were taken from the soil surrounding the grave (unit 1628), from the upper and lower layers of the grave fill (unit 1636 and 1638, respectively, both dry-sieved with 100% coverage,[53] and from some of the grave gifts. These included a miniature *trozzella*, a miniature *krater*, two black gloss plates, a black gloss oil lamp, a loom weight and three knucklebones of a sheep/goat. The samples from the *trozzella*, *krater* and one of the plates are included in sample 1638.

The samples from the grave fill (unit 1636, 1638) included emmer wheat, some chaff remains and unidentified cereals, grape pips, olive stones, broad beans and bitter vetches. The lower layer also contained some heavily damaged charcoal, of which only one fragment could be identified, which appeared to be olive wood. The samples from the uppermost layer of the grave fill (unit 1624) contained 30 grape pips, free-threshing wheat, olive stones, barley, emmer wheat, and broad beans. All of

---

[52] Akkerman 2002, p. 27.

[53] Unfortunately, sieves with rather wide meshes (2.5 and 5 mm) were used.

these may be interpreted as (carbonized) food offerings deposited during the burial. The grave goods offered only a very limited amount of plant remains. The black gloss plate contained some charcoal, which was, unfortunately, unidentifiable. The charcoal in the *krater* was also partly unidentifiable, but one fragment appeared to be olive wood. The *trozzella* contained unidentifiable charcoal as well, along with a spikelet fork that probably belonged to emmer wheat.

Two other finds of possible ritual depositions of carbonized food were made in units 1689 and 2551. Unit 1689 consists of the dark soil around a 4th-century BC drinking cup. This cup was found underneath one of the walls (unit 18) in room 2, and was interpreted as a possible sacrifice. The dark soil around it contained a lot of ash and one wheat grain, which might indicate that the cup was filled with burned food remains. Unit 2551 was also interpreted as a sacrifice, but here the plain ware pot was positioned in the middle of two division walls between the different burial clusters. Since it was probably already broken in antiquity, and a stone was put right in and through it, it is also possible that this vase actually contains the remains of a ritual meal that was associated with one of the burials rather than with the walls. The soil within the pot was sampled, and contained some heavily damaged charcoal (cf. *Erica* sp.) and an olive stone.

Summarizing, it can be concluded that the burning of food was often part of burial rituals at Muro Tenente, and possibly also in other contexts of ritual origin. As far as the graves are concerned, this usage is remarkable, since the deceased were buried and not cremated. This means that the burning of food did not take place inside the grave. Indeed, the pottery containers in which the food remains were found were not burned, so it appears that the macroremains were carbonized before they were included in the burial. This also explains the presence of small charcoal fragments in the burials. The taxa spectrum found in these ritual contexts is remarkably similar to the finds from other parts of the site, including domestic contexts and waste dumps. It appears that no special or exotic foods or products with a certain special meaning were used for ritual sacrifices, at least not in the ones that were preserved and sampled. In short, it seems that the food of the dead was the same as the food of the living, consisting mainly of cereals, pulses, and fruits.

3.6 SUMMARY AND CONCLUSION

Since almost all of the archaeobotanical samples from Muro Tenente derive from a single phase, this second case study is mostly informative about the Early Hellenistic period. A distinction can be made between units of domestic and of ritual origin, but the samples were predominantly taken from layers that were formed between the middle of the 4th and the late 3rd century BC.

The charcoal assemblage from Muro Tenente shows considerable diversity. This indicates that the most important argument to select a certain wood species as fuel was its availability. In other words, there is no clear evidence of a deliberate choice of wood as fire fuel. *Erica* and olive wood dominate the charcoal assemblages in hearths and kilns, followed by olive and oak wood. There are some indications that oak was used as construction material, but the evidence is inconclusive.

The inhabitants' diet consisted mostly of plant foods and contained very little meat. There is evidence for the consumption of wheat and barley, such fruits as olives, grapes, pomegranates, apples and pears, and pulses, among which bitter vetch and broad bean. Free-threshing wheat and naked barley were apparently more common than hulled types. The absence of weeds and the scarcity of chaff in the samples indicates that cereal cleaning usually took place outside the settlement.

The abundant finds of transport vessels and fragments of pressing stones are indicative of wine and olive oil consumption at Muro Tenente. Olive charcoal is ubiquitous, and olive stones were found in various types of contexts. The same holds true for grape remains, of which a particularly large amount was found in the central excavation trench (C). This deposit, which contained 9 olive stones and 5175 grape pips, together with grape stems, skins, and flesh, possibly represents the carbonized remains of pressed fresh grapes. In short, there is some archaeobotanical evidence to support the hypothesis that the inhabitants of Muro Tenente practiced olei- and viticulture. I will return to this issue in the next chapter.

As also observed at l'Amastuola, the ritual offering of food was apparently common practice at Muro Tenente, and it appears that instead of rare crops or products, mostly everyday food was used for this purpose.

In the next chapter, I will discuss some of the remaining questions that the archaeobotanical research at Muro Tenente has raised. In contrast to l'Amastuola, I believe that there are several reasons to argue that agricultural production took place at relatively large scale at Muro Tenente, and was probably partly sold on a market. I will discuss these reasons in detail in chapter 4, where I will also address some other important aspects of Muro Tenente's surrounding landscape and rural economy.

Chapter 4 – Meso level: Landscape and land use around l'Amastuola and Muro Tenente

4.1 INTRODUCTION

The previous two chapters dealt with the analysis on a micro- or site level. I used archaeological, archaeobotanical, and archaeozoological data to reconstruct the various components of the inhabitants' diet, the way food was prepared, which types of wood were used to light fires, and the purpose of plants in ritual activities. The present chapter is still concerned with l'Amastuola and Muro Tenente, but will widen the geographical and chronological scope of the discussion. That is, it will focus more closely on what the sites' surrounding landscape looked like, and how it was exploited. In addition, I will investigate how this exploitation developed in the course of time. This stage is referred to as the analysis on a meso level.

The present chapter is divided into three parts. The first covers the rural economy and exploitation of the landscape around l'Amastuola, the second discusses the same topics at Muro Tenente, while the third combines both case studies in order to detect differences in landscape and land use. Were the rural economies of the two settlements in any way comparable in terms of scale and organization? Did the inhabitants cultivate the same crops? What about the local landscape? Did the land zones around l'Amastuola offer the same possibilities for agricultural use, hunting, fishing, and the collection of wild foods as the area around Muro Tenente? Another important aspect of the interpretation on a meso level is the detection of change and innovations over time. Were the systems of land use any different during the early stages of habitation at l'Amastuola in comparison to the later periods, when Greek influences on architecture, pottery forms, and burial customs had become increasingly apparent? In the same line of reasoning: can land use at Early Hellenistic Muro Tenente be considered to be more 'advanced' in comparison to Early Iron Age and Archaic/Classical l'Amastuola? If so, in what way? These observations will be the starting point for the interpretation on a macro level in chapters 5 and 6, in which it will be shown how l'Amastuola and Muro Tenente fit into long-term regional trends.

4.2 L'AMASTUOLA

4.2.1 THE LANDSCAPE

During the VU University excavation campaigns at l'Amastuola, several attempts were made to extract pollen samples.[1] Unfortunately, the environmental circumstances appeared to be unsuitable for pollen preservation.[2] This means that we have to rely on other sources of information to form an image of the wider landscape that surrounded the site of l'Amastuola between the 8th and 5th centuries BC. Anthracology, the study of charcoal from archaeological contexts, has much to offer in this respect, since charcoal does not need an oxygen-poor environment to survive in archaeological soils.[3] A large and growing body of literature has been published about charcoal assemblages from archaeological sites and their use for landscape reconstructions.[4] The results of the charcoal analysis from l'Amastuola include a broad spectrum of plant taxa that is indicative of several different landscape types. In the following paragraph, I will explore what the charcoal assemblage can tell us about this environment. This discussion is based on the role of specific plant species in so-called 'communities' (i.e. the entire array of plants inhabiting a particular ecosystem, see *Box 1*). Obviously, the charcoal assemblage from l'Amastuola does not include the remains of *all* the plants that grew around the settlement. A variety of factors has influenced the sample, including human selection and post-depositional processes, resulting in a small selection of plant species. These plants, however, should not be regarded as isolated species, but as typical parts of larger plant communities. The following account is based on the principle that we can derive the presence of an entire plant community from a few characteristic species.[5] The char-

---

[1] Cf. Storme 2008; Lelivelt 2013.

[2] The outer layer of pollen, the exine, is almost indestructible in wet contexts, but deteriorates rapidly when it is exposed to oxygen. In this part of Italy, permanently waterlogged contexts are rare, as water basins, lagoons and small streams often fall dry during the hot summer months. Even if such a dry phase only occurs once every hundred years, it destroys most of the pollen that have accumulated in the previous period. The unsuitable conditions for pollen preservation in a large part of Italy is definitely a factor that has influenced the archaeobotanical research tradition there (see section 5.2).

[3] Charcoal was usually not collected at excavations until the 1950s and early 1960s, when it was often used for carbon dating. It was not until the late 1960s that the potential of charcoal research to reconstruct prehistoric environments was fully understood (Vernet 2008, p. 299). Today, anthracology is an independent research discipline. The University of Montpellier in southern France is particularly involved in anthracological research. Every four years, international meetings are held to promote charcoal research, the most recent ones have been held in 2004 in Cavallino (Lecce, Italy), in 2008 in Brussels, and in 2011 in Valencia.

[4] See for example Chabal 1994; Figueiral 1995; Vernet 1992, 1997; Damblon 1997; Figueiral and Mosbrugger 2000; Nelle 2008; Delhon *et al.* 2009, among many others.

[5] See also Chabal 1994; Fiorentino 1998, pp. 211-212, 1995a, pp. 336-341, 1995b; Fiorentino and Colaianni 2005. Obviously, this method has its limits. As Vernet (1999, p. 25) puts it, 'It might seem overambitious of anthracology to attempt to reconstruct past landscapes and people-landscape interactions given the emphasis of recent studies on a multidisciplinary approach integrating earth sciences, human sciences and archaeology. However, anthracology has an original contribution to make in terms of perception of natural and humanly-affected ecosystems and the uses people have made of them.' Vernet also discusses the use of charcoal assemblages from hearths and ovens for this purpose, noting that fires will provide a charcoal sample that should be reasonably representative of the territory exploited for its wood, but only if the 'duration requirement' is met. This means that many different fuel deposits from different phases and locations should be sampled. It is extremely difficult to avoid a certain bias towards certain species due to preferences made in collecting the wood. This can only be done by comparing as many archaeological charcoal deposits as possible.

coal assemblage from l'Amastuola indicates that the landscape surrounding the hill probably included several different exploitable land zones. Starting from the area directly around the site, these land zones may have consisted of arable land, a *macchia* and/or *gariga* zone, pastoral grounds, woodland and a marine environment.

Arable land
Structures and installations that were related to crop cultivation, such as sheds and other storage areas, presses and threshing floors, were probably located in the area outside the settlement. No trace of them was found in the excavated area and the archaeobotanical assemblage contains very little waste products from cereal cleaning (see above). Theoretically, these structures could have been located on a different point on the south terrace which has not been excavated, but as I pointed out above, this type of agricultural equipment is often invisible in the archaeological record.[6]

As such, it remains unclear where the crops were grown. The steeply sloping hillsides are unlikely to have been cultivated. The presence of arable fields or vegetable gardens inside the settlement is also improbable. This holds true for the early stages of habitation (in the Early Iron Age) as well as the later phases in the 6th and 5th centuries BC. Most of the Early Iron Age structures on the south terrace were built directly on top of the bedrock, which means that in many parts of the hill the soil was very thin and barren rock came to the surface.[7] The various phases of land movement during the later stages of habitation (the earliest colluvium layer was probably deposited in the 6th century BC) also testify to the hilltop's lack of vegetation.[8] In short, it appears that crop cultivation must have taken place downhill in the surrounding undulating sloping land.

We know from the field surveys that the surrounding landscape was almost void of other settlements in the period that the south terrace was inhabited.[9] These surveys were carried out in an area of some 2 km^2 around the site of l'Amastuola and also in sample zones in a transect crosscutting all relevant land systems in the Murge, the undulating karstic landscape surrounding the hilltop. Only a very limited number of isolated contemporary artefacts were found during these surveys.[10] For this reason, Burgers and Crielaard have suggested that the inhabitants worked their fields by commuting on a daily basis.[11] A similar interpretation has been proposed by Yntema for Archaic Oria. Here, the settlement may have functioned as a kind of agro-town, where the whole population lived, leaving the town in the morning to perform their daily duties in the fields, and returning in the evening.[12] Naturally, such a system of land use greatly diminished the usable amount of land, as the fields had to be located within walking distance, i.e. about 5 kilometres.

Given these restrictions and the diversity of crops that were found among the archaeobotanical remains (wheat, barley, pulses, fruits, garlic), agricultural fields are likely to have been rather small in scale. This hypothesis ties in with the characteristics of the landscape at l'Amastuola. The *gravine*, hills and heavily eroded rock formations and sediments of the *Mottola undulating sloping land system*[13] make this area unsuitable for large-scaled agricultural use.

The macchia zone
The plant assemblage from l'Amastuola seems to contain the remains of different forms of *macchia*. The characteristics of Mediterranean ecosystems have motivated the work of many students, and have focused mainly on the vegetation existing in different Mediterranean climate types (see *Box 1*).[14] The

---

[6] Foxhall 1993, p. 183.
[7] Burgers and Crielaard 2007, p. 102; Burgers and Crielaard 2011, pp. 133-134.
[8] Burgers and Crielaard 2007, pp. 101-102.
[9] Burgers and Crielaard 2007, pp. 92-99.
[10] Burgers and Crielaard 2007, p. 95.
[11] Burgers and Crielaard 2007, p. 111.
[12] Yntema 1993, p. 176, refers to Delano Smith, p. 37 ff., and literature cited there for the term agro-town and for the function of such settlements.

plant assemblage from l'Amastuola seems to contain the remains of all three forms of *macchia*. There are fragments of mastic wood and strawberry tree among the charcoal finds, which could belong to high *macchia* associations. In addition, the presence of myrtle, *Rhamnus/Phillyrea*, juniper and *Erica* is indicative of middle/low *macchia* and *gariga*. Grazing animals could have been a determining factor in the formation of these plant associations. The evidence of sheep/goat rearing and wool production at l'Amastuola is indirect, as the only indications are found in the form of sheep bones, loom weights, and spindle whorls. When we suppose that this combination of evidence actually is indicative of sheep/goat rearing, these animals are likely to have been left to graze in the nearby *macchia* zones.[15] It seems likely that only small numbers of livestock, which could have been maintained in the vicinity of the site all year round, were kept. Indeed, the great diversity of cultivated crops at l'Amastuola suggests that agriculture, rather than livestock, was the most important means of subsistence. There is no positive evidence for the seasonal herding of livestock away from the settlement. Indeed, long-distance transhumance may not have been necessary in this region, as the area outside the habitation core on the l'Amastuola hill was uninhabited, and the surrounding landscape presumably provided enough grazing areas.

Forest

Today, the presence of undisturbed woodland is hardly imaginable in the vicinity of the l'Amastuola hill, or in any part of southern Apulia, where the present-day landscape is the result of severe anthropogenic changes.[30] Indeed, the archaeobotanical evidence for the presence of such a forest is ambiguous, as oak and olive trees can both be found in degraded as well as climax vegetation. The dominance of oak and olive wood in the charcoal assemblage suggests that wood collection often took place in oak and olive forests or orchards. The charcoal analysis from fireplaces and hearths (see section 2.5.1) revealed that these two tree types were probably selected as fuel. Apparently, these trees were readily available for the inhabitants of l'Amastuola, either because they grew nearby or because they could easily be transported towards the settlement. This supports the hypothesis of the nearby presence of woodland.

Another clue is provided by the find of a piece of antler belonging to red deer (*Cervus elaphus*) in the floor matrix of building θ.[31] The red deer is one of the largest deer species, and also one of the largest game animals found in Europe. The animal originally mostly lived in open deciduous woodland, but nowadays its habitat has stretched into diverse woodlands, mountain forests and open moorland.[32] Its presence at l'Amastuola indicates that one such biotope had to be within walking distance from the settlement, and that it was accessible for hunting.

We know from illustrations on Daunian *stelai* (*Figure 4.1*) that indigenous populations in northern Apulia hunted deer, but it is unclear where they did it and at what scale. Interestingly, the archaeozoological research in the Metapontino has shown that this area was more forested in antiquity than it is

[13] See section 2.1.

[14] Di Castri 1981, p. 9.

[15] Goats are especially adapted to the environment of degraded Mediterranean forests, as they are extremely resistant to thirst and can find food even in the poorest vegetation zones. Together with fire, overgrazing is the principal enemy of the Mediterranean forests. Cf. Le Houérou 1981, p. 486 and pp. 499-502.

[30] Van Joolen 2003, p. 44. For example, many small hills have been levelled and removed, and fertile soils are often excavated and deposited elsewhere.

[31] Bones of red deer are not unusual in archaeozoological assemblages from sites in southeast Italy. For example, Sandór Bökönyi's (2010) investigations of the faunal material from six sites in the *chora* of Metaponto showed the presence of many wild species, including red deer, wild boar, fox, badger, weasel and wolf. Zeiler (1996, p. 4) also reports the presence of red deer in the early habitation period at Valesio, which is contemporary to the occupation of l'Amastuola (720-580/550 BC).

[32] Mitchell-Jones *et al.* 1999.

BOX 1: Mediterranean plant communities

Among the schools of thought concerning Mediterranean ecosystems, phytoecological (or phytosociological) studies have traditionally been very influential in the south of France and in Italy.[16] The two pillars of research on which it is based are the characterization of the different bioclimates and an exact description of plant associations. Regarding the latter type of research, phytosociologists have developed a number of theories about the composition and development of *macchia* communities.[17] In phytosociology, plant associations (the basic units) are classified into groups constituting higher units (alliance, order, class). The basic formation of Mediterranean shrub lands is divided into two classes, the Ononido-Rosmarinetea Class in the western Mediterranean and the Cisto-Micromerietea Class in the eastern Mediterranean.[18] The purpose of these classifications is to obtain information about the biogeography of a region, and to gain insight into its ecology. Another important aspect of phytosociology is the dynamics of plant associations, particularly their successional schemes. In most areas in the Mediterranean basin, including southeast Italy, climax vegetation usually consists of evergreen (holm) oak forest, a plant association called Quercetum illicis (*leccete*) or Oleo-Ceratonion, a plant group dominated by olive and carob trees.[19] It may be noted that such a climax situation is rarely encountered nowadays because of increasing human impact on the landscape.[20] It should be added, however, that the phytosociological plant associations that are described for the Mediterranean region run into the hundreds, and are very difficult to understand for anyone who is not a phytosociologist or is unfamiliar with the relevant literature.[21] In addition, such associations can differ from one another simply because of the presence of a single characteristic species. It is clear, then, that this method is not particularly practical for the study of archaeobotanical plant assemblages. For this reason, in the present study I will distinguish the encountered *macchia* types by height rather than phytosociological association. Such a subdivision is commonly used by both botanists[22] and archaeobotanists[23] working in Mediterranean countries. A similar system is proposed by Grove and Rackham,[24] who argue that cleared (by human impact, fire and grazing, or natural climatic aridity) woodland tends to give rise to different levels of sub-woodland vegetation:•
High macchia (*macchia alta*) can reach a height of over 5 metres and may be dominated by evergreen sclerophyllous (broad-leaved) plants or include conifers, depending on the location. The sclerophyllous type is usually found along the coast, whereas conifers generally grow further inland. In southeast Italy, the *macchia alta* is generally broad-leaved and consists of woody patches with evergreen oaks (but also *Calycotome spinosa, Pistacia lentiscus, Arbutus unedo, Cistus monspeliensis, C. incanus, C. salvifolius, Phillyrea media, Ph. angustifolia, Osyris alba, Rubia peregrina, Satureja calamintha*, etc.) with open spots that are dominated by *Cistus*. If this type of *macchia* is left untouched for a sufficient amount of time, it may develop into evergreen oak forest.

- High macchia (*macchia alta*) can reach a height of over 5 metres and may be dominated by evergreen sclerophyllous (broad-leaved) plants or include conifers, depending on the location. The sclerophyllous type is usually found along the coast, whereas conifers generally grow further inland. In southeast Italy,[25] the *macchia alta* is generally broad-leaved and consists of woody patches with evergreen oaks (but also *Calycotome spinosa, Pistacia lentiscus, Arbutus unedo, Cistus monspeliensis, C. incanus, C. salvifolius, Phillyrea media, Ph. angustifolia, Osyris alba, Rubia peregrina, Satureja calamintha*, etc.) with open spots that are dominated by *Cistus*. If this type of *macchia* is left untouched for a sufficient amount of time, it may develop into evergreen oak forest.
- Middle/low macchia (*macchia media/bassa*) does not grow higher than 2 metres and is often composed of mastic tree (*Pistacia lentiscus*), Italian buckthorn (*Rhamnus alaternus*), juniper (*Juniperus*), *Phillyrea*, and *Cistus*. In southeast Italy, *macchia media* is usually found in the form of associations with *Cistus monspeliensis*. Other species that grow in these groups may include *Calycotome spinosa, Daphne gnidium, Myrtus communis*, and over 70 other species. According to Curti and Lorenzoni,[26] this type of plant association in southern Apulia may be called Calycotomo-Myrtetum.

- *Gariga* (lower than 50 centimetres; plural: *garighe*; French: *garrigue*, Greek: *phryganà*) is the lowest form of Mediterranean vegetation, usually a degraded form of middle/low *macchia*. It is usually discontinuous and scattered and may consist of lavender (*Lavandula*), thyme (*Thymus vulgaris*), and *Cistus*.[27] Caniglia et al.[28] report that in Apulia, *gariga* is associated with *Coridothymus capitatus, Pistacia lentiscus, Myrtus communis*, and *Calicotome spinosa*. Grove and Rackham call this type of vegetation *undershrubs* and also distinguish another form of heavily degraded land, *steppe*, where bare rock is very prominent and thin grassland is mixed with spiky plants.[29]

Notes to BOX 1

[16] Di Castri 1981, p. 10.
[17] The phytoecological school has its conceptual roots in the work of Brown-Blanquet, Gaussen and particularly Emberger. For a more detailed discussion and extensive bibliography, see Di Castri 1981; Quézel 1981.
[18] Quézel 1981, pp. 88-89.
[19] Quézel 1981, p. 90; Gaudenzio and Peccenini 2002, p. 27; Caniglia *et al.* 1974-1975.
[20] Indeed, the term 'climax vegetation' has been challenged (e.g. Tobey 1981; Cook 1996). Several ecologists have pointed out that even if succession tends towards a steady state, the time required to achieve this state is often unrealistically long.
[21] Tomaselli 1981, p. 95.
[22] Cf. Tomaselli 1981.
[23] Vernet 1999; Fiorentino 1995b, p. 338; Fiorentino and Colaianni 2005, p. 98, Fiorentino *et al.* 2011, p. 237.
[24] Grove and Rackham 2001, p. 45.
[25] Curti and Lorenzoni 1969, p. 59.
[26] Curti and Lorenzoni 1969, pp. 60-61.
[27] Gaudenzio and Peccenini 2002, p. 33.
[28] Caniglia *et al.* 1974-1975.
[29] Grove and Rackham 2001, p. 45.

today (see chapters 5 and 6). Bökönyi stresses that the bones of *Cervus elaphus* that were found in the Metapontino belonged to particularly large individuals, which could only survive in large and dense forests. Only smaller forms develop in open woodland.[33]

The marine environment

The site of l'Amastuola is located at a distance of about 10 kilometres from the sea; the Gulf of Taranto dominates the view from the south terrace. It appears that the landscape between the l'Amastuola hill and the coast was characterized by lagoons and a peat land that was periodically flooded by the sea, resulting in a marshy environment.[34] These brackish lagoons may have been a rich source of (shell)fish, but there is no evidence that they were exploited for this purpose by the inhabitants of l'Amastuola. In fact, it seems that the lagoonal area was avoided altogether. It may have been off limits because of certain territorial boundaries, but more importantly, the lagoons probably formed an unhealthy, mosquito-plagued environment. Lelivelt concluded that the gastropod assemblages from the floodplain of the river Taras (about 3 kilometres southeast of l'Amastuola) are indicative of pools of stagnant water with

[33] Bökönyi 2010, p. 8.
[34] Lelivelt 2013.

Fig. 4.1. Decorations on Daunian stelai (c. 650-580 BC) showing deer hunting. Nava 1980, Tav. CCCXXVII (986B); Tav. CCCXXVIII (987Bd); LXXIII (248Bd).

low salinity levels.[35] Such an environment would have been the ideal breeding place for the malaria mosquito.[36] Malaria is a lethal disease that is known to have infested many of the low-lying marshy areas around spring issues and water bodies near the Apulian coast until recent times (i.e. Mussolini's

[35] Lelivelt 2013, pp. 101-102.   [36] Snowden 2006.

Bonifica Integrale in the 1930s and 1940s).[37] The Taras floodplain is situated within a zone where the deadliest form of malaria occurred on the malaria map by Luigi Torelli from 1882.[38] However, there is less clarity about the occurrence of malaria in antiquity.[39]

Remains of coastal vegetation were not found at l'Amastuola, but this in itself is not necessarily significant, since weed species do not abound in the archaeobotanical assemblage altogether. However, there is some evidence that the open sea, behind the possibly unhealthy coastal zone, was exploited. Shells and fish bones are very rare among the faunal remains, but considering the size of the fish hook from trench 6 (over 4 centimetres long), it seems likely that it was used for open sea fishing.

4.2.2 LAND USE

The archaeological, archaeobotanical, and archaeozoological evidence from chapter 2 raises several questions about the exploitation of the landscape around l'Amastuola. Considering the rural economy, we may ask ourselves whether the settlement's methods of land use were aimed at subsistence or surplus production. In addition, we might take a closer look at possible agricultural innovations that were introduced during the roughly three hundred years that the site was inhabited. Did the adoption of Greek customs also lead to the introduction of new crops, more efficient processing or harvesting methods, or other changes?

The crop spectrum
Hulled cereals appear to have been the most important cultivated crops at l'Amastuola. Even if we take into account that free-threshing wheat is usually underrepresented in the archaeobotanical record, it remains apparent that this cereal type was of minor importance in comparison to hulled cereals in all chronological phases. Whereas hulled wheat and barley were regularly found in large concentrations (e.g. hulled barley in units 67, 72, 74, 81, and 313; emmer wheat in units 320 and 626), free-threshing wheat was found only in small quantities (the largest concentrations were 11 grains in unit 159 in *oikos* ε and 8 in unit 533 in the domestic structure northwest of the potter's workshop). Free-threshing wheat may be considered a more 'advanced' cereal type since, unlike emmer or einkorn, it does not need to be parched before threshing and has larger grains. These advantages are also the main reason why free-threshing (bread) wheat is the dominant wheat type today. At the same time, the lack of a protective cover makes this wheat type more vulnerable to disease and fungi. Overall, free-threshing wheat is a more demanding crop compared to hulled wheats and barley, requiring relatively thick and fertile soils.[40] The absence of suitable soils could explain why *Triticum aestivum/compactum* was relatively rare at l'Amastuola.

No archaeobotanical evidence of grape cultivation was found at l'Amastuola, with the exception of three grape pips, which probably belonged to wild fruits (see section 2.5.3). The olive stone fragments were too small to produce statistically significant biometric measurements. However, in contrast to grape wood (which has not been found at l'Amastuola), olive charcoal abounds in the archaeobotanical assemblage from this site. It was encountered in samples covering the entire occupation period, as is

---

[37] Cf. Harding 1999, pp. 21-22.

[38] See Lelivelt 2013, pp. 51-52.

[39] The earliest literary references to malaria is probably made by Hippocrates (c. 460-370 BC). See Jones 1909. Both Strabo and Cicero report the rapid destruction of cities in Magna Graecia (Poseidonia, Taras and Kroton) due to malaria (e.g. 'But the city [Poseidonia] is rendered unhealthy by a river that spreads out into marshes in the neighbourhood.' Strabo, *Geography*, V.4.13.373. Translation by Horace Leonard Jones, penelope.uchicago.edu. See Shaw Briggs 1910.

[40] Renfrew 1973, pp. 65-66 and pp. 80-81.

Fig. 4.2. Pruned olive wood in San Pancrazio Salentino and Mesagne, province of Brindisi, winter 2010. Photo by the author.

Date	Early Iron Age Number of sampled units with charcoal= 20 (see Appendix 2)		Archaic period Number of sampled units with charcoal = 42		Classical period Number of sampled units with charcoal = 2	
	Frequency (number of units with olive charcoal)	Quantity (number of fragments)	Frequency	Quantity	Frequency	Quantity
Olive charcoal	14 (70%)	173	34 (81%)	422	2 (100%)	41
Olive stones					1	10

Table 4.1 L'Amastuola, olive (*Olea europaea*) remains from different habitation phases

illustrated in *Table 4.1*. Furthermore, olive wood also seems to be equally distributed in the different parts of the settlement, as it is strongly represented in the units in all the excavation trenches (see *Table 4.2*). This dominance can be explained in two ways. Either the olive trees were wild and (together with holm oak) part of middle/high *macchia* or climax vegetation (as I argued in section 4.1), or they were cultivated in olive groves, probably not too far from the settlement.[41] If we consider the latter possibility, the olive wood that was so abundantly used as fuel in the settlement may have derived from pruning and pollarding. Pruned olive branches are still widely used for this purpose in modern Italy, and can be seen in heaped-up piles lining the streets during the winter months (see *Figure 4.2*). Is there a way to determine whether the olive charcoal from l'Amastuola derived from pruning wood? In theory, the shape of the growth rings can provide an estimate of the original diameter of individual olive wood

---

[41] Cf. Nisbet and Ventura (1994, pp. 577-578) and Peroni (1994, p. 845), who interpret the olive wood from Broglio di Trebisacce as pruned branches of cultivated trees.

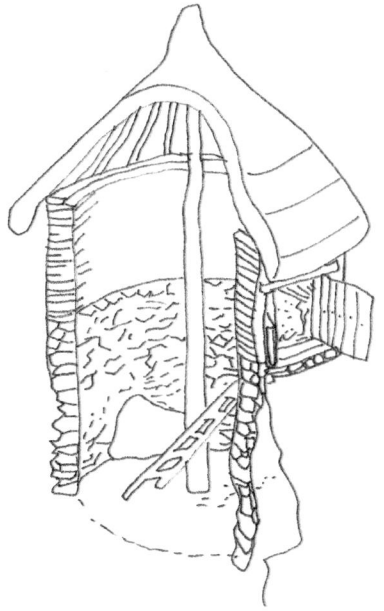

Fig. 4.3. Reconstruction of a granary from Old-Smyrna by R.V. Nicholls. Drawing by the author, after Mazarakis Ainian 1997, Figure 411.

Fig. 4.4. Clay models of granaries from the Temple of Artemis at Ano Mazaraki, Greece. Drawing by the author, after Mazarakis Ainian 1997, 120.

Fig. 4.4. L'Amastuola, artist's impression of the grain silos (?) in trench 5. Drawing by Bert Brouwenstijn.

	Frequency	Quantity
Trench 1 Number of units that contained charcoal: 4 Total number of samples: 7	2 (50%)	3
Trench 2 Number of units that contained charcoal: 21 Total number of samples: 33	13 (62%)	109
Trench 3 Number of units that contained charcoal: 6 Total number of samples: 9	6 (100%)	75
Trench 4 Number of units that contained charcoal: 17 Total number of samples: 31	13 (76%)	228
Trench 5 Number of units that contained charcoal: 25 Total number of samples: 61	20 (80%)	126
Trench 6 Number of units that contained charcoal: 32 Total number of samples: 80	25 (78%)	464

Table 4.2 L'Amastuola, olive (Olea europaea) charcoal from different excavation trenches.

Trench	5	5	5	6	6
Unit	32	33	63	332	509
Context	hearth?	fireplace	floor	part of kiln E?	feature on top of ritual deposition
Structure	building ζ	building ζ	building θ	Workshop	-
Date	VI BC	VI BC	VI BC	VI BC	VI BC?
Estimated diameter (cm)					
Fragment 1	1	4.5	11	30	50
Fragment 2		3.5			
Fragment 3		3			
Fragment 4		2.5			
Fragment 4		1.5			
Fragment 6		1.5			
Fragment 7		1.5			
Fragment 8		40			
Fragment 9		50			
Fragment 10		3			
Fragment 11		1.5			

Table 4.3 L'Amastuola, estimated original diameter of some of the Olea europaea charcoal finds

branches. If they had a generally small diameter, it can be assumed that the fire wood consisted mostly of small (pruning?) branches. However, this method is only suitable for charcoal fragments that are in a relatively good state of preservation, have visible growth rings *and* still contain at least a part of the bark or core. Unfortunately, none of the charcoal fragments from l'Amastuola fulfilled these requirements. Therefore, the estimates of the original diameter of olive branches in *Table 4.3* are no more than a rough indication. Nevertheless, the measuring results make it clear that the firewood contained small branches as well as larger ones. If the wood was collected by felling wild trees, it would have consisted predominantly of large trunks. The presence of small branches, then, suggests that at least part of the firewood derived from the pollarding or pruning of cultivated trees.

BOX 2 The storage capacity of the grain silos at l'Amastuola

Firstly, it must be emphasized that the exact function of the two stone platforms that were found at l'Amastuola is uncertain. But if their interpretation as silos is accepted, the next question is whether the storage capacity of the structures exceeds domestic requirements. The absence of the superstructure makes it rather difficult to estimate this. The western platform has a diameter of 1.87 metres, the eastern one a diameter of 1.93 metres (both measured north-south), but their original height is unknown. We may, however, attempt to provide a reconstruction of the silos by taking comparable structures from the Aegean as an example.[44] A reconstruction of a granary from Old-Smyrna (c. 900 BC) is shown in *Figure 4.3*.[45] Another useful comparison is provided by clay models of granaries[46] such as those found in the Artemis sanctuary at Ano Mazaraki, dating to the last quarter of the 8th century BC (*Figure 4.4*).[47] These models must be copies of actual, full-size granaries.

The proportions between the width and height of the Ano Mazaraki models is approximately 1 : 1.45 (diameter of 4 cm, height of 5.8 cm). Assuming that the silos from l'Amastuola have the same proportions, the one with a diameter of 1.87 metres would be about 2.71 metres high, and the one measuring 1.93 metres would be 2.80 metres high (1.45 x 187 = 271.15; 1.45 x 193 = 279.85). An artist's impression of what the silos may have looked like can be seen in *Figure 4.5*. Based on this hypothetical height, the contents of the silos would be 7,442,904 and 8,191,483 cm^3 ($\pi \times r^2 \times h$), or 7443 and 8191 litres, respectively. Of course, this reconstruction is only a tentative first step, the silos from l'Amastuola could have been more squat or slender in form than the clay models.

The silos could have contained any of the cereal types that were found at l'Amastuola, including emmer wheat, barley, naked wheat, or a combination of several cereals. Since naked cereals seem to have been less common (see section 2.5.2), I used a hulled cereal type as an example, in this case emmer wheat. Kooistra[48] calculated the ratio of volume to weight of modern emmer wheat after an initial threshing, leaving most of the grains in the chaff. The average outcome of six measurements was 272 grams per litre. Assuming, as Kooistra does, that 20% of the weight of grains and chaff of *Triticum dicoccum* is accounted for by chaff and 80% by grain, 272 grams of grain represents 218 grams of edible grains. Assuming that the silos were brim-full of wheat in its chaff, their joint capacity in terms of edible grains would have been approximately 3409 kilograms (7443 x 218 gram = 1,622,574 gram = 1623 kilo; 8191 x 218 gram = 1,785,638 gram = 1786 kilo; 1623 + 1786= 3409).

What would such an amount of emmer mean in economic terms? According to the FAO Food composition tables, one kilo of (unspecified) wheat yields about 3340 kCal.[49] A person's caloric requirements depend on a number of factors, such as age, sex, size, and rate of activity. For this exercise, the demographic profile suggested by Foxhall and Forbes was used.[50] Their estimated calorific requirement is 15,495 calories per day for a hypothetical household of six members.[51] If half of this energy requirement was met by cereal intake,[52] then the grain silos in trench 5 were sufficient to feed four such households for almost a year:

Total amount of kCalories provided by silos: 3409 x 3340= 11,386,060 kCal
Total amount of kCalories per day needed out of cereals by four households: [15,495/2] x 4= 30,990 kCal
Number of days silos can provide food for these households: 11,386,060 / 30,990 = *357 days*.

---

[42] As argued by Burgers and Crielaard (2007, p. 110).

[43] Burgers and Crielaard 2007, pp. 89-90, Crielaard 2011, pp. 57-59.

[44] Crielaard (2011, p. 67) has listed several such structures, and concluded that the stone platforms from l'Amastuola are comparable in context, date, diameter and construction technique with granaries in, for instance, Old-Smyrna in Asia Minor, Lefkandi on Euboia, Mende in Chalkidike and Halai in Phthiotis. See also Crielaard and Burgers 2012, pp. 72-75.

In conclusion, the archaeobotanical evidence from l'Amastuola is insufficiently explicit to conclude whether grapes were cultivated at the settlement, but it does not seem likely. The abundance of olive wood in the soil samples from l'Amastuola, on the other hand, does beg an explanation. Among the archaeological finds from the south terrace, there are both imported transport amphorae and olive stones. In addition, it appears that olive trees were omnipresent in the surrounding landscape. Combining these indications, I believe that the inhabitants of l'Amastuola were clearly familiar with the consumption of olives and olive oil. It is possible that they also cultivated olives, but it remains unlikely that this settlement was involved in large-scale olive oil production. We will see how this conclusion ties in with the overall image of olive and grape cultivation in southeast Italy in this period in section 5.3.3.

Self-sufficiency
Now that we have seen that the array of cultivated crops at l'Amastuola was relatively wide, we may raise the question of whether the inhabitants could depend on their own production or had to exchange foodstuffs with other areas and settlements. In other words, did l'Amastuola have a self-supporting rural economy?[42] At first glance, the diversity in the crop spectrum points to subsistence rather than surplus production. Can we assume that agricultural production at l'Amastuola was mostly aimed to fulfil the inhabitants' own needs?

In order to answer these questions, several categories of evidence need to be discussed. Firstly, it is necessary to take a look at the agricultural storage facilities at the site, since these can give insight into the scale of production. The excavations have revealed several examples of small-scale storage on a household level, such as the ceramic container full of bitter vetches that was found northwest of *oikos* γ (*Figure 2.25*), and storage vessels and amphorae in building δ, northwest of *oikos* γ, and in the upper floor of the potter's workshop. These finds suggest that small groups of people evidently managed their own food reserves. The diffusion of crop processing tools also indicates that cereal cleaning was mostly carried out at the household level. Mortars and grinding stones were retrieved from several domestic contexts within the settlement, for instance in building δ and *oikos* ε.[43] Two other mortars were discovered out of context at the site, one of them in the colluvium in trench 2 and another on the slope of the l'Amastuola hill (see section 2.5.2).

[45] Mazarakis Ainian 1997, figure 411. Reconstruction by R.V. Nicholls.

[46] Most of these models come from graves in the Athenian Agora and Kerameikos and can be dated between the middle of the 9th and the middle of the 7th centuries BC. This makes them only slightly older than the silos from l'Amastuola. The most impressive of the clay models from Athens, a chest with five model granaries on its lid, was found in the so-called 'Tomb of the Rich Lady' from the Agora (*c.* 850 BC). Smithson (1968, p. 92) mentions that there are many other model granaries known beside the ones from this tomb, listing ten other pointed structures that are probably or certainly from Attica.

[47] Mazarakis Ainian 1997, p. 120. A similar (and contemporary?) granary model was found at Phaleron.

[48] Kooistra 1996, p. 318.

[49] Chatfield 1954, *Table 1*, p. 10.

[50] Foxhall and Forbes 1982. Their source is FAO, Energy and protein requirements, WHO Technical Report Series No. 522, FAO Nutrition Meetings Report Series No. 52, Geneva, WHO (1973), pp. 12-13. Foxhall and Forbes mention that some authors consider the FAO caloric requirements on the high side for ancient peoples (cf. Dennell 1979).

[51] This hypothetical household consists of an elderly female, adult male, adult female, male child of 13-15 years, female child of 10-12 years, and another child of 7-9 years, all very active.

[52] Foxhall and Forbes (1982, p. 44) have pointed out that cereals especially form an essential part of the human diet when relatively little animal protein is consumed, as is, and always has been, the case in the Mediterranean region. As an example, the authors note that in Crete in the late 1940s, at a time when less grain than normal was eaten because of wartime disruptions, cereals supplied, on average, 39% of the total number of calories and 47% of the protein consumed.

Moreover, there is evidence of a comparable degree of diversification in small-scale craft activities, such as pottery and iron production. For example, the potter's workshop in trench 6 produced a wide array of products, varying from table wares to roof tiles.[53] The same holds true for the smithy in trench 4 (*oikos* ε), where craft production was combined with household activities.[54] Many different types of metal objects were found inside the workshop, including agricultural tools. Considering the archaeozoological finds at the site and the distribution of spindle whorls and loom weights, which were found in contexts from different phases,[55] we may assume that sheep were raised not only for meat consumption. It seems likely that they were also kept for the production of wool, especially since we have no evidence of the cultivation of fibre plants.[56] Wool production at a household level is certainly not unheard of in the Early Iron Age. Indeed, Hesiod included weaving in his description of a woman's monthly chores in *Works and Days* (Appendix 6, 1).[57]

In short, it seems that the inhabitants of l'Amastuola were not dependent on exchange to fulfil most of their everyday needs and produced their own metal tools and textiles as well. In addition, we have already seen that they did not focus on the production of a limited scope of agricultural crops, but rather aimed to cultivate the entire array of food plants that they needed. However, there are indications of surplus production. The first and most obvious one is the presence of imported objects, including pottery from adjacent regions in southern Italy, Corinth, eastern Greece and Attica. Some of the imported vases were transport amphorae, indicating that not only pottery, but also bulk goods such as wine and olive oil were among the imports. The inhabitants were clearly involved in external exchange. Given the nature of these imports, however, they should probably be interpreted as luxurious and, perhaps, prestigious additions to local production.

So how do the two stone platforms in trench 5, which were interpreted as the remains of grain silos, fit into this picture? Such silos are a clear example of excessive storage capacity,[58] which is an often used indicator of surplus production. As is shown in *Box 2*, however, this does not hold true for l'Amastuola, since the quantity of stored grain was probably too low for trade on any scale. Instead, I propose that the grain silos on the south terrace should be interpreted as the remains of storage areas that were used by only a few households, or possibly even just one. Obviously, for this hypothesis to work it has to be assumed that there were no other large storage structures on the south terrace of l'Amastuola. Unfortunately, this cannot be verified because only part of the settlement has been excavated. However, in combination with the additional evidence of craft activities, crop storage, and crop processing at the household level, it can be concluded that the site of l'Amastuola probably housed a largely self-sufficient community.

[53] Since the terracotta test pieces from trench 6 are square and rather thick (Crielaard and Burgers 2012, p. 97), it has been suggested that they were meant for testing products of a related shape, namely roof tiles.

[54] For example, a small double-axe, a pickaxe and a long knife or small dagger, Burgers and Crielaard 2007, p. 90, Figure 17-18.

[55] Evidence of textile production in pre-Roman Italy is altogether rare. Gleba (2008, p. 42) reports that a considerable number of linen textile fragments has been preserved in various Neolithic and Bronze Age sites in the Alpine region in northern Italy. However, such finds are much less common in southern Italy. Flax (*Linum usitatissimum*) seeds have exclusively been found in northern Italy, although Gleba (2008, p. 69) states that 'the south also seems to have had a flax-growing tradition going back to the prehistoric period, albeit the evidence is scarcer than in North Italy.' Even less is known about the use of other plant fibres, such as hemp (*Cannabis sativa*), nettle (*Urtica dioica*), tree bark and esparto grass (*Stipa tenacissima*) in southern Italy, although it can be assumed that their use also goes back to pre-Roman times.

[56] Gleba (2008, pp. 27-33) has collected a considerable corpus of iconographic evidence for the use of textile production in pre-Roman Italy. It contains an illustration on a Daunian *stele* from northern Apulia (datable between the middle of the 7th and the early 6th centuries BC), which shows a human figure working at a standing loom (Gleba 2008, p. 31; Nava 1980, Tav. CCXLVI (748 A Sin.)).

[57] *W&D* 770-779.

[58] Bakels 1996, pp. 331-332; cf. Groot and Lentjes 2013.

Change and innovations

Summarizing the previous two sections, a number of conclusions can be drawn. The landscape surrounding the l'Amastuola hill was quite varied and included several different exploitable land zones (arable land, a *macchia* and/or *gariga* zone, pastoral grounds, woodland, and a marine environment). The inhabitants of l'Amastuola cultivated cereals, pulses, fruits, and vegetables on small agricultural fields that were located within a close distance to the settlement. There is no conclusive evidence of wine production, but olive cultivation may have been practiced on a small scale as well. The inhabitants of l'Amastuola catered mostly for their own needs. We may ask ourselves, however, if this situation remained unchanged during the entire habitation period of the site. Greek influences on architecture, pottery forms, and burial customs became increasingly apparent at l'Amastuola during the later 7th and 6th centuries BC. Did this influence also extend to the inhabitants' diet and agricultural practices?

In order to answer this question, we need to take another look at the archaeobotanical assemblage. Appendix 2 lists the analysis results of all the seeds and fruits that are found in each chronological phase at l'Amastuola. The chronological subdivision in these tables makes it clear that the samples are not equally distributed across the different phases. For example, the Archaic period is well represented, whereas there is only one unit from the latest habitation phase (5th century BC) that contained the remains of seeds and fruits. The unequal distribution may well have influenced the assemblage. For instance, certain species may be over- or underrepresented, and differences between the distinguished chronological phases could be hidden from our view. Indeed, these differences appear to be minimal. In all four phases, it seems that the people in the settlement lived on a diet of hulled wheat and hulled barley and pulses such as bitter vetches, broad beans, and lentils. The important conclusion that can be drawn is that the crop spectrum does not show any signs of substantial change in the course of four centuries of habitation.

However, the adaptation of new customs may have taken place in different forms. Many differences may be hidden from our view, such as changes in the sowing season and/or harvesting method (especially of cereal crops) and the scale and intensity of production. As we have seen above, however, there is no conclusive evidence of large-scale surplus production in any of the habitation phases at l'Amastuola. As far as changes in the sowing season or harvesting method are concerned, the cereal spectrum in itself is not particularly informative about these processes. However, some information can be inferred from wild plant remains that are found in association with the cereals. The presence of certain weed seeds may be significant for the reconstruction of the growing circumstances. For instance, the ripening period of the weed seeds could indicate whether cereals were harvested in early summer (planted from September to December, i.e. winter grain or Secalinetea) or late summer (planted in March, i.e. summer grain or Chenopodietea).[59] I will show in chapter 5 that a few other sites in southeast Italy provided weed seeds of 'late bloomers' (*Chenopodium album* and *Polygonum*, which produce ripe seeds in the period between mid-summer through fall), but such weeds were not found at l'Amastuola. In short, it is not possible to establish whether the cultivated cereals at this site were winter or summer grains, let alone whether the growing season changed over the course of time.

The presence of cereal weeds can also be used as an indicator of the harvesting method.[60] Cereals usually reach a height between 50 and 120 centimetres. If the cereal sample is mixed with seeds from weed species that grow considerably less tall, this may indicate that the cereals were harvested near the root or in its entirety, including the stalks (and roots?) that may have been used to produce straw. The presence of (autumn) adonis in the archaeobotanical assemblage from l'Amastuola may be significant in this connection. *Adonis* was found in four stratigraphic units (67, 72, 534 and 626), often in combination with cereals (especially in units 67 and 72). Unit 67 is probably a modern disturbance; unit 72 represents the floor of building θ; unit 534 was a charcoal spot in trench 6, outside of the pottery workshop; and unit 626 con-

---

[59] Hillman 1981, pp. 146-147. Cf. Fiorentino 1998, p. 217.

tains the possible remains of the Iron Age hut that was found in this same trench. Although the sample is small, it can be concluded that *Adonis* grew in and around the site in the earlier habitation phases (unit 626) as well as in the more recent ones (units 67 and 534). *Adonis* is a short plant that reaches a height of no more than 35 centimetres, suggesting that low harvesting took place at l'Amastuola. Unfortunately, the available data do not suffice to detect chronological developments.

Returning to the question posed at the beginning of this section, it is now possible to state that no significant agricultural innovations or changes in food preparation and diet took place during the occupational history of l'Amastuola (at least, none were reflected in the archaeobotanical assemblage). No clear breaks, agricultural innovations or notable changes in the natural vegetation or cultivated plants around the site have been detected. This result may be explained in a number of ways. In any case, it appears that the system of land use was well adapted to the local landscape. As we have seen above, the l'Amastuola landscape is very diverse, intersected with *gravine*, rocks and hills, and therefore not particularly suitable for the layout of large agricultural fields. Indeed, the charcoal assemblage shows that during the habitation period of the settlement on the south terrace, the site's environs were mostly covered with middle/high *macchia*. There may even have been a relatively undisturbed forest nearby. The most natural way to exploit such a landscape would have been to use a mixed farming system, in which the yields from small agricultural fields were combined with the products of sheep/goat rearing. This system of land use, however, also had certain restrictions. Burgers and Crielaard have argued that when Taras' agricultural territory took its final shape in the 5th century BC, the settlement on the l'Amastuola hilltop was abandoned.[61] A much larger new settlement, that was probably incorporated in the *chora* of Taras, emerged on the lower terraces north and east of the hill. The survey results from the area around the l'Amastuola hill show that a different system of land use was practiced around this more recent site. Numerous small rural sites started to appear in the 4th and 3rd centuries BC, suggesting a clear break in the organization and exploitation of the landscape.[62] Apparently, the 'old ways' of land use did not survive the period of economic growth and prosperity that characterized the Greek settlements in southeast Italy in the Classical and Early Hellenistic periods.

4.3 MURO TENENTE

Most of the archaeobotanical samples from Muro Tenente were retrieved from stratigraphic levels from the Early Hellenistic period, when the rural hinterland of Muro Tenente was apparently no longer exclusively exploited by the inhabitants of the settlement, but also by farmers who lived permanently in rural hamlets or isolated farmsteads. This means that in comparison to earlier periods, the landscape around the settlement may have been used in a much more efficient way. In this section, I will examine whether these innovations are reflected in the archaeobotanical assemblage. Although the interpretation of this assemblage is complicated by the absence of archaeobotanical data from earlier periods, I will show that it is possible to detect some changes in the landscape, crop spectrum and scale of agricultural production.

4.3.1 THE LANDSCAPE

Pollen coring conducted around Muro Tenente provided just as little results as at l'Amastuola. Therefore, the charcoal assemblage is of crucial importance for the reconstruction of the surrounding land-

---

[60] Hillman 1981, pp. 148-153.
[61] Burgers and Crielaard 2007, p. 107.
[62] Alessio and Guzzo 1989-1990; Burgers and Crielaard 2007, pp. 92-99. See also section 6.4.

scape. The great majority of charcoal fragments from Muro Tenente belongs to the genus *Erica* and to olive wood, but there is also evidence of climax vegetation in the form of oak wood. Based on this archaeobotanical assemblage, we can postulate the presence of two or, possibly, three landscape types, namely cultivated fields, low shrub lands and perhaps also a forest zone.

Arable land
The survey results leave little doubt about the location of the areas where the inhabitants of Muro Tenente cultivated their crops in the Early Hellenistic period. On the one hand, the open spaces between the habitation nuclei in the settlement area were probably used for small-scale horticulture. On the other hand, the immediate surroundings of the settlement were exploited intensively by people living in isolated farms and small rural hamlets. The area around Muro Tenente can be compared to other survey areas in the Brindisino, namely those around Oria, Valesio San Pancrazio Salentino, Masseria Mea and Muro Maurizio, which all show an infill of the countryside in the Early Hellenistic phase.[63] Most of these rural sites were rather small and located on thick soils. Only a handful of sites on marginal grounds were discovered, indicating that the farmers probably practiced arable cultivation rather than keeping livestock.[64] The Valesio survey has shown that the distribution of rural sites around the settlement is remarkably regular, with an average distance of about 500 metres between one farm and another.[65] This pattern suggests that a certain level of central organization of the Brindisino landscape existed in this period.

There are also indications that travelling became easier, because new roads were built in previously uncultivated areas. This road system has been discussed at considerable length by Giovanni Uggeri.[66] According to Yntema, these roads must have 'surpassed the humble status of mere paths through the wild, given the fairly considerable surplus production of the area.'[67]

Cereals and pulses must have been prominent among the cultivated crops on these fields, but considering the archaeological and archaeobotanical evidence, it is likely that grapes and olives also played an important role. For l'Amastuola, I proposed that the abundance of olive wood could have been gathered in olive groves with cultivated trees. At Muro Tenente, olive wood also formed a dominant part of the charcoal assemblage, but as we will see below, the evidence that this wood can be associated with cultivated trees is much stronger.

Low shrublands
The dominance of *Erica* wood in the charcoal assemblage from Muro Tenente is striking. Almost 40% (792 out of 1984) of the identified charcoal fragments belonged to this genus, and it was found in 15 of the 41 sampled stratigraphic units. Only olive wood is found more frequently, but in much smaller quantities. Most *Erica* species, and particularly tree heath (*Erica arborea*), are considered to be important pioneer plants on recently cleared or burned grounds. Together with strawberry tree, tree heath can dominate the new vegetation that is formed after a destructive fire for years. In the absence of subsequent burning, it can take up to ten years for the original vegetation to recover.[68] *Erica* is also a

---

[63] Burgers 1998, p. 227.
[64] Yntema 1993, p. 186.
[65] Burgers 1998, p. 255.
[66] Uggeri 1975, 1983.
[67] Cf. Yntema, 1982, 1993, 2006, p. 100.
[68] Minelli 2002, p. 38. When the forest cover is disturbed, for instance by deforestation, crop cultivation and the grazing of sheep and goats, it gradually recovers in a number of stages. Firstly, the fallow land is colonized by steppe vegetation, i.e. grasses. After a while, the *gariga* species, low shrubs such as kermes oak (*Quercus coccifera*), lavender (*Lavandula*), thyme (*Thymus vulgaris*) and *Cistus* take over (Smith and Gillett 2000, p. 6). The third stage is *macchia secondaria*, which may contain different plant types and compositions., such as *Phillyreo angustofoliae-Ericetum multiflorae* (combinations of false olive and Mediterranean heath). See Gaudenzio and Peccenini 2002, p. 67.

Trench	C	A	C	C	C	C
Unit	370	15	253	455	458	503
Context	-	domestic	domestic	domestic	Domestic	Domestic
Structure	-	refuse dump	ash deposit	kiln fuel	kiln fuel	ash deposit
Date	unknown	Early Hellenistic	Early Hellenistic	Early Hellenistic	Early Hellenistic	Early Hellenistic
Taxa						
Erica sp.	1	17	23	65	45	10
Erica arborea					55	
Erica multiflora						

Trench	C	C	C	C	C	E	E
Unit	593	1702	2258	441	805	20011	20063
Context	domestic	domestic	domestic	grave	grave	domestic	domestic
Structure	floor matrix	kiln fuel	floor matrix	grave 25	grave 27	burned structure?	floor matrix
Date	Early Hellenistic	Early Hellenistic	Early Hellenistic	Early Hellenistic	Early Hellenistic	Late Hellenistic	Late Hellenistic
Taxa							
Erica sp.	6	102	10	8	11	5	1
Erica arborea							
Erica multiflora		100					

Table 4.4 Muro Tenente, find contexts of *Erica* charcoal

pyrophile plant. Similar to pine trees, it contains a chemical to make the plant more flammable. This feature is probably part of the plant's strategy to beat rivalling plants in the battle for space, nutrients and sunlight.[69]

Considering these properties, one might suggest that the *Erica* vegetation originated from the layers associated with the site's abandonment, and, therefore, does not represent the vegetation of a phase when the settlement was still inhabited. However, the samples that contained *Erica* charcoal were not taken from such layers, but originated from all the larger excavation trenches and a variety of different contexts, including graves, house floors, rubbish dumps, and fireplaces (see *Table 4.4*). This variety of find contexts of *Erica* charcoal also makes it less likely that its presence is related to its use as construction material, for example to cover the roofs and walls of houses. As I pointed out in section 3.5.1, *Erica* charcoal is often found in contexts that can be associated with hearths or furnaces at Muro Tenente (see *Table 3.1*), which renders it likely that it was also regularly selected to use as firewood.

In short, the abundance of *Erica* charcoal in the samples from Muro Tenente probably reflects a dominant part of the surrounding landscape, which consisted of low *macchia*. As we have seen, this vegetation type is largely the result of human impact on the landscape. Indeed, *Erica*-vegetation can be associated with a number of practical uses. Most importantly, it can be interpreted as an indicator for grazing. Grazing is one of the main reasons for the growth of *macchia* after deforestation, because it prevents most plant species from growing and therefore stands in the way of the formation of young forests.[70] *Erica*, however, is a particularly tough plant and fairly resistant to grazing sheep/goats. It can be argued, therefore, that the dominance of *Erica* wood in the charcoal assemblage from Muro Tenente is indicative of the vicinity of pastoral lands. This hypothesis ties in with the archaeological evidence of sheep rearing and wool production at the site. If wool production was indeed part of the rural

---

[69] Grove and Rackham 2001, pp. 219-220.

[70] Cf. Veenman 2002, pp. 94-98; Grove and Rackham 2001, pp. 48-49.

economy, various facilities would have been needed in and around the settlement area to accommodate the sheep.[71] Possibly, the animals were moved over short distances in the area around the settlement to graze in a system that Veenman,[72] Hofmeister,[73] and De Vooys[74] have called 'small-' or 'short-distance' transhumance. There are several plausible reasons for keeping sheep in the vicinity of the settlement.[75] First, sheep could be used to manure the nearby arable grounds. Second, goats and sheep that were kept for their milk needed to be kept close and possibly even grazed in the open spaces between the habitation clusters of the settlement.

Forest
According to Coco,[76] the Brindisino was, until recently, covered by a dense forest, the so-called *foresta Oritana*. The archaeobotanical remains from Muro Tenente, however, have revealed little evidence of the presence of woodland in this area. Theoretically, the oak and olive trees from the archaeobotanical assemblage could be indicative of the presence of climax vegetation. However, since oak and olive trees can also be found in degraded vegetation, this evidence is rather ambiguous. While it is true that indications of woodland vegetation are often underrepresented in settlement contexts,[77] it is important to consider that evidence for the nearby presence of forests is considerably stronger at l'Amastuola (i.e. the absence of contemporary settlements in the site's environs; dominance of oak and olive wood in the charcoal assemblage, especially in fireplaces and hearths (*Table 2.1*); find of red deer antler). In comparison, it seems less likely that Muro Tenente was surrounded by a *foresta Oritana* during its habitation period, although the existence of such a forest cannot be excluded based on the current evidence. Indeed, even the considerable quantities of wild animal bones that were found in contemporary contexts in the nearby settlement of Valesio (see *Table 5.3*) do not supply conclusive evidence for the presence of woodlands. The species that were found here, including brown hare (*Lepus europaeus*), red deer (*Cervus elaphus*), and fox (*Vulpes vulpes*) thrive in a wide variety of habitats.

4.3.2 LAND USE

Surplus production
In view of the changes in settlement patterns during the Early Hellenistic Period at Muro Tenente, I formulated the hypothesis that this development probably led to a more efficient way of land use. Indeed, it can be argued that these innovations made it possible to produce an agricultural surplus. Archaeological evidence for this is found in the distribution of crop processing and storage facilities. According to Burgers, these storage areas may have been used for agricultural produce, which is why they were deliberately located in peripheral zones within easy distance of the entrance ways of the settlement.[78] One of the northernmost rooms of the houses in the northern peripheral excavation trench (A) contained a series of large storage vessels (*dolia*) still *in situ* (*Figure 3.4*). During the urban survey, dense concentrations of amphorae were collected along the inner side of the outer fortification wall (*Figure 4.6*). Storage vessels were occasionally also found in the central excavation trench, but not in large quantities. The burned wooden structure near the fortification wall in the southern trench (unit 20011) may also have been a

---

[71] Such facilities, such as sheep pens and trails, were found in Archaic Cavallino. See section 6.4.
[72] Cf. Veenman 2002, pp. 13-16.
[73] Hofmeister 1961, p. 125.
[74] De Vooys 1959.
[75] Cf. Veenman 2002, p. 130.
[76] Coco 1919.
[77] Since the archaeobotanical assemblage in a settlement context is inevitably the result of human selection, it is much more likely to contain crops and other useful plants than forest species (unless they could be used as fuel or in construction). Pers. comm. L.I. Kooistra.
[78] Burgers 1998, p. 258.

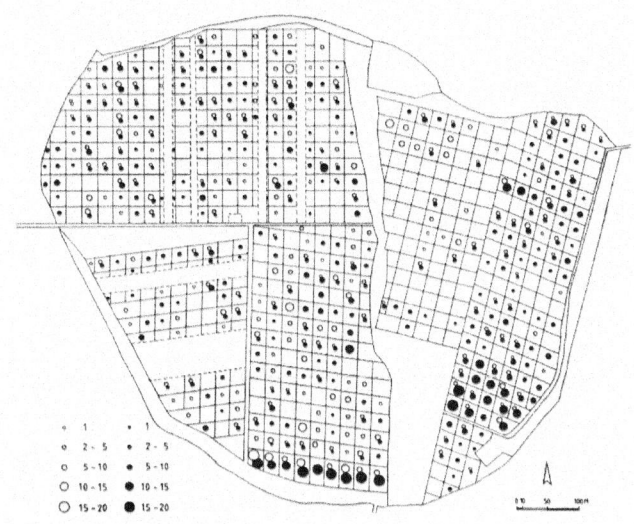

Fig. 4.6. Muro Tenente, density per square of amphorae sherds picked up during the field surveys. Burgers 1998, 256.

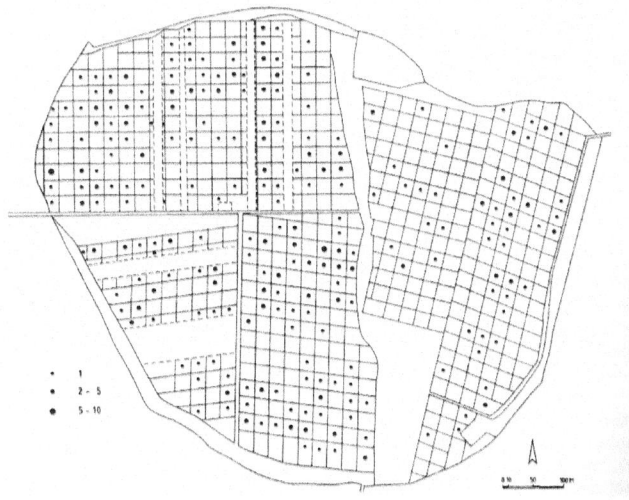

Fig. 4.7. Muro Tenente, density per square of loomweights picked up during the field surveys. Burgers 1998, 252.

storage building, or can perhaps be associated with crop processing activities, such as harvesting, cereal cleaning, weeding, and pruning. This interpretation is partly based on the large and varied collection of seeds and charcoal that was found in the soil samples (see *Figures 3.18* and *3.19*), and included crop remains (emmer wheat, barley, olives, pulses, and grapes) as well as agricultural waste products, such as cereal weeds (*Avena*) and a mastic tree berry. Among the charcoal fragments were mostly (evergreen) oak and olive wood remains. The nearby 'rooms' that were built parallel to the fortification wall (*ambiente* 1 and 2) have been interpreted as temporary refuges instead of permanently inhabited houses, as they were built when this part of the settlement was already abandoned. At the same time, they might also be connected with such seasonal crop processing activities as harvesting.

This begs the question what type of products were stored in these storage areas. Possible candidates are cereals and other arable crops, but also wool. There is evidence of wool production at Muro Tenente in the form of loom weights, which were found in abundance in all excavation trenches, and also during the field surveys.[79] These loom weights cannot usually be dated with much precision, but judging from

[79] Burgers 1998, p. 253.

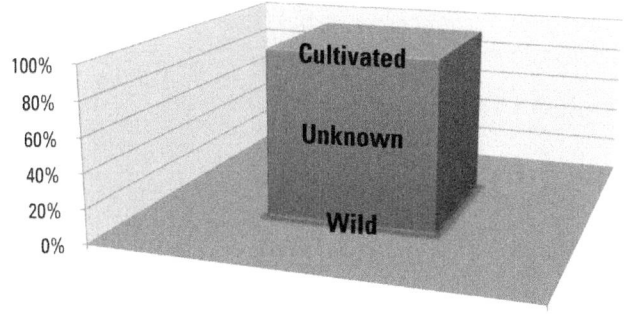

Fig. 4.8. Muro Tenente, morphological measurements of the grape pips from unit 89 compared to the index of Stummer 1911. Drawing edited by Bert Brouwenstijn.

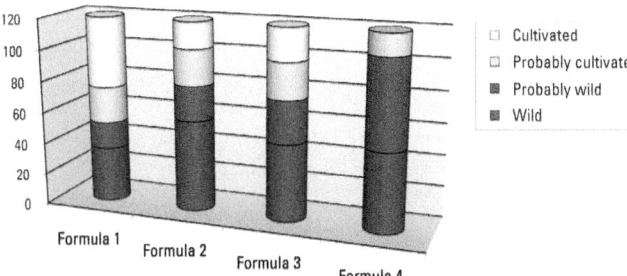

Fig. 4.9. Muro Tenente, morphological measurements of the grape pips from unit 89 compared to the formulae by Mangafa and Kotsakis 1996. Drawing edited by Bert Brouwenstijn.

the information gained from the field surveys, it seems that they were fairly evenly spread across the Early Hellenistic habitation units (*Figure 4.7*).

Wine and olive oil production
Apart from cereals and wool, a large part of the storage areas at Muro Tenente may have been used to store olive oil and wine. I already discussed the evidence for local wine and olive oil production at Muro Tenente in chapter 3. Most importantly, this evidence is supplied by the presence of olive/wine presses.[80] Olive stones were found in all the excavated areas in various types of contexts, including graves, ritual contexts, and refuse deposits (see Appendix 3).[81] Grapes were also found in abundance, including the remains of grape or possibly wine pressings in the central excavation trench (C) (*Figure 3.21*). Moreover, olive charcoal is the second most common wood type after *Erica* (in absolute numbers), and was found in even more units (see Appendix 3). It is possible that the wood derived from pruning and pollarding and it could, therefore, be interpreted as indicative of olive cultivation. Unfortunately, the problem with the state of conservation of the growth rings that we saw at l'Amastuola also applies here, because hardly any fragments contained parts of the bark or core. Nevertheless, combining the archaeological and archaeobotanical evidence, it seems likely that wine and olive oil were produced locally and at a relatively large scale at Muro Tenente.

Unfortunately, it is not possible to support this argument with morphometric analysis of the olive stones and grape pips from this site. Measurements of most of the olive stones' length and width are assembled in *Table 4.5*, but the total number of measured fragments (14 in total) is too small to provide any statistically significant outcomes. Grape remains, however, are found in abundance at Muro Tenente, especially in the large deposit of 'grape-pressings' (unit 89). Since this grape deposit may represent the remains of wine production, morphological measurements of the grape pips have been

[80] Burgers 1998, p. 254.
[81] Units 89, 253, 805, 1624, 1636, 1638, 2551, 20011, and 20067.

Trench	C	C	C	C	C	C	C
Unit	89	89	89	253	805	1624	1624
Findnr	10745	10745	10745	201029	4377	11931	11931
Context	domestic	domestic	domestic	ash deposit	fill+ grave gifts	fill	fill
Structure	-	-	-	-	grave 27	grave 30	grave 30
Date	Early Hellenistic	Early Hellenistic	Early Hellenistic	Early Hellenistic	Early Hellenistic	Early Hellenistic	Early Hellenistic
Fragmented Minimal length (mm)	5	4	5.2	?	5.1		8
Fragmented Minimal width	4		4		4		
Complete Length (mm)						10.2	
Complete Width (mm)		4.2		5.5		5	6

Trench	C	C	C	C	C	C	C
Unit	1624	1624	1624	1624	1624	1638	2551
Findnr	11931	11931	11931	11931	11931	7545	203175
Context	fill	fill	fill	fill	fill	lower layer fill	sacrifice?
Structure	grave 30	grave 30	grave 30	grave 30	grave 30	grave 30	division walls necropolis
Date	Early Hellenistic	Early Hellenistic	Early Hellenistic	Early Hellenistic	Early Hellenistic	Early Hellenistic	?
Fragmented Minimal length (mm)	6		7	5.5		4	5.3
Fragmented Minimal width	5			4.2		4.5	4
Complete Length (mm)		6.2			6.5		
Complete Width (mm)		3.8	4.8		4.5		

Table 4.5 Muro Tenente, measurements of olive stone fragments.

carried out to determine whether they belong to a wild or cultivated variety (*Vitis vinifera* var. *sylvestris* or *Vitis vinifera* var. *vinifera*). These measurements have, however, led to certain difficulties for interpretation. The results were compared to the index of Stummer (see section 2.5.3). The required measurements for this method were taken from a sample of 120 of the 5175 grape pips from unit 89. However, as can be seen from *Figure 4.8*, the Stummer formula was not suitable for the grapes from Muro Tenente, as almost all measurements provided indices that could belong to both wild and cultivated grapes. Therefore, it was decided to apply the formulae by Mangafa and Kotsakis instead of the Stummer Index. The outcomes can be found in Appendix 5, and are assembled in *Figure 4.9*. Unfortunately, the results of these calculations are not conclusive either, since the grapes once more fall within a range that encompasses both the wild and cultivated species.

In short, both methods fail to bring us any closer to discovering whether the grapes found at Muro Tenente were cultivated or wild. This problem is not caused by the data set: analysing the outcomes with the statistical analysis program SPSS (see *Box 3*), I was able to conclude that the sample is both large enough and reliable. The problem, therefore, seems to be the methods. The formulae by Mangafa and Kotsakis were only tested against seeds of (northeast) Greek origin. The growing circumstances for the Greek vines are, however, very different from those in southeast Italy, possibly resulting in morphological differences. Moreover, it is not unlikely that the grapes from Muro Tenente belong to a different variety, and contain characteristics that do not fit these formulae. The same holds true for the

Stummer Index, which was developed in the Austrian Danube area. Several authors have argued that the Stummer Index does not allow separation of wild grapevines and cultivars,[82] and the methodological debate about morphometric methods to distinguish between the two is still on-going.[83]

Box 3: Confronting the grape measurements from Muro Tenente (unit 89) with the statistical analysis program SPSS[84]

The tests of normality showed that the data are normally distributed in all four formulae. This means that the sample size was probably big enough and the outcomes would not differ much if it were enlarged. The grape population also needs to be normally distributed to compare the mean scores in SPSS. For this reason, a t-test was conducted. For each formula, the ranges that are provided by Mangafa and Kotsakis were replaced by one score. For example, for the range in formula 1 the mean score of 0.2 was used, where a score lower than -0.2 represents wild grapes, a score between -0.2 and 0.2 wild grapes with great (64.7%) probability, between 0.2 and 0.8 cultivated grapes with great (76.2%) probability, and higher than 0.8 cultivated grapes. In other words, if the outcome is higher than 0.2, the grape is considered to be of the cultivated type. If it is lower, the grape has to be wild. With the t-test, I tried to determine whether this mean score differed significantly from the actual average of the data set. This is just a different way of representing the outcomes of the formulae, but the difference is that the t-test also confirms whether the outcomes are statistically significant or not. It turned out that in all four formulae, the chosen score differed significantly from the average of the data set. In formula 1, the average was significantly higher, and in the other three the average was significantly lower. In other words, the t-test confirms that according to formula 1, the grape population is cultivated, and that according to formulae 2, 3, and 4, the grape population is wild. Mangafa and Kotsakis[85] describe the use of the second and the third formulae as more appropriate for the identification of charred archaeological grapes. According to these formulae, the grapes are most likely to be wild, but the outcomes remain somewhat ambiguous.

4.4 CONCLUSION: LANDSCAPE AND LAND USE AT L'AMASTUOLA AND MURO TENENTE COMPARED

The first observation that comes to mind when we review this chapter, is that the crop spectra at l'Amastuola and Muro Tenente are fairly similar; roughly the same cereals, pulses, and fruits were cultivated. However, there are also a few apparent differences. The most striking one is the dominance of hulled cereals at l'Amastuola, as opposed to the high frequency of naked cereals at Muro Tenente. Furthermore, hardly any evidence is found of the consumption of bitter vetches at the latter site, while it apparently did function as a common foodstuff at l'Amastuola. In general, pulses are fairly rare at Muro Tenente. These results may partly be due to sampling problems, but we should consider the possibility that they are indicative of a marked difference in eating habits between the inhabitants of the two sites.

---

[82] For example Rivera et al. 2007; Orrù et al. 2007.
[83] Cf. Fiorentino 2011, pp. 19-20.
[84] I am grateful to Sanne Iris Lentjes for her help with the use of this program.
[85] Mangafa and Kotsakis 1996, p. 417.

Furthermore, both the scale on which cultivation took place as well as the cultivation methods differed. The landscape surrounding Early Hellenistic Muro Tenente was exploited in a much more intensive way than the area around Archaic l'Amastuola. There is both archaeological evidence (diversity in craft activities, distribution of crop storage, and processing facilities) and archaeobotanical evidence (diversity in the crop spectrum) to suggest that the site of l'Amastuola housed a largely self-sufficient community. Agricultural production was primarily aimed at subsistence, not at surplus production for a market. If olives and grapes were cultivated at all, it did not happen on a large scale. Local production of wine and olive oil cannot be excluded, but it seems unlikely that the inhabitants of l'Amastuola were involved in such time- and capital-demanding activities. Some agricultural surplus may have been generated, but the grain silos found in trench 6 should probably not be interpreted as an indication of centralized surplus storage.

The situation was clearly different at Early Hellenistic Muro Tenente. The distribution and scale of storage deposits shows that this settlement was involved in surplus production, and it appears that this surplus included locally produced wine and olive oil. Several new developments in the Early Hellenistic Period had made it possible to change the methods and scale of production in this way. There is evidence that the agricultural system as a whole became more efficient and rational in its organization. The countryside surrounding Muro Tenente was filled in with isolated farms and small rural hamlets, and crop processing and storage areas were built in the settlement's periphery. As a result, human impact on the landscape also became increasingly apparent at Muro Tenente. New settlements and roads were built, previously untilled grounds were cleared, and existing fields were cultivated more intensively. Indeed, the charcoal samples from Early Hellenistic Muro Tenente are dominated by low *macchia* species and other indicators of landscapes that are degraded by human impact.

The process of rural infill also took place at l'Amastuola, but this happened in the late Classical Period, after the abandonment of the south terrace.[86] The survey data show that the Early Hellenistic period was the phase of maximum expansion in this area, with isolated and clustered rural sites distributed throughout the landscape. In contrast, no rural settlements existed in the area around the l'Amastuola hill during the Early Iron Age, the Archaic, and much of the Classical Period, i.e. during the entire time that the settlement on the south terrace was inhabited. This ties in with the archaeobotanical data from l'Amastuola, which show that there was a strong connection between the opportunities and restrictions of the landscape (which made it unsuitable for the layout of large agricultural fields) on the one hand, and the systems of (small-scale) land use on the other. The survey data and the charcoal assemblage suggest that the strategies of land use caused only limited stress for the surrounding landscape. The abundant presence of oak and olive wood in fireplaces and hearths on the south terrace suggests that there may also have been a forest zone nearby. The find of a piece of antler indicates that this forest may have been used for hunting activities. The land zones that surrounded l'Amastuola may also have included arable fields, a *macchia* and/or *gariga* zone, pastoral grounds, and a marine environment. Most of these landscapes were easy to reach and were probably exploited on a small scale.

In conclusion, the interpretation of the archaeobotanical data from l'Amastuola and Muro Tenente on a meso level reveal a number of differences in the way the landscape was exploited. These differences tie in with the general picture of settlement dynamics in the periods when the two settlements were inhabited. The main question that we are faced with now is how these results fit into the general framework of long-term developments in landscape and land use in southeast Italy. I will deal with

---

[86] Burgers and Crielaard 2007, p. 98.

Chapter 5 – Macro level: Part one

5.1 INTRODUCTION

In the present chapter, both the research area and the chronological framework of this study will be widened by combining the research data from all sites in southeast Italy where archaeobotanical sampling has taken place. This chapter will start with a short introduction to archaeobotanical research in southeast Italy and to the archaeological sites that I will use in order to put the case studies in a broader regional context. This overview is necessary, because the differences in the crop and livestock spectrum can often be explained by, for example, the sites' location, exchange contacts, or its status in the regional settlement pattern. The locations of these sites are indicated in *Figure 5.1*.

As a next step, the archaeobotanical data will be integrated with other sources of information, including archaeological excavation data, field surveys, archaeozoological studies, and ancient written texts. After the introduction to the archaeological sites, the structure of the remaining part of this chapter will consist of four paragraphs, each covering the usual research aspects: 1) the use of wood, 2) food preparation and diet, 3) the cultivation of grapes and olives, and 4) the use of plants in ritual activities. The final purpose of this analysis is to detect long-term developments in the rural economy and landscape, which will be discussed in detail in the next chapter.

Before proceeding with the introduction to the archaeological sites, I will address the reliability of one of the sources of information that is frequently used in this chapter, i.e. ancient written texts. There are very few contemporary written records that deal specifically with land use and the consumption and production of food, but the following ancient texts provide a useful context for the finds:

a) agricultural treatises by Greek and Roman authors, including Hesiod (8th century BC) and Aristotle (c. 384-322 BC). The Roman agronomists wrote their treatises on agriculture in more recent times. Among these texts, Cato's *De Agri Cultura* (written in the middle of the 2nd century BC), Publius Terentius Varro's *Rerum Rusticarum* (published in 37 BC), Columella's *De Re Rustica* and *De Arboribus* (middle of the 1st century AD) and Pliny the Elder's *Naturalis Historiae* (c. 77-79 AD) are the most important ones;[1]

b) casual references to food, land use and landscape in various texts, including Greek poetry by Archilochus (c. 680-645 BC), Semonides (7th century BC), Stesichorus (c. 640-555 BC), Sappho (c. 630-570 BC), Anacreon (582-485 BC), Hipponax of Ephesus (6th century BC), Euripides (c. 480-406 BC), Aristophanes (c. 446-386 BC), and Leonidas of Taras (330/320- 260 BC), and Roman authors such as Horace (65-8 BC), Dionysius of Halicarnassus (60 BC- after 7 BC), Livy (59 BC- 17 AD), Ovid (43 BC- 17/18 AD), Pausanias (2nd century AD), and Athenaeus (late 2nd-early 3rd century AD);

c) the so-called Herakleia tablets.[2] These two bronze plaques were discovered in 1732 in inland Basilicata, at the confluence of the rivers Salandrella and Cavone. They can probably be dated between 350 and 300 BC. The writings are in Greek, but on one of the tablets the original text was erased for the purpose of transcribing a law in Latin. The Greek inscriptions address a new division of two land plots that were sacred to Athena and Dionysos, and describe in some detail what these lands looked like and which crops were cultivated.

---

[1] For a more extensive discussion of the literary sources that concern Roman agriculture, see White 1970.

[2] Uguzzoni and Ghinatti 1968.

I do not intend to give an exhaustive overview of all references to the use of plant products in ancient literature; the main purpose of these examples is to supplement the archaeobotanical and archaeological evidence. In fact, ancient literary texts will only be used in combination with other sources of information. The reason for this is that their interpretation is often problematic. This is due, in part, to these classical authors living in different time periods and geographical areas, but also to the fact that they often had a personal agenda. Columella, for example, extensively discusses the bad state of agriculture in Roman Italy, but blames this situation on mismanagement rather than soil exhaustion due to careless tending.[3] As we do not have any other contemporary sources, we do not know whether this was actually the case, or whether Columella needed to make this point in order to support his account of 'proper' ways to supervise a slave-run estate.

5.2 A SHORT INTRODUCTION TO ARCHAEOBOTANICAL RESEARCH IN SOUTHEAST ITALY, AND THE ARCHAEOLOGICAL SITES

Until recently, archaeobotanical analyses were rarely an integral part of archaeological investigations in southeastern Italy.[4] There are several explanations for this, including the environmental circumstances for the preservation of plant remains, which are usually much less favourable in comparison to those in northern Europe. For example, it appears that most archaeological contexts in southeast Italy are unsuitable for pollen preservation. A quick glance at the European fossil pollen database makes it clear that most of the available pollen data from Italy are from the north.[5] It can also be noted that archaeobotanical samples are unevenly distributed between northern/central and southern Italy,[6] and also between sites with waterlogged and dry conditions.

---

[3] White 1970, p. 34.

[4] Archaeobotanical research was introduced in Italy at a later stage than in most northern European countries. The first time that more or less systematic archaeobotanical soil sampling was incorporated as an integral part of an excavation project in southeast Italy was in the 1970s, at Passo di Corvo on the Tavoliere plateau in northern Apulia (Follieri 1973). This was also the first site in Italy where a flotation tank was used. In contrast, archaeobotanical analyses of waterlogged plant remains were performed as early as the middle of the 19th century in Switzerland by Osvald Heer, in the 1950s by Grahame Clark at the excavations at Star Carr in Yorkshire, and by Hans Helbaek in Denmark.

[5] www.europeanpollendatabase.net. Pollen analyses seem to be carried out on a less regular basis in central Italy, and cores from the south are even rarer. The pollen database only lists two such cores, from the lakes of Vico and Monticchio. It should be immediately added that there are other known pollen cores from Pompeii (Dimbleby and Grüger 2002), Pomarico Vecchio (Caramiello and Siniscalco 1997), the Lago d'Averno (Grüger et al. 2002), Aspromonte (Schneider 1985), Coppa Nevigata (Sargent 1987; Fiorentino and Magri 1999), Pantanello (Sullivan 1983; Carter 2006), Laghi di Monticchio (Watts et al. 1996), Lago Monterosi (Bonatti 1966), the Laghi Alimini (Harding 1999; Di Rita and Magri 2009), Herdonia (Heim 1995) and Arpi Montarozzi (Accorsi et al. 1995). Nevertheless, the difference between the north and south remains salient.

[6] Hopf 1991, p. 243; Rottoli 1993, p. 305; Carter and Costantini 1994, p. 104: 'In contrast with the great interest that historians and archaeologists have shown for reconstructions of the Roman agrarian landscape, studies which focus on the vegetational history, the pollen and seed remains have only rarely been undertaken and developed.' Burgers 1998, p. 254: 'Especially troublesome to the study of the nature of the agricultural system in ancient Salento is the virtual lack of archaeobotanical research.' Cf. the dataset presented by Mercuri et al. in press, particularly Figure 1.

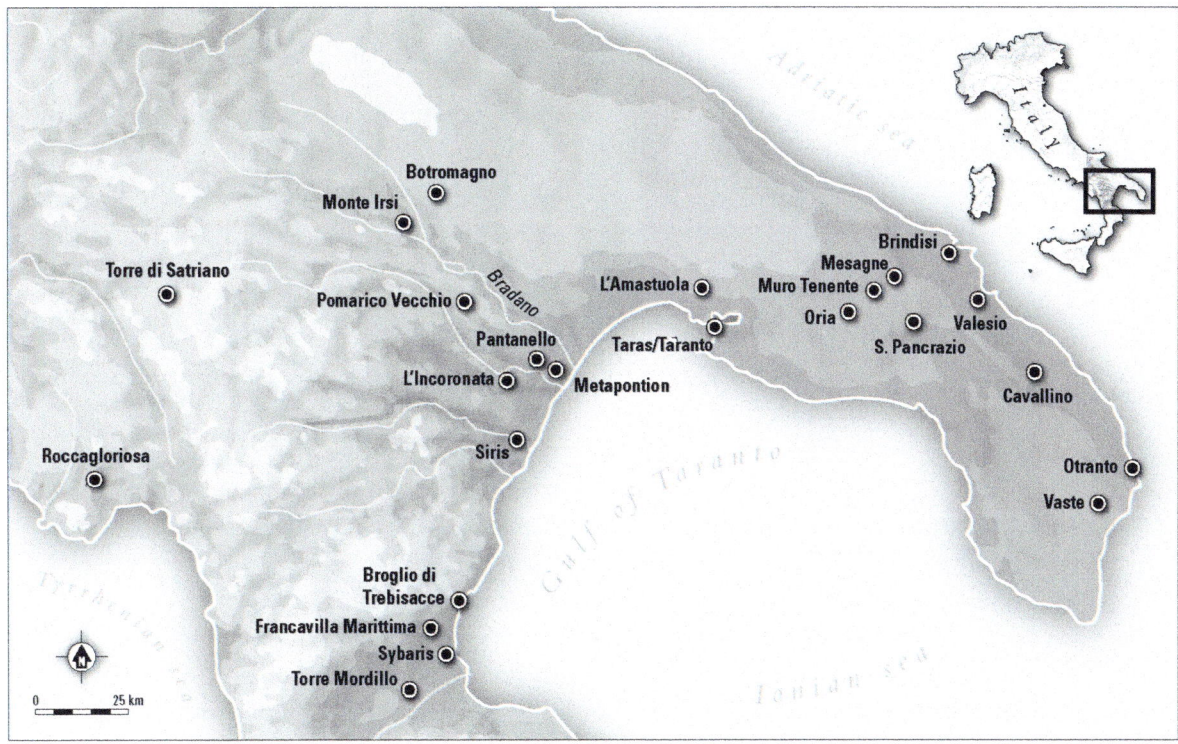

Fig. 5.1. Locations of the archaeological sites in southeast Italy that are discussed in chapters 5 and 6. Map by Bert Brouwenstijn.

However, as I pointed out in chapter 1, archaeobotanical research is slowly coming of age in Italy. In recent years, the traditional focus on (Greek) urban sites of archaeological research has gradually been counterbalanced by an increasing interest in rural sites and landscapes.[7] This development has also caused an upsurge in interdisciplinary research, combining archaeology with natural sciences such as biology, geology, and chemistry. The rise of archaeobotany in southeast Italy owes particularly to the ongoing research projects of the Archaeobotanical and Palaeoecological Laboratory of the Università del Salento in Lecce.[8] Nevertheless, most of the archaeobotanical researchers in this region take the local context into consideration, analysing the archaeobotanical data from one particular site, without putting them in a larger regional perspective. This is especially true for the period under study here, namely the first millennium BC. In the past two decades, synthesizing papers have been published on long-term landscape developments in the Neolithic period[9] and the Bronze Age.[10] Another research theme that has received much scholarly attention in Italy is Roman agriculture.[11] However, the period between the end of the Bronze Age and the Roman period is still largely *terra incognita*.

The present study aims to fill this gap by comparing the case studies from the previous chapters with those from other sites from southeast Italy where archaeobotanical and archaeozoological analyses have taken place. These sites are Broglio di Trebisacce, Torre Mordillo, Otranto, Valesio, Francavilla Marittima, l'Incoronata, Botromagno/Gravina, Monte Irsi, Cavallino, Monte Papalucio, Pantanello, Vaste, Roccagloriosa, and Pomarico Vecchio.[12] The following overview is a short introduction to these sites, in chronological order. The archaeobotanical and archaeozoological data are assembled in *Tables 5.1, 5.2,* and *5.3* at the end of this chapter.

[7] Yntema 1993, pp. 3-6; Burgers 1998, pp. 20-24; Burgers *et al.* 2010, pp. 119-120.
[8] www.unisalento.it.
[9] Costantini and Stancanelli 1994.
[10] Fiorentino 1998, 2002.
[11] For example, Jashemski and Meyer 2002.
[12] In this discussion, the sites are listed in chronological order.

Broglio di Trebisacce[13] and **Torre Mordillo**[14] are among the most prominent protohistorical sites in the Sibaritide. They are both located on the natural sand and conglomerate terraces of the central region (150-180 metres above sea level). Both sites were inhabited from the Middle Bronze Age onwards and abandoned in the 8th century BC. There is abundant evidence of trade contacts between the indigenous populations of the Sibaritide and Mycenaean seafarers, especially in the form of Mycenaean pottery and prestige goods. These articles may have been acquired *in exchange for* metal objects such as axes, swords, and pins. Such objects have been found in numerous archaeological contexts in Greece, for instance at the House of the Oil Merchant at Late Helladic III-Mycenae.[15]

Otranto[16] is the most eastern town in modern Italy, located on the Adriatic coast of Salento. Its geographical position makes the settlement particularly suited for trade and exchange with the opposite shore of the Adriatic. Indeed, ceramic evidence indicates that as early as the late 9th century BC Otranto was involved in exchange networks characterized by the presence of Corinthian fine wares and container vessels.[17] These contacts became particularly frequent towards the end of the 8th century BC, to such an extent that it has been suggested that a small group of Greeks lived at Otranto on a more or less permanent basis.[18] Animal bone samples were retrieved from Iron Age contexts (9th-7th centuries BC), but no archaeobotanical research was carried out at Otranto.

The settlement of **Valesio**,[19] in the province of Brindisi, was inhabited from the Iron Age until well within Roman Imperial times. Its settlement history has been studied in detail by a combination of urban- and field surveys and excavations in the 1980s by VU University Amsterdam.[20] Unfortunately, these projects did not include archaeobotanical research, but Zeiler[21] has carried out a detailed study of the animal remains from Valesio.

Torre di Satriano[22] was one of the principal habitation centres in northern Basilicata in the Iron Age. One of the most notable structures that were excavated in the settlement area is a monumental building with a semicircular end (or apsis) on one side, known as the *residenza ad abside* (absidal residence). It is thought to have functioned as an elite dwelling with a food storage area. The archaeobotanical data from Torre di Satriano were collected in this building, and date to the late 8th and early 6th centuries BC.

l'Incoronata[23] occupies a large terrace-like hill, some 40 to 50 metres above sea level between the Cavone and Basento rivers in Basilicata.[24] G.A. Maruggi used l'Incoronata as a model for the interpretation of the archaeological data from l'Amastuola, pointing out the similarities in both sites' occupational history. During the earliest phase, referred to as *l'Incoronata indigena* (late 9th-early 7th century BC), the settlement had a dispersed character and consisted of several groups of oval huts that occupied various parts of the terrace. In the second phase, conventionally designated as *l'Incoronata greca* (c. 690/680 BC- 620/610 BC), large quantities of Greek pottery started to appear, and most of the huts were replaced by rectangular buildings. These data have traditionally been interpreted in the

---

[13] Site: Peroni 1984; Moffa 2002. Archaeobotanical research: Nisbet 1984; Vallino and Ventura 1984; Nisbet and Ventura 1994; Celant 2002.

[14] Site: Arancio, Trucco and Vagnetti 2001. Archaeobotanical research: Coubray 2001.

[15] Peroni 1994, p. 853.

[16] Site: D'Andria 1991, 1995. Archaeozoological research: Veenman 2002, pp. 5-52.

[17] Yntema 2000, p. 23.

[18] Yntema 2000, p. 23; D'Andria 1996, p. 410.

[19] Site: Boersma and Yntema 1978. Archaeozoological research: Zeiler 1996.

[20] Boersma and Yntema 1978.

[21] Zeiler 1996.

[22] Site: Ross Holloway 1970; Osanna and Sica 2005. Archaeobotanical research: Novellis 2009.

[23] Site: Adamesteanu and Castoldi 1986. The preliminary results of the archaeobotanical research at l'Incoronata were published in Carter 1980, pp. 10-13, but this publication is no longer available. A short summary can be found in Carter 2006, pp. 78-79. Archaeozoological research: Bökönyi 2010.

[24] Adamesteanu and Castoldi 1986.

light of presumed Greek aggression towards the indigenous inhabitants.[25] However, further excavations provided indications of a pattern of peaceful coexistence.[26] The archaeobotanical samples from l'Incoronata that were taken from several late 8th-early 7th-century pits and a domestic structure, only cover a small part of the site's occupational history. The archaeozoological samples roughly date to the same period, between the 8th and 6th centuries BC.[27]

The sites of **Botromagno/Gravina**[28] and **Monte Irsi**[29] are both indigenous hilltop settlements. The first one is situated immediately to the west of the modern town of Gravina in Puglia, the latter 20 kilometres further to the southwest in the province of Matera. Among the most prominent features that the excavations at Monte Irsi have brought to light are an Iron Age settlement and a large Roman farmstead. The (scarce) archaeobotanical macroremains were found in one of the earliest layers of the settlement from the Early Iron Age, probably dating to the middle of the 7th century BC.[30] The site of Botromagno was occupied for most of the first millennium BC and reached its maximum extension in the 4th century BC. Although the site is located inland, at about 100 kilometres distance from the Greek colony at Taras and 70 kilometres from Metapontion, it is interesting that no Greek influence can be detected in the material culture at Botromagno until around 500 BC.[31] Twenty-six soil samples were taken from a range of contexts, including occupation deposits, pot burials, postholes, construction layers, and tomb fills, dating between the 9th and 4th centuries BC.[32] The archaeozoological samples from Botromagno were examined by John Watson; those from Monte Irsi were examined by Graeme Barker. The Monte Irsi samples derive from three different chronological layers, dating to the Early Iron Age, the Early Hellenistic, period and the Late Hellenistic period, respectively. The animal bones from Botromagno date to the period between the 6th and the late 1st centuries BC.[33]

Cavallino[34] in inland southern Apulia reflects two clearly distinct phases. The first dates to the Middle Bronze Age (c. 1600-1400 BC), the second to the Iron Age and the Archaic period (c. 750-480/450 BC). A series of major changes can be observed in the settlement history of Cavallino in the latter period.[35] Between 570 and 550 BC, the Iron Age hut settlement was replaced by groups of rectangular houses with tiled roofs and limestone foundations. Although the newly built houses still appeared to be grouped in dispersed nuclei, they were interconnected by a radial pattern of paved streets. At the end of the 6th or in the early 5th century, the settlement was also surrounded by a monumental fortification wall. The archaeobotanical and archaeozoological samples from this site were taken from these Archaic layers.

The overview includes two sites where the archaeobotanical and archaeozoological samples were collected in Early Hellenistic levels only, namely the fortified Lucanian centres of **Roccagloriosa**[36] (Campania) and **Pomarico Vecchio**[37] (Basilicata). These settlements were near the Tyrrhenian coast

[25] Maruggi 1996, p. 217.
[26] Yntema 2000, p. 13; Carter 2006, pp. 56-57; Denti 2009a, pp. 356-357, 2009b.
[27] Bökönyi 2010, p. 6.
[28] Site: Small 2000. Archaeobotanical research: Colledge 2000.
[29] Site: Small 2000. Archaeobotanical research: Hjelmqvist 1977. Archaeozoological research: Barker 1977.
[30] Hjelmqvist 1977.
[31] Small 2000, 8.
[32] Colledge 2000.
[33] Watson 1992.
[34] Site: Pancrazzi 1979; D'Andria 2005. Archaeobotanical research: Fiorentino and Colaianni 2005. Archaeozoological research: Sorrentino 1979.
[35] D'Andria 1996, 2005.
[36] Site: Gualtieri and Fracchia 1990, 2001; Fracchia and Ortolani 1993. Archaeobotanical and archaeozoological research: Bökönyi et al. 1990, 1993; Costantini 2001. Note: Only 4 macroremains, 1 of *Triticum* sp. and 3 of *Vitis vinifera*, were retrieved from earlier (Archaic) levels at Roccagloriosa. These taxa are also present in the Early Hellenistic contexts. In *Table 5.1*, at the end of this chapter, Roccagloriosa is categorized under the Early Hellenistic sites.
[37] Site: Barra Bagnasco 1997. Archaeobotanical research: Caramiello and Siniscalco 1997.

and inland in the province of Matera, respectively. The territory of Roccagloriosa has been surveyed by a Canadian team of the University of Alberta in the 1980s, indicating that during the settlement's main occupation period (c. 350-250 BC) the area experienced a boom in rural settlement.[38] The archaeobotanical macroremains from Pomarico were retrieved from one single context, a closed amphora datable between the late 4th and early 3rd century BC. The research at this site also included pollen coring.

Finally, this overview includes four sites where the archaeobotanical samples were collected in contexts of a ritual character. **Francavilla Marittima**[39] is the name of the modern Calabrian village near the hill called Timpone della Motta, which has three plateaus on which traces of human activities were found. The animal bone samples were collected from the sanctuary on one of the plateaus, and date from the period between 730 and 650 BC.[40] There are no archaeobotanical samples from this site.

The sanctuary of **Monte Papalucio**[41] is located next to a cave, 150 metres above sea level on a hill near Oria. The structures are built on two artificial terraces, containing a natural cavity that is now filled with debris. Monte Papalucio has two phases, the first one Late Archaic (mid-6th-beginning of the 5th century BC), the second phase Early Hellenistic (second half of the 4th-first half 3rd century BC). The countless finds of small clay figurines, antefixes, and drinking and pouring vessels indicate that the sanctuary may have been dedicated to Demeter or Persephone.[42] The great variety of Greek pottery has been interpreted as evidence of native trade and contact with Greeks,[43] although it has been also be suggested that the imported pottery may represent votives offered by the local people rather than foreign visitors.[44] Apart from the ceramic offerings, the votive deposits at Monte Papalucio also contained food remains, including carbonized cakes and biscuits in a variety of sizes and shapes.[45]

Located in the territory of Metapontion, the sanctuary of **Pizzica Pantanello** represents a clear case of a rural place of worship belonging to the Greek colonial world.[46] A large quantity of animal bones was found in the Pantanello complex, which includes the sanctuary, the *necropoleis* located to the west, and a so-called 'Greek pit'. All these contexts were in use between the 6th and 3rd centuries BC.[47] The archaeobotanical assemblage from the Pantanello sanctuary is even richer than the one from Monte Papalucio[48] and also includes a pollen core.[49] The deposit can be divided into three levels: level I (4th century BC), level II (early 3rd century BC) and level III (late 3rd century BC). It is possible that the macroremains partly represent what is left of ritual meals or offerings to Persephone and Dionysus, the gods worshipped here. The archaeozoological samples from Pantanello have recently been published in a detailed monograph on the animal finds from the *chora* of Metapontion.[50]

Excavations at the site of **Vaste**[51] (province of Lecce, southeast Salento) have been carried out since the early 1980s, unearthing an indigenous settlement with habitation traces from prehistoric

---

[38] Costantini 2001; Gualtieri and Fracchia 1990, pp. 323-328.

[39] Site: Maaskant-Kleibrink 1993. Archaeozoological research: Veenman 2002, pp. 52-53.

[40] Veenman 2002, pp. 52-53.

[41] Site: D'Andria 1990a. Archaeobotanical research: Ciaraldi 1997, 1999; Fiorentino 2008.

[42] D'Andria 1990a, p. 240.

[43] Whitehouse and Wilkins 1989, p. 110.

[44] Burgers 1998, pp. 216-217.

[45] Ciaraldi 1999, pp. 86-87.

[46] Site and archaeobotanical research: Costantini 1983c; Carter *et al.* 1985; Costantini and Biasini Costantini 2001; Carter 2006, pp. 23-29 and pp. 163-173. Archaeozoological research: Bökönyi 2010.

[47] Bökönyi 2010, p. 7 (*Tables 1.7-1.9*).

[48] Indeed, in the words of Joseph Carter (2006, p. 17), 'the largest and best-preserved collection of ancient organic remains known from the Archaic, Classical, and Early Hellenistic periods of Greek history.'

[49] The pollen data from Pantanello have never been completely published. They appeared in an unpublished report from the University of Texas in Austin (Sullivan 1983) and are discussed in various publications that concern the *chora* of Metaponto, including Carter *et al.* 1985, pp. 290-296, *Figures 16.5, 16.6* and *16.7*, and Carter 2006, pp. 26-27.

[50] Bartosiewicz 2010.

times until the Roman period. The structures that were found at Piazza Dante probably represent the remains of a cultic building that was in use in the Early Hellenistic period. Inside the building, three pits were found that may have been used for ritual depositions in the Early Hellenistic period (4th-3rd century BC). Soil samples were taken from the bottom of one of these pits, in which a large, pierced stone was discovered that could have been used as an *omphalos* for libations. The bone samples from Vaste date from two different phases, the Early Hellenistic Period (middle of the 3rd century BC) and the Late Hellenistic Period (2nd-1st centuries BC). They were retrieved from domestic contexts, including a cistern and a refuse pit.[52]

5.3 RESEARCH ASPECTS

5.3.1 THE USE OF WOOD

As discussed in chapters 2 and 3, a considerable quantity of publications has been dedicated to the problem of charcoal production and the use of wood as fuel, especially in connection with metal production.[53] Feugère and Serneels have presented an overview of Roman sites in the north-western Mediterranean that can be associated with metal working.[54] Charcoal analyses are not included in their study, but in the introduction Serneels specifically states that charcoal is the typical fuel used in ancient metal working.[55] It should be added that it is not always possible to distinguish between charcoal that was produced deliberately in charcoal burners, and carbonized wood from open fires. According to Castelletti,[56] the former is characterized by an extremely hard texture and shiny, clean fractures. As we have seen in chapter 3, however, recent studies show that vitrified charcoals do not result from high temperature charring.[57]

The use of wood as fuel is also occasionally mentioned in ancient texts. The Herakleia tablets report that one fifth of the land in the *chora* of Dionysus was occupied by *macchia* and oak forests, and that it was forbidden to fell these trees.[58] This rule may have been imposed because of the sacred character of the area, but it has also been interpreted as an attempt to slow down the rapid process of deforestation that was going on in the densely wooded regions of Magna Graecia in this period, such as the Sila (a mountainous plateau and modern national park in Calabria).[59]

Obviously, wood was also used for other purposes, such as the production of agricultural tools and furniture. The farmer/poet Hesiod describes how midsummer is the best period to cut and collect wood, which can be used to manufacture a mortar and pestle and parts of a wagon and a plough.[60] He specifically mentions that the latter needs to be made of holm oak wood. Yoke poles, on the other hand, needed to be made from laurel or elm, since these are 'most worm-free'.[61] The lyric poet Leonidas of Taras (330/320-260 BC) describes the work of the carpenter, which was apparently highly valued, in two of his dedicatory epigrams (Appendix 6, A 6.12 and 6.13).

---

[51] Site: D'Andria 1990b; Mastronuzzi 2005a. Archaeobotanical research: Solinas 2008. Archaeozoological research: Albarella 1995.
[52] Albarella 1995, pp. 289-290.
[53] See sections 2.5.1 and 3.5.1 for bibliographical references.
[54] Feugère and Serneels 1998.
[55] Serneels 1998, p. 18.
[56] Castelletti 1990.
[57] McParland *et al.* 2010.
[58] Uguzzoni and Ghinatti 1968, pp. 91-92.
[59] Forti and Stazio 1983, p. 676.
[60] *W&D* 420-436, translation by Tandy and Neale 1996, pp. 93-97.
[61] *W&D* 435, translation by Tandy and Neale 1996, p. 97.

Charcoal assemblages from sites in southeast Italy

There is still only a limited amount of charcoal assemblages from archaeological sites in southeast Italy, but a few new publications have become available in recent years.[62] Among the sites that are discussed in this chapter, Torre di Satriano, the sanctuary of Monte Papalucio, and the Archaic settlement of Cavallino are the only ones providing charcoal data from contexts postdating the Bronze Age (see *Table 5.5*, which comprises all the charcoal data).[63] At Satriano, the charcoal samples were collected in various contexts including fill layers, floor levels and a hearth inside of the monumental absidal residence. The samples consisted of deciduous oak (*Quercus* cf. *cerris*, 32%), silver fir (*Abies alba*, 26%), beech (*Fagus sylvatica*, 16%), poplar/willow (*Populus/Salix*, 15%), and some fruit trees (*Prunus* sp., *Cornus* sp., Rosaceae and Pomoideae).

At Cavallino, part of a habitation quarter from the Archaic period ('Zona G-Fondo Casino') was systematically sampled using a grid system.[64] The damaged state of some of the charcoal led the researchers to suggest that a considerable part of the charcoal must have derived from high-temperature fires, possibly metal smelting furnaces. The charcoal consisted mostly of evergreen oak and olive wood, with some mastic, *Erica*, *Cistus*, and myrtle.[65]

The charcoal assemblage from Monte Papalucio included over 300 fragments. This charcoal was collected from 13 soil samples, three of which came from levels dated to the Archaic period, four from the Early Hellenistic period and six were of uncertain date, providing a total of 21 wood species (see *Table 5.5*). The taxonomic variability per unit was not very high, particularly in the Archaic contexts, suggesting that they represent the remains of mono-phased fires.[66] The samples from the Early Hellenistic period showed more variation, perhaps because fires were reused or because the samples include removed and re-deposited remains. Olive pruning wood may have been selected as fuel. The charcoal assemblage also contains various fragments of wood from fruit trees, including *Pyrus/Malus* and even a vine branch. The finds of beech (*Fagus*) wood are noteworthy, since it has not been found at any of the other sites, suggesting that it may have been imported.

Furthermore, a few charcoal samples dating to the period between the 4th and the 2nd century BC have been collected at the settlement of Li Castelli (I Castiedd'), in the territory of San Pancrazio Salentino (located only a few kilometres from Muro Tenente, see Appendix 4).[67] The great majority (58%) of the identified charcoal fragments belongs to olive wood. Other species that were found in the soil samples include mastic (14%), *Rhamnus/Phillyrea* (10%), *Erica* sp. (9%), and the Rosaceae/Maloideae family (4%). Furthermore, small amounts of myrtle, oak (evergreen and deciduous), juniper, and species from the families of Leguminosae and Prunoideae (including what appears to be wild almond, *Prunus* cf. *dulcis*) were found.

Finally, an additional parallel for the charcoal assemblages from south-eastern Italy can be found in the pyrotechnic structures from the Late Roman period (3rd/4th century AD) at two archaeological sites in Lecce (Salento).[68] The charcoal from these sites, P.tta Epulione, and P.tta Castromediano, was collected from hearths and metal smelting ovens. It included eight wood species, including olive (46%), evergreen

---

[62] See for example D'Oronzo *et al.* 2013.

[63] The investigations at Broglio di Trebisacce did include charcoal sampling, but these data are left out of the present discussion because they were collected from Bronze Age levels. The samples from the Iron Age levels at Torre Mordillo contained such a limited amount of charcoal that these data are left out as well. Finally, the wood remains from Pantanello are also excluded because they were not carbonized and cannot be associated with hearth or oven contexts.

[64] Fiorentino and Colaianni 2005.

[65] Fiorentino and Colaianni 2005, p. 98.

[66] Fiorentino 2008, p. 100.

[67] The archaeobotanical assemblage from Li Castelli, which was analysed in 2008 by the author, is rather small and consisted of 969 charcoal fragments and only 27 seeds. The results, which have not been published before, are included in Appendix 4.

oak (22%), mastic tree (17%), tree heath (*Erica* cf. *arborea*, 6%), myrtle (5%), *Prunus* (2%), *Rhamnus/Phillyrea* (1%), and pine (*Pinus* cf. *pinea/halepensis*, 1%). In addition, numerous grape pips were found.

Discussion

Based on these charcoal data, only tentative conclusions can be drawn. There are some general trends worth noting, such as the preference for olive and oak wood as fuel. In chapters 2 and 3, I noted that olive and oak were found more frequently than most other wood types at l'Amastuola and Muro Tenente. These two wood types are known for their extremely robust and dense structure, which provides them with a particularly high heating value (i.e. the amount of heat released during combustion). Olive wood that is used as fuel often consists of prunings, which are usually collected in early spring.[69] The charcoal finds from the smelting ovens in Lecce show that this preference had not changed by the Late Roman period. Oak and olive wood were apparently the preferred fuel for fires that had to generate intense heat, for instance in order to reach temperatures for smelting metal.[70] *Erica*, the most strongly represented wood type at Muro Tenente, was also found at all the other sites discussed here. This type of wood is extremely flammable and therefore particularly suitable to light and revive fires (which makes it rather remarkable that so much of it is left in the form of charcoal, and not turned to ashes). At the Late Roman sites in Lecce, *Erica* wood was possibly used for the same purpose.[71] The numerous grape pips that were found in the pyrotechnic structures at these same sites were also used to light fires, because such pips are particularly oil-rich and burn easily. This provides an interesting parallel with the grape deposition from Muro Tenente. It is possible that these pressings were also used as fuel.

Overall, the charcoal analyses from the sites discussed here show a similar pattern, i.e. even though olive and oak appear to be the preferred fuel types, most of the charcoal assemblages show considerable taxonomic diversity. In most cases, there seems to have been no deliberate selection of wood species to use as fuel. It appears that fire wood was usually collected in the nearby woodland or *macchia*. Only the charcoal samples from Satriano seem to be indicative of nearby forests (represented by oak, fir, and beech wood). In the other cases, the charcoal assemblage rather points toward *macchia*-type vegetation, consisting of beech, strawberry tree, rockrose (*Cistus*), ephedra, juniper, myrtle, pine, *Rhamnus/Phillyrea*, mastic, rosemary, and sage. Occasionally, the pruning wood from fruit trees was also added.

5.3.2 FOOD PREPARATION AND DIET

Introduction

As we have seen in the previous chapters, the crop spectrum in l'Amastuola and Muro Tenente changed relatively little over the 500-year habitation period that is covered by these two sites (late 8th to late 3rd century BC). However, a few changes can be observed. First, hulled cereals dominate the crop spectrum at l'Amastuola, whereas naked cereals were found much more frequently at Muro Tenente. Furthermore, pulses are fairly rare in the archaeobotanical assemblage from Muro Tenente, while bitter vetches in particular were apparently a common foodstuff at l'Amastuola. With regard to the latter site, it was also concluded at the end of chapter 4 that the arrival of Greek colonists had no notable effect on the crop spectrum. The question remains, however, whether the results from the case studies are similar to archaeobotanical data from other sites in southeast Italy. In order to answer this question, I will

---

[68] Primavera *et al.* 2011.

[69] The main period of growth of olive trees is between April and September. The tree is at rest between November and March. Flowers open in May and June. Cf. Foxhall 2007, pp. 5-7.

[70] Cf. Horne 1982, p. 8.

[71] Primavera *et al.* 2011.

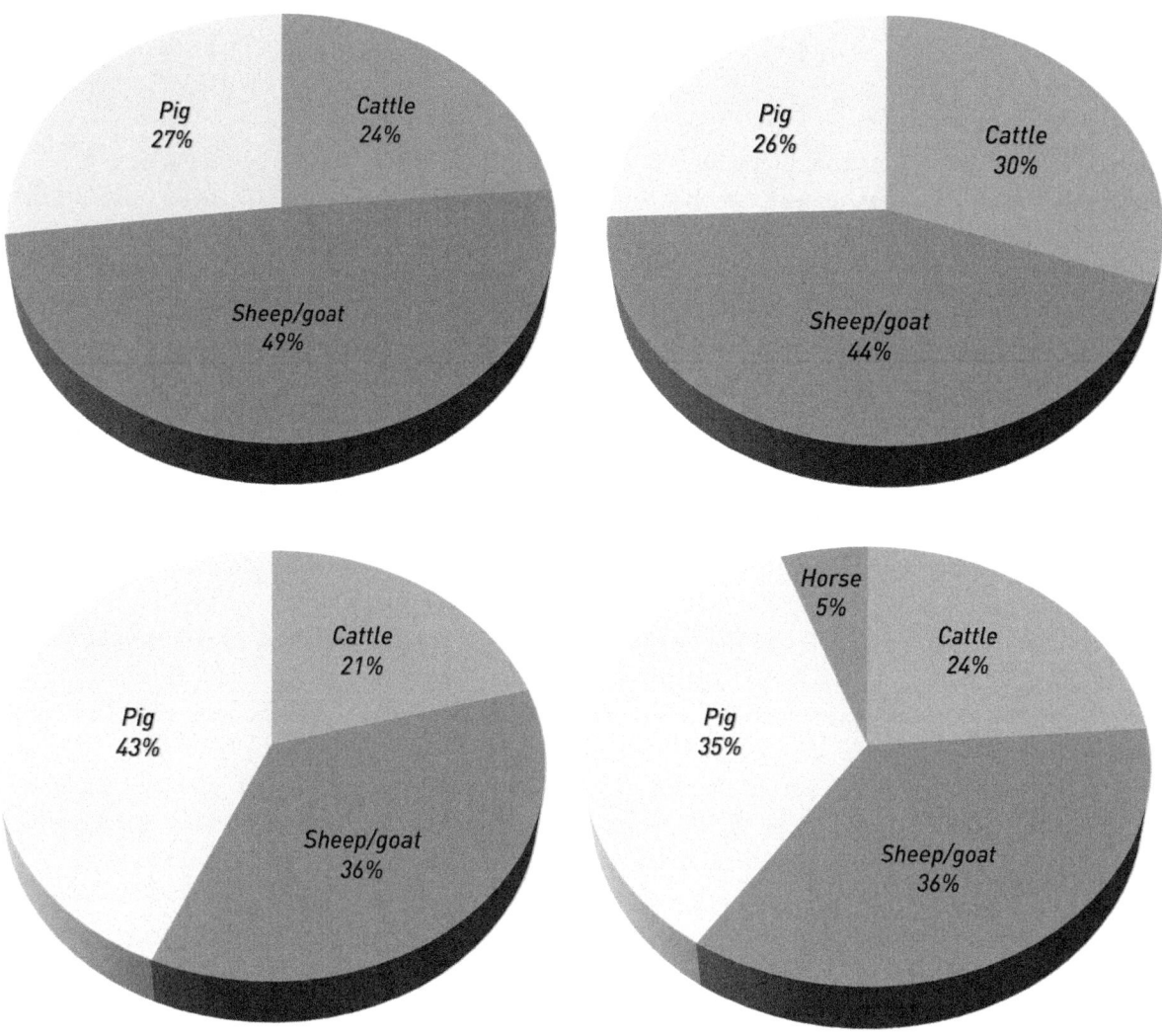

Fig. 5.2. Archaeozoological remains from Early Iron Age (a), Archaic/Classical (b), Early Hellenistic (c) and Late Hellenistic (d) contexts in southeast Italy. Charts by Bert Brouwenstijn.

discuss the archaeobotanical and archaeozoological remains from the sites that have been introduced above. A comprehensive overview of these data can be found in *Tables 5.1* and *5.3*. Many differences between these sites can be discerned, both in the number of macroremains and the variety of species. These differences may be caused by the difference in environment, the sampling strategy, and how the samples are cleaned. For example, among the 14 sites that are introduced above, Pantanello is the only one with waterlogged conditions. In all the other sites, the preservation of macroremains depended on their carbonization. Moreover, Pantanello is one of the few sites where systematic archaeobotanical sampling took place. Furthermore, the samples were cleaned using a flotation tank with sieves with 4, 2, 1, and 0.5 millimetre meshes, which means that only the smallest (< 0.5 mm) archaeobotanical macroremains were lost during sieving. As a result, the archaeobotanical assemblage from this site may contain many species that were absent at other sites. It is important to keep these biasing factors in mind throughout this chapter, in which five categories of archaeobotanical and archaeozoological remains will be discussed. The overview starts with animal foods and will subsequently cover fodder plants, cereals and bread, pulses, vegetables and fruits (except for olives and grapes, which will be discussed separately in the next paragraph), and nuts.

Animal foods: Meat, fish and dairy

Most information about the livestock composition is provided by archaeozoological data. In recent years, two regional comparative studies of animal bones from sites in southeast Italy have been carried out. One is Froukje Veenman's[72] review of the zoological data from 10 archaeological sites in southern and central Italy.[73] The other is Sándor Bökönyi's[74] analysis of six sites in the *chora* of Metapontion. The outcomes of these two studies have been combined with archaeozoological research data from other sites in southeast Italy in *Table 5.3* and *Figure 5.2*. Throughout the first millennium BC, sheep/goats, cattle, and pigs remained the most important domesticated animals. Goat's or sheep's milk was probably a common source of protein; this is also suggested by the Herakleia tablets. These tablets mention (sheep/goat) dairy farms that were supposedly located in the hills along the major traffic routes in the *chora*. According to Uguzzoni and Ghinatti,[75] these farms probably belonged to indigenous people that lived in the inland areas, who may have sold part of their produce (milk, cheese, wool) on the Herakleia market.

There are many indications that in the settlements near the coast livestock keeping was often supplemented by fishing and the collection of shellfish.[76] As we have seen in chapter 2, the inhabitants of l'Amastuola were probably involved in occasional sea fishing, but did not collect shellfish and avoided the lagoonal zone near the coast. At the same time, several contemporary sources confirm that the Gulf of Taranto was a rich source of large fish, such as tuna, which constituted one of the most important diet components at Taras.[77] Both Aristoteles and Leonidas of Taras praise these rich waters, which supposedly provided so much tuna that it could be exported.[78] According to Aristotle, no less than 93 types of fish could be found in the Gulf of Taranto. Leonidas of Taras describes the life and work of a Tarantine fisherman in one of his poems (A 6.8). Wuilleumier[79] lists a wide variety of sea creatures associated with Taras in ancient written sources and on Tarantine coinage, including tuna, squid, mussels, and oysters.

Fodder

The fourteen sites that are discussed here also provided remains of crops that may have been cultivated as fodder plants, namely oat, medick, and rye. These plants may also have been cereal weeds. Only one species from the genus *Medicago*, alfalfa (*Medicago sativa*), is regarded as a specific fodder plant.[80] Carter lists medick, oat, and darnel (*Lolium temulentum*) among the forage crops from Pantanello.[81] It is unlikely, however, that the latter was used as such, although *Lolium temulentum* does grow in the same production zones as wheat and can be considered a weed.[82] However, the seeds can contain a fungus that is considered extremely poisonous to humans and animals. Carter also mentions that the *Medicago* seeds from Pantanello form the earliest evidence for alfalfa in Italy. However, this claim is debatable, firstly since the seeds from Pantanello were not identified on the species level (the genus *Medicago* con-

[72] Veenman 2002.
[73] Valesio, Otranto, Francavilla Marittima, Monte Irsi, Cavallino, l'Incoronata, Pizzica Pantanello, Vaste, San Biagio and San Giovanni di Ruoti.
[74] Bökönyi 2010.
[75] Uguzzoni and Ghinatti 1968, p. 118.
[76] Forti and Stazio 1983, p. 677.
[77] Forti 1988, p. 312. Dunbabin (1968, p. 90) points out that 'considerable information about the objects of Tarantine commerce may be derived from the terra-cotta moulds for cakes, which are crowned with symbols. Many of them refer to natural products, wool, oil and wine, corn, and various kinds of sea-life, including the famous murex [purple dye for textiles]'.
[78] Forti 1988, p. 312.
[79] Wuilleumier 1987, pp. 218-219.
[80] According to White (1970, p. 217), alfalfa was introduced into Greece at the time of the Persian Wars by the invading Medes (hence the name *medica*, by which it was also known). It is mentioned as a superior fodder crop by several Roman authors who wrote treatises on agriculture.
[81] Carter 2006, p. 24.
[82] Polunin 1969, p. 539.

tains 82 other species besides alfalfa, *M. sativa*), and secondly because seeds of *Medicago* were also found in earlier contexts at l'Amastuola and at contemporary Vaste. Costantini also reports finds of alfalfa from the Roman farm site at San Giovanni di Ruoti in Basilicata, and adds that bitter vetch had also been grown on the same site for the animals.[83]

Cereals and bread consumption

When we examine the overview of archaeobotanical crop remains in *Table 5.1*, several conclusions can be drawn. Most importantly, it appears that the crop spectrum did not notably change during the roughly 1000 years that are covered by the samples. For instance, there was no shift from a barley- towards a wheat-dominated cereal spectrum over time. We know from literary evidence, as well as archaeobotanical data, that (emmer) wheat had completely replaced barley as the principal cereal crop in Roman Italy,[84] but this development is not reflected in the archaeobotanical samples that date to earlier periods. Wheat and barley are found equally frequently throughout the first millennium BC. Nevertheless, barley is strongly represented at some of the sites, such as at l'Amastuola, where the great majority of the cereals consisted of hulled barley.

It is generally assumed that in most of Europe and North Africa glume wheats were replaced by free-threshing ones during the 1st millennium BC,[85] but at the sites in southeast Italy, there is no sign of such a development. Einkorn appeared in the earliest layers at Torre Mordillo and not in the most recent ones, but it was also found in Early Hellenistic Vaste and Roccagloriosa, at Classical/Early Hellenistic Botromagno and possibly also at Monte Papalucio.[86] As for the free-threshing wheat species, this category was not found in some of the older sites (Broglio di Trebisacce and l'Incoronata). In contrast, bread wheat did appear in Recent Bronze Age Torre Mordillo.[87] In short, based on the cereal remains from these southeast Italian sites, it appears that einkorn became rare in archaeological contexts after the Bronze Age, but it certainly did not disappear altogether. At the same time, free-threshing wheats apparently became more common from the Early Iron Age onwards, but they were already in use in much earlier periods.

In order to put this cereal spectrum in a wider regional context, I will first compare it to what is known about cereal cultivation in contemporary Greece. Subsequently, I will compare the archaeobotanical data from southeast Italy to other parts of Italy.

Athens, Volos and Kalapodi are the only three sites in Greece that are represented in Kroll's overview of archaeobotanical finds from Early Iron Age contexts (10th-9th centuries BC).[88] They include hulled barley (*Hordeum vulgare, Hordeum distichum*), free-threshing wheat, einkorn (*Triticum monococcum*), emmer, spelt, millet (*Panicum*), and oat. The most interesting aspects of this list are the presence of spelt wheat and *Panicum*, which are both rare in contemporary Italy (see below). For the Archaic and Classical periods (8th-5th centuries BC), Kalapodi is the only site in Kroll's overview. The archaeobotanical samples from this site contain hulled barley, free-threshing wheat, emmer, and einkorn. No spelt or millet were found. These cereals did appear in later times, namely in Early Hellenistic levels at Demetrias (Thessaly). The samples from Kalapodi also included hulled barley, free-threshing wheat and emmer. Kroll's overview was published as early as 1991, but the more recent summary of archaeobotanical assemblages in Greece by Megaloudi (2006) offers hardly any new information. Additional

[83] Costantini 1983b.
[84] Cf. White 1970, p. 39. As Braun (1995, p. 33) has demonstrated, 'it does not seem that barley was valued as human food by the Romans at any time of which we have record.'
[85] It is generally assumed that in most of Europe and North Africa glume wheats were replaced by free-threshing ones during the 1st millennium BC. Van Der Veen 2007, p. 985.
[86] Ciaraldi 1999; Fiorentino 2008; Coubray 2001.
[87] See also chapter 2, note 57 for possible alternative reasons why free-threshing cereals are found less frequently in archaeological contexts than hulled ones.
[88] Kroll 1991, pp. 176-177.

data from Nichoria (Early Iron Age), Delphi (Early Iron Age-Archaic period), Krania (Early Iron Age), the Archaic sites of Ipsili, Phylla Vrachos (Euboia) and the Heraion on Samos, and two sites from the Classical period, Limenas Thasos, and Corinth, do not include other cereal species than the ones that had already been found earlier.[89] On the basis of these data, we can draw the preliminary conclusion that the cereal spectrum in Greece was roughly the same as in contemporary southeast Italy.

How does the cereal crop spectrum from southeast Italy compare to archaeobotanical data from other parts of Italy? Hopf[90] reports that although einkorn was the first cultivated cereal in Italy (together with emmer), it remained in use until the Medieval period, despite the introduction of naked wheat species. Naked barley was thought to have disappeared from Italy after the Middle Neolithic period,[91] but it was found in Recent Bronze Age levels at Broglio di Trebisacce and at Muro Tenente. At the latter site, naked barley was found more frequently than hulled barley in eight different units (hulled barley in five). At the other sites, barley is usually found in the form of hulled *Hordeum vulgare*.[92] On the whole, hulled barley, free-threshing wheat, and emmer wheat seem to have been the dominant cereal species.[93]

It should be noted that some of the seeds from Pantanello, Monte Papalucio, Roccagloriosa, and Torre Mordillo were in such a good state of conservation that they could be identified on the species level as club wheat (*Triticum compactum*), macaroni wheat (*Triticum durum*), and bread wheat (*Triticum aestivum*), instead of the more generic free-threshing wheat. Spelt (*Triticum spelta*) was rare: it was only found in the earliest phase of Botromagno, at Roccagloriosa and possibly at Monte Papalucio.[94] Oat and rye are counted as forage crops in *Table 5.1*, although it is possible that they were cultivated for human consumption. However, at Muro Tenente, l'Amastuola, Vaste, and Roccagloriosa, *Avena* and *Secale* appear in such small amounts that they are unlikely to have been cultivated at all, but rather grew here as weeds in cereal fields.[95] The same holds true for the scarce finds of *Avena* in level III at Pantanello, although Carter lists them among the forage crops (see below).[96]

We know from the Herakleia tablets of the existence of large-scale cereal cultivation in the *chora* of Herakleia, but it is not known whether such cereal fields were common, or unique to the territories of the Greek colonial towns. Little is known about the scale of cereal cultivation in southeast Italy in this period, but we may take a look at weed seeds from the archaeobotanical assemblages to find information about the way cereals were grown and harvested.[97] The presence of white goosefoot at Cavallino and Roccagloriosa and knotweed (*Polygonum*) at Broglio di Trebisacce, Pantanello, Roccagloriosa, and Pomarico Vecchio (see *Table 5.4*) suggests that the cereals were summer grains. These plant types produce ripe seeds in the period between mid-summer through fall, so the association with cereal samples from these sites could mean that the cereals were harvested in late summer (and, therefore, planted in the

---

[89] Megaloudi 2006, pp. 50-52.

[90] Hopf 1991, p. 246, p. 248. It should be added that even today, emmer wheat (*farro*) is consumed regularly in Italy; it is used to make bread (*pane di farro*), and as an ingredient in soups and salads.

[91] Hopf 1991, p. 247.

[92] In the archaeobotanical publication of Botromagno (Colledge 2000), hulled barley remains are referred to as Hordeum sativum.

[93] As Colledge (2000, p. 60) notes in her publication of the archaeobotanical analyses of Botromagno, cereal samples of similar composition are recorded at Bronze Age lakeside settlements in northern Italy. For instance, at Fiavé-Carera on Lake Garda, the diversified cereal culture is interpreted as advantageous for coping with interannual variations in the environment (Jones and Rowley-Conwy 1984, p. 339). This interpretation seems less likely for the south-eastern part of the country, however, since winters are much less severe there.

[94] Finds of *Triticum spelta* are not listed in all the publications of Monte Papalucio. They are mentioned in Ciaraldi 1997, but not in Ciaraldi 1999.

[95] A single seed of cf. *Avena* is listed among the cereal finds from Roccagloriosa (Bökönyi et al. 1993, p. 306), one of *Secale* and four of *Avena* at Vaste (Solinas 2008, p. 240).

[96] Carter 2006, p. 25.

[97] Cf. Hillman 1981, pp. 148-153.

spring). As for the harvesting method, we have seen in chapter 2 that low harvesting may have taken place at l'Amastuola. Fiorentino has shown that the same harvesting method, cutting the cereal stems off near the root, can be witnessed at the Apulian Bronze Age sites of Coppa Nevigata, Madonna del Petto, Monopoli, and Torre Santa Sabina.[98] Combining the average heights of the cereal weeds (especially *Adonis annua* (<35 cm), *Buglossoides arvensis* (<50 cm), *Lathyrus sativus/cicera* (<60 cm) and *Lolium temulentum* (<70 cm), see *Table 5.4*) that were found at Broglio di Trebisacce, Botromagno, Pomarico, and Pantanello, it can be suggested that the same method was used at these sites. Interestingly, Hesiod also describes a method of low harvesting of what appears to be summer grain[99] in *Works and Days* (A 6.2).

In sum, we know very little of the methods of cultivation and harvesting. There is some archaeobotanical evidence of spring sowing (i.e. summer grain) and harvesting near the root, possibly to produce straw. Throughout the first millennium BC, cereal cultivation in southeast Italy concentrated mainly on hulled barley, emmer, and bread wheat. Naked barley, einkorn, club wheat, and macaroni wheat were not uncommon, either. However, it appears that spelt wheat and millet were relatively rare. Interestingly, these two cereal types did occur in samples from contemporary Greece. It has to be added, however, that it can be very difficult to distinguish the grains of emmer and spelt wheat if there are no chaff remains present.[100] Therefore, it is possible that spelt wheat was not as rare as the archaeobotanical records from southeastern Italy suggests. However, the near absence of both types of millet – broomcorn millet (*Panicum miliaceum*, possibly found at Roccagloriosa) and the aptly named Italian millet (*Setaria italica*) – is striking. Both cereals were found in contemporaneous sites in central and northern Italy,[101] as well as in Greece (at Early Iron Age Volos and Kalapodi, and in levels dating to the 5th century BC at Corinth). Moreover, millet is ideally suited for the climate in southern Italy.[102] And yet, the earliest finds of both broomcorn and Italian millet were found in Herculaneum and date to Roman Imperial times. By this period, Pliny reports that millet flourished in Campania, where it was used for white porridge and sweet bread.[103] It remains unclear when this apparently successful millet cultivation was introduced in southern Italy.

Now that we have seen what cereal types were cultivated in southeast Italy, it is time to take a look at how these grains were consumed. How were cereals cleaned and prepared? The most obvious answer to this question is that they were sieved and milled, producing flour that could be used to bake bread. Do we know anything about bread consumption in pre-Roman southeast Italy? I have already discussed the series of ovens at l'Amastuola that were interpreted as bread ovens on the basis of their size and location (see section 2.5.2). Indeed, most bread baking in pre-Roman Italy seems to have taken place under a cover placed on the hearth, in domed clay ovens or 'cooking bells',[104] and under coarse pottery covers known in Early Republican Italy as *clibani*.[105]

[98] Fiorentino 1998, p. 217.
[99] According to Tandy and Neale (1996, p. 105) the fragment 'If you plow the glorious ground at the turnings of the sun [...]' (*W&D* 479) refers to the summer solstice. Cf. *W&D* 597, 'Urge your slaves to thresh out Demeter's holy grain, whenever strong Orion first appears [i.e. around June 20].'
[100] Jacomet 2006.
[101] Hopf (1991, pp. 247-248) reports finds of broomcorn millet from Monte Cóvolo (Late Neolithic, 5th and 4th millennium BC) and Valeggio (Polada culture, 14th-13th century BC), both in Lombardy, and Monte Leoni in Emilia-Romagna (Final Bronze Age). At the latter site, Italian millet has also been identified. Additional finds of *Setaria italica* are reported at Terramare di Parma in Emilia-Romagna (Bronze Age). During the Iron Age, it was well represented in northern and central Italy.
[102] Millet has a short growing season of 60-65 days (*Panicum*) or about 70 days (*Setaria*), but requires plenty of warmth and no (night) frost in this period. Renfrew 1973, p. 102.
[103] Plin. *Nat.* 18.24.
[104] Cubberley *et al.* 1998, 99; Scheffer 1981.
[105] Examples of this type of baking cover have been found at the Matrice villa near Campobasso in Molise, Monte Irsi and San Giovanni di Ruoti. Cubberley *et al.* 1998, 107.

Unfortunately, no direct archaeobotanical evidence for the processing of cereals was found in the vicinity of these ovens. No clear indications of bread baking were found at Muro Tenente, either. Fortunately, we know something about bread and biscuits in this period from the food offerings at Monte Papalucio.[106] The bread fragments that were found here included a compact and airy type, possibly indicating the use of yeast, with impressions of seeds (poppy, and possibly sesame seeds) on the surface.

References concerning the consumption of bread can also be found in ancient texts, such as some of the poems by Leonidas of Taras (A 6.9 and 6.10). In one of them (A 6.10), Leonidas refers to 'flour-less' 'rich barley-cakes'. The addition of 'flour-less' is particularly telling here, since it seems to suggest that instead of flour, these cakes were made of whole barley grains, possibly glued together with honey, comparable to modern sesame or almond bars.[107] Wheat is generally considered as the cereal of choice to make bread; barley is less suitable because it contains less gluten and results in a relatively flat, unrisen loaf. In addition, Leonidas (or his poetic persona) identifies himself as a 'pauper', indicating that the offered foods were of little value and that 'flour-less' cakes are apparently an indication of poverty. Indeed, the translation of ψαιστα τε πιηεντα as '**rich** barley cakes' in this poem should probably be read as 'fat' (πιων).[108] Being a 'wanderer', the I-figure may not have had access to flour, as its production requires a sedentary lifestyle. Indeed, Leonidas of Taras generally refers to himself as a poor man who can barely scrape together *a living*.[109] In one poem, he addresses the mice that attempt to share his food, reminding them that he only has so little of it to begin with (A 6.11). There is also a reference to barley-cakes as poor man's food in this poem.

There are other literary references to bread consumption from ancient Greece that may be used to put the poems by Leonidas in a broader context. Crielaard[110] has pointed out the contrast between a description of a luxurious breakfast by Anacreon (554-469 BC) and of the countryman's diet by his contemporary Hipponax of Ephesus. The former boasts how he had breakfast 'in luxury' with 'a bit of sweet sesame cake' (A 6.16). Hipponax, on the other hand, complains how instead of 'tarting up pancakes with sesame, or dripping waffles into honeycombs' he is 'munching modestly on a few figs and barley cobs - slave's fodder' (A 6.18). There are other indications that to Hipponax, barley-cakes had a negative connotation.[111] For example, he also lists them among the food items that a 'scapegoat' was given to eat (A 6.19).[112] In contrast, Anacreon's desired sesame-cakes are generally associated with wealth and luxury,

---

[106] Ciaraldi 1999, pp. 86-87; Fiorentino 2008, p. 100.

[107] Braun 1995, p. 27.

[108] Michiel van der Keur kindly suggested this alternative translation to me. I am also grateful to Gerard Boter, who pointed out that Hermann Beckby (ed., 1957-1958, Anthologia graeca, München) translates these words with 'Kuchen, gebacken in Öl' and Pierre Waltz (1960, Anthologie grecque, Paris) as 'des gateaux onctueux'. Gow and Page (1965, Hellenistic epigrams, Cambridge, AP 6.334.5) note that ψαιστά should be interpreted as 'a form of cake, used as offerings'. Since such offering cakes were prepared with olive oil, they may very well have been 'fat' in the sense that they were dripping with oil. Indeed, Liddell and Scott's Thesaurus Linguae Graeca lists 'fat' as the primary meaning of the word πιήεντα/πίων.

[109] Cf. also *Anth*. VII 715 ('Far from the Italian land I lie, far from my country Tarentum, and this is bitterer to me than death. Such is the life of wanderers, ill to live [...]')

[110] Crielaard 2009, p. 358.

[111] According to Braun (1995, p. 31), not all barley-cakes are to be considered poor man's food. In his view, the cakes described by Hipponax 'may have been the worst kind of *maza*, which was black, with chaff mixed in the kneading, 'prepared with a view to cheapness'.'

[112] In the Ionian 'scapegoat' ritual, which was performed to purify the town, someone was first given a meal and then driven out of town. West 1993, p. 206. Cf. also Columella's references to barley, which he seems to consider an inferior cereal in comparison to wheat, and more suitable as animal fodder ('Next to these [wheat] grains in utility is that variety of barley which country people call *hexastichum* [six-rowed barley], some also call it *cantherinum* because it is a better food than wheat for all animals that belong on a farm'), although he admits that it is 'more wholesome for humans than is bad wheat'. *RR* II, 14, translation by Bill Thayer, penelope.uchicago.edu.

for example in a dedication by Stesichorus (c. 640-555 BC), listing gifts for a girl (A 6.17). In short, it is evident that different types of bread existed, ranging from rough barley loaves that were eaten by slaves to sweet white bread that was considered an expensive delicacy. In any case, bread also seems to have been a staple food in Greece, indeed 'the marrow of men' in the words of Homer,[113] which was eaten on a daily basis, for example by the soldier/poet Archilochus (c. 680-645 BC) who refers to his 'daily bread' (A 6.19). Bread must also have been a daily staple for agricultural labourers. If we are to follow Hesiod's (8th/7th century BC) recommendation, one 'brisk fellow of forty years' needed to be fed a loaf 'of four quarters and eight slices for his dinner' (A 6.3).[114] West[115] also includes two work songs by anonymous writers that may have been used by labourers who harvested and milled the grain (A 6.21 and A 6.22).[116]

Brumfield[117] discusses the various forms of cereal consumption that are mentioned by ancient Greek authors, including loaves of bread made with yeast and baked in the oven (αρτος), but also several types of gruels and porridges made from coarsely ground wheat or barley soaked in goat's or sheep's milk (μαζα and τραγος).[118] Baked bread also came in different forms and qualities, the cheapest ones having a rougher consistency and containing the whole of the wheat or barley grain or even ground pulses. It is also mentioned in a children's begging-chant of unknown date from Rhodes (A 6.23). The children would carry a (model?) swallow with them, singing this chant and collecting alms in a 'trick-or-treat' kind of way. It can be assumed that the proposed donations – wine, cheese, and bran-or pulse-bread – were considered humble foodstuffs.[119]

In contrast, the more luxurious bread types were often reserved for the wealthy, or even as food offerings to the gods. It also appears on pottery decorations (*Figure 5.3*). The deposition of sacrificial cakes and biscuits has also been reported at several sanctuaries in Greece and southern Italy other than Monte Papalucio, often in connection with the cult of Demeter. Prominent among the bread offerings in this cult is the so-called *plakous*, a cheesecake-type of delicacy that was described by Athenaeus (2nd/3rd century AD) as honey and goat's milk cheese alternating with thin layers of pastry dough. Athenaeus described it as an irresistible delight (A 6.26 and A 6.27). Such delicacies, however, seem to have been a privilege of the rich and, indeed, the divine. Judging from the written sources, everyday food consisted of cereal porridge and coarse, dense barley and pulse bread. Leavened loaves, made with white flour, were much more labour-intensive and therefore, probably, expensive.[120]

Summarizing this section, we can conclude that the crop spectrum does not reveal any remarkable innovations during the period under study. Hulled barley, emmer, bread wheat, club wheat, and macaroni wheat continue to dominate the archaeobotanical samples from the Early Iron Age until the Late Hellenistic period. There are also hardly any differences in cereal crop cultivation between the Greek colonies and indigenous settlements, but many differences may be archaeologically invisible, such as the scale and intensity of production. As far as cereal cultivation in other parts of Italy is concerned, it is worth mentioning that the finds of naked barley at Broglio di Trebisacce and Muro Tenente are

---

[113] *Od.* XX 108. In contrast, a savage creature, like the Cyclops Polyphemos, is 'not like a man, an eater of bread' (*Od.* IX 190-191).

[114] W&D 442, translation by Evelyn-White, ancienthistory.about.com.

[115] West 849.

[116] Although grain milling was also carried out on a household level: cf. Semonides' satiric account of different types of women (7th century BC), in which he complains about the type that 'baulks at chores or anything that's hard/and wouldn't touch a millstone, lift a sieve' (A 6.26, West 7).

[117] Brumfield 1997, pp. 153-154.

[118] Cf. *W&D* 583 (A 6.7). Brumfield (1997, p. 153, note 33) reports that in Greece until recently the last of the goat's or sheep's milk was boiled with coarsely ground grain, especially barley, and dried in the sun to make a modern version of *trachos*, *trachanas*. This dried, milky product could be heated in liquid to make a porridge and was a simple way to store milk for use during the winter. Apparently, commercially prepared *trachanas* is still available in Greek grocery stores.

[119] West 848.

[120] Flour may have become easier to come by in the Roman period, after the invention of the rotating mill (around the 2nd century BC, cf. Jasny 1950).

Fig. 5.3. Characters in a *phlyax* (theatre) depiction stealing cakes. Decoration on Apulian red-figure pottery, c. 400-325 BC. Photo by Ervina Boeve/Hekman Digital Archive.

rather unusual, considering that this cereal type does not occur elsewhere in Italy after the Middle Neolithic period.

Based on the general image of the status of cereal consumption that emerges from the ancient written sources, we may hypothesize that porridges, gruels, and coarse barley-cakes were considered to be poor man's food which, nevertheless, was more likely to be served than leavened wheat bread. In view of this, the barley porridge that was found at l'Amastuola (see chapter 2) should probably be interpreted as a meal of low value, which ties in with the evidence of the consumption of bitter vetch at this site (see below).

Pulses
Broad beans, bitter vetches, and lentils seem to be the most common pulse species that were consumed in pre-Roman southeast Italy, but some of the samples also contained chickpeas, field peas, and vetchling. The seed assemblages from Monte Papalucio and Pantanello show more variety than most of the other samples. Only two types of legumes, broad beans, and bitter vetches, were found among the archaeobotanical macroremains at Muro Tenente. The same varieties were found at l'Amastuola, with the addition of lentils, whereas the samples from Cavallino, Monte Papalucio, Torre di Satriano, and Pantanello also yielded chickpeas and/or field peas (*Pisum* cf. *sativum*). On the whole, pulses (and especially broad beans) seem to occur more frequently in contexts that can be associated with funerary and commemorative rituals, as is the case at Muro Tenente (see *Table 3.3*).

Although bitter vetches have been found at several sites from this period, they are nowhere as abundant as at l'Amastuola. Indeed, a storage jar full of bitter vetches was found northwest of the 'terrace wall' in trench 3 (see chapter 2). This is significant, since, at least since Roman times, bitter vetches have been primarily utilized as fodder, or used to nourish people in times of extreme poverty or starvation. According to Zohary and Hopf,[121] it is exclusively consumed by the very poor, or in times of famine. We have no reason to believe that the inhabitants of l'Amastuola were starving, but as we have seen in the previous section, their diet included several elements that can be regarded as poor man's food.

Generally speaking, the rarity of pulses is a common characteristic in archaeobotanical samples from Italy.[122] Pulses are not mentioned on the Herakleia tablets. Hopf notes that *Vicia faba* has been by

---

[121] Zohary and Hopf 2000, pp. 116-118.

[122] Indeed, this problem is not just encountered in Italy. In their interpretation of crop remains from several sites of Swifterbant in the Netherlands, Cappers and Raemakers (2008, p. 387) list several reasons why pulses are underrepresented in the archaeobotanical record.

far the most common type throughout the ages, whereas the evidence of *Vicia ervilia* is much more limited. She mentions the Middle Neolithic strata of the Grotta dell'Uzzo in Sicily (c. 4800 BC[123]) as the earliest evidence of bitter vetch, after which it appeared again in the Iron Age at Monte Irsi.[124] However, it was also found in a considerably older context at Recent Bronze Age Torre Mordillo. The Monte Irsi find is contemporary to the earliest discoveries of bitter vetch at l'Amastuola. In more recent contexts, it appears at Pantanello, Vaste, and Muro Tenente. The oldest evidence of lentils was also found in the Grotta dell'Uzzo. According to Hopf, they reappeared during the Iron Age and the Roman period in central and southern Italy. Indeed, the samples from l'Amastuola provided the earliest finds of lentils in post-Bronze Age southeast Italy. They remained fairly rare at the later sites (the only finds are from level III at Pantanello, Vaste, and Roccagloriosa). Chickpeas are also very rare in Italy. Hopf mentions only two finds from pre-Roman contexts, namely Monte Irsi and Acquarossa in Etruria. Monte Papalucio and Pantanello can be added to this brief overview. The same holds true for vetchling (*Lathyrus*, found only at Recent Bronze Age Broglio and at Roccagloriosa), which is difficult to distinguish from other small leguminous seeds and therefore often listed as *Vicia/Lathyrus*.[125]

When we look at archaeobotanical samples from pre-Roman Greece, most sites seem to have more variety in the crop spectrum where pulses are concerned, but the species that are represented are basically the same. In the overviews by Kroll and Megaloudi, which I referred to above, Early Iron Age levels at Athens, Volos, Delphi, Krania, and Kalapodi yielded lentils, vetchling (*Lathyrus sativus*), bitter vetch, chickpeas (*Cicer*), peas (*Pisum sativum*), and broad beans.[126] These species continue to be present in the later phases at Kalapodi, Samos, Delphis and Corinth as well. It is of interest to note that chickpeas and the genus *Pisum* (pea) have not been found at any site in southeast Italy before the Archaic period, whereas they were apparently quite common in Archaic Greece.[127] Nevertheless, it is probably too far a stretch to argue that the chickpea was brought to Italy by Greek colonists, since the earliest finds of both chickpeas and peas are from native sites (Monte Irsi and Cavallino).

The cultivation of broad beans is not mentioned on the Herakleia tablets, but it is clear that for a long time they were a major component in the Mediterranean diet, especially before the introduction of common beans and lima beans (*Phaseolus vulgaris* and *Phaseolus lunatus*, originally from the Americas). We know from several ancient texts that the broad bean was highly regarded as food by the Romans who considered them to be healthy and nourishing.

Fruits and vegetables
Hopf[128] states that fruit remains will generally only be contained in faeces, and they decay very quickly unless preserved under waterlogged conditions. Since fruits are generally eaten fresh and do not require a process of toasting or charring before consumption, there is little chance of survival in the archaeological record. Also, it is difficult to detect the often extremely small-sized seeds of wild fruits and berries. Only hard stones, for instance of plums and Cornelian cherries, or ligneous nutshells such as hazelnut are more resistant to decay, but these are also lacking at the southern sites. Like with the pulses, the reason for their absence may be due to a combination of factors, such as preservation conditions, sampling strategies, and the number of investigated sites.

These reasons may partly explain why fruits are relatively rare in the archaeobotanical sample from southeast Italy. Grapes and olives (which will be discussed in detail in the next section) are the only fruits that were found at l'Amastuola and Muro Tenente, although the samples also contained charcoal

---

[123] Costantini 1981.
[124] Hopf 1991, p. 249.
[125] Hopf 1991, p. 249.
[126] Kroll 1991, pp. 176-177; Megaloudi 2006, p. 50.
[127] Cf. Sappho, 'chickpeas grew there golden on the banks [...]' (West 143, A 6.51).
[128] Hopf 1991, p. 250.

from pomegranate, strawberry tree, and apple/pear trees. The absence of figs is remarkable, since they appear at Torre Mordillo, Monte Papalucio, Roccagloriosa, and Pantanello.[129] Figs are also commonly found in archaeobotanical samples in Greece, for example at Early Iron Age (10th-9th centuries BC) Athens, both Early Iron Age and Archaic Kalapodi, at Early Hellenistic Demetrias, and in enormous quantities (over 100,000 fruits) at the Heraion at Samos.[130] As we have seen above in the writings of Hipponax and Leonidas of Taras, figs were considered a poor man's food. They are easy to grow and collect, high in calories and can be dried and stored to use throughout the year. The samples from Monte Papalucio also contained crab apples and dates.[131] The latter must have been imported; it can be assumed that they had some sort of ritual significance (see below). Pomegranates were found at Monte Papalucio and Vaste, and possibly, in the form of charcoal (cf. *Punica granatum*), at Muro Tenente. Pomegranates are among the earliest domesticated fruit trees in the Levant. There is archaeobotanical evidence of well-established cultivation in Early Bronze Age Israel.[132] When the fruit arrived in Italy is unclear, because finds of pomegranates on Italian sites are rare. In fact, the Monte Papalucio finds are the earliest in Italy.[133] Another possible wild fruit, the crab apple, was also found at Monte Papalucio. Jashemski and Meyer[134] list pomegranates, apples, and pears among the species found at Pompeii, and note that all these fruits were grown intensively in antiquity.[135]

The seed and fruit assemblages from the above mentioned sites in central and northern Italy and in Greece also included numerous wild fruits, such as Cornelian cherries (*Cornus mas*), wild cherries (*Prunus avium*), sloes (*Prunus spinosa*), damson plums (*Prunus insititia*), hawthorn (*Crataegus monogyna*), crab apples (*Malus* cf. *sylvestris*), wild pears (*Pyrus* sp.), wild grapes, and various genera of berries such as wild strawberry (*Fragaria*), blackberry (*Rubus*), blueberry (*Vaccinium*), and elderberry (*Sambucus*). In contrast, wild fruits are very rare in the archaeobotanical assemblages from southern Italy, with the exception of grapes and olives. The question remains, however, whether these fruits were wild or cultivated. I will discuss this matter in detail in the next section. The only other wild fruits that were found at these sites were crab apples from Monte Papalucio.

According to Forti and Stazio,[136] Taras was known for its garden crops, which included turnips, leeks, and lettuce. Unfortunately, archaeobotanical evidence of the cultivation of these types of crops is unlikely to survive. The only garden crops represented at sites in southeast Italy are the garlic cloves from l'Amastuola and remains of beetroot (*Beta vulgaris*) and borage (*Borago officinalis*) from Broglio di Trebisacce. The earliest archaeological finds of garlic were made in Egypt, including several well preserved dry garlic bulbs from the tomb of Tutankhamen (c. 1325 BC).[137] Although we will see below that garlic was already well known to the Egyptians in much earlier times, its large scale cultivation was introduced by the Greeks in the 3rd century BC, especially in the area of the Fayum.[138] Among the more recent finds of garlic in Italy are the carbonized remains of 50 well-preserved cloves from Herculaneum.[139] Garlic is occasionally found in Central European cemeteries from the Roman period

---

[129] At first glance, it appears that the mesh width of the sieves that were used to retrieve the macroremains is a determining factor here. This, however, is evidently not the case, since figs also appeared at Monte Papalucio, where sieves with relatively large meshes (2 mm) were used.

[130] Kroll 1991, pp. 176-177; Megaloudi 2006, pp. 50-52.

[131] Curiously, the dates that were supposedly found at Monte Papalucio appear in the first publication of the archaeobotanical analyses (cf. *Phoenix dactylifera* in Ciaraldi 1997), but are left out of the second one (Ciaraldi 1999). The identification was confirmed, however, by Fiorentino (2008, p. 99).

[132] Zohary and Hopf 2000, p. 171.

[133] Ciaraldi 1999, p. 79. However, pomegranates are frequently found in much earlier contexts in the form of terracotta models (see section 5.3.4).

[134] Jashemski and Meyer 2002, pp. 124-125, 152, 154-155.

[135] Zohary and Hopf 2000, pp. 174 and 177.

[136] Forti and Stazio 1983, p. 673.

[137] Nicholson and Shaw 2000, pp. 630-631.

[138] Crawford 1973.

[139] Jashemski and Meyer 2002, pp. 87-88. Garlic is also mentioned in two graffiti from Pompeii.

(1st-4th centuries AD), where it is usually interpreted as a 'Romanized' dietary custom.[140] Indeed, garlic was highly praised as a food condiment in Rome, but also in Classical Greece.[141]

Nuts

The remains of nuts are not particularly abundant at the sites in southeast Italy. The only specimens found hitherto are acorns, walnuts and beech-nuts (at Torre di Satriano). The former two appear only in Bronze Age contexts.[142] The consumption of acorns was demonstrated in the earliest Bronze Age strata of Torre Mordillo and Broglio di Trebisacce, and walnuts exclusively at the latter site. Acorns and hazelnuts (*Corylus avellana*) are not uncommon at Neolithic and Bronze Age sites in other parts of Italy, such as Neolithic La Marmotta[143] in Lazio, Santa Maria in Belverde[144] in Tuscany, and Gran Carro[145] in Lazio (Lake Bolsena). The acorns from Gran Carro showed signs of grinding, which may indicate that they were processed into flour. According to Hopf, chestnut (*Castanea sativa*) and walnut were not taken into cultivation in Italy before Roman imperial times.[146] Evidently, this is in accordance with the archaeobotanical evidence from pre-Roman southern Italy.

Summary and conclusion

Summarizing this section, it can be concluded that there is a certain amount of uniformity in the archaeobotanical assemblages from these sites. The cereal spectra usually include hulled barley, emmer, and bread wheat, and occasionally also naked barley, einkorn, club wheat, and macaroni wheat. Apparently, spelt wheat and the millets (*Panicum miliaceum* and *Setaria italica*) were relatively rare. Other crop remains that are regularly found in archaeobotanical assemblages in southeast Italy include pulses, mainly broad beans, bitter vetches, and lentils, with the occasional chickpea, field pea and vetchling. Among the fruits, there are usually grapes and olives, but also figs, crab apples (*Malus sylvestris*), pomegranates and even dates (*Phoenix dactylifera*). The only garden crops that have been found in southeast Italy are garlic, beetroot, and borage. Finally, a few acorns and walnuts were retrieved from Bronze Age contexts.

---

[140] Kreuz 2000, p. 47. But as Bakels and Jacomet (2003, p. 547) pointed out, its rarity is probably due to the poor chances of successful preservation of the cloves.

[141] Rome: Jashemski and Meyer 2002, pp. 87-88: *De re coquinaria* 9.13.3 (to make a sort of stuffed bread) and 4.1.3 (as a condiment based on fish sauce (liquamen) that would help to cure a sick stomach).
Greece: *Ra.* 554, 987, *Ec.* 288, *V.* 679, *Th.* 494, *Lys.* 458, 688, *Eq.* 600. Apparently, Megara was regarded as the centre of garlic cultivation in this period: see for example *Peace* 236-250, *A.* 521, 550, 761-3, *Pax* 502: 'Men of Megara, why don't you go to hell? The goddess [of Peace] remembers you with hatred, for you were the first to daub her with garlic'. Aristophanes also suggests that garlic bulbs were an acceptable form of payment, although that may have been a joke. In *Acharnenses* (*A.* 813), an Athenian man buys a piglet from a Megarian for the price of one bunch of garlic. Herodotus also refers to garlic as legal currency (in ancient Egypt), but his testimony is equally questionable: 'On the pyramid it is declared in Egyptian writing how much was spent on radishes and onions and garlic for the workmen, and if I rightly remember that which the interpreter said in reading to me this inscription, a sum of one thousand six hundred talents of silver was spent [...]' *Histories*, II, 125. Translation by H.W. Henderson (2002).

[142] Hopf (1991) makes no mention at all of almonds (*Amygdalus communis*, syn. *Prunus dulcis*), although this is probably one of the earliest domesticated trees in Old World agriculture (Zohary and Hopf 2002, pp. 185-187). The earliest finds of charred almond shells from Greece date back as far as the Mesolithic period (in the Franchthi Cave in the south-eastern Argolid), and they were also found at Early Hellenistic Demetrias (Kroll 1991, pp. 176-177). By contrast, archaeobotanical remains of almonds were evidently never found in pre-Roman Italy.

[143] Rottoli 1993, p. 308.

[144] Carra *et al.* 2003.

[145] Costantini and Costantini Biasini 1995, p. 330.

[146] Hopf 1991, p. 250.

Obviously, the daily diet did not consist solely of plant foods. Archaeozoological studies show that livestock keeping concentrated mainly on sheep/goats, cattle, and pigs. Although sheep/goats were probably mainly kept for their wool and cattle for traction, they undoubtedly served as a source of meat as well. Fodder crops such as oat, medick, and rye were cultivated to feed these domestic animals. There is additional archaeozoological and textual evidence that game, fish, and (goat) dairy provided additional protein.

We know disappointingly little about crop harvesting and cleaning methods in this period, but there is some information about the way these products were eventually consumed. As far as the consumption of cereals is concerned, it can be inferred from a combination of archaeological and textual sources that there was a variety of bread types. These ranged from the more expensive and luxurious leavened loaves of bread that were made of white flour, to coarse, dense barley and pulse bread. In addition, cereals were consumed in the form of biscuits that were made of whole grains, such as the barley-cakes that are mentioned frequently as poor man's food by Leonidas of Taras. Another way to consume whole grains is to soak them in water or milk to make a sort of porridge or gruel, which, for example, was found at l'Amastuola. Apart from the production of wine and olive oil, which will be discussed in detail in the next section, we have little other direct evidence for food preparation in this period.

5.3.3 GRAPE AND OLIVE CULTIVATION

Introduction
One may ask why, after an entire section about food preparation and diet, olive and grape cultivation is discussed in a separate paragraph. The reason is that since prehistoric times, the production of wine and olive oil has occupied a major place in the culture of Mediterranean peoples.[147] According to Colin Renfrew's hypothesis concerning the origin of Mediterranean polyculture (i.e. the combined cultivation of olive, vine, and wheat),[148] the systematic exploitation of olive trees and vines transformed the traditional Neolithic subsistence economy. Until the Early Bronze Age, subsistence was based on cereals, pulses, and livestock. The intensive cultivation of grapes and olives made it possible to colonize marginal land, which, in turn, led to the production of surplus, permitting a new flexibility in subsistence and storage strategies, and opening up the possibility of agricultural specialization.[149] Renfrew also emphasized the role of olive oil and wine as commodities that could be stored and transported, creating opportunities for exchange.

In addition, the prominent social role of olive oil and wine consumption in Mediterranean societies can hardly be underestimated.[150] Wine drinking in particular has often been associated with the emergence of elites, for whom it played an important part in hospitality and feasting.[151] According to Gilman,[152] olive- and viticulture were a key factor in the emergence of Bronze Age elites in yet another

---

[147] For a recent investigation of the connection between olive and grape cultivation and changes in the social organisation of ancient communities in southern Italy, see Lentjes and Saltini Semerari in press.

[148] Renfrew 1972. Since its first publication, Renfrew's subsistence/redistribution model has been widely criticized (see particularly Barrett and Halstead 2004). As Paul Halstead (2004, p. 192) has reminded us, far more and better information is available on the prehistoric economy than was the case in 1972. Current methods of investigation are both more diverse and more powerful, and our understanding of the dynamics and historical context of 'traditional' Mediterranean land use has greatly advanced.

[149] Renfrew 1972, p. 280.

[150] Renfrew 1972; Sherratt 1997.

[151] See for instance Gilman 1981; Milano 1994; and more recently Margaritis, Renfrew and Jones 2009.

[152] Gilman 1981, p. 6.

way. The high demands of these crops tied people to the land and rendered them more vulnerable to controlling power. Compared to the traditional cereal crops in prehistoric Europe, tree crops constitute a capital-intensification of subsistence. Grapevines need at least three years of careful nurturing before they yield any usable fruit. Olive trees need an even longer period of tending before they come into full production, at least fifteen to twenty years. However, they can produce fruit for centuries.[153] Even today, olive oil remains a valuable commodity in Mediterranean societies, which is used for cooking, personal hygiene, and as fuel.[154] Furthermore, since both fruits can be converted into storable commodities (wine, raisins, olive oil, pickled olives), the vine and olive tree provided additional security to subsistence farmers.[155]

The introduction of olive and grape cultivation is fundamental to our discussion of the effect of the Greek colonization process on landscape and land use. It is often assumed that Greek migrants introduced grape and olive cultivation in southern Italy. However, we will see in this section that there is an increasing amount of evidence to suggest that it already existed for many centuries before the arrival of Greek migrants.

Furthermore, the introduction of wine and olive oil production is also connected to the central research theme of this study, i.e. developments in land use in southeast Italy, especially with regard to changes in the scale and organization of agricultural production. I have already touched upon this research topic in the previous chapters, but we are still left with at least two important questions in respect of the introduction of olei- and viticulture:

When?

The cultivation of olives had already started in the Near East in the 5th millennium BC.[156] Observations from several submerged sites off the Carmel Coast in Israel demonstrate that olive oil was produced there as early as 4500 BC.[157] Archaeological finds of olive oil production equipment make it clear that

---

[153] Cf. Foxhall 2007, pp. 75-77.

[154] Foxhall 2007, pp. 85-97. It has to be added that we know very little of the use of other herbaceous oil plants, such as flax (*Linum usitatissimum*), poppy (*Papaver somniferum*), gold-of-pleasure (*Camelina sativa*) and rape (*Brassica camprestris*) in pre-Roman southeast Italy. None of these species were found at the sites discussed in this chapter. Indeed, oil seeds are notoriously underrepresented at archaeological sites because they generally do not carbonize (cf. for example Gleba 2008, p. 66). Instead, the oil in the seeds starts to boil when heated and causes the seed to explode. This is why oil plants are usually only found in archaeobotanical samples from waterlogged contexts, although clearly not in all of them, since they are also missing at Pantanello (Carter *et al.* 1985, p. 286, p. 290). In contrast, gold-of-pleasure, as well as some rape and mustard seeds, were recovered from the lakeside dwellings at Fiavé-Carera in northern Italy (Jones and Rowley-Conwy 1984, p. 329). Hopf (1991) lists finds of poppy, rape and flax seeds, as well as linen cloth, at Late Neolithic Lagozza di Besnate in Lombardy. Rottoli (1993, p. 306) reports the presence of poppy and possibly also flax seeds at Neolithic La Marmotta in Lazio. Flax seeds were also found at a few other sites in central and northern Italy, including Valeggio in Lombardy (Bronze Age), Monte Bibele in Emilia-Romagna and Isola Virginia in Lombardy (both Iron Age). The samples from Early Iron Age Kalapodi in Greece also included a few herbaceous oil plants, namely *Camelina*, *Linum* and *Papaver* (Kroll 1991, pp. 176-177; Megaloudi 2006, p. 50). These finds are remarkable, since most of the seeds were carbonized. More recently, Valamoti (2011) reported finds of charred flax seed concentrations from five prehistoric sites from Macedonia in northern Greece (Makriyalos, Mandalo, Arkadikos, Dikili Tash, Archondiko).

[155] Indeed, it has been argued that the cultivation of olives and grapes was fundamental to the emergence of state-level complex societies and the development of Minoan and Mycenaean palace economies from the Middle Bronze Age onwards. See debate in Barrett and Halstead 2004.

[156] Zohary and Spiegel-Roy 1975; Kislev 1995.

[157] Galili *et al.* 1997, p. 1147.

olive cultivation was already well known in Greece in the Early Bronze Age.[158] The earliest evidence of grape cultivation is of a much later date, although wild grapes were apparently utilized long before the domestication of the grapevine.[159] According to Zohary and Hopf, the earliest convincing signs come from a single Chalcolithic site and several Early Bronze Age sites in the Levant.[160] In the Aegean, grape cultivation appeared somewhat later, but there is good evidence for it in Lerna (2200-2000 BC) and several other Greek Early and Middle Bronze Age sites.[161]

It is still largely unclear when olive and grape cultivation were introduced in southeast Italy, and how long it took before olei- and viticulture were practiced in the Greek colonial territories as well as the indigenous areas. In fact, there are several reasons why collecting the research data required to answer these questions is complicated. Firstly, it has proved to be difficult to distinguish wild olives (*Olea europaea* subsp. *sylvestris*, 'oleaster') and wild grapes from domesticated ones based on the form of the stones or pips alone. The distinction is based on the overall dimensions and other morphological characteristics of the seeds. The wild varieties appear to be somewhat smaller and more globular than the domesticated ones.[162] The problem is that it is unknown at what point in the domestication process this change in morphology took place, and there seem to be some 'transitional phases'.[163] Second, additional evidence in the form of processing equipment is needed to prove that olive or grape cultivation has taken place, but such finds are very rare.[164]

How?

According to the traditional view, grape and olive cultivation spread into the central and western Mediterranean as a result of Greek, Etruscan, and Phoenician colonization during the first half of the first millennium BC.[165] However, there is much disagreement about this issue. Many authors believe that in the 7th and 6th centuries BC, the time of the consolidation and expansion of Greek colonial activities, the Greeks carried their vines and olive trees westwards.[166] According to Sallares, for instance, the Greek colonists were primarily interested in acquiring land for growing crops that were suited to coastal regions – which may also explain why Greek colonization in the Mediterranean was confined to the coast and never penetrated further inland. 'They also took with them the crops with which they were familiar. In other words, they were not merely founding new colonies, but creating new ecosystems modelled as closely as possible on those at home.'[167]

[158] Renfrew 1972, p. 285.
[159] Carbonized pips of grapes, that were evidently collected from the wild, appeared in numerous prehistoric sites in Europe, particularly northern Greece, Yugoslavia, northern Italy, Switzerland, Germany, and France. See Renfrew 1973, p. 127.
[160] Zohary and Hopf 2000, pp. 157-158.
[161] Zohary and Hopf 2000, p. 158.
[162] Smith and Jones 1990 (*Vitis*); Runnels and Hansen 1986.
[163] For example, some of the grape pips from Early Bronze Age Crete are believed to have belonged to such a transitional variety, being neither wild nor domesticated. See Renfrew 1995.
[164] Foxhall 1993. See also Vandermersch 1994, p. 36.
[165] Vallet 1962, p. 1554; Boardman 1976, p. 190; Zohary and Hopf 2000, pp. 150-151; Renfrew 1973, p. 127; Helbaek 1956, pp. 292-293.
[166] Vallet 1962, p. 1554: 'Il est certain che l'olivier, en tant qu'arbre cultivé, fut acclimaté en Italie par les colons grecs.' Boardman 1976, p. 190; Zohary and Hopf 2000, pp. 150-151.
[167] Sallares 1991, p. 92.

In recent years, however, much innovative research has explored the diffusion of olive cultivation based on genetic diversity in modern olive trees.[168] In addition, the combination of olive stone[169]/grape pip[170] shape analysis with statistical analyses has led to promising results. Both research directions confirm that olive domestication started in Italy long before the alleged introduction of oleiculture by Greek or Phoenician colonists. Unfortunately, however exciting these new insights may be, there is still very little archaeological and archaeobotanical evidence to support them. Furthermore, the morphometric (shape analysis) models that have been created to distinguish wild from domesticated fruits have considerable limitations. This is partly due to the fact that these models require elaborate measurements of various parts of the pips and stones, whereas most archaeobotanical studies only include the breadth and length.[171] Moreover, as we saw in chapter 4, these models are generally only suited to the analysis of grapes and olives from the area in which they were developed.[172] Additional biometric research of grape varieties in south-eastern Italy is much needed to overcome this omission.

In the following pages, three sources of evidence will be used to address the when and how questions, i.e. literary, archaeological, and archaeobotanical evidence. In the first part of this section, a survey of contemporary written sources will be carried out. I will not offer a complete overview of all the references to oil and wine in classical literature, as these have already been compiled by several other authors.[173] Instead, I have made a selection of fragments that are particularly informative about the region and period under study. It will become clear that the information about olive and grape cultivation that is supplied by ancient authors is not particularly helpful, since it is not only fragmented, but at times even unreliable. This problem can partly be solved with the aid of archaeological evidence, which I will discuss in the second part. Subsequently, I will address the archaeobotanical evidence and try to demonstrate that the combined information from these three sources can lead to a new understanding of the development of grape and olive cultivation in southeast Italy.

---

[168] Besnard and Bervillé (2000) studied DNA from 121 cultivated olive trees and 300 oleasters (sampled in 27 populations from all around the Mediterranean) to create a geographical distribution map of Mediterranean olive mitotypes (i.e. combinations of DNA sequences), revealing two different centres of origin for the domesticated olive, one in the eastern and one in the western Mediterranean. In the oleasters, two distinct genetic groups were distinguished: an eastern group (mitotype ME1, occurring from Turkey to the Near East) and a western group (mitotypes MOM and MCK, occurring from Libya to the Maghreb and Spain). Mitotype ME1 of the eastern oleaster group was also found in most (73%) of the cultivars, suggesting an origin for domesticated olives in the eastern Mediterranean. Three other mitotypes were distinguished in cultivars: ME2, MOM and MCK. ME2 was found in 11% of the cultivars from east to west, and is likely to have derived from ME1 by genetic replacement. MOM and MCK, on the other hand, were found only in the western Mediterranean. Besnard and Bervillé argue that it is unlikely that these mitotypes derived from ME1 in the same way as ME2 did. This suggests that the MOM and MCK mitotypes represent two other centres of origin for the domesticated olive, in the western Mediterranean.

[169] Terral *et al.* 2004. Analysing olive stones from various Mediterranean regions, this group of researchers proposed a model of diffusion of olive cultivation that is remarkably similar to the results of DNA studies. They used patterns of morphological variation in wild and archaeological olive stones and concluded that olive stones with a 'cultivated shape' occurred in the Chalcolithic in Spain, and in Bronze Age Italy.

[170] Mangafa and Kotsakis 1996.

[171] See, for example, Rottoli 1993, p. 310 and Costantini and Costantini Biasini 1995, pp. 330-331.

[172] This especially holds true for the formulas by Mangafa and Kotsakis. Cf. Perret 1997.

[173] For ancient written texts on Salento, see Lombardo 1992. For wine consumption in the Greek colonies in southern Italy, Vandermersch 1994, pp. 27-34. For olive oil, Brun 2004.

Literary evidence

Pliny (23-79 AD) gives an account of the introduction of the olive tree and vine in Italy in *Natural History* (A 6.30 and A 6.31). According to Pliny, the vine is an indigenous plant in Italy, but the olive tree is not. In Pliny's own words, the olive tree was introduced in more recent times, spreading quickly across France and Spain. He also mentions that Italy started to export olive oil from c. 50 BC onwards. As we will see below, archaeological evidence indicates that none of these statements are correct. Indeed, it is difficult to get a clear picture of the introduction of olives and grapes on the basis of ancient written sources. The earliest references to wine and olive oil production can be found in Greek texts. Hesiod (8th century BC) describes the best ways to prune vines and store wine (A 6.4 and A 6.5), and mentions the use of olive oil for personal hygiene (A 6.6). Surprisingly, he does not refer to the cultivation of olives or to olive oil production.

Greek texts are also informative about wine production in southern Italy. Especially the famous vineyards of Sybaris are frequently mentioned, for instance by the Greek historian Timaeus of Tauromenium (modern Taormina) in Sicily (c. 345 BC-250 BC) (A 6.29). The Sybarites were said to be extremely wealthy, their lifestyle synonymous with pleasure and luxury. Apparently, they also produced some of the finest wines in Magna Graecia. Given that Sybaris is said to have been destroyed around 510 BC, the production of Sybaritan wine was apparently in full bloom in the 6th century BC.

Information about wine production in other colonial Greek contexts is sparse. Pliny notes that the old temple of Hera at Metapontion, in use between the late 7th and early 6th century BC, was partly made out of vine stems.[174] For later periods, there is evidence of grape and olive cultivation from the Herakleia tablets.[175] The tablets make it clear that grapes and olives were the most profitable crops in the area. The rent that had to be paid for a vineyard was much higher than that for a cereal field. Several epigrams by Leonidas of Taras also refer to wine production and consumption (e.g. A 6.14 and A 6.15). Allegedly, the Tarantines were heavy wine drinkers, especially during festivities celebrating Dionysus. Leonidas' poems contain numerous references to excessive wine consumption.

Southeast Italian vineyards and olive groves are frequently mentioned by Roman authors from the 2nd century BC onwards.[176] These vineyards and orchards clearly had more than regional fame by this time. The earliest reference can be found in *De Agricultura* by Marcus Porcius Cato, written around the middle of the 2nd century BC. Interestingly, he mentions table olives, instead of olive oil production, from southern Apulia (A 6.36). Dionysius of Halicarnassus (c. 60 BC-after 7 BC) is particularly enthusiastic about Apulian olives, claiming that the Apulian orchards are superior to all others (A 6.38). Varro (116 BC-27 BC) mentions the vineyards of Brundisium in *Res Rusticae*[177] and also refers to the transport of wine, olive oil and cereals with mule trains through inland Apulia to the harbour of Brundisium (A 6.39). The Salentine roads must have been vital to the transportation of agricultural products to Brindisi, where they could be consumed or packed and shipped across the seas.[178] Horace (65-8 BC) talks of the vineyards of Aulon, which are also believed to have been situated in the *chora* of Taras (A 6.39). The Napolitan poet P. Papinius Statius (*c.* 45-96 AD) also mentions the 'illustrious vineyards of Galesi [Taras]' in the second book of the *Silvae*.[179] Finally, returning to Pliny, he shares the wines from southern Italy among the finest (A 6.32). Interestingly, his list of cities producing good-quality wines includes Thourioi, the town that was founded in the area of former Sybaris, which was destroyed around 510

---

[174] See also Carter 2006, p. 233. HN XIV 9: 'At Metapontum, the temple of Juno has long stood supported by pillars formed of the like material [the vine].' Translation by John Bostock and H.T. Riley, www.perseus.tufts.edu.

[175] Uguzzoni and Ghinatti 1968, pp. 91-92, p. 117.

[176] Cf. Hitchner 1993, p. 500.

[177] Lombardo 1992, pp. 50-52, nos. 81, 82 and 84; Burgers 1998, p. 257. Translation by W. D. Hooper and H. B. Ash (1934), penelope.uchicago.edu.

[178] Yntema 2006, p. 101, note 14.

[179] Vandermersch 1994, p. 34. *Silv.*, II, 2, 111.

BC. Apparently, the production of the renowned Sybaritan wines somehow continued or was resumed after the town had reportedly ceased to exist and lived on as the *apoikia* of Thourioi (since 444 BC).

These references to wine and olive oil in Roman texts illustrate that by the 2nd century BC, viti- and oleiculture in Apulia had acquired more than regional fame. Large-scale wine and olive oil production was obviously not restricted to the Greek colonial areas in this period. On the basis of the frequent references to Apulian olives in the Roman sources, Burgers[180] has argued that the domesticated olive tree was introduced in indigenous southeast Italy in a much earlier phase. Given that it takes 10 to 15 years for olive trees to bear fruit, it undoubtedly would have taken much longer to acquire a reputation.

In short, acknowledging that the information about the development of olive and grape cultivation in Italy shows several lacunae, the first reference to olive cultivation can be found in the Herakleia tablets (350-300 BC). The earliest evidence of grape cultivation (at Sybaris and Metapontion) that is provided by the ancient written sources dates to the late 6th century BC.

Archaeological evidence

Additional indications for grape and olive cultivation can be found in two main categories of archaeological evidence, namely pottery (and decorations on ceramic vessels) and processing equipment. The pottery remains that may be associated with grapes, olives, wine, and olive oil include storage containers, such as *amphorae* and *pithoi*, but also table ware, pouring vessels, cups, lamps, and small flasks for scented oil.

Indeed, in recent years there has been a growing tendency to place the introduction of viticulture and oleiculture in Italy in an earlier period than was previously thought, i.e. the Recent Bronze Age instead of the Early Iron Age. This is especially true for oleiculture, since there is only archaeological evidence of wine *consumption* in the period before the Early Iron Age, and not of local wine *production*. Evidence of wine consumption in Recent Bronze Age southeast Italy is supplied by Mycenaean painted wares, especially *kraters* and stemmed cups. Almost every site where Mycenaean pottery was found also provided local imitations,[181] suggesting that wine drinking was not uncommon in this period.

In contrast, there is clear evidence of large-scale olive oil production in Recent Bronze Age-Broglio di Trebisacce in the form of huge ceramic *pithoi*. At Broglio, two Recent Bronze Age storage complexes with *pithoi* have been excavated, which were probably used contemporaneously. Scatters of *pithoi* shards elsewhere on the site suggest that there may have been more of these complexes.[182] Chemical analyses have shown that the *pithoi* from Broglio used to contain olive oil.[183] Given the enormous storage capacity of these containers (one of them could contain over 5,000 litres), it can be assumed that the oil was produced locally.

Levi and Jones list many other examples of similar *pithoi* from archaeological sites in southeast Italy, including Torre Mordillo, Otranto, and Rocavecchia.[184] These containers could theoretically have contained wine or even cereals, but at Rocavecchia, traces of a 'greasy substance' were found on

---

[180] Burgers 1998, p. 257.

[181] A good example of this is Recent Bronze Age Termitito (near the river Cavone in Basilicata). De Siena (1986, p. 45, cf. Vagnetti and Jones 1988) reports that ceramics were found here that have parallels in contemporary Greece. However, while the decoration styles and pottery forms are similar, not a single vase was found that was exactly the same in form and decoration style and as its Mycenaean counterparts. This indicates that at least a part of the pottery at Termitito was modelled after Mycenaean ceramics, but produced locally.

[182] Peroni 1994, p. 856; Tenaglia 1994.

[183] Peroni 1994, pp. 855-859, *Figure 231*.

[184] Levi and Jones 1999, pp. 108-109. The listed sites in Apulia also include Mannaccora, Madonna di Ripalta, Madonna del Petto, Capo Colonna, Leuca, Torre Castelluccia, Porto Perone and San Domenico. In Basilicata: Toppo Daguzzo, Timmari, Matera and Tursi. In the Sibaritide: Amendolara, Timpone Motta, Belloluco e Santa Maria del Castello, La Prunetta, Mastro Raffo and Basili.

the outer surface of the *pithoi* that appeared to be olive oil.[185] Given their size, it has been suggested that these *pithoi* were part of communal storage areas, similar in nature (if not in scale) to those of the Mycenean palaces.[186] Chemical and petrographic analyses of the clay have shown that they had been made in at least three different production centres in southern Italy.[187] Most of the sites listed by Levi and Jones had trade contacts with Mycenaean Greece, so even though they were produced locally, the *pithoi* could have been modelled after Greek examples.[188] It must also be added that Broglio di Trebisacce, Torre Mordillo, and Rocavecchia can all be regarded as fortified regional centres in the Bronze Age.[189] The special status of these centres is essential to the interpretation of the storage facilities they housed. The presence of these storage areas implies that olive oil was produced on a fairly large scale, and organized in such a way that it could be centrally stored and redistributed. A major factor explaining the considerable degree of socio-economic complexity that would have been required, is the settlements' participation in Mediterranean exchange networks.[190] This is an important point to which I will return in the following chapter. For the present discussion, the most important conclusion is that large-scale olive oil production took place in southern Italy as early as the Recent Bronze Age. This scale of production seems to be limited to the regional centres that showed a relatively high degree of social and economic complexity.

Evidence of local large-scale olive oil storage in southeast Italy gradually becomes scarce in the Final Bronze Age and is even entirely absent in the Early Iron Age. The transition from the Final Bronze Age to the Early Iron Age (11th-9th centuries BC) is an eventful period. Interregional exchanges decreased considerably, and trade contacts with the eastern Mediterranean were almost completely interrupted (see section 6.2). Archaeological remains from these 'Dark Ages' are rare.[191] In fact, it is unclear whether smaller and more localized forms of olei- and viticulture continued to be practiced in this period, especially since these forms of land use tend to be archaeologically invisible. Archaeological evidence of olive oil and wine production is notoriously hard to find, unless it is practiced on a considerable scale.[192] For southeast Italy, this means that production may very well have continued after

---

[185] Gugliemino 2002, p. 184.

[186] Guglielmino 2002, pp. 185-186; Peroni 1994, pp. 852-853.

[187] Levi and Jones 1999, pp. 111-113. According to Brun (2004, p. 81), the *pithoi* from Broglio di Trebisacce and Torre Mordillo were initially imported from Crete and Cyprus, and subsequently replaced by local imitations. However, Tabò (1998, pp. 157-173; 162-163 and 165-166) and Levi and Jones (1999, p. 208) show in their studies of the pottery from Broglio di Trebisacce that only a few imports from Broglio can be traced back to the eastern Mediterranean. Levi and Jones have calculated that no less than 70% of the *pithoi* from the Recent Bronze Age and 80% from the Final Bronze Age/Early Iron Age were produced locally. The other 30% and 20%, respectively, generally do not originate from the Aegean, but were imported from the southern Sibaritide. The few sherds of imported *pithoi* are the smallest and most damaged ones, and are generally not found in association with storage areas. They seem to belong to smaller (transport?) containers.

[188] Peroni 1994, pp. 852-853; Guglielmino 2002, p. 185 ('Né i dolii di Roca né quelli degli altri siti italiani possono definirsi egei; giustamente è stato osservato che il confronto con i possibili modelli egei non consente di ipotizzare rapporti che vadano oltre il semplice echeggiamento'); Forni 2002, p. 116.

[189] For Rocavecchia, see Pagliara 2005 and Guglielmino 2002, 2005.

[190] Cf. Peroni's model for Final Bronze Age socio-economic and political complexity in the Sibaritide (1994, pp. 850-853).

[191] As Maaskant-Kleibrink (1997, p. 66) has pointed out, the archaeological time-scale in southern Italy for the transition between the Bronze Age to the Iron Age (11th-9th centuries BC) is usually divided into a very dark period, when no Greek seafarers are thought to have been about, and a pre-colonial period. Clearly, this 'light/dark' metaphor operates entirely in favour of the Greek settlers, and basically ignores what happened after the end of the Bronze Age before the first colonial settlements appeared.

[192] Cf. Foxhall 1993.

Fig. 5.4. Silver diobols of the Serdaioi (Lucania?) depicting grapes and olives, late 6th/early 5th century BC. Drawing by the author.

the storage complexes from the Recent and Final Bronze Age had fallen into disuse. Indeed, the continuity of oleiculture on a small local scale in this period ties in with the literary evidence from Greece, especially Hesiod's *Works and Days*. As I demonstrated above, Hesiod tended his own vineyard but does not mention the cultivation of olives.[193] Yet, he was clearly familiar with the use of olive oil.[194] Apparently, localized forms of oleiculture existed in Archaic Greece as well.

In any case, the archaeological evidence of wine and olive oil consumption reappears in the late 8th century BC. Matt-painted pottery forms that can be associated with wine drinking, such as cups, *kraters*, *askoi* (small pouring vessels), strainers, and other pouring vessels, started to appear throughout southern Italy.[195] This type of pottery is also found in areas without evidence of wine import,[196] suggesting that the wine that was consumed here was locally produced. The re-emergence of olive oil consumption in the archaeological record can be deduced from the distribution of smaller vases for perfumed oil[197] and of larger transport vessels from the Aegean, such as the so-called SOS and Corinthian A amphorae.[198] This type of transport vessel has been found in many Early Iron Age contexts in southern Italy. For instance, the excavations at Otranto have supplied hundreds of Corinthian A amphorae (8th–7th centuries BC).[199] However, their number gradually decreased in the Archaic Period. Corinthian A amphorae are rare in contexts that date after the 6th century BC. Some authors have argued that this development can be related to the development of local wine and olive oil production.[200]

Indeed, in this period we see the appearance of the Corinthian B amphora, which represents a different type of transport vessel. These amphorae were produced from the middle of the 6th century BC onwards in the 'Corinthian orbit', i.e. the area including the Albanian, north-western Greek and southern Italian coasts.[201] There is additional evidence of wine production in this period, particularly in colonial Greek contexts. For instance, the remains of possible wine plantations were unearthed near Megara Hyblaea, Syracuse, Pithekoussai, and perhaps also at Taras.[202] Grapes and olives are also fre-

[193] *W&D* 479, 570.

[194] *W&D* 521.

[195] Cf. Yntema 1979, 1990. Examples are Daunian strainers (late 8th–early 7th centuries BC onwards), *askoi* (rare among Geometric matt-painted ceramics, but increasingly common in later periods, especially in the Bari district), *kraters* and local imitations of Greek *oinochoai* and drinking cups.

[196] For example, matt-painted *kraters*, dippers and strainers have been found in abundance on the Tavoliere plain and in the area around Canosa (both located in northern Apulia, outside of the area under study here). Imported Greek pottery is extremely rare here, the indigenous population apparently focused their trade contacts on Campania and the areas that are now Croatia and Slovenia. See Yntema 1979. Considerable numbers of matt-painted strainers were found at l'Amastuola as well (see Crielaard and Burgers 2012, p. 83).

[197] Forni 2002, pp. 116-117.

[198] Brun 2004, p. 86.

[199] D'Andria 1995, pp. 466-67, *Figure 2*. The same type of transport vessel was also found in the earliest layers at l'Amastuola. See Burgers and Crielaard 2007, p. 104.

[200] Brun 2010, p. 426.

[201] Gassner 2011; Sourisseau 2012, in press.

[202] For Pithekoussai, see Gialanella 1994, p. 170, *Figure 4*. For Taras: a reference to possible traces of vineyards was presented on the poster exposition 'La vigna di Dioniso. Vite, vino e culti in Magna Grecia', held between 15 July and 10 October 2009 at the Museo Nazionale Archeologico

Fig. 5.5. Bronze, lead and clay funerary crown in the shape of grapes and grape leafs from the southern *necropolis* at Herakleia, 3rd century BC. Drawing by the author after Vandermersch 1994, 39.

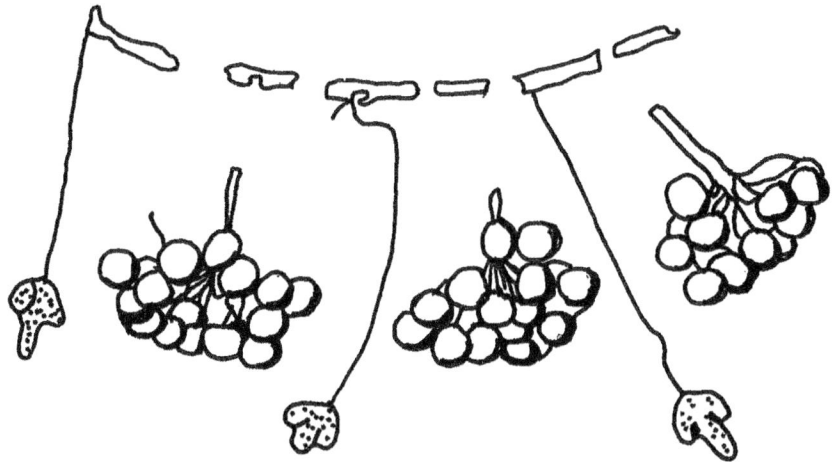

Fig. 5.6. Grape leaves on a Lucanian *oinochoe*, c. 380-360 BC. Drawing by the author, after Dentzer 1982; Vandermersch 1994, 40.

di Taranto. This exhibition was connected to the 49th Convegno di Studi sulla Magna Grecia (24-28 September 2009) of which the proceedings were published in 2011. For Megara Hyblaea and Syracuse, see Gras 1975, pp. 43-46. In the *necropolis* area at Megara Hyblaea, NW/SE oriented canals were discovered that were cut into the rock. The canals were laid out parallel to each other, at a distance of 2.4 and 3.5 metres, not interconnected, and sometimes interrupted for dozens of centimetres without apparent reason. The canals were generally less than a metre wide and 20 to 40 centimetres deep. Some of them could be followed for over 100 metres. Gras (1975, p. 44) refers to descriptions by Pliny for his interpretation of the canals as trenches to plant vineyards. The chronology of the canals poses a problem, since the vineyard and the *necropolis* (which was in use between the 7th century BC and the destruction of Megara around 483 BC) were obviously not in use at the same time. Since some of the canals cut through 6th century BC tombs, and some seem to be interrupted to avoid areas that are intensively used to place tombs, it was concluded that the vineyard was planted when the *necropolis* was no longer in use. Another argument for this chronology is provided by the find of a comparable system of canals in a *necropolis* between Syracuse and Megara that was excavated by Giuseppe Voza in the 1970s. Here, the oldest graves (4th century BC) provide a *terminus antequem* for the vineyard. In other words, both vineyards may have been in use in the 5th century BC.

[203] Horsnæs 2002, p. 121.

quently depicted on coinage from the Serdaioi, an indigenous tribe that probably lived in the hinterland of Sybaris (*Figure 5.4*).[203] These coins can be dated between the late 6th and early 5th centuries BC.[204]

Vandermersch reports finds of terracotta ex-votos from the Early Hellenistic Period in the form of a variety of fruits, including grapes, in a rural sanctuary near the Sinni river, about 4 km from Herakleia.[205] In addition, some of the bronze funerary wreaths and crowns that were discovered in 4th-and 3rd-century BC tombs at the southern *necropolis* of Herakleia were made in the shape of grape leafs (*Figure 5.5*).[206] Other indications for the importance of wine consumption can be found on locally produced pottery decorations showing symposia, grapevines, and wine in general, such as the Lucanian *oinochoe* shown in *Figure 5.6*.[207] In addition, grapes, olives and, more in general, the head of Dionysus, occasionally appear on colonial Greek coinage, including some coins from Taras.[208]

However, olive oil and wine production were clearly not restricted to colonial Greek contexts in the Early Hellenistic Period. Brun lists several examples of olive oil and/or wine presses that were found *in situ* in indigenous inland areas, among which the farmstead of Montegiordano in Calabria.[209] At this site, a press installation and two *pithoi* were found that were probably in use between 350 and 275 BC. This is also the period when the production of Graeco-Italic amphorae took off. These two developments are likely to be related, with local production of wine and olive oil going hand in hand with the local manufacturing of transport vessels to export it in.

Wine and olive oil were produced on a larger scale after the arrival of the Romans in southeast Italy. Soon after its foundation in 244 BC, the Roman colony of Brundisium (Brindisi) developed into a major centre for overseas trade.[210] The surveys by the University of Siena have detected the presence of late Republican kiln sites near Brindisi, producing amphorae for the transport of wine and olive oil. Large production centres of amphorae were found at the sites of Apani, Giancola, Marmorelle, and La Rosa.[211] There are indications that similar workshops, although probably of more modest dimensions, existed in southern Salento, for instance at the site of *masseria* Ramanno near present-day San Cataldo (Lecce) and Felline in the southern tip of Salento. Amphorae from these sites have been found throughout the Mediterranean, indicating that Brundisium became engaged in large-scale wine and olive oil export.[212]

The vineyards and olive groves that produced these export products were evidently also located in the rural hinterland of Brundisium.[213] There is archaeological evidence of wine and olive oil production in other parts of southeast Italy as well, for instance at the Late Hellenistic farms from Monte Moltone (Basilicata) and Posta Crusta (northern Apulia).[214] The excavations at Monte Moltone revealed the presence of numerous *pithoi* shards in a room that may have been a wine cellar. At the *villa rustica* of Posta Crusta, Ordona (Foggia), the remains of a complete installation for the production of olive oil were excavated, including a crusher, a press, a decantation basin, and several large *dolia*.[215]

In sum, it can be assumed that wine and olive oil were produced on a large enough scale in the Early and Late Hellenistic periods that they could be sold at market. There are indications that grapes, olives, wine, and olive oil vessels travelled fairly large distances over land.[216] On a terracotta sculpture

---

[204] Brousseau 2010, p. 275.

[205] Vandermersch 1994, pp. 40-41, note 146.

[206] Vandermersch 1994, p. 42; De Lachenal 1992, p. 55.

[207] Dentzer 1982, *Figure 119*.

[208] Wuilleumier 1987, p. 214.

[209] Brun 2004, pp. 167-168.

[210] Yntema 1993, p. 201, 2006, p. 101. For the increase of wine production in Roman southern Italy, see especially Tchernia 1986 and Purcell 1985.

[211] Yntema 2006, p. 109.

[212] Aprosio and Cambi 1997; Cambi 2000, p. 176.

[213] Cf. Yntema 2006, p. 110: 'Products from Salento were marketed in large parts of the Mediterranean with remarkable success. The district must therefore have generated very substantial surpluses indeed.'

[214] Brun 2004, pp. 167-168.

[215] Brun 2004, pp. 171-172.

Fig. 5.7. Terracotta horse carrying baskets of fruit, from Policoro, Museo della Siritide, 2nd half 4th century BC. Forti and Stazio 1983, Figure 672

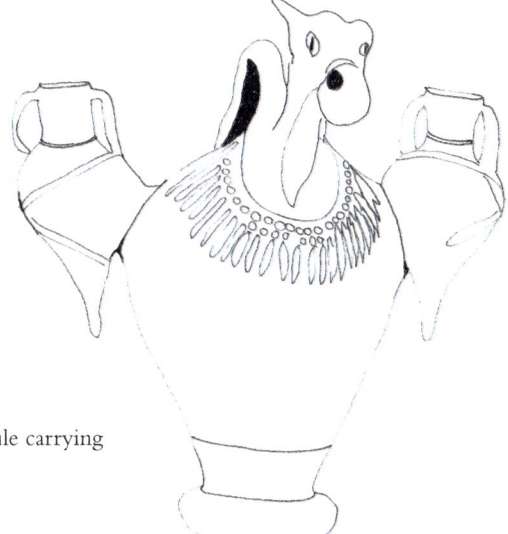

Fig. 5.8. Gnathia-style *askos* (small pouring vessel) in the form of a mule carrying two transport amphorae, c. 280-240 BC. Museo Archeologico di Bari. Drawing by the author.

from Herakleia (second half of the 4th century BC), a horse is carrying baskets of fruit (*Figure 5.7*). Another telling artefact in this context is a Gnathia-style *askos*, now in the collection of the Museo Archeologico di Bari, in the form of a mule carrying two transport amphorae (*Figure 5.8*).[217]

The main conclusion that can be drawn from the archaeological evidence is that there are clear indications of wine and olive oil consumption and of local olive oil production in the Recent and Final Bronze Age. But in the early centuries of the first millennium BC, evidence of wine and olive oil production is almost completely absent from the archaeological records. This situation lasted until the late 8th century BC, but the earliest indications of local olive oil and wine production after the Final Bronze Age date to the 6th and 5th centuries BC and are largely restricted to settlements that were nodal points in the exchange networks involving both southern Italy and the eastern Mediterranean.

The widespread production of Graeco-Italic amphorae suggests that this situation changed notably in the Early Hellenistic period. By this time, a form of specialized production had developed that made it possible to export wine and olive oil. The discovery of amphora production sites and specialized farms show that wine and olive oil were produced and traded on a considerable scale in the last three to four centuries of the first millennium BC.

---

[216] Varro (82-35 BC) mentions mule trains that 'are usually formed by the traders, as, for instance, those who pack oil or wine and grain or other products from the region of Brundisium or Apulia to the sea' (A 6.38). Cf. Lombardo 1992, pp. 50-52, nos. 81, 82 and 84; Burgers 1998, p. 257.

[217] The origin of this vase is unknown, but according to Douwe Yntema (personal comm.), the decoration style indicates that it was made between c. 280 and 240 BC.

Archaeobotanical evidence

The introduction and development of viti- and oleiculture in Italy has a long history of research.[218] Starting with the evidence of grape cultivation, as early as the 1950s Hans Helbaek argued that the Etruscans were responsible for the diffusion of the cultivated grape in Italy, but that viticulture was first introduced by Aegean colonists. As Helbaek reports, no grape pips were found among the plant remains in pre-Etruscan tombs in Rome.

Thus it may be concluded that they were a novelty connected with this foreign [Etruscan] cultural influence. Whereas the wild vine, *Vitis silvestris* Gm., was very common in the Alps, and grape pips occur abundantly in plant deposits of the Bronze Age in northern Italy, probably coming from non-cultivated plants, the Iron Age people of the Rome district do not seem to have had access to these attractive fruits. It may, therefore, be suggested that their occurrence in the late deposits is a result of introduction of viticulture, *Vitis vinifera* L., in Italy, brought about by the growing sea trade connection between the eastern and western Mediterranean.[219]

This view on the introduction of viticulture in Italy has been dominant for over 50 years.[220] As recently as 2002, Forni argued that the Greek colonists in southern Italy planted their own vineyards on foreign soil. Their success is believed to be reflected in the name they gave to modern Basilicata and northern Calabria, namely Oenotria ('the land of the trained vines').[221]

However, recent archaeobotanical investigations have shown that this traditional picture needs some fine-tuning. There is ample proof for grape consumption from Italian Neolithic and Bronze Age sites, but the identified grapes almost exclusively belong to the wild form (see *Table 5.6* at the end of this chapter for an overview of the archaeobotanical finds of grape and olives that are discussed here).[222] There are a few possible exceptions, e.g. the grape finds from the Middle Bronze Age site of Portella[223] (Salina, Aeolian Islands) and the Villanovan site of Gran Carro[224] (Lake Bolsena, Lazio).[225] In any case, the earliest finds of cultivated grapes and other evidence of grape cultivation still pre-date the period of Greek colonization. A particularly interesting case is provided by Longola di Poggiomarino in Campania, a site with habitation traces from the Early Iron Age until the early 6th century BC.[226] The settlement was located along the Sarno river and has been completely immersed since the 4th century BC. Here, numerous grape pips, pruned grapevines, and grape pressings were found that unmistakably

---

[218] See Helbaek 1956; Vallet 1962; Renfrew 1973; Lacroix Phippen 1975; Boardman 1976; Castelletti 1976; Pals and Voorrips 1979; Ampolo 1980, p. 31; Costantini 1981, 1983a, b, c, Forti and Stazio 1983, p. 313; Castelletti *et al.* 1987; Zohary and Hopf 2000, among many others.

[219] Helbaek 1956, pp. 292-293.

[220] See for example Renfrew 1973, p. 127, about the *Vitis* finds at Campo Servirola and pre-urban Rome. She refers to Helbaek to support her hypothesis that viticulture was introduced in Italy by the Etruscans.

[221] McGovern 2009, p. 193.

[222] Rivera Nuñez and Walker 1989, p. 224. The earliest finds of wild grape pips were probably made in the Grotta dell'Uzzo on Sicily (8th millennium BC, Costantini 1981, 1989) and, subsequently, at Torre Canne in Apulia (6th millennium BC, Brun 2004, p. 81).

[223] Fiorentino 2005, Fiorentino *et al.* 2011. A recent publication by Martinelli *et al.* (2010, pp. 297-298) reports the discovery of a considerable quantity of carbonized grape pips from the Early Bronze Age hut settlement of Filo Braccio on one of the other Aeolian islands, Filicudi. No morphometric results are included in the publication, so it is unclear whether they belong to wild or cultivated fruits.

[224] Costantini and Costantini Biasini 1995; Hopf 1995. Cf. Forni (2002, p. 114) who argues that the early *Vitis* finds from Gran Carro represent a point of arrival rather than one of diffusion, and that viticulture probably ended up here after various travels that all started from the earliest point of exchange with Egyptian, Minoan, and Mycenaean traders in the south of the country.

[225] According to Gras (1985, p. 267) and Peroni (1994, p. 845), carbonized grape pips were also found at the Bronze Age site on Vivara (Phlaegrean islands), but the results have apparently not been published.

[226] Cicirelli and Albore-Livadie 2008, p. 475.

point at viticulture and winemaking, datable between the late 10th and early 9th centuries BC.[227] Not far from Poggiomarino, at S. Maria Capua Vetere, a large number of pruned vines from Final Bronze Age layers were found in a rubbish pit.[228]

These finds demonstrate that grape cultivation was already practiced in Bronze Age Italy, but the scant evidence is restricted to a few areas. Indeed, cultivated grape remains or other indications of viticulture have never been found in southeast Italy. Grape remains were also absent at Broglio di Trebisacce, which is striking, since there was an abundance of drinking services and wine pouring vessels among the pottery finds. According to Peroni, there can be no doubt that wine consumption took place at Broglio, but this wine was apparently imported.[229] There is a pollen core from Aspromonte in southern Calabria that shows several *Vitis* (and *Olea*) peaks in the first millennium BC, but there are also peaks in the 5th, 4th, and 3rd millennia BC, so it is not evident how these data should be interpreted.[230]

What about the archaeobotanical evidence of olive cultivation during the Bronze Age in Italy? As I explained above, it is difficult to distinguish between wild and cultivated olives. Their interpretation is often based on the chronological context. Therefore, the earliest archaeological finds of olives in southern Italy, such as those from the Grotta dell'Uzzo, are commonly qualified as collected fruits of wild origin.[231] We have seen above, however, that there is archaeological evidence of large-scale olive oil production in Recent Bronze Age-Broglio di Trebisacce and other sites in southern Italy. Do these data tie in with the archaeobotanical evidence? Indeed, the earliest cultivated olives make their appearance in layers dating to the Recent Bronze Age. The number of remains, however, is still very limited. In southeast Italy, stones of cultivated olives have only been found at Broglio di Trebisacce and Monopoli/Piazza Palmieri.[232] Brun also mentions that carbonized stones were found at Castello di Tursi (Basilicata, 12th century BC), which may have belonged to cultivated olives.[233]

The olive remains from Broglio di Trebisacce have been studied particularly well because of their association with the *pithos* finds at this site. Olive stones were found here in contexts of the Recent Bronze as well as Final Bronze Age/Early Iron Age. Furthermore, the olive wood in the charcoal assemblage (see *Table 5.5*) has been interpreted as evidence of olive tree pruning.[234] Vallino and Ventura state that the olive stones from Broglio show 'a significant spectrum of biometric variability that may lead to the hypothesis that they derived from the cultivated variety.'[235] The length/breadth ratio of the stones is around 1.83[236] which, according to these authors, is similar to the dimensions of cultivated

---

[227] Cicirelli *et al.* 2008, p. 574. These dates are based on dendrochronological analyses. The wooden objects that were found in the same stratigraphic level as the grape pips can be dated to 905/864 BC.

[228] Castiglioni and Rottoli 1996.

[229] Peroni 1994, p. 845.

[230] Schneider 1994, *Figure 2*.

[231] Costantini 1981.

[232] For Monopoli/Piazza Palmieri, see Fiorentino 1995 ('I resti di olive [...] sono probabilmente da riferirsi a forme di *raccolta selettiva/incipiente coltivazione* [my emphasis, DL] che non ha ancora determinato modificazioni dimensionali dei frutti'; Terral *et al.* 2004, p. 72 ('The first occurence of a 'cultivated shape' appears during the Chalcolithic in Spain and the Bronze Age at Palmieri (Italy). This means that cultivated morphotypes appeared in Spain and Italy long before the introduction of oleiculture.').

Vallino and Ventura (1984, p. 274) refer to the site of Tufariello di Buccino (Salerno) in Campania as another Bronze Age context where domesticated olive stones were found. Unfortunately, in the publication of the archaeobotanical remains from Tufariello (Lacroix Phippen 1975, p. 79), no such statements are made. Lacroix Phippen mentions numerous olive stones and also reports that 'All olive pits belong to a single species', but not whether this 'single species' was domesticated or wild.

[233] Brun 2004, p. 81. Unfortunately, these finds have never been published. Brun reports that this information appeared in a poster presentation by the Soprintendenza per i Beni Archeologici della Basilicata on the Taranto Conference in 2002.

[234] Namely by Nisbet and Ventura (1994, pp. 577-578) and Peroni (1994, p. 845).

[235] Vallino and Ventura 1984, p. 274.

olive stones from Myrtos, Volos and Cyprus.[237] In wild olives, the length/breadth ratio is supposedly lower (the stones are less elongated).[238] Therefore, it is likely that the olive stones from Broglio belong to cultivated fruits. However, no archaeobotanical remains of olives were found at contemporary Torre Mordillo (only in the Final Bronze Age/Early Iron Age layers), although the charcoal assemblage from this site did contain some olive wood. According to Coubray,[239] the exploitation of olive trees at Recent Bronze Age Torre Mordillo cannot be excluded, but there is not nearly enough evidence to support this view.

There is also palynological evidence of an increase in olive pollen in this period. Apart from the Aspromonte core, which I discussed above, there is a remarkable *Olea* peak between 3600 and 3100 cal. BP (i.e. in the Middle, Recent and Final Bronze Age) in the pollen core from the Laghi Alimini in southeast Salento.[240] These lakes are located at a distance of less than 10 kilometres from Rocavecchia, where Bronze Age-storage complexes were found, with *pithoi* filled with olive oil.[241] It is tempting to associate the *Olea* peak from the Laghi Alimini with large-scale olive cultivation in the area, although Di Rita and Magri have proposed an alternative explanation. A general Late-Holocene increase of evergreen vegetation has been largely recognized in the Mediterranean basin, and ascribed to either human activity or climatic trends.[242] The *Olea* peak from the Laghi Alimini could possibly be associated with this increase of evergreen vegetation rather than the spread of oleiculture.[243]

Summarizing the archaeobotanical evidence for olive and grape cultivation in Bronze Age southeast Italy, I believe that the example of Broglio di Trebisacce makes it clear that oleiculture was practiced at a considerable scale near the larger centres in the Recent Bronze Age. It is mainly due to this large-scale production that the cultivation of olives is particularly evident at Broglio. Olive oil production may have taken place at some of the smaller Bronze Age settlements too, but the lack of large scale storage and/or production facilities makes it much more difficult to find archaeological evidence to *substantiate* this *hypothesis*.

The same observation holds true for viticulture, but at this point it can *be plausibly argued* that grape cultivation was not commonly practiced in Bronze Age southeast Italy. However, *as* Brun[244] has noted, the grape finds from Longola in Campania not only prove that a form of viticulture was practiced by the indigenous populations of southern Italy before the arrival of the Greek colonists, but also make it clear that it takes an archaeological site with exceptional environmental circumstances to find such traces. In other words, the fact that no remains of grape cultivation and wine making have been found

---

[236] Vallino and Ventura 1984, p. 275.

[237] Cf. Renfrew 1973, p. 133, reporting length/breadth ratios of supposedly cultivated olive stones from EBA Myrtos (2,13), BA Lachish (1,96), BA Apliki (1,65), IA Lachish (1,77), RBA Volos (between 1.92 and 2.3) and IA Salamis (1.82).

[238] Cf. Kislev 1995. Nisbet and Ventura refer to remarkably outdated literature, including G. Buschan, *Vorgeschichtliche Botanik der Kultur- und Nutzpflanzen der Alten Welt auf Grund prähistorischer Funde* (Breslau, 1895) and A. De Candolle, *Origine des plantes cultivées* (Paris, 1883), pp. 222-227.

[239] Coubray 2001, p. 430. The only olive stone from Torre Mordillo was found in the most recent stratigraphical layers (Early Iron Age). Nevertheless, Brun (2010, p. 425) lists it among the earliest cultivated olives in Italy.

[240] At least three separate pollen cores were retrieved from the Alimini lakes, i.e. one from the larger lake and the other from the small one, both published in 1999 by Harding, and another one from the small lake that was recently published by Di Rita and Magri (2009). In the pollen cores that were studied by Harding (1999, pp. 121, 93-94), the lower limit to pollen preservation, and hence of the chronology for vegetation change represented by the cores, lies within the aeolian sand layer of proposed mid-Holocene age. In the more recently published core from Di Rita and Magri (2009, p. 297) 57 samples were collected between 8 cm and 232 cm deep. The earliest samples were carbon dated around 5600-5200 cal. BP.

[241] Gugliemino 2002, p. 184.

[242] Di Rita and Magri 2009, with further references.

[243] Cf. Di Rita and Magri 2009, pp. 301 and 303-304.

[244] Brun 2010, p. 426.

at more (indigenous) sites in southern Italy from this period, does not necessarily mean that viticulture was not practiced.[245]

If viticulture was practiced, however, it was on a local scale. The archaeobotanical finds of grapes from Early Iron Age contexts seem to confirm this. The earliest carbonized grape pips from southeast Italy date to the late 8th and early 7th century BC and were found at l'Incoronata and l'Amastuola. Grape remains were particularly rare at the latter site, consisting of three pips only (and no charcoal). Only two of the pips could be measured, resulting in a 58 and 64 score on the Stummer Index. According to the Mangafa and Kotsakis formulas, the pips belong to wild fruits. It is not known what the grape pips from l'Incoronata looked like and whether the fruits from this site were cultivated or wild.[246] The sample from l'Incoronata is quite small, which may explain why several other crops, such as olives, but also bread wheat, are absent. However, there is also a distinct possibility that these crops were simply not cultivated at this settlement. There are other sites from this period, such as Monte Irsi[247] and Botromagno[248] where no grape or olive remains were found in the Early Iron Age levels. Interestingly, imported pottery vessels that can be associated with wine consumption have been found in the wealthy tombs at the latter site. This suggests that the inhabitants, or at least a privileged few of them, were familiar with wine consumption.

However, it appears that this wine was mostly imported, rather than produced locally. The same holds true for olive oil. Archaeobotanical evidence of local olei- and viticulture is particularly scarce in the Early Iron Age. It becomes increasingly common, however, for the Archaic/Classical periods. Three grape pips (but no olive stones) were found at excavation levels from the Archaic period at Roccagloriosa. At Monte Papalucio, both olives and (entire) grapes were present in all phases, from the middle of the 6th until the first half of the 3rd century BC. According to Ciaraldi, the olives probably belonged to the domesticated variety but this hypothesis is based on references in ancient written sources, not on biometric analysis.[249] Nevertheless, the strong presence of olive wood at this site is also indicative of olive cultivation, especially since most of the fragments consisted of small branches, possibly from pruning wood. Among the charcoal fragments was also a single wood fragment of a vine branch from the Archaic period.[250] Ciarallo reports that since the grapes from Monte Papalucio were carbonized in its entirety, it was not possible to measure the pips.[251] However, she adds that since the fruits were quite large (on average 12.5 x 10.5 mm) they appear to be of the domesticated type.[252] Furthermore, the samples from Archaic layers at Torre di Satriano also included grape pips, and both grapes and olives were found at Cavallino and l'Amastuola.[253] In addition, the pollen spectrum from Pantanello contains traces of olives from the Archaic/Classical periods (late 6th and early 5th centuries BC) onward, but not of grapes – possibly because grapevines generally produce little pollen.[254] The same holds true for the pollen core from the Laghi di Monticchio in northern Basilicata, which shows a peak in olive pollen around 2460 BP.[255]

---

[245] Blitzer (1993, p. 165) makes a comparable point for olive cultivation in Minoan Crete: '[...] when archaeologists have looked seriously for organic evidence of olive cultivation at Bronze Age sites on Crete they have found it. When they have made no attempt to collect carbonized remains (and this applies to over 90% of the excavations carried out on Crete in the last fifty years), they have not.'

[246] Carter 2006, p. 78.

[247] Hjelmqvist 1977.

[248] Colledge 2000, p. 60.

[249] Ciaraldi 1997, p. 214, 1999, p. 84 ('The record of olive cultivation in the Eraclea tablets as well as the mention of the exportation of oil from Apulia in the Late Republican period (Varro RR 2.6.5) suggests that the finds at MP belong to the domesticated form.')

[250] Fiorentino 2008, p. 102.

[251] Ciaraldi 1997, p. 213.

[252] This hypothesis is supported by Fiorentino (2008, p. 102), who states that the finds from MP (entire grapes and grape wood) attest to the 'probable grape cultivation in the territory as early as the Archaic period.'

[253] Fiorentino and Colaianni 2005, p. 98.

[254] Turner and Brown 2004, p. 131.

[255] Watts et al. 1996, 124.

Interestingly, olive and grape remains have been found in all the archaeological sites with habitation levels from the Early Hellenistic period. These finds tie in well with the archaeological evidence and the information from ancient written sources, which both show that wine and olive oil were produced and traded on a large scale in the Early Hellenistic period. The sampled amphora from Pomarico Vecchio only contained grape pips and no olive stones, but the pollen spectrum from this site indicates the presence of both viticulture and oleiculture. Brun also reports the finds of olive stones in food offerings from the sanctuary of Demeter at Herakleia (4th-3rd century BC).[256] Grapes and olives also abound in the samples from the sanctuary of Pantanello, all of which were taken from Early Hellenistic layers. Apart from the macroremains, these layers also contained waterlogged olive wood and vines, both with pruning cuts. Furthermore, the olive pollen from Pantanello show a peak around the middle of the 4th century BC.[257]

Conclusion
Taking all three categories of evidence together, several conclusions can be drawn. As we have seen, the traditional view on the introduction of olive cultivation is outdated. Archaeological and archaeobotanical evidence show that the methods to cultivate olives and produce olive oil were already known to the indigenous Italian populations before the arrival of the first Greek colonists in the 8th century BC. There is an increasing body of evidence indicating that the cultivation of olives in southeast Italy started as early as the Recent Bronze Age, and continued to be practiced throughout the first millennium BC. Bronze Age oleiculture is especially well attested in the regional centres that were part of larger exchange networks, such as Broglio di Trebisacce, Torre Mordillo, and Rocavecchia. Oleiculture may have been practiced at other sites as well, but because of the small scale, the visibility of these activities is low.

The same holds true for the cultivation of olives in the Early Iron Age. Evidence of olive oil production is almost completely absent in the archaeological record in the early centuries of the first millennium BC. This does not exclude that oleiculture continued to be practiced on a small, local scale in this period, but it appears that a large part was imported from the eastern Mediterranean in SOS and Corinthian A amphorae. Wine was also imported. There is no evidence of viticulture in Bronze Age and Early Iron Age southeast Italy, although wild grapes were consumed and some (elite) groups had access to imported wine. We have seen abundant archaeological evidence of this in the form of transport amphorae and pottery shapes that are related to wine consumption. Such amphorae were found, for instance, at l'Amastuola, where grape cultivation was apparently unknown or practiced on a small scale. Since there are indications of wine consumption at this site (i.e. the huge amount of cups and strainers in the ritual deposition in trench 6), these amphorae are likely to have contained imported wine.

The replacement of Corinthian A amphorae by mostly locally produced Corinthian B vessels in the Archaic period is probably related to the development of local wine and olive oil production. Indeed, this is the period when the first clear evidence of post-Bronze Age olive cultivation appears in the archaeobotanical record, notably at Monte Papalucio and Pantanello. At the same time, a form of local viticulture developed around these sites. According to the written sources, wine was already produced at a considerable scale in the Greek colonial towns in this period. We have also seen some archaeological evidence for this, i.e. traces interpreted as wine plantations and depictions of grapes and olives on coinage.

This brings us to the effect of Greek colonization on the development of oleiculture and especially wine production in southern Italy. The Greek colonization process no doubt was a catalytic agent in

---

[256] Brun 2004, p. 166, note 20.   [257] Carter *et al.* 1985, pp. 290-296.

the spread of viticulture in the inland areas by introducing wine drinking rituals.[258] As we have seen, in the early centuries of the first millennium BC these rituals were mostly performed with imported wine. In the Classical and particularly in the Early Hellenistic Period, however, cultivation techniques and pottery types to store, pour, and consume wine also reached the inland areas and indigenous settlements started to produce their own wines. Nevertheless, the import of wines from the Aegean continued even in the following centuries. A possible explanation for this might be that drinking expensive imported wines, even though much cheaper local ones were available, was a matter of prestige.[259] Indeed, there is archaeological evidence of wine import from Greece even in the Roman period, when local wines had become easily available throughout the Italian peninsula.[260]

Archaeological, textual, and archaeobotanical evidence are all indicative of a clear increase in the scale of production of wine and olive oil from the 4th century BC onward. By this time, these products had obviously become a key element of southeast Italy's agricultural economy. As we have seen, this was the case at Muro Tenente, where locally produced wine and olive oil was exported in Graeco-Italic amphorae. It will be argued in chapter 6 that this development was probably connected with the process of rural infill that took place in this period, which allowed an expansion and rationalization of agricultural production. In addition, newly built roads and rural hamlets in between the larger centres facilitated travelling. As a result, it became easier and much more profitable to exchange agricultural products on a market. Judging from the numerous references to Apulian olei- and viticulture in ancient written texts, the impact of these developments became even more evident in the Roman period. As Hitchner has noted, the 'boom' in olive production in the western Roman provinces may be attributed to the prior existence of olive cultivation in these areas, and of long distance trade in other agricultural and non-agricultural commodities.[261] This certainly seems to apply to Roman southeast Italy, where wine and olive oil were exported on a large scale, especially after the foundation of the Latin colony of Brundisium.

5.3.4 THE USE OF PLANTS IN RITUAL ACTIVITIES

In this section, two categories of contexts that can be associated with ritual activities will be discussed, namely 1) sanctuaries and ritual depositions and 2) graves. This may seem to distract from our discussion of landscape and land use in southeast Italy, but quite the opposite is true. The ritual significance of plants and food offerings is a research theme that has received much scholarly attention.[262] However, an important point that studies often tend to overlook, is that such remains also provide excellent opportunities to investigate agricultural practices and other forms of land use. Archaeobotanical assemblages

---

[258] Cf. Fiorentino 2011, p. 17.

[259] In an almost laughable parallel, it was brought to my attention that at prestigious parties and receptions at the foreign embassies in Rome in the 1970s and 1980s, the served wine was always French, and never Italian.

[260] For example, Rhodian wine amphorae dating to the late 3rd and 2nd centuries BC in several sites in southern Italy, for instance in a wealthy elite burial that was excavated in the southern *necropolis* of Mesagne (first half/middle of the 2nd century BC), see Yntema 2009, p. 151. A parallel from a much earlier period can be found in Hesiod's *Works and Days* (*W&D* 583, 8th century BC) where the author, who tended his own vineyards, takes a break from work in midsummer and enjoys a flask of imported ('biblian') wine instead of his own product (A 6.7)

[261] Hitchner 1993, p. 501. 'The olive was a well-established crop along the coast of southern Gaul, Africa, and Tripolitania [*southern Italy is not mentioned, DL*] well before the Roman conquest. Moreover, with the rise of grain shipments to Rome and the army from Africa as early as the 2nd century BC, regular shipping routes and supply and distribution mechanisms were initiated which olive producers in the imperial period could exploit to their own advantage.'

[262] For southeast Italy, see for example Mastronuzzi 2005b; D'Andria, De Grossi Mazzorin and Fiorentino 2008.

from sanctuaries and graves offer a perspective on the crop spectrum that differs significantly from domestic contexts. Whereas the composition of the latter is usually based on coincidence, offering pits and graves often contain intentional depositions of food, flowers, fragrant wood, and other products. Studying their contents, therefore, provides information about the perceived value of particular items. Moreover, the ritual deposits from sanctuaries are often particularly rich in macroremains, and therefore provide much more information about the crop spectrum than domestic contexts. Comparing these two types of contexts can be particularly revealing. This is the main reason why I will discuss the archaeobotanical data from sanctuaries and graves in more detail in this section. The second reason is that studying these ritual contexts adds a new dimension to our understanding of the role of food products. It illustrates that food is not only used for consumption, but also tends to have ritual connotations, such as associations with certain deities.

In this section, I will first give a list of the crop and wood remains from sanctuaries, ritual depositions, and graves at the sites that were introduced earlier in this chapter. Subsequently, I will demonstrate the ways in which these assemblages differ from those from domestic contexts, and discuss the implications of these differences. Finally, I will dedicate a section to the ritual connotations of some of the food products and wood types that were found at these sites.

Plant remains from contexts of ritual origin
The ritual depositions that are discussed in this paragraph are divided into two categories, i.e. graves and ritual depositions. The archaeobotanical finds from these two types of contexts are included in *Table 5.7*.[263] Samples from the graves at Botromagno and Muro Tenente included hulled and naked barley, free-threshing wheat, emmer, einkorn, broad bean, bitter vetch, vetchling, grapes, and olives. In the samples from Botromagno, a few weed seeds were found as well, namely corn gromwell, canarygrass (*Phalaris*), and bulrush (*Scirpus*).

No doubt the most surprising find that was made in a ritual deposition consisted of the 27 carbonized cloves of garlic from l'Amastuola. However, several other types of food remains were found as well. All the ritual depositions contained cereal remains, among which hulled barley, bread wheat, emmer, einkorn, and possibly even spelt (*T. spelta*). The sanctuaries of Vaste (*bothroi*) and Monte

[263] Perhaps it comes as a surprise that the Pantanello sanctuary is not included in this overview. The excavation levels from which the archaeobotanical samples were retrieved, can be dated to the 4th century BC. In the previous phases, the Pantanello water basin had been used to deposit votive figurines, and probably also other types of ritual offerings (Carter 2006, pp. 164-173). In the course of the 5th century, however, the spring and collecting basin went out of use and were filled with soil. This is confirmed by the Pantanello pollen core (Sullivan 1983; Carter *et al.* 1985, pp. 290-296, *Figures 16.5, 16.6* and *16.7*; Carter 2006, pp. 26-27) showing that the sanctuary's water basin gradually turned into a swamp until it had completely silted up in the first quarter of the 3rd century BC. The earliest phase of the sanctuary is characterized by aquatic plants and weeds such as coontail (*Ceratophyllum demersum*), horned pond weed (*Zannichellia*, which can be found in both still and slow-flowing water) and sedge (*Carex*, usually in marshy places and on damp fields). In the later phases, the remains of plants that may have been weeds in arable fields, such as vetchling (*Lathyrus*), knotweed (*Polygonum*) and darnel became more numerous. However, the site was revived for a few decades in the second half of the 4th century BC, when the collecting basin was cleared down to its cobble pavement. In this phase, the *oikos* of Dionysos from the Archaic period was replaced by a new structure that was probably a farmhouse. Although Carter (2006, pp. 164 and 168) has pointed out that the collecting basin continued to receive votive vessels in this period, the nature of the archaeobotanical finds suggests that they consisted mostly of agricultural waste products rather than votive depositions. A telling example is the presence of pruning wood, including waterlogged fig wood, which is particularly unsuitable to use a fuel, as it produces poisonous smoke. This may in part be the reason why it has not been encountered at any of the other sites that are discussed in this chapter.

Papalucio (*eschara*) bear a strong resemblance in their votive deposits, as both are dominated by cereals, cakes, and biscuits.[264] Cereals are often found in large quantities. For example, at Vaste, about 60% of the macroremains were cereals, and they were also particularly abundant at Monte Papalucio. The archaeobotanical assemblage from Vaste also contained several (cereal) weed seeds, including oat, brome, medick, and rye.

Apparently, pulses also played an important role in ritual activities at these sites, but some species are more dominant than others. Chickpeas and field peas, for example, were only found at Monte Papalucio, and lentils only at Vaste. On the other hand, bitter vetches and broad beans appeared more frequently (at l'Amastuola, Monte Papalucio, and Vaste).

Fruits are among the most interesting components of the archaeobotanical assemblages from these sites, since most of the types are rarely found in excavations in southeast Italy. For example, figs appeared at four of the sites that are discussed in this chapter, usually in the form of seeds. Only the Monte Papalucio deposits contained complete carbonized fruits. Some of the cakes from Monte Papalucio also had fig as one of their main ingredients, the seeds being clearly visible in the dough. The two fruits that were discussed in the previous paragraph, the olive and the grape, appear in both sanctuaries and graves. According to Ciaraldi, the olive was unimportant from a symbolic point of view – in sharp contrast to its important economic role.[265] But this observation is not confirmed by the ritual deposits discussed in this section, since olives were found in the votive deposits at Monte Papalucio (although, admittedly, only in small quantities), and in relative abundance in the cult place at Vaste.[266] The ritual depositions at Monte Papalucio also contained two fruit types that were not found at any of the other sites, namely crab apples (*Malus* cf. *sylvestris*) and dates. The few charred crab apples were rather small, with a diameter of only a few centimetres.[267] Since the fruits of the date palm do not mature in Italy, the dates from Monte Papalucio were probably imported from Africa or Asia Minor.[268]

Olive is the only wood type that was found in all the contexts discussed here. Most of the other wood types only appeared in one or two contexts, and included oak, silver fir (*Abies alba*), ephedra, erica, beech (*Fagus* sp.), fig, myrtle, mastic, poplar/willow (*Populus/Salix*), *Rhamnus/Phillyrea*, grapevine, and a few other fruit trees (*Prunus* sp., cf. *Punica granatum*, *Pyrus/Malus*).

Clearly, there are differences in the archaeobotanical assemblages from these two types of contexts. Not only do the samples from ritual depositions contain far more plant remains than the ones from graves, the types of plants that are deposited also differ in character. Several tombs contained the remains of plants that that can be interpreted as agricultural waste, namely weeds and chaff remains (spikelet forks in all the tombs at Botromagno and grave 30 at Muro Tenente). The cereal depositions in the graves at Botromagno were also occasionally mixed with weed seeds. It is tempting to interpret this as a sign that the ritual meals that were deposited in these graves were not as carefully prepared as the ones for the deities. It can be counter argued that weeds are also present in the ritual deposit at Vaste, but on the other hand, most weed types from this assemblage (oat, brome, and rye) are edible grasses that are often found as 'contaminations' in cereal fields. It appears, therefore, that funerary contexts are similar to domestic ones in the sense that the composition of their archaeobotanical assemblages is also largely based on coincidence. This marks an important difference with the intentional deposition of food offerings and other ritual contexts.

---

[264] Solinas 2008, pp. 237 and 240. The cakes from Vaste consisted of small fragments of carbonized dough, characterized by a heterogeneous and loose structure, possibly indicating the use of rising agents. They were interpreted as pieces of bread or *focaccia*.

[265] Ciaraldi 1999, p. 84.

[266] Solinas 2008, p. 238.

[267] Ciaraldi 1999, p. 79.

[268] Ciaraldi 1997, pp. 219-220; Zohary and Hopf 2000, pp. 165-170. There has been some confusion about the presence of the dates in the ritual deposits of Monte Papalucio, but the most recent analyses by Fiorentino (2008, p. 106) confirm their presence.

Discussion: Differences between archaeobotanical finds in domestic contexts and contexts of ritual origin
The archaeobotanical finds support the hypothesis that intentional deposits often contain macroremains that are not, or rarely, found in domestic contexts, such as the carbonized bread and biscuits from the food offerings at Monte Papalucio.[269] Some of the bread fragments also had impressions of poppy and possibly sesame seeds on the surface. In addition, einkorn was used as decoration. Given that einkorn is one of the rarest cereal types in southeast Italy in this period (see section 5.3.2), it is interesting to note that it was found in ritual contexts at Vaste and in the graves of Botromagno.[270]

Without the finds from Monte Papalucio, we would have had little evidence of the cultivation and/or gathering of garlic, figs, pomegranates, and apples in this period. It needs to be added, however, that there are quite a few examples of terracotta replicas of these crops from ritual deposits in Italy and Greece (see below). Pomegranates were also found at Monte Papalucio and Vaste, while carbonized pomegranate wood was possibly present in grave 45 at Muro Tenente. Rather than explaining their rareness by a possible ritual significance, I would argue that these special contexts with large and varied archaeobotanical assemblages show that crops such as einkorn and fruits were, in fact, more common than the archaeobotanical records of other types of sites suggest. Several reasons can be given for why these assemblages are richer than those from domestic contexts. Firstly, since their original purpose was to serve as a last meal for the deceased or food offering for a deity, it can be assumed that these ritual depositions were assembled with care. This may be reflected in the presence of rare species or particularly abundant quantities of food. Secondly, ritual food offerings often involve the use of fire, which likely causes some of the food to carbonize and, hence, to remain preserved in the archaeological record. As Burkert[271] notes, the burning of food was an especially important part of the cult activities involving deities that were associated with the underworld, such as Demeter, Kore (Persephone), and Hades. Sacrifices to the gods and/or the dead often involved the butchering of animals, and the burning of fruits, vegetables, grains, and cakes, which were deposited in a pit (*bothros*) or hearth (*eschara*).[272]

Ritual connotations
The archaeobotanical assemblages from sanctuaries and graves illustrate that food is not only used for consumption, but also tends to have ritual connotations. In the present section, I will discuss the ritual use of cereals and bread, followed by pulses, fruits, and garlic. In addition, I will briefly examine plants that were used for medical purposes. The discussion is by no means meant to provide an exhaustive overview of all the references to the ritual use of plant products in ancient literature, but rather to highlight some interesting examples.

Firstly, a few remarks must be made about the wood fragments in these contexts. Most of the wood that was found in graves and ritual depositions can be interpreted as the remains of firewood that was used for the ritual burning of food offerings. It will be clear from the carbonized food remains that are discussed in this section that burning food was a common form of sacrifice, as fire played a purifying

---

[269] Ciaraldi 1999, pp. 86-87; Fiorentino 2008, p. 100.

[270] Colledge 2000, p. 60.

[271] Burkert 1977, p. 200. A considerable quantity of literature has been published on the use of animal and offerings in the ancient Greek and Roman world. See for example Bremmer 1994; Pedley 2005; Stavrianopoulou 2006; Schultz and Harvey 2006; Warrior 2009. For some of the bibliographical references in this paragraph, I am grateful to Kimberley van den Berg.

[272] Pedley 2005, p. 80.

[273] Cf. Sfameni Gasparro 1986, pp. 123-136.

[274] Apart from their possible ritual connotations, wood remains from these contexts can be used in the same way as the anthracological assemblages from other sites, i.e. to reconstruct the natural environment. For example, Fiorentino (2008, p. 103) has used the charcoal remains from Monte Papalucio to draw conclusions about climatic differences between the Archaic and Early Hel-

role.²⁷³ The only wood type that was found in all the contexts discussed here is olive, which is, as we have seen in section 5.3.1, particularly suitable and therefore widely used as fuel. The same holds true for oak. Most of the other wood types were only found in one or two different contexts.

It is possible, however, that some of this wood was not merely used as fuel but also because of its ritual significance.²⁷⁴ Pliny (A 6.33), and many other ancient writers report that trees were dedicated to one or several deities. Myrtle, which was found in abundance at Monte Papalucio, was used for funerary branches and wreaths and to decorate steles of the dead in ancient Greece.²⁷⁵ Moreover, myrtle symbolized immortality and, because it was sacred to Aphrodite, goddess of love and beauty, it symbolized love.²⁷⁶ The deposition of flowers and tree branches in graves is not unusual in the ancient Mediterranean. When the Pythagoreans buried their dead, they placed them on leaves of black poplar, olive, and myrtle, all trees sacred to underworld deities. These wood species have all been found at Monte Papalucio, but it is unclear how their presence must be interpreted, since the fragments are carbonized. Another type of wood that is associated with commemorative rituals is the pine tree, of which some charcoal fragments were found in grave 27 at Muro Tenente. Pine trees are very flammable but well adapted to fire, as the trees grow back very swiftly from the popped seeds released from their cones (see section 4.3.1). It is perhaps for this reason that in the ancient Mediterranean, the pine cone was associated with the wine god Dionysos.²⁷⁷ Dionysos is usually depicted holding a staff with a pine-cone on top.²⁷⁸ Pine nuts (*Pinus pinea*) were also a symbol of fertility and, as can be seen in a fragment from Ovid's *Art of Love* (A 6.41), known as an aphrodisiac.

I discussed the consumption of bread in ancient Greece, and the social status that may have been associated with different cereal preparations, in section 5.3.2. Apart from the common everyday meals that consisted of coarse wholemeal bread, porridges, gruels, and barley-cakes, more luxurious types of bread existed that were made of white flour and possible additions of cheese, honey, nuts, and olive oil. The use of cereals, bread and cakes as votive offerings is well attested in the ancient written sources.²⁷⁹ Especially relevant for our subject is a poem by Leonidas of Taras (A 6.10) that mentions the offering of barley cakes, and references the bread offerings that were associated with the cult of Demeter. As we have seen, Athenaeus describes a specific type of delicacy, *plakous*, as a 'golden, sweet, large, round, thick child of Demeter'²⁸⁰ that was 'luxuriating in countless delicately-compounded wrappings'²⁸¹(A 6.27 and 6.28). *Plakous* is on a list of foods that is described by Athenaeus as products that are customarily carried in the *liknophoria*, or carrying of the *liknon*, in a procession associated with the mysteries of Demeter. These foods include white poppy seeds, wheat, barley, peas, lentils, beans, emmer wheat, oats, honey, olive oil, wine, milk, and unwashed sheep's wool.²⁸² It was originally thought that there were carbonized remains of *plakous* among the food remains from Monte Papalucio,²⁸³ but this turned out not to be the case.²⁸⁴

Nevertheless, many other products from Athenaeus' list were found in the sanctuaries of Monte Papalucio and Vaste. For example, impressions of poppy- and possibly sesame seeds were found on the surface of one of the bread types from Monte Papalucio. These recall the sesame cakes that are

---

²⁷³ lenistic period. When comparing the two phases of the sanctuary, it appears that the more distinctly xerotermic elements (*Erica, Pistacia, Myrtus*, Leguminosae) predominate in the Hellenistic phase, whereas the charcoal assemblage from the Archaic phase is characterized by indicators of evergreen woodland (holm oak, Pomoideae).

²⁷⁵ Simoons 1998, p. 209: Plin. *HN* 35.160, Plu. *Arist.* 21.

²⁷⁶ Simoons 1998, p. 421, note 147.

²⁷⁷ Simoons 1998, p. 279.

²⁷⁸ Jashemski and Meyer 2002, p. 144.

²⁷⁹ Burkert 1977, pp. 115-119.

²⁸⁰ Athen. 137b-c, translation by Brumfield 1997, p. 152.

²⁸¹ Athen. 449c, translation by Charles Burton Gulick.

²⁸² Brumfield 1997, p. 148.

²⁸³ Ciaraldi 1999, pp. 86-87.

²⁸⁴ When these fragments were re-examined by Fiorentino (2008, p. 100), it was discovered that they were in fact not the remains of dough but heavily damaged charcoal fragments.

described as luxury food by Stesichorus, Anacreon, and Hipponax of Ephesus (A 6.16-18). Hipponax mentions them in contrast to 'barley cobs', which he considers 'slave's fodder' (A 6.18). The deposition of clay models of sacrificial cakes is known from several Greek sites, including the Sanctuary of Demeter and Kore on Acrocorinth.[285] Presumably, the terracotta cakes were dedicated as a memorial of the ceremony in which real cakes were sacrificed. The clay cakes from the Acrocorinth are similar in form to those from Monte Papalucio, and also include a bread type that looks like *plakous*.[286]

Apparently, Leonidas of Taras did not think much of barley-cakes either, because they are the first item on the list of offerings that he associates with his 'pauper' self (A 6.10). Does this mean that we should consider all barley products 'pauper' food that was unfit for the gods? Probably not. Barley was found in the votive deposits in all the sanctuaries in southeast Italy that are discussed here. Moreover, there are also references to barley offerings in the ancient texts. Pausanias reports that at Eleusis, there were sacred fields where barley was grown to make such sacrificial cakes (A 6.42).[287] In several of Euripides' 'tragedies', barley grains are thrown on the altar, or more precisely into the fire that is already burning on it (A 6.45-47).[288] The same ritual is mentioned by Pausanias (A 6.43)[289] and in Aristophanes' *Peace*[290] (A 6.48). The existence of sacred fields, as mentioned by Pausanias, has also been suggested for Monte Papalucio. Einkorn grains that were used as decorations on some of the carbonized cakes and biscuits were, according to Ciaraldi, cultivated exclusively for religious purposes.[291]

Pulses that are extremely rare in domestic contexts, such as peas and chickpeas, do appear in the votive deposits at Monte Papalucio and Pantanello. This suggests, again, that they may not have been as rare as the archaeological record suggests. In ancient Greece and Rome, broad beans were associated with funerary and commemorative rituals. They are indeed found in contexts at all the sites discussed in this section, with the exceptions of Botromagno and Vaste. In book 18 of his *Natural History*, Pliny dedicates an entire chapter to broad beans, describing their use as food as well as the particularities that were associated with them (A 6.33). As Simoons has pointed out, the association of beans with the underworld and its use in funerary rituals is also described by many other Roman and Greek authors.[292]

---

[285] These clay cakes were placed in miniature clay likna, or winnowing baskets. Votive likna were dedicated in the sanctuary from the early 6th century BC, if not earlier, until the 2nd century BC. Brumfield 1997, p. 147.

[286] Athen. 449b-c, interpretation by Brumfield (1997, p. 152). As we have seen above, one of the types of dough from Monte Papalucio was originally also interpreted as the remains of *plakous*, but was eventually identified as charcoal (Fiorentino 2008, p. 100).

[287] Ciaraldi 1999, p. 32.

[288] Van Straten 1995, p. 38 (notes 77 and 78).

[289] Pausanias I 24, 4. Cf. Van Straten 1995, p. 51.

[290] Van Straten 1995, pp. 33-40.

[291] Ciaraldi 1999; Coubray 2001.

[292] Simoons 1998, p. 200, note 50: Lucian. *DMort* 6 (20).3, Plu. 4.286 *E*95, Cic. *Div*. 2.119. The ban on beans among Pythagoreans is particularly interesting. Apparently, followers of Pythagoras (580-500 BC) at the Achaean colony Kroton (modern Crotone in Calabria) were forbidden to eat broad beans. According to Aristotle, there were several reasons for this ban, all relating to life, reproduction and death. Simoons (1998, pp. 199-200) lists several of these reasons, such as the belief that their form resembles the universe, which might mean that they were regarded as living matter; that they are similar to 'the gates of Hades' in that they alone are 'unjointed'; that they look like testicles in their internal structure; that they harbour the souls of the dead, and much more. It has also been suggested that the ban had a political connotation, or rather an apolitical one. Since beans were used in voting, in place of balls or pebbles, the recommendation not to eat them could be interpreted as Pythagoras asking his disciples to abstain from politics (cf. John Bostock and H.T. Riley, www.perseus.tufts.edu, *NH* 18.30 (12), note 5). The Pythagorean ban on beans has also been interpreted from a much more practical point of view, i.e. to avoid illness among followers suffering from favism (Simoons 1998, pp. 218-249). Favism is a disorder characterized by a haemolytic reaction (the abnormal breakdown of red blood cells) to consumption of broad beans. The underlying cause is an enzyme defect called glucose-6-phosphate dehydrogenase (G6PD) deficiency.

 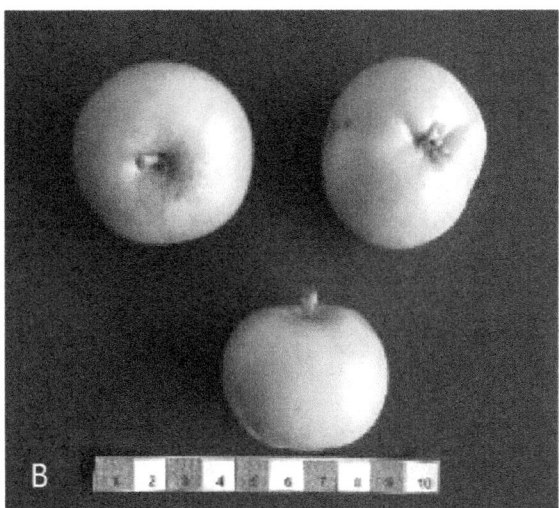

Fig. 5.9a. Terracotta 'San Giovanni' Apples from the Mannella Sanctuary at Lokroi Epizephyrioi. Meirano 2008, 142, Figure 6.
Fig. 5.9b. Modern San Giovanni apples.

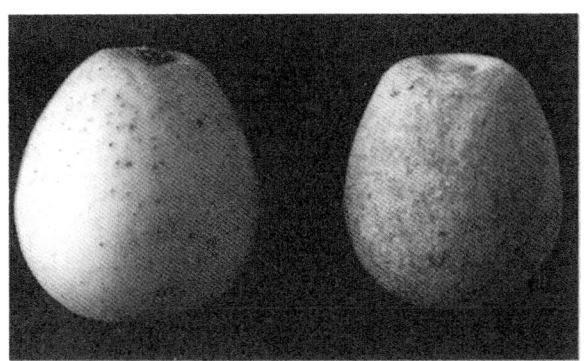 

Fig. 5.10. Terracotta 'Limoncella' apples from the Mannella Sanctuary at Lokroi Epizephyrioi. Meirano 2008, 142, Figure 7.

Fig. 5.11. Terracotta apple from Olympia. Drawing by the author after Furtwängler 1890, no. 1183, pl. LXVIII.

Fig. 5.12. Terracotta fruit (apple?) from Lindos, 525-400 BC. Drawing by the author after Blinkenberg 1931, no. 2441.

Fig. 5.13. Terracotta pomegranate from the Prytaneion in Olympia. Drawing by the author after Bol 1978, 668, 130, pl. 61.

The archaeobotanical assemblages from ritual depositions are especially informative regarding the consumption of fruits. In particular, grape pips and olive stones often appear in sanctuaries and funerary contexts. Olives were found in the votive deposits at Monte Papalucio (although only in small quantities) and in grave 30 at Muro Tenente. In addition, olive stones appeared in relative abundance in the cult place at Vaste, although the total quantity of fragments (59) probably represents no more than about 15 stones.[293] The 'olives easy to store' that are mentioned in the poem by Leonidas of Taras (A 6.10) must have been fresh or, more likely, pickled. Beside fresh grapes, wine was probably often used in rituals. Drinking cups, pouring vessels, and other pottery shapes that are related to wine consumption were found, for instance, in the ritual meal deposition at l'Amastuola, in the *bothroi* at Vaste, and at Monte Papalucio. In addition, there are numerous references to libations in the ancient texts. At the same time, it can be concluded from the Homeric hymn that wine drinking was forbidden during the mysteries of Demeter (A 6.25).[294] The ritual deposits from this site reflect the common use of fruit offerings. Ritual depositions of fruit are also frequently mentioned in ancient texts including, again, the same poem by Leonidas. According to Pausanias, the fig was sacred to Demeter (A 6.44).

Terracotta replicas of apples and pomegranates are also found in sanctuaries. For example, at the sanctuary of Mannella near Lokroi Epizephyrioi small spherical terracotta objects with deep vertical grooves were found that bear a strong resemblance to a type of green apple (named San Giovanni) that is still cultivated today in Italy (*Figure 5.9*). Another type of apple-like terracotta from the same sanctuary rather looks like the modern 'limoncella' apple (*Figure 5.10*).[295] Raubitschek reports the finds of several apple-like votives from Olympia and Lindos (*Figures 5.11-5.13*).[296] Comparable terracotta votives in the shape of apples or pomegranates have been found in southeast Italy, for instance at Taranto (*Figure 5.14*) and in a grave at Oria (tomb 1973-3), datable to the middle of the 2nd century BC (*Figure 5.15*).[297] In some cases, it is hard to say whether these models are supposed to represent apples, pomegranates, or even garlic bulbs. The spherical object in *Figure 5.13*, which was found north of the Prytaneion at Olympia, is tentatively identified as a pomegranate. Depictions of pomegranates can also be found on tomb paintings, notably at Paestum, but also at Taras (*Figure 5.16*).[298] Apart from its association with funerary rituals, the pomegranate was also considered to be a symbol of fertility.[299] It is associated with the myth of Persephone, since Demeter's daughter ate a few grains of a pomegranate when she was abducted by Hades into the underworld. This is probably the reason why fasting women during the Thesmophoria were only allowed to eat pomegranate seeds.[300]

Since this defect is hereditary, it is possible that it was common among Pythagoreans and/or that Pythagoras himself suffered from it. In any case, the ban on beans was not exclusive to Pythagoreans. Their consumption was also forbidden among participants in the Haloa festival in honour of Demeter, Persephone and Dionysus, and initiates of the Eleusinian mysteries of Demeter.

[293] Solinas 2008, p. 238: experiments have shown that olive stones generally break into 4 pieces when they are fractured.

[294] Fiorentino (2008, p. 105) suggests that the presence of grapes in the votive deposits of Monte Papalucio may indicate that it was Persephone rather than Demeter who was worshiped here, even though the taboo applied to wine and not to grapes.

[295] Meirano 2008, p. 142.

[296] Raubitschek 1998, p. 11.

[297] This tomb is believed to have been fundamentally early 3rd-century with secondary interment of the first half to mid-2nd century BC, but Yntema (2009, *Figure 9*, p. 155) interprets them as mid-2nd century tombs in which much older objects were purposely incorporated.

[298] Ciaraldi 1999, p. 85; Pontrandolfo, Rouveret and Cipriani 1992.

[299] Zohary and Hopf 2000, p. 17.

[300] '[...] just as the women, in celebrating the Thesmophoria, abstain from eating the seeds of the pomegranate which have fallen on the ground, from the idea that pomegranates sprang from the drops of the blood of Dionysus.' Clement of Alexandria, Protrepticus 2.22. Translation by Alexander Roberts and James Donaldson, www.ellopos.net. Cf. Lazongas 2005, p. 104.

Fig. 5.14. Terracotta votive objects, Museo Nazionale di Taranto. Drawing by the author after Forti and Stazio 1983, Figures 728, 703.

Fig. 5.15. Terracotta pomegranates and garlic bulbs (?) from a grave in Oria (tomb 1973-3), middle of the 2nd century BC. Yntema 2009, Figure 9, 155.

The connotation with funerary rituals is also evident for garlic. The garlic cloves from l'Amastuola are another example of a food item from a ritual deposition that has never been found in a domestic context. Although archaeobotanical finds of garlic are rare, several clay and ivory models of garlic bulbs are known from Greek sanctuaries, including the Temple of Poseidon at Isthmia (*Figure 5.17*) and that of Hera Limenia at Perachora (*Figure 5.18*).[301] Other fruit models from sanctuaries that may be interpreted as garlic bulbs, were found near Lousoi in Greece (*Figure 5.19*) and at Olympia (*Figure 5.20*), and in Egypt (*Figures 5.21* and *5.22*).

[301] Raubitschek 1998, p. 11.

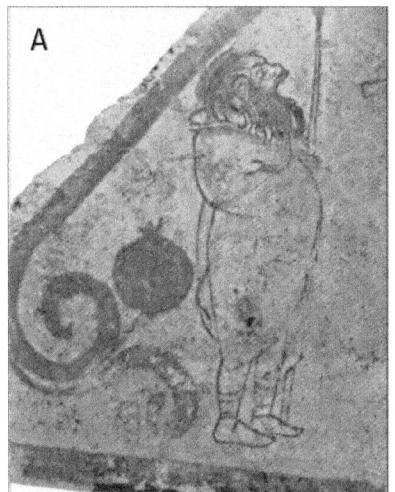

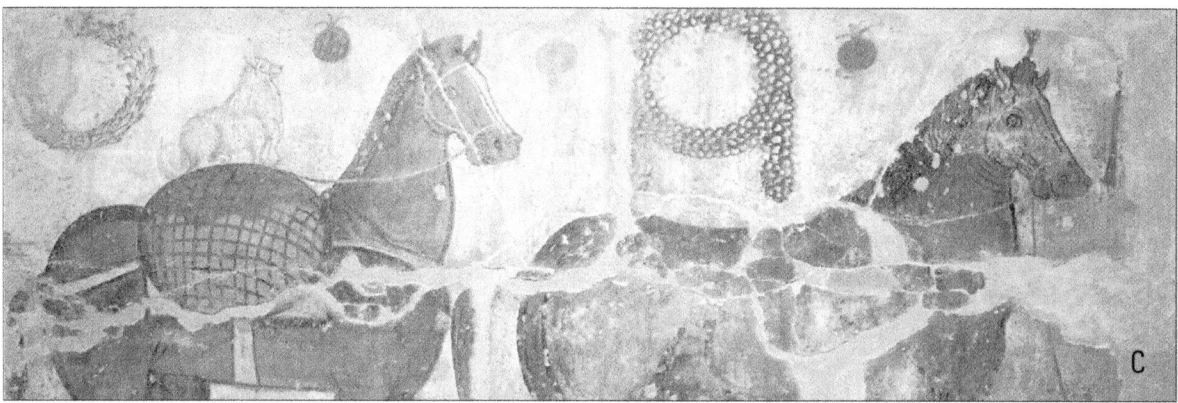

Fig. 5.16 The pomegranate in tomb paintings. Pontrandolfo, Rouveret and Cipriani 1992, 56, Figure 55; 34, Figure 28; 72, Figure 71.

A Paestum, *necropolis* of Andriulo: Braggart soldier (tomb 53, east wall);

B Paestum, *necropolis* of Vannullo: Return of the warrior (tomb 4, west wall).

C Taranto, *necropolis* of Spinazzo, left wall of a tomb: Cortege of horses, late 4th century BC.

Indeed, the association of garlic with underworld forces, darkness, and evil goes much further back than Bram Stoker's *Dracula* (1897). In many cultures, garlic and its relatives are considered impure and linked to the underworld, which means that they are usually suitable for offering to underworld deities, in seeking their protection, divining their intentions, repelling them, or eliminating the evil they brought on.[302] Pliny remarks that Egyptians took oaths on garlic (and onions), a habit that may be comparable to the present-day Mediterranean custom of swearing by bread and salt.[303] There is also an inscription from the 4th century BC that refers to the use of garlic by the chief priestesses at the Thesmophoria in the *deme* Cholargos in Attica. Unfortunately, the inscription is incomplete. The part that explains what the purpose of these goods was (to be used for a ritual meal, or as a food offering?) is missing (A 6.24).

---

[302] Simoons (1998, pp. 136-157) discusses garlic as an impure food in numerous areas from Europe to China.

[303] Darby *et al.* 1976, p. 660. 'Garlic and onions are invoked by the Egyptians, when taking an oath, in the number of their deities.' Pl. *HN* 19.XXXII. Translation by John Bostock and H.T. Riley, www.perseus.tufts.edu. Most references to garlic in ancient texts that I quote in this paragraph are taken from Crawford 1973.

Fig. 5.17. Lead garlic bulb from Isthmia, Greece (Sanctuary of Poseidon), 4th century BC. Raubitschek 1998, pp. 11 (nr. 40); courtesy of the American School of Classical Studies at Athens.

Fig. 5.18. Lead 'knob of uncertain use' (garlic bulb?) from the sanctuary of Hera Limenia at Perachora. Drawing by the author after Payne and Dunbabin 1940, p. 186, pl. 85:12.

Fig. 5.19. Bronze 'poppy' (garlic bulb?) with votive inscription (meaning unknown), 3rd-2nd century BC. Drawing by the author after Mitten and Doeringer 1967, nr. 152 (p. 146).

Fig. 5.20. Terracotta object (garlic bulb?) from Olympia. Drawing by the author after Furtwängler 1890, p. 186, no. 1261.

Fig. 5.21. Clay models of garlic bulbs (?) from Egypt. Drawing by the author after Flinders Petrie 1920, pl. 46, no. 23-24.

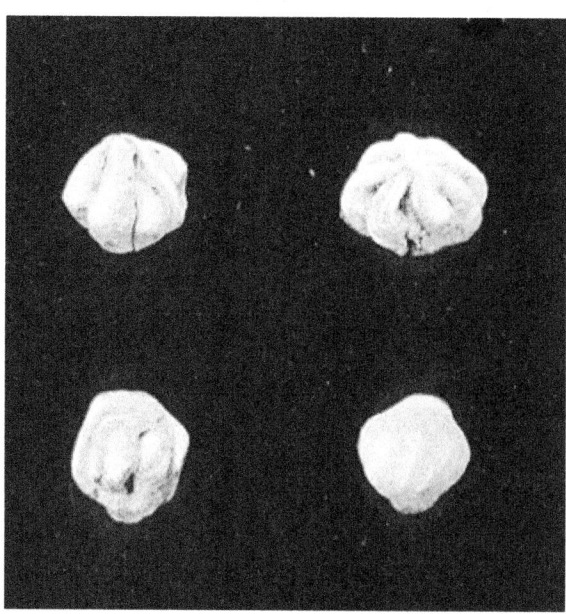

Fig. 5.22. Clay models of garlic bulbs (?) from the Predynastic cemetery at El Mahasna, Egypt. Ayrton and Loat 1911, pl. 17.

Garlic was also used for medical purposes, some of which are listed by Aristophanes.[304] Dioscurides also lists countless medical applications for the cloves,[305] and the entire twenty-third chapter of the twentieth book of Pliny's *Natural history* is dedicated to it, mentioning that 'the very smell of it drives away serpents and scorpions' (A 6.35). The Romans may also have considered garlic as an aphrodisiac. In Ovid's *Art of Love*, several stimulants are listed, including eggs, honey and pine nuts, and a 'white bulb from Megara' (*'candidus Alcathoi urbe Pelasga bulbus'*). This passage is usually translated as 'white onion'[306] or even 'grape-hyacinth',[307] but in my opinion the reference to Megara (which was regarded as the centre of garlic cultivation in Classical Greece, see note 141) probably indicates that Ovid is talking about garlic, and not onion.

Conclusion

Archaeobotanical assemblages from ritual depositions and graves offer a perspective on the crop spectrum that differs significantly from those offered by domestic contexts. In fact, it can be argued that both types of contexts complement each other in studies of land use. The former type offers a different perspective on the use of plant materials that goes beyond their role as daily foodstuffs. As we have seen, this creates exciting new insights into the availability of certain crops (e.g. dates, figs, chickpeas, and crab apples) and into food preparations (e.g. bread and cakes). Especially the discovery of garlic cloves in a ritual meal deposition at l'Amastuola is striking. The plant remains from ritual depositions shed light on the ritual connotations assigned to various fruits, types of wood, and ways of food preparation. For example, the association of broad beans and garlic with the underworld is

[304] *A.* 163-6 and *Eq.* 494 (as a stimulating ointment), *Pl.* 714-25 and *Ec.* 404 (to soothe a black eye: 'Grind up garlic and figs and add Spartan spurge, and rub it on your eyelids at bedtime'), *V.* 1172 (to cure a skin boil).

[305] Jashemski and Meyer 2002, pp. 87-88. *Dsc.* 2.152.

[306] Translation by J. Lewis May, www.sacred-texts.com.

[307] Translation by Andrew Dalby, dalby.pagesperso-orange.fr.

particularly clear and ritual food offerings to the gods often included apples, pomegranates, grapes and/or wine. Although we know of these foods from ancient written sources, they have never been found in archaeobotanical samples from domestic contexts. This can partly be explained by the frequent use of fire in ritual food offerings, but we can also assume that the meals that were prepared as offerings to the dead or the divine were assembled with considerable care.

Indeed, we have seen many examples of rare ingredients in these offerings. For example, in the food depositions from Monte Papalucio einkorn and impressions of poppy and possibly sesame seeds were found. On the other hand, ritual meals that were deposited in graves were usually rather poor and included weed seeds and chaff remains. It appears that archaeobotanical assemblages from funerary contexts are similar to the ones from domestic contexts, which marks an important difference between the two types of samples that I discussed in this section.

TABLES CHAPTER 5

period	Recent Bronze Age		Final Bronze Age and Early Iron Age		
site	Broglio di Trebisacce 1	Torre Mordillo 2	Broglio di Trebisacce 2	Torre Mordillo 3	
conservation of macroremains	carbonized	carbonized	carbonized	carbonized	
sampling method	random	random	random	random	
sieving method	wet sieving: 5, 2.5, 1.5 and in one case 0.5 mm meshes	flotation	wet sieving: 5, 2.5, 1.5 and in one case 0.5 mm meshes	flotation	
context	settlement	settlement	settlement	settlement	
location	coastal area of northern Calabria	inland Basilicata	coastal area of northern Calabria	inland Basilicata	
date	1350-1200 BC	1350-1000 BC	1200-700 BC	1200-700 BC	
cereals					**common name**
Hordeum vulgare		*			hulled barley
Hordeum sp.	*			*	barley
Hordeum vulgare var. nudum	*				naked barley
Triticum aestivum	*	*		*	bread wheat
Triticum dicoccum		*		*	emmer wheat
Triticum cf. durum	*				macaroni wheat
Triticum sp.	*	*	*		wheat
pulses					
Lathyrus sp.	*				vetchling
Lens culinaris	*				lentil
Vicia cf. cracca	*				bird vetch
Vicia faba var. minor		*			broad bean
Vicia ervilia	*	*			bitter vetch
Vicia/Lathyrus	*				vetch/vetchling
fruits					
Ficus carica		*			fig
Olea europaea	*		*	*	olive
nuts					
Juglans regia	*				walnut
Quercus sp.	*	*		*	acorn

Table 5.1. Part 1: Archaeobotanical macroremains of cultivated plants from southeast Italy. Part 1: Recent-Final Bronze Age; Early Iron Age (c. 1350-700 BC).

period	Early Iron Age						
site	Botromagno 1	l'Incoronata	L'Amastuola 1	Torre di Satriano 1	Monte Irsi	Cavallino	
conservation of macroremains	carbonized	carbonized	carbonized	carbonized	carbonized	carbonized	
sampling method	random	random	systematic	random	random	systematic (in one area)	
sieving method	flotation: 1.18 mm and 300 μm meshes	unknown	flotation: 5 and 1 mm meshes	unknown	unknown	flotation: 4 and 0.5 mm meshes	
context	settlement	settlement	settlement	settlement	settlement	settlement	
location	inland area of northern Apulia	inland Basilicata	Province of Taranto, northwestern Apulia	Province of Potenza, Basilicata	Province of Matera, Basilicata	inland Salento, province of Lecce	
date	900-600 BC	late 8th- early 7th century BC	late 8th -end of the 7th century BC	late 8th- early 7th century BC	Mid-7th century BC	750-480/450 BC	
cereals							**common name**
Hordeum vulgare	*	*	*		*	*	hulled barley
Hordeum sp.			*	*			barley
Triticum aestivum/compactum	*		*			*	free-threshing wheat
Triticum dicoccum	*	*	*	*	*	*	emmer wheat
Triticum monococcum/ dicoccum	*						einkorn/ emmer wheat
Triticum monococcum	*						einkorn
Triticum cf. spelta	*						spelt wheat
Triticum sp.	*						wheat
pulses							
Cicer arietinum					*?		chickpea
Lens sp.				*			
Pisum sativum				*		*	field pea
Vicia faba var. minor		*	*	*	*	*	broad bean
Vicia ervilia			*		*	*	bitter vetch
Vicia/Lathyrus	*	*					vetch/vetchling
Vicia sp.		*	*				vetch
fruits							
Olea europaea						*	olive
Vitis vinifera		*	*			*	grape
nuts							
Fagus sylv.				*			beech-nut
condiments							
Allium sativum			*				garlic
forage crops							
Avena			*				oat
Medicago			*				medick
Secale cereale			*				rye

Table 5.1. Part 2: Early Iron Age (c. 900–600 BC).

site	Torre di Satriano 2	l'Amastuola 2	Botromagno 2	Monte Papalucio 1	Botromagno 3	Pizzica Pantanello 1	
conservation of macroremains	carbonized	carbonized	carbonized	carbonized	carbonized	waterlogged	
sampling method	random	systematic	random	random (early excavations) systematic (recent excavations)	random	systematic	
sieving method	unknown	flotation: 5 and 1 mm meshes	flotation: 1.18 mm and 300 μm meshes	dry sieving: 2 mm meshes (early excavations) flotation: 0,2 mm meshes (recent excavations)	flotation: 1.18 mm and 300 μm meshes	flotation: 4, 2, 1 and 0.5 mm meshes	
context	settlement	settlement	settlement	sanctuary	settlement	refuse deposit?	
location	Province of Potenza, Basilicata	Province of Taranto, northwestern Apulia	inland area of northern Apulia	inland Salento, province of Brindisi	inland area of northern Apulia	Metapontino, Basilicata	
date	6th century BC	early 6th-first half 5th century BC	600-400 BC	Mid-6th-early 5th century BC	400-300 BC	4th century BC	
cereals							common name
Hordeum vulgare		*	*	*	*	*	hulled barley
Hordeum sp.	*	*					barley
Triticum aestivum/compactum		*	*	*	*		free-threshing wheat
Triticum aestivum/durum				*			bread/ macaroni wheat
Triticum compactum						*	club wheat
Triticum dicoccum	*	*		*		*	emmer wheat
T. monococcum/dicoccum			*	*	*		einkorn/ emmer wheat
Triticum monococcum					*		einkorn
Triticum cf. spelta				*			spelt wheat
Triticum sp.			*		*		wheat
pulses							
Cicer arietinum				*			chickpea
Lathyrus sp.							vetchling
Lens culinaris	*	*					lentil
Pisum sativum	*			*		*	field pea
Vicia faba var. minor	*	*		*			broad bean
Vicia ervilia		*					bitter vetch
Vicia/Lathyrus				*			vetch/vetchling
Vicia sp.		*					vetch
fruits							
Ficus carica				*		*	fig
Malus cf. sylvestris				*			crab apple
Olea europaea		*		*		*	olive
Cf. Phoenix dactylifera				*			date
Punica granatum				*			pomegranate

site	Torre di Satriano 2	l'Amastuola 2	Botromagno 2	Monte Papalucio 1	Botromagno 3	Pizzica Pantanello 1	
conservation of macroremains	carbonized	carbonized	carbonized	carbonized	carbonized	waterlogged	
sampling method	random	systematic	random	random (early excavations) systematic (recent excavations)	random	systematic	
sieving method	unknown	flotation: 5 and 1 mm meshes	flotation: 1.18 mm and 300 μm meshes	dry sieving: 2 mm meshes (early excavations) flotation: 0,2 mm meshes (recent excavations)	flotation: 1.18 mm and 300 μm meshes	flotation: 4, 2, 1 and 0.5 mm meshes	
context	settlement	settlement	settlement	sanctuary	settlement	refuse deposit?	
location	Province of Potenza, Basilicata	Province of Taranto, northwestern Apulia	inland area of northern Apulia	inland Salento, province of Brindisi	inland area of northern Apulia	Metapontino, Basilicata	
date	6th century BC	early 6th-first half 5th century BC	600-400 BC	Mid-6th-early 5th century BC	400-300 BC	4th century BC	
cereals							common name
Vitis vinifera	*	*		*		*	grape
nuts							
Fagus sylv.	*						beech-nut
forage crops							
Avena		*					oat
Medicago		*					medick

Table 5.1. Part 3: Archaic/Classical Periods.

site	Monte Papalucio 2	Vaste, Piazza Dante	Roccagloriosa	Pomarico vecchio	
conservation of macroremains	carbonized	carbonized	carbonized	carbonized	
sampling method	random (early) systematic (recent)	100%	systematic	100%	
sieving method	dry sieving: 2 mm meshes (early) flotation: 0,2 mm meshes (recent)	flotation: 4 and 0.5 mm meshes	wet sieving: mesh width unknown	flotation: mesh width unknown	
context	sanctuary	sanctuary	settlement	settlement	
location	inland Salento, province of Brindisi	inland Salento, province of Lecce	southern Campania	inland Basilicata, province of Matera	
date	2nd half 4th-1st half 3rd century BC	4th-3rd century BC	4th-3rd century BC	4th-3rd century BC	
cereals					**common name**
Hordeum vulgare	*		*	*	hulled barley
Hordeum sp.		*	*		barley
Hordeum vulgare var. nudum					naked barley
Triticum aestivum/compactum	*			*	free-threshing wheat
Triticum aestivum/ durum	*	*			bread/ macaroni wheat
Triticum compactum			*		club wheat
Triticum dicoccum		*	*		emmer wheat
Triticum monococcum/ dicoccum	*				einkorn/ emmer wheat
Triticum monococcum		*	*		einkorn
Triticum sp.		*	*		wheat
Panicum sp.			*		millet
pulses					
Cicer arietinum	*				chickpea
Lathyrus sp.			*		vetchling
Lens culinaris		*	*		lentil
Pisum sativum	*				field pea
cf. Pisum sp.			*		pea
Vicia faba var. minor	*		*		broad bean
Vicia ervilia		*			bitter vetch
Vicia/Lathyrus	*				vetch/vetchling
Vicia sp.		*			vetch
fruits					
Ficus carica	*		*		fig
Malus cf. sylvestris	*				crab apple
Olea europaea	*	*	*		olive
Punica granatum	*	*			pomegranate
Vitis vinifera	*	*	*	*	grape
Rosaceae					
forage crops					
Avena		*			oat
Medicago		*			medick
Secale cereale		*			rye

Table 5.1 Part 4: Early Hellenistic Period (a).

site	Pizzica Pantanello 2	Pizzica Pantanello 3	Muro Tenente	
conservation of macroremains	waterlogged	waterlogged	carbonized	
sampling method	systematic	systematic	systematic	
sieving method	flotation: 4, 2, 1 and 0.5 mm meshes	flotation: 4, 2, 1 and 0.5 mm meshes	flotation: 5 and 1 mm meshes	
context	refuse deposit?	refuse deposit?	settlement	
location	Metapontino, Basilicata	Metapontino, Basilicata	inland Salento, province of Brindisi	
date	early 3rd century BC	late 3rd century BC	4th-2nd century BC	
cereals				common name
Hordeum vulgare	*	*	*	hulled barley
Hordeum sp.			*	barley
Hordeum vulgare var. nudum			*	naked barley
Triticum aestivum/compactum			*	free-threshing wheat
Triticum aestivum/durum				bread/ macaroni wheat
Triticum compactum	*	*		club wheat
Triticum dicoccum		*	*	emmer wheat
Triticum monococcum/dicoccum				einkorn/ emmer wheat
Triticum monococcum				einkorn
Triticum sp.				wheat
Panicum sp.				millet
pulses				
Cicer arietinum		*		chickpea
Lathyrus sp.				vetchling
Lens culinaris		*		lentil
Pisum sativum		*		field pea
cf. Pisum sp.				pea
Vicia faba var. minor	*	*	*	broad bean
Vicia ervilia		*	*	bitter vetch
Vicia/Lathyrus				vetch/vetchling
Vicia sp.			*	vetch
fruits				
Ficus carica	*	*		fig
Malus cf. sylvestris				crab apple
Olea europaea	*	*	*	olive
Punica granatum				pomegranate
Vitis vinifera	*	*	*	grape
Rosaceae			*	
forage crops				
Avena		*	*	oat
Medicago	*	*		medick
Secale cereale			*	rye

Table 5.1 Part 5: Early Hellenistic Period (b).

period	Recent and Final Bronze Age	Final Bronze Age and Early Iron Age	Early Iron Age			
site	Broglio di Trebisacce 1	Broglio di Trebisacce 2	Botromagno 1	Cavallino	l'Amastuola 1	
date	1350-1200 BC	1200-700 BC	900-600 BC	750-480/450 BC	late 8th -end of the 7th century BC	
taxa						common name
weeds in arable fields						
Agrostemma githago				*		corncockle
Adonis sp./ cf. annua					*	(autumn) adonis
Ajuga/Teucrium			*			bugleweed/germanders
Avena sp.					*	wild oat
Buglossoides arvensis			*			corn gromwell
Consolida regalis	*					forking larkspur
Hordeum sp. (weed type)			*			wild barley
Lathyrus sp.	*					vetchling
Lolium cf. perenne/ rigidum			*		*	ryegrass
Polygonum sp.	*		*			knotweed
Secale cereale					*	rye
Umbelliferae			*			carrot family
Vicia narborensis		*				purple broad vetch
uncultivated or abandoned zones						
Arnoseris minima		*				lamb's succory
Borago officinalis		*				borage
Chenopodium urbicum		*				upright goosefoot
Fumaria capreolata	*					white ramping-fumitory
Lepidium campestre		*				field pepperweed
Malva sp.					*	mallow
Rumex sp.		*	*			sorrel
cultivated ground, waste places, waysides						
Chenopodium album				*		white goosefoot
Medicago hispida					*	bur medick
wetlands						
Sagittaria sp.	*					arrowhead
Scirpus sp.			*			bulrush
Possible forage crops						
Bromus sp.	*					brome
Phalaris sp.			*		*	canarygrass
Other						
Brassica sp.	*					cabbages/mustards
Euphorbiaceae	*					spurge family
Rosa sp.	*					rose

Table 5.2 Archaeobotanical micro- and macroremains of wild plants from southeast Italy. Part 1: Recent Bronze Age, Final Bronze Age, Early Iron Age.

period	Archaic/Classical periods				
site	Botromagno 2	l'Amastuola 2	Botromagno 3	Pizzica Pantanello 1	
date	600-400 BC	early 6th-first half 5th century BC	400-300 BC	4th century BC	
taxa					common name
weeds in arable fields					
Adonis sp./ cf. annua		*			(autumn) adonis
Avena sp.		*			wild oat
Arenaria sp.			*		sandwort
Buglossoides arvensis			*		corn gromwell
Lolium cf. perenne/rigidum	*		*		ryegrass
Lolium temulentum				*	darnel
Sonchus sp.				*	sow thistle
uncultivated or abandoned zones					
Euphorbia helioscopia				*	sun spurge
Liguliflorae (pollen)				*	subfamily of Compositae
Rumex sp.	*	*			sorrel
cultivated ground, waste places, waysides					
Heliotropium sp.		*			heliotrope
Medicago hispida		*			bur medick
wetlands					
Alisma sp. (pollen)				*	water-plantain
Carex sp.				*	sedge
Ceratophyllium demersum				*	coontail
Lythrum sp. (pollen)				*	loosestrife
Sagittaria sp. (pollen)				*	arrowhead
Scirpus sp.	*		*		bulrush
Typha (pollen)				*	cattail
Zannichellia sp.				*	horned pond weed
grazing indicators					
Centaurea sp. (pollen)				*	knapweed
Plantago sp. (pollen)				*	plantain
Mediterranean macchia					
Phillyrea sp. (pollen)				*	phillyrea
Pistacia sp. (pollen)				*	
Pistacia lentiscus		*			mastic
Possible forage crops					
Bromus sp.		*			brome
Phalaris sp.	*		*		canarygrass
Other					
Acer (pollen)				*	maple
Chenopodium	*		*		goosefoot
Compositae (pollen)				*	aster, daisy, or sunflower family
Cyperaceae (pollen)				*	sedges family
Euphorbiaceae		*			spurge family

period	Archaic/Classical periods				
site	Botromagno 2	l'Amastuola 2	Botromagno 3	Pizzica Pantanello 1	
date	600-400 BC	early 6th-first half 5th century BC	400-300 BC	4th century BC	
taxa					common name
Labiatae (pollen)				*	mint family
Liliaceae (small seeded)		*			lily family
Pinus sp. (pollen)				*	pine
Quercus sp. (pollen)				*	oak
Ranunculus sp.				*	buttercup family
Rubus sp.				*	blackberry

Table 5.2 Part 2: Archaic/Classical periods (c. 600-325 BC).

period	Early Hellenistic Period			
site	Roccagloriosa	Vaste	Pomarico vecchio	
date	4th-3rd century BC	4th-3rd century BC	4th-3rd century BC	
taxa				common name
weeds in arable fields				
Adonis sp./ cf. annua			*	(autumn) adonis
Avena sp.	*	*		wild oat
Galium aparine	*			stickyweed
Lathyrus sativus/cicera	*			grass/red pea
Lathyrus sp.				vetchling
Lolium temulentum				darnel
Polygonum sp.	*		*	knotweed
Secale cereale				rye
Sonchus sp.				sow thistle
Umbelliferae			*	carrot family
Umbelliferae (pollen)			*	carrot family
Dry, stony grounds				
Echium sp.			*	bugloss
Lathyrus aphaca	*			yellow vetch
uncultivated or abandoned zones				
Euphorbia helioscopia	*			sun spurge
Fumaria sp.			*	fumitory
Liguliflorae (pollen)				subfamily of Compositae
Malva sp.			*	mallow
cultivated ground, waste places, waysides				
Chenopodium album	*			white goosefoot
grazing indicators				
Centaurea sp. (pollen)				knapweed
Dipsacaceae (pollen)			*	teasel family
Plantago sp. (pollen)			*	plantain
Mediterranean macchia				
Phillyrea sp. (pollen)				phillyrea
Pistacia sp. (pollen)				
Pistacia lentiscus				mastic
Possible forage crops				
Bromus sp.		*		brome
Medicago sp.				medick
Other				
Acer (pollen)				maple
Bifora sp.			*	?
Cannabaceae (pollen)			*	hemp family
Chenopodium sp.			*	goosefoot
Compositae (pollen)				aster, daisy, or sunflower family
Cyperaceae (pollen)				sedges family
Galium sp.				bedstraw
Labiatae (pollen)				mint family
Liliaceae (pollen)			*	lily family

period	Early Hellenistic Period			
site	Roccagloriosa	Vaste	Pomarico vecchio	
date	4th-3rd century BC	4th-3rd century BC	4th-3rd century BC	
taxa				common name
Pinus sp. (pollen)				pine
Quercus sp. (pollen)				oak
Rubus sp.				blackberry

Table 5.2 Part 3: Early Hellenistic Period (c. 325-200 BC) (a).

period	Early Hellenistic Period			
site	Muro Tenente	Pizzica Pantanello 2	Pizzica Pantanello 3	
date	4th-2nd century BC	early 3rd century BC	late 3rd century BC	
taxa				common name
weeds in arable fields				
Adonis sp./ cf. annua			*	(autumn) adonis
Avena sp.	*		*	wild oat
Galium aparine				stickyweed
Lathyrus sativus/cicera				grass/red pea
Lathyrus sp.		*	*	vetchling
Lolium temulentum		*	*	darnel
Polygonum sp.		*	*	knotweed
Secale cereale	*			rye
Sonchus sp.		*		sow thistle
Umbelliferae				carrot family
Umbelliferae (pollen)				carrot family
Dry, stony grounds				
Echium sp.				bugloss
Lathyrus aphaca				yellow vetch
uncultivated or abandoned zones				
Euphorbia helioscopia		*	*	sun spurge
Fumaria sp.				fumitory
Liguliflorae (pollen)		*	*	subfamily of Compositae
Malva sp.				mallow
cultivated ground, waste places, waysides				
Chenopodium album				white goosefoot
wetlands				
Alisma sp. (pollen)		*		water-plantain
Carex sp.		*		sedge
Ceratophyllium demersum		*		coontail
Lythrum (pollen)		*		loosestrife
Sagittaria sp. (pollen)		*		arrowhead
Typha (pollen)		*	*	cattail
Zannichellia sp.		*		horned pond weed
grazing indicators				
Centaurea sp. (pollen)		*	*	knapweed
Dipsacaceae (pollen)				teasel family
Plantago sp. (pollen)		*	*	plantain
Mediterranean macchia				
Phillyrea sp. (pollen)		*		phillyrea
Pistacia sp. (pollen)		*		
Pistacia lentiscus	*			mastic
Possible forage crops				
Bromus sp.				brome
Medicago sp.		*	*	medick
Other				
Acer (pollen)		*	*	maple

period	Early Hellenistic Period			
site	Muro Tenente	Pizzica Pantanello 2	Pizzica Pantanello 3	
date	4th-2nd century BC	early 3rd century BC	late 3rd century BC	
taxa				common name
Compositae (pollen)		*	*	aster, daisy, or sunflower family
Cyperaceae (pollen)		*	*	sedges family
Galium sp.		*	*	bedstraw
Labiatae (pollen)		*	*	mint family
Liliaceae (pollen)				lily family
Pinus sp. (pollen)		*	*	pine
Quercus sp. (pollen)		*	*	oak
Rubus sp.		*	*	blackberry

Table 5.2 Part 4: Early Hellenistic Period (c. 325-200 BC) (b).

period	Early Iron Age					
site	l'Incoronata	Otranto	Valesio 1	Monte Irsi 1	Francavilla Marittima	
context	settlement	settlement	settlement	settlement	sanctuary	
location	inland Basilicata	Adriatic coast of Salento	inland Salento, province of Brindisi	Province of Matera, Basilicata	Timpone della Motta hill, Calabria	
date	Iron Age/Archaic period (8th-6th centuries BC)	Early Iron Age (late 8th- early 7th century BC)	Early Iron Age (8th-7th centuries BC)	Early Iron Age	730-650 BC	
Domesticated animals	95.2%	100%			100%	**common name**
Bos taurus	24%	34%	14.8%	25.1%	18%	cattle
Ovis/Capra	41.81%	45%	52.1%	57.6%	46%	sheep/goat
Sus scrofa dom.	32.62%	21%	26.6%	16.6%	36%	pig
Equus caballus	0.63%					horse
Canis familiaris	0.88%					dog
Gallus domesticus	0.06%					hen
Wild animals	4.8%					
Capra ibex	2.5%					ibex
Capreolus capreolus	1.25%					roe deer
Cervus elaphus	66.25%		3.3%	0.7%		red deer
Chelonia	20%					turtle
Lepus europaeus	2.5%		1.2%			brown hare
Sus scrofa fer.	7.5%					wild boar
Birds						
Alectoris rufa			0.4%			red-legged partridge
Circus aeruginosus			0.4%			western marsh-harrier

Table 5.3 Archaeozoological remains from southeast Italy. Part 1: Early Iron Age.

period	Archaic/Classical periods			6th-3rd centuries BC			
site	Valesio 2	Cavallino	Botromagno 1	Pizzica Pantanello 1	Pizzica Pantanello 2	Pizzica Pantanello 3	
context	settlement	settlement	settlement	sanctuary	*necropolis*	refuse deposit	
location	inland Salento, province of Brindisi	inland Salento, province of Lecce	inland northern Apulia	Metapontino, Basilicata			
date	6th-5th centuries BC)	8th-5th centuries BC)	600-400 BC	6th-3rd centuries BC			
domesticated animals				100%	100%	100%	**common name**
Bos taurus	25.5%		29.5%	52.74%	3.57%	13.64%	cattle
Ovis/Capra	44.8%	70%	57%	22.06%	33.44%	40.91%	sheep/goat
Sus scrofa dom.	22.4%	30%	29.5%	5.63%	0.97%	40.91%	pig
Equus caballus				14.38%	48.7%		horse
Equus asinus				0.78%	20.13%	4.54%	ass/mule
Canis familiaris	1.9%			3.01%			dog
Felis catus				0.1%			cat
Gallus domesticus				0.19%			hen
Wild animals				100%	100%		
Bos primigenius				7%			aurochs
Canis lupus					100%		wolf
Capra ibex				0.64%			ibex
Capreolus capreolus	0,4%			1.27%			roe deer
Cervus elaphus	0.8%		2%	57.95%			red deer
Chelonia				12.10%			turtle
Lepus europaeus	0.8%			1.27%			brown hare
Meles meles				0.64%			badger
Rodentia				1.27%			rodent
Sus scrofa fer.	0.8%			3.18%			wild boar
Testudo hermanni	0.4%						tortoise
Birds							
Aegypius monachus				5.09%			black vulture
'fauna occasionale' (Sorrentino (1979, 308)		1%					
	100%	99%	100%	100%			

Table 5.3 Part 2: Archaic/Classical Periods.

site	Valesio 3	Botromagno 2	Vaste 1	Roccagloriosa	Monte Irsi 2	
context	settlement	settlement	sanctuary	settlement	settlement	
location	inland Salento, province of Brindisi	inland northern Apulia	inland Salento, province of Lecce	southern Campania	Province of Matera, Basilicata	
date	4th-3rd century BC	400-150 BC	mid-3rd century BC	4th-3rd century BC	4th-3rd century BC	
domesticated animals			100%	domestic to wild ratio: 98% : 2%		common name
Bos taurus	14.8%	22%	1%	35.8%	27.1%	cattle
Ovis/Capra	43%	57%	1%	45.8%	45.7%	sheep/goat
Sus scrofa dom.	28.8%	18%	98%	15.9%	22.9%	pig
Equus caballus				0.8%	2.5%	horse
Equus asinus	0.2%			0.8%		ass/mule
Canis familiaris	0.9%			1.3%		dog
Gallus domesticus	1%			0.3%		hen
Wild animals			100%			
Bos primigenius				11.1%		aurochs
Cervus elaphus	2.9%	3%		30.6%	0.9%	red deer
Cervus/Dama				8.3%		Red/fallow deer
Chelonia				11.1%		turtle
Dama dama				0.6%		fallow deer
Lepus europaeus	0.2%					brown hare
Rodentia				2.8%		rodent
Testudo hermanni			100%		0.9%	tortoise
Vulpes vulpes	0.2%					fox
Birds						
Avis sp.				8.3%		wild bird
Anatidae	0.2%					duck family
Anser anser	0.2%					graylag goose
Columba palumbus	0.7%					wood pigeon
Columba sp.	0.2%					pigeon
	100%			100%	100%	

Table 5.3 Part 3: Early Hellenistic Period.

	Late Hellenistic period					
site	Valesio 4	Vaste 2	Pizzica Pantanello 4	Monte Irsi 3	Pizzica Pantanello 5	
context	Settlement	sanctuary	refuse deposition	settlement	refuse deposition	
location	inland Salento, province of Brindisi	inland Salento, province of Lecce	Metapontino, Basilicata	Province of Matera, Basilicata	Metapontino, Basilicata	
date	3rd-2nd century BC	2nd-1st century BC	2nd century BC	2nd-1st century BC	early 1st century AD	
domesticated animals			100%			**common name**
Bos taurus	12%	4.8%	50.7%	29.8%		cattle
Ovis/Capra	30%	15.9%	6%	27.6%	66.6%	sheep/goat
Sus scrofa dom.	44.9%	50.8%	1.3%	36.2%	11.8%	pig
Equus caballus		20.5%		2.1%		horse
Equus asinus	0.1%					ass/mule
Equus sp.		1.6%	25.3%		2%	horse/mule/ass
Canis familiaris	1.5%	1.6%	16.7%			dog
Felis catus						cat
Gallus domesticus	1%					hen
Wild animals						
Cervus elaphus	0.1%	1.6%			19.6%	red deer
Cervidae	0.1%					deer
Lepus europaeus	0.3%					brown hare
Sus scrofa fer.	0.7%					wild boar
Testudo hermanni		1.6%				tortoise
Vulpes vulpes	0.1%					fox
Birds						
Avis sp.		1.6%		4.3%		wild bird
Anas platyrhynchos	0.3%					wild duck
Anatidae	0.3%					duck family
Anser anser						graylag goose
Columba palumbus	0.3%					wood pigeon
Vanellus vanellus	0.1%					peewit
	100%	100%		100%	100%	

Table 5.3 Part 4: Late Hellenistic Period.

site	flowering period according to Pignatti 1982	height according to Pignatti 1982	Broglio di Trebisacce 2	Botromagno 1	l'Amastuola 1	Cavallino	l'Amastuola 2	Botromagno 3	Pizzica Pantanello 1	
date			1200-700 BC	900-600 BC	late 8th –end of the 7th century BC	750-480/450 BC	early 6th-first half 5th century BC	400-300 BC	4th century BC	
taxa										common name
Adonis (cf. annua)	March-June	15-35 (60) cm			*		*			(autumn) adonis
Agrostemma githago	May-June	30-100 cm				*				corn-cockle
Avena	April-June	20-120 cm			*		*			oat
Buglossoides arvensis	January-June	10-50 cm		*				*		corn gromwell
Chenopodium album	June-September	10-200 cm				*				white goose-foot
Consolida regalis	May-June	30-80 cm	*							forking larkspur
Hordeum	May-June	5-150		*						barley
Lolium temulentum	April-June	20-70 cm							*	darnel
Polygonum	April-October	10-100 cm	*	*						knotweed
Secale cereale	May-July	100-180 cm			*					rye

Table 5.4 Archaeobotanical macroremains of cereal weeds from southeast Italy. Part 1: Final Bronze Age-Classical Period.

site	flowering period according to Pignatti 1982	height according to Pignatti 1982	Pizzica Pantanello 2	Pizzica Pantanello 3	Vaste	Roccagloriosa	Pomarico Vecchio	Muro Tenente	
date			early 3rd century BC	late 3rd century BC	4th-3rd century BC	4th-3rd century BC	4th-3rd century BC	4th-2nd century BC	
taxa									common name
Adonis (cf. annua)	March-June	15-35 (60) cm					*		(autumn) adonis
Agrostemma githago	May-June	30-100 cm							corncockle
Avena	April-June	20-120 cm		*	*	*		*	oat
Chenopodium album	June-September	10-200 cm				*			white goosefoot
Lathyrus sativus/cicera	March-May March-June	10-60 cm				*			grass/ red pea
Lolium temulentum	April-June	20-70 cm	*	*					darnel
Polygonum	April-October	10-100 cm	*	*		*	*		knotweed
Secale cereale	May-July	100-180 cm						*	rye

Table 5.4 Part 2: Early Hellenistic Period.

Period	Final Bronze Age and Early Iron Age	Early Iron Age and Archaic/Classical Periods				Early Hellenistic Period		
site	Torre Mordillo 3	Torre di Satriano	L'Amastuola	Cavallino	Monte Papalucio	Li Castelli di San Pancrazio	Muro Tenente	
date	1200-700 BC	Late 8th- 6th century BC	late 8th - first half 5th century BC	750-480/450 BC	mid-6th- 1st half 3rd century BC	4th-3rd century BC		
taxa								common name
Abies alba		*						silver fir
Arbutus unedo			*					strawberry tree
Cistus sp.				*				rockrose
Cornus sp.		*						
Ephedra sp.					*		*	ephedra
Erica sp. (incl. cf. multiflora and cf. arborea)			*	*	*	*	*	Mediterranean/ tree heath
Euonymus sp.					*			spindle tree
Fagus sp.		*			*			beech
Juniperus sp.			*			*	*	juniper
cf. Leguminosae					*	*		legumes
Maloideae (incl. Sorbus sp.)			*			*		Maloideae
Myrtus communis			*		*	*	*	myrtle
Olea europaea	*		*	*	*	*	*	olive
Pinus sp.			*		*	*	*	pine
Pistacia sp. (cf. lentiscus)			*	*	*	*	*	mastic
Pomoideae		*			*			Pomoideae
Populus/ Salix		*			*		*	poplar/willow
Prunus sp. (incl. cf. dolcis)		*	*	*	*	*		prune
cf. Punica granatum							*	pomegranate
Pyrus / Malus					*		*	pear/apple
Quercus sp. (deciduous type)	*	*	*			*	*	oak
Quercus sp. (evergreen type)			*	*	*	*	*	oak
Rhamnus/Phillyrea			*		*	*	*	Rhamnus/Phillyrea
Rosaceae/Maloideae		*	*			*		
Rosmarinus officinalis			*					rosemary
Salvia sp.							*	sage
Ulmus cf. campestris	*							elm
Viburnum opulus					*			water elder
Vitis vinifera					*			grape

Table 5.5 Charcoal finds from southeast Italy.

period	grape	olive
Neolithic	Grotta dell'Uzzo (8th millennium BC)	Grotta dell'Uzzo (8th millennium BC)
	Torre Canne (6th millennium BC)	
Bronze Age	Filo Braccio (EBA)	Broglio di Trebisacce 1 (1350-1200 BC)
	Vivara (MBA)	Broglio di Trebisacce 2 (1200-700 BC)
	Portella (MBA)	Monopoli/Piazza Palmieri
	Maria Capua Vetere (FBA)	Castello di Tursi (12th century BC)
		Torre Mordillo 3 (1200-700 BC)
Early Iron Age	Longola di Poggiomarino (late 10th and early 9th century BC)	Cavallino (750-480/450 BC)
	l'Incoronata (late 8th- early 7th century BC)	
	l'Amastuola (late 8th -end of the 7th century BC)	
	Cavallino (750-480/450 BC)	
Archaic/Classical periods	l'Amastuola (early 6th-first half 5th century BC)	l'Amastuola (early 6th-first half 5th century BC)
	Monte Papalucio 1 (mid-6th-early 5th century BC)	Monte Papalucio 1 (mid-6th-early 5th century BC)
	Torre di Satriano (6th century BC)	Pizzica Pantanello 1 (4th century BC)
	Roccagloriosa (6th /5th century BC)	
	Pizzica Pantanello 1 (4th century BC)	
Early Hellenistic period	Monte Papalucio 2 (2nd half 4th-1st half 3rd century BC)	Monte Papalucio 2 (2nd half 4th-1st half 3rd century BC)
	Vaste, Piazza Dante (4th-3rd century BC)	Vaste, Piazza Dante (4th-3rd century BC)
	Roccagloriosa (4th-3rd century BC)	Roccagloriosa (4th-3rd century BC)
	Pomarico vecchio (4th-3rd century BC)	Pizzica Pantanello 2 (early 3rd century BC)
	Pizzica Pantanello 2 (early 3rd century BC)	Pizzica Pantanello 3 (late 3rd century BC)
	Pizzica Pantanello 3 (late 3rd century BC)	Muro Tenente (4th-2nd century BC)
	Muro Tenente (4th-2nd century BC)	

Table 5.6 Early archaeobotanical evidence of grape and olive cultivation in southern Italy.

site	L'Amastuola	Monte Papalucio	Vaste	Muro Tenente	
date	early/middle 7th century BC	middle of the 6th until the first half of the 3rd century BC	4th -3rd century BC	4th century BC	
taxa					common name
cereals					
Hordeum vulgare	*	*			hulled barley
Hordeum sp.			*		barley
Triticum aestivum/compactum	*	*			free-threshing wheat
Triticum aestivum/ durum		*	*		bread/ macaroni wheat
Triticum dicoccum	*	*	*		emmer wheat
Triticum monococcum/ dicoccum		*			einkorn/ emmer wheat
Triticum monococcum			*		einkorn
Triticum cf. spelta		*			spelt wheat
Triticum sp.			*	*	wheat
pulses					
Cicer arietinum		*			chickpea
Lens culinaris			*		lentil
Pisum sativum		*			field pea
Vicia faba var. minor	*	*			broad bean
Vicia ervilia	*		*		bitter vetch
Vicia/Lathyrus		*			vetch/ vetchling
Vicia sp.			*		vetch
fruits					
Ficus carica		*			fig
Malus cf. sylvestris		*			crab apple
Olea europaea		*	*	*	olive
Cf. Phoenix dactylifera		*			date
Punica granatum		*	*		pomegranate
Vitis vinifera		*	*		grape
condiments					
Allium sativum	*				garlic
forage crops and/or weeds					
Avena			*		oat
Bromus sp.			*		brome
Medicago			*		medick
Secale cereale			*		rye
charcoal					
Ephedra sp.		*			ephedra
Erica sp.		*		*	heath
Fagus sp.		*			beech
Myrtus communis		*			myrtle
Olea europaea	*	*			olive
Pistacia cf. lentiscus		*			mastic
Prunus sp.		*			prune
Pyrus / Malus		*			pear/ apple

site	L'Amastuola	Monte Papalucio	Vaste	Muro Tenente	
date	early/middle 7th century BC	middle of the 6th until the first half of the 3rd century BC	4th-3rd century BC	4th century BC	
taxa					common name
Quercus sp. (deciduous type)	*				oak
Quercus sp. (evergreen type)	*	*			oak
Rhamnus/Phillyrea	*	*			Rhamnus/Phillyrea
Vitis vinifera		*			grape

Table 5.7 Archaeobotanical macroremains from sites in southeast Italy that can be associated with ritual activities. Part 1: ritual depositions.

site	Botromagno	Muro Tenente	
dat	7th-4th century BC	4th and 3rd century B	
taxa			common name
cereals			
Hordeum vulgare	*		hulled barley
Hordeum vulgare var. nudum		*	naked barley
Triticum aestivum/compactum	*	*	free-threshing wheat
Triticum dicoccum		*	emmer wheat
Triticum monococcum/ dicoccum	*		einkorn/ emmer wheat
Triticum monococcum	*		einkorn
Triticum sp.	*	*	wheat
pulses			
Vicia faba var. minor		*	broad bean
Vicia ervilia		*	bitter vetch
Vicia/Lathyrus	*		vetch/ vetchling
Vicia sp.		*	vetch
fruits			
Olea europaea		*	olive
Vitis vinifera		*	grape
forage crops and/or weeds			
Buglossoides arvensis	*		corn gromwell
Phalaris sp.	*		canarygrass
Scirpus sp.	*		bulrush
charcoal			
Erica sp.		*	heath
Olea europaea		*	olive
Pinus pinea/halepensis		*	umbrella/ Aleppo pine
cf. Punica granatum		*	pomegranate

Table 5.7 Part 2: Graves.

Chapter 6 – Macro level: Part two

6.1 INTRODUCTION

An important aim of this study was to demonstrate that archaeobotany offers possibilities for a different approach to study the occupational history of pre-Roman southeast Italy. This different approach focuses on developments in landscape exploitation, agricultural production, and human impact on natural landscapes. We have seen examples of this interaction in the previous chapters, both on a micro- and meso level. In chapter 4, it was explained how the local landscape determined certain choices in the crop spectrum and the exploitation of the natural landscape around l'Amastuola and Muro Tenente. At the same time, it was described how the inhabitants altered the landscape in order to exploit it more effectively. This happened on a large scale in the Early Hellenistic Period, when the previously uninhabited areas around the sites were filled in by isolated farms and rural hamlets. I examined this development by investigating what the landscape around l'Amastuola and Muro Tenente looked like and how it was exploited. This analysis on a meso level revealed a number of differences between the two sites, particularly in the scale and organization of agricultural production. It appears that the landscape surrounding Muro Tenente was exploited in a much more intensive way than that of l'Amastuola. At the latter site, agricultural production was mostly aimed at subsistence. At Muro Tenente, an agricultural surplus was produced for a market. This raised the question of how these results fit into the general framework of long-term developments of landscape and land use in southeast Italy.

In order to answer this question, archaeobotanical studies from other sites in southeast Italy were integrated with other types of research data, from archaeological excavations, field surveys, archaeozoological research, and ancient written texts in chapter 5. This chapter focuses on the second part of the macro level analysis. In the following sections, I will integrate the research data that were presented in the previous chapter into a diachronic overview of developments in landscape and land use. Moving from the interpretation on site level to the wider region, and combining a variety of sources, the multidisciplinary research data from southeast Italy will be viewed in a broader diachronic context.[1] The purpose of this exercise is to remedy one of the main problems of archaeobotanical research in southeast Italy, i.e. a lack of synthesizing, regional studies that integrate archaeobotanical data with information from excavations, field surveys, ancient written sources, and archaeozoological studies.

This chapter has been divided into five parts, each dealing with a well-defined chronological period. As explained in chapter 1, the focus of this overview will be on the first millennium BC, but some developments in the Recent and Final Bronze Age are essential to our understanding of the following centuries. For this reason, I will start with the Final Bronze Age (c. 1200-1000 BC), followed by the Early Iron Age (c. 1000-600 BC), the Archaic/Classical periods (c. 600-325 BC) and the Early Hellenistic period (325-200 BC). Finally, a short epilogue will be dedicated to land use in southeast Italy in the Late Hellenistic/ Early Roman period (200-30 BC). Each part of the chronological overview will be concluded with a short summary that focuses on three main points:

---

[1] There is a large volume of published studies describing settlement and land-use dynamics in pre-Roman southeast Italy. The present overview is based on the most complete syntheses to date, including Yntema 2013; D'Andria 1991; Peroni 1994; Attema, Burgers and Van Leusen 2010.

1. Regional diversity in settlement patterns, especially between the coastlands (where Greek migrants settled) and inland areas;
2. Agricultural strategies: the introduction of new crops, changes in consumer/producer relations, agricultural expansion, rationalization, and specialization;
3. Human impact on the natural landscape, and the contrast between 'wild' unexploited and cultivated areas.

6.2 THE FINAL BRONZE AGE (C. 1200-1000 BC)

The general picture for southeast Italy in the Final Bronze Age is that of continuity of habitation.[2] Most of the important sites with Bronze Age roots, such as Timmari, Scoglio del Tonno, and Rocavecchia, continued to exist in the Iron Age. The Bronze Age sites of Broglio di Trebisacce and Torre Mordillo also continued to be inhabited.[3] However, a loss of monumental features (such as fortifications) in settlements can be witnessed.[4] Bronze Age settlements such as Santa Maria d'Anglona[5] and San Teodoro/l'Incoronata[6] consisted of several hut clusters and probably housed no more than a few hundred inhabitants. Settlements in this period were mainly concentrated along the 30 to 40 km-wide coastal strip of southern Apulia, Basilicata, and northern Calabria, and inland in the Materano (around present-day Matera).[7] The larger part of the inland area displays hardly any trace of habitation. There are a few exceptions, including the settlements of Oria in the Brindisino and Monte Salete in the Tarantino.[8] Settlement locations often appear to be determined by strategic considerations, such as a dominant and well-defensible position in the landscape and a proximity to overseas transport routes. The material evidence for contacts with Greece and other areas of the eastern Mediterranean is particularly thin between the end of the 11th and the late 9th century BC, especially in comparison to earlier and later periods (i.e. the Recent Bronze Age and the second half of the Early Iron Age).[9] The Final Bronze Age, however, was not a period of general crisis. In fact, the production of matt-painted pottery[10] and metal[11] testifies to dynamic local communities.

The only palynological data from this phase come from the Laghi Alimini in southern Apulia. The pollen spectrum from these lakes starts around 5600-5200 cal. BP, when dry conditions seem to have prevailed, until the considerably moister and warmer present day. Interestingly, the most evident changes in the landscape that are reflected in the Alimini record took place before the period discussed in this study. A deforestation phase is recorded for the Early Bronze Age (between 4350 and 3900 cal. BP), which resulted in a landscape with low *macchia* type shrubs and open herbaceous vegetation. The presence of *Rumex*, *Plantago*, and *Artemisia* pollen suggests a partial reduction to grassland. It should be emphasized, however, that these developments were probably caused by a combination of increasing human impact and climate change.[12] There is a considerable amount of evidence for the latter, including a transition from *Quercion ilicis* to *Oleo-Ceratonion* communities, possibly as a result of precipitation

---

[2] Yntema 2013.

[3] Broglio di Trebisacce: Buffa 1984; Torre Mordillo: Arancio 2001, pp. 275-292.

[4] Cf. Saltini Semerari 2010, p. 21, with additional bibliography.

[5] For Santa Maria d'Anglona, see Yntema 2000, p. 29, with further references.

[6] There is a huge bibliography on l'Incoronata: see Yntema 2000, p. 29, for further references.

[7] D'Andria 1991, p. 396 (Figure 2), p. 403. In Apulia, such sites have been indentified at Scoglio del Tonno, Torre Castelluccia, Torre Saturo, Taranto-Borgo Nuovo and Torre Guaceto.

[8] Burgers 1998, p. 174.

[9] Bietti Sestieri 1985, pp. 104-113.

[10] Yntema 1990.

[11] Bietti Sestieri 1973.

[12] Harding 1999, p. 93; Di Rita and Magri 2009, pp. 301-302.

or temperature changes.[13] A more reliable indication of increasing human activity in the Early Bronze Age is the continuous presence of cereals. A peak of *Olea* pollen can also be observed around 3600 cal. BP, reaching its maximum around 3100 cal. BP (i.e. around 1150 BC, in the Final Bronze Age). This is also the period when the large storage facilities for olive oil at Broglio di Trebisacce, Torre Mordillo, Rocavecchia, and several other sites were in use, so the peak can probably be associated with olive cultivation.[14] No other major changes are visible in the pollen record in the period between the Early Bronze Age and the Early Iron Age, so it can be assumed that at the start of the first millennium BC, the landscape around the Laghi Alimini was still characterized by low *macchia* vegetation and grassland. Unfortunately, we do not know to what extent this type of vegetation was typical of other parts of southeast Italy.

The Sibaritide stands out from most of the other areas in southeast Italy in this period. Our knowledge of the settlement patterns in the Sibaritide owes much to the excavations and surveys in this area that were directed by Renato Peroni, who modelled the developments in protohistoric habitation.[15] Peroni emphasizes that settlement patterns in northern Calabria are indicative of a continuous process of increasing complexity in the Bronze Age. One of his hypotheses is that the landscape in the Sibaritide suffered from a considerable economic pressure, and certain landscape zones may have reached the limits of their carrying capacity already at the end of the Middle Bronze Age.[16] According to Peroni's analysis of the relation between settlements and geological units, sites from this period were preferably located on the natural sand and conglomerate terraces, which were well-adapted to dry farming.[17] In the Final Bronze Age, several new sites appeared while others were abandoned, especially in the south-eastern part of the Sibaritide. There are indications that the new sites, as well as the surviving Middle Bronze Age ones such as Torre Mordillo, Amendolara, Broglio di Trebisacce, and Timpone della Motta/Timpa del Castello (Francavilla Marittima), functioned as central places and started to command larger territories than before. In the territory of Torre Mordillo, for instance, several new sites appeared, including Pietra Castello di Cassano Ionio and Cozzo Michelicchio. According to Peroni, these settlements can be interpreted as 'satellite sites' that had an agricultural function, but were also part of the defensive system of Torre Mordillo.[18] In Peroni's view, the changes in the settlement pattern were imposed by local elites wishing to strengthen their military and productive potential. In the southern Sibaritide there was also a tendency to occupy sites located at higher altitudes, possibly for strategic reasons. Both developments have been interpreted by Peroni as indications of considerable demographic growth and increasing territoriality.[19] These interpretations, however, are mainly based on survey data. Since settlements in this period are highly dispersed, the growth of settlement areas (as indicated by surface scatters) does not necessarily imply population growth.[20]

According to Burgers, Final Bronze Age communities were probably relatively autarchic within their small territories.[21] The settlements were not only dispersed, they probably consisted of a relatively small number of households. This means that agricultural production did not need to exceed domestic requirements. It is perhaps telling that habitation was mainly concentrated in the coastal areas in this period, although the best soils for agriculture were located inland.[22]

---

[13] Di Rita and Magri 2009, p. 301.

[14] Although Di Rita and Magri (2009, pp. 301 and 303-304) argue that the *Olea*-peak can be explained by an increase of evergreen vegetation rather than the spread of oleiculture.

[15] Peroni 1994.

[16] Peroni 1994, p. 835.

[17] Peroni 1994, pp. 843-845.

[18] Peroni 1994, p. 877.

[19] Peroni 1994, pp. 863-865, 869.

[20] Cf. Vanzetti 2002, p. 44.

[21] Burgers 1998, p. 174.

[22] Cf. Burgers 1998, p. 174: 'The inland hills and plains of the peninsula may have been exploited for extensive pastoralism, if they were exploited at all.'

Few archaeobotanical data are available that can be used to reconstruct land use practices in this period. According to Peroni, the crop spectrum from Recent Bronze Age levels at Broglio di Trebisacce (consisting of cereals, grasses and pulses, while there is also evidence of the consumption of figs, walnuts and olives – see *Table 5.1*) was particularly adapted to cultivation in an arid climate. The cereal spectrum at Torre Mordillo was supplemented by a hulled wheat type, i.e. emmer, perhaps because this type of wheat is less demanding compared to hulled wheats and barleys.[23]

As indicated in section 5.3.3, there is good reason to believe that the cultivation of olives continued to take place throughout the first millennium BC in southeast Italy, but that these activities are only visible in the archaeological record when carried out on a large scale. This was the case, for instance, at Recent Bronze Age Broglio di Trebisacce and Torre Mordillo, but also at Rocavecchia in southern Apulia. It appears, however, that the scale of production decreased in the Final Bronze Age, and production came to a halt in the Early Iron Age.[24] In Peroni's view, this phenomenon can be explained by the emerging elites in this period. During the transition from the Final Bronze Age to the Early Iron Age, land possession gradually became the privilege of a few families, which would explain why the practice of collective olive oil storage was abandoned.[25]

In fact, the large-scale production of olive oil in the Recent Bronze Age requires an explanation, rather than the fact that the scale of production diminished in the Final Bronze Age. Ethnoarchaeological studies show that the cultivation of olives and vines has often been a small-scale activity and the consumption of wine and oil was more or less restricted to prestigious or ritual contexts.[26] Farmers with limited involvement in the market tended to grow a mixture of crops to reduce the risk of total crop failure. Large-scale (i.e. archaeologically visible) olei- and viticulture, however, were a risky business that required stable settlements and settled conditions.[27] Indeed, it is worth reiterating that compared to cereals and pulses, olives and vines constitute a capital-intensification of subsistence, demanding years of careful nurturing before they yield fruit. Such an investment could eventually be profitable if the fruit was produced on a large scale. It could be converted into storable commodities such as wine and oil, and sold at market. But, whereas some of the larger regional centres in the Recent and Final Bronze Age were actively involved in external exchanges, such a market is unlikely to have existed in the Early Iron Age. As a result, large-scale oleiculture was no longer a profitable activity and was mostly abandoned.

---

[23] Renfrew 1973, pp. 65-66 and 80-81.

[24] The same development can be witnessed in contemporary Greece, where viti- and oleiculture soon regained their positions of economic importance after the Dark Ages, but were still not produced in quantities as large as in the Bronze Age. Runnels and Hansen 1986, pp. 302-304.

[25] Peroni 1994, p. 877.

[26] For example, Forbes 1976, p. 237, 1989, p. 90, 1993, pp. 217-218; Foxhall 1993, p. 199; Hamilakis 1996, pp. 21-22. Cf. Halstead 2004, p. 191, and Forbes 1993, p. 216, where he points out that prior to the Second World War, olive cultivation in the southern Argolid in Greece was small-scaled because it was considered much more of a cash-generating, rather than subsistence-oriented, activity.

[27] Renfrew 1972, p. 280. This argument is often used to explain the decrease of olive oil and wine production in the early Middle Ages, for example by Grieco (1993, p. 298: 'The fall of the Roman empire and the consequent social, economic and demographic collapse brought about, in many places, an abandoning of arboriculture in general and of olive tree growing in particular'). Cf. Hitchner 1993, p. 501.

SUMMARY: THE FINAL BRONZE AGE (C. 1200-1000 BC)

Regional diversity and settlement patterns
The first contrast in this period is the difference in habitation density between coastal zone and inland areas. Stable settlements mainly concentrated along the coast, whereas the inland shows only faint traces of habitation. In addition, a clear contrast can be noted between the Sibaritide and other parts of southeast Italy, where habitation remained isolated and rather dispersed. In contrast, there is evidence that local centres such as Torre Mordillo and Broglio di Trebisacce functioned as central places in the Sibaritide. According to Peroni, the emergence of smaller rural sites in the territory of Torre Mordillo may even be interpreted as evidence of increased settlement hierarchy. This view is debatable, but there can be no doubt that compared to other regions of southeast Italy, the inland of the Sibaritide was exploited more intensively.

Agricultural strategies
Agricultural strategies may have included pastoral land use as well as arable cultivation, but there is very little archaeobotanical and archaeozoological evidence to support this hypothesis. The archaeobotanical assemblage from Broglio di Trebisacce is indicative of a rather varied spectrum of cereals as well as pulses. In addition, it can be assumed that olives and grapes were still cultivated, but large-scale production of olive oil was restricted to a few sites that functioned as regional centres.

Human impact on the natural landscape
The palynological data from the Laghi Alimini in Salento indicate that the landscape in this part of Apulia was characterized by low *macchia* and grasslands. This is indicative of considerable human impact on the natural vegetation. At the same time, this indication clearly conflicts with the archaeological record for the most part of southeast Italy. Most settlements were located in rather isolated positions and there is little evidence of trade and exchange in this period. It can be assumed, therefore, that communities were mostly self-supporting. The absence of isolated farms and rural hamlets outside of the larger centres indicates that exploitable land zones had to be located within walking distance from each settlement. In other words, areas that were more than about 5 kilometres away from a site are likely to have remained untouched. Human impact must have been limited in the inland areas as well, since only a few traces of habitation have been found there.

6.3 THE EARLY IRON AGE (C. 1000-600 BC)

The Early Iron Age in southeast Italy is marked by the arrival of Greek migrants and other peoples from the eastern Mediterranean. Evidence of renewed trade contacts became increasingly evident from the end of the 9th century BC onwards. In the second half of the 8th century BC, imported Greek ceramics (both fine wares and transport vessels) started to appear at almost every site along the Strait of Otranto and the Gulf of Taranto, including large parts of Salento and the coastal zones of Basilicata and northern Calabria.[28] The pottery from Otranto[29] indicates that the settlement participated in an exchange network that involved at least three districts on the Ionian Sea, the 'Corinthian' orbit with the Gulf of Corinth, north-western Greece/southern Albania, the Salento peninsula itself, and possibly also eastern Sicily, through which the Tyrrhenean Sea and the Greek *emporion* Pithekoussai on Ischia could be reached.[30]

[28] Semeraro 1997; Yntema 2013, p. 56.
[29] D'Andria 1995, p. 403.
[30] For Pithekoussai, see Ridgway 1992, with further references.

In some areas, small groups of Greek migrants settled permanently. This happened, for example, at present-day Taranto. The area at the entrance to the Mar Piccolo, a small lagoon-like bay just off the Gulf of Taranto, was continuously inhabited from the Middle Bronze Age to the present day. The earliest traces of habitation were found at the large site of Scoglio del Tonno and at a few other find spots within the modern city of Taranto (San Domenico, Borgo Nuovo).[31] According to later written sources, Greek immigrants founded the colony of Taras here in 706 BC, but the intense post-classical occupation of the Taranto area has made it difficult to collect evidence of this phase. In any case, only a small number of cremation burials dating from the end of the 8th or the early 7th century BC were found in the Taranto area.[32] Since the native groups of southern Italy did not cremate their dead, and the graves often contained Greek pottery, they have been interpreted as Greek burials. It is important to emphasize that the settlement at Taras did not show any urban characteristics in this period. The evidence shows that occupation was dispersed in the same way as at contemporary Early Iron Age sites elsewhere, and probably consisted of several small groups of huts.[33]

This was also the case in the Metapontino.[34] Underneath the future urban centre of Metapontion, traces of a dispersed hut settlement, the so-called 'Andrisani' plot, were found. There is also evidence of Iron Age occupation at San Teodoro and l'Incoronata, and further south at the settlement of Santa Maria d'Anglona. But the situation changed in the 2nd half of the 7th century BC, when the Andrisani site and l'Incoronata were abandoned.[35] This is probably the moment that the colonial town came into existence.

Two other Greek settlements arose in the coastal areas of Basilicata and northern Calabria, namely Siris and Sybaris. Sybaris is believed to have been founded by Achaean colonists in the early 7th century BC. Very little is known about this town, because the abundant fluviatile deposits that cover it have made archaeological research very problematic.[36] However, some information about Sybaris' indigenous hinterland and Greek-indigenous relationships in this area is provided by the sanctuary of Timpone della Motta (Francavilla Marittima) and the *necropolis* of Macchiabate. The excavations by Groningen University demonstrated that the cult place on the Timpone della Motta hill was continuously in use from the Middle Bronze Age onwards.[37] During this time, several cult buildings were built, including a wooden temple in which indigenous and Greek elements were combined (built around 725/700 BC). Such continuity can also be found in the Macchiabate cemetery, where the community living in the settlement at Timpone della Motta buried their dead. The chronological analysis of the grave goods further shows that the deposition of sets of indigenous pottery continued despite the increasing presence of Greek pottery, which demonstrates that the indigenous population only gradually adopted Greek material culture in their grave inventories.[38]

---

[31] The spectacular Borgo Nuovo or Pozzo d'Eredità deposit, which was discovered in the 19th century, contained hundreds of matt-painted and impasto vessels. The pots can all be dated between the middle of the 9th and the final decades of the 8th centuries BC. According to Yntema (2000, p. 19), they probably stem from carefully removed native burial plots. This removal could have happened somewhere during the 7th century BC with the introduction of the Greek concept of a strict separation between the area of the living and the area of the dead.

[32] Neeft (1994, p. 187) has shown that graves from the earliest phase (the first half of the 7th century BC) are very rare; the majority of the tombs is datable between 640 and 620 BC. The number of burials considerably increased from the end of the 7th century BC onwards.

[33] Yntema 2000, p. 22.

[34] Carter 2006, pp. 51-90.

[35] Carter 2006, p. 199.

[36] Cf. Yntema 2013, p. 104, with further references.

[37] See Kleibrink 1993, with references. Cf. Attema, Burgers and Van Leusen 2010, pp. 98-99.

[38] Vink 1995. Cf. Attema, Burgers and Van Leusen 2010, p. 99.

Siris, on the other hand, was founded by Ionian colonists from Colophon (in modern Turkey) towards the end of the 8th or the early 7th century BC.[39] Siris was located in a previously uninhabited area between the rivers Agri and Sinni in Basilicata that was known for its fertile soils. For example, the poet Archilochus (middle of the 7th century BC) compares the island of Thasos in the northern Aegean with the countryside of Siris and states that 'It's not a beautiful or lovely place or charming like the Siris river lands.'[40] In this earliest phase of its existence, Siris had a decidedly dispersed character, consisting of various small nuclei of dwellings that are often supposed to have functioned as a kind of trading post.[41] The settlement changed in character sometime after the middle of the 7th century BC, when it was surrounded by a mud-brick wall and one or possibly two sacred buildings were constructed. This was probably the time when Siris became a *polis* in the physical and socio-political sense.[42]

According to some authors, the Early Iron Age can also be seen as the period when the formation of proto-urban centres took place in the indigenous areas.[43] Signs of human presence in the landscape become more numerous, and land use more intensive. Settlement patterns became increasingly stable, and population numbers grew considerably. However, these developments showed much regional variety. In fact, regional features become steadily more pronounced during the 8th century BC in southeast Italy.[44] A process of 'regionalization' is apparent in the production of pottery and metal, the funerary customs, the character of the dwellings and the settlement types. For instance, whilst the material culture of the coastal area on the Gulf of Taranto displays signs of the exponential increase of trade and exchange with Greeks, northern Apulia had strong links with the northern Adriatic and eastern Hallstatt world. The results of this differentiation are particularly evident when we look at pottery production in this period. Various regional styles developed in the course of the 8th century BC. For instance, decoration patterns derived from southern Albania and north-western Greece can be witnessed on matt-painted pots from Salento.[45]

Nevertheless, a few similar trends can be noted, namely gradual infill of the inland areas, and settlement expansion. The field surveys that were carried out in the context of the l'Amastuola project have detected very few Bronze Age scatters in this area, and no continuity between this Bronze Age occupation and the late 8th century settlement at l'Amastuola was found. It was concluded, therefore, that in this period the landscape was reclaimed for human occupation after a long phase of marginality.[46] Indeed, a substantial number of new settlements, such as Muro Tenente, Li Castelli di San Pancrazio, Cavallino, Vaste, Valesio, and many others, was founded in Early Iron Age southern Apulia. Whereas during the Bronze Age the majority of habitation centres was located on the coast, these new settlements came into existence in the inland areas.[47] This means that many 'wild' landscapes were reclaimed for human occupation. The new habitation centres were built almost exclusively near fertile, well-watered soils that were very suitable for agricultural activities. In contrast, the Bronze Age centres were located on much thinner soils in the coastal zone. This suggests that this 'colonization' process was primarily driven by the search for farmland. As D'Andria[48] and Burgers[49] have demonstrated, the

---

[39] The information from the ancient written sources about Siris suggests a foundation date in the second quarter or, more likely, the middle of the 7th century BC (Lombardo 1992, p. 58). However, the earliest habitation traces that were unearthed in the archaeological excavations at Siris/Policoro date to a slightly earlier period, around the end of the 8th or beginning of the 7th centuries BC.

[40] West 1993, p. 7.

[41] Cf. Yntema 2000, p. 9, with further references.

[42] Yntema 2000, p. 11.

[43] Attema, Burgers and Van Leusen 2010, p. 113; Yntema 2013, pp. 45-47.

[44] Yntema 2013, p. 92.

[45] Yntema 2013, p. 93.

[46] Burgers and Crielaard 2007, pp. 94-96.

[47] D'Andria 1991, p. 398 (*Figure 3*), 400 (*Figure 4*), 405; Yntema 1993, pp. 159-161, Burgers 1998, pp. 186-191.

[48] D'Andria 1991, pp. 398, 400 and 405.

[49] Burgers 1998, pp. 186-191.

number of new settlements in Salento was surprisingly large. Between 770 and 720 BC, some 15 to 20 settlements came into existence, which means that in a relatively short time the number of settlements more than doubled and formerly uninhabited inland areas became 'colonized'. Moreover, the larger coastal sites (Otranto, Brindisi) and the few inland sites with Bronze Age roots that were continuously inhabited, also expanded in size. A good example of this development can be found in the settlement of Oria in the Brindisino plain. In the Final Bronze Age, Oria occupied some 6 to 8 hectares. By the late 8th century BC, occupation was much more dispersed, and covered an area of 70 to 90 hectares.[50] By this time, Oria may have had approximately the same number of inhabitants as the large coastal sites on the Basilicata coast, i.e. between 300 and 500 persons.[51]

It appears that parallel developments occurred in contemporary Basilicata. There is evidence that several coastal sites with Bronze Age roots, such as Santa Maria d'Anglona and San Teodoro/l'Incoronata expanded considerably in this period, up to several hundreds of hectares. Like Oria, these settlements consisted of several hut clusters, but probably housed no more than a few hundred inhabitants.

Several hypotheses have been proposed to explain this infill of the inland areas in the Early Iron Age. According to D'Andria, demographic growth is likely to have been the determining factor.[52] The establishment of new settlements in previously unexploited areas can then be seen as a strategy to mobilize new resources.[53] Yntema, on the other hand, stresses that the peninsula was not densely inhabited and that there are no signs of population pressure in this period.[54] He argues that the emergence of elite groups and increasing contacts with foreigners may have caused social unrest within the tribal groups in Salento, ultimately leading to fission and to the birth of new settlements in different areas: 'Small groups were thrown out or went away on their own initiative in order to build up a new existence. They did so by clearing patches in the woods at a considerable distance from the settlement they came from.'[55]

In any case, the hypothesis of demographic growth ties in with the second general trend that characterizes the settlement patterns in southeast Italy in this period, namely the expansion of some of the larger regional centres. This is particularly evident in the Sibaritide. Surveys have revealed that, although the number of sites from this period is not much higher in comparison to the Final Bronze Age (18 vs 14), the total surface covered by these sites is almost twice as large (>200 hectares).[56] Some of the larger sites also show indications of craft specialization and the existence of a sub-regional market. At Broglio di Trebisacce, for instance, 50% of the fine wares was imported from the south and central Sibaritide.[57] Interestingly, however, site location in these parts still seemed to be mostly determined by strategic considerations, with settlements preferably built on hilltops and other prominent locations. Yntema has added that the mountainous parts of the region were probably colonized by people coming from the relatively low-lying coastal areas, who must have been familiar with these uplands since the region contained important summer pastures.[58]

After this eventful period of settlement expansion and 'native' colonization of the inland areas in the 8th century BC, the 7th century shows distinct signs of stabilization.[59] The inland settlements retained their highly dispersed character and often grew considerably in size, especially in the areas in

---

[50] Yntema 1993, p. 155.
[51] Yntema 1993, p. 158.
[52] D'Andria 1991, p. 405.
[53] Cf. Burgers 1998, p. 190.
[54] Yntema 1993, p. 161.
[55] As Yntema has argued, there is another possible explanation for the apparent shift in settlement locations. Formerly archaeologically invisible groups, such as pastoralist members of Salento societies, may have contributed to the landscape infill of the plains by becoming sedentary, archaeologically traceable as farmers. Yntema 2013, p. 51.
[56] Peroni 1994, p. 869.
[57] Vanzetti 2002, p. 44.
[58] Yntema 2013, p. 52.
[59] Yntema 2013, p. 64; D'Andria 1991, p. 403.

Salento that had recently been reclaimed for agriculture.[60] As Yntema has put it, the small, 8th-century human 'enclaves' in the forests of southeast Italy became substantial patches of manmade landscape in the 7th century BC. In this period the impact of man on the natural environment of southeast Italy increased substantially.[61]

Nevertheless, it is important to emphasize the rural character of the dispersed Iron Age sites. As Yntema has pointed out, dispersed settlements like Iron Age Oria were fairly mobile within a more or less defined area.[62] Huts were abandoned every 30 to 40 years, and replaced by new ones that were built on different spots. In this way, the location of habitation nuclei changed from time to time. These nuclei were often hundreds of meters apart. The empty spaces in between are likely to have been used for intensive agricultural cultivation, to graze livestock and perform communal rites. The archaeozoological research that was carried out by Veenman (see section 5.3.2) shows that sheep and goats were one of the pillars of domestic economy of Iron-Age southeast Italy, supplying wool, milk, cheese, meat and skins. Cattle were needed for traction, but also supplied meat and hides. Pigs were also held to provide meat and skins, but their percentages vary considerably between sites. Horses, on the other hand, are uncommon in the bone samples, but this does not necessarily imply that they were rare. It is possible that, in contrast to cattle, sheep/goats and pigs, horses were not eaten, and therefore buried in different contexts than the garbage pits from which most bone samples have been retrieved.

Most settlements were not surrounded by fortifications, although there may have been archaeologically invisible earthworks, bushes or palisades. A minimum of such barriers would have been necessary to protect the grazing fields and arable lands from wild animals; the archaeozoological samples from Iron Age sites in southeast Italy (*Table 5.3*) also contain bones of wild boar, fox and wolf, to name but a few. Apparently, these wild animals' habitat could be found in close vicinity of the inhabited areas. This, in its turn, suggests that there was only limited human impact on the regional natural landscape in this period, which is, in fact, also the conclusion that can be drawn from the survey data. Even though a gradual infill of some previously marginal landscapes can be observed, southeast Italy still seems to be thinly populated in this period. Settlements were located at some distance from each other, and even though there may have been paths connecting them, much of the landscapes in between are likely to have remained basically untouched by man and can be considered as 'wild' grounds.

In chapter 4, it was discussed in detail what these 'wild grounds' around l'Amastuola and Muro Tenente may have looked like, consisting of different forms of *macchia* and undisturbed woodland. I also mentioned the archaeozoological samples from the Metapontino, which have shown that this area was more densely forested in Antiquity than it is today. Bökönyi has used faunal material to reconstruct different landscape types in the Metaponto area between the Late Neolithic and the Late Roman Imperial periods.[63] Based on the presence of certain species, he argued that there must have been at least four types of habitats (see *Table 6.1*). This reconstruction, however, applies to the entire archaeozoological assemblage from the Metapontino (i.e. it is not site- or period-specific). There is only one site that yielded wild animal bones from the Early Iron Age, namely l'Incoronata (see *Table 5.3*). The low percentage of wild species in comparison to domesticated animals indicates that hunting was not of great importance here. This is different at sites from earlier and later periods in the Metapontino. For example, the ratio of wild animal bones at Final Bronze Age Termitito was much higher (15.9%).[64] Nevertheless, at l'Incoronata the bones of six wild species were found, the majority belonging to red deer (*Cervus elaphus*), followed by turtle (*Chelonia*), and small ratios of wild boar (*Sus scrofa*), ibex (*Capra ibex*), brown hare (*Lepus europaeus*) and roe deer (*Capreolus capreolus*). Outside the Metapontino, the excavations in Early Iron Age-Valesio and Monte Irsi also produced

---

[60] Burgers 1998, pp. 186-191.
[61] Yntema 2013, p. 65.
[62] Yntema 1993, p. 157.
[63] Bökönyi 2010, pp. 6-9.
[64] Bökönyi 2010, p. 5.

Habitat	Indicator species
grassland with forested spots (*Parklandschaft*)	aurochs (*Bos primigenius*) wild ass (*Equus hydruntinus*) brown hare (*Lepus europaeus*) Greek tortoise (*Testudo hermanni*) fallow deer (*Dama dama*) roe deer (*Capreolus capreolus*) wild cat (*Felis silvestris*) badger (*Meles meles*) fox (*Vulpes vulpes*))
large, dense forests	red deer (*Cervus elaphus*) wild boar (*Sus scrofa*) fox (*Vulpes vulpes*)
gallery forests along rivers or watercourses	wild duck (*Anas*) wolf (*Canis lupus*) weasel (*Mustela nivalis*) fallow deer (*Dama dama*) roe deer (*Capreolus capreolus*) wild cat (*Felis silvestris*)
medium range or high mountains	black vulture (*Aegypius monachus*) ibex (*Capra ibex*) chamois (*Rupicapra rupicapra*) fox (*Vulpes vulpes*) wolf (*Canis lupus*) weasel (*Mustela nivalis*)

Table 6.1 Habitat types for the encountered animal species in the Metapontino between the Late Neolithic and the Late Roman Imperial periods, after Bökönyi 2010

small numbers of wild animal bones. At the former site, red deer, brown hare, red-legged partridge (*Alectoris rufa*), and western marsh-harrier (*Circus aeruginosus*) were found. At Monte Irsi, the presence of red deer has also been attested.

Following Bökönyi's proposed habitat types, the landscapes around l'Incoronata, Valesio, and Monte Irsi may have been characterized by grasslands and forests in this period. The presence of ibex indicates that the inhabitants made longer hunting excursions, as the terrain in the Metapontino would have been too flat and too densely populated to accommodate this animal. Such hunting trips may have been a privilege of the leisure class, who could afford to be away from home for a long time and bring back valuable and no doubt status-enhancing prey (a single full-grown male ibex can weigh as much as 110 kg). The huntsmen on horseback that can be seen on many Daunian *stelai* (see for example *Figure 4.1*) could be interpreted as an illustration of these practices, although it is unclear what type of landscape is pictured here.

Based on the archaeobotanical and archaeozoological evidence, it can be hypothesized that beside the extensive exploitation of 'wild grounds' at a long distance from the settlements, there would have been another 'ring' of uncultivated landscapes that was easier to reach. Beside the evidence of hunting activities that can be found in the archaeozoological data, the charcoal assemblages from the Early Iron Age phases at Torre Mordillo and l'Amastuola are also indicative of the exploitation of woodlands and *macchia* zones (see *Table 5.5* and chapter 4). The samples from Iron Age levels at Torre Mordillo also contained a limited amount of charcoal, that was identified as olive, deciduous oak and elm wood. The latter two can probably be associated with forests, which supplied firewood and possibly also building material (section 5.3.1). Moreover, these areas must have functioned as foraging zones for sheep/goats, pigs and possibly cattle and provided additional food, such as game and wild fruits and nuts. Wild fruit gathering was apparently quite common in the Bronze Age. Nuts are rare in Iron Age samples from southeast Italy, but there were some remains of acorns among the finds from the most recent levels (Final Bronze Age/Early Iron Age) at Torre Mordillo.

Another indication of the presence of woodland is provided by the palynological evidence from the Laghi Alimini, which suggest that the oak-dominated woodland around the lakes recovered, and even slightly expanded in the Early Iron Age.[65] Lower charcoal frequencies in the cores suggest that clearance by burning was less widespread, allowing high *macchia* or scrub to re-establish in some areas. There is also an increased presence of pollen from evergreen oak species, indicating the recovery of high *macchia* vegetation.

In contrast, most of the weed seeds that are found in Early Iron Age levels at Broglio di Trebisacce and Botromagno can be associated with cultivated zones and/or (abandoned) crop fields including, for instance, (upright) goosefoot (*Chenopodium urbicum*), canarygrass, ryegrasses (*Lolium*), knotweed (*Polygonum*), sandwort (*Arenaria*), and corn gromwell. Indeed, the macroremains also indicate that at least parts of the Iron Age landscapes were already cleared and used for crop cultivation. The diverse crop spectra from Broglio di Trebisacce, Torre Mordillo, l'Incoronata, Botromagno, and l'Amastuola (including hulled barley, free-threshing wheat, emmer, einkorn, spelt, broad bean, bitter vetch, vetchling, and possibly also chickpea and garlic) suggest that these settlements were mainly focused on subsistence agriculture, limiting the risk of individual crop failure. Indeed, I already proposed the hypothesis that olive and grape cultivation was probably practiced on a small and localized scale in this period, if such risky, time- and capital- demanding activities were carried out at all. Olive stones from Early Iron Age contexts are rare, the only two sites where they were found are Broglio di Trebisacce and Torre Mordillo. The earliest carbonized grape pips appear in the archaeobotanical assemblages from l'Incoronata and l'Amastuola (both datable between the late 8th and early 7th century BC). At other sites, such as Botromagno, archaeobotanical sampling did not provide any grape or olive remains.

SUMMARY: THE EARLY IRON AGE (C. 1000–600 BC)

Regional diversity and settlement patterns
We will see in the next section that the increasing intensity of contacts between southeast Italy and the Greek world clearly set some areas apart. However, it would take at least two or three generations before the colonization process resulted in distinct changes in town planning and architecture, and even longer before its effect became notable in the landscape and the way it was exploited. Archaeological evidence from the Early Iron Age shows that the Greek settlements at Taras and Metapontion were of the dispersed type and consisted of several small groups. This feature also contributes to an image of relative uniformity. Nevertheless, in the course of the 8th century BC regional features become steadily more pronounced. A process of 'regionalization' is apparent in the production of pottery and metal, funerary customs, character of the dwellings and settlement types.

Agricultural strategies
Settlement dynamics in Early Iron Age southeast Italy are characterized by at least two general trends. First, new settlements were established on good arable soils further inland, and second, some of the larger regional centres expanded considerably. The reclamation of the previously unexploited inland is a clear sign of agricultural expansion, especially since the new habitation centres were built almost exclusively in areas with fertile, well-watered soils. The archaeobotanical evidence is also indicative of clearances and arable cultivation. The crop spectra from Early Iron Age sites show much variety, probably because a wide array of crops was cultivated at each site to ensure that subsistence needs were met. Olive and grape finds are rare, probably because in this period their cultivation only took place on a

---

[65] Harding 1999, p. 74.

relatively small and localized scale, or not at all. Meanwhile, the archaeozoological data illustrate that sheep/goat herding was probably the most important type of livestock keeping in this period.

Human impact on the natural landscape
Signs that human impact on the landscape became more intense are easy to detect in the earliest phase of the Early Iron Age. Both the infill of the inland areas and the gradual process of settlement expansion are clear indications of this trend. Although it is unlikely that the peninsula was densely inhabited in this period, it can be assumed that the changes were at least partially catalyzed by demographic growth. On the other hand, the impact of forest clearances should certainly not be overestimated. The palynological data from the Laghi Alimini suggest that the forest zones around the lakes even slightly expanded. This ties in with the archaeological evidence from the more recent part of the Early Iron Age (the 7th century BC), which shows distinct signs of stabilization after the 'colonization' of the inland areas. The charcoal data from Torre Mordillo and l'Amastuola also provide evidence of the exploitation of woodlands and high *macchia* zones. There are indications that these 'wild' areas were used to collect additional food (e.g. game, wild fruit, or nuts) and raw materials, such as wood, and to graze livestock.

6.4 THE ARCHAIC/CLASSICAL PERIODS (C. 600-325 BC)

The Archaic/Classical periods include a major phase of social and economic innovations in southeast Italy which started in the 6th century BC. This period not only saw the rise of four Greek colonial settlements in southeast Italy (Taras, Metapontion, Siris/Herakleia and Sybaris), but also witnessed the formalization of their rural territories. A move towards increasing complexity in settlement structure occurred in the inland areas as well.

The coastal areas
Land use in the coastal areas of southeast Italy in the Archaic and Classical periods was closely intertwined with the formalization and organization of Greek rural territories. This was especially the case in the Metapontino. The earliest substantial structures (a small temple known as Sacellum C and the first phase of Temple D) at this site date to about 620/600 BC.[66] Within the course of the 6th century BC, the town grew considerably and acquired distinct urban features, such as an orthogonal street plan, city walls, an *ekklesiasterion* with room for 8,000 people, and several monumental temples.[67] By the end of the 6th century BC, Metapontion showed strong resemblances to contemporary urban centres in Greece and other parts of Magna Graecia.

In this same period, Metapontion also began to organize its agricultural territory. One of the most distinct features of this territory is the systems of land division, which consist of parallel linear 'anomalies' that were discovered on aerial photographs in the 1950s.[68] The lines are located approximately 210 metres apart, beginning just outside the ancient city and running approximately. 14 kilometres inland, and were probably laid out in the first half of the 5th century BC at the latest.[69] There is still no consensus as to how to interpret these features. It has been argued that some were roads or canals dug

---

[66] Carter 1998, p. 7. Cf. Yntema 2000, p. 14.

[67] According to Carter (2006, p. 101), the new urban plan of Metapontion, with all its essentials, was envisioned, if not completely realized, by the middle of the 6th century BC.

[68] These photos were taken during a complete survey of the Italian peninsula (*volo di base*) in 1954-1955 by the Italian air force. Adamesteanu 1973.

[69] The main axis of the division of the Metapontine *chora* has an orientation that appears to be only a few degrees different from that of Plateia A, the main street of the *asty*, and may therefore be contemporary. Obviously, it is quite

to drain parts of the countryside.[70] According to Carter, the lines indicate a division of the *chora* into rectangular plots that might represent equal-sized holdings.[71]

The field surveys in the area between the Bradano and Basento rivers have shown that this strictly organized territory soon became littered with farmsteads, but small rural *necropoleis* and sanctuaries were also present, for instance at Pantanello.[72] In the area covered by the surveys, the density of farm sites developed as follows:[73]

Period	Number of farm sites in the survey transect
600-550 BC	5
550-500 BC	66
500-450 BC	116
450-400 BC	53
400-350 BC	46
350-300 BC	128
300-250 BC	73

Following Carter's[74] calculations for the Early Hellenistic period (see below), there would be as many as 789 farm units operating in the entire *chora* between 500 and 450 BC, resulting in a rural population of between 4,000 and 8,700 individuals. Assuming, as Carter does, that the total area of the territory measured about 20,000 ha, the resulting population density would be between 20 and 43 persons per square km and every farm would have over 25 ha of land at its disposal.[75]

The land divisions in the Metapontino tie in with Ian Morris' exploitation model for Archaic Greece, in which farmers lived in the *chora* of their *polis* on plots of roughly the same size, i.e. between 5 and 15 hectares.[76] As Foxhall[77] has pointed out, minimal estimates of a viable 'peasant' holding have clustered roughly around 4-5 hectares, which is also close to the maximum area which a single household without access to extra labour could cultivate.[78] In other words, the average plot size in the Metapontino (of over 25 ha) is rather large. Assuming that Carter's calculations are correct, Foxhall suggests that this anomaly may be explained by the fact that larger holdings were more extensively worked, with only a relatively small proportion being used to plant arable crops.[79] Long fallow periods, grazing, and tree crops might have been useful alternatives when land was not in short supply in rela-

---

difficult to date the division lines themselves, but on the basis of the chronology of the central road system, it can be argued that they were laid out in the first half of the 5th century BC at the latest. If this date is correct, the land division system at Metapontion is the oldest known example in Magna Graecia, but it is by no means unique. Similar regular, orthogonal grid systems have been found in the *chora* of Chersonesus Taurica in modern Ukraine on the Black Sea coast, on ancient Pharos (Hvar) in the Adriatic Sea (founded in 384 BC), and at Megara Hyblaea, Syracuse and Selinous on Sicily. Carter *et al.* 2004; Carter 2006, p. 202.

[70] Carter *et al.* 1985, pp. 303-305.
[71] Carter 2006, p. 94. Cf. De Siena 2001, p. 766.
[72] For example, Carter 1980, 1998; Carter *et al.* 1985; Carter 2001, pp. 779-781.
[73] Table reproduced from Carter 1990, p. 410.
[74] Carter 1990, p. 410.
[75] Carter 2006, p. 120.
[76] Morris points out that the spacing of Classical rural sites in Metapontion as well as Boeotia, Haliesis, the Nemea valley, Kea and Chios points to contiguous blocks of land averaging five to fifteen hectares. Morris 1994, p. 364. Cf. Hanson 1995, pp. 51-89.
[77] Foxhall 2003, p. 83. Farm units under the management of a single household with one yoke of cattle could have cultivated a maximum of 5-6 hectares per year as arable crops over 20-30 days' ploughing per year at a rate of 0.2-0.3 hectare per day.
[78] See bibliography in Foxhall 2003, note 39.
[79] Foxhall 2003, p. 83.

tion to human and animal labour. This could have been the case in the Metapontino. Such a system with long fallow periods would only work for cereal cultivation, and not for viticulture and oleiculture since vines and olive trees need to be tended for several years before they produce fruit. Indeed, there are indications that the rural economy at Metapontion was mostly based on cereal cultivation, to such an extent that a head of six-rowed barley is represented on Metapontine coins (*Figure 6.1*), which were issued from the third quarter of the 6th century BC onwards.

Apart from its practical use, the land divisions may also have had a social-political motivation. It has been argued that they can be associated with political reforms, in the sense that after a long period of oligarchy or even tyranny, it suddenly became possible for an individual family to own a parcel of land.[80] In Aristotle's *Politics*, reference is made to the Greek statesman Phaleas of Chalcedon (4th century BC?) who argued that an equal division of land and equal education for all citizens would eliminate civil strife (A 6.49).

In any case, the spread of rural farmsteads is probably indicative of population growth, and definitely of an increase in scale and efficiency of production.[81] The *chora* of Metapontion was considerably productive in the late Archaic and early Classical period. Indeed, on the basis of pottery distribution patterns, Carter argues that produce such as timber, animals and most of all, cereals also appealed to a market beyond the *chora*. Archaic Metapontine pottery and terracotta objects were widely distributed outside the *chora*, both at other Greek sites and in the indigenous centres in the basins of the Bradano and Basento rivers.[82] Another interesting indication of trade was brought forward by Mertens, who pointed out that the building stones for the large structures in the urban centre of Metapontion originate from the area between Ginosa, Castellaneta and Laterza (about 40 kilometres to the northeast, in Apulia).[83]

The survey data suggest that something drastic happened in the Metapontine countryside in the middle of the 5th century BC. According to Carter, the sudden decrease in the number of sites (from 116 to 53 sites in the surveyed area) can probably be explained by a sudden rise of the groundwater level. Geomorphologist James Abbott has shown that human activity, especially agriculture and forest clearances, may have caused episodes of alluviation and erosion in the Metapontino that can be dated back as far as the mid-Neolithic.[84] Indeed, groundwater levels were already high in the Metapontino when the colonial *chora* was arranged, which may explain why the area's cereal cultivation was based on barley instead of wheat.[85] However, the erosion started to have serious implications for human life in the *chora* in the Archaic/Classical periods, as the mouths of the rivers Bradano and Basento became blocked and caused a rise of the water table between 50 centimetres and 1 metre along the whole coastal plain. Carter and Abbott have both argued that the effects of this phenomenon are clearly demonstrated by the decrease in the number of rural sites, but also by the excavations in the *asty* of Metapontion, where no new monumental buildings were erected in the 5th century BC and the existing ones quickly deteriorated.[86] According to these authors, this may be related to the fact that the river valleys turned into swamps, and apparently also into breeding grounds for the *Anopheles* mosquito, the vector of malaria.[87]

However, this account of the events in the Metapontino in the 5th century BC can be challenged on several grounds. First, it seems rather odd that after the temporary dip, the *asty* and *chora* of Meta-

---

[80] Carter 2006, pp. 91-132.

[81] See Hanson 1995, pp. 51-89, on the intensification of agriculture in Classical Greece and the necessity for the farmer to live on or near his land.

[82] Carter 2006, pp. 113-114, note 56.

[83] Mertens 1998, pp. 123-124.

[84] Abbott 1997.

[85] Wheat does not thrive well on wet clays, see Renfrew 1973, p. 66.

[86] Carter 2006, pp. 230-231.

[87] Carter 2006, p. 43. The study of the anthropological remains from the rural *necropolis* at Pantanello by Henneberg and Henneberg (1992, p. 455) shows that malaria was endemic in the population of the chora over the

pontion suddenly regained prosperity between the later 4th and early 3rd century BC. Indeed, the number of farm sites from the second half of the 4th century BC is without precedent. How does this tie in with the perceived period of decline, only fifty years earlier? Second, it is not entirely true that no new monumental buildings were erected in the *asty* of Metapontion in the 5th century BC, since the construction of another big temple in the Ionic order started around 470 BC.[88] In fact, the 'dip' in the number of farmsteads may not represent an archaeological reality. As Yntema has pointed out, the middle of the 5th century BC is altogether poorly represented in southeast Italy, probably as a result of methodological issues (i.e. problems with pottery sequences that make it difficult to distinguish archaeological contexts from this period).[89]

In comparison to Metapontion, much less is known about the other Greek settlements in southeast Italy. This especially holds true for Sybaris, since the remains of this town are buried under more than four meters of alluvial sediment. We are dependent on ancient written sources for information about its agricultural territory. I already discussed references to grape cultivation and wine production in Sybaris/Thourioi in section 5.3.3. The vineyards of Sybaris enjoyed more than regional fame, and produced some of the finest wines in Magna Graecia. We do not know how this wine production was organized, but it was probably produced on a large enough scale to allow the export of a part of the surplus. Indeed, several authors refer to Sybaris' overseas trade contacts, for instance with Miletus.[90]

Sybaris was destroyed by neighbouring Kroton in 510 BC (after 444 BC, the town was revived as Thourioi). Several reconstructions and explanations have been offered for this fall, including Strabo's account that the Crotoniates diverted the course of the river Crathis to submerge Sybaris.[91] However, analysis of sediment facies in two cores from the Sybaris archaeological park has not provided any evidence of fluvial sandy conglomerates deposited directly on top of the site.[92] The burial of Sybaris more likely resulted from natural processes such as fluvial overbank alluviation. Another version of the events that presumably led to Sybaris' decline is offered by Diodorus Siculus, who connects the fall of the town to an episode of social strife.[93] In his account, the oligarchic government of the city was overthrown, the 500 richest citizens were sent into exile, and their wealth was confiscated.

Siris was also destroyed, by its neighbours Metapontion, Sybaris and Kroton, around 550 BC. However, the territory continued to be inhabited, and regained its *polis* status in the 5th century BC when a new Greek town, Herakleia, was founded. As far as its agricultural territory is concerned, too little is known about early Siris to establish whether its *chora* was organized like Metapontion's. No archaeological evidence of land divisions has been found around Herakleia, either. However, the Herakleia tablets do supply some information about a system of land redistributions in the latter *chora*. Apparently, at some point during the first half of the 4th century BC previously occupied lands were re-measured and redistributed to new owners. Uguzzoni and Ghinatti have argued that in the preceding period (i.e. before the 4th century BC), most of the land was apparently under the control of a few people.[94] The fact that the tablets specifically state that the new owners had to build a farmstead on their rented plots, also suggests that these did not exist yet. Indeed, the *tavole* do not mention any isolated farms or small rural settlements in the detailed description of the *chora* of Herakleia, so the people that worked on the land probably lived in the city and travelled up and down to their fields on a daily basis.[95] However, an alternative interpretation can be proposed, namely that the developments

---

whole period that this burial ground was in use (i.e. from the early 6th to the early 3rd centuries BC). It may also have been the primary cause for the population decline from the 3rd century BC onwards. The chora lay virtually abandoned from the 6th century AD until relatively recent times (Carter 2006, p. 224).

[88] Carter 1998, p. 11.

[89] Yntema 1997, pp. 105-107.

[90] Athen. 519; Herodotus, *Hist.* 6.21.1.

[91] *Geographica* 6.1.13.

[92] Stanley and Bernasconi 2009, p. 82.

[93] Diodorus Siculus, *Bibliotheca historica* 12.9-10.

[94] Uguzzoni and Ghinatti 1968, pp. 91-92.

[95] Uguzzoni and Ghinatti 1968, pp. 116-117.

that are described on the tablets represent a return to an earlier situation, when the *chora* of Siris had already been formally organized. Archaeological surveys would add enormously to our knowledge of the territories of Siris/Herakleia.

This is also largely the case at Taras, although we know that by the early 6th century BC this town started to show the first physical aspects of a Greek *asty*, with a temple, a regular layout and a *necropolis* outside the habitation area. The city had also started issuing its own coins, displaying its eponymous hero sitting on the back of a dolphin.[96] The Tarantino is studied well enough to be fairly certain that the *chora* was not divided into regular plots.[97] No trace of such lines was found on aerial photographs, during the topographic prospections in the *chora* that were carried out by the Soprintendenza per i Beni Archeologici della Puglia in the 1970s and 1980s, or the archaeological surveys by the Università del Salento and ACVU.[98] Although these surveys did not cover the entire *chora*, the north-western and south-eastern parts of the area around Taranto have been well covered. Interestingly, these two parts of the *polis'* territory did not develop in the same way at all. Based on documentary evidence and chance finds of ritual and funerary nature, Alessio and Guzzo[99] have argued that from the 6th century BC onwards the southern side of the Tarantine *chora* gradually became occupied by small rural sites. In contrast, Burgers and Crielaard have shown that until the 5th century BC, l'Amastuola was the only site in the sample areas north-west of Taranto.[100] According to these authors, Taras expanded only east- and southwards.[101] This conclusion is partly based on the ACVU survey data from the area around the l'Amastuola hill, which is located to the north-west of Taras. Small rural sites started to appear only in the later 5th century BC, when a remarkable reorganization and expansion of the settlement on the l'Amastuola hilltop can be witnessed. The site's south terrace was abandoned, and a new settlement was built on the slopes north and east of the hill. Burgers and Crielaard connect these changes to the incorporation of the territory of l'Amastuola into the *chora* of Taras. Literary and epigraphic sources indicate that during the first decades of the 5th century a series of violent confrontations took place between the Greeks of Taras and indigenous peoples. Herodotus reports that a confederacy of indigenous peoples led by Iapyges annihilated an army of Taras and Rhegion.[102] After this defeat, which must have taken place around 473 BC, democratic reforms were carried through at Taras. These reforms possibly included the expropriation of rural estates that belonged to elite figures that were sent into exile.[103]

Summarizing, the formalization and organization of rural territories did not follow the same course in the various Greek colonies. However, literary sources indicate that they had at least one factor in common. In all the Greek towns, there are indications of social/political reforms that resulted in the confiscation of land belonging to wealthy elite groups. If we assume that the chronology of the land division system is correct, these reforms started to take place at Metapontion in the first half of the 5th century BC. It may have happened even earlier at Sybaris, where the fall of the town may be connected to an episode of social strife and the richest citizens were sent into exile. There are also references to

[96] Yntema 2000, p. 21.

[97] As we have seen above, the land divisions at Metapontion may have had a political motivation. We know from the Herakleia tablets that a similar revolution took place in at least one other *chora*, but matters may have been different at Taras.

[98] Cf. Burgers and Crielaard 2007, pp. 92-99, with further references listed under note 33.

[99] Alessio and Guzzo 1989-1990, p. 366.

[100] Burgers and Crielaard 2007, p. 95.

[101] Burgers and Crielaard 2007, p. 107.

[102] *Histories* 7.170.3: 'The result was that no one has ever heard of so great a slaughter of Greeks as that of the Tarentines and Rhegians; three thousand townsmen of the latter, men who had been coerced by Micythus son of Choerus to come and help the Tarentines, were killed, and no count was kept of the Tarentine slain.' Translation by A. D. Godley, www.perseus.tufts.edu.

[103] Arist. *Pol.* 5.3.7 [1303a.3]): '[...] for instance at Tarentum when a great many notables were defeated and killed by the Iapygians a short time after the Persian wars a constitutional government was changed to a democracy [...]' Translation by H. Rackham, www.perseus.tufts.edu.

democratic reforms at Herakleia and Taras, which must have taken place before the 4th century and during the first decades of the 5th century, respectively. We know from the Herakleia tablets that the confiscated lands were redistributed among a larger group of agricultural smallholders. This may also have happened at the other towns. Such a change could partly explain the apparent prosperity of the colonial agricultural economies in the Classical and Early Hellenistic periods (see below).

But what was the agricultural basis of these economies? The pollen from the Pantanello core are indicative of a diversified crop spectrum, with some cereal and olive pollen. In the late 6th and early 5th century BC, however, a significant increase of grazing indicators such as knapweeds (*Centaurea*) and plantain (*Plantago*) can be observed,[104] providing an indirect indication that sheep and goat herds were also numerous in this period.[105] The archaeozoological samples from the Pantanello sanctuary are dominated by cattle (52.74%), followed by sheep/goats, horses and pig.[106] According to Carter,[107] the dominance of cattle (presumably for traction) reflects the importance of cereal cultivation. This is debatable, however. As can be seen in *Table 5.3*, the archaeozoological samples from the Pantanello sanctuary are the only ones that contain high percentages of cattle bones. In other parts of the site, such as the *necropoleis* and a refuse dump that is referred to as the 'Greek pit', the animal remains included a much smaller number of cattle bones. It can be concluded that the high percentage of cattle is rather related to the ritual character of this context, i.e. that bovines were sacrificed in the sanctuary.[108] Indeed, the reliance on pastoralism rather than arable cultivation is confirmed by the recently published results from another pollen core from the Metapontino, taken in an Archaic farmhouse at Ponte Fabrizio.[109] This pollen spectrum indicates that grazing lands were prevalent and more extensive than cereal fields on the slopes near the site. According to Florenzano,[110] pastoral management was a major activity during the 4th century BC, probably continuing traditions that were already established in the area at least as early as the 6th century BC. In addition, the development of shrubby vegetation strongly suggests that the predominant domesticated animals were ovicaprines.

By the middle of the 4th century BC, however, the grazing indicators in the Pantanello core decline. Instead, *macchia* species such as *Pistacia* and *Phillyrea* start to appear, and olive, cereals and legumes peak. There may be a connection between the proliferation of *macchia* species and the livestock composition in the Metapontino, e.g. when the sheep/goat population declined.[111] The contemporary peak of olive, cereal and legume pollen suggests that pastoralism was replaced by arboriculture and arable cultivation. Interestingly, the animal remains from the Pantanello complex (6th-3rd centuries BC, see *Table 5.3*) yielded the highest number of wild species of all the sample areas in the Metapontino. As Bökönyi has noted, this high number is surprising for this period, because one would expect less reliance on hunting in a 'civilized' Greek colonial town.[112] Apparently, there were still enough 'wild areas' in the Metapontino to allow the local population to engage in hunting activities. Indeed, Bökönyi also reports several indications of the introduction of new domesticated animal breeds in the *chora* of Metapontion.[113] For instance, a clear difference in size can be noted between the small 'prehistoric' sheep at pre-colonial

[104] Carter *et al.* 1985, p. 290.
[105] Carter 2006, p. 31.
[106] Bökönyi 2010, *Table 1.7*, p. 10.
[107] Carter 2006, p. 29.
[108] Indeed, Bökönyi (2010, p. 19) has noted that it is fruitless to examine the Pantanello samples to learn more about the development of the domestic fauna, since they are too small to be representative.
[109] Florenzano 2014.
[110] Florenzano 2014, p. 138.
[111] Carter 2006, p. 31. These animals thrive on *macchia* vegetation, and may have eaten the plants' inflorescences and in this way prevented it from releasing pollen. Conversely, an increase of *macchia* pollen could indicate that less *macchia* flowers were eaten by browsers, possibly because there were less of them. Unfortunately, there are insufficient archaeozoological data to confirm this hypothesis.
[112] Bökönyi 2010, p. 6. It should be added that the number of wild species is this high in the Pantanello sanctuary only, and may be related to the ritual character of this context.
[113] Bökönyi 2010, p. 20.

l'Incoronata and a larger species that was found in layers that were datable to the 6th century BC. The latter might have been a superior breed, possibly introduced by the Greek colonists.[114]

Unfortunately, on the basis of the current evidence it is difficult to establish whether the prosperity of the Metapontino is characteristic of the *chorai* of Greek settlements in southeast Italy in this period. As Carter[115] has pointed out, Metapontion may have been a relatively wealthy *polis* and in that sense perhaps not easily comparable to Sybaris, Siris and Taras. On the other hand, Sybaris was generally known as one of the richest cities in the Archaic Greek world. It is also said to have exported fine wines, which would require a rather evolved rural economy. Another indication is the evidence of overseas transport in Corinthian B amphorae. Such vessels were made in several production centres along the southern Italian coast, suggesting that a highly developed agricultural economy had developed there.[116] In other words, the evidence hints at regional specialization among the Greek towns (cereals at Metapontion, wine at Sybaris), but we do not have enough information to support that hypothesis.

The inland areas
Meanwhile, land use in the contemporary inland areas was not nearly as large-scale and strictly organized as in the Greek *chorai* on the coast. Yet, here, too, we can observe a tendency towards urbanization or, in any case, increasing complexity in settlement forms.[117] In the second half of the 6th century BC, some of these settlements contracted, lost much of their dispersed character and acquired a more town-like appearance. The Iron Age huts were replaced by houses in almost every part of southeast Italy, in such sites as l'Amastuola (see chapter 2), l'Incoronata[118] and Cavallino.[119] At the latter site, huts were replaced by rectangular houses with stone foundations and tiled roofs, a radial pattern of paved streets was laid out, and a monumental fortification wall was built.[120] Another example of an Archaic site that underwent a major transformation in this period is Serra di Vaglio in the uplands of Basilicata. This site changed from a dispersed hut settlement to a small town with distinct urban features in the second half of the 6th century BC.[121] Monumental architecture has also been found at several other inland sites. The discovery of a large Doric capital on the highest part of the central hill at Oria in southern Apulia shows that in the end of the 5th or early 4th century BC a monumental building was constructed here.[122] Another telling example is the construction of four Archaic temples with stone foundations, as well as several houses with stone foundations on the Timpone della Motta near Francavilla Marittima.[123]

Moreover, some of the traditional burial grounds, which were located between habitation clusters in the highly dispersed Iron Age settlements, were replaced by a new type of *necropolis*. This new type of *necropolis* was located outside of the habitation areas, consisted of several (family?) clusters and was usually in use for a very long time.[124] Interestingly, formal burials made their appearance in Salento (southern Apulia) in this same period. Before the late 7th century BC, the dead were apparently buried in an archaeologically invisible way.[125]

However, it should be noted that considerable differences continued to exist between individual settlements. Whereas sites such as Cavallino were surrounded by fortifications, and an aristocratic dining hall (the so-called Braida building) was erected near the foot of the Serra di Vaglio plateau, other sites remained relatively small and continued to display many of their Early Iron Age features. This

---

[114] Carter (2006, p. 29) regards these finds as evidence of 'biological imperialism'.
[115] Carter 1998, pp. 8-9.
[116] Gassner 2011; Sourisseau 2012, in press.
[117] Yntema 2013, p. 115.
[118] See section 5.2, with further references.
[119] D'Andria 1996, p. 412.
[120] Pancrazzi 1979; D'Andria 2005.
[121] Cf. Yntema 2013, p. 120, with further references.
[122] Yntema 1993, p. 169.
[123] Maaskant-Kleibrink 2003; 2006, with further references.
[124] The *necropoleis* of Schirone and Madonelle at Siris-Herakleia and the one at Taras are good examples of this new type of burial ground. Cf. Yntema 2013, p. 60, with further references.
[125] D'Andria 1991, p. 409.

development has been interpreted as an indication of increasing site hierarchy and regionalization.[126] In this period, the settlements in the inland areas were vastly different from the Greek settlements on the coast. For example, whereas Sybaris, Siris, Metapontion and Taras were laid out according to a very strict, orthogonal plan, the traditional settlement layout remained basically intact at Cavallino, despite the increased use of stone architecture.[127] Another example is the Archaic settlement at Timpone della Motta, where houses with stone foundations were built. However, these houses were not part of an urban lay-out with paved streets, nor did they have tile-covered roofs.[128]

Other differences between the coast and the inland areas occur in the organization of the countryside. While the rural areas around some of the Greek settlements, notably Metapontion, became strictly organized and littered with small rural farmsteads, the countryside around the inland centres remained uninhabited. For example, during the Archaic/Classical periods Oria functioned as a kind of agro-town.[129] The whole population and part of the livestock lived inside the fortified settlement. In the mornings, the inhabitants left for their fields, which must have been at close distance from the town and in the empty spaces between the habitation nuclei of the settlement, to return to their homes in the evenings. Obviously, this is not the most economical way of tilling the soil, as a farmer has to spend a considerable amount of time and energy on traveling each day.[130] Farmers at Archaic/Classical Oria were probably not involved in agriculture and stock raising in order to supply goods to large external markets, but rather to gain subsistence for their own family units.[131] In effect, this situation is a continuation of the land use strategies current in the Early Iron Age.

I believe that this holds true for most parts of the rural economy in the inland areas of southeast Italy in this period, including l'Amastuola. We have seen in chapters 2 and 4 that the inhabitants of l'Amastuola were not dependent on exchange to fulfil most of their everyday needs. There are a few indications of surplus production, such as the presence of imported objects, but these should probably be interpreted as luxurious and perhaps prestigious additions to local production. There are a few other examples of imported foodstuffs in indigenous contexts from this period, including the dates that were found in the 6th- and 5th-century BC votive deposits in the sanctuary of Monte Papalucio.[132] According to Harding, the appearance of walnut in the fossil record from the Laghi Alimini in the Archaic period may also represent an element of increasing trade contact with Greece.[133] This assumption, however, has not been confirmed by other archaeobotanical finds.

This does not mean, however, that the inland centres did not engage in exchanges at all. On the contrary, imports from Greece and the Greek coastal settlements in southern Italy are fairly common in indigenous inland centres. A case in point is the Archaic Metapontine pottery and terracotta objects that were found in abundance in indigenous centres further inland in Basilicata.[134] Carter believes that Metapontion also exported cereals to these areas. Does this mean that these communities did not produce enough grain themselves? And if so, what did they offer in return? Whitehouse and Wilkins

---

[126] Yntema 2013, p. 128, with further references.

[127] Yntema 2013, p. 121.

[128] Maaskant-Kleibrink 2006.

[129] Yntema 1993, pp. 174-176.

[130] In Greece, the problem of 'farm fragmentation' (as Thompson calls it), has persisted until modern times. Thompson reported that many modern Greek farmers claimed they lost three weeks a year by simply walking to their disparate fields. Similarly, on the Aegean island of Melos survey archaeologists found that modern Greek farmers averaged a mean time of two hours fifty-five minutes travelling to work each day (Hanson 1995, p. 53).

[131] Yntema 1993, p. 175.

[132] Ciaraldi 1997, pp. 219-220; Fiorentino 2008, p. 106. See also section 5.3.4.

[133] Walnut is widely believed to have been imported to Europe in the early Holocene, becoming palynologically evident in north-western Greece around 3200 BP and on the Dalmatian coast in association with Roman activities. In Italy, walnut pollen was found in sediments dated to the early Holocene at Lago di Martignano, see Harding 1999, p. 91.

[134] Carter 2006, pp. 113-114, note 56. Cf. Lo Porto 1973.

identified wool as one of the most important export products of the indigenous areas of southern Apulia.[135] Since southeast Italy lacks useful raw materials such as metals or minerals, domestic products were probably the only items available for exchange. This could either be actual subsistence goods or secondary products such as textiles, skins, objects made of bone, etc. Apulia was famous for its wool production in Roman times; loom weights found in large numbers at indigenous sites in southeast Italy suggest that wool was a likely export product in the Archaic/Classical periods too. According to Whitehouse and Wilkins, the Greek towns could not produce much wool themselves, as it would have been impossible to keep large flocks of sheep all year round within their small territories, assuming that they did not have access to the upland summer pastures. The ancient written sources mention that both Taras and Sybaris were famous for their textile production.[136] If it is true that their rural territory was unsuitable for large-scale pastoral activities, the wool had to be imported. Indeed, the importance of pastoralism is evident at indigenous sites in this period. When we look at the archaeozoological remains from Cavallino and Valesio (see *Table 5.3*), it appears that sheep/goat herding remained the most important form of livestock keeping in the Archaic/Classical Periods.[137] It is not known, however, if this was different in the colonial towns since we have no archaeozoological samples from these sites.

There may have been other forms of exchange in addition to the ones that Whitehouse and Wilkins mention. I already referred to the transport of building stone from southwest Apulia towards Metapontion. Apart from goods, services could have been of great significance as well, although these are not archaeologically visible. For instance, whereas Whitehouse and Wilkins assume that the Greek cities did not have access to upland summer pastures, it is quite possible that the indigenous peoples in the inland areas allowed them to graze their sheep there. In addition, the inland areas could have provided seasonal labourers, for instance during harvests.

One would expect to find clear differences in the crop spectra between the coastal and inland areas, given that the Greek *chorai* were organized in a much more efficient way and there is evidence of agricultural rationalization and specialization. However, this is not the case. The pollen core from the Laghi di Monticchio in inland Basilicata is remarkably similar to the Pantanello one, showing clear evidence of deforestation and a steady increase of arable crops over a few hundred years between about 2500 and 2200 years ago.[138] The archaeobotanical assemblages from Archaic/Classical levels (from l'Amastuola, Botromagno, Monte Irsi, Cavallino, and Monte Papalucio; an overview can be found in the second part of *Table 5.1*) indicate that crop cultivation concentrated mostly on cereals in the inland settlements. Additional evidence can be found in the weed finds from Cavallino, which included

---

[135] Whitehouse and Wilkins 1989, p. 115.

[136] Theocr. vii 785. Cf. Dunbabin 1968, p. 78, p. 90.

[137] The site of Cavallino is an especially interesting example. Pancrazzi 1979 and Veenman 2002 report that in the earliest phase (Middle Bronze Age, c. 1600-1400 BC), this settlement's livestock spectrum is apparently dominated by cattle (*Bos taurus*). The high culling ages suggest that most of these animals were used for traction, although they undoubtedly also provided meat. The percentages of *Bos taurus* drop significantly in the Iron Age. Although cattle is still very well represented, the livestock is dominated by sheep/goat in this period. It is important to note that this shift in animal husbandry took place in the same period that other major changes can be observed in the settlement history of Cavallino (D'Andria, 'Le trasformazioni dell'insediamento', see elsewhere in this section). Interestingly, there are also archaeological indications for the importance of sheep and goat rearing in this period, such as the numerous finds of loom weights and spindle whorls. In addition, recent excavations at Cavallino also revealed the remains of a pathway that evidently formed a direct connection between the living quarters and the countryside. According to D'Andria (2005, p. 40), this 7 metres wide, so-called 'strada V' served as a sheep trail, flanked by the sort of *a secco* walls that can still be found in rural contexts in modern Salento. The trail opened into spacious animal pens that were also delimited by *a secco* walls, in the middle of a living quarter ('Zona G- Fondo Casino').

[138] Watts *et al.* 1996, p. 126: 'The last phase of the Holocene shows the decline to extinction of *Abies* and *Tuxus*. If we accept the 2460 BP date, then the extinctions took place

corncockle (*Agrostemma githago*), which is a common weed in cereal fields, and white goosefoot, which thrives on all soil types, but especially on fertile disturbed grounds. Interestingly, olive stones and grape pips are still relatively rare at these inland sites, appearing only in small amounts in the samples from Cavallino, l'Amastuola, and Monte Papalucio. If we compare these results with the Pantanello pollen core, it appears that the crop spectra in the Greek *chorai* and the indigenous inland areas are more or less the same. No clear differences can be noted in the livestock composition either. At the inland sites of Cavallino and Valesio, as well as the 'Greek pit' from Pantanello, the archaeozoological data continue to be dominated by sheep/goats.[139]

We saw in the previous section that the dispersed Iron Age sites in southeast Italy had a distinctly rural character, and human impact on the natural landscape was probably still limited in this period. Considering the urbanization trends at some settlements in the ensuing Archaic/Classical periods, one would expect to see changes in the exploitation of the landscape as well. However, archaeobotanical and archaeozoological data suggest that the situation remained more or less the same. Firstly, the macroremains assemblages from the Archaic/Classical periods show that wild fruit collecting was still a common way to supplement daily meals. There is also archaeozoological evidence of the extensive exploitation of 'wild grounds'. At Valesio, for instance, the archaeozoological finds of roe deer, red deer, brown hare and wild boar are indicative of hunting being important. Unfortunately, we have to rely mostly on these indirect sources of information for the vegetation around the inland settlements, since anthracological and palynological data from this period are particularly scarce. Nevertheless, the charcoal assemblages from the Archaic/Classical periods at Cavallino and Monte Papalucio (*Table 5.5*) confirm that uncultivated landscapes with climax vegetation were found close to the settlement areas. The assemblage from Cavallino suggests that firewood was collected in a landscape with olive-dominated *macchia* and *leccete* (evergreen oak forest) which, according to the researchers, were situated just outside the settlement.[140] The charcoal assemblage from Monte Papalucio also included mostly Mediterranean *macchia*-type vegetation, dominated by olive wood, evergreen oak, mastic, *Rhamnus/Phillyrea*, erica, myrtle, and *Ephedra*.

SUMMARY: THE ARCHAIC/CLASSICAL PERIODS (C. 650-325 BC)

Regional diversity in settlement patterns

One or two centuries after Greeks settled on the coast of southeast Italy, the differences between the coastal and inland regions became truly apparent. In the coastal areas, the Greek settlements of Metapontion, Siris, Sybaris, and Taras grew considerably and acquired some distinct urban features. In the

over a few hundred years between about 2500 and 2200 years ago. [...] *Olea*, probably the cultivated olive, has a peak at 184 cm, recording local olive groves. *Juglans* and *Castanea* both appear for the first time. Among the herbs, cereal-type pollen remains at low values but there is an increase in wild grasses, especially towards the surface. *Plantago* species, *Rumex* and *Pteridium* (bracken) probably indicate invasion of weeds after forest cutting. There is no very clear pattern of alternating periods of cutting and re-growth, but the general spread of weedy plants, plants of cultivation, and shrubs and trees of secondary woodland point to extensive forest clearance from the Roman period onward.'

[139] Yntema (2013, p. 71) has pointed out that the percentage of *Bos taurus* in bone samples from southeast Italy is often much higher than strictly necessary for economic purposes. A possible reason for this is that cattle were equivalent to wealth, and the ownership of a few cows and/or oxen was considered a matter of prestige. Therefore, a decrease in the amount of cattle bones in the samples does not necessarily indicate that less animals were needed for traction, but rather that the number of oxen at each site started to be more closely associated with the amount of land that was tilled.

[140] Fiorentino and Colaianni 2005, p. 98.

course of the 6th and 5th centuries BC, Metapontion began to organize its agricultural territory as well, which soon became littered with farmsteads, small rural *necropoleis* and sanctuaries. A system of ditches or canals was made in order to divide the *chora* into regular plots. Such division lines have not been found in the *chorai* of Siris, Sybaris, and Taras, indicating that Metapontion may have been an atypical Greek settlement and regional differences existed within the coastal regions, too.

Increasing regional diversity can also be witnessed in the inland areas. Innovations, such as the replacement of oval huts by rectangular houses with a stone foundation, are found at sites in almost every part of inland southeast Italy. But as in the Early Iron Age, some settlements were considerably larger than others. A few of these sites, including Cavallino, Serra di Vaglio, and Oria, acquired a few urban features such as paved streets and fortifications. In spite of that, these centres differed considerably from the Greek settlements on the coast in terms of scale and spatial organization. Differences are also apparent in the organization of the countryside. The rural infill in the colonial *chorai* and the land divisions around Metapontion appear to have no parallels in the inland areas.

Agricultural strategies
The system of land division and the rural infill in the Metapontino suggest an increasing level of agricultural rationalization, expansion, and intensification. The Pantanello pollen cores are indicative of a diversified farming economy in the *chora* of Metapontion in this period, dominated by cereal cultivation. On the basis of the number of farms, pottery distribution patterns and archaeobotanical evidence, it can be argued that the agricultural production around Archaic/Classical Metapontion was thriving on a considerable scale. Although the *chorai* of the other Greek settlements have not been studied as intensely as Metapontion's, it is safe to assume that they also experienced a period of economic prosperity. The ancient written sources contain many references to the fertile soils and wealth of the Greek colonies in southern Italy. The production of Corinthian B amphorae at Sybaris, Taras, and Metapontion is also indicative of a considerably evolved agricultural economy. This wealth may partly be connected with social/political reforms, which led to the confiscation of land belonging to wealthy elite groups and a more important role of agricultural smallholders.

We have only little information about the basis of this thriving agricultural economy, but it can be hypothesized that some of the Greek settlements started to engage in agricultural specialization. Part of the cereal surplus from the *chora* of Metapontion, for instance, may have been exported to inland and overseas markets. Archaeobotanical data from Greek *chorai* in southeast Italy are particularly scarce, but, on the basis of the Pantanello pollen core, ancient written sources and ceramic evidence, it can be assumed that wine and olive oil production played a significant role in their agricultural economies. This is an important difference compared to the inland areas, where smaller and more localized forms of olei- and viticulture took place which tend to be obscure in the archaeological record.

Another difference in agricultural strategies between the coastal areas and inland regions concerns the scale and efficiency of production. Whereas the Greek *chorai*, especially at Metapontion, were strictly organized and filled in with farmsteads, settlements in the inland areas continued to function as agro-towns. Based on this distinction, I argued that inland farmers were generally not involved in market-oriented surplus production. Instead, they aimed to be self-supporting and gain subsistence for their own families. This hypothesis ties in with the archaeobotanical and archaeozoological evidence, which suggests a considerable degree of continuity in land use methods between the Early Iron Age and the Archaic/Classical periods. However, even though the inland settlements probably had no large agricultural surpluses to trade with, other forms of exchange may have taken place between the Greek coastal settlements and indigenous inland centres. Wool is likely to have been an important trade product, along with building materials such as stone and wood, and services such as seasonal labourers and access to grazing areas.

Human impact on the natural landscape

The organization of agricultural territories along the coast is the most evident sign of increased human influence on the landscape in the Archaic/Classical periods. This phenomenon is especially evident in the Metapontino, where forests were felled in order to expand the area that could be used as arable ground. As a side effect of these practices, increasing episodes of alluviation and erosion can be witnessed in the geomorphological record. In contrast, survey data indicate that settlement patterns in the inland areas changed very little in comparison to the Early Iron Age. The territories of the inland centres, even the largest ones such as Oria, show no traces of rural settlement. It appears that agricultural fields existed only in the direct vicinity (i.e. 5 kilometres walking distance) of towns.

The high number of wild animal remains from Valesio and the Pantanello complex confirms the extensive exploitation of 'wild' landscapes in the form of hunting activities. It is interesting to note that hunting existed in both the inland areas and the *chora* of Metapontion, where one presumably had to travel some distance to reach actual 'wild grounds'. Apparently, even after the organization of the *chorai*, the inhabitants of the Greek settlements were accustomed to exploit the landscape outside of their agricultural territories.

6.5   THE EARLY HELLENISTIC PERIOD (325-200 BC)

In the previous section, I started the general discussion with an overview of developments in and around the coastal areas with the Greek settlements. These underwent some remarkable changes during the Archaic/Classical periods. In the following section, however, I will start with the inland areas of southeast Italy. The Early Hellenistic period (325-200 BC), was a period of notable change for these areas in particular. Two general, and probably interconnected, trends can be discerned, i.e. a process of rural infill and a process of urban expansion. Land use practices underwent a major transformation, leading not only to agricultural expansion and intensification, but also to specialization. As a result, the regional differences between the coastal zones and the inland areas that developed during the preceding period became considerably less marked.

As far as rural infill is concerned, the ACVU surveys in the Brindisino have attested the appearance in this period of rural settlements, rural burial sites, and isolated farmsteads in the countryside outside the larger centres. This pattern is observed throughout the survey area and dates between the late 4th and early 3rd century BC. For example, around Valesio, 3rd century BC farmsteads covered the entire survey area at regular intervals of approximately 500 metres. A higher density in rural occupation is also observed in field surveys at Oria, the Murge hills,[141] the Tarantino and the Sibaritide (see below). The field surveys demonstrate that even in marginal areas with less fertile soils, rural settlements came into existence. This indicates that the rural infill reached a point where even infertile soils were taken into cultivation. This happened, for instance, at the hamlet Masseria Mea.[142] Most of the rural settlements, however, were located near good arable soils, indicating that agriculture rather than stock-raising was the prime economic activity.[143] The presence of rural burial grounds shows that rural dwellers were buried near their farms, where they lived on a permanent basis.[144] This does not apply to all the farm sites, however, as some may have been only seasonally inhabited, for example during the harvesting period, or not inhabited at all, functioning as storage sheds (see below).

If we are to follow descriptions in ancient written sources, the settlement dynamics in native southeast Italy were accompanied, or rather caused, by the development of larger and more powerful tribal entities such as the Lucanians in Basilicata.[145] Apparently, these peoples started to become a continuous

---

[141] Attema, Burgers and Van Leusen 2010, p. 149.

[142] Burgers 1998, p. 255; Yntema 1993, p. 186.

[143] Yntema 1993, p. 186.

[144] Burgers 1998, p. 243.

threat to the Greek *poleis* in this period, resulting in a strengthening of Greek political forces in the Italiote League under the leadership of Taras. In the early 3rd century, however, a coalition was forged of both Greek states and indigenous Italic polities, possibly as a reaction to the increasing influence of Rome. Indeed, Taras had become particularly wealthy and powerful in this period.[146] As we have seen in the previous paragraph, the *chora* of Taras was shaped in a long drawn-out process of territorial expansion. The survey data from this area show significant transformations towards the late 4th century BC. The Early Hellenistic period was the phase of maximum expansion, with isolated and clustered rural sites distributed throughout the landscape. Burgers and Crielaard have argued that these developments are indicative of a second phase of northward and westward expansion of the Tarentine *chora*.[147]

At Herakleia, we have direct evidence of a newly imposed system of land use in the *chora*, where land was redistributed and new farms were built. The Herakleia tablets refer to considerably advanced agricultural practices, such as the use of irrigation systems with small canals that led water from the hills towards the lower-lying fields. They also mention that the Greek city had trade contacts with indigenous people who lived in the inland areas, and acquired (goat) dairy products and wool from them.[148] As we have seen in the previous section, exchanges between the inland areas and the Greek settlements on the coast were already quite common in the Archaic/Classical periods.

Meanwhile, in the Sibaritide the urban function of Sybaris had been taken over by its successor, the *polis* of Thourioi. Archaeological research in this area is almost impossible due to large scale alluvial flooding, which has completely covered the remains of not only Sybaris but also Thourioi and their environs. Nevertheless, topographic and selective field surveys in the Sibaritide produced evidence of rural occupation in the hinterland of Thourioi and its Roman successor Copia in the Early Hellenistic period.[149]

In addition to a major increase in rural settlements, the Early Hellenistic period in southeast Italy is also characterized by a regional trend toward urban expansion. Some of the indigenous settlements acquired increasingly urban features, such as public buildings and orthogonal street plans, which are found for instance at Pomarico Vecchio.[150] The urban expansion is perhaps best illustrated by the growth of settlement areas in this phase. The ACVU surveys at Muro Tenente, Muro Maurizio, San Pancrazio, and Valesio confirm that these sites all expanded considerably during the late 4th and early 3rd centuries BC.[151] The excavations at Muro Tenente provide a more detailed picture of this development. An orthogonal grid was used during the construction of at least two new habitation quarters in the settlement's periphery. In addition, an inner defensive wall was constructed around the central habitation area, and a larger enceinte around the whole settlement.

Comparable developments of rapid settlement expansion and the emergence of urban features, took place at many other sites in southeast Italy. Monumental fortification walls were built around quite a number of settlements, such as Roccagloriosa, Oria, Manduria, Li Castelli di San Pancrazio, and Valesio.[152] The dimensions of the space that was enclosed by these walls differed greatly; for example, the intra-mural spaces of Muro Tenente and Li Castelli measured about 52 ha, whereas Oria had a walled area of about 118 ha. According to D'Andria, these differences are indicative of developing settlement hierarchy, as the largest sites may have been tribal centres.[153] Such centres may have fulfilled urban functions for a larger rural area, such as producing craft products, offering facilities for the processing, storage and exchange of agricultural products, and supplying religious/ceremonial and political services.

---

[145] Cf. Yntema 2006.
[146] See De Juliis 1988, p. 15.
[147] Crielaard and Burgers 2012, p. 98.
[148] Uguzzoni and Ghinatti 1968, p. 118.
[149] Attema, Burgers and Van Leusen 2010, p. 149.
[150] Barra Bagnasco 1997, p. 12.
[151] Burgers 1998, p. 227.
[152] D'Andria 1991, p. 445.
[153] D'Andria 1991, p. 447.

The number of archaeobotanical samples from the Early Hellenistic period (see the third part of *Table 5.1*) is higher than for any other phase, rendering a comparison with earlier periods difficult. What we may safely do, however, is compare the samples from sites in the coastal and inland areas in order to investigate whether there are differences in the crop spectrum between indigenous and 'Greek' sites. Such differences may be informative about diverse methods of land use. For this comparison, we will take a closer look at Pantanello, located in the *chora* of Metapontion, and Roccagloriosa, which was a fortified centre in inland Lucania with only weak links with the Greek colonial world. The samples from both sites contained hulled barley, club wheat and emmer wheat. Einkorn and millet were found at Roccagloriosa, whereas the Pantanello assemblage contained neither of these cereals.[154] The fruit assemblage from Roccagloriosa and Pantanello is much the same, and consists of figs, olives, and grapes; chickpeas and bitter vetches were found at Pantanello, vetchling at Roccagloriosa. Legumes are rare at sites in southeast Italy, but the assemblages from Pantanello show a larger variety of pulses in comparison to most other sites. It is remarkable that chickpeas and the genus *Pisum* (pea) only occur in the Archaic period, but this should not be taken to indicate that they were introduced by Greek colonists, since the earliest finds of both chickpeas and peas are from native sites (Monte Irsi and Cavallino). In conclusion, we can say that these data do not show any pronounced differences in the crop spectrum of Greek colonies and indigenous settlements for the period under discussion.

However, there may be differences hidden from our view. The survey data from the Metapontino, the information from the Herakleia tablets and the pollen samples from Pantanello together present an image of a developed system of land use in the Greek *chorai*, which is unlikely to have existed in the contemporary indigenous territories. The *chora* of Metapontion is probably unique in one aspect, however, namely the dominance of cereal cultivation. Carter has hypothesized that a cereal monoculture developed in the *chora* as a less risky alternative for oleiculture and viticulture in this politically instable period.[155] This was supposedly caused by the emergence of a powerful native tribe, the Lucanians, who according to ancient written sources,[156] formed a continuous threat for the Greek colonies of Magna Graecia in the 4th and 3rd centuries BC.[157]

It can be doubted, however, that Metapontion suffered much under this period of 'political instability', as the sanctuary at Pantanello was renovated and a new sanctuary of Apollo was built at the agora.[158] As I showed above, the perceived drop in the number of inhabited farmsteads in the *chora* may not represent an archaeological reality and cannot be taken as evidence of profound change in the organization of the countryside. In fact, Yntema[159] has shown that there is no archaeological evidence of a severe crisis or a Dark Age in Lucania. Rather, the 'rise' of the Lucanians – who were probably a coalition of several tribal units – should perhaps be seen as the result of an increasing organizational complexity within the tribal world of Basilicata, stimulated by many years of regular contacts with

---

[154] It should be added that evidence of einkorn and millet cultivation is limited at all the sites in southeast Italy. Indeed, millet was found at none of the other sites beside Roccagloriosa, so this find is rather unusual. Other finds of einkorn, on the other hand, were made at Botromagno phase 1 (900-600 BC) and 3 (400-300 BC) and at Vaste. According to Small (2000, p. 8), Botromagno shows many signs of Greek influence in its latest phase (3). The same holds true for the sanctuary at Vaste (D'Andria 1990b, p. 62-64). These two sites are both contemporary to Roccagloriosa, so I am not convinced that einkorn should be qualified as part of a 'typical indigenous' diet.

[155] Carter 2006, pp. 26-27.

[156] These include mainly citations of Greek authors living in southern Italy in the 5th and 4th centuries BC by Roman authors, such as Athenaeus, Pliny, and Strabo.

[157] Carter 1998, p. 15. These Lucanians had already captured several Greek towns, including Paestum in Campania, in the 5th century BC. Since they continued to form a threat in the following century, the Greek towns invited Greek mercenary leaders (*condottieri*) to fight the Lucanians on their behalf. Cf. Bottini 1987; Lomas 1993.

[158] Cf. Carter 1998, pp. 13-15.

[159] Yntema 1997, pp. 105-108.

Fig. 6.1. Metapontion, silver stater representing a hexaploid (six-rowed) head of barley, 6th century BC. Photo by Vera Massaro, courtesy of the Institute of Classical Archaeology, University of Texas, US.

their colonial Greek neighbours.[160] The Italiote Greeks had been accustomed to the native tribes outside their territories, but somewhere in the 5th century BC, they were suddenly confronted with a 'supertribe' which had both the manpower and the organization to oppose them successfully in military confrontations.

We may take a critical look at the 'cereal monoculture' scenario as well. Carter argues that the monoculture of cereals may even have contributed to the economic decline of the *chora* and *asty* of Metapontion after 300 BC. This hypothesis is based on palynological evidence, i.e. a peak in the number of grasses in the pollen diagrams in the late 4th-early 3rd century BC, and second, the representation of barley on Metapontine coins (*Figure 6.1*).[161] As we have seen, the latter does not point at a cereal monoculture in the Early Hellenistic Period specifically, since this type of coin was issued from the third quarter of the 6th century BC onwards. We may interpret this as an indication of long-lasting cereal monoculture, but the palynological evidence for this is rather weak. The percentage of cereal pollen in the Pantanello core never exceeds 4%. This is not a particularly small figure considering that levels of cereal pollen are relatively low when compared with the pollen of arboreal and other non-arboreal species, but it does not convincingly point at cereal monoculture.[162] Nevertheless, the palynological evidence shows that cereal cultivation was a continuous, and probably important, part of the agricultural system in the Metapontino. Several cereal peaks can be noted in the Pantanello core, for instance in the late 7th century BC and again in the middle of the 4th century BC. In other words, while I am not convinced that the Metapontine farmers went so far as to engage in a cereal monoculture, there is reason to believe that specialization in cereal cultivation took place in the *chora* of Metapontion.

Agricultural production apparently flourished greatly in the Early Hellenistic Period. In the late 4th and early 3rd century BC, the density of farm sites in the Metapontino reached an unprecedented height.[163] Carter calculated that, if the 128 Early Hellenistic farm sites found in the survey area were typical of the whole territory between the Bradano and the Cavone rivers, there would have been as many as 870 farm units operating between 350 and 300 BC. This would result in a population for the territory of between 4,500 and 9,000 and a population density between 22 and 44 persons per square kilometre.[164] Dividing the total number of discovered farm sites by the total area surveyed, Carter calculated that in the 4th century BC, the average plot size in the Metapontino was 21.2 hectares, of which 16.6 hectares were arable. This is considerably less than in the Classical Period, when the average agricultural plot measured over 25 ha (see above). Nevertheless, if we follow Foxhall's analysis of plot size, this is still over three times as much as the maximum area that could be cultivated as arable land by a single household.[165] It is possible that these large plots continued to be extensively worked, with long fallow periods, as was probably the case in the Archaic/Classical periods. However, we

---

[160] Yntema 1997, p. 110.

[161] Carter 2006, pp. 26-27.

[162] Vuorela (1973) found that the concentration of cereal pollen was highest in samples taken close to the cultivated area. Cf. Bower 1992, p. 236.

[163] Carter 1990, p. 410.

[164] As opposed to c. 789 farm units and an estimated rural population of between 4,000 and 8,700 individuals in the Archaic/Classical Periods (see section 6.4). Carter 2006, p. 120.

[165] Foxhall 2003, p. 83.

should also consider the possibility that in the Early Hellenistic Period, family households had ceased to be the primary production units and part of the work was carried out by agricultural labourers. Carter mentions a political decision from this period that noncitizens – especially the thoroughly Hellenized barbarians of the surrounding areas – were given permission to work in the *chora*.[166] This may have increased the quantity of labour available, and possibly even resulted in an influx of seasonal workers. There is no hard evidence to support this hypothesis, but such developments would certainly explain Metapontion's great economic prosperity in the Early Hellenistic Period, and the ability to successfully engage in specialized cereal production for a market.

There are other examples of agricultural specialization in the Early Hellenistic Period, both in the Greek *chorai* and the inland areas. For example, Veenman has argued that many of the local centres in the Early Hellenistic period engaged in their own form of specialization, such as pork production at Vaste[167] and later also at Valesio,[168] and sheep rearing in inland Lucania.[169] Indeed, it can be argued that a complementary economic system started to emerge in this period, with individual towns or areas specializing in specific products that were sold on a regional market.

The most prominent examples of this emerging agricultural specialization are grape- and olive cultivation, especially in the inland areas. Grapes and olives are found at practically every site in the Early Hellenistic Period, except for the ones where sampling was limited (latest phase at Botromagno, Pomarico Vecchio). There is considerable evidence for an increase in the production of wine and olive oil from the 4th century BC onward (see section 5.3.3). This coincides with the rural infill in the inland areas, which facilitated and increased agricultural production. Agriculture in the Archaic/Classical periods was probably characterized by the agro-town system, of farmers living in fairly populous urban centres and travelling back and forth to their fields. It needs no further elucidation that skipping this daily trip would have saved a lot of time and energy, which could be invested in production processes instead. Yntema has proposed that beside the numerically dominant group of peasants who lived in modest farm buildings and tilled small agricultural plots, local elites may have owned fairly substantial stretches of farmland.[170] Funerary evidence is clearly indicative of the rise of such new elites, who must have been wealthy enough to build monumental *hypogaea* tombs and cist graves.[171] These elite groups may have been the first to engage in large-scale olive oil and wine production, which requires considerable financial investments (e.g. purchasing pressers, crushers and *pithoi*), not to mention the input of labour that was needed to nurture the trees or vineyards and harvest the fruits.[172] Moreover, grapevines need at least three years of careful nurturing before they become productive, and olive trees at least fifteen years. After these initial investments, both can yield fruit for centuries and, under the right circumstances and in the proximity of a market, wine and olive oil production can be extremely profitable. It can be argued that the process of rural infill created better opportunities for the transport of agricultural products, facilitating their way to reach a market.[173] Indeed, the prosperity of some of the larger regional centres, such as Oria, may be indicative of this development. As I argued above, these larger settlements may have performed 'urban' functions for a larger rural area, including its function as a distribution centre and market for the exchange of agricultural products.

It can be concluded that in the Early Hellenistic period southeast Italy saw great prosperity, the emergence of a complementary agricultural economy, and probably a substantial population growth. Settlement growth and rural infill are clear indicators of the latter. Yntema addressed additional evidence of population growth, including the unprecedented quantity of tombs dating to the later 4th

---

[166] Carter 2006, pp. 230-231.
[167] Veenman 2002, pp. 84-86.
[168] Zeiler 1996, *Table 1d*.
[169] Uguzzoni and Ghinatti 1968, p. 118.
[170] Yntema 1993, p. 190.
[171] For example, Yntema 2009.
[172] Cf. Foxhall 1993, pp. 183-192, 2007, pp. 121-124.
[173] Cf. Attema, Burgers, Kleibrink and Yntema 1998, p. 355; Yntema 1993, p. 194.

and earlier 3rd centuries BC,[174] and an apparent increase in the number of *trozzellas* (a type of pot that is exclusively found in female graves).[175] This increase implicitly points at an increase in the number of (female) burials, indicating that the population as a whole was growing. If the combined indirect evidence is accepted, it is interesting to theorize about the consequences that this population growth may have had for the exploitation of the landscape. Firstly, more people need more food. At the same time, more people can also produce more food, since the quantity of available labour increases. This may have led to two possible results, namely 1) more economic agricultural production (rationalization), and/or 2) clearing new areas for cultivation (expansion). The infill of the rural landscape with newly built farms and hamlets clearly indicates that the latter solution was adopted, which must have had enormous effects on the landscape in many parts of southeast Italy.[176] The survey results from the Brindisino, Tarantino, and Murge show that previously uninhabited areas were exploited for cultivation on a massive scale.[177] Since some of these areas had never been touched by human hands before, they may have contained climax vegetation such as evergreen oak forest that had to be felled.

The charcoal assemblage from Muro Tenente is a good illustration of the effects of increasing human impact on the landscape. The dominance of *Erica* vegetation suggests that the landscape around the settlement had severely degraded, probably as a result of deforestation and subsequent grazing. The contemporary charcoal assemblage from Li Castelli also contains a fair amount of low shrub land species (see section 5.3.1 and *Table 5.5*). In addition, there is palynological evidence of increasing human impact on the landscape. The pollen core from Pomarico Vecchio shows indicators of grazing in the Early Hellenistic period (notably plantain (*Plantago* sp.) and the teasel family (Dipsacaceae), but there are also signs of agricultural activity in the form of cereals, pulses and the carrot (Umbelliferae) and lily (Liliaceae) families, and fruit trees, including *Prunus* sp., *Vitis* sp., and *Olea* sp.[178] Pollen sequences from northern Apulia (Herdonia[179] and Arpi[180]) also indicate a landscape that is considerably degraded because of human intervention, with elements of *macchia* and evergreen woodlands. Furthermore, the weed seeds from Early Hellenistic levels equally point at increased human influence on the natural vegetation. At Roccagloriosa,[181] the weed assemblage included white goosefoot, sun spurge (*Euphorbia helioscopia*), stickyweed (*Galium aparine*), yellow vetch (*Lathyrus aphaca*), grass/red pea (*Lathyrus sativus/cicera*), knotweed (*Polygonum*), and catchfly (*Silene*). Most of these weeds grow on arable fields and disturbed grounds. At Pomarico Vecchio, the macroremains were retrieved from an amphora that, besides bread wheat and a grape pip, contained numerous weeds that are mostly plants characteristic of (abandoned) cultivated zones and crop fields (including *Adonis, Chenopodium, Fumaria, Malva,* and *Polygonum*).[182] The weed assemblages from Vaste and Muro Tenente also contained a few probable cereal weeds, such as oat, rye, and brome. In short, the archaeobotanical assemblages all seem to be indicative of intensive arable cultivation.

---

[174] Yntema 1993, p. 186. A good example is the nucleated *necropolis* at the site of Manduria (Burgers 1998, p. 241).

[175] Yntema 1993, pp. 177 and 186-189. Note that the increase in the number of *trozzellas* can be explained in different ways; it may also indicate that more people were formally buried.

[176] Cf. Yntema 2013, p. 187.

[177] Although it must be emphasized that the absence of a farm does not necessarily imply that an area was not cultivated. Indeed, arable cultivation in pre-Hellenistic times, when the agro-town method was commonly used, is likely to be archaeologically invisible.

[178] It also contained some traces of pollen from the Cannabaceae family, but since the various genera in this family (including hemp, hop and hackberries) cannot be distinguished from each other from pollen alone, it is unclear whether this is the earliest testimony of hemp in Italy. *Cannabis sativa* L., hemp, was cultivated in Roman Italy for its fibres, but most authors believe that it was not introduced here before *c.* 100 BC. Godwin 1967; Zohary and Hopf 1993; Mercuri *et al.* 2002.

[179] Heim 1995.

[180] Accorsi *et al.* 1995.

[181] Bökönyi, Costantini, and Fitt 1990, p. 328.

[182] Caramiello and Siniscalco 1997.

However, it also needs to be emphasized that large patches of 'wild', uncultivated landscape clearly remained intact. The surveys show that in this period there still existed 'empty' areas that were void of human occupation. Although a part of these landscapes may have been exploited in an archaeologically invisible way, the archaeozoological samples from Early Hellenistic levels at Valesio, Roccagloriosa, and Monte Irsi indicate that at least some woodland must have survived the process of rural infill. The bone samples (*Table 5.3*) include red deer (*Cervus elaphus*), brown hare (*Lepus capensis*), and fox (*Vulpes vulpes*) in percentages that hardly differ from earlier periods. At Roccagloriosa, even fallow deer (*Dama dama*) and aurochs (*Bos primigenius*) were encountered.

SUMMARY: THE EARLY HELLENISTIC PERIOD (C. 325-200 BC)

Regional diversity and settlement patterns

In the previous paragraphs, we have seen that in the Archaic/Classical periods there were considerable differences between the coastal and inland regions. In the Early Hellenistic period, however, the differences between these micro-regions gradually started to vanish. This is largely due to the interconnected processes of urbanization, expansion of the rural economy, and increasing interconnectivity between the inland and coastal areas and overseas markets. As a result of this, two important trends can be witnessed in this period: settlements in the inland areas increasingly acquired urban features, and the surrounding countryside became filled in with rural habitation. The rural infill of the inland areas also facilitated long-distance trade. As a consequence, we witness increasing site differentiation, agricultural expansion and intensification, market-oriented agrarian production in the inland districts, and – probably as a result of the rise of these markets – agricultural specialization.

Agricultural strategies

The rural infill also resulted in the organization of agricultural production on a larger scale and in a much more efficient way. Together with an improvement of the infrastructure, it became easier and much more profitable to produce agricultural surplus for a market. This may be the main reason why large-scale olive oil and wine production really took off in the inland areas in the late 4th and 3rd centuries BC. With this clear manifestation of a typical Mediterranean polycultural system (cereals, olives, grapes) in the inland areas, another important difference between agricultural strategies in the coastal and inland regions disappeared – in addition to its scale and efficiency of production. In contrast to the previous periods, it became more common for farmers to supply goods for a market, whether they resided in the inland areas or in the Greek *chorai* on the coast. As a result, a complementary economic system started to emerge.

Human impact on the natural landscape

The processes of rural infill and urban expansion affected the natural landscape in many parts of southeast Italy in a drastic way. The survey results from Apulia are indicative of large-scale clearances, and the transformation of formerly 'wild' areas into human landscapes of fields and farmsteads. An increasing amount of agricultural products reached a regional market in this period, which suggests that exchanges between settlements and farmland intensified. Indeed, there is evidence that a network of roads was laid out in this period, no doubt crossing previously unexploited areas. Pollen and charcoal assemblages also confirm the increasing human impact on the landscape in this period. The dominance of *Erica* vegetation around Muro Tenente is a case in point, but the palynological analyses from northern Apulia also point towards a considerable degradation of the landscape. There is also evidence of the extensive exploitation of woodlands, so apparently considerable patches of uncultivated landscape remained intact.

6.6 EPILOGUE: SOUTHEAST ITALY IN THE LATE HELLENISTIC/ EARLY ROMAN PERIOD (200-30 BC). NOTHING BUT SHEEP AND OLIVE TREES?

Although the Early Roman period is outside the scope of this study, a few words must be said about the way land use developed in southeast Italy in the 2nd and 1st centuries BC. According to the traditional point of view, southeast Italy was largely abandoned after the devastating Hannibalic war (218-201 BC). When we look at the archaeological evidence, however, it appears that this image is exaggerated.

According to A.J. Toynbee, the Hannibalic wars had left southeast Italy in a pitiful state, thinly populated and devastated. Toynbee cites Cato and Varro as evidence that after the Roman conquest, completed in 266 BC, the traditional peasant subsistence economy was superseded by two new forms of land utilization: a nomadic livestock industry, in combination with an intensive plantation agriculture.[183] The Roman state expropriated large tracts of privately owned land, creating freedom for moving flocks and herds. In the Late Hellenistic period and Roman Imperial times, the Apulian pastoral economy and its products gathered a fine reputation. Several Roman authors refer to Tarentine and Daunian wool production.[184] Wool from Roman Taras was reportedly the softest and glossiest kind that could be found anywhere in Italy.

There are a few archaeozoological studies in southeast Italy that confirm this image. For example, the most recent excavation levels at Pantanello show high percentages of sheep/goats (see *Table 5.3*). These layers were formed in a period when the sanctuary had lost its function, between the 2nd century BC and the 1st century AD. The number of cattle bones in the deposit drops progressively. They are still numerous at the lowest level (middle of the 2nd century BC), but in the layers that were formed in the 1st century AD, there are none. Instead, sheep/goat numbers show a sudden increase around the 1st century BC. This shift has been interpreted as a reflection of changing land use practices. The decline of cattle, whose primary use was for traction and ploughing, could mean that arable farming gradually lost its importance in comparison to pastoralism.[185] In the latest phase of the Roman occupation of the *chora* of Metapontion, evidenced at 4th century AD San Biagio, sheep/goats still outnumber all other animals.[186] The archaeological evidence also suggests that the Roman occupation of southeast Italy led to conflicts with the local populations, resulting in the destruction and abandonment of many settlements.[187] Moreover, the surveys in Salento and inland Basilicata have demonstrated that most of the sites that made their appearance during the economic 'boom' between c. 330 and 280 BC were abandoned after the Hannibalic war.[188] The untilled fields were gradually reclaimed by natural vegetation.[189] The surveys and excavations in the Metapontino also suggest both urban and rural decline.[190] The effects of the Roman conquests were reflected first by dramatic changes in the urban centre of Metapontion. In the early 3rd century BC, a Roman fort (*castrum*) was constructed in the southeast corner of the city. The silver coinage of Metapontion disappeared in the same period. All the known rural sanctuaries in the *chora* and most of the farmhouses were abandoned by the middle of the 3rd century BC.

However, it can be counter argued that quite a number of settlements survived, and often expanded considerably in size. These higher plot sizes are in the right order of magnitude for the large rural estates that are described by Cato (A 6.37). Similar developments are witnessed in the countryside around Oria, where 12 of the 30 farmsteads discovered during the field survey had been abandoned

---

[183] Toynbee 1965, p. 309. See also Brunt 1971, pp. 282-284.
[184] Morel 1978.
[185] Carter *et al.* 1985, p. 298.
[186] Carter 1987, p. 187, *Figure 268*.
[187] Cf. Burgers 1998, pp. 276-277.
[188] Yntema 1993; Burgers 1998, pp. 270-271.
[189] Yntema 2013, pp. 243-252.
[190] Carter 2006, pp. 240-247.

around the middle of the 2nd century BC.[191] But the town of Oria does not show any trace of decline, and intensive surveying has demonstrated that the remaining 18 farms in the countryside more than doubled in size. Yntema[192] has also compared these large farmsteads, that could house some 20 to 30 people, with Catonian rural estates. Overall, survey data provide reasons to believe that the image of southern Italy as a depopulated rural hinterland of Rome has clearly been exaggerated.[193]

Nevertheless, some modifications in the landscape must have taken place. The last, most recent part of the Pantanello pollen core shows peaks of pioneer plants (Liguliflorae) and pine, which suggests that fields had been abandoned and evergreen forests were on the rise. The evidence for abandoned fields and forests in the Metapontino is indirectly supported by the faunal record from Pantanello. The archaeozoological samples from this site (see *Table 5.3*) show a sudden increase in sheep/goat numbers around the 1st century BC. In addition, the studies by Bökönyi also suggest that the Metapontino was more forested in antiquity than today. For example, the archaeozoological record from Pantanello includes a high percentage (19.6%) of red deer bones.[194] In addition, population shifts can be observed from the inland areas towards the newly founded Roman colonies of Brentesion (Brindisi, founded in 244 BC), Copia (Sybaris/Thourioi, 193 BC), Neptunia/Tarentum (Taras, 122 BC), and Buxentum (Pyxous, 194 BC). Especially Brundisium grew exponentially and became a centre of supra-regional importance. Massive production of amphorae (of the so-called 'Brindisi' or 'Apulian' type) is attested in the area surrounding Brundisium, starting around 170/160 BC.[195]

As we have seen in section 5.3.3, Varro not only mentions the vineyards of Brundisium, but also refers to the transport of wine, olive oil, and cereals with mule trains through inland Apulia to the harbour of Brundisium. Here, the agricultural produce was packed in the locally-made transport amphorae and shipped to overseas destinations.[196] Clearly, these amphorae were filled with the olive oil and/or wine produced in the new large rural estates in the Brindisino.[197] The large output of the pottery workshops suggests that large quantities of Brindisine oil and/or wines were exported.[198] Moreover, agricultural production for faraway markets may not have been restricted to wine and olive oil. Livy mentions that during the Hannibalic war, (northern) Apulia provided grain to the Roman army, which was shipped overseas (A 6.50).

There are also indications of specialization in livestock production. In fact, not all archaeozoological data confirm the image of a pastoralism-based rural economy (see *Table 5.3*). Graeme Barker reports a very clear bias towards sheep and goats in all habitation phases at Monte Irsi, except for the most recent ones (after the middle of the 2nd century BC).[199] In this period, pigs seem to have gradually increased in importance at the expense of sheep and goats. Pig bones also dominate the archaeozoological samples from the Roman period at San Giovanni di Ruoti,[200] Vaste, and Valesio. In Veenman's[201] view, these changes can be interpreted as indications of specialization, contrasting strongly with the mixed farming system in earlier periods. In the Early and particularly Late Hellenistic period, many of the villages with Iron Age roots had become local centres, each specializing in their own products (agricultural or pastoral). Moreover, the cattle bones from the Pantanello kiln deposit of the 2nd century BC show indications of selected breeding for size.[202] Metapontion was famous for its horses in the Archaic period,

[191] Yntema 1993, pp. 198-202.
[192] Yntema 2006, p. 109.
[193] Cf. Yntema 2006.
[194] Bökönyi 2010, p. 10 (*Table 1.7*).
[195] Large-scale production of amphorae has also been reported from the sites of Apani, Giancola, Marmorelle, La Rosa, *masseria* Ramanno, and Felline. See section 5.3.3.
[196] Yntema 2006, p. 101, note 14.
[197] Yntema 2006, p. 110.
[198] Cf. Hitchner 1993, p. 501 for the role of the expanding transport network in Roman Italy and for the 'boom' in olive production.
[199] Barker 1977, p. 265.
[200] MacKinnon *et al.* 2002, p. 26.
[201] Veenman 2002, p. 85.
[202] Bökönyi 2010, pp. 19 and 26.

but horses and cows of unusually large size were raised at Pantanello in the 2nd and 1st centuries BC. Evidently, the rural economy was not as completely ruined as the ancient written sources would make us believe.[203]

Indeed, the pollen cores from the Laghi Alimini and Pantanello both show that land use remained largely unchanged during the last two centuries of the first millennium BC. Carter[204] has already drawn attention to the fact that the information of land use given by the Pantanello pollen core does not tie in with the survey data, which suggest that the *chora* was virtually abandoned in this period. An explanation for this paradox is the expansion of the remaining farmsteads. The most recent part of the Pantanello core shows no dramatic new developments except for a moderate increase in grazing indicators, although these are still lower than they were in the early years of the colonial *chora*.[205] Di Rita and Magri[206] report a stronger human impact on the landscape around the Laghi Alimini, illustrated by the continuous presence of Cannabaceae and cereal pollen, which may represent agricultural activity.

In short, the period covering the late 3rd and the 2nd centuries BC was a time of great changes. However, in contrast to the traditional view of a ruined post-Hannibalic southern Italy, the archaeological evidence shows that in some respects it was a time of prosperity. The complementary economic system that had started to emerge in the Early Hellenistic Period became firmly established, especially when the increasing Roman influence on southern Italy facilitated the possibilities of long-distance trade. As a result of this, agricultural specialization further developed and led to a series of successful export products, including corn, wine, olive oil and wool.[207]

---

[203] An interesting parallel for the archaeozoological data from southeast Italy, and especially the dominance of pigs, is the work of De Grossi Mazzorin (2001, pp. 325-329) in the area around Rome. Comparing the animal bones from sites that were occupied between the Middle Bronze Age and the Roman Imperial period, De Grossi observes a clear increase in herding activity in the final phase of the Bronze Age. In the Early Iron Age, the mortality curves of the sheep and goats are indicative of the importance of wool production. Eventually, sheep rearing made way for the breeding of pigs. The percentages of pig bones increase in the Early Iron Age, and even more during the Archaic period. Still higher numbers can be witnessed in the 3rd and 2nd centuries BC, probably due to increasing urbanization and population growth. Pig breeding apparently reached its peak in the full Imperial period, when the city of Rome was at its largest. Evidently, the fact that a pig can produce meat at the fastest rate possible, and that this meat is easy to preserve and store (in the form of bacon), made it a very desirable animal to keep, especially in times of demographic stress.

[204] Carter 2006, pp. 243-248.

[205] Carter 2006, p. 243.

[206] Di Rita and Magri 2009, p. 301.

[207] For the development of large-scale rural estates in Roman Apulia, see Kuzišin 1982.

Chapter 7 – Conclusions

7.1 INTRODUCTION, RESTATEMENT OF RESEARCH AIMS AND METHOD

In the present study, I aimed to investigate the mutual relationship between the people and the landscapes in southeast Italy during the first millennium BC. The area witnessed a series of unprecedented changes in this period, including the processes of Greek colonization, urbanization, and incorporation in the Roman state. On the one hand, it was investigated what consequences these changes had on the landscape and the way it was exploited. On the other hand, it was assessed how the landscape affected human behaviour. The secondary aim was to demonstrate that this type of research should preferably be carried out using a multidisciplinary research method, combining archaeobotany with information from archaeological excavations and field surveys, ancient written sources, and archaeozoological studies.

In order to achieve these two aims, I focused on three research themes in particular: (1) the long-term developments in landscape and land use between c. 1000 and 200 BC, (2) long-term developments in the scale and organization of agricultural production, and (3) the effect of Greek colonization on the exploitation and organization of the landscape. In this final chapter, I will summarize my conclusions for each of these themes. In addition, the significance of these results will be discussed and I will give some recommendations for future research.

7.2 LONG-TERM DEVELOPMENTS IN LANDSCAPE AND LAND USE

Human impact on the natural landscape of southeast Italy increased considerably in the course of the first millennium BC, but it did not develop in the same way throughout the entire area under study. Considerable regional differences can be noted even in the Recent and Final Bronze Age, when a few larger centres had developed in the Sibaritide and southern Apulia. Such centres as Broglio di Trebisacce, Torre Mordillo, and Rocavecchia displayed a considerable degree of socio-economic complexity. For instance, these sites were involved in the production and redistribution of olive oil on a fairly large scale. This suggests that at least part of the surrounding landscapes was exploited for olive cultivation. This contrasts considerably with the general pattern for Recent and Final Bronze Age southeast Italy, which is one of relatively isolated settlements concentrating in the coastal areas, even though the best soils for agriculture are located inland. This is indicative of extensive arable farming, which was probably complemented with pastoral land use. However, there is too little archaeobotanical and archaeozoological evidence from Final Bronze Age contexts to get a clear picture of land use practices in this period.

This also holds true for the first two centuries of the Early Iron Age (c. 1000-800 BC). This period is commonly considered to be a 'Dark Age' in which interregional exchanges decreased considerably, and trade contacts with the eastern Mediterranean were almost completely interrupted. Archaeological remains from this period are rare, and archaeobotanical and archaeozoological data are completely absent. This makes it difficult to detect changes in land use between the Final Bronze Age and the Early Iron Age, which is especially unfortunate for our understanding of the spread of olive cultivation. Oleiculture probably continued on a smaller, local scale in the following centuries, but archaeological evidence of these practices is notoriously hard to find.

There is more clarity on land use and environmental change in the second half of the Early Iron Age (i.e. 800-600 BC). This was an eventful period, in which regional features became steadily more pronounced because of the arrival of Greek migrants and other peoples from the eastern Mediterranean. New settlements were established on good arable soils further inland, and some of the larger regional centres expanded considerably. However, in spite of these changes, the principal way of land use, i.e. small-scale subsistence agriculture, remained the same. The archaeobotanical and archaeozoological evidence shows that farmers in these new settlements operated mixed farming systems, combining small-scale arable cultivation and sheep/goat herding in order to provide subsistence and reduce the risk of crop failure, which is characteristic of farmers with limited involvement in the market. Indeed, it appears that such risky businesses as the large-scale cultivation of olives and grapes were largely avoided in this period. There is archaeological evidence of wine and olive oil consumption, but these products were, for the most part, imported rather than produced locally. The oldest post-Bronze Age grape remains from southeast Italy (found at l'Incoronata and l'Amastuola) date to the late 8th and early 7th century BC, while the earliest indications of local wine production (in the Greek colonial towns, see below) date to the Archaic Period. In other words, viticulture may not have been practiced at all in the Early Iron Age.

Archaeological and archaeobotanical evidence from the Early Iron Age indicates that the infill of the inland areas certainly did not result in a largely man-made landscape. The palynological data from the Laghi Alimini suggest that the forest zones around the lakes even slightly expanded. The case study of l'Amastuola is illustrative of the general picture of land use practices in the Early Iron Age. The natural opportunities and restrictions of the landscape largely dictated the manners of land use around the settlement on the south terrace. The charcoal data provide evidence of the exploitation of woodlands and high *macchia* zones. There are indications that these 'wild' areas were used to collect additional food (e.g. game, wild fruit, or nuts) and raw materials such as wood, and to graze livestock. There is no reason to assume that this was different in the coastal areas where the Greek migrants had recently settled. In the first decades of their existence, these 'Greek' settlements did not have any distinctive features. Like all settlements in this period, they were of the dispersed type and consisted of several small groups of huts.

However, dramatic changes took place at the end of the 7th century BC. By this time, a few settlements on the coast started to differentiate from the inland areas in several important ways. Not only did the settlements acquire more 'urban' characteristics, such as monumental architecture and a predefined street plan, the surrounding landscapes were modified as well. The most salient example is Metapontion. Around 600 BC, a small temple (Sacellum C) was built. In the course of the 6th century BC, the town grew considerably and numerous public building and construction works were undertaken. What is more, Metapontion began to reorganize its agricultural territory, which soon became littered with farmsteads, small rural *necropoleis* and sanctuaries. A system of ditches or canals was made, dividing the *chora* into regular plots. We can assume that these developments together served the same purpose, i.e. to facilitate agricultural surplus production (see section 7.3). These innovations obviously affected the natural landscape. The consequences of deforestation, which caused episodes of alluviation and erosion, can be witnessed in the geomorphological record.

Drastic new developments took place in the other Greek colonial towns as well, and it can be assumed that their agricultural territories were reorganized and filled in in the same way as Metapontion's. Unfortunately, much less is known about this development, since the *chorai* of Sybaris, Siris, and Taras have never been as systematically investigated. However, the ancient written sources contain many references to the fertile soils and opulence of the Greek towns in southern Italy. Furthermore, the surveys in the southern part of the *chora* of Taras indicate that it was filled in with rural settlements. The local production of Corinthian B amphorae is also indicative of a relatively highly developed agricultural economy. Although the formalization and organization of rural territories may not have followed the same course in the various Greek colonies, literary sources indicate that they were all connected to social/political reforms in the Archaic/Classical periods. These reforms involved the confiscation of land belonging to wealthy elite groups and its redistribution among a larger group of agricultural smallholders.

Meanwhile, survey data indicate that in the inland areas settlement patterns changed very little in comparison to the Early Iron Age. The territories of the inland centres, even the largest ones such as Oria, show no traces of rural settlement. Agricultural fields were apparently only laid out in the direct vicinity (i.e. 5 kilometres walking distance) of towns in this period. In short, it appears that land use was still largely determined by the opportunities and restrictions of the landscape. Whereas human impact on the landscape became much more intensive around the colonial settlements, the archaeozoological data from inland settlements such as Valesio confirm that 'wild' landscapes were still exploited for hunting activities, which is not what one would expect in a 'civilized', man-made landscape. Agricultural production continued to be aimed primarily at subsistence, not at surplus production for a market.

This changed in the Early Hellenistic Period, when land use practices in the inland areas underwent a major transformation, leading not only to agricultural expansion and intensification, but also to specialization (see below). The survey results from Apulia are indicative of large-scale clearances and the transformation of formerly 'wild' areas into human landscapes of fields and farmsteads. The dominance of *Erica* vegetation around Muro Tenente is a case in point, and the palynological analyses from northern Apulia also point towards a considerable degradation of the landscape. As a result, the regional differences between the coastal zones and the inland areas became considerably less marked. By the end of the Early Hellenistic Period, large parts of the natural landscape in southeast Italy were skilfully exploited for settlement, agriculture, pastoralism, and traffic routes.

7.3 LONG-TERM DEVELOPMENTS IN THE SCALE AND ORGANIZATION OF AGRICULTURAL PRODUCTION: EXPANSION, RATIONALIZATION, SPECIALIZATION

The relatively highly developed rural economy that had come into existence in the Early and particularly in the Late Hellenistic Period did not develop overnight. In fact, many examples of agricultural expansion, rationalization, and specialization can be detected in earlier periods, starting in the Recent Bronze Age. I will first illustrate this point with a few examples, and then argue how these episodes differ from the developments in the Early and Late Hellenistic Period.

Large-scale olive oil production at Broglio di Trebisacce (Recent/Final Bronze Age)
The earliest evidence of agricultural specialization and surplus production dates to the Recent Bronze Age and is best illustrated by the storage complexes containing huge ceramic *pithoi* that were found at Broglio di Trebisacce. Chemical analyses have shown that these *pithoi*, which had a storage capacity of over 5,000 litres, used to contain olive oil. Furthermore, carbonized stones of cultivated olives were found at this site in contexts of the Recent Bronze as well as Final Bronze Age/Early Iron Age. The charcoal assemblage is dominated by olive wood. At the same time, there is palynological evidence of peaks in olive pollen in the Middle, Recent and Final Bronze Age around the Laghi Alimini in southeast Salento and the Aspromonte mountains in southern Calabria. In sum, it can be concluded that there is clear evidence of large-scale olive oil production at Broglio di Trebisacce in this period.

Broglio di Trebisacce is not unique in this respect. There are other Recent and Final Bronze Age sites where large storage facilities for olive oil were found, such as Torre Mordillo and Rocavecchia. These data tie in with the archaeobotanical evidence, since the earliest cultivated olives make their appearance in layers dating to the Recent Bronze Age – not only at Broglio di Trebisacce, but also at Monopoli/Piazza Palmieri and Castello di Tursi. It appears that olive oil was produced and centrally stored on a fairly large scale, probably in order to be redistributed and/or exchanged. Although we have no evidence of large scale storage of other crops in this period, it can be assumed that olive oil production was not the only form of agricultural specialization.

However, this degree of socio-economic complexity developed only in a few larger centres. Most Bronze Age settlements, such as Santa Maria d'Anglona and San Teodoro/l'Incoronata, were of the dispersed type and probably housed no more than a few hundred inhabitants. Agricultural production at these settlements was primarily aimed at subsistence, not at surplus production for a market. Olive oil production may have been carried out here too, but clearly not on the same scale. In other words, large parts of southeast Italy did not participate in the process of agricultural specialization that took place in this period.

Wine production at Sybaris (Archaic Period)

In the late Archaic Period, we again witness agricultural specialization and surplus production in the Greek colonial towns and their territories, for instance at Sybaris, which was founded by Achaean colonists in the early 7th century BC. The Sibaritide was already relatively densely populated before the arrival of Greek migrants, especially in the elevated parts of the landscape, where the important Bronze- and Iron Age settlements of Torre Mordillo, Timpone della Motta, and Broglio di Trebisacce were located. Apparently, living conditions were no less favourable in the coastal area, as Sybaris soon became known as one of the richest cities in the Archaic Greek world. Especially its famous vineyards are frequently mentioned by ancient authors. It is said that they produced some of the finest wines in Magna Graecia, before Sybaris was destroyed by neighbouring Kroton around 510 BC. The production of these renowned wines even continued or was resumed after the town had reportedly ceased to exist and lived on as the *apoikia* of Thourioi (since 444 BC).

We do not know how this wine production was organized, but it was probably produced on a large enough scale to allow the export of a part of the surplus in Corinthian B amphorae. Such vessels were made in several production centres along the southern Italian coast, including Sybaris, Taras, and Metapontion. Grapes and olives were also frequently depicted on coinage from the Serdaioi, an indigenous tribe that probably lived in the hinterland of Sybaris. These coins can be dated between the late 6th and early 5th centuries BC. Additional archaeological evidence of wine production in the Greek colonial towns is provided by the remains of possible wine plantations, which were found near Taras.[1] The chronology of these plantations poses a problem, but they were definitely in use in the 5th century BC.

In short, it appears that most of the Greek colonial towns were involved in wine production in the Archaic Period, and also produced transport vessels to export their surpluses to overseas markets. However, large-scale (i.e. archaeologically visible) viticulture is a risky business that requires stable settlements and settled conditions. It can be profitable enough to take this risk if the fruits can be converted into storable commodities (i.e. wine), and sold at market. But whereas the Greek colonial towns were actively involved in external exchanges, such a market is unlikely to have existed in the inland areas. As a result, viticulture was still in its infancy in the inland areas in this period. There is archaeological evidence of wine consumption and grape collecting, for example at Roccagloriosa,

---

[1] Traces of wine plantations were also found at several other Greek towns that are located outside of the area here under study, i.e. Megara Hyblaea, Syracuse and Pithekoussai.

Cavallino, l'Amastuola, and Monte Papalucio. The wine in question, however, was for the most part imported, rather than produced locally.

Cereal specialization at Metapontion (Archaic/Classical and Early Hellenistic periods)
Another example of agricultural specialization, expansion and rationalization is provided by Archaic Metapontion. In the course of the 6th century BC, Metapontion began to organize its agricultural territory. The survey data from the Metapontino, the information from the Herakleia tablets and the pollen samples from Pantanello together present an image of a developed system of land use in the Metapontine *chora*. Since the agricultural plots are relatively large, it has been argued that a sort of crop rotation system with long fallow periods was used. Another possibility is that part of the work was carried out by agricultural labourers. There are indications that the rural economy at Metapontion was mostly based on cereal cultivation, to such an extent that a head of six-rowed barley is represented on Metapontine coins. The Pantanello pollen core contains a steady percentage of cereal pollen for Metapontion's entire habitation period, with a few peaks in the late 7th century BC and again in the middle of the 4th century BC. In short, agricultural production around Archaic/Classical Metapontion displayed a high level of organization and specialization, producing a surplus that was probably shipped to overseas and possibly inland markets. The layout of agricultural plots is also indicative of agricultural rationalization. Again, this system appears to have no parallels in the inland areas, and is even difficult to compare to the other Greek *chorai* in this period.

It is tempting to connect the remarkable innovations in the Metapontino to environmental circumstances. The thick, fertile soils may have been particularly suited to cereal cultivation. However, we should also consider the possibility that social factors contributed to Metapontion's economic prosperity in an important way. It has been argued that the land divisions in the Metapontino were established after a long period of oligarchy or even tyranny. When this system came to an end, it suddenly became possible for an individual family to own a parcel of land. Similar social/political reforms took place in the other Greek towns. We know from the Herakleia tablets that the confiscated lands were redistributed among a larger group of agricultural smallholders. This may also have happened at Metapontion, where even noncitizens were eventually given permission to occupy the *chora*. This may have increased the quantity of labour available, and possibly even resulted in an influx of seasonal workers. Such developments would certainly explain Metapontion's great economic prosperity in the Early Hellenistic Period, and the ability to successfully engage in specialized cereal production for a market.

The development of a complementary market economy (Early Hellenistic Period)
In contrast to the three examples that I described above, the developments in the Early Hellenistic Period took place on a regional scale. Several important changes can be detected in this period, including the infill of previously uninhabited inland areas and a regional trend toward urban expansion. Some of the larger settlements started to fulfill urban functions for a wider rural area. Regional centres such as Oria presumably furnished the hinterland with craft products and offered facilities for the processing, storage and exchange of agricultural products. These developments had far-reaching consequences for the scale, diversity, and organization of agricultural production in the inland areas. The changes in the settlement hierarchy – with the larger sites functioning as regional centrers – made it easier and much more profitable to exchange agricultural produce on a market. In this way, a greater demand for agricultural products was created, which the newly built rural settlements were able to provide. The increased inter-regional mobility and interconnectivity created the background for agricultural specialization and the production of cash-crops.

The most prominent example of such agricultural specialization is the sudden 'boom' in wine and olive oil production that took place in the late 4th and 3rd centuries BC. Olive and grape remains have been found in all the archaeological sites from southeast Italy with habitation levels from the Early Hellenistic period. These finds tie in well with the archaeological evidence and the information from ancient written sources, which both show that wine and olive oil were produced and traded on a large scale in this period. Pork and wool can probably be added to the list of successful export products that transformed the rural economy in southeast Italy in the last centuries of the first millennium BC. Indeed, it can be argued that a complementary economic system started to emerge in this period, with individual towns or areas specializing in specific products that were sold on regional and external markets. Both the inland and coastal regions were involved in this development. This degree of socio-economic complexity had no precedent in southeast Italy. The focus of the rural economy shifted from subsistence- to market-oriented, paving the way for large-scale land exploitation after the Roman conquest. In contrast to the traditional view of a ruined post-Hannibalic southern Italy, the archaeological evidence shows that in some respects it was a time of prosperity. The increasing Roman influence on southern Italy facilitated long-distance trade. As a result of this, agricultural specialization and a series of successful export products, including cereals, wine, olive oil, and wool, were firmly established. Seen in this light, the emergence of large rural estates that produced wine and olive oil for overseas markets in the 1st century AD was clearly not the result of a sudden transformation in land use practices. Rather, it followed the same process of change that had already started centuries earlier.

7.4 THE EFFECT OF GREEK COLONIZATION

During the 8th and 7th centuries BC, small groups of Greek migrants settled along the coast of southeast Italy, especially at Taras, Metapontion, Siris/Herakleia and Sybaris. Initially, these 'Greek' settlements hardly differed from other habitation centres in the area, which were of the dispersed type and consisted of several small groups of huts. The crop spectrum from such settlements, for instance at l'Amastuola, is indicative of small-scale and diverse farming, directed at self-sufficiency. It took many decades before some of the coastal settlements started to display distinct changes in town planning and architecture, and even longer before its effect became notable in the landscape and the way it was exploited. Meanwhile, the other settlements such as l'Amastuola, persisted in their traditional ways of land use, in which the yields from small agricultural fields were combined with the products of sheep/goat rearing. This system of land use, however, had certain restrictions. It did not allow l'Amastuola to participate in the period of economic growth and prosperity that characterized the Greek settlements in southeast Italy in the Archaic/Classical periods. Around c. 600 BC, these new colonial settlements started to acquire more urban characteristics, rearranged their agricultural territories and developed various forms of agricultural specialization. For example, Sybaris exported fine wines and Metapontion was involved in large-scale cereal production. Some of the Greek colonial towns had a relatively highly developed agricultural economy, but their methods of surplus production, agricultural specialization and rationalization did not reach beyond the borders of the *chora*. In the most part of southeast Italy, settlements continued to function as agro-towns and subsistence economies.

As we have seen, this changed rather dramatically in the Early Hellenistic Period, when land use practices in the inland areas underwent a major transformation and a complementary market economy started to develop. l'Amastuola did not participate in this development, either, as the site had already been abandoned by this time. A much larger new settlement, that was probably incorporated in the *chora* of Taras, emerged on the lower terraces north and east of the l'Amastuola hill. The survey results from the area around the l'Amastuola hill show that this settlement did participate in the 'new ways' of land use, since numerous small rural sites started to appear in the 4th and 3rd centuries BC.

In conclusion, it can be argued that the Greek colonization had a far-reaching effect on land use practices in southeast Italy, but this effect was far from immediate. The spread of olei- and viticulture provides an illustrative example. It is often assumed that Greek migrants introduced grape and olive cultivation to Italy, but this view is clearly outdated. Grape and olive cultivation already existed before the arrival of the Greeks, and oleiculture was even practiced on a large scale in the Recent Bronze Age. However, the Greek colonization process was no doubt a catalytic agent in the spread of viticulture in the inland areas by introducing wine drinking rituals. In the early centuries of the first millennium BC, these rituals were mostly performed with imported wine. Starting in the late Classical period, however, cultivation techniques and pottery types made to store, mix, pour, and consume wine also reached the inland areas, and indigenous settlements started to produce their own wines.

7.5 FUTURE RESEARCH

This research has raised many questions in need of further investigation. Firstly, more research is clearly needed to investigate the effect of the Greek colonization process on land use practices in Italy. We still know very little about the agricultural basis of the colonial foundations in Italy, and to what extent the migrants adapted their farming methods to local circumstances. As I have attempted to show in this study, a better understanding of agricultural practices, dietary habits and land exploitation in this period needs to be developed, comparing the evidence from Greek colonies in southern Italy to that of Archaic Greece. Such an investigation touches on some core issues in the current debate about the character of the Greek colonization process that I discussed in chapter 2, namely the colonists' means of subsistence in their new homelands, their relationship with indigenous societies, and the impact of the colonization.

In addition, more work has to be done to produce a more detailed picture of the landscape in southeast Italy in the period under study, and of the opportunities and restrictions it created for the people who inhabited it. The only way to move forward is to carry out integrated interdisciplinary research. In this study, I have shown that the combination of archaeology, archaeobotany and archaeozoology can lead to significant new insights, but several follow-ups of this kind can be proposed. Firstly, the analysis of organic residues on pottery and kitchen tools could lead to real progress in our understanding of the dietary habits of the inhabitants of pre-Roman southeast Italy. Thus far, such analyses have only occasionally been carried out in this area,[2] mainly to study the contents of Bronze Age vessels (*dolia*).[3] The same holds true for stable isotope research on skeletons, which has the potential to represent a considerable step forward in our understanding of the variety of natural resources available for both human and animal consumption. In order to develop a better understanding of the landscape itself, it is strongly recommended that geomorphological research acquires a more prominent role in future archaeological projects. Van Joolen made a useful start with the evaluation of land systems in the southern part of Apulia, but her basic classification is in urgent need of further investigation.

The results of this study also show that considerably more work has to be done to determine how and when oleiculture and viticulture were introduced in southern Italy. The limited amount of archaeobotanical finds of grapes and olives is problematic, especially for the Bronze Age, Early Iron Age, and Archaic/Classical periods.[4] In addition, further experimental investigations are needed to distinguish between the archaeological remains of wild and cultivated grape pips and olive stones. For instance, the Stummer index and formulae by Mangafa and Kotsakis turned out to be of little use for the analysis of the grape remains from Muro Tenente. Indeed, the question arises whether such morphometric methods add much to our understanding of early grape and olive cultivation in Italy.

---

[2] See particularly Notarstefano 2012.

[3] For example, Peroni 1994; Gugliemino 2002; Evans and Recchia 2001-2003.

[4] Cf. Lentjes and Saltini Semerari in press.

List of figures

Fig. 1.1 The research area of this study. Map by Bert Brouwenstijn.
Fig. 2.1 Aerial view of the l'Amastuola hilltop. Photo: Società Kikau.
Fig. 2.2a L'Amastuola, south terrace: Location of the excavation trenches. Map by Jaap Fokkema.
Fig. 2.2b L'Amastuola, south terrace: Location of the excavation trenches. Map by Bert Brouwenstijn.
Fig. 2.3 L'Amastuola, trench 6: Digital reconstruction of the cultic structure by Bert Brouwenstijn.
Fig. 2.4 L'Amastuola, trench 4: Burnt loam showing wood impressions. Burgers and Crielaard 2007, 89 (Fig. 16).
Fig. 2.5a L'Amastuola, trench 1: Location of the archaeological finds. Drawing by Jaap Fokkema.
Fig. 2.5b L'Amastuola, trench 1: Location of the archaeobotanical samples. Drawing by Jaap Fokkema.
Fig. 2.6a L'Amastuola, trench 2: Location of the archaeological finds. Drawing by Jaap Fokkema.
Fig. 2.6b L'Amastuola, trench 2: Location of the archaeobotanical samples. Drawing by Jaap Fokkema.
Fig. 2.7a L'Amastuola, trench 3: Location of the archaeological finds. Drawing by Jaap Fokkema.
Fig. 2.7b L'Amastuola, trench 3: Location of the archaeobotanical samples. Drawing by Jaap Fokkema.
Fig. 2.8a L'Amastuola, trench 4: Location of the archaeological finds. Drawing by Jaap Fokkema.
Fig. 2.8b L'Amastuola, trench 4: Location of the archaeobotanical samples. Drawing by Jaap Fokkema.
Fig. 2.9a L'Amastuola, trench 5: Location of the archaeological finds. Drawing by Jaap Fokkema.
Fig. 2.9b L'Amastuola, trench 5: Location of the archaeobotanical samples. Drawing by Jaap Fokkema.
Fig. 2.10a L'Amastuola, trench 6: Location of the archaeological finds. Drawing by Jaap Fokkema.
Fig. 2.10b L'Amastuola, trench 6: Location of the archaeobotanical samples. Drawing by Jaap Fokkema.
Fig. 2.11 L'Amastuola, trench 6: Black semicircular area (units 501 and 510). Burgers and Crielaard 2011, 69 (Figures 3-32).
Fig. 2.12 L'Amastuola, trench 5: Possible silos for grain storage. Burgers and Crielaard 2011, 65 (Figures 3-28).
Fig. 2.13 L'Amastuola, results of the charcoal analysis: Frequency of wood taxa (i.e. the number of stratigraphical units in which it was found). Chart by Bert Brouwenstijn.
Fig. 2.14 L'Amastuola, results of the charcoal analysis: Total number of fragments of wood taxa. Chart by Bert Brouwenstijn.
Fig. 2.15 L'Amastuola, results of the analysis of seeds and fruits: Frequencies. Chart by Bert Brouwenstijn.
Fig. 2.16 L'Amastuola, results of the analysis of seeds and fruits: Total number of fragments. Chart by Bert Brouwenstijn.
Fig. 2.17 L'Amastuola, results of the charcoal analysis: Wood taxa from hearths and fireplaces (fuel?). Chart by Bert Brouwenstijn.

Fig. 2.18 L'Amastuola, south terrace: Location of the samples from hearths and fireplaces (units 265, 274, 112, 148, 166, 170, 32, 33, 332, 335, 346, 373, 537, 542). Drawing by Jaap Fokkema.

Fig. 2.19 L'Amastuola, trench 4: Stone mortar from building δ. Burgers and Crielaard 2011, 150 (Figures 8-14).

Fig. 2.20 L'Amastuola, trench 2: Terracotta mortar from the colluvium layer. Burgers and Crielaard 2007, 102 (Figure 39e).

Fig. 2.21 L'Amastuola, all trenches: Grinding stones. Burgers and Crielaard 2011, 151-152 (Figures 8-15).

Fig. 2.22 Decorations on Daunian stelai showing cereal parching with mortars and pestles. Nava 1980, Figures CCLVII (775B) and CCCLXXXI (1157AB). Cf. Burgers and Crielaard 2011, 153 (Figures 8-17b).

Fig. 2.23a L'Amastuola, south of the hill: Stone mortar. Photo by Jan Paul Crielaard (cf. Burgers and Crielaard 2011, 153 (Figures 8-17a).

Fig. 2.23b San Pancrazio Salentino, Apulia: Stone mortar of unknown origin. Photo by the author.

Fig. 2.24 L'Amastuola, trench 6: Cooking pot with rounded base and relatively narrow neck. Burgers and Crielaard 2007, 102 (Figure 39a).

Fig. 2.25 L'Amastuola, trench 3, unit 107: Storage jar. Photo by Jan Paul Crielaard.

Fig. 2.26 L'Amastuola, trench 6: Fragmented olive stones from cooking pot. Photo by the author.

Fig. 2.27a L'Amastuola, trench 6: Carbonized garlic cloves (Allium sativum). Photo by Mark van Waijjen, courtesy of Biax consult.

Fig. 2.27b SEM image showing epidermal surface. Photo by Lucy Kubiak-Martens, courtesy of Biax consult.

Fig. 2.27c SEM image showing epidermal surface. Photo by Lucy Kubiak-Martens, courtesy of Biax consult.

Fig. 2.27d SEM image showing attachment scar. Photo by Lucy Kubiak-Martens, courtesy of Biax consult.

Fig. 3.1 Aerial view of Muro Tenente, showing the outlines of the Early Hellenistic fortification wall (cf. Figure 3.2). Burgers and Napolitano 2010, 8.

Fig. 3.2 Muro Tenente, location of the excavation trenches and soundings. Map by Jaap Fokkema.

Fig. 3.3 Muro Tenente, inner face of the southern section of the fortification wall. Burgers and Napolitano 2010, 43.

Fig. 3.4 Muro Tenente, northern excavation trench (A). Burgers and Yntema 1999, 114 (Figure 3), with additions by Jaap Fokkema.

Fig. 3.5 Muro Tenente, central excavation trench (C). Burgers and Napolitano 2010, 4, with additions by Jaap Fokkema.

Fig. 3.6 Muro Tenente, southern excavation trench (E). Drawing by Jaap Fokkema.

Fig. 3.7 Muro Tenente, archaeobotanical samples from the northern excavation trench (A). Drawing by Jaap Fokkema.

Fig. 3.8 Muro Tenente, archaeobotanical sample from test trench B. Drawing by Jaap Fokkema.

Fig. 3.9 Muro Tenente, archaeobotanical samples from the central excavation trench (C). Drawing by Jaap Fokkema

Fig. 3.10 Muro Tenente, archaeobotanical samples from the southern excavation trench (E). Drawing by Jaap Fokkema.

Fig. 3.11 Muro Tenente, ashy layer in the southern excavation trench (E), units 20009 and 20011. Photo by Lucia Di Noi.

Fig. 3.12 Muro Tenente, results of the charcoal analysis: Frequency of wood taxa (i.e. the number of stratigraphical units in which it was found). Chart by Bert Brouwenstijn.

Fig. 3.13 Muro Tenente, results of the charcoal analysis: Total number of fragments of wood taxa. Chart by Bert Brouwenstijn.

Fig. 3.14   Muro Tenente, results of the analysis of seeds and fruits: Frequencies. Chart by Bert Brouwenstijn.
Fig. 3.15   Muro Tenente, results of the analysis of seeds and fruits: Total number of fragments. Chart by Bert Brouwenstijn.
Fig. 3.16   Muro Tenente, results of the charcoal analysis: Wood taxa from hearths and fireplaces (fuel?). Chart by Bert Brouwenstijn.
Fig. 3.17a   Muro Tenente, charcoal fragment from unit 455. Photo by the author.
Fig. 3.17b   Muro Tenente, charcoal fragment from unit 455, 100x magnification. Photo by the author.
Fig. 3.18   Muro Tenente, results of the analysis of seeds and fruits from unit 20011. Chart by Bert Brouwenstijn.
Fig. 3.19   Muro Tenente, results of the charcoal analysis from unit 20011. Chart by Bert Brouwenstijn.
Fig. 3.20   Muro Tenente, location of archaeobotanical samples that contained chaff remains. Drawing by Jaap Fokkema.
Fig. 3.21   Muro Tenente, carbonized grape (*Vitis vinifera*) remains from unit 89. Photo by the author.
Fig. 3.22   Muro Tenente, central excavation trench (C) with the location of graves 22, 25, 27 and 30. Drawing by Jaap Fokkema.
Fig. 3.23   Muro Tenente, northern excavation trench (A) with the location of grave 45. Drawing by Jaap Fokkema.
Fig. 4.1   Decorations on Daunian stelai (c. 650-580 BC) showing deer hunting. Nava 1980, Tav. CCCXXVII (986B); Tav. CCCXXVIII (987Bd); LXXIII (248Bd).
Fig. 4.2   Pruned olive wood in San Pancrazio Salentino and Mesagne, province of Brindisi, winter 2010. Photo by the author.
Fig. 4.3   Reconstruction of a granary from Old-Smyrna by R.V. Nicholls. Drawing by the author, after Mazarakis Ainian 1997, Figure 411.
Fig. 4.4   Clay models of granaries from the Temple of Artemis at Ano Mazaraki, Greece. Drawing by the author, after Mazarakis Ainian 1997, 120.
Fig. 4.5   L'Amastuola, artist's impression of the grain silos (?) in trench 5. Drawing by Bert Brouwenstijn.
Fig. 4.6   Muro Tenente, density per square of amphorae sherds picked up during the field surveys. Burgers 1998, 256.
Fig. 4.7   Muro Tenente, density per square of loomweights picked up during the field surveys. Burgers 1998, 252.
Fig. 4.8   Muro Tenente, morphological measurements of the grape pips from unit 89 compared to the index of Stummer 1911. Drawing edited by Bert Brouwenstijn.
Fig. 4.9   Muro Tenente, morphological measurements of the grape pips from unit 89 compared to the formulae by Mangafa and Kotsakis 1996. Drawing edited by Bert Brouwenstijn.
Fig. 5.1   Locations of the archaeological sites in southeast Italy that are discussed in chapters 5 and 6. Map by Bert Brouwenstijn.
Fig. 5.2   Archaeozoological remains from Early Iron Age (a), Archaic/Classical (b), Early Hellenistic (c) and Late Hellenistic (d) contexts in southeast Italy. Charts by Bert Brouwenstijn.
Fig. 5.3   Characters in a *phlyax* (theatre) depiction stealing cakes. Decoration on Apulian red-figure pottery, c. 400-325 BC. Photo by Ervina Boeve/Hekman Digital Archive.
Fig. 5.4   Silver diobols of the Serdaioi (Lucania?) depicting grapes and olives, late 6th/early 5th century BC. Drawing by the author.
Fig. 5.5   Bronze, lead and clay funerary crown in the shape of grapes and grape leafs from the southern *necropolis* at Herakleia, 3rd century BC. Drawing by the author after Vandermersch 1994, 39.
Fig. 5.6   Grape leaves on a Lucanian oinochoe, c. 380-360 BC. Drawing by the author, after Dentzer 1982; Vandermersch 1994, 40.

Fig. 5.7   Terracotta horse carrying baskets of fruit, from Policoro, Museo della Siritide, 2nd half 4th century BC. Forti and Stazio 1983, Figure 672

Fig. 5.8   Gnathia-style *askos* (small pouring vessel) in the form of a mule carrying two transport amphorae, c. 280-240 BC. Museo Archeologico di Bari. Drawing by the author.

Fig. 5.9a   Terracotta 'San Giovanni' Apples from the Mannella Sanctuary at Lokroi Epizephyrioi. Meirano 2008, 142, Figure 6.

Fig. 5.9b   Modern San Giovanni apples.

Fig. 5.10   Terracotta 'Limoncella' apples from the Mannella Sanctuary at Lokroi Epizephyrioi. Meirano 2008, 142, Figure 7.

Fig. 5.11   Terracotta apple from Olympia. Drawing by the author after Furtwängler 1890, no. 1183, pl. LXVIII.

Fig. 5.12   Terracotta fruit (apple?) from Lindos, 525-400 BC. Drawing by the author after Blinkenberg 1931, no. 2441.

Fig. 5.13   Terracotta pomegranate from the Prytaneion in Olympia. Drawing by the author after Bol 1978, 668, 130, pl. 61.

Fig. 5.14   Terracotta votive objects, Museo Nazionale di Taranto. Drawing by the author after Forti and Stazio 1983, Figures 728, 703.

Fig. 5.15   Terracotta pomegranates and garlic bulbs (?) from a grave in Oria (tomb 1973-3), middle of the 2nd century BC. Yntema 2009, Figure 9, 155.

Fig. 5.16   The pomegranate in tomb paintings. Pontrandolfo, Rouveret and Cipriani 1992, 56, Figure 55; 34, Figure 28; 72, Figure 71.

Fig. 5.16a Paestum, *necropolis* of Andriulo: Braggart soldier (tomb 53, east wall);

Fig. 5.16b Paestum, *necropolis* of Vannullo: Return of the warrior (tomb 4, west wall).

Fig. 5.16c Taranto, *necropolis* of Spinazzo, left wall of a tomb: Cortege of horses, late 4th century BC.

Fig. 5.17   Lead garlic bulb from Isthmia, Greece (Sanctuary of Poseidon), 4th century BC. Raubitschek 1998, pp. 11 (nr. 40); courtesy of the American School of Classical Studies at Athens.

Fig. 5.18   Lead 'knob of uncertain use' (garlic bulb?) from the sanctuary of Hera Limenia at Perachora. Drawing by the author after Payne and Dunbabin 1940, p. 186, pl. 85:12.

Fig. 5.19   Bronze 'poppy' (garlic bulb?) with votive inscription (meaning unknown), 3rd-2nd century BC. Drawing by the author after Mitten and Doeringer 1967, nr. 152 (p. 146).

Fig. 5.20   Terracotta object (garlic bulb?) from Olympia. Drawing by the author after Furtwängler 1890, p. 186, no. 1261.

Fig. 5.21   Clay models of garlic bulbs (?) from Egypt. Drawing by the author after Flinders Petrie 1920, pl. 46, no. 23-24.

Fig. 5.22   Clay models of garlic bulbs (?) from the Predynastic cemetery at El Mahasna, Egypt. Ayrton and Loat 1911, pl. 17.

Fig. 6.1   Metapontion, silver stater representing a hexaploid (six-rowed) head of barley, 6th century BC. Photo by Vera Massaro, courtesy of the Institute of Classical Archaeology, University of Texas, US.

BIBLIOGRAPHY

Abbott, James T. *Late quaternary alluviation and soil erosion in Southern Italy* (Unpublished PhD thesis, University of Texas at Austin, 1997).

Accorsi, Carla, A., Marta Bandini Mazzanti, Marco Marchesini and Silvia Marvelli, 'Ricerche archeoambientali nella Daunia antica. Dati pollinici sull'insediamento di Arpi e sulla villa Romana di Ascoli Satriano', in *Agricoltura e commerci nell'Italia antica*, ed. by Lorenzo Quilici and Simona Quilici Gigli (Rome: L'Erma di Bretschneider, 1995), pp. 103-113.

Adamesteanu, Dinu, 'Le suddivisioni di terra nel Metapontino', in *Problèmes de la terre en Grèce ancienne*, ed. by Moses I. Finley (Paris: Mouton, 1973), pp. 49-61.

Adamesteanu, Dinu, *La Basilicata antica: Storia e monumenti* (Cava dei Terreni: Di Mauro, 1974).

Adamesteanu, Dinu and Marina Castoldi, *I Greci sul Basento. Mostra scavi archeologici all'Incoronata di Metaponto, 1971-1984* (Como: New Press, 1986).

Akkerman, Erik N., *Fysisch antropologisch onderzoek van de Messapische necropolen van Muro Tenente* (Unpublished doctoral thesis, University of Groningen, 2002).

Albarella, Umberto, 'Vaste, Fondo S. Antonio - I reperti faunistici dalle cisterne e dalla buca di scarico', *Studi di Antichità*, 8 (2) (1995), pp. 289-304.

Alessio, Arcangelo and Pietro Giovanni Guzzo, 'Santuarie fattorie ad est di Taranto. Elementi archeologici per un modello di interpretazione', *Scienze dell'Antichità*, 3-4 (1989/1990), pp. 363-396.

Amouretti, Marie-Claire and Jean-Pierre Brun, *La production du vin et de l'huile en Méditerranée* (Athens: École Française d'Athènes, 1993).

Ampolo, Carmine, 'Le condizioni materiali della produzione. Agricoltura e paesaggio agrario', *Dialoghia di Archeologia*, 1 (1980), pp. 15-46.

Anderberg, Anna-Lena, *Atlas of seeds and small fruits of Northwest-European plant species, Part 4: Resedaceae-Umbelliferae* (Stockholm: Swedish Natural Science Research Council, 1994).

Aprosio, Maria and Franco Cambi, 'La ricognizione archeologica nell'agro brindisino', in *Metodologie di catalogazione dei beni archeologici. Beni Archeologici - Conoscenza e Tecnologie, Quaderno 1.2*, ed. by Francesco D'Andria (Martano: Edipuglia, 1997), pp. 177-180.

Arancio, Maria Letizia, 'La prima età del ferro', in *Torre Mordillo 1987-1990, Le relazioni egee di una comunità protostorica della Sibaritide*, ed. by Maria Letizia Arancio, Flavia Trucco and Lucia Vagnetti (Rome: CNR, Istituto per gli Studi Micenei ed Egeo-Anatolici, 2001), pp. 275-292.

Arancio, Maria Letizia, Flavia Trucco and Lucia Vagnetti (eds), *Torre Mordillo 1987-1990, Le relazioni egee di una comunità protostorica della Sibaritide*, (Rome: CNR, Istituto per gli Studi Micenei ed Egeo-Anatolici, 2001).

Attema, Peter A.J., Gert-Jan L.M. Burgers, Marianne Maaskant-Kleibrink and Douwe G. Yntema, 'Case studies in indigenous developments in early Italian centralization and urbanization, a Dutch perspective', *Journal of European Archaeology* 1 (3) (1998), pp. 326-381.

Attema, Peter A.J., Gert-Jan L.M. Burgers and Martijn Van Leusen, *Regional pathways to complexity. Settlement and land-use dynamics in early Italy from the Bronze Age to the Republican period* (Amsterdam: Amsterdam University Press, 2010).

Bakels, Corrie, 'Growing grain for others, or how to detect surplus production', *Journal of European Archaeology*, 4 (1996), pp. 329-336.

Bakels, Corrie, 'Plant remains from Sardinia, Italy, with notes on barley and grape', *Vegetation History and Archaeobotany*, 11 (2002), pp. 3-8.

Bakels, Corrie and Stéphanie Jacomet, 'Access to luxury foods in Central Europe during the Roman period: The archaeobotanical evidence', *World Archaeology*, 34 (3) (2003), pp. 542-57.

Barker, Graeme, 'Animal husbandry and economic change at Monte Irsi', in *Monte Irsi, Southern Italy. The Canadian excavations in the Iron Age and Roman sites, 1971-1972*. BAR Supplementary series 20274-281, ed. by Alastair Small (Oxford: British Archaeological Reports, 1977), pp. 265-273.

Barker, Graeme, 'Early neolithic land use in Yugoslavia', Proceedings of the Prehistoric Society, 41 (1975).

Barker, Graeme, *Prehistoric farming in Europe* (Cambridge: Cambridge University Press, 1985).

Barker, Graeme, 'Two Italys: One valley', in *The Annales school and archaeology*, ed. by John Bintliff (London and New York: Leicester University Press, 1991), pp. 34-56.

Barker, Graeme, *A Mediterranean valley: Landscape archaeology and Annales history in the Biferno valley* (London: Leicester University Press, 1995).

Barker, Graeme, *The Biferno Valley survey: The archaeological and geomorphological record* (London, New York: Leicester University Press, 1995).

Bagnasco, Marcella Barra (ed.), *Pomarico vecchio Vol. 1*, (Dep. St. Pat. Lucania, Quaderni di Archeologia e Storia antica, 10°, 1997).

Barrett, James C. and Paul Halstead (ed.), *The emergence of civilisation revisited*, (Oxford: Oxbow Books, 2004).

Bartosiewicz, László (ed.), *The chora of Metaponto 2. Archaeozoology at Pantanello and five other sites* (Austin, Texas: University of Texas Press, 2010).

Berggren, Greta, *Atlas of seeds and small fruits of northwest-European plant species, part 2: Cyperaceae* (Stockholm, Naturhistoriska riksmuseet, 1969).

Berggren, Greta, *Atlas of seeds and small fruits of northwest-European plant species, part 3: Salicaceae-Cruciferae* (Stockholm, Naturhistoriska riksmuseet, 1981).

Besnard, Guillaume and André Bervillé, 'Multiple origins for the Mediterranean olive (*Olea europaea* L. subsp. *europaea*) based upon mitochondrial DNA polymorphisms', *Comptes Rendus de l'Académie des Sciences de Paris*, III, 323 (2000), pp. 173-181.

Bietti Sestieri, Anna Maria, 'The metal industry of continental Italy, 13th to 11th century BC, and its connections with the Aegean', *Proceedings of the Prehistoric Society* 39 (1973), pp. 383424.

Bietti Sestieri, Anna Maria, 'Rapporti e scambi fra le genti indigene fra l'età del bronzo e la prima età del ferro nelle zone della colonizzazione', in *Magna Grecia I, Il Mediterraneo, le metropoleis e la fondazione delle colonie*, ed. by Giovanni Pugliese Carratelli (Milan: Electa, 1985), pp. 85-126.

Bietti Sestieri, Anna Maria, 'L'età del Bronzo finale nella penisola italiana', *Bollettino del centro Polesanodi studi storiciarcheologici ed etnografici*, 127 (2008), pp. 7-54.

Bintliff, John, *The Annales school and archaeology* (London and New York: Leicester University Press, 1989).

Bintliff, John, 'Time, structure and agency: The Annales, emergent complexity, and archaeology', in *A companion to archaeology*, ed. by John Bintliff (London & New York: Blackwell, 2004), pp. 174-194.

Bintliff, John, Phil Howard and Anthony Snodgrass, *Testing the hinterland: The work of the Boeotia survey (1989-1991) in the southern approaches to the city of Thespiai* (Cambridge: McDonald Institute for Archaeological Research, 1991).

Blinkenberg, Christian, *Lindos: Fouilles et recherches, 1902-1914, Les petits objets* (Berlin: De Gruyter & Libraires-Éditeurs, 1931).

Blitzer, Harriet, 'Olive cultivation and oil production in Minoan Crete', in *La production du vin et de l'huile en Méditerrannée*, ed. by Marie-Claire Amouretti and Jean-Pierre Brun (Athens: École Française d'Athènes, 1993), pp. 163-75.

Boardman, John, 'The olive in the Mediterranean: Its culture and use', *Philosophical Transactions of the Royal Society of London*, 275 (1976), pp. 187-96.

Boardman, John, *The Greeks overseas. Their early colonies and trade (third edition, with Epilogue)* (London: Thames and Hudson, 1998).

Boardman, Sheila and Glynis Jones, 'Experiment on the effects of charring on cereal plant components', *Journal of Archaeological Science,* 17 (1990), pp. 1-11.

Boersma, Johannes and Douwe G. Yntema, *Valesio. History of an Apulian settlement from the Iron Age to the Late Roman period* (Fasano di Puglia: Montedipe, 1987).

Boersma, Johannes (ed.), *Mutatio Valentia. The Late Roman baths at Valesio, Salento*, (Amsterdam: Thesis Publishers, 1995).

Bökönyi, Sandór, Lorenzo Costantini and Jane Fitt, 'The farming economy', in *Fourth century BC Magna Grecia - A case study*, ed. by Maurizio Gualtieri (Jonsered: Åström, 1993), pp. 281-307.

Bökönyi, Sandór, 'Animal husbandry from the Late Neolithic through the Roman period', in *The chora of Metaponto 2. Archaeozoology at Pantanello and five other sites*, ed. by László Bartosiewicz (Austin, Texas: University of Texas Press, 2010), pp. 1-33.

Bonatti, Enrico, 'I sedimenti del lago di Monterosi', *Experientia* 15. VI. Volume 17, Issue 6 (1961), pp. 252-253.

Bol, Peter C., *Grossplastik aus Bronze in Olympia* (Berlin: Walter de Gruyter, 1978).

Bottini, Angelo, 'I Lucani', in *Magna Grecia II, Lo sviluppo politico, sociale ed economico*, ed. by Giovanni Pugliese Caratelli (Milan: Electa, 1987), pp. 259-280.

Bouby, Laurent, 'L'orge à deux range (*Hordeum distichum*) dans l'agriculture Gallo-Romaine: Données archéobotaniques', *Revue d'Archéométrie* 25 (2001), pp. 35-44.

Bower, Mim, 'Cereal pollen dispersal: A pilot study', *Cambridge Archaeological Journal,* 2 (1992), pp. 236-41.

Braadbaart, Freek and Imogen Poole, 'Morphological, chemical and physical changes during charcoalification of wood and its relevance to archaeological contexts', *Journal of Archaeological Science* 35 (2008), pp. 2434-2445.

Braudel, Fernand P., *La Méditerrannée et le monde Méditerranéen à l'époque de Philippe II* (Paris: Colin, 1949).

Braun, Thomas, 'Barley cakes and emmer bread', in *Food in antiquity*, ed. By John Wilkins,

David Harvey, Mike Dobson and Michael J. Dobson (Exeter: University of Exeter Press, 1995), pp. 25-35.

Bremmer, Jan, *Greek Religion* (Cambridge: Cambridge University Press, 1994).

Brothwell, Don R. and Patricia Brothwell, *Food in antiquity: A survey of the diet of early peoples* (London: Thames and Hudson, 1969).

Brousseau, Louis, 'La monnayage des Serdaioi revisité', *Revue Numismatique,* 166 (2010), pp. 257-85.

Brumfield, Allaire, 'Cakes in the *liknon*: Votives from the Sanctuary of Demeter and Kore on Acrocorinth', *Hesperia* 66 (1) (1997), pp. 147-72.

Brun, Jean-Pierre, *Archéologie du vin et de l'huile: de la préhistoire à l'époque Hellénistique* (Paris: Editions Errance, 2004).

Brun, Jean-Pierre, 'Viticulture et oléiculture grecques et indigènes en Grande Grèce et en Sicile', in *Grecs et indigènes de la Catalogne à la Mer Noire*, ed. by Henri Tréziny (Aix-en-Provence: Centre Camille Jullian, 2010), pp. 425-32.

Brunt, Peter A., *Italian manpower, 225 BC - AD 14* (Oxford: Clarendon Press, 1971).

Buffa, Vittoria, 'I materiali del Bronzo finale e della prima età del ferro', in *Nuove ricerche sulla protostoria della Sibaritide*, ed. by Renato Peroni (Rome: Paleani, 1984), pp. 212-221.

Burgers, Gert-Jan L.M., 'The Salento Isthmus Project, Second interim report', *Babesch,* 69 (1994), pp. 145-154.

Burgers, Gert-Jan L.M., 'The settlement of Muro Tenente, Southern Italy. First interim report', *Babesch*, 71 (1996), pp. 103-113.

Burgers, Gert-Jan L.M., *Constructing Messapian landscapes. Settlement dynamics, social organization and culture contact in the margins of Graeco-Roman Italy* (Amsterdam: Gieben, 1998).

Burgers, Gert-Jan L.M. and Douwe G. Yntema, 'The settlement of Muro Tenente, Southern Italy. Second interim report', *Babesch,* 73 (1998), pp. 115-124.

Burgers, Gert-Jan L.M. and Douwe G. Yntema, 'The settlement of Muro Tenente, Southern Italy. Third interim report', *Babesch,* 74 (1999), pp. 111-132.

Burgers, Gert-Jan L.M. and Jan Paul Crielaard, 'Greek colonists and indigenous populations at L'Amastuola, southern Italy', *Babesch,* 82 (2007), pp. 77-114.

Burgers, Gert-Jan L.M. and Daphne M. Lentjes, 'Charcoals in context: Anthracological analysis at Muro Tenente, South-Eastern Italy', in *Charcoals from the past: Cultural and palaeoenvironmental implications. Proceedings of the Third International Meeting of Anthracology, Cavallino-Lecce (Italy) June 28th - July 1st 2004,* BAR International Series 1807, ed. by Girolamo Fiorentino and Donatella Magri (Oxford: Archaeopress, 2008), pp. 39-45.

Burgers, Gert-Jan L.M., Jan Paul Crielaard and Douwe G. Yntema, 'L'area centrale dell'abitato di Muro Tenente', in *L'insediamento Messapico di Muro Tenente. Scavi e ricerche 1998*-2009, ed. by Gert-Jan L.M. Burgers and Christian Napolitano (Mesagne: Locopress, 2010), pp. 15-30.

Burgers, Gert-Jan L.M. and Jitte Waagen, 'Excavations at I Castiedd' di San Pancrazio Salentino, Southern Italy', *Babesch,* 85 (2010), pp. 69-85.

Burgers, Gert-Jan L.M., 'Il sito di Muro Tenente: ricerca e valorizzazione', in *L'insediamento Messapico di Muro Tenente. Scavi e ricerche 1998-2009,* ed. by Gert-Jan L.M. Burgers and Christian Napolitano (Mesagne: Locopress, 2010), pp. 9-13.

Burgers, Gert-Jan L.M. and Christian Napolitano (ed.), *L'insediamento Messapico di Muro Tenente. Scavi e ricerche 1998-2009,* (Mesagne: Locopress, 2010).

Burgers, Gert-Jan L.M. and Jan Paul Crielaard (ed.), *Greci e indigeni a l'Amastuola* (Mottola: Stampa Sud, 2011).

Burkert, Walter, *Griechische Religion der archaischen und klassischen Epoche* (Stuttgart: Kohlhammer, 1977).

Butzer, Karl W., Juan F. Mateu, Elisabeth K. Butzer and Pavel Kraus, 'Irrigation agrosystems in Eastern Spain: Roman or Islamic origins?', *Annals of the Association of American Geographers,* 75, (4) (1985), pp. 479-509.

Butzer, Karl, 'Geomorphology and stratigraphy of the Paleolithic site of Budino (Prov. Pontevedra, Spain)', *Quaternary Science Journal,* 18, No. 1, A. 04 (1967), pp. 82-103.

Butzer, Karl W. and Sarah E. Harris, 'Geoarchaeological approaches to the environmental history of Cyprus: Explication and critical evaluation', *Journal of Archaeological Science,* 34, (11) (2007), pp. 1932-1952.

Cambi, Franco, 'Pottery and territory: A tormented relationship', in *Extracting meaning from ploughsoil assemblages. The archaeology of Mediterranean landscapes 5,* ed. by Riccardo Francovich, Helen Patterson and Graeme Barker (Oxford: Oxbow Books, 2000), pp. 174-184.

Caniglia, Giovanni, Francesca Chiesura, Luigino Curti, Giovanni Lorenzoni and Silvano Marchiori, 'Inquadramento fitosociologico di una cenosi a *Sarcopoterium spinosum* (L.) Spach del Salento (Puglia)', *Atti dell'Istituto Botanico dell'Università e Laboratorio Crittogamico di Pavia,* 6 (10) (1974-1975), pp. 241-267.

Cappers, René T.J., Renée M. Bekker and Judith E. Jans, *Digital seed atlas of the Netherlands* (Groningen Archaeological Studies 4; Eelde: Barkhuis Publishing, 2006).

Cappers, René T.J. and Daan C.M. Raemaekers, 'Cereal cultivation at Swifterbant? Neolithic wetland farming on the North European Plain', *Current Anthropology* 49-3 (2008), pp. 385-402.

Caramiello, Roberto and Consolata Siniscalco, 'Studio archeobotanico nell'abitato di Pomarico vecchio (Matera)', in *Pomarico vecchio Vol. 1,* ed. by Manuela Barra Bagnasco (Dep. St. Pat. Lucania, Quaderni di Archeologia e Storia antica, 10a, 1997), pp. 253-268.

Carandini, Andrea, *Storie dalla terra. Manuale dello scavo archeologico* (Bari: Einaudi, 1981).

Carra, Marialetizia, Laura Cattani and Carlotta Zanni, 'Aspetti paletnobotanici dell' area insediativa protostorica di S. Maria in Belverde sul Monte Cetona (Siena)', *Rivista di Scienze Preistoriche,* LIII (2003), pp. 505-518.

Carter, Joseph C., *Excavations in the territory, Metaponto, 1980* (Austin, Texas: University of Texas Press, 1980).

Carter, Joseph C., Lorenzo Costantini, Cesare D'Annibale, J.R. Jones, R.L. Folk and Donald Sullivan, 'Population and agriculture: Magna Grecia in the fourth century BC', in *Papers in Italian Archaeology IV. The Cambridge Conference. Part I: The Human Landscape*, ed. by Simon Stoddart and Caroline Malone (Cambridge: BAR International Series 243, 1985), pp. 281-312.

Carter, Joseph C., 'Agricoltura e pastorizia in Magna Grecia tra Badano e Basento', in *Magna Grecia II. Lo sviluppo politico, sociale ed economico*, ed. by Giovanni Pugliese Carratelli (Milan: Electa, 1987), pp. 173-212.

Carter, Joseph C., 'Metapontum: Land, wealth, and population', in *Greek colonists and native populations: Proceedings of the first Australian Congress of Classical Archaeology held in honour of emeritus professor A. D. Trendall, Sydney, 9-14 July 1985*, ed. by Jean-Pierre Descoeudres (Oxford: Clarendon Press, 1990), pp. 405-441.

Carter, Joseph C. and Lorenzo Costantini, 'Settlement density, agriculture, and the extent of productive land cleared from forest in the time of the Roman Empire in Magna Grecia', in *Evaluation of land surfaces Cleared from forests in the Mediterranean region during the time of the Roman Empire*, ed. by Burkhard Frenzel (Stuttgart/New York: G. Fischer Verlag, 1994), pp. 101-118.

Carter, Joseph C., *The Chora of Metaponto. The necropoleis* (Austin: University of Texas Press, 1998).

Carter, Joseph C., 'La chora di Metaponto. Risultati degli ultimi 25 anni di ricerca archeologica', in *Problemi della* chora *coloniale dall'Occidente al Mar Nero. Atti del XL Convegno di Studi sulla Magna Grecia*, ed. by Attilio Stazio and Stefania Ceccoli (Taranto: Istituto per la Storia e l'Archeologia della Magna Grecia, 2001), pp. 771-92.

Carter, Joseph C., Steve M. Thompson and Jessica Trelogan, 'The system of land division in the *chorai* of Metaponto and Chersonesos', in *Chora and polis (Kolloquien des Historischen Kollegs 5 bis 8 April 2000)*, ed. by Frank Kolb (Munich: Oldenbourg Verlag, 2004), pp. 127-47.

Carter, Joseph C., *Discovering the Greek countryside at Metaponto* (Ann Arbor: University of Michigan Press, 2006).

Carter, Joseph C., Alberto Prieto and Jessica Trelogan, *The Chora of Metaponto 3: Archaeological field survey Bradano to Basento* (University of Texas at Austin. Institute of Classical Archaeology: University of Texas Press, 2011).

Cartwright, Caroline R., 'Grapes or *raisins?* An Early Bronze Age larder under the microscope', *Antiquity*, 77 (296) (2003), pp. 345-348.

Castelletti, Lanfredo, 'Contributo alle ricerche paletnobotaniche in Italia', *Istituto Lombardo Rendiconti*, 106 (1972), pp. 331-374.

Castelletti, Lanfredo, 'Rapporto preliminare sui resti vegetali macroscopici della serie neolitico bronzo di Pienza (Siena)', *Rivista archeologica della antica provincia e diocesi di Como*, 156/157, (1976), pp. 243-51.

Castelletti, Lanfredo, 'I carboni della grotta 'Latronico 3' (Latronico, Provincia di Potenza)', (Firenze, 1978), pp. 228-39.

Castelletti, Lanfredo *et al.*, 'Considerazioni sull'ambiente e l'economia durante il Neolitico', *Atti della XXVI Riunione Scientifica dell'Istituto Italiano di Preistoria e Protostoria* (Firenze, 1987), pp. 37-55.

Castelletti, Lanfredo, 'Legni e carboni in Archeologia', in T. Manoni and A. Molinari (eds), *Scienze in archeologia. Il ciclo di lezioni sulla ricerca applicata in archeologia, Certosa di Pontigliano (Siena) 7-19 Novembre 1988* (Firenze: Edizioni all'Insegna del Giglio, 1990), pp. 321-94.

Castelletti, Lanfredo, Elisabetta Castiglioni and Mauro Rottoli, 'L'agricoltura dell'Italia settentrionale dal Neolitico al Medioevo', in *Le piante coltivate e la loro storia. Dalle origini al transito in Lombardia nel centenario della riscoperta della genetica di Mendel*, ed. by Osvaldo Failla and Gaetano Forni (Milan: Franco Angeli, 2001), pp. 33-84.

Castiglioni, Elisabetta and Mauro Rottoli, 'Capua (Caserta). Località Strepparo e Cento Moggie. Scavi nell'area del CIRA. Resti botanici da un pozzo dell'età del Bronzo', *Bollettino di Archeologia*, 37-38 (1996), pp. 62-67.

Castiglioni, Elisabetta, Michela Cottini and Mauro Rottoli, 'I resti botanici di Santa Giulia a Brescia', in *S. Giulia di Brescia; gli scavi dal 1980 al 1992. Reperti preromani, romani e alto medievali*, ed. by Gian Pietro Brogiolo (Florence: All'Insegna del Giglio, 1999), pp. 401-424.

Castiglioni, Elisabetta, Michela Cottini and Mauro Rottoli, 'I resti archeobotanici', in *Archeologia a Monte Barro, vol. II- Gli scavi 1990-97 e le ricerche al S. Martino di Lecco*, ed. by Gian Pietro Brogiolo and Lanfredo Castelletti (Lecco: Editrice Stefanoni, 2001), pp. 223-247.

Celant, Alessandra, 'Risultati delle indagini paleobotaniche eseguite su impronte e resti vegetali incombusti relativi a frammenti di intonaco di capanna e di fornelli dell'abitato protostorico di Broglio di Trebisacce (CS)', in *L'organizzazione dello spazio sull'acropoli di Broglio di Trebisacce: Dallo studio delle strutture e dei manufatti in impasto di fango all'analisi della distribuzione dei reperti*, ed. by Claudio Moffa (Firenze: All'Insegna del Giglio, 2002), Appendice 2.

Chabal, Lucie, 'Apports récents de l'anthracologie à la connaissance des paysages passés: Performances et limites', *Histoire & Mesure,* IX (3/4) (1994), pp. 317-338.

Chatfield, Charlotte, *Food composition tables for international use; Minerals and vitamins* (FAO Nutritional Studies; Rome: Food and Agriculture Organization of the United Nations, 1954).

Ciaraldi, Marina, 'I resti vegetali delle offerte di età arcaica e ellenistica', in *Metodologie di catalogazione dei beni archeologici. Beni archeologici- Conoscenza e tecnologie, Quaderno I.1*, ed. by Francesco D'Andria (Lecce/Bari: CNR, 1997), pp. 211-228.

Ciaraldi, Marina, 'Food offerings at the Archaic/Hellenistic sanctuary of Demeter and Persephone at Monte Papalucio', *Accordia Research Papers*, 7 (1999), pp. 75-91.

Cicirelli, Caterina and Claude Albore-Livadie, 'Stato delle ricerche a Longola di Poggiomarino: Quadro insediamentale e problematiche', in *Nuove ricerche archeologiche nell'area vesuviana, scavi 2003-2006: Atti del Convegno Internazionale, Roma, 1-3 febbraio 2007. Studi della Soprintendenza Archeologica di Pompei, 25*, ed. by Pietro Giovanni Guzzo and Maria Paola Guidobaldi (Napoli: Electa, 2008), pp. 473-487.

Cicirelli, Caterina, Claude Albore Livadie, Lorenzo Costantini and Matteo Delle Donne, 'La vite a Poggiomarino, Longola: un contesto di vinificazione dell'Età del Ferro', in *Nuove ricerche archeologiche nell'area vesuviana, scavi 2003-2006: Atti del Convegno Internazionale, Roma, 1-3 febbraio 2007. Studi della Soprintendenza Archeologica di Pompei, 25*, ed. by Pietro Giovanni Guzzo and Maria Paola Guidobaldi (Napoli: Electa, 2008), pp. 574-575.

Coco, Antonio Primaldo, *La foresta Oritana e i suoi antichi casali* (Lecce: Spacciante, 1919).

Colledge, Sue, 'Charred plant remains', in *Botromagno. Excavation and Survey at Gravina in Puglia 1979-1985*, Acordia Research Studies on Italy, vol. 9, ed. by Ruth D. Whitehouse, John B. Wilkins and Edward Herring (London: Accordia Research Institute), pp. 53-60.

Cook, James E., 'Implications of modern successional theory for habitat typing: A review', *Forest Science*, 42(1) (1996), pp. 67-75.

Costantini, Lorenzo, 'Monte San Mauro di Caltagirone. Analisi paleoetnobotaniche dei semi contenuti nei pithoi 4 e 6', *Bollettino d'Arte,* 4 (1979), pp. 43-44.

Costantini, Lorenzo, 'The evidence for Metapontine agriculture (seeds and bones)', in *Excavations in the territory of Metaponto 1980*, ed. by Joseph C. Carter (Austin, Texas: University of Texas Press, 1980), pp. 10-13.

Costantini, Lorenzo, 'Semi e carboni del mesolitico e neolitico della Grotta dell'Uzzo, Trapani', *Quaternaria,* XXIII (1981), pp. 233-247.

Costantini, Lorenzo, 'Analisi paleoetnobotaniche nel comprensorio di Camarina', *Bollettino d'Arte,* 17 (1983), pp. 49-56.

Costantini, Lorenzo, 'Piante spontanee e piante coltivate a S. Giovanni di Ruoti, Potenza', in *Lo scavo di S. Giovanni di Ruoti ed il periodo tardonantico in Basilicata: Atti della tavola rotonda, Roma 4 luglio 1981,* ed. by Maurizio Gualtieri, Mariarosaria Salvatore and Alastair Small (Bari: Adriatica, 1983), pp. 85-90.

Costantini, Lorenzo, 'Indagini bioarcheologiche nel sito di Pizzica Pantanello', in *Magna Grecia e il mondo miceneo, Atti del XXII Convegno di Studi sulla Magna Grecia, Taranto 7-11 ottobre 1982,* ed. by Lucia Vagnetti (Taranto: Istituto per la Storia e l'Archeologia della Magna Grecia, 1983), pp. 487-492.

Costantini, Lorenzo and Loredana Costantini Biasini, 'Bolsena, Gran Carro', in *L'alimentazione nel mondo antico: Gli Etruschi* (Rome: Ministero per i Beni Culturali e Ambientali, 1987), pp. 61-67.

Costantini, Lorenzo, 'Plant exploitation at Grotta dell'Uzzo, Sicily', in *The territory of Metaponto 1981-1982,* ed. by Joseph C. Carter (Austin, Texas: University of Texas Press, 1989), pp. 32-36.

Costantini, Lorenzo and Mauro Stancanelli, 'La preistoria agricola dell'Italia centro-meridionale: Il contributo delle indagini archeobotaniche', *Origini,* XVIII (1994), pp. 149-244.

Costantini, Lorenzo and Loredana Biasini Costantini, 'I resti vegetali del villaggio del 'Gran Carro', Bolsena (VT): scavo 1974', in *Un abitato villanoviano perilacustre. Il 'Gran Carro' sul lago di Bolsena (1959-1985),* ed. by Pietro Tamburini (Rome: Giorgio Bretschneider Editore, 1995), pp. 325-333.

Costantini, Lorenzo and Loredana Biasini Costantini, 'La ricerca archeobotanica nella *chora* di Metaponto: Quadro storico e prospettive future', in *Problemi della chora coloniale dall'Occidente al Mar Nero, Atti del XL Convegno di Studi sulla Magna Grecia, Taranto 20 settembre-3 ottobre 2000,* ed. by Giovanni Pugliese Carratelli and Aleksandra Wasowicz (Taranto: Istituto per la Storia e l'Archeologia della Magna Grecia, 2001), pp. 423-434.

Costantini, Lorenzo, 'Italia Centro-Meridionale', in *Storia dell'agricoltura italiana/Accademia dei Georgofili, Florence. I: L'età Antica,* ed. by Gaetano Forni and Nicola Marcone (Firenze: Polistampa, 2001), pp. 221-234.

Costantini, Lorenzo, Biasini Lorenzo Costantini and Matteo Delle Donne, 'I resti vegetali e le impronte delle piante alimentari', in *Nola quattromila anni fa'. Il villaggio dell'Età del Bronzo Antico di Nola distrutto dal Vesuvio (1800-1600 a.C.)* (www.meridies-nola.org/nola/villagiopreistorico.htm, 2005), pp. 13-15.

Coubray, Sylvie, 'Étude paléobotanique des macrorestes végétaux provenant de Ischia', in *Apoikia: I più antichi insediamenti greci in Occidente: funzioni e modi dell'organizzazione politica e sociale: scritti in onore di Giorgio Buchner,* ed. by Bruno D'Agostino and David Ridgway (Naples: Istituto Universitario Orientale, 1994), pp. 205-209.

Coubray, Sylvie, 'Étude anthracologique et carpologique' in *Torre Mordillo 1987-1990, Le relazioni egee di una comunità protostorica della sibaritide,* ed. by Maria Letizia Arancio, Flavia Trucco, Lucia Vagnetti (Rome: CNR, Istituto per gli Studi Micenei ed Egeo-Anatolici, 2001), pp. 419-431.

Crawford, Dorothy, 'Garlic-growing and agricultural specialization in Graeco-Roman Egypt', *Chronique d'Egypte,* 96 (1973), pp. 136-146.

Crielaard, Jan Paul, *Muro Tenente 2001,* unpublished preliminary report (VU University Amsterdam, 2001).

Crielaard, Jan Paul, 'Cities', in *A companion to Archaic Greece,* ed. by Kurt A. Raaflaub and Hans van Wees (Malden, MA Wiley-Blackwell, 2009), pp. 349-372.

Crielaard, Jan Paul Crielaard and Gert-Jan L.M. Burgers, 'Communicating identity in an Italic-Greek community: The case of L'Amastuola (Salento)', in *Communicating identity in Italic Iron Age communities. Papers from the international symposium held in Copenhagen, 2008,* ed. by Margarita Gleba and Helle W. Horsnæs (Oxford: Oxbow, 2010), pp. 73-89.

Crielaard, Jan Paul, 'Le indagini di scavo sulla collina de l'Amastuola (2003-2008)', in *Greci e indigeni a l'Amastuola,* ed. by Gert-Jan L.M. Burgers and Jan Paul Crielaard (Mottola: Stampa Sud, 2011), pp. 47-92.

Crielaard, Jan Paul and Gert-Jan L.M. Burgers, 'Greek colonists and indigenous populations at L'Amastuola, southern Italy – II', *Babesch,* 87 (2012), pp. 69-106.

Crielaard, Jan Paul, 'The 'wanax to basileus model' reconsidered: Authority and ideology after the collapse of the Mycenaean palaces', in *The 'Dark Ages' Revisited. Proceedings of an international conference in memory of William D.E. Coulson, University of Thessaly, Volos, 14-17 June 2007,* ed. by Alexander Mazarakis Ainian (Volos: University of Thessaly, 2012), pp. 83-112.

Crielaard, Jan Paul, *Hygra keleutha.* Maritime matters and the ideology of seafaring in the Greek epic tradition, in *Alle origini della Magna Grecia. Mobilità, migrazioni, fondazioni. Atti del L Convegno di Studi sulla Magna Grecia, Taranto 1-4 ottobre 2010* (Taranto: Istituto per la Storia e l'Archeologia della Magna Grecia, 2013), pp. 135-157.

Cubberley, Anthony L., John A. Lloyd and Paul C. Roberts, 'Testa and clibani: The baking covers of Classical Italy', *Papers of the British School at Rome,* 56 (1988), pp. 98-119.

Dabas, Michel, Nadine Dieudonne-Glad and Philippe Poirier, 'Caractérisation des structures d'une forge antique: Approche Archéologique, Géophysique et Anthracologique', *Revue d'Archéométrie,* 26 (2002), pp. 141-54.

D'Agostino, Bruno, 'Le genti della Basilicata antica', in *Italia omnium terrarum parens,* ed. by Giovanni Pugliese Caratelli (Milan: Scheiwiller, 1989), pp. 191-246.

Dalby, Andrew, *Siren feasts; A history of food and gastronomy in Greece* (London: Routledge, 1996).

Damblon, Freddy, 'Anthracology and past vegetation reconstruction', in *Pavlov I- Northwest. The Upper Paleolithic burial and its settlement context: The Dolní Věstonice studies,* ed. by Jiří Svoboda (Brno: Academy of Sciences of the Czech Republic, Institute of Archaeology, 1997), pp. 437–442.

D'Andria, Francesco, 'Messapi e Peuceti', in *Italia Omnium Terrarum Alumna,* ed. by Giovanni Colonna and Bruno D'Agostino (Milan: Scheiwiller, 1988), pp. 653-715.

D'Andria, Francesco, 'Monte Papalucio', in *Archeologia dei Messapi, Catalogo della mostra,* ed. by Francesco D'Andria (Bari: Edipuglia, 1990), pp. 239-240.

D'Andria, Francesco, 'Vaste', in *Archeologia dei Messapi, Catalogo della mostra,* ed. by Francesco D'Andria (Bari: Edipuglia, 1990), pp. 49-190.

D'Andria, Francesco, 'Insediamenti e territorio: L'età storica', in *I Messapi. Atti del XXXI Convegno di Studi sulla Magna Grecia,* ed. by Francesco D'Andria (Taranto: Istituto per la Storia e l'Archeologia della Magna Grecia, 1991), pp. 393-478.

D'Andria, Francesco, 'Corinto e l'Occidente: La costa adriatica', in *Corinto e l'Occidente, Atti del XXXIV Convegno di Studi sulla Magna Grecia,* ed. by Giovanni Pugliese Carratelli (Taranto: Istituto per la Storia e l'Archeologia della Magna Grecia, 1995), pp. 457-508.

D'Andria, Francesco, 'La casa in Messapia', in *Ricerche sulla casa in Magna Grecia e in Sicilia,* ed. by Francesco D'Andria and Katia Mannino (Galatina: Congedo editore, 1996), pp. 403-438.

D'Andria, Francesco, 'Ricerche recenti sugli insediamenti indigeni di Puglia e Basilicata', in *La forma della città e del territorio: Esperienze metodologiche e risultati a confronto. Atti dell'Incontro di studio, S. Maria Capua Vetere 27-28 novembre 1998,* ed. by Lorenzo Quilici and Simona Quilici Gigli (Rome: L'Erma di Bretschneider, 1999), pp. 103-118.

D'Andria, Francesco, 'Le trasformazioni dell'insediamento', in *Cavallino. Pietre, case e città della Messapia arcaica,* ed. by Francesco D'Andria (Ceglie Messapica: Schirone & Co., 2005), pp. 34-43.

D'Andria, Francesco, Jacopo De Grossi Mazzorin and Girolamo Fiorentino (eds), *Uomini, piante e animali nella dimensione del sacro: Seminario di Studi di Bioarcheologia (28-29 giugno 2002) Convento dei Domenicani, Cavallino (Lecce)* (Bari: Edipuglia, 2008).

Darby, William Jefferson, Paul Ghalioungui and Louis Grivetti, *Food: The gift of Osiris* (London: Academic Press, 1976).

Davidson, Iain, 'Can we study prehistoric economy for fisher - gatherer - hunters? An historical approach to Cambridge 'Palaeoeconomy'', in *Economic Archaeology*, ed. by Alison Sheridan and Geoff Bailey (Oxford: BAR International Series 96, 1981), pp. 17-33.

Davidson, Iain, 'Site variability and prehistoric economy in Levante', in *Hunter-gatherer economy in Prehistory: A European perspective*, ed. by Geoff Bailey (Cambridge: Cambridge University Press), pp. 79-95.

De Cleene, Marcel and Marie Claire Lejeune, *Compendium van rituele planten in Europa* (Ghent: Stichting Mens en Kultuur, 1999).

De Grossi Mazzorin, Jacopo, 'Archaeozoology and habitation models: From a subsistence to a productive economy in Central Italy', in *From huts to houses. Transformations of ancient societies (Proceedings of an International Seminar organized by the Norwegian and Swedish* Institutes in Rome, 21-24 september 1997), ed. by J. Rasmus Brandt and Lars Karlsson (Rome: Paul Aströms Förlag, 2001), pp. 323-330.

De Juliis, Ettore M., *Gli Japigi* (Milan: Longanesi, 1988).

De Lachenal, Lucilla (ed.), *Da leukania a Lucania: La Lucania centro-orientale fra Pirro e i Giulio-Claudii*, (Rome: Istituto Poligrafico e Zecca dello Stato, 1992).

Delano Smith, Catherine, *Western Mediterranean Europe. A historical geography of Italy, Spain, and Southern France since the Neolithic* (London: Academic Press, 1979).

Delhon, Claire, Stephanie Thiébault and Jean-François Berger, 'Environment and landscape management during the Middle Neolithic in Southern France: Evidence for agro-sylvo-pastoral systems in the Middle Rhone valley', *Quaternary International* 200, (2009), pp. 66-76.

Dennell, Robin W., 'Prehistoric diet and nutrition', *World Archaeology*, 11.2 (1979), pp. 121-135.

Dennell, Robin W., Europaean economic prehistory: A new approach, (London: Academic Press, 1983).

Denti, Mario, 'Nouvelles perspectives à l'Incoronata. Les phases oenôtres du VIIIe et une zone artisanale gréco-indigène du VIIe siècle avant J.-C.', *Mélanges de l'École française de Rome* 1 (2009), pp. 350-60.

Denti, Mario, 'Des Grecs très indigènes et des indigènes très grecs. Grecs et Oenôtres au 7e siècle av. J.-C.', in *Portraits de migrants, Portraits de colons*, ed. by Pierre Rouillard (Coll. Colloques de la Maison René-Ginouvès, 5; Paris: De Boccard, 2009), pp. 77-89.

Dentzer, Jean-Marie, *Le motif du banquet couché dans le Proche-Orient et le monde Grec du VII au IV siècle avant J.C.* (Rome: École Française de Rome, 1982).

De Siena, Antonio, 'Termitito', in *Traffici micenei nel mediterraneo. Problemi storici e documentazione archeologica, Atti del Convegno di Palermo 1984, Taranto 1986*, ed. by Massimiliano Marazzi (Taranto: Istituto per la Storia e l'Archeologia della Magna Grecia, 1986), pp. 41-54.

De Siena, Antonio, 'Il territorio di Metaponto', in *Problemi della chora coloniale dall'Occidente al Mar Nero, Atti del XL Convegno di Studi sulla Magna Grecia, Taranto 20 settembre-3 ottobre 2000*, ed. by Giovanni Pugliese Carratelli and Aleksandra Wasowicz (Taranto: Istituto per la Storia e l'Archeologia della Magna Grecia, 2001), pp. 757-70.

De Vooys, Andriaan C., 'Uitholling van geografische begrippen: de transhumance', *Geografisch Tijdschrift*, XII (1959), pp. 193-99.

Di Castri, Francesco, 'Mediterranean-type shrublands of the world', in *Mediterranian-type shrublands. Ecosystems of the world, 11*, ed. by Francesco Di Castri, David W. Goodall and Raymond Louis Specht (Amsterdam: Elsevier scientific, 1981), pp. 1-52.

Di Noi, Lucia and Gert-Jan L.M. Burgers, 'La cinta muraria esterna', in *L'insediamento Messapico di Muro Tenente. Scavi e ricerche 1009-2009*, ed. by Gert-Jan L.M. Burgers and Christian Napolitano (Mesagne: Locopress, 2010), pp. 41-52.

Di Rita, Franco and Donatella Magri, 'Holocene drought, deforestation and evergreen vegetation development in the central Mediterranean: A 5500 year record from Lago Alimini Piccolo, Apulia, southeast Italy', *The Holocene* 19, 2 (2009), pp. 295-306.

Dimbleby, Geoffrey W. and Eberhard Grüger, E. 'Pollen analysis of soil samples from the AD 79 level. Pompeii, Oplontis, and Boscoreale', in *The natural history of Pompeii*, ed. by Wilhelmina F. Jashemski and Frederick Meyer (Cambridge: Cambridge University Press, 2002), pp. 181-216.

D'Oronzo, Cosimo, Giampiero Colaianni, Anna Maria Grasso, Daniela Martella, Angela Stellati and Girolamo Fiorentino, 'Decoding wood exploitation in archaeological sites in south-eastern Italy', in *Proceedings of the Fourth International Meeting of Anthracology, Brussels, 8-13 September 2008*, ed. by Freddy Damblon (Oxford: Archaeopress, 2013), 51-56.

Dunbabin, Thomas J., *The Western Greeks* (Oxford: Oxford University Press, 1968).

Evans, John and Giulia Recchia, 'Pottery function: Trapped residues in Bronze Age pottery from Coppa Nevigata (southern Italy)', *Scienze dell'Antiquità*, 11 (2001-2003), pp. 187-201.

Feugère, Michel and Vincent Serneels (eds), *Recherches sur l'économie du fer en Méditerranée nord-occidentale*, (Monographies Instrumentum, 4; Montagnac: Ed Monique Megoil, 1988).

Figueiral, Isabel, 'Evidence from charcoal analysis for environmental change during the interval Late Bronze Age to Roman, at the archaeological site of Castro De Penices, NW Portugal', *Vegetation History and Archaeobotany*, 4 (1995), pp. 93-100.

Figueiral, Isabel and Volker Mosbrugger, 'A review of charcoal analysis as a tool for assessing quaternary and tertiary environments: Achievements and limits', *Palaeogeography, Palaeoclimatology, Palaeoecology*, 164 (2000), pp. 397-407.

Fiorentino, Girolamo, 'Primi dati archeobotanici dall'insediamento dell'età del Bronzo di Monopoli-Piazza Palmieri', in *Taras* XV (2) (1995): *L'età del Bronzo lungo il versante adriatico pugliese, Atti del Seminario di Studi (Bari 1995)*, ed. by Francesca Radina, pp. 335-373.

Fiorentino, Girolamo, 'New perspectives in anthracological analysis. Palaeoecological and technological implications of charcoals found in the Neolithic flint mine at La Defensola (Vieste, Apulia, Italy)', *Quaternaria Nova* 5 (1995), pp. 99-128.

Fiorentino, Girolamo, 'Le risorse vegetali', in *Documenti dell'età del Bronzo. Ricerche lungo il versante adriatico pugliese*, ed. by Angela Cinquepalmi and Francesca Radina (Fasano di Brindisi: Schena editore, 1998), pp. 211-221.

Fiorentino, Girolamo and Donatella Magri, 'Flora', in *Primi risultati di una ricerca paleoambientale nell'area di Coppa Nevigata (Foggia), Atti 19 Convegno Nazionale sulla Preistoria - Protostoria - Storia della Daunia*, ed. by Armando Gravina (San Severo, 1999), pp. 217-226.

Fiorentino, Girolamo, 'Paleo-ambiente e paleo-economia nel Golfo di Taranto durante l'età del Bronzo', in *Strutture e modelli di abitanti del Bronzo tardo da Torre Castelluccia a Roca Vecchia*, ed. by Mariantonia Gorgoglione (Manduria: Filo editore, 2002), pp. 141-154.

Fiorentino, Girolamo, Elisabetta Castiglioni, Mauro Rottoli and Renato Nisbet, 'Le colture agricole in Italia nel corso dell'età del Bronzo: sintesi dei dati e linee di tendenza', in *L'età del Bronzo recente in Italia, Atti del Congresso Nazionale di Lido di Camaiore, 26-29 ottobre 2000*, ed. by Daniela Cocchi Genick (Viareggio: M. Baroni, 2004), pp. 219-226.

Fiorentino, Girolamo and Giampiero Colaianni, 'L'analisi archeobotanica', in *Cavallino. Pietre, case e città della Messapia arcaica*, ed. by Francesco D'Andria (Ceglie Messapica: Schirone & Co., 2005), pp. 96-99.

Fiorentino, Girolamo, 'Analisi archeobotanica', in *Il villaggio dell'età del Bronzo medio di Portella a Salina nelle Isole Eolie*, ed. by Maria Clara Martinelli (Firenze: L'Erma di Bretschneider, 2005), pp. 263-273.

Fiorentino, Girolamo, 'Paleoambiente e aspetti rituali in un insediamento archeologico tra fase arcaica ed ellenistica: nuove analisi archeobotaniche ad Oria- Papalucio (Br)', in *Uomini, piante e animali nella dimensione del sacro. Seminario di Studi di Bioarcheologia (28-29 giugno 2002), Convento dei Domenicani-Cavallino (Lecce)*, ed. by Francesco D'Andria, Jacopo De Grossi Mazzorin and Girolamo Fiorentino (Bari: Edipuglia, 2008), pp. 97-109.

Fiorentino, Girolamo and Donatella Magri (eds), *Charcoals from the past: Cultural and palaeoenvironmental implications. Proceedings of the Third International Meeting of Anthracology, Cavallino - Lecce (Italy), June 28th-July 1st 2004*, ed. by (BAR International Series 1807; Oxford: Archaeopress, 2008).

Fiorentino, Girolamo, Giampiero Colaianni, Anna Maria Grasso and Angela Stellati, 'Caratteristiche del paleoambiente e modalità di sfruttamento dei vegetali a Salina nel corso dell'età del Bronzo', in *Archeologia delle Isole Eolie. Il villaggio dell'età Del Bronzo Medio di Portella a Salina. Ricerche 2006-2008*, ed. by Maria Clara Martinelli (La Spezia: Rebus Edizioni, 2011), pp. 235-241.

Fiorentino, Girolamo, 'Vite e vitigni nel mondo antico: Il contributo dell'archeobotanica', in *La vigna di Dioniso. Vite, vino e culti in Magna Grecia, Atti del XLIX Convegno di Studi sulla Magna Grecia, 24-28 settembre 2009*, ed. by Mario Lombardo, Aldo Siciliano and Arcangelo Alessio (Taranto, Istituto per la Storia e l'Archeologia della Magna Grecia, 2011), pp. 9-31.

Flinders Petrie, William, *Prehistoric Egypt* (London: British School of Archaeology in Egypt, 1920).

Florenzano, Assunta, Archaeobotany at Fattoria Fabrizio, in *The Chora of Metaponto 5*, ed. By Elisa Lanza Catti, Joseph Coleman Carter and Keith Swift, (Austin, Texas: University of Texas Press, 2014), 133-138.

Follieri, Maria, 'I vegetali del pozzo di età repubblicana nell'area sacra di vesta al Foro Romano', *Annali di Botanica,* 30 (1971), pp. 85-99.

Follieri, Maria, 'Cereali del villaggio neolitico di Passo di Corvo (Foggia)', *Annali di Botanica,* 32 (1973), pp. 49-61.

Follieri, Maria, 'Resti vegetali macroscopici nel collettore ovest del Colosseo', *Annali di Botanica,* 34 (1975), pp. 123-141.

Follieri, Maria and Giuseppe Coccolini, 'I carboni dei *bothroi* dell'area sacra di Locri Epizefiri (VI-IV sec. A.C)', *Geoarcheologia,* 2 (1979), pp. 9-27.

Follieri, Maria, 'Le più antiche testimonianze dell'agricoltura neolitica nell'Italia meridionale', *Origini,* 11 (1982), pp. 337-344.

Forbes, Hamish A., '"We have a little of everything': The ecological basis of some agricultural practices in Methana, Trizinia', *Annals of the New York Academy of Sciences,* 268 (1976), pp. 236-250.

Forbes, Hamish A., 'Ethnoarchaeology and the place of the olive in the economy of the southern Argolid, Greece', in *La production du vin et de l'huile en Méditerrannée*, ed. by Marie Claire Amouretti and Jean-Pierre Brun (Athens: École Française d'Athènes, 1993), pp. 213-226.

Forni, Gaetano, 'L'agricoltura: coltivazione ed allevamento', in *Storia dell'agricoltura italiana/Accademia dei Georgofili, Florence. I: L'età Antica*, ed. by Gaetano Forni and Nicola Marcone (Firenze: Polistampa, 2001), pp. 7-157.

Forti, Lidia and Attilio Stazio, 'Vita quotidiana dei Greci d'Italia', in *Megale Hellas: Storia e civiltà della Magna Grecia*, ed. by Giovanni Pugliese Carratelli (Milano: Scheiwiller, 1983), pp. 643-713.

Forti, Lidia, 'La vita quotidiana', in *Magna Grecia Pt. 3: Vita religiosa e cultura letteraria, filosofica e scientifica*, ed. by Giovanni Pugliese Carratelli (Milan: Electa, 1988), pp. 285-326.

Foxhall, Lin and Hamish A. Forbes, 'Sitometreia: The role of grain as a staple food in classical antiquity', *Chiron,* 12 (1982), pp. 41-90.

Foxhall, Lin, 'Oil extraction and processing equipment in classical Greece', in *La production du vin et de l'huile en Méditerrannée*, ed. by Marie Claire Amouretti, Jean-Pierre Brun (Athens: École Française d'Athènes, 1993), pp. 181-200.

Foxhall, Lin, 'Cultures, landscapes, and identities in the Mediterranean world', *Mediterranean Historical Review,* 18 (2) (2003), pp. 75-92.

Foxhall, Lin, *Olive cultivation in ancient Greece: Seeking the ancient economy* (Oxford: Oxford University Press, 2007).

Fracchia, Helena and Franco Ortolani, 'The regional landscape', in *Fourth century BC Magna Grecia - A case study*, ed. by Maurizio Gualtieri (Jonsered: Paul Åström förlag, 1993), pp. 227-254.

Furtwängler, Adolf, *Die Bronzen und die übrigen kleineren Funde von Olympia* (Berlin: A. Ascher, 1890).

Gale, Rowena and David F. Cutler, *Plants in archaeology: Identification manual of vegetative plant materials used in Europe and the southern Mediterranean to c. 1500* (Otley, West Yorkshire Westbury, 2000).

Galili, Ehud, Daniel Jean Stanley, Jacob Sharvit and Mina Weinstein-Evron, 'Evidence for earliest olive-oil production in submerged settlements off the Carmel Coast, Israel', *Journal of Archaeological Science*, 24 (1997), pp. 1141-1150.

Garcia, Jaume and Climent Quintana-Domeque, 'The evolution of adult height in Europe: A brief note', *Economics and Human Biology*, 5 (2) (2007), pp. 340-349.

Gassner, Verena, 'Amphorae production of the Ionic-Adriatic region', *FACEM*, version 06/06/2011, www.facem.at/project-papers.php.

Gaudenzio, Paola and Simonetta Peccenini, 'Aspetti vegetazionali', in *La macchia mediterranea. Formazioni sempreverdi costiere*, ed. by Alessando Minelli (Udine: Museo Friuliano di Storia Naturale, 2002), pp. 13-74.

Gialanella, Costanza, 'Pithecusa: Gli insediamenti di Punta Chiarito', in *Apoikia: i più antichi insediamenti greci in Occidente: funzioni e modi dell'organizzazione politica e sociale: scritti in onore di Giorgio Buchner*, ed. by Bruno D'Agostino and David Ridgway (Naples: Istituto Universitario Orientale, 1994), pp. 169-204.

Gilman, Antonio, 'The development of social stratification in Bronze Age Europe', *Current Anthropology*, 22 (1) (1981), pp. 1-8.

Gleba, Margarita, *Textile production in pre-Roman Italy* (Oxford: Oxbow Books, 2008).

Godwin, Harry, 'The ancient cultivation of hemp', *Antiquity*, 41 (1967), pp. 42-49.

Gras, Michel T., 'Nécropole et histoire: quelques réflections à propos de Mégara Hyblaea', *Kókalos: Studi pubblicati dall'Istituto di Storia Antica dell'Università di Palermo*, 21 (1975), pp. 37-53.

Gras, Michel T., *Trafics tyrrhéniens archaïques* (Rome: École Française de Rome, 1985).

Grieco, Allen, 'Olive tree cultivation in Late Medieval Italy', in *La production du vin et de l'huile en Méditerrannée*, ed. by Marie Claire Amouretti, Jean-Pierre Brun (Athens: École Française d'Athènes, 1993), pp. 297-306.

Groot, Maaike and Daphne M. Lentjes, 'Studying subsistence and surplus production', in Barely surviving or more than enough? The environmental archaeology of subsistence, specialisation and surplus food production, ed. by Maaike Groot, Daphne M. Lentjes and Jørn Zeiler (Leiden: Sidestone, 2013), pp. 7-28.

Grove, A.T. and Oliver Rackham, *The nature of Mediterranean Europe: An ecological history* (New Haven: Yale University Press, 2001).

Grüger, Eberhard, Barbara Thulin, Jens Müller, Jürgen Schneider, Joachim *Alefs and* Francisco W. Welter-Schultes, 'Environmental changes in and around lake Avernus in Greek and Roman times. A study of plant and animal remains preserved in the lake's sediments', in *The natural history of Pompeii*, ed. by Wilhelmina F. Jashemski, Frederick Meyer (Cambridge: Cambridge University Press, 2002), pp. 240-73.

Gualtieri, Maurizio and Helena Fracchia (eds), *Roccagloriosa I. L'Abitato: Scavo e ricognizione topografica (1976-1986)*, (Naples: Publications du Centre Jean Bérard, 1990).

Gualtieri, Maurizio and Helena Fracchia (eds), *Roccagloriosa II. L'oppidum Lucano e il territorio*, (Naples: Centre Jean Bérard, 2001).

Gualtieri, Maurizio and François De Polignac, 'A rural landscape in western Lucania', in *Roman Landscapes. Archaeological Survey in the Mediterranean Region*, ed. by Graeme Barker and John Lloyd (Archaeological Monographs of the British School at Rome 2, 1991), pp. 194-203.

Gualtieri, Maurizio and Helena Fracchia, 'Excavation and survey at Masseria Ciccotti, Oppido Lucano: Interim report 1989-1992', *Echos du Monde Classique/Classical Views* (1993), pp. 313-38.

Guarino, Carmine and Maria Rosaria Sciarillo, 'Attuali tendenze nello studio dei resti archeobotanici: La creazione di un nuovo modello ecologico', in *Ambiente e paesaggio nella Magna Grecia: Atti del XLII Convegno di Studi sulla Magna Grecia, Taranto 5-8 ottobre 2002*, ed. by Attilio Stazio and Stefania Ceccoli (Taranto: Istituto per la Storia e l'Archeologia della Magna Grecia, 2003), pp. 199-208.

Guglielmino, Riccardo, 'Rocavecchia: Nuove testimonianze di relazioni con l'Egeo e il Mediterraneo orientale nell'età del Bronzo', in *Emporia. Aegeans in the Central and Eastern Mediterranean. Proceedings of the 10th International Aegean Conference, Aegeum, 25, Athens*, ed. by Robert Laffineur and Emanuele Greco (Liège: Université de Liège, Histoire de l'art et archéologie de la Grèce antique, 2005), pp. 637-652.

Gugliemino, Riccardo, 'Ceramiche egee ed egeizzanti da Roca Vecchia (Melendugno, Lecce)', in *Strutture e modelli di abitanti del Bronzo tardo da Torre Castelluccia a Roca Vecchia*, ed. by Mariantonia Gorgoglione (Manduria: Filo Editore, 2002), pp. 171-92.

Hakbijl, Tom, 'The traditional, historical and prehistoric use of ashes as an insecticide, with an experimental study on the insecticidal efficacy of washed ash', *Environmental archaeology*, 7 (2002), pp. 13-22.

Halstead, Paul, 'Life after Mediterranean polyculture: The subsistence subsystem and the emergence of civilisation revisited', in *The emergence of civilisation revisited*, ed. by James C. Barrett and Paul Halstead (Oxford: Oxbow Books, 2004), pp. 189-206.

Halstead, Paul and James C. Barrett (eds), *Food, cuisine and society in prehistoric Greece*, (Oxford: Oxbow Books, 2004).

Hamilakis, Yannis, 'Wine, oil and the dialectics of power in Bronze Age Crete: A review of the evidence', *Oxford Journal of Archaeology* 15 (1996), pp. 1-32.

Hanson, Victor D., *The other Greeks: The family farm and the agrarian roots of western civilisation* (New York: Free Press, 1995).

Harding, Jenny, *Environmental change during the Holocene in south-east Italy: An integrated geomorphological and palynological investigation* (Sheffield: Larix Books, 1999).

Heim, Jean, 'Il paesaggio vegetativo', in *Herdonia: Scoperta di una città*, ed. by Joseph Mertens (Bari: Edipuglia, 1995), pp. 321-324.

Helbaek, Hans, 'Appendix I: Vegetables in the funeral meals of pre-urban Rome', in *Early Rome, II, The tombs*, ed. by Einar Gjerstad (Lund: Håkan Ohlssons Boktryckeri, 1956), pp. 287-294.

Helbaek, Hans, 'Plant collecting, dry-farming, and irrigation agriculture in prehistoric Deh Luran', in *Prehistory and human ecology of the Deh Luran Plain. An early village sequence from Khuzistan, Iran*, ed. by Frank Hole, Kent V. Flannery, and James A. Neely (Ann Arbor: University of Michigan Museum of Anthropology, 1969), pp. 383-428.

Henneberg, Maciej, Renata J. Henneberg and Joseph C. Carter, 'Health in colonial Metaponto', *National Geographic research & exploration*, 8 (1992), pp. 446-459.

Henneberg, Maciej and Renata J. Henneberg, 'Analysis of human skeletal and dental remains from Metaponto (7th-2nd c. BC)', in *Problemi della chora coloniale dall'Occidente al Mar Nero, Atti del XL Convegno di Studi sulla Magna Grecia, Taranto 20 settembre-3 ottobre 2000*, ed. by Giovanni Pugliese Carratelli and Aleksandra Wasowicz (Taranto: Istituto per la Storia e l'Archeologia della Magna Grecia, 2001), pp. 461-474.

Higgs, Eric Sidney (ed.), *Palaeoeconomy*, (Cambridge: Cambridge University Press, 1975).

Hillman, Gordon C., 'Reconstructing crop husbandry from charred remains of crops', in *Farming practice in British prehistory*, ed. by Roger J. Mercer (Edinburgh Edinburgh University Press, 1981), pp. 123-162.

Hillman, Gordon C., 'Interpretation of archaeological plant remains: The application of ethnographic models from Turkey', in *Plants and ancient man: Studies in palaeoethnobotany. Proceedings of the sixth symposium of the International Work Group for Palaeoethnobotany, Groningen, 30 May-3 June 1983*, ed. by Willem Van Zeist and Willem A. Casparie (Groningen: Balkema, 1984), pp. 1-41.

Hitchner, Robert B., 'Olive production and the Roman economy: The case for intensive growth in the Roman empire', in *La production du vin et de l'huile en Méditerrannée*, ed. by Marie Claire Amouretti, Jean-Pierre Brun (Athens: École Française d'Athènes, 1993), pp. 499-508.

Hjelmqvist, Hakon, 'Economic plants of the Italian Iron Age from Monte Irsi', in *Monte Irsi, Southern Italy. The Canadian excavations in the Iron Age and Roman sites, 1971-1972. BAR Supplementary series 20274-281*, ed. by Alastair Small (Oxford: British Archaeological Reports, 1977), pp. 274-81.

Hofmeister, Burkhard, 'Wesen und Erscheinungsformen der Transhumance', *Erdkunde*, XV (1961), pp. 121-135.

Hopf, Maria, 'South and southwest Europe', in *Progress in Old World Palaeoethnobotany*, ed. by Willem Van Zeist, Krystyna Wasylikowa, Karl-Ernst Behre (Rotterdam: Balkema, 1991), pp. 241-277.

Hopf, Maria, 'Determinazione dei resti vegetali del villaggio del 'Gran Carro' (Lago di Bolsena, Viterbo): scavo 1980', in *Un abitato villanoviano perilacustre. Il 'Gran Carro' sul Lago di Bolsena (1959-1985)*, ed. by Pietro Tamburini (Rome: L'Erma di Bretschneider, 1995), pp. 336-338.

Horne, Lee, 'Fuel for the metal worker. The role of charcoal and charcoal production in ancient metallurgy', *Expedition*, 25 (1982), pp. 6-13.

Horsnæs, Helle W., *The cultural development in North-Western Lucania c. 600-273 BC* (Rome: L'Erma di Bretschneider, 2002).

Jacomet, Stephanie, *Identification of cereal remains from archaeological sites* (Basel: Archaeobotany Lab IPAS, Basel University, 2006).

Jarman, Michael, 'Culture and economy in the North Italian Neolithic', *World Archaeology*, 3 (1971), pp. 255-265.

Jarman, and Derek Webley, 'Settlement and land use in Capitanata, Italy', in
Palaeoeconomy, ed. by Eric Sidney Higgs (Cambridge: Cambridge University Press, 1975), pp. 177-221.

Jashemski, Wilhelmina F and Frederick Meyer, *The natural history of Pompeii*, (Cambridge: Cambridge University press, 2002).

Jasny, Naum, 'The daily bread of the Ancient Greeks and Romans', *Osiris*, 9 (1950), pp. 227-253.

Jones, William H. S., *Malaria and Greek history* (Manchester: The University Press, 1909).

Jones, Glynis and Peter Rowley-Conwy, 'Plant remains from the North Italian lake dwellings of Fiave (1400-1200 BC)', in *Scavi archeologici nella zona palafitticola di Fiave-Carera. Parte I – Campagne 1969-1976*, ed. by Renato Perini (Trento: Provincia Autonoma di Trento, 1984), pp. 323-355.

Keeley, John E., 'Fire intensity, fire severity and burn severity: A brief review and suggested usage', *International Journal of Wildland Fire*, 18 (2009), pp. 116-126.

Kelley, Don W., *Charcoal and charcoal burning* (Buckinghamshire: Shire publications, 2002).

Kislev, Mordechai, 'Wild olive at submerged Chalcolithic Kfar Samir, Haifa, Israel', *Journal of the Israel Prehistoric Society* 26 (1994-1995), pp. 134-145.

Kok, Raphaëlle-Anne, 'La cinta muraria interna', in *L'insediamento Messapico di Muro Tenente. Scavi e ricerche 1009-2009*, ed. by Gert-Jan L.M. Burgers and Christian Napolitano (Mesagne: Locopress, 2010), pp. 31-40.

Kooistra, Laura I., *Borderland farming. Possibilities and limitations of farming in the Roman period and Early Middle Ages between the Rhine and Meuse* (Assen: Van Gorcum, 1996).

Kooistra, Laura I., 'Organische materialen', in *Veldhandleiding Archeologie, Leidraad 1*, ed. by Arnold Carmiggelt and Paul J.W.M. Schulten (Zoetermeer: College voor de Archeologische Kwaliteit, 2002), pp. 7-30.

Körber-Grohne, Udelgard, *Bestimmungsschlüssel für subfossile Juncus-samen und Gramineen-Früchte* (Hildesheim: A. Lax, 1964).

Körber-Grohne, Udelgard, *Bestimmungsschlüssel für subfossile Gramineen-Früchte* (Hildesheim: A. Lax, 1991).

Kreuz, Angela, 'Functional and conceptual archaeobotanical data from Roman cremations', in *Burial, society and context in the Roman world*, ed. by John Pearce, Martin Millett and Manuela Struck (Oxford: Oxbow Books, 2000), pp. 45-51.

Kroll, Helmut, 'Südosteuropa', in *Progress in Old World Palaeoethnobotany*, ed. by Willem Van Zeist, Krystyna Wasylikowa and Karl-Ernst Behre (Rotterdam: Balkema, 1991), pp. 161-77.

Kubiak-Martens, Lucyna, 'New evidence for the use of root foods in pre-agrarian subsistence recovered from the late Mesolithic site at Halsskov, Denmark', *Vegetation History and Archaeobotany*, 11 (2002), pp. 23-32.

Kuzišin, V.I., 'L'espansione del latifondo in Italia alla fine della Repubblica', in *L'agricoltura romana*, ed. by Luigi Capogrossi Colognesi (Bari: Laterza, 1982), pp. 4163.

LaCroix Phippen, William, '8. Vegetal Remains', in 'Buccino: the Early Bronze Age Village of Tufariello', ed. by Robert Ross Holloway, *Journal of Field Archaeology*, 2 (1975), pp. 79-80.

Lazongas, E.G. (2005), 'Side: The personification of the pomegranate', in E. Stafford, Herrin, J. (eds.), *Personification in the Greek world: From antiquity to Byzantium* (Ashgate: Aldershot), 99-109.

Le Houérou, H.N., 'Impact of man and his animals on Mediterranean vegetation', in *Mediterranian-type shrublands. Ecosystems of the world, 11*, ed. by Francesco Di Castri, David W. Goodall and Raymond Louis Specht (Amsterdam: Elsevier scientific, 1981), pp. 479-521.

Lelivelt, Ruben, *Landscape evolution during the Greek period in the Taras floodplain, Apulia, Italy. A literature overview and landscape reconstruction, using lithological and (micro)faunal criteria, GIS and present environmental conditions* (unpublished MSc thesis, VU University Amsterdam, 2013).

Lentjes, Daphne M., 'La fioritura dell'ambiente. I risultati preliminari del recupero dei resti archeobotanici a Muro Tenente', in *L'insediamento Messapico di Muro Tenente. Scavi e ricerche 1009-2009*, ed. by Gert-Jan L.M. Burgers and Christian Napolitano (Mesagne: Locopress, 2010), pp. 53-60.

Lentjes, Daphne M., 'Risultati delle analisi del materiale botanico recuperato nelle campagne di scavo', in *Greci e indigeni a l'Amastuola*, ed. by Gert-Jan L.M. Burgers and Jan Paul Crielaard (Mottola: Stampa Sud, 2011), pp. 93-104.

Lentjes, Daphne M. and Giulia Saltini Semerari, 'Big debates over small fruits. Wine and oil production in protohistoric Southern Italy (c. 1350-750 BC)', *Babesch*, in press.

Leroy-Ladurie, Emmanuel, *The peasants of Languedoc* (Urbana: University of Illinois Press, 1966).

Leroy-Ladurie, Emmanuel, *Montaillou* (Paris: Editions Gallimard, 1975).

Levi, Sara T., 'Produzione e circolazione della ceramica nella Sibaritide protostorica', in *Broglio di Trebisacce 1990-1994. Elementi e problemi nuovi dalle recenti campagne di scavo*, ed. by Renato Peroni and Alessandro Vanzetti (Soveria Mannelli: Rubbettini editore, 1998), pp. 175-212.

Levi, Sara T. and Richard E. Jones, 'Dolii al di fuori della Sibaritide', in *Produzione e circolazione della ceramica nella Sibaritide protostorica I. Impasto e dolii*, ed. by Sara T. Levi (Firenze: All'Insegna del Giglio, 1999), pp. 108-113.

Liphschitz, Nili, Ram Gophna, Moshe Hartman and Gideon Biger, 'The beginning of olive (*Olea europaea*) cultivation in the Old World: A reassessment', *Journal of Archaeological Science*, 18 (1991), pp. 441-453.

Lo Porto, Felice G., 'Civiltà indigena e penetrazione greca nella Lucania orientale', *Monumenti antichi*, 48 (1973), pp. 145-251.

Lo Porto, Felice G., 'Gli scavi di Muro Tenente presso Mesagne', in *Atti del VII Convegno di Studi dei Comuni dei Messapi, Peuceti e Dauni* (Bari: Laterza, 1976), pp. 9-21.

Lomas, Kathryn, *Rome and the Western Greeks 350 BC-AD 200: Conquest and acculturation in southern Italy* (London: Routledge, 1993).

Lombardo, Mario, *I Messapi e la Messapia nelle fonti letterarie greche e latine* (Galatina: Congedo editore, 1992).

Maaskant-Kleibrink, Marianne, 'Religious activities on the Timpone della Motta, Francavilla Marittima', *Babesch,* 68 (1993), pp. 1-47.

Maaskant-Kleibrink, Marianne, 'Dark Age or Ferro I? A tentative answer for the Sibaritide and Metapontine plains', *Caeculus,* III (1976), pp. 63-90.

Maaskant-Kleibrink, Marianne, *Van wol tot water, cultus en identiteit in het Athenaion van Lagaria, Francavilla Marittima (Calabrië, Italië)* (Rossano: Grafosud, 2003).

Maaskant-Kleibrink, Marianne, *Oenotrians at Lagaria near Sybaris, a native proto-urban centralized settlement. A preliminary report on the excavation of two timber dwellings on the Timpone della Motta near Francavilla Marittima, southern Italy* (London: Accordia Specialist Studies on Italy, vol. II, 2006).

MacKinnon, Michael R. and Alastair Small (eds), *The excavations of San Giovanni di Ruoti. Volume III, The faunal and plant remains,* (Toronto, University of Toronto Press, 2002).

Mangafa, Maria and Kostas Kotsakis, 'A new method for the identification of wild and cultivated charred grape seeds', *Journal of archaeological Science,* 23 (1996), pp. 409-418.

Margaritis, Evi and Martin Jones, 'Beyond cereals: Crop processing and *Vitis vinifera* L. Ethnography, experiment and charred grape remains from Hellenistic Greece', *Journal of Archaeological Science,* 33 (2006), pp. 784-805.

Margaritis, Evi, Colin Renfrew and Martin Jones (eds), *Wine confessions: Production, trade and social significance of wine in ancient Greece and Cyprus,* (Hesperia Supplements, 2009).

Martinelli, Maria Clara, Girolamo Fiorentino, Benedetta Prosdocimi, Cosimo D'Oronzo, Sara T. Levi, Gabriella Mangano, Angela Stellati and Nicholas Wolff, 'Nuove ricerche nell'insediamento sull'istmo di Filo Braccio a Filicudi. Nota preliminare sugli scavi 2009', *Origini,* XXXII (2010), pp. 285-314.

Maruggi, Grazia A., 'Crispiano (Taranto), L'Amastuola', in *Ricerche sulla casa in Magna Grecia e in Sicilia,* ed. by Francesco D'Andria and Katia Mannino (Galatina: Congedo editore, 1996), pp. 197-218.

Mastronuzzi, Giovanni, 'L'archeologia di un luogo di culto in Messapia: Vaste-Piazza Dante', in *Lo spazio del rito. Santuari e culti in Italia meridionale tra indigeni e greci. Atti delle giornate di studio (Matera, 28 e 29 giugno 2002),* ed. by Maria Luisa Nava and Massimo Osanna (Santo Spirito: Edipuglia, 2005), pp. 235-247.

Mastronuzzi, Giovanni, *Repertorio dei contesti cultuali indigeni in Italia meridionale 1. Età arcaica* (Bari: Edipuglia, 2005).

Mazarakis Ainian, Alexander, *From ruler's dwellings to temples. Architecture, religion and society in Early Iron Age Greece (1100-700 BC)* (Jonsered: Paul Aströms Förlag, 1997).

McGovern, Patrick E., *Ancient wine. The search for the origins of viticulture* (Princeton and Oxford: Princeton University Press, 2003).

McGovern, Patrick E., *Uncorking the past: The quest for wine, beer, and other alcoholic beverages* (Berkeley, CA University of California Press, 2009).

McParland, Laura C., Margaret E. Collinson, Andrew C. Scott and Gill Campbell, 'The use of reflectance for the interpretation of natural and anthropogenic charcoal assemblages', *Archaeological and Anthropological Sciences,* 1 (2009), pp. 249-261.

McParland, Laura C., Zoe Hazell, Gill Campbell, Margaret E. Collinson and Andrew C. Scott, 'How the Romans got themselves into hot water: Temperatures and fuel types of a Roman hypocaust fire', *Environmental Archaeology,* 14 (2009), pp. 172-179.

McParland, Laura C., Margaret E. Collinson, Andrew C. Scott, Gill Campbell and Robyn Veal, 'Is vitrification in charcoal a result of high temperature burning of wood?', *Journal of Archaeological Science*, 37 (10) (2010), pp. 2679-2687.

Megaloudi, Fragkiska, *Plants and diet in Greece from Neolithic to Classical periods. The archaeobotanical remains* (Oxford: Archaeopress, 2006).

Meiggs, Russell, *Trees and timber in the ancient Mediterranean world* (Oxford: Clarendon Press, 1982).

Meirano, Valeria, 'I vegetali eduli nella dimensione del sacro: l'apporto degli studi iconografici', in *Uomini, piante e animali nella dimensione del sacro. Seminario di Studi di Bioarcheologia (28-29 giugno 2002), Convento dei Domenicani- Cavallino (Lecce)*, ed. by Francesco D'Andria, Jacopo De Grossi Mazzorin and Girolamo Fiorentino (Bari: Edipuglia, 2008), pp. 137-146.

Mercuri, Anna Maria, Carla A. Accorsi and Marta Bandini Mazzanti, 'The long history of *cannabis* and its cultivation by the Romans in central Italy, shown by pollen records from Lago Albano and Lago di Nemi', *Vegetation History and Archaeobotany*, 11 (2002), pp. 263-76.

Mercuri, Anna Maria, Emilia Allevato, Daniele Arobba, Marta Bandini Mazzanti, Giovanna Bosi, Roberto Caramiello, Elisabetta Castiglioni *et al.*, , 'Pollen and macroremains from Holocene archaeological sites: A dataset for the understanding of the bio-cultural diversity of the Italian landscape', *Review of Palaeobotany and Palynology* (in press).

Mertens, Dieter, 'L'architettura e l'urbanistica di Metaponto nel quadro dell'economia locale e dell'evoluzione generale nella Magna Grecia', in *Siritide e Metapontino. Storie di due territori coloniali*, ed. by Dinu Adamesteanu (Naples/Paestum: Cahiers Centre Jean Bérard XX, 1998), pp. 123-140.

Meurers-Balke, Jutta and Jens Lüning, 'Some aspects and experiments concerning the processing of glume wheats', in *Préhistoire de l'agriculture: Nouvelles approches expérimentales et ethnographiques*, ed. by Patricia C. Anderson (Paris: Éd. du CNRS, 1992), pp. 341-362.

Milano, Lucio (ed.), *Drinking in ancient societies: History and culture of drinks in the ancient Near East: Papers of a symposium held in Rome, May 17-19 1990*, (Padova: Sargon, 1994).

Minelli, Alessandro (ed.), *La macchia mediterranea-Formazioni sempreverdi costiere*, (Quaderni habitat, Museo Friulano di Stroria Naturale, Udine: Ministero dell'Ambiente e della Tutela del Territorio, 2002).

Mitchell-Jones, Anthony J., *The atlas of European mammals*, (London: London Academic Press, 1999).

Mitten, David G. and Suzannah F. Doeringer, *Master bronzes from the classical world* (Mainz: Von Zabern, 1967).

Moffa, Claudio (ed.), *L'organizzazione dello spazio sull'acropoli di Broglio di Trebisacce: Dallo studio delle strutture e dei manufatti in impasto di fango all'analisi della distribuzione dei reperti*, (Firenze: All'Insegna del Giglio, 2002).

Morel, Jean-Paul, 'La laine de Tarente', *Ktema*, 3 (1978), pp. 93-110.

Morel, Jean-Paul, 'Greek colonization in Italy and the West. Problems of evidence and interpretation', in *Crossroads of the Mediterranean: Papers delivered at the International Conference on the Archaeology of Early Italy, Haffenreffer Museum Brown University, 8-10 May 1981*, ed. by Tony Hackens, Nancy D. Holloway and Ross R. Holloway (Louvain-la-Neuve: Institut Supérieur d'Archéologie et d'Histoire de l'Art, Collège Érasme Providence: Brown University R.I., 1984), pp. 123-162.

Morris, Ian, 'The Athenian economy twenty years after the ancient economy', *Classical Philology* (1994), pp. 351-366.

Nava, Maria Luisa, *Stele Daunie* (Florence: Sansoni, 1980).

Neeft, Cornelis W., 'Tarantine graves containing Corinthian Pottery', in *Catalogo del Museo Nazionale Archeologico di Taranto, III.1. Taranto, La necropoli: aspetti e problemi della documentazione archeologica dal VII al I sec. a.C.*, ed. by Giuseppe Andreassi (Taranto: Scorpione, 1994), pp. 185-237.

Nelle, Oliver, 'Combining charcoal and pollen analysis: Holocene vegetation dynamics, tree species composition and woodland use in the Bavarian Forest', in *Charcoals from the past: Cultural and palaeoenvironmental implications. Proceedings of the Third International Meeting of Anthracology, Cavallino - Lecce (Italy), June 28th -July 1st 2004*, ed. by Girolamo Fiorentino and Donatella Magri (BAR International Series 1807; Oxford: Archaeopress, 2008), pp. 183-91.

Nenci, Giuseppe and Georges Vallet, *Bibliografia Topografica della colonizzazione Greca in Italia e nelle Isole Tirreniche* (Pisa-Rome: Byvanck, 1977-2005).

Nicholson, Paul T. and Ian Shaw, *Ancient Egyptian materials and technology* (Cambridge: Cambridge University Press, 2000).

Nisbet, Renato, 'Dati archeobotanici dal Broglio: I carboni', in *Nuove ricerche sulla protostoria della Sibaritide*, ed. by Renato Peroni (Rome: Paleani, 1984), pp. 266-271.

Nisbet, Renato and Giulia Ventura, 'I dati archeobotanici', in *Enotri e Micenei nella Sibaritide*, ed. by Flacia Trucco and Renato Peroni (Taranto: Paleani, 1994), pp. 577-585.

Notarstefano, Florinda, *Ceramica e alimentazione. L'analisi chimica dei residui organici nelle ceramiche applicata ai contesti archeologici* (Bari: Edipuglia, 2012).

Novellis, Donatella, 'Archeobotanica a Torre di Satriano. Aggiornamenti e novità dallo scavo 2008', in *Lo spazio del potere. La residenza ad abside, l'anaktoron, l'episcopio a Torre di Satriano*, ed. by Massimo Osanna, Lucia Colangelo and Gianfranco Carollo (Venosa: Osanna, 2009), pp. 217-226.

Orrù, Martino, Oscar Grillo, Gianni Lovicu, Gianfranco Venora and Gianluigi Bacchetta, 'Morphological characterisation of *Vitis vinifera* L. seeds by image analysis and comparison with archaeological remains', *Vegetation History and Archaeobotany* (2012), 1-12.

Osanna, Massimo and Maria Maddalena Sica (eds), *Torre di Satriano I. Il santuario lucano*, (V e n o s a : Osanna, 2005).

Pagliara, Cosimo, 'Rocavecchia (Lecce): Il sito, le fortificazioni e l'abitato dell'età del Bronzo', in *Emporia. Aegeans in the Central and Eastern Mediterranean. Proceedings of the 10th International Aegean Conference, Aegeum, 25, Athens*, ed. by Robert Laffineur and Emanuele Greco (Liège: Université de Liège, Histoire de l'art et archéologie de la Grèce antique, 2005), pp. 629-635.

Pals, Jan Peter and Albertus Voorrips, 'Seeds, fruits and charcoals from two prehistoric sites in Northern Italy', in *Festschrift Maria Hopf: zum 65. Geburtstag am 14. September 1979*, ed. by Udelgard Körber-Grohne (Bonn: Rheinisches Landesmuseum, Bonn, 1979), pp. 217-235.

Pancrazzi, Orlanda, *Cavallino,* (Galatina: Congedo, 1979).

Payne, Humfry and Thomas J. Dunbabin, *Perachora I: The sanctuaries of Hera Akraia and Limenia: Excavations of the British school of archaeology at Athens, 1930-1933* (Oxford: Clarendon Press, 1940).

Pedley, John, *Sanctuaries and the sacred in the ancient Greek world* (Cambridge: Cambridge University Press, 2005).

Peroni, Renato (ed.), *Nuove ricerche sulla protostoria della Sibaritide*, (Rome: Paleani, 1984).

Peroni, Renato, 'Le communità enotrie della Sibaritide ed i loro rapporti con i navigatori egei', in *Enotri e Micenei nella Sibaritide*, ed. by Flacia Trucco and Renato Peroni (Taranto: Paleani, 1994), pp. 831-879.

Perret, M., 'Caractérisation et évaluation du polymorphisme des génotypes sauvages et cultivés de *Vitis vinifera* L. à l'aide de marqueurs RAPD et de certains traits morphologiques', *Bulletin de la Société Neuchâteloise des Sciences Naturelles*, CXX (1997), pp. 45-54.

Pignatti, Sandro, *Flora d'Italia*, 3 vols. (Bologna: Edagricole, 1982).

Polunin, Oleg, *Flowers of Europe. A field guide* (London: Oxford University Press, 1969).

Polunin, Pleg and Anthony J. Huxley, *Flowers of the Mediterranean* (London: Chatto and Windus, 1974).

Pontrandolfo Greco, Angela, *I Lucani: Etnografia e archeologia di una regione antica* (Milan: Longanesi, 1982).

Pontrandolfo, Angela, Agnès Rouveret and Marina Cipriani, *The painted tombs of Paestum* (Paestum: Pandemos, 2004).

Primavera, Milena, Girolamo Fiorentino and Giampiero Colaianni, 'Il combustibile delle attività metallurgiche nelle forge di Lecce tardo-antica: caratteristiche della vegetazione e sfruttamento dell'ambiente', in *Archeometallurgia : dalla conoscenza alla fruizione: atti del workshop, 22-25 maggio 2006, Cavallino (LE), Convento dei domenicani*, ed. by Claudio Giardino (Santo Spirito: Edipuglia, 2011), pp. 321-332.

Purcell, Nicholas, 'Wine and wealth in Roman Italy', *Journal of Roman Studies*, 75 (1985), pp. 1-19.

Pye, Vanessa and Bruno Ancel, 'Archaeological experiments in fire setting: Protocol, fuel and anthracological approach', in *Charcoal analysis: new analytical tools and methods for archaeology. Papers from the table-ronde held in Basel 2004*, ed. by Alexa Dufraisse (Oxford: Archaeopress, 2006), pp. 71-82.

Quézel, P., 'The study of plant groupings in the countries surrounding the Mediterranean: Some methodological aspects', in *Mediterranian-type shrublands. Ecosystems of the world, 11*, ed. by Francesco Di Castri, David W. Goodall and Raymond Louis Specht (Amsterdam: Elsevier scientific, 1981), pp. 87-93.

Ræder Knudsen, Lise, 'La tessitura con le tavolette nella tomba 89', in *Guerriero e sacerdote. Autorità e comunità nell'età del ferro a Verrucchio*, ed. by Patrizia Von Eles (Firenze: All'Insegna del Giglio, 2002), pp. 220-234.

Raubitschek, Isabelle K., *Isthmia VII. The metal objects (1952-1989)* (Princeton: American School of Classical Studies at Athens, 1998).

Renfrew, Colin A., *The emergence of civilisation: The Cyclades and the Aegean in the third millennium B.C.* (London: Methuen, 1972).

Renfrew, Jane M., *Palaeoethnobotany. The prehistoric food plants of the Near East and Europe* (New York: Columbia University Press, 1973).

Renfrew, Jane M. (ed.), *New light on early farming: recent developments in palaeoethnobotany*, (Edinburgh: Edinburgh University Press, 1991).

Renfrew, Jane M., 'Palaeoethnobotanical finds of *Vitis* from Greece', in *The Origins and ancient history of wine*, ed. by Patrick E. McGovern, Stuart Fleming, Solomon Katz (New York: Gordon & Breach, 1995), pp. 255-267.

Renfrew, Colin A. and Paul Bahn, *Archaeology: Theories, methods and practice* (4th edition, London: Thames & Hudson, 2004).

Richter, Augusta, *The furniture of the Greeks, Etruscans and Romans* (London: Phaidon Press, 1966).

Ridgway, David, *The First Western Greeks* (Cambridge: Cambridge University Press, 1992).

Riley, F.R., 'Olive oil production on Bronze Age Crete: nutritional properties, processing methods and storage life of Minoan olive oil', *Oxford Journal of Archaeology*, 21 (2002), pp. 63-75.

Rivera, Diego B. Miralles, Concepción Obón, Encarna Carreño, José A. Palazón, 'Multivariate analysis of *Vitis* subgenus *Vitis* seed morphology', *Vitis* 46 (4) (2007), pp. 158-167.

Rivera, Diego Nuñez and Michael J. Walker, 'A review of palaeobotanical findings of early *Vitis* in the Mediterranean and of the origins of cultivated grape-vines, with special reference to new pointers to prehistoric exploitation in the western Mediterranean', *Review of Palaeobotany and Palynology*, 61 (1989), pp. 205-237.

Roberto, Claude, James A. Plambeck and Alastair Small, 'The chronology of the sites of the Roman period around San Giovanni: Methods of analysis and conclusions', in *Archaeological field survey in Britain and abroad. The Societies of Antiquaries of London, Occasional Paper 6*, ed. by Sarah Macready and Frederick H. Thompson (London: Thames and Hudson, 1985), pp. 136-145.

Roberto, Claude and Alastair Small, 'The Field Survey', in *The excavations of San Giovanni di Ruoti. Volume III, The faunal and plant remains*, ed. by Michael R. MacKinnon, Alastair Small (Toronto, University of Toronto Press, 2002), pp. 19-22.

Ross Holloway, R. *Satrianum: The archeological investigations conducted by Brown University in 1966 and 1967* (Providence: Brown University Press, 1970).

Rottoli, Mauro, 'La Marmotta, Anguillara Sabazia (RM), Scavi 1989. Analisi paletnobotaniche: Prime risultanze', *Bullettino di Paletnologia Italiana*, 84 (1993), pp. 305-315.

Rottoli, Mauro, 'Italia settentrionale', in *Storia dell'agricoltura italiana/Accademia dei Georgofili, Florence. I: L'età Antica*, ed. by Gaetano Forni and Nicola Marcone (Firenze: Polistampa, 2001), pp. 235-246.

Ruas, Marie-Pierre and Laurent Bouby, 'Carbonization, preservation and deformation of carpological remains', in *The taphonomy of burned organic residues and combustion features in archaeological contexts. Proceedings of the round table, Valbonne, May 27-29 2008*, ed. by Isabelle Théry-Parisot, Lucie Chabal, Sandrine Costamagno (P@lethnologie, 2010), pp. 69-78.

Runnels, Curtis and Julie Hansen, 'The olive in the prehistoric Aegean: The evidence for domestication in the Early Bronze Age', *Oxford Journal of Archaeology* 5(3) (1986), pp. 299-308.

Russo Tagliente, Alfonsina, *Edilizia domestica in Apulia e Lucania: Ellenizzazione e società nella tipologia abitativa indigena tra VIII e III secolo A.C.* (Galatina: Congedo, 1992).

Sallares, Robert, *The ecology of the ancient Greek world* (London: Duckworth, 1991).

Saltini Semerari, Giulia, *Towards the Greek colonisation: The interaction between Greece and Italy from the end of the Bronze Age to the Iron Age* (Unpublished PhD thesis, University of Oxford, 2010).

Sargent, A., 'Relazione sui resti paleobotanici di Coppa Nevigata', in *XXVI Atti della Riunione Scientifica dell'Istituto Italiano di Preistoria e Protostoria 1985*, ed. by A. Revedin (Firenze: Istituto Italiano di Preistoria e Protostoria, 1987), pp. 761-764.

Scheffer, Charlotte, 'Cooking and cooking stands in Italy, 1400-400 BC', *Acta Inst. Rom. Reg. Suec.*, XXXVIII, II, 1 (Stockholm, 1981).

Schneider, R., 'Analyse palynologique dans l'Aspromonte en Calabre (Italie meridionale)', *Cahiers Ligures de Préhistoire et de Protohistoire*, 2 (1985), pp. 279-288.

Schultz, Celia and Paul B. Harvey Jr., *Religion in republican Italy* (Yale Classical Studies 33, Cambridge University Press, 2006).

Schweingruber, Fritz, H., *Mikroskopische Holzanatomie* (Zürich: Zürger, 1982).

Schweingruber, Fritz, H., *Anatomie europäischer Hölzer* (Haupt, Bern and Stuttgart: Sieber, 1990).

Scott, Andrew and Freddy Damblon (eds), 'Charcoal and its use in palaeoenvironmental analysis. Selected papers from the 4th International Meeting of Anthracology, Brussels, 8-13 September 2008', *Palaeogeography, Palaeoclimatology, Palaeoecology,* 291 (1-2) (2010), pp. 1-166.

Seltmann, Charles T., *Wine in the ancient world* (London, 1957).

Semeraro, Grazia, *En neusi: Ceramica greca e società nel Salento arcaico* (Lecce: Martano, 1997).

Sfameni Gasparro, Giulia, *Misteri e culti mistici di Demetra* (Rome: L'Erma di Bretschneider, 1986).

Shaw Briggs, Martin, *In the heel of Italy: A study of an unknown city* (London: Duffield and Co., 1910).

Sherratt, Andrew, 'Climatic cycles and behavioural revolutions: The emergence of modern humans and the beginning of farming', *Antiquity* 71 (1997), pp. 271-328.

Simoons, Frederick J. *Plants of life, plants of death* (Madison, Wisconsin: The University of Wisconsin Press, 1998).

Small, Alastair *et al.*, 'A pit group of c. 8070 BC from Gravina di Puglia', *Papers of the British School at Rome,* 62 (1994), pp. 197260.

Small, Alastair, Ian Campbell, Michael MacKinnon, Tracy Prowse and Charmaine Sipe, 'Field survey in the Basentello Valley on the Basilicata-Puglia Border', *Echos du Monde Classique/Classical Views*, XLII (1998), pp. 337-371.

Small, Alistair (ed.), *An Iron Age and Roman republican settlement on Botromagno, Gravina di Puglia: Excavations of 1965-1974*, (London: British School at Rome, 2000).

Small, Alastair, 'Changes in the pattern of settlement and land use around Gravina and Monte Irsi', in *Modalità insediative e strutture agrarie nell'Italia meridionale in età Romana*, ed. by Elio Lo Cascio and Alfredina Storchi Marino (Bari: Edipuglia, 2001), pp. 35-53.

Smith, Helen and Glynis Jones, 'Experiment on the effect of charring on cultivated grape seeds', *Journal of archaeological science,* 17 (1990), pp. 317-327.

Smith, Gemma and Harriet Gillett, *European forests and protected areas: Gap analysis. Technical report* (UNEP World Conservation Monitoring Centre Cambridge, UK, 2000).

Smithson, Evelyn Lord, 'The tomb of a rich Athenian lady, ca. 850 BC', *Hesperia,* 37 (1968), pp. 77-116.

Snowden, Frank M., *The conquest of malaria: Italy, 1900-1962* (New Haven: Yale University Press, 2006).

Solinas, Francesco, 'Il Megaron delle meraviglie: Culti ctoni ed offerte vegetali nell'area sanctuariale di Vaste-Piazza Dante (LE) nel corso del IV-III sec. a.C.', in *Uomini, piante e animali nella dimensione del sacro. Seminario di Studi di Bioarcheologia (28-29 giugno 2002), Convento dei Domenicani- Cavallino (Lecce)*, ed. by Francesco D'Andria, Jacopo De Grossi Mazzorin and Girolamo Fiorentino (Bari: Edipuglia, 2008), pp. 235-243.

Sorrentino, Claudio, 'La fauna', in *Cavallino*, ed. by Orlanda Pancrazzi (Galatina: Congedo, 1979), pp. 294-309.

Sourisseau, Jean-Christophe, 'Documents archéologiques et réseaux d'échanges en Méditerranée centrale (VIIIe-VIIe s. a.C.)', in *Mobilités grecques. Mouvements, réseaux, contacts en Méditerranée, de l'époque archaïque à l'époque hellénistique*, ed. by Laurent Capdetrey and Julien Zurbach (Bordeaux : Ausonius Eds., 2012), pp. 179-197.

Sourisseau, Jean-Christophe, 'La diffusion des vins grecs d'Occident du VIIIe au IVe s. av. J.-C., sources écrites et documents archéologiques', in *La vigna di Dioniso. Vite, vino e culti in Magna Grecia, Atti del XLIX Convegno di Studi sulla Magna Grecia, 24-28 settembre 2009*, ed. by Mario Lombardo, Aldo Siciliano, Arcangelo Alessio (Taranto, Istituto per la Storia e l'Archeologia della Magna Grecia, 2011), pp. 145-252.

Stanley, Jean-Daniel and Maria P. Bernasconi, 'Sybaris-Thuri-Copia trilogy: Three delta coastal sites become land-locked', *Méditerranée* 112 (2009), pp. 75-86.

Stavrianopoulou, Eftychia, *Ritual and communication in the Graeco-Roman world* (Liège: Centre International d'Étude de la Religion Grecque Antique, 2006).

Storme, Annelies, *Preliminary report on the study of the paleo-landscape in the coastal plain west of Taranto, Southern Italy* (Unpublished internal report, VU University Amsterdam, 2008).

Stummer, Albert, 'Zur Urgeschichte der Rebe und des Weinbans', *Mitteilungen der Anthropologischen Gesellschaft in Wien,* 41 (1911), pp. 283-296.

Sullivan, Donald G., *Pollen evidence for land use and vegetation change at Pizzica-Pantanello* (Unpublished internal report, Institute of Classical Archaeology, University of Texas at Austin, 1983).

Syred, Caroline and Anthony J. Griffiths, 'A clean, efficient system for producing charcoal, heat and power (CHaP)', *Fuel,* 85 (2006), pp. 1566–1578.

Tabò, D., 'I nuovi dolii dell'età del bronzo recente', in *Broglio di Trebisacce 1990-1994. Elementi e problemi nuovi dalle recenti campagne di scavo*, ed. by Renato Peroni and Alessandro Vanzetti (Soveria Mannelli: Rubbettini editore, 1998), pp. 157-174.

Tandy, David W. and Walter C. Neale, *Hesiod's Works and Days. A translation and commentary for the social sciences* (Berkeley: University of Berkeley Press, 1996).

Tchernia, André, *Le vin de l'Italie romaine: Essai d'histoire économique d'après les amphores* (Rome: École Française, 1986).

Tenaglia, Paola, 'I dolii cordonati', in *Enotri e Micenei nella Sibaritide*, ed. by Flacia Trucco and Renato Peroni (Taranto: Paleani, 1994), pp. 347-371.

Terral, Jean-Frédéric, Natalia Alonso, Ramon Buxó I Capdevilla, Noureddine Chatti, Laurent Fabre, Girolamo Fiorentino, Philippe Marinval et al., 'Historical biogeography of olive domestication (*Olea europaea* L.) as revealed by geometrical morphometry applied to biological and archaeological material', *Journal of Biogeography*, 31 (2004), pp. 63-77.

Terrenato, Nicola, 'Surface thoughts: Future directions in Italian field surveys', in *The future of surface artefact survey in Europe*, ed. by John L. Bintliff, Martin Kuna, Natalie Venclová (Sheffield: Sheffield Academic Press, 2000), pp. 21-28.

Tetteroo, Corine and Jitte Waagen, 'Le sepolture di Muro Tenente 1993-2002', in *L'insediamento Messapico di Muro Tenente. Scavi e ricerche 1009-2009*, ed. by Gert-Jan L.M. Burgers and Christian Napolitano (Mesagne: Locopress, 2010), pp. 85-140.

Théry-Parisot, Isabelle, *Économie des combustibles au paléolithique. Expérimentation, taphonomie, anthracologie* (Dossier de Documentation Archéologique n°20; Paris: CNRS Editions, 2001).

Thiébault, Stephanie (ed.), *Charcoal analysis. Methodological approaches, palaeoecological results and wood uses. Proceedings of the 2nd International Meeting of Anthracology, Paris, September 2000*, (Oxford: Archaeopress, 2002).

Thompson, Kenneth, *Farm fragmentation in Greece: The problem and its setting* (Athens, Center of Economic Research, 1963).

Thurmond, David L., *A handbook of food processing in classical Rome: For her bounty no winter* (Leiden: Brill, 2006).

Tobey, Ronald C., *Saving the prairies: The life cycle of the founding school of American plant ecology, 1895-1955* (Berkeley: University of California Press, 1981).

Tomaselli, R., 'Main physiognomic types and geographic distribution of shrub systems related to Mediterranean climates', in *Mediterranian-type shrublands. Ecosystems of the world, 11*, ed. by Francesco Di Castri, David W. Goodall and Raymond Louis Specht (Amsterdam: Elsevier scientific, 1981), pp. 95-106.

Tomlinson, Philippa, 'Vegetative plant remains from waterlogged deposits identified at York', in *New light on early farming: Recent developments in palaeoethnobotany*, ed. Jane M. Renfrew (Edinburgh: Edinburgh University Press, 1991), pp. 109-119.

Toynbee, Arnold J., *Hannibal's legacy: The Hannibalic war's effects on Roman life* (London: Oxford University Press, 1965).

Turner, Simon D. and Anthony G. Brown, '*Vitis* pollen dispersal in and from organic vineyards. I: Pollen trap and soil pollen data', *Review of Palaeobotany and Palynology*, 129 (2004), pp. 117-132.

Tutin, T.G, (ed.), *Flora Europaea. Volume 5, Alismataceae to Orchidaceae (monocotyledones)*, (Cambridge: Cambridge University Press).

Uggeri, Giovanni, 'La viabilità preromana della Messapia', *Studi e ricerche del Museo Provinciale di Brindisi*, 8 (1975), pp. 74-104.

Uggeri, Giovanni, *La viabilità romana del Salento* (Fasano: Grafischena, 1983).

Uguzzoni, Arianna and Franco Ghinatti, *Le tavole greche di Eraclea* (Rome: L'Erma di Bretschneider, 1968).

Vagnetti, Lucia and Richard E. Jones, 'Towards the identification of local Mycenaean pottery in Italy', in *Problems in Greek prehistory, Papers presented at the Centenary Conference of the British School of Archaeology at Athens, Manchester April 1986*, ed. by Elizabeth B. French, K.A. Wardle (Bristol: Bristol Classical Press, 1988), pp. 335-348.

Valamoti, Sultana-Maria, 'Grain versus chaff: Identifying a contrast between grain-rich and chaff-rich sites in the Neolithic of northern Greece', *Vegetation History and Archaeobotany*, 14 (2005), pp. 259–267.

Valamoti, Sultana-Maria, Maria Mangafa, Ch. Koukouli-Chrysanthaki and D. Malamidou, 'Grape-pressings from northern Greece: The earliest wine in the Aegean?', *Antiquity*, 81 (2007), pp. 54-61.

Valamoti, Sultana-Maria, 'Flax in Neolithic and Bronze Age Greece: Archaeobotanical evidence', *Vegetation History and Archaeobotany*, 20.6 (2011), pp. 549-560.

Vallet, Georges, 'L'Introduction de l'olivier en Italie centrale d'après les données de la céramique', *Hommages à Albert Grenier* (vol. LVIII; Brussels: Latomus, 1962), pp. 1554-1563.

Vallino, Fabienne O. and Giulia Ventura, 'Dati archeobotanici dal Broglio: Semi ed altri reperti', in *Nuove ricerche sulla protostoria della Sibaritide*, ed. by Renato Peroni (Rome: Paleani, 1984), pp. 272-280.

Van Alberda, Karel, Gert-Jan L.M. Burgers, Harry Burgers, Dick Karel, Douwe G. Yntema, *Muro Tenente. Centro Messapico nel territorio di Mesagne: Le ricerche Olandesi, 1992-1997*, a cura di A. Nitti (Mesagne: Amministrazione Communale, Assessorato Cultura e Turismo, 1999).

Van Joolen, Ester, 'Archaeological land evaluation. A reconstruction of the suitability of ancient landscapes for various land uses in Italy focused on the first millennium BC', (Unpublished PhD thesis, Groningen University, 2003).

Van der Veen, Marijke, *Crop husbandry regimes. An archaeobotanical study of farming in northern England 1000 BC-AD 500* (Sheffield: J. R. Collis Publications, 1992).

Van der Veen, Marijke, 'Formation processes of desiccated and carbonized plant remains- the identification of routine practice', *Journal of archaeological science*, 34 (2007), pp. 968-990.

Van Straten, Folkert T., Hiera kala. *Images of animal sacrifice in Archaic and Classical Greece* (Leiden: E.J. Brill, 1995).

Vandermersch, Christian, *Vins et amphores de Grande Grèce et de Sicile, IVe-IIIe s.avant J.-C.* (Rome: L'Erma di Bretschneider, 1994).

Vanzetti, Alessandro, 'Some current approaches to protohistoric centralization and urbanization in Italy', in *New developments in Italian landscape archaeology*, ed. by Peter Attema, Gert-Jan L.M. Burgers, Ester van Joolen, Martijn van Leusen, Benoît Mater (Oxford: Archaeopress, 2002), pp. 36-51.

Veenman, Froukje A., *Reconstructing the pasture. A reconstruction of pastoral landuse in Italy in the first millennium BC* (Unpublished PhD thesis, VU University Amsterdam, 2002).

Vernet, Jean-Louis, *Les charbons de bois, les anciens écosystèmes et le rôle de l'homme* (Paris: Société botanique de France, 1992).

Vernet, Jean-Louis, *L'homme et la forêt Méditerranéenne de la préhistoire à nos jours* (Paris: Editions Errance, 1997).

Vernet, Jean-Louis, 'Reconstructing vegetation and landscapes in the Mediterranean: The contribution of anthracology', in *Mediterranean landscape archaeology 2: Environmental reconstruction in Mediterranean landscape archaeology*, ed. by Philippe Leveau (Oxford: Oxbow Books, 1999), pp. 25-36.

Vernet, Jean-Louis, 'Anthracology and Mediterranean landscape, classical and new approaches', in *Charcoals from the past: Cultural and palaeoenvironmental implications. Proceedings of the Third International Meeting of Anthracology, Cavallino - Lecce (Italy), June 28th -July 1st 2004*, ed. by Girolamo Fiorentino and Donatella Magri (BAR International Series 1807; Oxford: Archaeopress, 2008), pp. 299-306.

Vink, Marja, 'Confrontatie of coexistentie? De verhouding tussen lokale bewoners en Griekse kolonisten in Zuid-Italië', *Tijdschrift voor Mediterrane Archeologie* 14 (1994-1995), pp. 16-24.

Vita-Finzi, Claudio and Eric Sidney Higgs, 'Prehistoric economy in the Mount Carmel area of Palestine: Site catchment analysis', *Proceedings of the Prehistoric Society*, 36 (1970), pp. 1-37.

Vuorela, Irmeli, 'Relative pollen rain around cultivated fields', *Acta Botanica Fennica*, 102 (1973), pp. 2-27.

Warrior, Valerie M., *Greek religion: A sourcebook* (Newburyport, MA: Focus Publishing, R. Pullins & Company, 2009).

West, Martin L., *Greek lyric poetry: The poems and fragments of the Greek iambic, elegiac, and melic poets (excluding Pindar and Bacchylides) down to 450 BC* (Oxford: Clarendon, 1993).

White, Kenneth D., *Roman farming* (London: Thames and Hudson, 1970).

White, Kenneth D., 'Cereals, bread and milling in the Roman world', in *Food in antiquity*, ed. by John *Wilkins*, David Harvey, Michael J. Dobson (Exeter: University of Exeter Press, 1995), pp. 38-43.

Whitehouse, Ruth D. and John B. Wilkins, 'Greeks and natives in south-east Italy: Approaches to the archaeological evidence', in *Centre and periphery. Comparative studies in archaeology*, ed. by Timothy C. Champion (London: Unwin Hyman, 1989), pp. 102-126.

Willerding, Ulrich, 'Methodische Probleme bei der Untersuchung und Auswertung von Pflanzenfunden. Vor- und frühgeschichtlichen Siedlungen', *Nachrichten aus Niedersachsens Urgeschichte*, 40 (1971), pp. 180-198.

Willerding, Ulrich, 'Präsenz, Erhaltung un Repräsentation von Pflanzenresten im archäologischem Fundgut', in *Progress in Old World palaeoethnobotany*, ed. by Willem Van Zeist, Krystyna Wasylikowa, Karl-Ernst Behre (Rotterdam: Balkema, 1991), pp. 25-51.

Wuilleumier, Pierre, *Taranto dalle origini alla conquista romana* (Taranto: Mandese, 1987).

Yntema, Douwe G., 'Background to a South Daunian Krater', *Babesch*, 54 (1979), pp. 1-48.

Yntema, Douwe G., 'Notes on Greek influence on Iron Age Salento', *Studi di Antichità*, 3 (1982), pp. 83-131.

Yntema, Douwe G., *The matt-painted pottery of Southern Italy: A general survey of the matt-painted pottery styles of Southern Italy during the Final Bronze Age and the Iron Age* (Galatina: Congedo, 1990).

Yntema, Douwe G., *In search of an ancient countryside: The Amsterdam Free University field survey at Oria province of Brindisi South Italy (1981-1983)* (Amsterdam: Thesis Publishers, 1993).

Yntema, Douwe G., Constructing a Dark Age. The 5th century BC in Southern Italy, in: *Caeculus III, Debating Dark Ages* (1997), pp. 103-111.

Yntema, Douwe G., 'Mental landscapes of colonization: The ancient written sources and the archaeology of early colonial-Greek southeastern Italy', *Babesch*, 75 (2000), pp. 1-49.

Yntema, Douwe G., *Pre-Roman Valesio. Excavations of the Amsterdam Free University at Valesio, province of Brindisi, southern Italy. Vol. I.: The Pottery* (Amsterdam: Institute of Archaeology, 2001).

Yntema, Douwe G., 'The birth of a Roman Southern Italy: A case study. Ancient written sources and archaeological evidence on the early Roman phase in the Salento district, southern Italy (3rd-1st century BC)', *Babesch*, 81 (2006), pp. 95-137.

Yntema, Douwe G., 'Material culture and plural identity in early Roman Southern Italy', in *Ethnic constructs in antiquity. The role of power and tradition*, ed. by Ton Derks and Nico Roymans (Amsterdam: Amsterdam University Press, 2009), pp. 145-166.

Yntema, Douwe G., *South-east Italy in the first millennium BC* (Amsterdam: Amsterdam University Press, 2013).

Zancani Montuoro, Paolo, 'I vini di Sibari e Thuri', in Aparchai: *Nuove ricerche e studi sulla Magna Grecia e la Sicilia antica in onore di Paolo Enrico Arias*, ed. by Maria Letizia Gualandi (Pisa: Giardini editori, 1982), pp. 559-562.

Zeiler, Jørn, *De vleespotten van Valesio. Archeologisch onderzoek van een Zuiditaliaanse nederzetting, ca. 720-90/80 v. Chr.* (Unpublished internal report, VU University Amsterdam, 1996).

Zohary, Daniel and Pinhas Spiegel-Roy, 'Beginnings of fruit growing in the Old world', *Science*, 187 (1975), pp. 319-327.

Zohary, Daniel and Maria Hopf, *Domestication of plants in the Old world. The origin and spread of cultivated plants in West Asia, Europe and the Nile Valley* (Third edition; Oxford: Oxford University Press, 2000).

Appendices

APPENDIX I, ARCHAEOBOTANICAL SAMPLE PROCESSING

A I.I METHODOLOGY: GENERAL INTRODUCTION AN RECOMMENDATIONS

Archaeobotanical remains are best preserved in an oxygen-poor or very dry environment, in which the activities of decomposition bacteria are slowed down or stopped altogether. Examples of such environments are bogs, pits, wells, lakes, cesspits, deserts, and sometimes tombs, especially when they are sealed off from the outside air and contain a very dry or wet environment. Archaeobotanical remains also thrive in nutrient-poor and acid soils (but not too acid), in the presence of manganese and the absence of calcium.[1] Sandy soils are usually less suitable. That said, archaeobotanical material is often saved from degradation because it was carbonized before deposition. In most cases, carbonized plant remains are almost indestructible, at least from a chemical point of view (they can easily be pulverized by mechanical pressure). Therefore, hearths and ovens are particularly suitable contexts for collecting archaeobotanical remains. For the same reason, sites that were destroyed by fire or other sources of heat, such as the Vesuvian sites and Akrotiri in Greece, are usually relatively rich in plant remains.

The nature of archaeobotanical remains in an archaeological context can vary between microscopic plant parts, such as pollen, and entire (carbonized) trees. The first category is referred to as microremains, i.e. plant remains that are not visible to the naked eye and have to be magnified at least a hundred times under a microscope to become visible.[2] The latter category is called macroremains and includes all plant remains that are visible to the naked eye or under a microscope with a magnification of less than a hundred times. Both categories require their own methods of sampling and identification.

Archaeobotanical macroremains and charcoal can be collected by conducting systematic soil sampling. The size of these samples depends entirely on the archaeological context, but there are some general rules that should always be followed. Most importantly, it is recommendable to take soil samples from different types of structures throughout the excavated area, as agricultural activities and food preparation might have taken place at different locations in and around the settlement. For the same reason, it is usually advised to take soil samples from as many excavated structures as possible, and to select the most significant ones for analysis later.[3] A standard sample contains ten litres of soil, but it can be decided to take a larger sample from material-rich archaeological features, or a smaller sample when it is not possible to collect enough soil, for instance when the contents of a pottery container are sampled.

A frequently used method for recovering ancient plant remains from the soil is wet sieving by means of a flotation machine. This laboratory technique for segregating plant remains from mineral samples by means of buoyancy was first used by Hans Helbaek in 1961 at the excavation of Tepe Ali Kosh in

---

[1] Kars and Smit 2003, p. 45; Moore and Webb 1978, p. 8–15.
[2] Kooistra 2002.
[3] Kooistra 2002, p. 15.

Iran.[4] The system consists of a water tank, a source of running tap water and two sieves, one inside and one outside the tank. The soil sample is added to the flotation machine in the sieve inside the tank, after which it is filled with water. When the tank is full, the overflowing water pours through the second sieve. When this happens, the floating charred archaeobotanical remains are caught. Although the success of this method depends entirely on the soil type (heavy clays and moist soils tend to clot together and stop the carbonized plant parts from floating), it has proved to be quite effective in dry sandy environments, and also on the calcareous soils of southern Italy. Among the macroremains that can be collected in this way are charcoal fragments (carbonized wood) and carbonized fruits and seeds. Strictly speaking, plant stems, fibres, leaves and roots also fall into the category of archaeobotanical macroremains, but until now these have not been found at Muro Tenente, l'Amastuola and Li Castelli.

A I.2 ARCHAEOBOTANICAL SAMPLING AT L'AMASTUOLA, MURO TENENTE AND LI CASTELLI

At the excavations of l'Amastuola, Muro Tenente and Li Castelli, the location of archaeobotanical samples was chosen at random; no grid sample system was used. The volume differed between c. 10 and 40 litres of soil. Larger units, or the ones that seemed more interesting, were often sampled more thoroughly, whereas units that appeared disturbed were almost never sampled. All samples were floated by means of a flotation machine, four of which were built specifically for use at these sites by the Laboratorio di Archeobotanica e Paleoecologia (LAP) of the Università del Salento in Lecce. These machines contained two sieves with meshes of 2.5 and 1 mm. After flotation, the residue in the large sieve was checked for further carbonized remains that for some reason had not come to the surface. Subsequently, the two fractions (from the 1 mm sieve and remaining carbonized remains from the 2.5 mm sieve) were united and left to dry. The analysis was carried out at the palaeobotanical laboratories of the Università del Salento, Lecce, and of Biax *Consult*, Zaandam. For the analysis of the charcoal fragments, a reflective light microscope with a magnification range between 100 and 400 times was used and for the carbonized fruits and seeds a basic binocular microscope with 4 to 40 times magnification. The seeds and charcoal collection at the Lecce Laboratory and Biax *consult* were used as reference material, as well as the standard literature for the analysis of archaeobotanical macroremains (including charcoal).[5]

A I.3 RECOMMENDATIONS

Much work still remains to be done to make archaeobotanical research projects 1) more compatible with each other and 2) more integrated into archaeological studies. A great example of well-integrated research can be found in the rural hinterland of Metapontion, which is one of the best studied countrysides of the Greek world.[6] The Metapontino project demonstrates that multidisciplinary studies can generate new insights into classic research themes such as Greek/indigenous relationships, the

---

[4] Helbaek 1969, p. 385: the floating technique employed in the field was initially just a makeshift arrangement. The principle of segregation is to exploit the difference in specific weight between the plant matter and the fluid. This difference is not very great when water is used. Carbon tetrachloride is 1.8 times heavier than water and is therefore the agent used in the laboratory.

[5] Berggren 1969, 1981; Anderberg 1994; Cappers *et al.* 2006, Körber-Grohne 1964, 1991; Jacomet 2006; Schweingruber 1982, 1990.

[6] Carter 2006, p. 16.

development of socio-economic complexity, and urbanization. Future archaeological projects will be able to generate a larger and more complete data set by including archaeobotanical research. In order to successfully combine these two research disciplines, I would like to make the following recommendations.

1. A suitable protocol for collecting archaeobotanical soil samples should be made *before* the start of an excavation, and preferably maintained throughout the duration of the project. Only in this way will it be possible to compare soil samples from different parts of the excavated area. Comparison becomes notoriously difficult when some structures are sampled more thoroughly than others.

2. It is recommended to take soil samples from different types of structures throughout the excavated area, as agricultural activities and food preparation might have taken place at different locations in and around the settlement. For the same reason, it is usually advised to take soil samples from as many excavated structures as possible, and to select the most significant ones for analysis later. It should be added, however, that archaeobotanical sampling is only useful in contexts that have a more or less clear place in the chronology of the site. If this is not the case, it is hardly possible to interpret the plant remains.

3. A standard archaeobotanical sample contains 10 litres of soil, but it can be decided to take a larger sample from material-rich archaeological features, or a smaller sample when it is not possible to collect enough soil (for instance when the contents of a pottery container are sampled), or to collect by hand small amounts of material that are clearly visible in the field. Samples should be collected using a clean (!) trowel, shovel or dustpan, and placed in clean, preferably airtight closable containers.

4. The most important aspect in any sampling strategy is data recording. It may seem obvious why and how a sample was taken in the field during the excavation, but it often takes several months before the samples are analysed in the laboratory, possibly by a specialist who was not present at the excavation. It is useful to keep a central list of all the samples from the different excavation trenches, and to make someone in the excavation team responsible for updating this list and keeping track of the samples (i.e. who took them, where they are now, if they are sieved yet, if all the necessary information is included in the excavation reports, etc.).

5. Make sure that the following information is recorded in the daily excavation reports, or in a separate administration system for the soil samples:
    - Basic information: date, trench, unit number, etc.
    - Reasons for taking the sample, e.g. many carbonized plant remains are visible in the field; nature of the unit (tomb, surface, ritual deposition, other contexts that may contain food and/or other plant remains), etc.
    - Precise location of the sample. A unit number does not suffice, since units can be very large, and it may be important to know whether the sample was taken in the vicinity of any neighbouring units and/or next to a specific feature. Be as precise as possible. Making a sketch is always helpful, but determining a more precise location, e.g. with a Total Station, is preferable, especially when more than one sample is collected from the same unit.
    - Sampling method: at random, using a grid system (often a useful strategy to sample house floors), 100% (for small charcoal concentrations, the contents of pottery containers, *enchytrismos* graves), etc. Again: a sketch often clarifies matters.
    - f necessary: record how the sample should be treated. Most samples will probably be sieved in water (see below), but if, for some reason, this particular sample needs to be treated differently, make sure this is described in the daily report and, more importantly, on the sample bag or find tag.
    - If there is more than one sample bag from one unit, write down why and if there is any difference between the bags. It is important to distinguish samples that were simply too large to fit into one bag (in that case, write 1:2 and 2:2 on the find tickets) from samples that, for instance,

were taken from different features or places within the same unit. Make sure every sample bag has its own find tag.

Charcoal concentrations are often easily recognizable as single carbonized wood fragments in the field, but break into smaller pieces when they are sampled. These smaller pieces all have to be studied separately by the archaeobotanist in the lab. Thus, if charcoal concentrations are individually sampled, it saves a lot of time to make a note on the find ticket bag that the contents originally consisted of one single fragment.

6. Sieving by means of a flotation machine has proved to be a useful method for Mediterranean contexts, but it is important to keep in mind that the mesh width of the smallest sieve has to be small enough to collect chaff remains and small weed seeds. Ideally, a flotation tank has at least two sieves, one inside with large meshes (usually 1 mm) and one outside with 0.5 mm meshes, or smaller (but not larger!). A combination of several sieves, for instance with 0.5 and 0.25 mm meshes, would be even better.

APPENDIX 2, ARCHAEOBOTANICAL ANALYSES FROM L'AMASTUOLA, COMPLETE RESULTS

A 2.1 RESULTS: SEEDS AND FRUITS

period	unknown																			
unit	3	8	15	16	20	43	67	74	78	111	151	157	158	217	218	219	302	320	529	535
trench	1	1	7	7	5	5	5	5	5	3	4	4	4	2	2	2	6	6	6	6
context	colluvium/ fill/ disturbed layers																			
taxa																					common name
cereals																					
Hordeum vulgare	9		4	8	3	13	559	1176			26	6	12		6	3		10		6	hulled barley
Triticum dicoccum	1	1	1	1						1	2		1	1	1			153		4	emmer wheat
Triticum dicoccum *spikelet fork*																	1				emmer wheat
Triticum sp.	1	1	1													1					wheat
Cerealia	6					3	26	297			3	4	2						1		cereals
pulses																					
Lens culinaris																				3	lentil
Vicia faba var. minor				4			16	3	5		6										broad bean
Vicia ervilia				9	1		17			3			2		1	1				12	bitter vetch
Vicia sp.												1									vetch
Fabaceae							14													3	legumes
forage crops																					
Avena sp.								2					1								oat
Wild plants																					
Adonis cf. annua							1														(autumn) adonis
Subrecent contaminations	*	*		*						*			*	*			*				

Period	Early Iron Age										
Units	80	85	107	122	220	229	513	620	624	626	
Trench	5	5	3	4	2	2	6	6	6	6	
Context	Floor matrix	Floor matrix (?)	? Burned outdoors area	Levelling material for building δ	Man-made beaten earth surface	Ritual deposition?	Ritual deposition	Floor	Rubble on top of hut	Hut	
Taxa											common name
Cereals											
Hordeum vulgare	48	127		8	6			3	64	380	hulled barley
Triticum aestivum/compactum						2				2	free-threshing wheat
Triticum dicoccum				8	2	1			32	331	emmer wheat
Triticum dicoccum *spikelet fork*										2	emmer wheat
Triticum sp.				11					7	10	wheat
Cerealia	20	54		7				4	120	752	cereals
Pulses											
Vicia faba var. minor	6	1						13	11	1	broad bean
Vicia ervilia	3		685		8	3		4	49	130	bitter vetch
Fabaceae								5	22	37	legumes
Fruits											
Vitis vinifera										1	grape
Condiments											
Allium sativum							27				garlic
forage crops											
Secale cereale										1	rye
Wild plants											
Adonis cf. annua										2	(autumn) adonis
Lolium cf. perenne/rigidum										6	ryegrass
Malva sp.										1	mallow
Phalaris sp.									1		Canary grass
Poaceae									1		grass family

period	Archaic																						
units	26	33	61	63	72	81	105	109	144	148	152	159	164	166	170	265	274	319	336	346	373	533	534	537	627	
trench	5	5	5	5	5	5	3	3	4	4	4	4	4	4	4	2	2	6	6	6	6	6	6	6	6	
context	Outdoor area building ζ	Fireplace building ζ	Part of building θ	Floor building θ	Floor building θ	Floor building ζ	Outdoor surface	Floor matrix	Refuse dump	Oven outside building δ	Refuse dump	Floor oikos ε	Work bench (?) oikos ε	Burned soil related to /170\	Metal oven oikos ε	Burnt/dried clay; hearth? Storage pit?	Fill of /265\	Courtyard potter's workshop	Potter's wheel (?)	Ash deposit from kiln D	Ash deposit from kiln E	Surface in structure NE of potter's workshop	Charcoal spot	Kiln (?)	Burnt layer	
taxa																										common name
cereals																										
Hordeum vulgare		2	1		133	332	1		112				2	1	2	4						34	926	3	15	hulled barley
Triticum aestivum/compactum									1													8	1		6	free-threshing wheat
Triticum dicoccum					1				24	1	3	11			1	1		2				5	*			emmer wheat
Triticum dicoccum *spikelet fork*																										emmer wheat
Triticum sp.						1	1															14				wheat
Cerealia					7	139			39		14			3	2				1			35	49	1	42	cereals
pulses																										
Lens culinaris									1													10	16	5		lentil
Vicia faba var. minor						3						12				1						2	25	1		broad bean
Vicia ervilia	3	186			14	44		71	8		2	3	1		4							3	6	98	4	bitter vetch
Vicia sp.									5		3	23		1												vetch
Fabaceae		42			2	7																	19	30	5	legumes
fruits																										
Olea europaea																										olive
Pistacia lentiscus															1											mastic
Vitis vinifera												2													1	grape
Rosaceae																										Rosaceae
forage crops																										
Avena sp.								1	13		1		1	5												oat

period	Archaic																					
units	26	33	61	63	72	81	105	109	144	148	152	159	164	166	170	265	274	319	336	346	373	533	534	537	627
trench	5	5	5	5	5	5	3	3	4	4	4	4	4	4	4	2	2	6	6	6	6	6	6	6	6
context	Outdoor area building ζ	Fireplace building ζ	Part of building θ	Floor building θ	Floor building θ	Floor building ζ	Outdoor surface	Floor building	Refuse dump	Oven outside building δ	Refuse dump	Floor oikos ε	Work bench (?) oikos ε	Burned soil related to /170\	Metal oven oikos ε	Burnt/dried clay: hearth? Storage pit?	Fill of /265\	Courtyard potter's workshop	Potter's wheel (?)	Ash deposit from kiln D	Ash deposit from kiln E	Surface in structure NE of potter's workshop	Charcoal spot	Kiln (?)	Burnt layer
taxa																										common name
Secale cereale																										rye
Wild plants																										
Adonis cf. annua				1																		15				(autumn) adonis
Medicago hispida									1																	bur medick
Rumex sp.													1													sorrel
Subrecent contaminations									*		*	*	*		*		*									

Period	Classical	
Units	313	
Trench	6	
Context	Floor potter's workshop	
Taxa		common name
Cereals		
Hordeum vulgare	170	hulled barley
Triticum aestivum/compactum	1	free-threshing wheat
Triticum dicoccum	20	emmer wheat
Triticum sp.	2	wheat
Pulses		
Vicia faba var. minor	1	broad bean
Vicia ervilia	1	bitter vetch
Fabaceae	4	legumes
Fruits		
Olea europaea	10	olive
Wild plants		
Bromus sp.	3	brome
Subrecent contaminations	*	

A 2.2 RESULTS: CHARCOAL

period	unknown (part 1)																			
unit	3	4	5	8	15	16	18	20	34	38	67	74	77	78	111	116	120	151	157	158
trench	1	1	1	1	7	7	5	5	5	5	5	5	5	5	3	4	4	4	4	4
context	colluvium/ fill/ disturbed layers																			
taxa																				common name
Arbutus unedo																		2		strawberry tree
Erica sp.																			1	heath
Juniperus sp.				1							1									juniper
Olea europaea	1			2	2	1	2	6	2	1	20	6	6	10	6			3	7	3	olive
Pistacia sp. (cf. lentiscus)		1	1																		mastic
Quercus sp. (deciduous type)				1	1		2					258		1							oak
Quercus sp. (evergreen type)							1												1		oak
Quercus sp.	4								7				4								oak
Rhamnus/ Phillyrea											15		12								Rhamnus/ Phillyrea
indet. hardwood	1	3		2							27			3	4	1	4			1	indet. hardwood

period	unknown (part 2)																							
unit	210	212	215	217	218	219	231	232	234	235	236	238	240	251	259	302	305	320	341	529	534	535	545	
trench	2	2	2	2	2	2	2	2	2	2	2	2	2	2	2	6	6	6	6	6	6	6	6	
context	colluvium/ fill/ disturbed layers																							
taxa																								common name
Erica sp.																	2							heath
Juniperus sp.				1	1						5						1		1	1				juniper
Maloideae (incl. cf. Sorbus sp.)																	1	1						Maloideae
Myrtus communis																					13			myrtle
Olea europaea			1	4	19	6		1			17		2	10	5		19	201			22	3	2	olive
Pistacia sp. (cf. lentiscus)											9		4				2							mastic
Prunus sp.																		10						prune
Quercus sp. (deciduous type)			1		2	1		1			1								3		2	11		oak
Quercus sp. (evergreen type)																					1		13	oak
Quercus sp.	1				4												3	4	1		1			oak
Rhamnus/ Phillyrea																		2		3	2		5	Rhamnus/ Phillyrea
Rosmarinus officinalis																								rosemary
indet. hardwood	2	4		5	1	3	12		2	1							1	7		2		5		indet. hardwood

period	Early Iron Age																			
unit	31	80	83	84	85	107	122	125	127	163	167	229	233	270	509	513	519	620	624	626	
trench	5	5	5	5	5	3	4	4	4	4	4	2	2	2	6	6	6	6	6	6	
context	Wall foundation	Floor matrix	Floor matrix (?)	Floor matrix	Floor matrix	? Burned outdoors area	Levelling material for building δ	Eroded soil under floor matrix	Dump/fill connected to /122\	Outdoor surface	Outdoor surface	Ritual deposition?	= /229\	Floor matrix	Circular feature on top of /513\	Ritual deposition	Burned layer	Floor	Rubble on top of hut	Hut	
taxa																					common name
Arbutus unedo																					strawberry tree
Erica sp.							1														heath
Juniperus sp.				1			1			1										3	juniper
Maloideae (incl. cf. Sorbus sp.)							1														Maloideae
Myrtus communis																					myrtle
Olea europaea		1	5		7	7	33			26	1	13		1	2		1	4	5	67	olive
Pistacia sp. (cf. lentiscus)							1	1											1	2	mastic
Quercus sp. (deciduous type)							30		1		4			5				2		71	oak
Quercus sp. (evergreen type)		8					4	4	8					1		158				5	oak
Quercus sp.			2		1		3					4					1			49	oak
Rhamnus/ Phillyrea	1				1		3			1							5		3	32	Rhamnus/ Phillyrea
indet. hardwood			3	1	4	5	5			1	1						3		15	143	indet. hardwood

period	Archaic (1)																						
unit	26	27	32	33	36	46	61	63	72	75	81	82	105	108	109	112	122	125	144	148	152	159	164	166
trench	5	5	5	5	5	5	5	5	5	5	5	5	3	3	3	3	4	4	4	4	4	4	4	4
context	Outdoor area building ζ	floor matrix	hearth?	Fireplace oikos ζ	floor matrix	unknown	Part of building θ	Floor building θ	floor building θ	floor matrix building θ	floor building ζ	floor building θ	outdoor surface	refuse dump?	floor matrix	furnace	levelling material	eroded soil under floor matrix building δ	refuse dump	oven outside building δ	refuse dump	floor oikos ε	Work bench (?) oikos ε	Burned soil related to /170\

taxa																									common name
Arbutus unedo																						118	2		strawberry tree
Erica sp.													2				1								heath
Juniperus sp.		1															1		13			8		4	juniper
Maloideae (incl. cf. Sorbus sp.)													3				1								Maloideae
Myrtus communis						1						5													myrtle
Olea europaea	3	10	11	13	3	2	4	8		6			36	17	3	6	33		45	12	8	77	4	3	olive
Pistacia sp. (cf. lentiscus)																	1	1							mastic
Quercus sp. (deciduous type)				3	1		1	166									30		1		1	5	5		oak
Quercus sp. (evergreen type)			3		1							7					4	4							oak
Quercus sp.					4	13			2	5			1				3		10			6		3	oak
Rhamnus/ Phillyrea								12			1		1				3					2			Rhamnus/ Phillyrea
indet. hardwood				9	2			2	1	26		5					5		6		2	15			indet. hardwood

unit	170	220	265	274	328	329	332	335	336	346	348	373	522	533	537	542	625	627	
trench	4	2	2	2	6	6	6	6	6	6	6	6	6	6	6	6	6	6	
context	Metal oven oikos ε	beaten earth surface	Burnt/dried clay: hearth? Storage pit?	Fill of /265\	clay deposit	part of kiln?	part of kiln E?	kiln E	Potter's wheel (?)	Ash deposit from kiln D	floor/cooking stones	Ash deposit from kiln E	part of potter's workshop	Surface in structure NE of potter's workshop	Kiln (?)	Ash refuse from kiln /537X?	unknown	Burnt layer	
taxa			1																common name
Arbutus unedo								1											strawberry tree
Erica sp.				25		3			1		9								heath
Juniperus sp.		7					3		2					4					juniper
Myrtus communis																			myrtle
Olea europaea	6	12	18	6	6	1	17		1	1				6	19	15	9	1	olive
Pistacia sp. (cf. lentiscus)		1					3										1		mastic
Quercus sp. (deciduous type)							2							1		118	10	19	oak
Quercus sp. (evergreen type)				1									6						oak
Quercus sp.		7	2												28				oak
Rhamnus/ Phillyrea				1			3	4	9	3				6	1	2		1	Rhamnus/ Phillyrea
indet. hardwood		1	5	36	1	5		2			10				11	1	24	10	indet. hardwood

period	Classical	Classical	Early Hellenistic	
unit	374	313	607	
trench	6	6	6	
context	preparation level for /313	Floor potter's workshop	Fill of dump pit cultic structure blocks	
taxa				common name
Arbutus unedo				strawberry tree
Erica sp.		1		heath
Juniperus sp.	1			juniper
Maloideae (incl. cf. Sorbus sp.)		2		Maloideae
Myrtus communis	3			myrtle
Olea europaea	19	22		olive
Pinus sp.		2		pine
Pistacia sp. (cf. lentiscus)		11		mastic
Prunus sp.				prune
Quercus sp. (deciduous type)		5		oak
Quercus sp. (evergreen type)	3	17	13	oak
Quercus sp.		9		oak
Rhamnus/Phillyrea	1	6	4	Rhamnus/Phillyrea
Rosmarinus officinalis		2		rosemary
indet. hardwood	3	11	1	indet. hardwood

APPENDIX 3, ARCHAEOBOTANICAL ANALYSES FROM MURO TENENTE, COMPLETE RESULTS

A 3.1 RESULTS: SEEDS AND FRUITS

Period	unknown									
Unit	0	364	365	370	1621	1734	1784	1792	20030	
Trench	-	C	C	C	C	C	C	C	E	
	disturbed layers/layers of unclear origin									
Taxa										common name
Cereals										
Hordeum vulgare		2				1				hulled barley
Hordeum vulgare var. nudum	2		2	16		1				naked barley
Triticum aestivum/compactum		20		2				8		free-threshing wheat
Triticum dicoccum				1						emmer wheat
Triticum dicoccum *spikelet fork*		2								emmer wheat
Triticum sp.				1						wheat
Cerealia		80				3				cereals
Pulses										
Vicia ervilia						1				bitter vetch
Fruits										
Pistacia lentiscus									1	mastic
Vitis vinifera					6		3			grape

Period	Early Hellenistic												
Unit	12	89	253	313	363	391	503	1702	2260	2268	1689	2551	
Trench	A	C	C	C	C	C	C	C	C	C	C	C	
Context	domestic										ritual?		
	floor	fireplace	ash deposit	part of courtyard	burned layer	Iron furnace?	ash deposit	charcoal deposit (from kiln /841\ and /598\?)	floor matrix room 3	floor matrix room 2	contents buried drinking cup	contents buried plainware pot	
Taxa													common name
Cereals													
Hordeum vulgare							6			1			hulled barley
Hordeum vulgare var. nudum				1			3			5			naked barley
Hordeum			1										barley
Triticum aestivum/compactum			4				8	2		15			free-threshing wheat
Triticum dicoccum				1	1		3		1				emmer wheat
Triticum dicoccum *spikelet fork*			1				3		1				emmer wheat
Triticum							10	3			1		wheat
Cerealia			31			2	10	1					cereals
Pulses													
Vicia faba var. minor				1									broad bean
Fruits													
Olea europaea		9	2									1	olive
Vitis vinifera	1	5175											grape
forage crops													
Secale cereale			5				1						rye

Period	Late Hellenistic		
Unit	20011	20067	
Trench	E	E	
Context	domestic		
	burned structure?	floor matrix ambiente 2	
Taxa			common name
Cereals			
Hordeum vulgare	6		hulled barley
Triticum dicoccum	12		emmer wheat
Cerealia	5		cereals
Pulses			
Vicia ervilia	1		bitter vetch
Vicia	4		vetch
Fruits			
Olea europaea	13	1	olive
Pistacia lentiscus	1		mastic
Vitis vinifera	2		grape
Rosaceae	2		Rosaceae
forage crops			
Avena	6		oat

Period	Early Hellenistic					
Unit	447	805	1624	1636	1638	
Trench	C	C	C	C	C	
Context	grave					
	around grave 22	fill + grave gifts grave 27	grave 30	upper layer grave 30	lower layer grave 30	
Taxa						common name
Cereals						
Hordeum vulgare						hulled barley
Hordeum vulgare var. nudum			1			naked barley
Hordeum						barley
Triticum aestivum/compactum	2		1			free-threshing wheat
Triticum dicoccum			1		1	emmer wheat
Triticum dicoccum *spikelet fork*				2	1	emmer wheat
Triticum	1					wheat
Cerealia	7		2	4		cereals
Pulses						
Vicia faba var. minor			2	1		broad bean
Vicia ervilia				11		bitter vetch
Vicia sp.	1					vetch
Fruits						
Olea europaea		2	8	1	1	olive
Vitis vinifera			30	36	2	grape

A 3.2 RESULTS: CHARCOAL

Period	unknown				
Unit	370	1689	20015	20030	
Trench	C	C	E	E	
Context	disturbed layers/layers of unclear origin				
Taxa					common name
Erica sp.	1				heath
Olea europaea			19	1	olive
Quercus sp. (deciduous type)			5	12	oak
indet. hardwood		8	3		indet. hardwood

period	Early Hellenistic																
unit	5	15	54	253	314	455	458	459	503	593	1603	1656	1702	2255	2258	2263	
trench	A	A	A	C	C	C	C	C	C	C	C	C	C	C	C	C	
context	Domestic																
	floor matrix	refuse dump	wall	ash deposit	wall room 3	charcoal from kiln /841\ and /598\	charcoal from kiln /841\ and /598\	charcoal from kiln /841\ and /598\	ash deposit	floor matrix room 3	foundation trench	refuse dump	charcoal deposit (from kiln /841\ and /598\?)	floor matrix (same as /593\ /2258\)	floor matrix (same as /593\ /2255\)	foundation trench	
taxa																	common name
Ephedra sp.	13																ephedra
Erica sp.		17		23		65	45	10	10	6			102		10		heath
Erica arborea							55										tree heath
Erica multiflora													100				Mediterranean heath
Myrtus communis										6				27			myrtle
Olea europaea	3			49	11					7	14				4		olive
Pistacia sp. (cf. lentiscus)				19													mastic
Pyrus/Malus													7				pear/ apple
Quercus sp. (evergreen type)																10	oak
Quercus sp.							201										oak
Rhamnus/Phillyrea												18					Rhamnus/Phillyrea
Salvia sp.			10														sage
indet. hardwood	40	15		136		86	364		28	62	14	2	1650		18	10	indet. hardwood

period	Late Hellenistic									
unit	20011	20022	20023	20028	20039	20054	20056	20063	20067	
trench	E	E	E	E	E	E	E	E	E	
context	Domestic									
	burned structure?	contents of pithos	Wall	floor matrix ambiente 2	contents of pithos	outside surface area	posthole	floor matrix ambiente 1	floor matrix ambiente 2	
taxa										common name
Erica sp.	5							1		heath
Juniperus sp.							373			juniper
Myrtus communis										myrtle
Olea europaea	55	2	7	2		1	10	5	16	olive
Pinus sp.							10			pine
Pistacia sp. (cf. lentiscus)	4	2			3					mastic
Quercus sp. (evergreen type)	62									oak
Quercus sp.	91	4				2		2	1	oak
Rhamnus/Phillyrea					1					Rhamnus/Phillyrea
indet. hardwood	53	4			2	1				indet. hardwood

period	Early Hellenistic					
unit	34	441	447	805	1638	
trench	A	C	C	C	C	
context	Grave					
	grave 45	grave 25	around grave 22	fill + grave gifts grave 27	lower layer grave 30	
taxa						common name
Erica sp.		8		11		heath
Olea europaea			7	2	1	olive
Pinus pinea/halepensis				29		umbrella/ Aleppo pine
Punica granatum	14					pomegranate
indet. hardwood	12	21	16	23	29	indet. hardwood
indet. softwood				107		indet. softwood

APPENDIX 4, ARCHAEOBOTANICAL ANALYSES FROM LI CASTELLI DI SAN PANCRAZIO SALENTINO, COMPLETE RESULTS

A 4.1 INTRODUCTION TO THE SITE[7]

The site known as Li Castelli, or I Castiedd', is located at a distance of about one kilometre east of the modern village of San Pancrazio Salentino. Its position on a natural platform, which reaches a height of 60 metres above sea level, gives it a somewhat elevated position overlooking the surrounding countryside. This landscape is mostly covered with vineyards, interrupted only occasionally by small olive groves and fields with cereals, tomatoes and artichokes. Large-scale archaeological research at Li Castelli started in 1991, when the VU University Amsterdam carried out a systematic field survey in the area.[8] The survey revealed a settlement that was occupied from the 8th century BC until the late 1st century AD. It was estimated that the whole habitation area extended over c. 50 hectares, but the absence of a standing fortification wall complicated the delineation of the site's contours.[9] It appears that the site reached its maximum expansion in the Early Hellenistic Period, when the settlement was probably composed of a series of separate habitation clusters.[10] These clusters all seem to circle around one hypothetical core, a land ridge of some 14 hectares. The excavations by the VU University Amsterdam concentrated on this ridge, which was thought to constitute the centre of the site. Two excavation campaigns were carried out in 1999 and 2001, in collaboration with the Soprintendenza per i Beni Archeologici della Puglia.

Among the structures brought to light was a road of hard-pressed calcareous grit from the Early Hellenistic period. In addition, several wall foundations were found that consisted of large limestone blocks. The walls formed a series of 'rooms', six of which were (partially) excavated in 2007. A second excavation campaign was started at Li Castelli in 2009, involving the extension of the 2007 excavation trench (1), and the opening of a second trench northeast of the previous excavations (2). The rooms, named A, B, C, D, E, and F, were all rectangular shaped and made up of large, neatly cut limestone blocks. The construction of room A, B, and C showed evidence for at least three building phases, with the pottery indicating a domestic function at least in the Hellenistic phase. Room E was added to room C in the latest phase, creating an L-shaped building. Rooms D and F are located in the south-eastern area of the trench, parallel to the north-eastern limit of the road. The upper part of the layers investigated in room D contained the remains of collapsed walls and a roof. In the middle of the room, a medium-sized *pithos* was found that was filled with pottery datable to the 4th/3rd centuries BC. Underneath the room, traces of an earlier phase of habitation came to light in the form of a curvilinear hut that was probably in use in the 7th/6th centuries BC.

In sum, room B remained the most interesting. It measured 7.1 x 6.3 metres and had walls that at least in the room's latest phase were decorated with red plaster, which was found in considerable quantities in the surface accumulation. However, the archaeological strata related to room B were also much disturbed, showing several intrusions that revealed materials ranging from the 7th/6th century BC to the 1st/2nd centuries AD. Most of these disturbances were probably caused by recent deep-ploughing

---

[7] This introduction is based on the preliminary excavation reports of A. Fontana, G. Carluccio and J. Waagen, personal communications from A. Fontana, and Burgers and Waagen 2010.

[8] Burgers 1998, p. 129–159. These surveys followed several reports of archaeological finds at Lo Castelli, for instance in the 1960s by Cosimo Pagliara, who collected a diverse collection of Iron Age pottery from the surface.

[9] Only faint traces of fortification walls were identified at Li Castelli. If the settlement did have a defensive system, it is likely to have been obliterated by modern agricultural practices and in particular the arrangement of the vineyards that dominate the present-day landscape. Burgers and Waagen 2010, p. 60.

[10] Burgers and Waagen 2010, p. 62.

activities. As a result, only a few remains were excavated in situ in room B, including a floor level that contained an *enchytrismos* child burial. The other 'rooms' showed similar signs of post-depositional disturbances, which often made the interpretation of their stratigraphy difficult.

During the 2009 excavation campaign, two other roads were found that were oriented NW–SE, and also seemed to be flanked by limestone drainage channels. The intersection with the Early Hellenistic road in the southwest of the trench was not found, but has to be located somewhere outside the trench. The 2007/2009 excavations also uncovered six burials, including the above-mentioned *enchytrismos*. The oldest two burials, I and III, are of the *fossa* (pit) type. They are located in the northern half of the trench and date between the early 5th and the first half of the 4th century BC. The remaining three burials, II, IV and T20, are relatively simple cist-graves with buried infants, datable to the 4th and the first half of the 3rd century BC, respectively.

Apart from the planned excavations in the large trench, a small rescue operation was carried out in an area where the municipality of San Pancrazio planned to place a series of drainage tubes. This small (6.52 x 2.54 metres) excavation trench revealed limestone wall foundations similar to the ones found in the central trench. Adjacent to one of these walls, a terracotta bath tub (/571\, fill /574\) was found. The bath tub probably dates from the same habitation phase as the impasto *pithos* (RA 26) that was found in situ next to it. The *pithos* was placed inside the layer of abandonment that covered the limestone walls, so both the bath tub and the *pithos* date from a period posterior to the use of the stone structures.

Summarizing, it can be stated that the excavations at Li Castelli confirm the existence of a substantial village with a long continuity of occupation, at least from the Early Iron Age to the Roman period. The investigations also made it clear, however, that deep-ploughing and other recent activities have had a devastating impact on the site.

Archaeobotanical samples were only taken during the field campaigns in 2007 and 2009. In 2007, 89 soil samples were collected in 37 different stratigraphical units, and in 2009, 19 samples from 13 units. The 89 soil samples from the excavation campaign in 2007 have provided 969 charcoal fragments and only 27 seeds. Unfortunately, it must be concluded that the results of the archaeobotanical analysis have limited value for the reconstruction of the characteristics of the surrounding vegetation. Based on the archaeobotanical evidence collected so far, we could propose as a working hypothesis that the settlement was surrounded by high and middle-high *macchia* vegetation, notably olive, oak trees, and *Rhamnus/Phillyrea*. As for the settlement's means of subsistence, we are almost completely in the dark. The samples contained sporadic finds of wheat, barley, pulses, and grape pips, but we have no idea how, where and on what scale these crops were cultivated. Charcoal remains from the Maloideae/Rosaceae and Prunoideae families were found, but the samples contained no actual fruit remains except for the above-mentioned grape pips. The present evidence is also too scarce to determine whether some of these crops were used as grave gifts.

A 4.2 RESULTS: SEEDS AND FRUITS

Period	Early Hellenistic			
Unit	763	901	905	
Trench				
Context	Grave			
	fill of Tomb 4	fill of tomb 3	contents of *trozzella* in Tomb 3	
Taxa				common name
Cereals				
Hordeum sp.			2	barley
Triticum aestivum/compactum	1			free-threshing wheat
Triticum dicoccum		1		emmer wheat
Pulses				
Vicia sp.	1		1	vetch
Fruits				
Vitis vinifera		5	1	grape

A 4.3 RESULTS: CHARCOAL

period	(Sub)recent/unknown																		
unit	500	501	517	566	572	573	574	593	599	731	760	773	782	784	790	791	843	852	858	864	913
trench	1	Salvage excavation	1	1	Salvage excavation	Salvage excavation	Salvage excavation	Salvage excavation	Salvage excavation	1	1	1	1	1	1	1	1	1	1	1	1
Context	Samples from the top layers, strata of abandonment and collapse, disturbed and more recent layers, including the well found at the north side of excavation trench 1																				
	Top layer	Contents of pithos (after abandonment)	Pottery dump	Pottery dump	Layer of abandonment	Wall collapse	Contents of bath tub (after abandonment)	Wall collapse	Unknown	Fill of a (sub)recent pit in room B	Layer underneath the top layer (/500) in room E.	Wall collapse	Fill of a (sub)recent pit in room B	Accumulation layer south of room C	Fill of a (sub)recent pit in room B	Fill of a (sub)recent pit in room B	Layer of abandonment	Wall collapse in room F	Wall collapse in room D	Layer underneath /858\	Fill of well

Taxa	500	501	517	566	572	573	574	593	599	731	760	773	782	784	790	791	843	852	858	864	913	common name
Erica sp.	2									4	7	8	4		6	2	1		1			heath
Juniperus sp.															2							juniper
Myrtus communis		1						25														myrtle
Olea europaea	4		1	41					2	6	9		1	16		3			1		204	olive
Pistacia sp. (cf. lentiscus)				31	12				1	1	1			1								mastic
Prunoideae																		2				Prunoideae
Quercus sp. (deciduous type)																						oak
Quercus sp. (evergreen type)			2																			oak
Quercus sp.											5					2	8					oak
Rhamnus/Phillyrea								1			2											Rhamnus/Phillyrea
indet. Hardwood	5	2		11	3	3			2	2	4	20	5	6	14	27	6		3		7	indet. hardwood

Period	Early/Late Hellenistic								
Unit	638	748	756	772	786	787	855	864	
Trench	1	1	1	1	1	1	1	1	
Context	Rubbish pit	Floor matrix room B	Floor matrix room D	Floor matrix room B	Floor matrix room B	Floor matrix room B	Fill of pithos in room D	Floor matrix room D	
Taxa									common name
Erica sp.	1	3					4	1	heath
Rosaceae/Maloideae					1				Rosaceae/Maloideae
Myrtus communis		2				1	1		myrtle
Olea europaea	40	7	9			1	1	1	olive
Pistacia sp. (cf. lentiscus)	42		4		1	2			mastic
Quercus sp. (deciduous type)			2						oak
Quercus sp.	4	1							oak
Rhamnus/Phillyrea	1	4	10			3			Rhamnus/Phillyrea
indet. hardwood	22	8	19	7	1	15	3	3	indet. hardwood

Period	5th century BC	Early Hellenistic	Early Hellenistic	Early Hellenistic	Early Hellenistic	Early Hellenistic	
Unit	568	763	764	769	901	905	
Trench	1	1	1	1	1	1	
Context	Grave						
	Contents of grave gifts Tomb 1	Fill of tomb 4	Contents of grave gifts Tomb 4	Contents of enchytrismos burial	Fill of tomb 3	Contents of *trozzella* in Tomb 3	
Taxa							common name
Erica sp.	1						heath
Myrtus communis		3					myrtle
Olea europaea	6	4			1		olive
Pistacia sp. (cf. lentiscus)			4				mastic
Prunoideae		1					Prunoideae
Quercus sp.	1	2					oak
Rhamnus/Phillyrea		1	2				Rhamnus/Phillyrea
indet. hardwood	2	5	7	2	6	3	indet. hardwood

APPENDIX 5, GRAPE MEASUREMENTS MURO TENENTE AND L'AMASTUOLA[11]

A 5.1 MORPHOMETRIC ANALYSIS METHODS TO DISTINGUISH BETWEEN CULTIVATED AND WILD GRAPES (VITIS VINIFERA VAR. VINIFERA VS VITIS VINIFERA VAR. SYLVESTRIS).

The Stummer Index[12] only requires breadth (B) and length (L) measurements. The four formulae by Mangafa and Kotsakis[13] require measurements of length (L), breadth (B), length of the stalk (LS) and the distance from the base of the chalaza (the spoon-shaped structure on the dorsal side of a grape pip), to the tip of the stalk (PCH).

		WILD	wild with great (64.7%) probability	cultivated with great (76.2%) probability	CULTIVATED
Mangafa and Kotsakis 1996 Formula 1	$-0.3801 + (-30.2LS/L + 0.4564PCH - 1.386L + 2.88PCH/L + 9.4239LS)$	< -0.2	between -0.2 and 0.2	Between 0.2 and 0.8	> 0.8
		WILD	wild with great (90.1%) probability	cultivated with great (63.8%) probability	CULTIVATED
Mangafa and Kotsakis 1996 Formula 2	$0.2951 + (-12.64PCH/L - 1.6416L + 4.5131PCH + 9.63LS/L)$	< -0.2	Between -0.2 and 0.4	Between 0.4 and 0.9	> 0.9
		WILD	wild with great (93.3%) probability	cultivated with great (63.3%) probability	CULTIVATED
Mangafa and Kotsakis 1996 Formula 3	$-7.491 + (1.7715PCH + 0.49PCH/L + 9.56LS/L)$	< 0	Between 0 and 0.5	Between 0.5 and 0.9	> 0.9
		WILD	wild with great (91%) probability	cultivated with great (76.5%) probability	CULTIVATED
Mangafa and Kotsakis 1996 Formula 4	$0.7509 + (-1.5748L + 5.297PCH - 14.47PCH/L)$	< -0.9	Between -0.9 and 0.2	Between 0.2 and 1.4	> 1.4
		WILD			CULTIVATED
Stummer index (Stummer 1911)	B/L	Between 0.44 and 0.53			Between 0.76 and 0.83

---

[11] These measurements were carried out in the Laboratorio di Archeobotanica e Paleoecologia (LAP) of the Università del Salento in Lecce, Italy, with the kind help of dr. Anna Maria Grasso.

[12] Stummer 1911.

[13] Mangafa and Kotsakis 1996.

A 5.2 RESULTS: MURO TENENTE

pip number	1	2	3	4	5	6	7	8	9	10
L	5.8	4.8	5.5	5.9	5.3	5.9	4.4	4.9	5.2	5.5
B	3	3.2	3.6	3.6	3.3	3.5	2.9	3.1	3.3	3.5
LS	1.6	1.4	1.8	1.,3	1.5	1.6	1.2	1.3	1.7	1.6
PCH	3	2.6	2.9	3.1	2.7	2.7	2.4	2.4	3	2.7
Formula 1	1.187161	0.098867	1.918389	-0.03261	0.56223	0.881156	-0.73991	-0.4267	1.590992	0.935784
Formula 2	0.431741	0.111563	0.841199	0.080778	0.066216	-0.37785	-0.36468	-0.55342	1.154042	0.048034
Formula 3	0.71419	0.16865	1.033441	0.364548	0.247333	0.10883	-0.36485	-0.46307	1.231577	0.313686
Formula 4	0.023577	-0.87386	-0.17884	0.277399	-0.66515	-0.86038	-1.35815	-1.34017	0.104863	-0.71205
Formula 5 (Stummer)	0.517241	0.666667	0.654545	0.610169	0.622642	0.59322	0.659091	0.632653	0.634615	0.636364

pip number	11	12	13	14	15	16	17	18	19	20
L	5.4	4.6	6.1	5.5	5.7	5.5	5.5	4.9	5.5	5
B	3.2	2.8	3.7	3.7	3.2	3.1	3.4	3.2	3.6	3.8
LS	1.8	1.4	2.1	1.6	1.7	1.6	1.5	1.2	1.5	1.5
PCH	3	2.3	3.1	3	2.9	2.9	3.1	2.7	2.9	2.6
Formula 1	2.001053	-0.26382	3.437215	1.229795	1.522136	1.131791	0.934499	-0.43952	0.738492	0.44999
Formula 2	1.157538	-0.26526	1.163589	0.712509	0.467198	0.491017	0.75891	-0.1699	0.315926	0.13736
Formula 3	1.282389	-0.26198	1.540814	0.871864	0.746876	0.685805	0.884105	-0.09673	0.511986	0.2377
Formula 4	0.099091	-1.54508	0.211713	0.087773	-0.22609	-0.17884	0.354382	-0.63699	-0.17884	-0.8753
Formula 5 (Stummer)	0.592593	0.608696	0.606557	0.672727	0.561404	0.563636	0.618182	0.653061	0.654545	0.76

pip number	21	22	23	24	25	26	27	28	29	30
L	5	5	4.6	5.1	5.6	5.4	4.5	5.7	5	5
B	3.1	3.2	2.9	3.2	3.1	3.5	3.5	3.3	2.8	2.9
LS	1.4	1.5	1.4	1.7	1.7	1.5	1.2	1.7	1.4	1.7
PCH	2.3	2.6	2.3	3	3.1	2.4	2.7	3	2.5	2.9
Formula 1	-0.19812	0.44999	-0.26382	1.568581	1.720199	0.257821	-0.40147	1.618302	0.00836	1.43649
Formula 2	-0.65077	0.13736	-0.26526	1.236946	1.019	-0.68088	0.07727	0.696754	-0.25375	1.11809
Formula 3	-0.51435	02377	-0.26198	1.298402	1.174043	-0.36607	0.135383	0.932623	-0.14045	1.18095
Formula 4	-1.5962	-0.8753	-1.54508	0.098655	0.342541	-1.47133	-0.7158	0.049751	-1.1156	-0.1544
Formula 5 (Stummer)	0.62	0.64	0.630435	0.627451	0.553571	0.648148	0.777778	0.578947	0.56	0.58

pip number	31	32	33	34	35	36	37	38	39	40
L	6	5.6	5	5.1	5.1	5.3	5.4	4.8	4.5	5.2
B	3.3	3.2	3.6	3.4	3.2	2.9	3.4	3.2	2.8	3.2
LS	2.5	1.7	1.7	1.7	1.6	1.7	1.6	1.4	1.2	1.2
PCH	3.4	3.3	3.1	2.7	2.8	3	2.8	2.5	2.2	2.4
Formula 1	5.464077	1.914336	1.64297	1.262249	1.014127	1.607326	1.036845	-0.00677	-0.94967	-0.82326
Formula 2	2.639873	1.470191	1.51511	0.626545	0.641189	1.068071	0.366399	-0.07641	-0.77484	-1.02132
Formula 3	2.7931	1.545843	1.55485	0.738128	0.737435	1.167274	0.555867	-0.01871	-0.80481	-0.80709
Formula 4	1.112233	0.885156	0.3262	-0.63927	-0.39329	0.104894	-0.42438	-1.1021	-1.75652	-1.40372
Formula 5 (Stummer)	0,55	0.571429	0,72	0.666667	0.627451	0.54717	0.62963	0.666667	0.622222	0.615385

pip number	41	42	43	44	45	46	47	48	49	50
L	5	5.5	5.1	5.7	5.6	5.1	5.5	5.6	5.2	5.2
B	3.1	3.3	3.1	3.2	3.1	3.2	3.4	3.6	3.1	3.2
LS	1.6	1.4	1.5	2	1.6	1.3	1.5	1.7	1.5	1.6
PCH	2.5	2.7	2.5	3.2	2.4	2.4	2.5	3	2.9	2.8
Formula 1	0.68514	0.149185	0.357562	3.048331	0.637614	-0.44502	0.346477	1.62313	0.766725	1.027322
Formula 2	0.13145	-0.30215	-0.15804	1.662707	-0.73213	-0.73915	-0.57004	0.793404	0.575424	0.552383
Formula 3	0.24195	-0.03395	-0.01029	1.807274	-0.29797	-0.57195	-0.23225	0.988143	0.677312	0.674585
Formula 4	-1.1156	-0.71205	-1.13122	0.601431	-1.55661	-1.37719	-1.24527	0.071234	-0.14657	-0.398
Formula 5 (Stummer)	0.62	0.6	0.607843	0.561404	0.553571	0.627451	0.618182	0.642857	0.596154	0.615385

pip number	51	52	53	54	55	56	57	58	59	60
L	5.6	5.7	4.3	5.2	5.5	5.2	4.9	4.6	5	5
B	3.2	3.4	3	3.3	3.1	2.9	3.2	2.9	3.2	3.1
LS	1.5	1.8	1	1.3	1.7	1.5	1.5	1.4	1.3	1.6
PCH	2.7	2.9	2.2	3	2.8	2.6	2.6	2.	2.8	2.5
Formula 1	0.525716	1.934701	-1.46169	0.144508	1.427086	0.463652	0.434255	-0.15558	-0.02031	0.68514
Formula 2	-0.22731	0.636145	-1.0624	0.413272	0.444616	-0.04928	0.22634	-0.08873	0.14918	0.13145
Formula 3	0.089014	0.914596	-1.11975	0.496192	0.673564	0.117592	0.301431	-0.07418	0.2292	0.24195
Formula 4	-0.74269	-0.22609	-1.7706	0.104863	-0.44545	-0.90086	-0.87138	-1.32995	-0.3947	-1.1156
Formula 5 (Stummer)	0.571429	0.596491	0.697674	0.634615	0.563636	0.557692	0.653061	0.630435	0.64	0.62

pip number	61	62	63	64	65	66	67	68	69	70
L	4.6	4.9	5.5	5.2	5.5	5.8	4.9	5.3	4.9	5.6
B	3.3	3.4	3.3	3.1	3.2	3.1	3.2	3.2	3.2	3.5
LS	1.2	1	1.7	1.4	1.5	2	1.5	1.6	1.4	1.5
PCH	2.2	1.9	2.8	2.2	2.8	3.1	2.4	2	2.3	2.8
Formula 1	-0.94381	-1.92697	1.427086	-0.30207	0.640488	2.969257	0.225424	0.234951	-0.20505	0.622784
Formula 2	-0.86048	-2.10977	0.444616	-1.0674	0.094435	1.329258	-0.16036	-1.24182	-0.55024	-0.00172
Formula 3	-0.86544	-1.98413	0.673564	-0.81255	0.325927	1.559098	-0.07287	-0.87706	-0.45512	0.274914
Formula 4	-1.76021	-2.51214	-0.44545	-1.90658	-0.44545	0.303794	-1.34017	-2.46192	-1.57456	-0.47138
Formula 5 (Stummer)	0.717391	0.693878	0.6	0.596154	0.581818	0.534483	0.653061	0.603774	0.653061	0.625

pip number	71	72	73	74	75	76	77	78	79	80
L	5.6	5.4	5.1	5.5	5.3	4.5	5.1	6.1	5.2	5.2
B	3.4	3.5	2.8	3	3.1	2.9	3.6	3.5	3.5	3.3
LS	2	1.3	1.3	1.5	1.3	0.9	1.5	1.9	1.3	1.7
PCH	3.2	2.6	2.6	3	2.6	2	3.1	3.4	2.9	2.8
Formula 1	3.02658	-0.31049	-0.24079	0.836495	-0.28291	-1.98279	0.970225	2.821159	0.043484	1.388942
Formula 2	1.760489	-0.60307	-0.33222	0.537418	-0.51	-1.75768	1.062766	1.580142	0.205039	0.737575
Formula 3	1.872086	-0.34769	-0.19843	0.698045	-0.29982	-1.81822	1.110258	1.78292	0.309619	0.858431
Formula 4	0.613849	-0.94786	-0.88524	0.087773	-0.92183	-2.17281	0.34463	1.089174	-0.14657	-0.398
Formula 5 (Stummer)	0.607143	0.648148	0.54902	0.545455	0.584906	0.644444	0.705882	0.57377	0.673077	0.634615

pip number	81	82	83	84	85	86	87	88	89	90
L	5.3	6.5	4.4	5.2	5	5.2	5.3	4.2	5	4.9
B	3.3	3	2.9	3.3	3.3	3	2.8	3.5	2.9	3
LS	1.3	1.4	1.1	1	1.2	1.5	1.5	1.3	1.3	1.9
PCH	2.7	3.2	2	2.5	2.5	2.6	2.9	2.4	2.7	2.5
Formula 1	-0.18293	0.178071	-1.44032	-1.44548	-0.66842	0.463652	0.762189	-0.55677	-0.12355	1.634094
Formula 2	-0.29718	-0.082	-1.23969	-1.18347	-0.63895	-0.04928	0.491855	-0.01032	-0.04933	0.819112
Formula 3	-0.11342	0.478108	-1.33527	-0.98821	-0.52285	0.117592	0.620124	-0.00035	0.04225	0.894689
Formula 4	-0.66515	0.341408	-2.16149	-1.15229	-1.1156	-0.90086	-0.15179	-1.41903	-0.635	-1.10577
Formula 5 (Stummer)	0.622642	0.461538	0.659091	0.634615	0.,66	0.576923	0.528302	0.833333	0.58	0.612245

pip number	91	92	93	94	95	96	97	98	99	100
L	4.9	5.1	4.6	4.7	4.3	5.3	4.9	5	5.6	5.6
B	3.2	3.4	3.2	3	2.8	3.6	3.3	3.4	3.4	3.8
LS	1.3	1.3	1.2	1.3	1.1	1.3	1.3	1.2	2.1	1.6
PCH	2.3	2.8	2.3	2.5	2	2.7	2.8	2.1	3.1	2.9
Formula 1	-0.53112	-0.03657	-0.83556	-0.32351	-1.44686	-0.18293	-0.00904	-1.08138	3.332616	1.122957
Formula 2	-0.74677	0.074718	-0.68396	-0.19746	-1.15316	-0.29718	0.219981	-1.43299	1.706857	0.395844
Formula 3	-0.65022	0.175082	-0.67764	-0.15736	-1.27451	-0.11342	0.285527	-1.27065	1.8569	0.631529
Formula 4	-1.57456	-0.39329	-1.54508	-1.10497	-2.15697	-0.66515	-0.40259	-2.0768	0.342541	-0.20007
Formula 5 (Stummer)	0.653061	0.666667	0.695652	0.638298	0.651163	0.679245	0.673469	0.68	0.607143	0.678571

pip number	101	102	103	104	105	106	107	108	109	110
L	4.9	5.5	5.5	5.9	5.1	4.5	5.8	5.4	5.1	4.7
B	3.2	3.1	3.5	3.8	3.5	2.7	3.2	3.5	3.1	2.8
LS	1.3	2	1.6	1.8	1.5	1.4	1.7	1.6	1.1	1.1
PCH	2.5	2.9	3	2.8	2.6	2.4	2.7	2.4	2.4	2.1
Formula 1	-0.32229	2.704987	1.229795	1.83666	0.459672	-0.18784	1.322976	0.640952	-1.14548	-1.35085
Formula 2	-0.36007	1.191381	0.712509	0.185662	0.045431	-0.00599	-0.10236	-0.50254	-1.1168	-1.33674
Formula 3	-0.27592	1.381077	0.871864	0.618353	0.176469	-0.00384	0.322222	-0.18903	-0.94685	-1.31447
Formula 4	-1.10577	-0.17884	0.087773	-0.57594	-0.88524	-1.34023	-0.81707	-1.47133	-1.37719	-1.99228
Formula 5 (Stummer)	0.653061	0.563636	0.636364	0.644068	0.686275	0.6	0.551724	0.648148	0.607843	0.595745

pip number	111	112	113	114	115	116	117	118	119	120
L	5.3	4.7	5	4.7	4.5	4.5	5.8	5.2	5.8	5.4
B	3	3.1	3.6	2.5	3	3.1	3.3	3.3	3.1	3.4
LS	1.8	1.3	1.2	1.2	1.2	1.2	1.7	1.6	1.7	1.5
PCH	2.5	2	2.4	2	2.2	2.2	3	2.8	2.9	2.7
Formula 1	1.480007	-0.85809	-0.77166	-1.15793	-0.94967	-0.94967	1.608861	1.027322	1.513566	0.554741
Formula 2	0.185672	-1.10933	-0.83746	-1.31422	-0.77484	-0.77484	0.597775	0.552383	0.364396	-0.02917
Formula 3	0.415675	-1.09523	-0.7098	-1.29864	-0.80481	-0.80481	0.879017	0.674585	0.693419	0.192606
Formula 4	-1.17851	-2.21411	-1.3559	-2.21411	-1.75652	-1.75652	0.023577	-0.398	-0.25664	-0.68612
Formula 5 (Stummer)	0.566038	0.659574	0.72	0.531915	0.666667	0.688889	0.568966	0.634615	0.534483	0.62963

A 5.3 RESULTS: L'AMASTUOLA

pip number	1	2
L	5	4.3
B	3.2	2.5
LS	0.9	1
PCH	2	2.1
Formula 1	-2.19979	-1.5743
Formula 2	-2.2093	-1.21976
Formula 3	-2.0312	-1.30829
Formula 4	-2.3171	-1.96378
Formula 5 (Stummer)	0.64	0.581395

APPENDIX 6 – ANCIENT WRITTEN TEXT FRAGMENTS[14]

HESIOD (8TH CENTURY BC)

A 6.1
Also the eleventh and twelfth [day of the month] are both excellent, alike for shearing sheep and for reaping the kindly fruits; but the twelfth is much better than the eleventh, for on it the airy-swinging spider spins its web in full day, and then the Wise One gathers her pile. On that day a woman should set up her loom and get forward with her work.[15]

A 6.2
If you plough the glorious ground at the turning of the sun [the summer solstice, 21 July], you will reap seated, grasping a little bit in your hand, tying together the sheaves head to foot, covered in dust, not overly rejoicing, and you will carry it off in a basket.[16]

A 6.3
Let a brisk fellow of forty years follow them [the oxen pulling the plough], with a loaf [of bread] of four quarters and eight slices for his dinner [...].[17]

A 6.4
After him the shrilly wailing daughter of Pandion, the swallow, appears to men when spring is just beginning. Before she comes, prune the vines, for it is best so.[18]

A 6.5
But when Orion and Sirius are come into mid-heaven, and rosy-fingered Dawn sees Arcturus [around September 9] then cut off all the grape-clusters, Perses, and bring them home. Show them to the sun ten days and ten nights: then cover them over for five, and on the sixth day draw off into vessels the gifts of joyful Dionysus.[19]

A 6.6
She [a tender-skinned virgin] washes her delicate neck well and rubs herself richly with olive oil [...].[20]

A 6.7
But then [in June] let me have shade from a rock and bibline wine and emmer [μαζα] soaked in milk [...].[21]

---

[14] These fragments are listed in order of appearance in this study, not in chronological order.

[15] *W&D* 770-779, translation by Evelyn-White, http://ancienthistory.about.com.

[16] *W&D* 479, translation by Tandy and Neale 1996, p. 105.

[17] *W&D* 442, translation by Evelyn-White, http://ancienthistory.about.com.

[18] *W&D* 570, translation by Evelyn-White, http://ancienthistory.about.com.

[19] *W&D* 616, translation by Evelyn-White, http://ancienthistory.about.com.

[20] *W&D* 521, translation by Tandy and Neale 1996, p. 109.

[21] *W&D* 583, translation by Tandy and Neale 1996, p. 113-115.

LEONIDAS OF TARAS (330/320–260 BC)

A 6.8
Theris the old, the waves that harvested,
More keen than birds that labour in the sea,
With spear and net, by shore and rocky bed
Not with the well-mannered galley, laboured he;
Him not the Star of Storms, nor sudden sweep
Of wind with all his years hath smitten and bent.
But in his hut of reeds he fell asleep,
As fades a lamp when all the oil is spent:
This tomb nor wife nor children raised, but we
His fellow-toilers, fishers of the sea.[22]

A 6.9
Vex not thyself if thou hast a little hut to cover thee, warmed by a little fire, if thou hast a poor cake of no fine meal kneaded by thy hands in a stone trough, if thou hast mint or thyme for a relish or even coarse salt not unsweetened.[23]

A 6.10
Lathrian goddess [Aphrodite], accept these offerings from Leonidas the wanderer, the pauper, the flour-less: rich barley-cakes, olives easy to store, and this green fig from the tree. Take, too, lady, these five grapes picked from a rich cluster, and this libation of the dregs of the cup.[24]

A 6.11
Out of my hut, ye mice that love the dark! Leonidas' poor meal-tub has not wherewith to feed mice. The old man is contented if he has salt and two barley-cakes.[25]

A 6.12
Theris, the cunning worker, on abandoning his craft, dedicates to Pallas his straight cubit-rule, his stiff saw with curved handle, his bright axe and plane, and his revolving gimlet.[26]

A 6.13
These are the tools of the carpenter Leontichus, the grooved file, the plane, rapid devourer of wood, the line and ochre-box, the hammer lying next them that strikes with both ends, the rule stained with ochre, the drill-bow and rasp, and this heavy axe with its handle, the president of the craft; his revolving augers and quick gimlets too, and these four screwdrivers and his double-edged adze—all these on ceasing from his calling he dedicated to Athene who gives grace to work.[27]

---

[22] Translated by Andrew Lang, www.blackcatpoems.com.
[23] *Anth.* VII 736, translation by W.R. Paton.
[24] *Anth.* VI 300, translation by W.R. Paton, www.ancientlibrary.com.
[25] *Anth.* VI 302, translation by W.R. Paton.
[26] *Anth.* VI 204. Translation by W. R. Paton, www.ancientlibrary.com.
[27] *Anth.* VI 205. Translation by W. R. Paton, www.ancientlibrary.com.

A 6.14
To the must-bibbing Satyrs and to Dionysus the planter of the vine did Heronax consecrate these three casks of fresh wine filled from three vineyards, the first-fruits of his planting. We, having first poured what is right from them to purple Dionysus and the Satyrs, will drink more than the Satyrs.[28]

A 6.15
Wine-bibbing old Maronis, the jar-drier, lies here, and on her tomb, significant to all, stands an Attic cup. She laments beneath the earth not for her husband and children whom she left in indigence, but solely because the cup is empty.[29]

ANACREON (582 BC–485 BC)

A 6.16
For breakfast I broke off a bit of sweet sesame cake; I've drunk a whole flagon of wine, and in luxury now, I play my sweet harp, making merry beside my dear girl.[30]

STESICHORUS (C. 640–555 BC)

A 6.17
[...] sesame-cakes and spelt, sweetflan and other bakes and yellow honey.[31]

HIPPONAX OF EPHESUS (6TH CENTURY BC)

A 6.18
[...] I have to dig the rocky hillside, munching modestly on a few figs and barley cobs—slave's fodder—not champing hare and francolin, not I, not tarting up pancakes with sesame, or dripping waffles into honeycombs.[32]

A 6.19
[...]figs, barley-cake, and cheese, like scapegoats[33] eat.[34]

---

[28] Vandermersch 1994, p. 28. *Anth.* VI 44. Translation by W.R. Paton, www.ancientlibrary.com.

[29] *Anth.* VII 455. Translation by W.R. Paton.

[30] F373 Page, F373 West.

[31] West 179a.

[32] F26–26a West.

[33] In the Ionian 'scapegoat' ritual, which was performed to purify the town, some friendless wretch was first given a meal and then driven out of town. West 1993, p. 206.

[34] West 8. Cf. also Columella's references to barley, which he seems to consider an inferior cereal in comparison to wheat, and more suitable as animal fodder ('Next to these [wheat] grains in utility is that variety of barley which country people call *hexastichum* [six-rowed barley]; some also call it *cantherinum* because it is a better food than wheat for all animals that belong on a farm'), although he admits that it is 'more wholesome for humans than is bad wheat'. *RR* II, 14, translation by Bill Thayer, penelope.uchicago.edu.

ARCHILOCHUS (C. 680–645 BC)

A 6.20
I am a servant of the lord god of war,
and one versed in the Muses' lovely gifts.
On my spear's my daily bread,
on my spear my wine [...].[35]

ANONYMOUS

A 6.21
Toss me the mostest sheaf, toss me a sheaf!

A 6.22
Grind, mill, grind:
even Pittacus [c. 640–568 BC] used to grind,
the ruler of great Mytilene.

A 6.23
The swallow, the swallow is here
bringing a fine new year
white belly, dark back;
so from your rich pack
roll out a fruit-pack,
a cup of wine, please
and a punnet of cheese;
or a bran-loaf or pulse-loaf or so [...].[36]

A 6.24
[...] and that both [female] archontes together give the offering for the festival and the care for the Thesmophoria one half ekteus [1/6 medimnos, a weight measure for corn] of barley, one half ekteus of wheat, one half ekteus of pearl barley, one half ekteus of dried figs, with a libation [probably refers to a measure here] of wine, half a libation of olive oil, two cups of honey, a choinix [a weight measure for (dry) corn] of white sesame, a choinix of black [sesame], a choinix of poppy [seeds?], of cheese two fresh cheeses, each weighing no less than a stater [both a weight measure and form of currency, so it could also mean 'a stater worth of [...]'] and two staters of garlic and pine wood.[37]

A 6.25
Then Metaneira filled a cup with sweet wine and offered it to her [Demeter] but she refused it, for she said it was not lawful for her to drink red wine.[38]

---

[35] F2 West.
[36] West 848.
[37] IG II² 1184, 15. For the translation and notes, I am grateful to Michiel van der Keur.
[38] Homeric Hymn to Demeter, 206-207. Translation by Hugh G. Evelyn-White, www.sacred-texts.com.

SEMONIDES (7ᵀᴴ CENTURY BC)

A 6.26
A fancy mare was mother to another [type of woman],
who baulks at chores or anything that's hard
and wouldn't touch a millstone, lift a sieve,
or clear the shit out, or sit at the stove
for fear of soot; and yet compels a man
to love her.[39]

ATHENAEUS (LATE 2ᴺᴰ–EARLY 3ᴿᴰ CENTURY AD)

A 6.27
[...] when I saw the golden, sweet, large, round, thick child of Demeter coming, a baked *plakous* [...].[40]

A 6.28
[...] a flat covering of the maiden daughter of chaste Demeter [flour] luxuriating in countless delicately-compounded wrappings [spices], or shall I say plainly to you, a *plakous*.[41]

A 6.29
[Quoting Timaeus:] And some of the roads which led to their villas in the country were covered with awnings all over; and a great many of them had [wine] cellars near the sea, into which their wine was brought by canals from the country, and some of it was then sold out of the district, but some was brought into the city in boats.[42]

PLINY THE ELDER (23–79 AD)

A 6.30
Theophrastus, one of the most famous among the Greek writers, who flourished about the year 440 of the City of Rome [c. 313 BC], has asserted that the olive does not grow at a distance of more than forty miles from the sea.[43] Fenestella tells us that in the year of Rome 173 [c. 580 BC], being the reign of Tarquinius Priscus, it did not exist in Italy, Spain, or Africa; whereas at the present day it has crossed the Alps even, and has been introduced into the two provinces of Gaul and the middle of Spain. In the year of Rome 505 [c. 248 BC], Appius Claudius, grandson of Appius Claudius Cæcus, and L. Junius being consuls, twelve pounds of oil sold for an as; and at a later period, in the year 680 [c. 73 BC], M. Seius, son of Lucius, the curule ædile, regulated the price of olive oil at Rome, at the rate of ten pounds for the as, for the whole year. A person will be the less surprised at this, when he learns that twenty-two years after [c. 51 BC], in the third consulship of Cn. Pompeius, Italy was able to export olive oil to the provinces.[44]

---

[39] West 7.
[40] Athen. 137b-c, translation by Brumfield 1997, p. 152.
[41] Athen. 449c, translation by Charles Burton Gulick.
[42] Zancani Montuoro 1982, p. 559. Athen. XII, 519d. Translation by C.D. Yonge (1854), www.attalus.org.
[43] Theophrastus does not literally mention this, but describes some other limiting factors in the cultivation of olive trees in Hist. Plant. IV, 14, 9.
[44] NH 15.1. Translation and notes by John Bostock and H.T. Riley, www.perseus.tufts.edu.

A 6.31
Those [fruit trees] which have been hitherto mentioned, are, nearly all of them, exotic trees, which it is impossible to rear in any other than their native soil, and which are not to be naturalized in strange countries. It is now for us to speak of the more ordinary kinds, of all of which Italy may be looked upon as more particularly the parent. [...] With what then ought we to begin in preference to the vine, the superiority in which has been so peculiarly conceded to Italy [...].[45]

A 6.32
The regions of Italy that are at a greater distance from the Ausonian Sea, are not without their wines of note, such as those of Tarentum, Servitia [San Severino?], and Consentia [Cosenza], and those, again, of Tempsa, Babia, and Lucania, among which the wines of Thurii hold the pre-eminence.[46]

A 6.33
Each kind of tree remains immutably consecrated to its own peculiar divinity, the beech to Jupiter, the laurel to Apollo, the olive to Minerva, the myrtle to Venus, and the poplar to Hercules.[47]

A 6.34
Beans are mostly eaten together with other food, but it is generally thought that they dull the senses, and cause sleepless nights attended with dreams. Hence it is that the bean has been condemned by Pythagoras; though, according to some, the reason for this denunciation was the belief which he entertained that the souls of the dead are enclosed in the bean: it is for this reason, too, that beans are used in the funereal banquets of the Parentalia [sacrifices offered to the spirits of deceased relations]. According to Varro, it is for a similar cause that the Flamen abstains from eating beans: in addition to which, on the blossom of the bean, there are certain letters of ill omen to be found.
There are some peculiar religious usages connected with the bean. It is the custom to bring home from the harvest a bean by way of auspice, which, from that circumstance, has the name of 'referiva' ['brought home']. In sales by public auction, too, it is thought lucky to include a bean in the lot for sale.[48]

A 6.35
The very smell of it [garlic] drives away serpents and scorpions, and, according to what some persons say, it is a cure for wounds made by every kind of wild beast, whether taken with the drink or food, or applied topically.[49]

MARCUS PORCIUS CATO (234–149 BC)

A 6.36
In heavy, warm soil plant olives—those for pickling, the long variety, the Salentine [...].[50]

---

[45] *NH* 14.1 and 14.2. Translation and notes by John Bostock and H.T. Riley, www.perseus.tufts.edu.

[46] Vandermersch 1994, p. 33. NH XIV 8, 41–47. Translation by John Bostock and H.T. Riley, www.perseus.tufts.edu.

[47] *NH* 12.2. Cf. also De Cleene and Lejeune 1999, p. 203–211, 608–621, 805–826, 740–751, 903–915.

[48] *NH* 18.30 (12). Translation and notes by John Bostock and H.T. Riley, www.perseus.tufts.edu.

[49] Pl. *NH* 20.XXIII. Translation by John Bostock and H.T. Riley, www.perseus.tufts.edu.

[50] Lombardo 1992, p. 38–39, no. 65; Burgers 1998, p. 257. Translation by W. D. Hooper and H. B. Ash (1922), penelope.uchicago.edu.

A 6.37
This is the proper equipment for an olive yard of 240 iugera [c. 65 ha]: An overseer, a housekeeper, 5 labourers, 3 teamsters, 1 muleteer, 1 swineherd, 1 shepherd—a total of 13 persons; 3 yoke of oxen, 3 pack-asses to carry manure, 1 ass for the mill, and 100 sheep; 5 complete oil-pressing apparatus [...].[51]—
This is the proper equipment for a vineyard of 100 iugera [c. 27 ha]: An overseer, a housekeeper, 10 laborers, 1 teamster, 1 muleteer, 1 willow-worker, 1 swineherd- a total of 16 persons [...].[52]

DIONYSIUS OF HALICARNASSUS (60 BC–AFTER 7 BC)

A 6.38
To what olive orchards are those of the Messapians, the Daunians, the Sabines and many others inferior?[53]

PUBLIUS TERENTIUS VARRO (VARRO ATACINUS) (82–35 BC)

A 6.39
There remains the question of number; but there really are no herds of these animals [asses] except of those which form pack trains, for the reason that they are usually separated and sent to the mills, or to the fields for hauling, or even for ploughing where the land is porous, as it is in Campania. The trains are usually formed by the traders, as, for instance, those who pack oil or wine and grain or other products from the region of Brundisium or Apulia to the sea in donkey panniers.[54]

HORACE (QUINTUS HORATIUS FLACCUS) (65–8 BC)

A 6.40
Long springs, mild winters glad that spot
By Jove's good grace, and Aulon, dear
To fruitful Bacchus, envies not
Falernian cheer.[55]

---

[51] Cato, *De Agricultura* X.1-2. Translation by W. D. Hooper and H. B. Ash, penelope.uchicago.edu.

[52] Cato, *De Agricultura* XI.1. Translation by W. D. Hooper and H. B. Ash, penelope.uchicago.edu.

[53] Lombardo 1992, p. 78, no. 133; Burgers 1998, p. 257. Translation by Earnest Cary (1950), penelope.uchicago.edu.

[54] Lombardo 1992, p. 50-52, nos. 81, 82 and 84, Burgers 1998, p. 257. Translation by W. D. Hooper and H. B. Ash (1934), penelope.uchicago.edu.

[55] Falernian wine came from Mt. Falernus, near the border of Latium and Campania. Vandermersch 1994, p. 32. Horace, *Od.*, II 6, 17–20. Translation by John Conington, ancienthistory.about.com/library.

OVID (PUBLIUS OVIDIUS NASO) (43 BC–17/18 AD)

A 6.41
One may try the white bulb that comes from the Pelasgian town of Alkathoos [Megara, Greece], or the lascivious leaf grown in gardens [rocket], or eggs, or honey from mount Hymettus, or the nuts that are found on the sharp fronds of pine trees.[56]

PAUSANIAS (2ND CENTURY AD)

A 6.42
They say that the plain called Rharium was the first to be sown and the first to grow crops, and for this reason it is the custom to use sacrificial barley and to make cakes for the sacrifices from its produce. Here there is shown a threshing-floor called that of Triptolemus and an altar.[57]

A 6.43
Upon the altar of Zeus Polieus they place barley mixed with wheat and leave it unguarded. The ox, which they keep already prepared for sacrifice, goes to the altar and partakes of the grain.[58]

A 6.44
There is a legend that in this place Phytalus welcomed Demeter in his home, for which act the goddess gave him the fig tree. This story is borne out by the inscription on the grave of Phytalus: "Hero and king, Phytalus here welcome gave to Demeter,
August goddess, when first she created fruit of the harvest;
Sacred fig is the name which mortal men have assigned it."[59]

EURIPIDES (C. 480–406 BC)

A 6.45
Send the maiden out to join her father, for the lustral water stands there ready, and barley-meal to scatter with the hand on the cleansing flame, and heifers to be slain before the marriage, in honour of the goddess.[60]

A 6.46
Begin the sacrifice with the baskets, let the fire blaze for the purifying meal of sprinkling, and my father pace from left to right about the altar [...].[61]

---

[56] *Ars Amatoria* 2, 420–424. Translation by Andrew Dalby, dalby.pagesperso-orange.fr.

[57] Pausanias I 1.38.6. Translation by W.H.S. Jones, www.theoi.com.

[58] Pausanias I 24, 4 and 28, 10. Translation by W.H.S. Jones and H.A. Ormerod, www.perseus.tufts.edu. Cf. Van Straten 1997, p. 51.

[59] Pausanias 1.37.2, cited in Ciaraldi 1999, p. 84. Translation by W.H.S. Jones and H.A. Ormerod, www.perseus.tufts.edu.

[60] *Iphigenia Aulidensis* 1111–2. Translation by E.P. Coleridge, www.perseus.tufts.edu.

[61] *Iphigenia Aulidensis* 1470–1. Translation by E.P. Coleridge, www.perseus.tufts.edu.

A 6.47
Then your mother's bed-fellow took barley for sprinkling, and cast it upon the altar with these words […].[62]

ARISTOPHANES (C. 446–386 BC)

A 6.48
Slave: 'Got everything here, Master! Let's see. The basket, the barleycorn, a wreath, a knife, kindling, me… nope, nothing's missing… Ah! Except the lamb!'
(Runs off to get it.) […]. Master (To the slave): 'Quick, now hand me some barleycorn.' (Slave obeys and Master sprinkles the barleycorn all over the lamb.)[63]

ARISTOTLE (C. 384–322 BC)

A 6.49
[…] for he [Phaleas of Chalcedon, 4th century BC?] says that the citizens' estates ought to be equal and he thought that this would not be difficult to secure at the outset for cities in process of foundation, while in those already settled, although it would be a more irksome task, nevertheless a levelling would most easily be effected by the rich giving dowries but not receiving them and the poor receiving but not giving them.[64]

LIVY (TITUS LIVIUS PATAVINUS) (59 BC–17 AD)

A 6.50
Sextius Digitius, T. Juventius, and M. Caecilius were sent into Apulia and Calabria to purchase corn for the fleet and army.[65]

SAPPHO (C. 630–570 BC)

A 6.51
And chick-peas grew there golden on the banks.[66]

---

[62] *Electra* 803–4. Translation by E.P. Coleridge, www.perseus.tufts.edu.

[63] Van Straten 1995, p. 33–40. Aristophanes, *Pax* 937–8 and 962. Translation by G. Theodoridis, www.poetryintranslation.com.

[64] Aristotle, *Politika*, Book 2 1266a-b. Translation by W.H. Fyfe, www.perseus.tufts.edu.

[65] Titus Livius, *Ab urbe condita*, 42.27.8. Translation by Canon Roberts, mcadams.posc.mu.edu

[66] West 143.

Index

A

Abbott, James 198
agricultural expansion 5, 186, 195, 207, 213, 219
agricultural rationalization 5, 204, 206, 221
agricultural specialization 5, 131, 186, 192, 204, 206, 207, 210, 215 216, 219, 220, 221, 222
agro-town 89, 203, 206, 211, 212, 222
Akkerman, Erik 60
Aleppo pine (*Pinus halepensis*) 30, 83
Amendolara 136, 187
amphora:
    SOS/Corinthian type-A 21, 138, 146
    Graeco-Italic 140, 141, 147
Anacreon 111, 112, 125, 152, 284
Andrisani 190
Ano Mazaraki 96, 98
Apani 140, 215
apple (*Malus*) 63, 69, 77, 118, 129, 130, 149, 162, 164, 165, 179, 181, 270
Archilochus 111, 126, 191, 285
Aristophanes 111, 130, 152, 158, 290
Aristotle 111, 121, 152, 198, 290
Arpi 112, 212
Aspromonte pollen core 112, 143, 144, 219
Athenaeus 111, 126, 151, 209
Athens 99, 122, 128, 129
aurochs (*Bos primigenius*) 174, 175, 194, 213
autumn adonis (*Adonis* cf. *annua*) 31

B

barley cakes 125, 127, 131, 151, 152, 283, 284
Basentello valley survey 2
beech (*Fagus sylvatica*) 118, 119, 130, 149, 161, 163, 179, 181, 287
beetroot (*Beta vulgaris*) 129
bitter vetch (*Vicia ervilia*) 32, 38, 41, 48, 75, 82, 128, 160, 161, 162, 164, 165, 181, 183, 257, 258, 259, 261, 267, 269
blackberry (*Rubus*) 129, 168, 170, 172
blueberry (*Vaccinium*) 129
Bökönyi, Sandor 90, 92, 114-116, 121, 123, 193, 194, 201, 215
borage (*Borago officinalis*) 129, 166
Botromagno/Gravina 113, 115, 122-124, 145, 148-150, 152, 161-163, 166-168, 174, 175, 177, 183, 195, 204, 209, 211
Braudel, Fernand 3, 4
bread 19, 33, 37, 77, 120, 122, 123-127, 130, 131, 149-152, 156, 158, 282, 285
bread wheat (*Triticum dicoccum*) 94, 123, 145, 148, 160, 162, 164, 165, 181, 212
broad bean flour (*lomentum*) 77
broad bean (*Vicia faba* var. *minor*) 32, 40, 41, 66, 77, 82-84, 101, 127, 128, 130, 148, 149, 152, 158, 160-162, 164, 165, 181, 183, 195, 257, 258, 259, 261, 268, 269
Broglio di Trebisacce 95, 113, 114, 118, 122-124, 126, 128-130, 136, 137, 143, 144, 146, 160, 166, 177, 180, 186-189, 192, 195, 217, 219, 220
brome (*Bromus* sp.) 31, 38, 39, 41, 166, 167, 169, 171, 181, 261
broomcorn millet (*Panicum miliaceum*) 124, 130, 209
brown hare (*Lepus europaeus*) 105, 173-176, 193, 194
Brundisium (Brindisi) 135, 140, 141, 147, 215, 288
bulrush (*Scirpus*) 148, 166, 167, 183
Burgers, Gert-Jan IX, 11, 12, 14, 15, 26, 27, 39, 40, 42-47, 54, 56, 57, 59, 89, 102, 105, 106, 136, 187, 191, 200, 208
bur medick (*Medicago hispida*) 32, 38, 121, 122, 161, 163-167, 169, 171, 181, 260

C

canarygrass (*Phalaris*) 148, 183, 258
Carter, Joseph Coleman 116, 121, 123, 197, 198, 201-203, 209-211, 216
catchfly (*Silene*) 212
Cato (Marcus Porcius) 111, 135, 214, 215, 287
Cavallino 13, 88, 105, 113, 115, 118, 121, 123, 127, 128, 145, 161, 166, 174, 177, 179, 180, 191, 202-206, 209, 221
cereal monoculture 209, 210
chaff 38, 39, 75, 76, 83, 84, 98, 124, 125, 149, 159, 227

chestnut (*Castanea sativa*) 130, 205
chickpea (*Cicer arietinum*) 40, 77, 78, 127, 128, 130, 149, 152, 158, 161, 162, 164, 165, 181, 195, 209, 290
chora 2, 5, 12, 14, 90, 102, 116, 117, 121, 123, 135, 196-202, 204-211, 213, 214, 216, 218, 219, 221, 222
Ciaraldi, Marina 145, 149, 152
cist tombs 60, 211, 273
clibani 124
club wheat (*Triticum compactum*) 123, 124, 126, 130, 162, 164, 165, 209
Colophon 191
Columella 111, 112, 125, 284
Corinth 45, 100, 123, 124, 128, 189
corn gromwell (*Buglossoides arvensis*) 124, 166, 167, 177, 183
Cornelian cherry (*Cornus mas*) 128, 129
Cozzo Michelicchio 187
crab apple (*Malus* cf. *sylvestris*) 49, 129, 130, 149, 158, 162, 164, 165, 181
Crielaard, Jan Paul 11-14, 16, 26, 27, 37, 39, 40, 42-44, 46, 47, 55, 81, 89, 98, 99, 102, 125, 200, 208

D

D'Andria, Francesco 1, 191, 192, 208
darnel (*Lolium temulentum*) 121, 148, 167, 169, 171, 177, 178
date (*Phoenix dactylifera*) 129, 130, 162, 181
Daunian *stelai* 13, 38, 43, 90, 93, 194, 226, 227
Delphi 123, 128
Demetrias 122, 129, 130
Dikili Tash 81, 132
Dionysius of Halicarnassus 111, 135, 288
Dioskouroi 14
dolia 60, 105, 140, 223

E

einkorn (*Triticum monococcum*) 94, 122-124, 130, 148, 150, 152, 159, 161, 162, 164, 165, 181, 183, 195, 209
elderberry (*Sambucus*) 129
emmer wheat (*Triticum dicoccum*) 31, 37-39, 41, 47, 48, 66, 76, 82-84, 94, 98, 106, 122-124, 126, 130, 148, 151, 160-162, 164, 165, 181, 183, 188, 195, 209, 257-259, 261, 267-269, 274, 282
Euripides 111, 152

F

Felline 140, 215
foresta Oritana 105
fossa (pit) grave 60, 83, 273
Foxhall, Lin 45, 98, 197, 210
fox (*Vulpes vulpes*) 90, 105, 175, 176, 193, 194, 213
Francavilla Marittima 113, 121, 173, 187, 190, 202
free-threshing wheat (*Triticum aestivum/compactum*) 31, 38, 39, 41, 49, 66, 74, 82-84, 94, 122, 123, 148, 161, 162, 164, 165, 181, 183, 195, 258, 261, 267, 269, 274

G

gariga 89, 90, 92, 101, 103, 110
garlic (*Allium sativum*) 32, 47, 48, 50, 89, 129, 130, 148, 150, 154, 155-158, 161, 181, 195, 258, 285, 287
Giancola 140, 215
goat (*Capra hircus*) 9, 41, 60, 77, 83, 90, 102-105, 121, 126, 131, 173-176, 193, 194, 196, 201, 204, 205, 208, 214-216, 218, 222
Gran Carro 130, 142
grape (*Vitis vinifera*) 6, 7, 30, 32, 33, 45, 46, 49, 50, 53, 60, 66, 68, 77-85, 94, 103, 106-111, 119, 120, 128-149, 154, 159, 161, 163-165, 179-183, 189, 195, 199, 205, 209, 211-213, 218, 220, 221, 223, 258, 259, 267-269, 273, 274, 277-283
grass/red pea (*Lathyrus sativus/cicera*) 124, 169, 171, 178, 212
grazing 90, 91, 103, 104, 167, 169, 171, 193, 197, 201, 206, 212, 216
Greek colonization 1, 5, 6, 12, 132, 133, 142, 146, 195, 217, 222, 223
Greek-style house (*oikos*) 13, 19-21, 23, 33, 35, 37, 38, 41, 94, 99, 100, 148, 259, 260, 264, 265
grinding stone 18, 20, 26, 37, 39, 42, 99
Grotta dell'Uzzo 128, 142, 143, 180

H

Hannibal 58, 214, 215, 216, 222
hawthorn (*Crataegus monogyna*) 32, 129
hazelnut (*Corylus avellana*) 128, 130
heath (*Erica* sp.) 29, 30, 33, 35, 37, 49, 63, 69, 70, 72, 73, 75, 82-84, 90, 103-105, 118, 119, 149, 151, 179, 181, 183, 205, 212, 213, 219, 261-266, 270, 271, 275, 276
Helbaek, Hans 112, 142
héliotrope (*Heliotropium* sp.) 32, 38, 167

Heraion, Samos   123, 128, 129
Herakleia tablets   111, 117, 121, 123, 127, 128, 135, 136, 145, 199-201, 208, 209, 221
Herdonia   112, 212
Hesiod   38, 100, 111, 117, 124, 126, 135, 138, 147, 282
Hipponax of Ephesus   111, 125, 129, 152, 284
Hopf, Maria   48, 123, 127, 128, 130, 133
hulled barley (*Hordeum vulgare*)   31, 37, 38, 39, 41, 75, 94, 101, 122, 124, 126, 130, 148, 160-162, 164, 165, 181, 183, 195, 209, 257-259, 261, 267-269
hydria (water container)   20, 21, 23

I
ibex (*Capra ibex*)   173, 174, 193, 194
impasto   12, 13, 15, 21, 54, 190, 273
interconnectivity   5, 213, 221
Ipsili   123
Italian millet (*Setaria italica*)   124, 130

J
Joolen, Ester van   9, 53, 223
juniper (*Juniperus* sp.)   29, 33-35, 37, 49, 63, 69, 72, 73, 90, 91, 118, 119, 179, 261-266, 271, 275

K
Kalapodi   122, 124, 128, 129, 132
knapweed *(Centaurea)*   71, 167, 169, 201
knotweed (*Polygonum*)   101, 123, 148, 166, 169, 171, 177, 178, 195, 212
Komboloi   81
Kooistra, Laura   16, 98, 105
Krania   123, 128
krater   83, 84, 136, 138
Kroll, Helmut   47, 122, 128
Kroton   94, 152, 199, 220

L
Laghi Alimini   112, 144, 186, 187, 189, 195, 196, 203, 216, 218, 219
l'Amastuola   3, 6, 7, 9-52, 54, 63, 68, 74, 75, 77, 85, 87, 88-103, 105, 107, 109, 110, 114, 119, 121, 122-124, 127-129, 131, 138, 145, 146, 148, 149, 154, 155, 158, 162, 163, 166-168, 177, 180, 185, 191, 193-196, 200, 202-205, 218, 221, 222, 254
Lamiaceae   63
land divisions   197-200, 206, 221
La Rosa   140, 215

leek (*Allium porrum*)   48, 129
Lelivelt, Ruben   9, 92
lentil (*Lens culinaris*)   32, 38, 40, 77, 101, 127, 128, 130, 149, 151, 160, 162, 164, 165, 181, 257, 259
Leonidas of Taras   111, 117, 121, 125, 129, 131, 135, 151, 152, 154, 283
Limenas Thasos   123
l'Incoronata   12, 113-115, 121, 122, 145, 161, 173, 180, 186, 190, 192-195, 202, 218, 220
Lindos   153, 154
Lokroi Epizephyrioi   153, 154
Longola di Poggiomarino   142, 180, 234
loom weight   14, 15, 18, 21, 25, 26, 62, 83, 90, 100, 106, 204
Lousoi   155
Lucanians   207, 209

M
macaroni wheat (*Triticum durum*)   123, 124, 126, 130, 160, 162, 164, 165, 181
macchia   28, 29, 30, 33, 63, 77, 89, 90-92, 95, 101, 102, 104, 110, 117, 119, 167, 169, 171, 186, 187, 189, 193-196, 201, 205, 212, 218, 273
Macchiabate *necropolis*   190
Macedonian oak (*Quercus trojana*)   27
Magna Graecia   1, 94, 117, 135, 196, 197, 199, 209, 220
malaria   93, 94, 198
mallow (*Malva* sp.)   31, 166, 169, 171, 258
Maloideae   30, 118, 179, 262-264, 266, 273, 276
Mangafa and Kotsakis formulae   46, 107-109, 134, 145, 223, 277
Marmorelle   140, 215
Maruggi, Grazia Angela   10, 12-14, 19, 114, 115,
masseria Ciccotti   2
masseria Mea   53, 103, 207
mastic (*Pistacia lentiscus*)   30, 32, 35, 37, 66, 69, 72, 73, 90, 91, 106, 118, 119, 149, 167, 169, 171, 179, 181, 205, 259, 261-267, 269-271, 275, 276
matt-painted pottery   12-15, 19, 21, 40, 47, 138, 186, 190, 191
Mediterranean heath (*Erica multiflora*)   30, 63, 103, 270
Megara Hyblaea   138, 139, 197, 220
Metapontion (Metaponto)   1, 2, 115, 116, 121, 135, 136, 190, 195-207, 209-211, 214, 215, 218, 220-222, 254
mixed farming system   9, 102, 215, 218

293

Monopoli/Piazza Palmieri 124, 143, 180, 220
Montegiordano 140
Monte Irsi 113, 115, 121, 124, 128, 161, 173, 175, 176, 193, 194, 204, 209, 213, 215
Monte Moltone 140
Monte Papalucio 113, 116, 118, 122, 123, 125-129, 145, 146, 148, 149, 150-152, 154, 159, 162-164, 179-182, 203-205, 221
mormon-tea (*Ephedra*) 63, 119, 149, 179, 181, 205, 270
mortar 19, 38, 39, 43, 44, 75, 99, 117
Muro Maurizio 3, 53, 103, 208
Muro Tenente 3, 6, 7, 13, 31, 53-87, 102-110, 118, 119, 123, 125-129, 147-151, 154, 165, 171, 172, 178-183, 185, 191, 193, 208, 212, 213, 219, 223, 254
myrtle (*Myrtus communis*) 30, 63, 90, 118, 119, 149, 151, 179, 181, 205, 262-266, 270, 271, 275, 276, 287

N
naked barley (*Hordeum vulgare* var. *nudum*) 31, 37, 66, 74, 82, 84, 109, 119, 123, 124, 126, 130, 148, 160, 164, 165, 183, 267-269
Nichoria 123

O
oak (*Quercus*) 27, 33-35, 37, 48-50, 63, 68-70, 72, 73, 84, 90, 91, 95, 103-106, 110, 117-119, 149, 151, 168, 170, 172, 179, 182, 194, 195, 205, 212, 261-266, 270, 271, 273, 275, 276
oat (*Avena*) 31, 38, 66, 75, 121-123, 131, 149, 151, 161, 163-167, 169, 171, 177, 178, 181, 212, 257, 259, 269
Oenotria 142
offering hearth (*eschara*) 149, 150
offering pit (*bothros*) 150
Old-Smyrna 96, 98, 99
olive oil 5, 41, 45, 50, 78, 84, 99, 100, 107, 110, 125, 131, 132, 134-138, 140, 141, 143-147, 151, 187-189, 206, 211, 213, 215-222, 282, 285, 286
olive (*Olea europaea*) 6, 7, 9, 27, 28, 32-35, 37, 39, 41, 45, 46, 48-50, 53, 66, 68, 69, 72, 73, 77-79, 81-84, 90, 94, 95, 97, 99, 101, 103, 105-108, 110, 111, 118-120, 128-149, 151, 154, 160-162, 164, 165, 179-181, 183, 188, 189, 194, 195, 198, 201, 205, 209, 211, 213, 218-221, 223, 243, 259, 261-266, 268-273, 275, 276, 283, 286-288

olive/wine presses 45, 78, 84, 107, 140, 211, 288
Olympia 153-155, 157
onion (*Allium cepa*) 48, 130, 156, 158
Oria 3, 53, 89, 103, 116, 154, 155, 186, 192, 193, 202, 203, 206-208, 211, 214, 215, 219, 221
Otranto 113, 114, 121, 136, 138, 173, 189, 192
Ovid (Publius Ovidius Naso) 111, 151, 158, 289

P
Pantanello 112, 113, 116, 118, 120, 121, 123, 124, 127-129, 132, 145, 146, 148, 152, 162, 163, 165, 167, 168, 171, 172, 174, 176-178, 180, 197, 198, 201, 204-207, 209, 210, 214-216, 221
pastoralism 89, 101, 104, 110, 187, 189, 192, 201, 204, 214, 215, 217, 219
Pausanias 111, 152, 154, 289
pear (*Pyrus*) 63, 69, 77, 84, 129, 179, 181, 270
Perachora 155, 157
Peroni, Renato 1, 143, 187-189
Phylla Vrachos 123
Pietra Castello di Cassano Ionio 187
pine (*Pinus* sp.) 30, 63, 69, 82, 83, 104, 119, 151, 158, 168, 170, 172, 179, 183, 215, 266, 271, 285, 289
Pisum (pea) 128, 209
Pithekoussai 138, 189, 220
pithos 143, 271-273, 275, 276
plakous 126, 151, 152, 286
Pliny the Elder 77, 111, 124, 135, 139, 151, 152, 156, 158, 209, 286
polis (pl. *poleis*) 12, 191, 197, 199, 200, 202, 208
pollen 88, 112, 116, 143-146, 148, 167-172, 186, 187, 189, 195, 196, 201, 203-206, 209, 210, 212, 213, 215, 216, 218, 219, 221, 253
Pomarico Vecchio 112, 113, 116, 123, 124, 146, 164, 169, 170, 178, 180, 208, 211, 212
pomegranate (*Punica granatum*) 63, 77, 82, 83, 84, 129, 130, 150, 153-155, 159, 162, 164, 165, 179, 181, 183, 271
Portella 142, 180
Posta Crusta 140
potter's workshop (l'Amastuola) 13, 23-26, 33-35, 39, 41, 45, 94, 97, 99, 100, 259-261, 265, 266
pruning 50, 95, 97, 106, 107, 118, 119, 135, 142, 143, 145, 146, 148, 282
Prunus 30, 118, 119, 129, 130, 149, 179, 181, 212, 262, 266

R

red deer (*Cervus elaphus*) 21, 90, 105, 173, 174, 176, 193, 194, 205, 213, 215

red-legged partridge (*Alectoris rufa*) 173, 194

Regional Pathways to Complexity (RPC) project 3

Rhamnus/Phillyrea 29, 33, 34, 49, 63, 69, 90, 118, 119, 149, 179, 182, 205, 261-266, 270, 271, 273, 275, 276

Roccagloriosa 2, 113, 115, 116, 122-124, 128, 129, 145, 164, 169, 170, 175, 178, 180, 208, 209, 212, 213, 220

roe deer (*Capreolus capreolus*) 173, 193, 194, 205

Rosaceae 30, 66, 75, 118, 164, 165, 179, 259, 269, 273, 276

rosemary (*Rosmarinus officinalis*) 30, 119, 179, 262, 266

ryegrass (*Lolium* cf. *perenne/rigidum*) 31, 166, 167, 195, 258

rye (*Secale cereale*) 31, 66, 75, 121, 123, 131, 149, 161, 164-167, 169, 171, 177, 178, 181, 212, 258, 260

S

San Biagio 121, 214

San Cataldo 140

sandwort (*Arenaria*) 167, 195

San Giovanni di Ruoti 121, 122, 124, 215

San Pancrazio Salentino 3, 44, 53, 95, 103, 118, 179, 191, 208, 272-276

Santa Maria Capua Vetere 143, 180

Santa Maria d'Anglona 186, 190, 192, 220

Sappho 111, 128, 290

Scanning Electron Microscope (SEM) 47

self-sufficiency 13, 99, 100, 110, 222

Semonides 111, 126, 286

Serdaioi 138, 140, 220

sheep (*Ovis aries*) 9, 41, 60, 77, 83, 90, 100, 102, 104, 105, 121, 126, 131, 151, 173-176, 193, 194, 196, 201, 204, 205, 211, 214-216, 218, 222, 282, 288

silos for grain storage 21, 22, 27, 96, 98, 99

silver fir (*Abies alba*) 118, 149, 179

Siris/Herakleia (Policoro) 1, 12, 139-141, 146, 190, 191, 196, 199-203, 205, 206, 208, 209, 218, 221, 222

socio-economic complexity 5, 137, 217, 220, 222, 254

Sorbus 30, 179, 262, 263, 264, 266

spelt wheat (*Triticum spelta*) 122-124, 130, 148, 161, 162, 181, 195, 284

spindle whorl 14, 15, 18, 20, 21, 90, 100, 204

Spurge family (Euphorbiaceae) 32, 166, 167

Stesichorus 111, 126, 152, 284

stickyweed (*Galium aparine*) 169, 171, 212

strawberry tree (*Arbutus unedo*) 29, 35, 49, 91, 179, 261, 263-266

Stummer index 46, 107-109, 145, 223, 277-281

summer grain (Chenopodietea) 101, 123, 124

sun spurge (*Euphorbia helioscopia*) 32, 167, 169, 171, 212

surplus production 5, 51, 94, 99-101, 103, 105, 110, 131, 140, 185, 199, 203, 206, 213, 218-222, 229, 240

Sybaris (Sibari) 1, 135, 136, 140, 190, 196, 199, 200, 202-206, 208, 215, 218, 220

Syracuse 138, 139, 197, 220

T

Taras (Taranto) 1, 6, 9. 10, 12, 40, 92, 94, 102, 115, 121, 129, 135, 138, 140, 154, 190, 195, 196, 200-206, 208, 214, 215, 218-220, 222

terebinth (*Pistacia terebinthus*) 30

Thesmophoria 154, 156, 285

Thourioi 135, 136, 199, 208, 215, 220

timber 30, 72, 198, 244

Timpone della Motta/Timpa del Castello (Francavilla Marittima) 113, 116, 121, 173, 187, 190, 202

Torre di Satriano 114, 118, 127, 130, 145, 161-163, 179, 180

Torre Mordillo 113, 118, 122, 123, 128-130, 136, 137, 144, 146, 160, 179, 180, 186-189, 194-196, 217, 220

Toynbee, Arnold J. 214

tree heath (*Erica arborea*) 29, 69, 103, 104, 119, 179, 270

trozzella 83, 84, 212, 274, 276

Turkey oak (*Quercus cerris*) 27, 118

U

Uggeri, Giovanni 103

umbrella pine (*Pinus pinea*) 30, 82, 83, 119, 151, 183, 271

upright goosefoot (*Chenopodium urbicum*) 166, 195

urbanization 1, 3, 5, 6, 202, 205, 213, 216, 217

V

Valesio 3, 53, 90, 103, 105, 113, 114, 121, 173-176, 191, 193, 194, 204, 205, 207, 208, 211, 213, 215, 219

Vallonea oak (*Quercus macrolepis*) 27
Vandermersch, Christian 139, 140
Varro (Publius Terentius) 111, 135, 141, 145, 214, 215, 287, 288
Vaste 113, 116, 117, 121-123, 128, 129, 148-152, 154, 164, 169, 170, 175, 176, 178, 180-182, 191, 209, 212, 215
Veenman, Froukje 105, 121, 193, 211, 215
vitrification (charcoal) 71, 117
Volos 122, 124, 128, 144

W

walnut (*Juglans*) 130, 160, 188, 203
western marsh-harrier (*Circus aeruginosus*) 173, 194
white goosefoot (*Chenopodium album*) 123, 166, 169, 171, 177, 178, 205, 212
Whitehouse, Ruth 203, 204
wild cherry (*Prunus avium*) 30, 129
wild olive (*Olea europaea* ssp. *sylvestris*) 28, 133, 134, 143, 144
wild strawberry (*Fragaria*) 129
Wilkins, John 203, 204
wine 5, 9, 16, 30, 41, 45, 50, 78, 81, 84, 100, 101, 107, 110, 121, 126, 131-147, 151, 154, 159, 188, 199, 202, 206, 211, 213, 215, 216, 218, 220-223, 282, 284, 285, 286, 288
winter grain (Secalinetea) 101
woodland 89-92, 101, 105, 119, 151, 193, 195, 205, 213
wool 14, 90, 100, 104, 106, 107, 121, 131, 193, 204, 206, 208, 214, 216, 222

Y

yellow vetch (*Lathyrus aphaca*) 169, 171, 212
Yntema, Douwe 38, 57, 89, 103, 141, 154, 155, 190, 192, 193, 199, 205, 209, 211, 215

Z

Zohary, Daniel 48, 127, 133